LINGUISTICS

LINGUISTICS

AN INTRODUCTION TO LANGUAGE AND COMMUNICATION

Fifth Edition

Adrian Akmajian
Richard A. Demers
Ann K. Farmer
Robert M. Harnish

The MIT Press
Cambridge, Massachusetts
London, England

This book was set in Times New Roman in 3B2 by Asco Typesetters, Hong Kong. Printed and bound in the United States of America.

Library of Congress Cataloging-in-Publication Data

Linguistics : an introduction to language and communication / Adrian Akmajian ... [et al.].—5th ed.
   p. cm.
  Includes bibliographical references and index.
  ISBN 0-262-01185-9 (alk. paper) — ISBN 0-262-51123-1 (pbk. : alk. paper)
  1. Linguistics. I. Akmajian, Adrian.
P121 .A4384 2001
410—dc21

00-053286

Contents

Acknowledgments   ix

Note to the Teacher   xi

PART I

THE STRUCTURE OF HUMAN LANGUAGE   1

INTRODUCTION   3

Chapter 1
What Is Linguistics?   5

Chapter 2
Morphology: The Study of the Structure of Words   11

2.1   Words: Some Background Concepts   11

2.2   Complex Words and Morphemes   16

2.3   Neologisms: How Are New Words Created?   23

2.4   Inflectional versus Derivational Morphology   42

2.5   Problematic Aspects of Morphological Analysis   46

2.6   Special Topics   49

The Meaning of Complex Words   49

More on Compounds   50

Morphological Anaphora   53

Classes of Derivational Affixes   54

Chapter 3
Phonetics and Phonemic Transcription   65

3.1   Some Background Concepts   65

3.2   The Representation of Speech Sounds   71

vi   Contents

3.3   Special Topics   97

Vowels before /ɹ/   97

Contractions in Casual Spoken English   100

Consonant Clusters   101

Chapter 4
Phonology: The Study of Sound Structure   109

4.1   What Is Phonology?   109

4.2   The Internal Structure of Speech Sounds: Distinctive Feature Theory   110

4.3   The External Organization of Speech Sounds   126

4.4   Special Topic   140

The Word-Level Tone Contour of English   140

Chapter 5
Syntax: The Study of Sentence Structure   149

5.1   Some Background Concepts   149

5.2   An Informal Theory of Syntax   156

5.3   A More Formal Account of Syntactic Theory   197

5.4   Special Topics   211

Wh-Questions   211

Sentence Structure and Anaphora   213

X-Bar Theory   215

Chapter 6
Semantics: The Study of Linguistic Meaning   227

6.1   Semantics as Part of a Grammar   227

6.2   Theories of Meaning   228

6.3   The Scope of a Semantic Theory   237

6.4   Special Topics   248

Mood and Meaning   249

Singular and General   253

Deictics and Proper Names   255

Definite Descriptions: Referential and Attributive   258

Natural Kind Terms, Concepts, and the Division of Linguistic Labor   261

Anaphora and Coreference   261

Contents

Chapter 7
Language Variation   275

7.1   Language Styles and Language Dialects   275

7.2   Some Rules of the Grammar of Informal Style in English   288

7.3   Other Language Varieties   295

Chapter 8
Language Change   315

8.1   Some Background Concepts   315

8.2   The Reconstruction of Indo-European, the Nature of Language Change, and Language Families of the World   319

8.3   The Linguistic History of English   339

PART II

COMMUNICATION AND COGNITIVE SCIENCE   355

INTRODUCTION   357

Chapter 9
Pragmatics: The Study of Language Use and Communication   361

9.1   Some Background Concepts   361

9.2   The Message Model of Linguistic Communication   363

9.3   The Inferential Model of Linguistic Communication   370

9.4   Discourse and Conversation   387

9.5   Special Topics   391

Performatives   391

Speech Acts   394

Meaning, Saying, and Implicating   397

Pragmatic Presupposition   400

Speaker Reference   403

Chapter 10
Psychology of Language: Speech Production and Comprehension   417

10.1   Psycholinguistics: Competence, Performance, and Acquisition   417

10.2   Speech Production   418

10.3   Language Comprehension   425

10.4   Special Topics   454

The McGurk Effect   454

Open- and Closed-Class Items   455

The Psychological Reality of Empty Categories   458

Connectionist Models of Lexical Access and Letter Recognition   460

Chapter 11
Language Acquisition in Children   477

11.1   Some Background Concepts   477

11.2   Is There a "Language Acquisition Device"?   490

11.3   Is the Human Linguistic Capacity Unique? Children and Primates
Compared   506

11.4   Special Topic   516

Principles and Parameters   516

Chapter 12
Language and the Brain   527

12.1   Where Is Language Localized in the Brain?   528

12.2   How Does the Brain Encode and Decode Speech and Language?   535

12.3   Are the Components of Language Neuroanatomically Distinct?   542

12.4   Special Topics   546

PET and MRI Imaging   546

Event-Related Potentials   550

Japanese Orthography and Graphic Aphasia   554

Appendix
The Written Representation of Language   561

Glossary   571

Index   591

Acknowledgments

For this fifth edition we would like to thank the many students whom we have taught and from whom we have learned. We would also like to express our special thanks to our colleagues at the University of Arizona and the State University of New York at Albany. We would especially like to mention Keith Allan, Andrew Barss, Lee Bickmore, Aaron Broadwell, Ken Forster, Bruce Fraser, Merrill Garrett, Ken Hale, Scott Jacobs, Eloise Jelinek, Anita Thurmond, and Frank Vellutino. Finally, thanks to Meghan O'Donnell for help with the index.

Note to the Teacher

This fifth edition of our text evolved from our continuing collaboration in teaching introductory linguistics at the University of Arizona. Classroom experience, as well as valuable feedback from students and colleagues, revealed ways in which the material from the fourth edition could be further improved.

Like the fourth edition, this one is divided into two parts. Part I deals with the structural and interpretive parts of language: morphology, phonetics, phonology, syntax, semantics, variation, and change. Part II is cognitively oriented and includes chapters on pragmatics, psychology of language, language acquisition, and language and the brain.

In this edition most chapters have been revised and/or updated. Many of them include sections on special topics of particular interest, which are set off at the end of the chapter so that the flow of discussion is not disturbed. The new structure of chapter 2, "Morphology," stresses the creative aspect of English vocabulary (or the vocabulary of any language, for that matter). The primary transcription system used in chapter 3, "Phonetics and Phonemic Transcription"—indeed, throughout the book —is now the International Phonetic Alphabet. A new section in chapter 4, "Phonology," discusses the interaction of full and reduced vowels and their relationship to metrical feet. This discussion will permit students to understand the patterns of full and reduced vowels in English and consequently to write any English word they know how to pronounce. Chapter 5, "Syntax"; chapter 6, "Semantics"; chapter 9, "Pragmatics"; chapter 11, "Language Acquisition in Children; and chapter 12, "Language and the Brain," have been reworked and updated. We have also added a "Further Reading" section at the end of chapters 2–12 and the appendix to assist the student in learning more about the topics discussed in those chapters.

Despite these revisions, certain aspects of the text remain unchanged. First, as in earlier editions, the chapter on morphology appears before the chapters on phonetics and phonology. Though this is not the "traditional" order of presentation, we have found it desirable for two reasons. First, it enables us to introduce students to the various fields of linguistics by virtue of the information encoded in words. And second, words and their properties are intuitively accessible to students in a way that sounds and their properties may not be.

Second, we must emphasize once again our concern with imparting basic conceptual foundations of linguistics and the method of argumentation, justification, and hypothesis testing within the field. In no way is this edition intended to be a complete survey of the facts or putative results that have occupied linguists in recent years. On the contrary, we have chosen a small set of linguistic concepts that we understand to be among the most fundamental within the field at this time; and in presenting these concepts, we have attempted to show how to argue for linguistic hypotheses. By dealing with a relatively small number of topics in detail, students can get a feeling for how work in different areas of linguistics is done. If an introductory course can impart this feeling for the field, it will have largely succeeded.

Third, we have drawn the linguistic examples in this edition, as in earlier ones, almost exclusively from English. Once again we should note that we recognize the great importance of studying language universals and the increasingly significant role that comparative studies play in linguistic research. However, in presenting conceptual foundations of linguistics to students who have never been exposed to the subject before, we feel it is crucial that they should be able to draw upon their linguistic intuitions when required to make subtle judgments about language, both in following the text and in doing exercises. This is not merely for convenience, to set up as few obstacles as possible in an introductory course; rather, we feel that it is essential that students be able to evaluate critically our factual claims at each step, for this encourages a healthy skepticism and an active approach toward the subject matter. Given that the majority of our readers are native speakers of English, our focus on English examples provides benefits that we feel far outweigh the lack of data from other languages. Obviously, the general principles we discuss must be applicable to all languages, and some teachers may wish to emphasize universals and crosslinguistic data in their lectures. Such material can be found in *A Linguistics Workbook* (4th ed.), by Ann K. Farmer and Richard A. Demers, also published by The MIT Press.

LESSON PLANS

We have organized this edition to give teachers maximum flexibility in designing a linguistics course for their own (and their students' own) special needs. The individual chapters are designed with numerous sub-sections and in such a way that core material is often presented first, with additional material following as special topics. In this way, teachers who can spend only a week on a certain chapter are able to choose various subsections, so that students are exposed to the material most relevant for that particular course—in short, the book can be used in a modular fashion. We will take up some specific examples.

For teachers working in the quarter system, this edition can be used easily for a one-quarter course. For a course oriented toward more traditional topics in linguistics, the following is a possible format (with variations depending on the teacher):

Chapter 2: Morphology
Chapter 3: Phonetics and Phonemic Transcription
Chapter 4: Phonology
Chapter 5: Syntax
Chapter 7: Language Variation
Chapter 8: Language Change

The chapters cited do not depend crucially on the ones that have been skipped over; thus, we have ensured that a traditional core exists within this edition.

For a one-quarter course with an emphasis on psycholinguistics, cognitive science, or human communication, the following is a possible format:

Chapter 2: Morphology
Chapter 5: Syntax
Chapter 6: Semantics
Chapter 9: Pragmatics
Chapter 11: Language Acquisition in Children
Chapter 12: Language and the Brain

Teachers working within the semester system (or teaching courses that run two quarters in the quarter system) will find that this edition can be used quite comfortably within a 14- or 15-week term. For example, for a one-semester linguistics course oriented toward more traditional topics, the following is a possible format:

Chapter 2: Morphology
Chapter 3: Phonetics and Phonemic Transcription
Chapter 4: Phonology
Chapter 5: Syntax
Chapter 6: Semantics
Chapter 7: Language Variation
Chapter 8: Language Change
Chapter 9: Pragmatics

Obviously, teachers with other interests will pick different modules. For example, for a course with a psycholinguistic, cognitive science, or human communication orientation, the following choice of topics seems reasonable:

Chapter 2: Morphology
Chapter 5: Syntax
Chapter 6: Semantics
Chapter 9: Pragmatics
Chapter 10: Psychology of Language
Chapter 11: Language Acquisition in Children
Chapter 12: Language and the Brain

In short, by varying the selection of chapters, subsections, and special topics, teachers from diverse backgrounds and in diverse academic departments will be able to design an introduction to linguistics that is custom-made for their purposes.

PART I
THE STRUCTURE OF HUMAN LANGUAGE

INTRODUCTION

In this section we will examine the structure of human language, and in doing so we will discover a system that is highly complex. Beginning students of linguistics are often surprised to find that linguists spend considerable time formulating theories to represent and account for the structure (as well as the functioning) of human language. What is there, after all, to explain? Speaking one's native language is a natural and effortless task, carried out with great speed and ease. Even young children can do it with little conscious effort. From this, it is commonly concluded that aside from a few rules of grammar and pronunciation there is nothing else to explain about human language.

But it turns out that there is a great deal to explain. If we "step outside" language and look at it as an object to be studied and described and not merely used, we discover an exciting sphere of human knowledge previously hidden from us.

In beginning the study of the structural properties of human language, it is useful to note a common theme that runs throughout part I: the structural analysis of human language can be stated in terms of (1) discrete units of various sorts and (2) rules and principles that govern the way these discrete units can be combined and ordered. In the sections on morphology (chapter 2), phonetics (chapter 3), phonology (chapter 4), and syntax (chapter 5), we will discuss the significant discrete units that linguists have postulated in the study of these subareas of linguistics. In addition to isolating discrete units such as morphemes, phonetic features, and syntactic phrases, we will be discussing the rules and principles by which words are formed, sounds are combined and varied, and syntactic units are structured and ordered into larger phrases.

In addition to discussing the core areas of morphology, phonology, syntax, and semantics (chapter 6), we will discuss two subfields of linguistics that draw heavily on those core areas, namely, language variation (chapter 7) and language change (chapter 8). In these chapters we will consider the ways in which language varies across individual speakers and dialect groups (regionally, socially, and ethnically) and how languages vary and relate to each other historically. Thus, having isolated important structural units and rules for combination in chapters 2–5, we will then examine how such units and rules can vary along a number of dimensions.

The subfields represented in chapters 2–6 form the core of what has classically been known as *structural linguistics* (as practiced in the United States from the 1930s to the 1950s), and they continue to form a central part of *transformational/generative linguistics*, the theoretical perspective we adopt here. The latter dates from the publication of Noam Chomsky's 1957 work *Syntactic Structures* and has been the dominant school of linguistics in the United States since that time. It has also come to be a dominant school in Western Europe and Japan and has increasing influence in several Eastern European countries as well.

Assuming that the majority of our readers are native speakers of English, we have drawn the language data used in this book almost exclusively from English (see *A Linguistics Workbook*, also published by the MIT Press, for exercises based on over 20 languages). We encourage you to use your native linguistic judgments in evaluating our arguments and hypotheses. It is important that you test hypotheses, since this is an important aspect of doing scientific investigations. We should also stress that the general aspects of the linguistic framework we develop here are proposed to hold for all languages, or at least for a large subset of languages, and we encourage you to think about other languages you may know as you study the English examples.

Chapter 1
What Is Linguistics?

The field of linguistics, the scientific study of human natural language, is a growing and exciting area of study, with an important impact on fields as diverse as education, anthropology, sociology, language teaching, cognitive psychology, philosophy, computer science, neuroscience, and artificial intelligence, among others. Indeed, the last five fields cited, along with linguistics, are the key components of the emerging field of cognitive science, the study of the structure and functioning of human cognitive processes.

In spite of the importance of the field of linguistics, many people, even highly educated people, will tell you that they have only a vague idea of what the field is about. Some believe that a linguist is a person who speaks several languages fluently. Others believe that linguists are language experts who can help you decide whether it is better to say "It is I" or "It's me." Yet it is quite possible to be a professional linguist (and an excellent one at that) without having taught a single language class, without having interpreted at the UN, and without speaking any more than one language.

What is linguistics, then? Fundamentally, the field is concerned with the nature of language and (linguistic) communication. It is apparent that people have been fascinated with language and communication for thousands of years, yet in many ways we are only beginning to understand the complex nature of this aspect of human life. If we ask, What is the nature of language? or How does communication work? we quickly realize that these questions have no simple answers and are much too broad to be answered in a direct way. Similarly, questions such as What is energy? or What is matter? cannot be answered in a simple fashion, and indeed the entire field of physics is an attempt to answer them. Linguistics is no different: the field as a whole represents an attempt to break down the broad questions about the nature of language and communication into smaller, more manageable questions that we can hope to answer, and in so doing establish reasonable results that we can build on in moving closer to answers to the larger questions. Unless we limit our sights in this way and restrict ourselves to particular frameworks for examining different aspects of language and communication, we cannot hope to make progress in answering the broad questions that have fascinated people for so long. As we will see, the field covers a surprisingly broad range of topics related to language and communication.

Part I of the text contains chapters dealing primarily with the structural components of language. Chapter 2, "Morphology," is concerned with the properties of words and word-building rules. Chapter 3, "Phonetics and Phonemic Transcription," introduces the physiology involved in the production of speech sounds as well as phonemic and phonetic transcription systems that are used to represent the sounds of English. Chapter 4, "Phonology," surveys the organizational principles that determine the patterns the speech sounds are subject to. Chapter 5, "Syntax," presents a study of the structure of sentences and phrases. Chapter 6, "Semantics," surveys the properties of linguistic meaning. Chapter 7, "Language Variation," deals with the ways speakers and groups of speakers can differ from each other in terms of the various forms of language that they use. Chapter 8, "Language Change," examines how languages change over time and how languages can be historically related.

Having examined certain structural properties of human language in part I, we turn to functional properties in part II. Chapter 9, "Pragmatics," explores some of the issues involved in describing human communication and proposes certain communication strategies that people use when they talk to each other. Chapter 10, "Psychology of Language," examines how language is produced and understood. Chapter 11, "Language Acquisition in Children," studies the stages involved in language acquisition by humans with normal brain function and reviews the evidence for positing a genetically endowed "Language Acquisition Device." Finally, chapter 12, "Language and the Brain," deals with how language is stored and processed in the brain.

To turn now from the particular to the general, what are some of the background assumptions that linguists make when they study language? Perhaps the most important fundamental assumption is that human language at all levels is rule- (or principle-) governed. Every known language has systematic rules governing pronunciation, word formation, and grammatical construction. Further, the way in which meanings are associated with phrases of a language is characterized by regular rules. Finally, the use of language to communicate is governed by important generalizations that can be expressed in rules. The ultimate aim in each chapter, therefore, is to formulate rules to describe and account for the phenomena under consideration. Indeed, chapter 7, "Language Variation," shows that even so-called casual speech is governed by systematic regularities expressible in rules.

At this point we must add an important qualification to what we have just said. That is, we are using the terms *rule* and *rule-governed* in the special way that linguists use them. This usage is very different from the layperson's understanding of the terms. In school most of us were taught so-called rules of grammar, which we were told to follow in order to speak and write "correctly"—rules such as "Do not end a sentence with a preposition," or "Don't say *ain't*," or "Never split an infinitive." Rules of this sort are called *prescriptive rules*; that is to say, they prescribe, or dictate to the speaker, the way the language supposedly should be written or spoken in order for the speaker to appear correct or educated. Prescriptive rules are really rules of style rather than rules of grammar.

In sharp contrast, when linguists speak of rules, they are not referring to prescriptive rules from grammar books. Rather, linguists try to formulate *descriptive rules* when they analyze language, rules that describe the actual language of some group of speakers and not some hypothetical language that speakers "should" use. Descriptive rules express generalizations and regularities about various aspects of language. Thus, when we say that language is rule-governed, we are really saying that the study of human language has revealed numerous generalizations about and regularities in the structure and function of language. Even though language is governed by strict principles, speakers nonetheless control a system that is *unbounded in scope*, which is to say that there is no limit to the kinds of things that can be talked about. How language achieves this property of *effability* (unboundedness in scope) is addressed in chapters 2 and 5, "Morphology" and "Syntax."

Another important background assumption that linguists make is that various human languages constitute a *unified phenomenon*: linguists assume that it is possible to study human language in general and that the study of particular languages will reveal features of language that are universal. What do we mean by universal features of language?

So far we have used the terms *language* and *human language* without referring to any specific language, such as English or Chinese. Students are sometimes puzzled by this general use of the term *language*; it would seem that this use is rarely found outside of linguistics-related courses. Foreign language courses, after all, deal with specific languages such as French or Russian. Further, specific human languages appear on the surface to be so different from each other that it is often difficult to understand how linguists can speak of language as though it were a single thing.

Although it is obvious that specific languages differ from each other on the surface, if we look closer we find that human languages are surprisingly similar. For instance, all known languages are at a similar level of complexity and detail—there is no such thing as a primitive human language. All languages provide a means for asking questions, making requests, making assertions, and so on. And there is nothing that can be expressed in one language that cannot be expressed in any other. Obviously, one language may have terms not found in another language, but it is always possible to invent new terms to express what we mean: anything we can imagine or think, we can express in any human language.

Turning to more abstract properties, even the formal structures of language are similar: all languages have sentences made up of smaller phrasal units, these units in turn being made up of words, which are themselves made up of sequences of sounds. All of these features of human language are so obvious to us that we may fail to see how surprising it is that languages share them. When linguists use the term *language*, or *natural human language*, they are revealing their belief that at the abstract level, beneath the surface variation, languages are remarkably similar in form and function and conform to certain universal principles.

In relation to what we have just said about universal principles, we should observe once again that most of the illustrative examples in this book are drawn from the English language. This should not mislead you into supposing that what we say is relevant only to English. We will be introducing fundamental concepts of linguistics, and we believe that these have to be applicable to all languages. We have chosen English examples so that you can continually check our factual claims and decide whether they are empirically well founded. Linguistics, perhaps more than any other science, provides an opportunity for the student to participate in the research process. Especially in chapter 5, "Syntax," you will be able to assess the accuracy of the evidence that bears on hypothesis formation, and after having followed the argumentation in the chapter, you will be in a position to carry out similar reasoning processes in the exercises at the end.

Finally, we offer a brief observation about the general nature of linguistics. To many linguists the ultimate aim of linguistics is not simply to understand how language itself is structured and how it functions. We hope that as we come to understand more about human language, we will correspondingly understand more about the processes of human thought. In this view the study of language is ultimately the study of the human mind. This goal is perhaps best expressed by Noam Chomsky in his book *Reflections on Language* (1975, 3–4):

Why study language? There are many possible answers, and by focusing on some I do not, of course, mean to disparage others or question their legitimacy. One may, for example, simply be fascinated by the elements of language in themselves and want to discover their order and arrangement, their origin in history or in the individual, or the ways in which they are used in thought, in science or in art, or in normal social interchange. One reason for studying language—and for me personally the most compelling reason—is that it is tempting to regard language, in the traditional phrase, as "a mirror of mind." I do not mean by this simply that the concepts expressed and distinctions developed in normal language use give us insight into the patterns of thought and the world of "common sense" constructed by the human mind. More intriguing, to me at least, is the possibility that by studying language we may discover abstract principles that govern its structure and use, principles that are universal by biological necessity and not mere historical accident, that derive from mental characteristics of the species. A human language is a system of remarkable complexity. To come to know a human language would be an extraordinary intellectual achievement for a creature not specifically designed to accomplish this task. A normal child acquires this knowledge on relatively slight exposure and without specific training. He can then quite effortlessly make use of an intricate structure of specific rules and guiding principles to convey his thoughts and feelings to others, arousing in them novel ideas and subtle perceptions and judgments. For the conscious mind, not specifically designed for the purpose, it remains a distant goal to reconstruct and comprehend what the child has done intuitively and with minimal effort. Thus language is a mirror of mind in a deep and significant sense. It is a product of human intelligence, created anew in each individual by operations that lie far beyond the reach of will or consciousness.

Bibliography

Chomsky, N. 1975. *Reflections on language*. New York: Pantheon Books.

Chapter 2

Morphology: The Study of the Structure of Words

2.1 WORDS: SOME BACKGROUND CONCEPTS

We begin our study of human language by examining one of the most fundamental units of linguistic structure: the word. Words play an integral role in the human ability to use language creatively. Far from being a static repository of memorized information, a human vocabulary is a dynamic system. We can add words at will. We can even expand their meanings into new domains.

How many words do we know? As it turns out, this is not an easy question to answer. We all have the intuition that our vocabulary cannot be too enormous since we don't remember having to learn a lot of words. Yet when we think about it, we realize that the world around us appears to be infinite in scope. How do we use a finite vocabulary to deal with the potentially infinite number of situations we encounter in the world? We will learn that the number of sentences at our disposal is infinite (chapter 5). Our vocabulary also has an open-endedness that contributes to our creative use of language.

So again, how many words do we know? According to Pinker (1999, 3), children just entering school "command 13,000 words.... A typical high-school graduate knows about 60,000 words; a literate adult, perhaps twice that number." This number (120,000) may appear to be large, but think, for example, of all the people and all the places (streets, cities, countries, etc.) you can name. These names are all words you know. In sum, anyone who has mastered a language has mastered an astonishingly long list of facts encoded in the form of words. The list of words for any language (though not a complete list, as we will see) is referred to as its *lexicon*.

When we think about our native language, the existence of words seems obvious. After all, when we hear others speaking our native language, we hear them uttering words. In reading a printed passage, we see words on the page, neatly separated by spaces. But now imagine yourself in a situation where everyone around you is speaking a foreign language that you have just started to study. Suddenly the existence of words no longer seems obvious. While listening to a native speaker of French, or Navajo, or Japanese, all you hear is a blur of sound, as you strain to recognize words you have learned. If only the native speaker would slow down a little (the eternal complaint of the foreigner!), you would be able to divide that blur of sound into individual words. The physical reality of speech is that for the most part the signal is continuous, with no breaks at all between the words. Pinker (1995, 159–160) notes, "We [native speakers] simply hallucinate word boundaries when we reach the edge of a stretch of sound that matches some entry in our mental dictionary." The ability to analyze a continuous stream of sound (spoken language) into discrete units (e.g., individual words) is far from trivial, and it constitutes a central part of language comprehension (see chapter 10). When you have "mastered" a language, you are able to recognize individual words without effort. This ability would not be possible if you did not know and understand many properties associated with words.

What *do* we know when we know a word? To put it another way, what kinds of information have we learned when we learn a word? It turns out that the information encoded in a word is fairly complex, and we will see that a word is associated with different kinds of information. In discussing these types of information, we will in fact be referring to each of the subfields of linguistics that will be dealt with in this book:

1. *Phonetic/Phonological information.* For every word we know, we have learned a pronunciation. Part of knowing the word *tree* is knowing certain sounds—more precisely, a certain sequence of sounds. *Phonetics* and *phonology* are the subfields of linguistics that study the structure and systematic patterning of sounds in human language (see chapters 3 and 4).

2. *Lexical structure information.* For every word we have learned, we intuitively know something about its internal structure. For example, our intuitions tell us that the word *tree* cannot be broken down into any meaningful parts. In contrast, the word *trees* seems to be made up of two parts: the word *tree* plus an additional element, -*s* (known as the "plural" ending). *Morphology* is the subfield of linguistics that studies the internal structure of words and the relationships among words.

3. *Syntactic information.* For every word we learn, we learn how it fits into the overall structure of sentences in which it can be used. For example, we know that the word *reads* can be used in a sentence like *Mark reads the book,* and the word *readable* (related to the word *read*) can be used in a sentence like *The book is readable.* We may not know that *read* is called a verb or that *readable* is called an adjective; but we intuitively know, as native speakers, how to use those words in different kinds of sentences. *Syntax* is the subfield of linguistics that studies the internal structure of sentences and the relationships among the internal parts (see chapter 5).

4. *Semantic information.* For virtually every word we know, we have learned a meaning or several meanings. For example, to know the word *brother* is to know that it has a certain meaning (the equivalent of "male sibling"). In addition, we may or may not know certain extended meanings of the word, as in *John is so friendly and helpful, he's a regular brother to me. Semantics* is the subfield of linguistics that studies the nature of the meaning of individual words, and the meaning of words grouped into phrases and sentences (see chapter 6).

5. *Pragmatic information.* For every word we learn, we know not only its meaning or meanings but also how to use it in the context of discourse or conversation. For instance, the word *brother* can be used not only to refer to a male sibling but also as a conversational exclamation, as in "Oh brother! What a mess!" In some cases, words seem to have a use but no meaning as such. For example, the word *hello* is used to greet, but it seems to have no meaning beyond that particular use. *Pragmatics* is the subfield of linguistics that studies the use of words (and phrases and sentences) in the actual context of discourse (see chapter 9).

In addition to being concerned with what we know when we know a word, linguists are interested in developing hypotheses that constitute plausible representations of this knowledge. As a starting point, one could ask if *Webster's II: New Riverside Dictionary* is a good representation of a speaker's knowledge of words. Do the dictionary entries represent what we know about words? For example, is the entry for the word *baker* a good representation of what we know about that word? Consider the following dictionary entry for *bake*:

bake (bāk) *v.* **baked, bak·ing. 1.** to cook, esp. in an oven, with dry heat. **2.** to harden and dry in or as if in an oven ⟨*bake* pottery⟩ —*n.* A social gathering at which baked food is served. —**bak'er** *n.*

At least three issues arise. First, the only information given for *baker* is that it is a noun; the entry provides neither a definition for *baker* nor a means for deducing its meaning from that of *bake*. (There is no other entry for *baker* where this information is given.) The meaning of the noun is somehow related to the meaning of the verb, but what exactly is the nature of this relationship? The dictionary does not specify. Intuitively we know that a *baker* is someone who bakes and not, for example, the thing that gets baked; yet again, the dictionary does not represent how or why we pick one option rather than the other.

Second, representing our knowledge of words as simply consisting of entries of the type offered above fails to capture the relatedness of words that have the same form—say, [verb] + *er*. Thus, *weave*, v./*weaver*, n., *pout*, v./*pouter*, n., and *bake*, v./*baker*, n. are independent, apparently unrelated entries. This is counterintuitive, however. In all cases the meaning of the verb is predictably related to the meaning of the noun: a [verb] + *er* is "one who [verb]s." The separate-entry approach fails to capture what all these words have in common.

Third, the dictionary is a finite list and the information it contains is finite as well. How novel words behave cannot be accounted for. For example, *gork* does not appear in *Webster's II*. Neither does *gorker*—and yet a native speaker of English, upon encountering this previously unheard and unseen pair, can tell you that a *gorker* is "one who gorks." *Webster's II*, then, cannot account for the scope of what humans are able to do in creating new words or analyzing existing ones.

Besides the types of information outlined here—information that we assume any native speaker must have learned about a word in order to know it—there are other aspects of words that linguists study, which may or may not be known to native speakers. For example, words and their uses are subject to variation across groups of speakers. In American English the word *bonnet* can be used to refer to a type of hat; in British English it can be used to refer, as well, to the hood of a car. Words and their uses are also subject to variation over time. For example, the English word *deer* was once the general word meaning "animal," but now it is used to refer only to a particular species of animal. These facts about word variation and historical change may not be known to most native speakers—even for highly educated speakers, the history and dialectal variation of most words remain obscure—but such facts form the subject matter of other important subfields of linguistics, namely, language variation and language change, which we will explore in chapters 7 and 8.

We have seen that words are associated with a wide range of information and that each type of information forms an important area of study for a subfield of linguistics. In this chapter we will be concerned with the subfield known as morphology. First we will introduce certain basic concepts of morphology. Then we will discuss how new words are created, and finally we will motivate the postulation of rules and principles of word formation that will address the problems discussed above with respect to the inadequacies of the dictionary as a representation of a speaker's knowledge of words.

Some Basic Questions of Morphology

Within the field of morphology, it is possible to pose many questions about the nature of words, but among the more persistent questions have been the following:

What are words?
What are the basic building blocks in the formation of complex words?
How are more complex words built up from simpler parts?
How is the meaning of a complex word related to the meaning of its parts?
How are individual words of a language related to other words of the language?

These are all difficult questions, and linguists studying morphology have not yet arrived at completely satisfactory answers to any of them. Once we begin to construct plausible answers, we quickly discover that interesting and subtle new problems arise, which lead us to revise those answers.

We can see this process of constructing and refining answers by looking at our first question, What are words? To begin to answer this question, we note that the word *brother* is a complex pattern of sounds associated with a certain meaning ("male sibling"). There is no necessary reason why the particular combination of sounds represented by the word *brother* should mean what it does. In French, Tohono O'odham (a Native American language of southern Arizona and northern Mexico), and Japanese, the sounds represented by the words *frère, we:nag,* and *otooto,* respectively, share the meaning "male sibling." Clearly, it is not the nature of the sound that dictates what the meaning ought to be: hence, the pairing of sound and meaning is said to be *arbitrary*. It is true that every language contains *onomatopoeic* words (i.e., words whose sounds imitate or mimic sounds in the world about us: *meow, bow-wow, splash, bang, hoot, crash*, etc.). But such words form a very limited subset of the words of any given language; for the vast majority of words the sound-meaning pairing is arbitrary. Thus, as a first definition, we might say that a word is *an arbitrary pairing of sound and meaning*.

However, there are at least two reasons why this definition is inadequate. First, it does not distinguish between words and phrases or sentences, which are also (derivatively) arbitrary pairings of sound and meaning. Second, a word such as *it* in a sentence such as *It is snowing* has no meaning. The word is simply a placeholder for the subject position of the sentence. Therefore, not all sound sequences are words, and not all sound sequences that native speakers would identify as words have a meaning. We have intuitions about what is and is not a word in our native language, but as yet we do not have an adequate definition for the term *word*.

In the next section we will consider initial answers to the second question on the list, What are the basic building blocks in the formation of complex words?

2.2 COMPLEX WORDS AND MORPHEMES

It has long been recognized that words must be classed into at least two categories: *simple* and *complex*. A simple word such as *tree* seems to be a minimal unit; there seems to be no way to analyze it, or break it down further, into meaningful parts. On the other hand, the word *trees* is made up of two parts: the noun *tree* and the plural ending, spelled *-s* in this case. The following lists of English words reveal that the plural *-s* (or *-es*) can be attached to nouns quite generally:

(1)

Noun	*Plural Form* $(+s)$
boy	boys
rake	rakes
lip	lips
dog	dogs
bush	bushes
brother	brothers

Not every noun in English forms its plural in this fashion; for example, the plural of *child* is *children*, not *childs*. However, for nouns such as those in (1), and others of this large class, we can say that complex plural forms (such as *trees*) are made up of a simple noun (such as *tree*) followed by the plural ending *-s*. The basic parts of a complex word—that is, the different building blocks that make it up—are called *morphemes*. Each of the plural nouns listed in (1) is made up of two morphemes: a *base* morpheme such as *boy* or *rake*, and a *plural* morpheme, *-s*, which is attached to the base morpheme. The meaning of each plural form listed in (1) is a combination, in some intuitive sense, of the meaning of the base morpheme and the meaning of the plural morpheme *-s*. In some cases a morpheme may not have an identifiable meaning. For example, *-ceive* in the word *receive* does not have an independent meaning, and yet it is recognizable as a unit occurring in other words (e.g., *per-ceive*, *con-ceive*, *de-ceive*). In short, we will say that morphemes are the minimal units of word building in a language; they cannot be broken down any further into recognizable or meaningful parts.

The process of distinguishing the morphemes in the continuous stream of sound can sometimes lead to a novel morpheme analysis. One example of reanalysis involves the alternation of the indefinite article between *a* and *an*. Consider the following words:

(2)
a nadder   →   an adder
a norange   →   an orange
a napron   →   an apron

In an earlier period of English the initial *n* in each of the nouns on the left was incorrectly interpreted as the final *n* of the indefinite article. A similar reanalysis may be taking place again, but the other way around. For example, have you heard (perhaps even said) something like "That's a whole nother ballgame?"

Another example of reanalysis involves the Spanish word *tamales*. On encountering this plural, English speakers—applying what they knew about English plural formation, in reverse—analyzed the singular as *tamale*. The singular in Spanish is, in fact, *tamal*.

A very interesting novel analysis comes from Swahili, involving the English-based expression *kipilefti* "traffic circle." If you pronounce the Swahili *i*'s like the *ee* in English *keep* and remember that cars do not drive on the right side of the road in every part of the world, you can determine why *kipilefti* means "traffic circle." An important characteristic of Swahili is that it possesses a rich set of prefix pairs that are used with different classes of nouns. One prefix pair is *ki-* and *vi-*, where *ki* is used in the singular and *vi-* is used in the plural. You now have enough information to form the Swahili plural meaning "traffic circles."

Morphemes are categorized into two classes: *free* morphemes and *bound* morphemes. A free morpheme can stand alone as an independent word in a phrase, such as the word *tree* in *John sat in the tree*. A bound morpheme cannot stand alone but must be attached to another morpheme—as, for example, the plural morpheme *-s*, which can only occur attached to nouns, or *cran-*, which must be combined with *berry* (or, more recently, with *apple*, *grape*, or some other fruit). Certain bound morphemes are known as *affixes* (e.g., *-s*), others as *bound base morphemes* (e.g., *cran-*). *Affixes* are referred to as *prefixes* when they are attached to the beginning of another morpheme (like *re-* in words such as *redo*, *rewrite*, *rethink*) and as *suffixes* when they are attached to the end of another morpheme (like *-ize* in words such as *modernize*, *equalize*, *centralize*). The morpheme to which an affix is attached is the *base* (or *stem*) morpheme. A base morpheme may be free (like *tree*; *tree* is thus both a free morpheme and a free base) or bound (like *cran-*). A basic classification of English morphemes is summarized in figure 2.1.

Certain languages also have affixes known as *infixes*, which are attached within another morpheme. For example, in Bonto Igorot, a language of the Philippines, the infix *-in-* is used to indicate the product of a completed action (Sapir 1921). Taking the word *kayu*, meaning "wood," one can insert the infix *-in-* immediately after the first consonant

Figure 2.1
A basic classification of English morphemes

k to form the word *kinayu*, meaning "gathered wood." In this way, the infix *-in-* fits into the base morpheme *kayu* in the internal "slot" *k- -ayu* (hence, *kinayu*). In addition, the infix *-um-* is used in certain verb forms to indicate future tense; for example, *-um-* can be added within a morpheme such as *tengao*, meaning "to celebrate a holiday," to create a verb form such as *tumengao-ak*, meaning "I will have a holiday" (the suffix *-ak* indicates the first person "I"). Here, the infix *-um-* fits into the base morpheme *tengao* in the internal "slot" immediately following the first consonant (*t- -engao*). Infixation is common in languages of Southeast Asia and the Philippines, and it is also found in some Native American languages.

It must be noted, in regard to figure 2.1, that not all bound morphemes are affixes or bound bases. For example, in English certain words have *contracted* ("shortened") forms. The word *will* can occur either as *will* in sentences such as *They will go*, or in a contracted form, spelled *'ll*, in sentences such as *They'll go*. The form *'ll* is a bound morpheme in that it cannot occur as an independent word and must be attached to the preceding word or phrase (as in *they'll* or *The birds who flew away'll return soon*, respectively). Other contractions in English include *'s* (the contracted form of *is*, as in *The old car's not running anymore*), *'ve* (the contracted from of *have*, as in *They've gone jogging*), *'d* (the contracted form of *would*, as in *I'd like to be rich*), and several other contracted forms of auxiliary verbs. These contracted forms are all bound morphemes in the same sense as *'ll*.

To sum up, then, we have seen that words fall into two general classes: simple and complex. Simple words are single free morphemes that cannot be broken down further into recognizable or meaningful parts. Complex words consist of two or more morphemes in combination.

Grammatical Categories (Parts of Speech)

Each word belongs to a grammatical category. For example, *daffodil* is a noun, *compute* is a verb, *famous* is an adjective, *up* is a preposition, and *quickly* is an adverb. A word such as *daffodil* shares various properties with the word *disk*. For example, the plural suffix *-s* can be attached to each of these words, to form the plural *daffodils* and *disks*. This suffix attaches to words classified as *nouns* and produces *plural* nouns. Though there are exceptions—for instance, irregular plurals (*children* and not *childs*) and mass nouns (*rice* and not *rices*)—most nouns can be plural-

ized in this fashion, whereas a word such as *famous* cannot be. Thus, there exists morphological evidence for distinguishing nouns from words belonging to other categories.

Morphological evidence also exists that differentiates the other categories from one another.

Verbs take the suffix *-s* (as in *bake–bakes, walk–walks, hit–hits*) in the present tense. This is known as the "third person singular" form, because this is the form of the verb that occurs when the subject of the sentence is third person singular. The following present tense verb forms illustrate this:

(3)

	Singular	*Plural*
1st person	I walk.	We walk.
2nd person	You walk.	You walk.
3rd person	She *walks*.	They walk.
	He *walks*.	
	It *walks*.	

Notice that the verb form remains the same in all cases, except when the subject is third person singular.

Verbs can also take the suffix *-ing*, as in *bake–baking, walk–walking, hit–hitting, sing–singing*, illustrated in sentences such as *They are baking, She is singing*.

Adjectives can usually take the suffixes *-er* and *-est* (as in *big–bigger–biggest, red–redder–reddest, wise–wiser–wisest*). Some adjectives occur not with *-er* or *-est* but with the comparative words *more* and *most* (*beautiful–more beautiful–most beautiful*).

Adverbs share many of the properties of adjectives and are often formed from adjectives by the addition of the suffix *-ly*. For example, the adjective *quick* can be converted into an adverb by adding *-ly*, to form *quickly* (and similarly for pairs such as *easy–easily, ferocious–ferociously, obvious–obviously*). (But note that adverbs are not the only class of words in English that can end in *-ly*. Adjectives can too: witness *lonely man, loneliest man*.)

Prepositions have no positive morphological evidence for their classification.

The question now arises, Are these categories (part-of-speech classes) found in all languages, or just in English? The answer is by no means simple. However, linguists generally assume that certain "major" cate-

gories—in particular, nouns and verbs—exist in most, if not all, languages. (Evidence exists, though, that in the lexicon of some of the Native American languages of the Northwest, the noun/verb distinction is instantiated in a very abstract fashion.)

By and large, the grammatical properties of a given part-of-speech class are quite specific to a given language or small group of languages. For example, the property particular to nouns of taking a plural suffix, which defines English nouns, obviously cannot be used as a general defining property for nouns across languages. Although some other languages have a plural suffix for nouns (note, e.g., German *Frau* "woman" vs. *Frauen* "women"), other languages have no special affix for indicating a plural form for nouns. For example, in Japanese a noun like *hon* "book, books" can be used with either singular or plural meaning. In other languages the plural form for nouns is derived by a process known as *reduplication*, in which a specific part of the singular form is reduplicated (repeated) to construct the plural form. For example, in Tohono O'odham we find pairs such as *daikuḍ* "chair"–*dadaikuḍ* "chairs," *kawyu* "horse"–*kakawyu* "horses," *gogs* "dog"–*gogogs* "dogs," in which the first consonant + vowel sequence of the singular form is repeated at the beginning of the word to construct the plural form. Hence, there is no single affix to indicate plurality in these cases. We see, then, that in some languages there is no morphological indication of plural form for nouns; in other languages the plural is morphologically indicated by an affix or by reduplication (among other ways). In short, in terms of our intuitive notions we can probably say that nouns exist in many languages; but it must be kept in mind that the specific grammatical properties associated with nouns can vary across languages.

Though it may be true that most, if not all, languages share the categories noun and verb (and possibly a few others), it is also clear that other categories are found in some languages but not others. For example, Japanese has a class of bound morphemes known as *particles*, which are attached to noun phrases to indicate grammatical function. In a Japanese sentence such as *John-ga hon-o yonda* "John read the book(s)," the particle *-ga* indicates that *John* functions as the subject of the sentence (the "doer" of the action), and the particle *-o* indicates that *hon* "book, books" functions as the object (that which "undergoes" the action) of the verb *yonda* "read." English has no such particles to indicate subject or object; instead, such grammatical functions are indicated most often by word order. The subject of an English sentence typically precedes the verb and the object typically follows it, as in *John read the book*.

Conversely, English has grammatical categories not found in Japanese. For example, English has a class of words known as *articles*, including *the* (the so-called definite article) and *a* (the so-called indefinite article), as in *the book* or *a book*. Articles are not found in Japanese, as the example sentence *John-ga hon-o yonda* illustrates. The noun *hon* is followed by the particle *-o* (indicating its object function), but it is accompanied by no morphemes equivalent to the English articles. This is not to say that Japanese speakers cannot express the difference in meaning between *the book* (definite and specific) and *a book* (indefinite and nonspecific). In Japanese this difference is determined by the context (both linguistic and nonlinguistic) of the sentence. For example, if a certain book has been mentioned in previous discourse, speakers of Japanese interpret *John-ga hon-o yonda* as meaning "John read the book" rather than "John read a book."

To sum up, whether or not all languages share certain part-of-speech categories, we nevertheless expect to find groups of words within any given language that share significant grammatical properties. To account for these similarities, we hypothesize that words sharing significant properties all belong to the same category. Such categories are traditionally labeled *noun*, *verb*, and so on, but we must remain open to the possibility that a given language may have a grammatical category not found in others. The existence of part-of-speech categories shows that the lexicon of a language is not simply a long, random list. Rather, it is structured into special subgroups of words (the various grammatical categories).

Open- versus Closed-Class Words

In discussions about words, a distinction is sometimes made between *open-class words* and *closed-class words* (sometimes referred to as *content words* and *function words*, respectively). Examples of open-class words include the English words *brother, run, tall, quickly*. The open-class words are those belonging to the major part-of-speech classes (nouns, verbs, adjectives, and adverbs), which in any language tend to be quite large and "open-ended." That is, an unlimited number of new words can be created and added to these classes (recall *gork/gorker*).

In contrast, closed-class words are those belonging to grammatical, or function, classes (such as articles, demonstratives, quantifiers, conjunctions, and prepositions), which in any language tend to include a small number of fixed elements. Function words in English include conjunctions (*and*, *or*), articles (*the*, *a*), demonstratives (*this*, *that*), quantifiers (*all*, *most*, *some*, *few*), and prepositions (*to*, *from*, *at*, *with*). To take one specific case, consider the word *and*. The essential feature of the word *and* is that it functions grammatically to conjoin words and phrases, as seen in the combination of noun phrases *the woman and the man*. Any change in membership of such a class happens only very slowly (over centuries) and in small increments. Thus, a speaker of English may well encounter dozens of new nouns and verbs during the coming year; but it is extremely unlikely that the English language will acquire a new article (or lose a current one) in the coming year (or even in the speaker's lifetime).

One familiar variety of language in which the distinction between open-class words and closed-class words is important is known as *telegraphic speech* (or *telegraphic language*). The term *telegraphic* derives from the kind of language used in telegrams, where considerations of space (and money) force one to be as terse as possible: HAVING WONDERFUL TIME; HOTEL GREAT; RETURNING FLIGHT 256; SEND MONEY; STOP. Generally speaking, in telegraphic forms of language the open-class words are retained, whereas the closed-class words are omitted wherever possible. Telegraphic forms of language are not limited to telegrams and postcards but can also be observed in early stages of child language, in the speech of people with certain brain disorders known as aphasic brain syndromes, in classified advertising, in certain styles of poetry, in newspaper headlines, and generally in any use of language where messages must be reduced to the essentials.

The morpheme classifications discussed in this section are summarized in figure 2.2. Note, incidentally, that affixes could also be classified as belonging to "closed classes." For example, the classes of prefixes and suffixes also consist of a small number of fixed elements, augmented or changed only very slowly over time. Both are sometimes grouped together and referred to as *grammatical morphemes*. It has been customary to use the term *closed class* to refer to function words (rather than to bound affixes), however, and we adopt that usage in figure 2.2.

2.3   NEOLOGISMS: HOW ARE NEW WORDS CREATED?

How can our finite vocabulary be expanded and altered to deal with our potentially infinite world? First, new words can be added, and the meaning of already existing words can be changed. Second, new words can

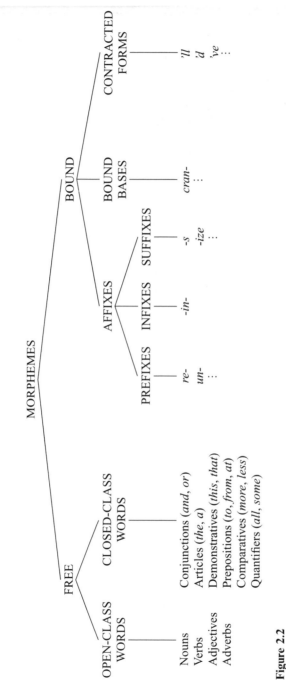

Figure 2.2
Summary of the classification of morphemes. (All examples are from English except the Bonto Igorot infix *-in-*, used to indicate the product of a completed action.)

enter a language through the operation of word formation rules. (The part of language study that deals with word formation rules is also called *derivational morphology*.)

Creating New Words and Changing the Meaning of Words

Creating New Words (Neologisms)

Speakers continually create new words using the processes listed below. Under the right conditions these can be adopted by the larger linguistic community and become part of the language.

Coined Words   Entirely new, previously nonexistent words keep entering a language. This often happens when speakers invent (or *coin*) new words. (In terms of the two components of words (sound and meaning), speakers coin a new word by inventing a new sound sequence and pairing it with a new meaning.) For example, adolescent slang has given us words such as *geek* and *dweeb*.

Acronyms   The words *radar* and *laser* are *acronyms*: each of the letters that spell the word is the first letter (or letters) of some other complete word. For example, *radar* derives from *radio detecting and ranging*, and *laser* derives from *light amplification (by) stimulated emission (of) radiation*. It is important to note that even though such words are originally created as acronyms, speakers quickly forget such origins and the acronyms become new independent words. The world of computers offers a wealth of acronyms. Here are just a few:

(4)

Acronym	Source
URL (pronounced "earl")	uniform resource locator
GUI (pronounced "gooey")	graphical user interface
DOS (pronounced "doss")	disk operating system
SCSI (pronounced "skuzzy")	small computer system interface
LAN (pronounced "lan")	local area network
GIF (pronounced "jiff")	graphics interchange format

Acronym formation is just one of the abbreviation, or shortening, processes that are increasingly common in American society (and perhaps internationally) as a means of word formation.

Alphabetic Abbreviations   For many speakers of American English, one-time abbreviations such as *CD*, *ER*, and *PC* have entirely replaced longer words, such as *compact disc* (or *certificate of deposit*), *emergency room*, and *personal computer* (or *politically correct*), respectively, in most styles of speech; through this process new, previously nonexistent words have come into use. Characteristic of these *alphabetic abbreviations* (or *initialisms*) is that each of their letters is individually pronounced (they contrast with acronyms in this respect).

Computer-inspired alphabetic abbreviations now number in the thousands. Here are some well-known (and perhaps not so well known) examples:

(5)

Abbreviation	*Source*
www	World Wide Web
IT	information technology
HTML	hypertext markup language
OOP	object-oriented programming
HDL	hardware description language
I/O	input/output
IP	Internet Protocol
FTP	file transfer protocol/file transfer program

Clippings   *"Clipped"* abbreviations such as *prof* for *professor*, *fax* for *facsimile*, and *photo op* for *photographic opportunity* are now in common use. There are also *orthographic abbreviations* such as *Dr.* (*doctor*), *Mr.* (*mister*), *AZ* (*Arizona*), and *MB* (*megabyte*), where the spelling of a word has been shortened but its pronunciation is not (necessarily) altered.

Blends   New words can also be formed from existing ones by various *blending* processes: for example, *motel* (from *motor hotel*), *infomercial* (from *information* and *commercial*), *edutainment* (from *education* and *entertainment*), *brunch* (from *breakfast* and *lunch*), *cafetorium* (from *cafeteria* and *auditorium*), *Monicagate* (from *Monica (Lewinsky)* and *Watergate*), *netiquette* (from *network etiquette*), *trashware* (from *trash* and *software*), and *bit* (from *binary* and *digit*).

Generified Words   The words *kleenex* and *xerox* illustrate another technique for creating new words, namely, using specific brand names of products as names for the products in general (*generification*). Hence, *kleenex*, a brand name for facial tissue, has come to denote facial tissue in general. *Xerox* is the name of the corporation that produces a well-known photocopying machine, and much to the dismay of the company, the term *xerox* has lost its specific brand-name connotation and has come to be used to describe the process of photocopying in general (*I xeroxed a letter*). Hence, in casual speech we can commit the grave sin of talking about buying a Canon xerox machine.

Proper Nouns   Not infrequently, a trait, quality, act, or some behavior associated with a person becomes identified with that person's name, typically his or her last name: for example, *hooker* (from the prostitutes who followed the troops of General George Hooker) and *guillotine* (an instrument of execution named after its inventor, Dr. Joseph Guillotin). Thousands of such words are now part of English; in many cases the word remains and the connection to the person has been lost.

Borrowings: Direct   Yet another way to expand our vocabulary is to "*borrow*" words from other languages. Speakers of English aggressively borrow words from other languages. We have *kindergarten* (German), *croissant* (French), *aloha* (Hawaiian), and *sushi* (Japanese), among many others. We have even borrowed words that were themselves borrowed. The Aztec language contributed many words to Spanish, which have now become part of English. The following Aztec words are known to most English speakers living in the United States:

(6)

avocado	guava	saguaro
cocoa	macho	taco
chocolate	maize	tamale
coyote	mesquite	tequila
enchilada	Mexico	tomato
guacamole	ocelot	

And these Aztec words will be familiar to many English speakers living in the southwestern part of the United States:

(7)

cholla	ocotillo
horchata	pozole

javalina   pulque
metate   quetzal
mezcal   Tecate
mole (pronounced
        MOH-lay)

Borrowings: Indirect   An interesting type of borrowing occurs when an expression in one language is translated literally into another language. For example, the borrowed terms *firewater* and *iron horse* are literal translations of Native American words meaning "alcohol" and "railroad train." Other such indirect borrowings (also known as *calques* or *loan translations*) are *worldview* and *superman* from German *Weltanschauung* and *Übermensch*.

Changing the Meaning of Words

A new meaning can become associated with an existing word. There are numerous ways this can come about:

· The grammatical category of the word changes (change in part of speech).
· The vocabulary of one domain is extended to a new domain (metaphorical extension).
· The meaning of a word broadens in scope (broadening).
· The meaning of a word narrows in scope (narrowing).
· The meaning of a complex word involves restricting the more general compositional meaning of the complex word (semantic drift).
· The meaning of a word changes to the opposite of its original meaning (reversal).

Change in Part of Speech   A word can be modified by changing its grammatical category. For example, the nouns *Houdini, porch, ponytail,* and *people* can be used as verbs: *to Houdini one's way out of a closet, to porch a newspaper, to ponytail her hair,* and *to people an island*. In this way a new meaning can be associated with and related to an existing word. For example, *ponytail,* the noun, refers to hair that is tied together at the back of the head, whereas *to ponytail,* the verb, refers to the process of making a ponytail. In cases involving proper names, the meaning of the new word does not derive from the meaning of the previously existing word (i.e., the name, which may not even have a meaning) but is based on associations with that name. *To Houdini* is one example. *To mesmerize* derives from the name "Mesmer."

Metaphorical Extension   *Metaphorical extension* is yet another way in which the meaning of an existing word is modified, thus resulting in new uses. When a language does not seem to have just the right expression for certain purposes, speakers often take an existing one and extend its meaning in a recognizable way. The language does not gain a new word as such, but since a word is being used in a new way, the language has been augmented, as though a new word had been added. To take one example: it is interesting to note that speakers of English have adopted many existing terms from the realm of ocean navigation to use in talking about space exploration. For instance, we use the word *ship* to refer to space vehicles as well as to ocean-going vessels; we speak of a spaceship *docking* with another in a way related to the way an ocean-going ship docks; we speak of *navigation* in both types of transportation; we could certainly speak of a spaceship *sailing* through space, even though no wind or sails are involved; we speak of certain objects as *floating* in space and of ships as floating on water; we speak of a *captain* and a *crew* for both kinds of ships; and we have carried over the names of ship parts, such as *hull, cabin, hatch,* and (at least on television shows) *deck*. It is striking that terms that basically derive from the historical epoch of wind-powered ocean navigation have with great ease been *extended* into the realm of space navigation. The technology in the two realms is radically different, yet we apparently perceive enough similarities to use already existing terms, in new ways, to describe the new phenomena. This is an important fact, for it shows that technological changes in a society will not necessarily result in the addition of previously nonexistent words to its language. Indeed, speakers of all human languages show great creativity and imaginative power in extending the existent language into new realms of experience. Just think of how the meanings of existing words have been extended to accommodate the rapidly changing world of high technology; for example, you "surf," or "navigate," the "web."

Another interesting case is the metaphorical extension of words from the physical realm of food and digestion into the mental realm of ideas and interpersonal exchange of ideas. For example, consider the following sentences:

(8)

a. I'll have to *chew* on that idea for a while.

b. They just wouldn't *swallow* that idea.

c. She'll give us time to *digest* that idea.

d. On the exam, please don't merely *regurgitate* what I've told you.

e. He *bit off* more than he could *chew*. (speaking of someone's research project)

f. Will you stop *feeding* me that old line!

g. All right, *spit* it *out*.

In these examples, one realm (roughly, a realm involving ideas) is described in terms of words from another realm (food and digestion). A feature of this particular case is that words from a physical realm are being extended into a mental realm, perhaps because the physical vocabulary provides a familiar and public frame of reference for discussing our private mental life.

Broadening   Metaphorical extension is not the only mechanism by which already existing words can be put to new uses. Sometimes the use of existing words can become *broader*. For example, the slang word *cool* was originally part of the professional jargon of jazz musicians and referred to a specific artistic style of jazz (a use that was itself an extension). With the passage of time, the word has come to be applied to almost anything conceivable, not just music; and it no longer refers just to a certain genre or style, but is a general term indicating approval of the thing in question.

Narrowing   Conversely, the use of a word can *narrow* as well. A typical example is the word *meat*. At one time in English it meant any solid consumable food (a meaning that persists in the word *nutmeat*), but now it is used to refer only to the edible solid flesh of animals.

Semantic Drift   Over time the meanings of words can change, or *drift*. A rather striking example of change has occurred in the word *lady*. This word was originally a compound made up of the two words *hlaf* and *dighe*. *Hlaf* was the Old English word for "bread" (related to the modern word *loaf*), and *dighe* was the word for "kneader" (related to the modern word *dough*). Thus, the original "kneader of bread" has experienced a rather remarkable increase in status. (Semantic drift is discussed more fully in "Special Topics: The Meaning of Complex Words.")

Reversals   Finally, *reversals* of meaning can occur. In certain varieties of American slang, the word *bad* has come to have positive connotations, with roughly the meaning "emphatically good." Hollywood movies of the 1930s and 1940s reveal that the words *square* and *straight* had positive connotations, meaning "honest" and "upright," meanings that survive in the phrases *square deal* and *play it straight*. During the late 1950s and into the 1960s, the word *square* came to have a negative connotation, referring to anyone or anything hopelessly conventional and uncomprehending of "in" things. By the late 1960s this use of *square* had itself come to be regarded as old-fashioned and the word dropped out of favor (which, incidentally, illustrates the rapid rate at which so-called slang terms enter and leave a language). In the same period the word *straight* came to be used in a wide range of areas, always with the general meaning of adhering to conventional norms: for example, a straight person is one who doesn't take drugs; who is heterosexual rather than homosexual; who is generally "out of it"; and so on.

We have discussed various kinds of extensions and modifications of meaning as a way to create new uses for already existing words. Although this is one of the most interesting areas of word meaning, we unfortunately have very little understanding of the exact mechanisms of meaning change and extension. For one thing, we have very little idea *what* the meaning of a word is: Is the meaning an abstract idea, a concept? Is it an image? When we describe the meaning of the word, are we describing the thing that the word denotes? Or is meaning best described neither as an idea nor as a referent, but as the use of a word in some context? We will discuss these possibilities in more detail in chapter 6, which deals with semantics. Suffice it to say here that because it is not known precisely what the meaning of a word is and because theories in the psychology of human thought are still at a rudimentary level, we can currently say very little about the exact nature of metaphorical extension or other meaning shifts. However, this area, especially the study of so-called slang, will be extremely important for future research because it provides fundamental evidence about speakers' linguistic creativity.

By way of summary, table 2.1 lists the mechanisms by which new words can enter a language and by which the meaning of existing words can change.

Table 2.1
Mechanisms by which new words can enter a language (left column) and by which the meaning of existing words can change (right column)

New words	Meaning change
Neologisms	Change in part of speech
Coining	Metaphorical extension
Acronym formation	Broadening
Alphabetic abbreviation	Narrowing
Clipping	Semantic drift
Blending	Reversal
Generification	
Appropriation of proper nouns	
Borrowing: direct	
Borrowing: indirect (calques)	
Derivational morphology	

Derivational Morphology (Word Formation Rules)

New vocabulary can also be added by following rules that incorporate specific derivational processes. For the most part, the core of each process is an already existing word, to which other words and affixes can be added. English has dozens of these rules, and we will discuss a few of the most common.

In the discussion to follow, we will see that compositionality (the property whereby the meaning of a whole expression is determined by the meaning of its parts) only partially holds in derivational morphology. Typically, the new words formed by these processes have a nuance of meaning that is not predictable from the meaning of their parts.

Compounds and Compounding

In English (as in many other languages) new words can be formed from already existing words by a process known as *compounding*, in which individual words are "joined together" to form a *compound* word, as illustrated in table 2.2. For example, the noun *ape* can be joined with the noun *man* to form the compound noun *ape-man*; the adjective *sick* can be joined with the noun *room* to form the compound noun *sickroom*; the adjective *red* can be joined with the adjective *hot* to form the compound adjective *red-hot*. (For examples of other types of compounds found in English, see table 2.2.)

Table 2.2
Some types of compounds in English

Noun + Noun	Adjective + Noun	Preposition + Noun	Verb + Noun
landlord	high chair	overdose	go-cart
chain-smoker	blackboard	underdog	swearword
snail mail	wildfire	underarm	scarecrow

Adjective + Adjective	Noun + Adjective	Preposition + Verb
red-hot	sky-blue	oversee
icy-cold	earthbound	overstuff
bittersweet	skin-deep	underfeed

Generally speaking, the part of speech of the whole compound is the same as the part of speech of the rightmost member of the compound, which is termed the *head* of the compound. For example, the rightmost member (the "head") of the compound *high chair* is a noun (the noun *chair*); hence, the whole compound *high chair* is also a noun. The rightmost member of the compound *overdo* is a verb (the verb *do*); hence, the whole compound is also a verb.

Compounds are not limited to two words, as shown by examples such as *bathroom towel-rack* and *community center finance committee*. Indeed, the process of compounding seems unlimited in English: starting with a word like *sailboat*, we can easily construct the compound *sailboat rigging*, from which we can in turn create *sailboat rigging design*, *sailboat rigging design training*, *sailboat rigging design training institute*, and so on.

You may wonder when compound words are to be written as single words (i.e., as long words with no spaces between the individual words), as hyphenated words, and as sequences of words separated by spaces. For instance, *bathroom*, *ape-man*, and *living room* are all compounds. Moreover, the high-tech world is bringing us compounds written in a heretofore decidedly *un*conventional way: two (or more) words are run together, and the first letter in the second word is capitalized (e.g., *FrameMaker*, *WordPerfect*, *netViz*, *GroupWise*). The conventions for writing two-word compounds in English are not consistent. Often, the hyphen is used when a compound has been newly created or is not widely used. When a compound has gained a certain currency or permanence, it is often spelled closed up, without the hyphen. The word *blackboard*, when it was first created, was written *black-board*, a spelling found in texts from the first part of the twentieth century. The rule in English for spelling multiword compounds, such as *community center finance committee*, is not to write them as a single word. In contrast, the conventions for writing German are much more consistent. Two-word and multiword compounds are written as a single word: *Unfallversicherungspflicht* (*Unfall* = accident; *Versicherung* = insurance; *Pflicht* = obligation) "obligation to insure against accidents."

Certain compounds have a characteristic stress pattern (accent pattern). For example, in compound nouns consisting of two words the main stress (position of heaviest accent) comes on the leftmost member of the compound. The compound *movie star* is pronounced *MOVIEstar* (where capital letters indicate the location of the heaviest accent), not *movie-STAR*; the compound noun *bathroom* is pronounced *BATHroom*, not *bathROOM*. The stress pattern can sometimes be a clue to whether a sequence of two words is a compound noun or not. For example, the sequence *high* and *chair* can be pronounced *HIGHchair*, in which case it is a compound noun denoting a special kind of chair that babies sit in; or it can be pronounced *highCHAIR*, in which case it is simply a noun phrase consisting of the noun *chair* modified by the adjective *high*, denoting some chair that happens to be high (not necessarily a baby's high chair). Other tests that can be used to disambiguate an adjective-noun sequence involve the suffixes (comparative) *-er* and (superlative) *-est* and the adverb *very. Higher chair, highest chair*, and *a very high chair* are compatible only with the phrasal (not compound) interpretation.

Although the meaning of a complex word such as *trees* is a combination of the meaning of its parts, the meaning of compounds cannot always be predicted in this way; that is, compounds are rarely completely compositional. For example, consider the contrast between the compounds *alligator shoes* and *horseshoes: alligator shoes* are shoes made from alligator hide; yet *horseshoes* are not shoes made from horsehide, but rather are iron "shoes" for horses' hooves. Similarly, a *salt pile* is a pile made of salt, but a *saltshaker* is not a shaker made of salt. The compound *Bigfoot* refers to a mythical creature with large feet; but the compound *bigwig* does not refer to a large wig. Nevertheless, certain generalizations can be made about the meaning of compounds. For example, an *apron string* is a kind of string, whereas a *string apron* is a kind of apron; in other words, the meaning of the head of the compound seems to be central in the meaning of the whole compound, at least for certain kinds of compounds.

Compounding is a rich source of new words in English, and many compounds—such as *letter carrier*, *hot tub*, *talk show*, *flight attendant*, *sanitation engineer*, and *channel surfing*—are numbered among recent additions to the language.

People often ask why the compound *maple leaf* has two plurals: the irregular form *maple leaves* (for the botanical entity) and the regular form *Maple Leafs* (for the Toronto hockey team). The answer lies in the fact that properties of the head of a compound become properties of the whole. Among the properties of the botanical compound *maple leaf*, with head *leaf*, are the meaning of the word *leaf* and its grammatical features, including its irregular behavior in the plural. In contrast, the hockey team and its members are not leaves, and the word *leaf* does not contribute its semantic and grammatical properties to the meaning of the compound. In other words, the word *leaf* is not the head of the compound; this compound is said to be "headless." The default (regular) morphology is thus applicable, and speakers use the plural *Maple Leafs*. Headless compounds are relatively rare, but many, such as *pickpocket* and *cutpurse*, are common English words. *Pickpocket* and *cutpurse* can be recognized as headless since they do not refer to pockets or purses.

The Agentive Suffix *-er*

Agentive nouns are formed by the word formation rule "Add the suffix *-er* to a verb." Here is a tiny sample of the nouns this rule derives:

(9)

Verb	$\rightarrow$	Agentive noun ($V + $ *-er*)
(to) write		writer
(to) kill		killer
(to) play		player
(to) win		winner
(to) open		opener

The derived noun form means roughly "one who does X" or "an instrument that does X," where X is the meaning of the verb. Suppose that a new verb enters the English language, such as the verb *to xerox* (recall that *xerox* was originally a trademark for a photocopying process). Native speakers of English automatically know that this verb can be converted into an agentive noun, *xeroxer*. This word would be perfectly natural in a sentence such as *If you want to get that copied, you'll have to see John, because he's our xeroxer around here.* Hence, the process of agentive noun formation (using the suffix *-er*) establishes a relationship between verbs and nouns.

The *-able* Suffix

Another word formation rule is illustrated by the following pairs of words:

(10)
(to) read	readable
(to) wash	washable
(to) break	breakable
(to) drink	drinkable
(to) pay	payable

In the left-hand column is a set of verbs; in the right-hand column those same verbs have the suffix *-able* attached to them. There is an obvious systematic relation between the words in the two columns. To native speakers of English who know the words listed in the left-hand column, many features of the words in the right-hand column are completely predictable. That is, the relation between *read* and *readable* is not arbitrary; rather, the suffix *-able* is a morpheme that is used in a highly systematic way.

What are the various effects of the *-able* suffix? In what basic ways are the verbs changed when *-able* is added?

Obviously, there is a phonological change, which in this case is quite straightforward: when the *-able* suffix is added, the pronunciation of the verb must be augmented by a certain sequence of sounds that we can transcribe with the symbols *-əbl* (where the phonetic symbol ə stands for the vowel sound, spelled as *a*, in the suffix *-able*). With other derivational suffixes the phonological changes that are triggered by the attachment of these suffixes are not so trivial. For example, when *-ion* is added to verbs, it triggers sound changes in the verb stem itself:

(11)
relate	relation
dictate	dictation
investigate	investigation
correlate	correlation
appreciate	appreciation

Two changes are taking place. The *t*-sound in the *-ate* words is pronounced as a *sh*-sound in the corresponding *-ion* words, and no matter where the main stress (emphasis) is located in the *-ate* words, it always occurs on the vowel just before *-ion* in the *-ion* words.

The suffix *-able* introduces another obvious change when it is added to a word. Note that when *-able* attaches to verbs, the resulting words are adjectives (and hence can modify nouns):

(12)
a. This book is readable. (Compare: This book is blue.)
b. a readable book (Compare: a blue book)

The suffix *-able* also introduces a new element of meaning, roughly "able to be *X*'d," where *X* is the meaning of the verb. For example, *breakable* means roughly "able to be broken," *movable* means "able to be moved," and so on. Thus, at least three changes are associated with this suffix:

(13)
a. a phonological change (sound change)
b. a category change (part-of-speech change)
c. a semantic change (meaning change)

Other facts reveal that there are certain restrictions on the use of *-able*. For example, if we wish to express the idea that man is mortal, we cannot say *Man is dieable*. If a car is able to go, we nevertheless cannot say that it is *goable*; if John and Mary are able to cry, they are still not *cryable*. It is all too tempting to suppose that these cases are somehow exceptions or that no rule or principle governs the data in question. But if we compare the columns in (14), a generalization emerges:

(14)

Verbs taking -able	*Verbs not taking* -able
read	die
break	go
wash	cry
ply	sleep
mend	rest
debate	weep
use	sit
drive	run

The verbs on the left are *transitive* (they occur with object noun phrases), whereas the verbs on the right are *intransitive* (they do not occur with objects). For example:

(15)

a. Pat <u>read</u> <u>the book</u>. (*read + the book = transitive verb + object*)

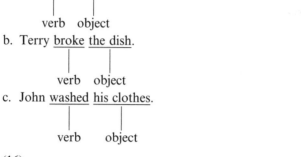

       verb object

b. Terry <u>broke</u> <u>the dish</u>.

       verb object

c. John <u>washed</u> <u>his clothes</u>.

       verb   object

(16)

a. Pat died. (*died = intransitive verb with no following object*)
b. Terry went.
c. John cried.

It seems to be the case that *-able* attaches only to transitive verbs, not to intransitive verbs. Nevertheless, just among the verbs listed in (14), there appears to be a counterexample. What about *runnable*? Consider the example in (17):

(17)
The race is runnable.

It will turn out that *run* is only an apparent counterexample, not a real one. Note that the verb *run* has both a transitive and an intransitive use:

(18)

a. Mary runs fast.
b. Mary will run the race.

The (a) example exhibits the intransitive use of *run*; the (b) example illustrates the transitive use. In a moment we will see that it is the transitive version of this verb that is available for the attachment of *-able*.

An interesting relation emerges between sentences with transitive verbs and sentences with corresponding *-able* words. A comparison of the following examples reveals what is going on:

(19)

a. We can read these books. (*these books* = object of the verb *read*)

b. These books are readable. (*these books* = subject of *are readable*)

(20)

a. We can wash these clothes.

b. These clothes are washable.

(21)

a. We can drive this car.

b. This car is drivable.

The relation that emerges is this: the subject of each (b) sentence corresponds to the object in the corresponding (a) sentence. In other words, the subject of V + *able* is always understood as the object (that which "undergoes" the action) of V. For this reason, if (at a tennis match) we say *Kim isn't beatable*, we mean that no other player can beat Kim (Kim is understood as the object of *beat*); we do not mean that Kim is unable to beat other players.

Returning to our "counterexample," we can now see that it in fact accords with the generalization just noted:

(22)

a. Mary ran the race.

b. The race is runnable.

We can now state the *-able* word formation rule as follows:

(23)

a. *Phonological change*: When *-able* is attached to a base, the pronunciation of the base is augmented by the phonetic sequence əbl.
b. *Category change*: *-able* is attached to transitive verbs and converts them into adjectives.
c. *Semantic change*: If X is the meaning of the verb, then *-able* adds the meaning "able to be X'd."

In general, then, whenever we postulate a systematic morphological relation between sets of words, we will describe (1) the systematic phonological changes, if any, (2) the category changes, if any, and (3) the semantic changes, if any, that characterize the relationship.

The Diminutive Suffix -*y*/-*ie*

Not all affixes cause the sorts of changes we have observed with the *-able* suffix. For example, English has a so-called diminutive suffix, usually spelled -*y* (or -*ie*), which is added to nouns such as those in the following pairs: *dad–daddy, mom–mommy, dog–doggy, horse–horsie.* Like *-able*, the suffix -*y* causes no phonological changes in the base word to which it is attached but does augment the base by adding its own sound. It does not change the part of speech of the base (both *dad* and *daddy* are nouns); and it causes no obvious semantic change (in the sense that both *dad* and *daddy* denote the same persons, except that the form *daddy* is used in baby talk or intimate family contexts). (Although -*y* does not cause a semantic change, it does change the context of appropriate use, which is a pragmatic change.) In other words, although affixes may cause the types of changes we have discussed in connection with *-able*, it is not generally the case that affixes *must* cause such changes, and indeed affixes vary in the types of changes they cause in the stem to which they are attached.

Given these remarks, we can observe that word formation rules state *predictable* information about complex words. We can see this very clearly from a different point of view. Suppose someone invents a nonsense word, such as *fleeb.* Even though we know nothing about the meaning of this word, if we are told that *-able* can be added to *fleeb* to form *fleebable*, we can in turn make a claim about another property of *fleeb*, namely, that it is a transitive verb. As for *fleebable*, we know that it means "able to be *fleebed*" and that it is an adjective.

Backformation

As we have seen, given a newly created verb such as *to xerox*, we can create another new word, *xeroxable*, based on the word formation rule for *-able*. In this way, word formation rules are not merely artificial creations of linguists; they correspond to processes used by speakers to create new words.

A particularly interesting case illustrating the "psychological reality" of morphological rules is a phenomenon known as *backformation*, in which word formation processes are "reversed." We can illustrate backformation with the following examples, taken from Williams 1975. It is a historical fact about English that the nouns *pedlar, beggar, hawker, stoker, scavenger, swindler, editor, burglar,* and *sculptor* all existed in the language before the corresponding verbs *to peddle, to beg, to hawk, to stoke, to scavenge, to swindle, to edit, to burgle,* and *to sculpt.* Each of these nouns denoted a general profession or activity, and speakers simply assumed that the sound at the end of each one was the agentive suffix *-er.* Having made this (mistaken) assumption, speakers could then subtract the final *-er* and arrive at a new verb—just as we can subtract the *-er* affix on *writer* and arrive at the verb *write.* In short, backformation is the process of using a word formation rule to analyze a morphologically simple word as if it were a complex word in order to arrive at a new, simpler form.

An interesting contemporary example of backformation involves the agentive suffix *-er. Laser* ends in *er* only because *e* stands for *emission* and *r* stands for *radiation* (*light amplification (by) stimulated emission (of) radiation*). Speakers quickly forget such origins, though, and before long physicists had invented the verb *to lase,* used in sentences such as *This dye, under the appropriate laboratory conditions, will lase,* where *to lase* refers to emitting radiation of a certain sort. The *er* on *laser* accidentally resembles the agentive suffix *-er,* and the word itself denotes an instrument; hence, physicists took this *er* sequence to be the agentive suffix and subtracted it to form a new verb.

Another recent example involves the plural suffix *-s.* The word in question is *kudos,* which is a synonym for "praise." The final *-s* in this word is not a plural morpheme. However, some speakers now use the word *kudo,* having mistakenly analyzed the *s* as a plural morpheme and removed it to derive a singular. In other words, they use the originally singular noun *kudos* as a plural, "praises," and their new backformation *kudo* as a singular, "praise." In the original pronunciation of *kudos,* the final *s* sounded like the *s* in *mouse.* Interestingly, the speakers who use both *kudos* and the backformation *kudo* pronounce the *s* in *kudos* like *z,* as in *dogs.* It turns out that this is no accident. Once the *s* in *kudos* has been analyzed as being the plural *-s,* it must be pronounced like *z* in this word. We will see the reason for this in chapters 3 and 4 when we discuss certain phonological properties associated with the English plural.

Other examples of backformation cited in Williams 1975 are as follows:

(24)

Existed earlier	*Formed later by backformation*
resurrection	to resurrect
preemption	to preempt
vivisection	to vivisect
electrocution	to electrocute
television	to televise
emotion	to emote
donation	to donate

It is ironic that even the word *backformation* is undergoing backformation. The technical linguistic term *backformation* existed in English first, and now one hears linguists saying *Speakers backformed word X from word Y*, creating a new verb in English, *to backform*. What is happening in all these cases is that speakers recognize that the ending *-ion* is used to create abstract nouns from verbs (e.g., *to instruct–instruction*). Hence, they can take a noun ending in *-ion*, factor out the ending, and arrive back at a verb, which has a simpler morphological shape (i.e., it lacks the ending).

Finally, a slightly different sort of backformation has applied to the word *cranberry*. Until very recently in American English, the *cran-* of *cranberry* existed in that word alone. In fact, linguists coined the term *cranberry morph* for bound bases, such as *cran-*, that occur in only one word of a language. Currently, however, even though the morpheme *cran-* is not yet an independent word, speakers of English have begun using it in other words besides *cranberry*. In particular, the fruit juice section of any supermarket will now reveal new linguistic blends such as *cranapple*, *cranicot*, and *cranprune*. By subtracting the recognizable morpheme *berry* from *cranberry*, speakers have extended the use of the morpheme *cran-* by backformation, using it in various new blends.

In sum, these cases show that morphological rules and analyses are not simply abstract aspects of morphological theory. In actuality, speakers produce (and hearers understand) new words using procedures corresponding to these rules and analyses.

2.4 INFLECTIONAL VERSUS DERIVATIONAL MORPHOLOGY

In the previous section we used the term *derivational morphology*. In the study of word formation, a distinction has often been drawn between *inflectional* and *derivational* morphology. The basis for the distinction has never been made entirely precise, but we can begin to explore it by listing the affixes of English that are referred to as *inflectional affixes* or *inflectional endings* (classified according to the part of speech each affix occurs with):

(25)

Noun inflectional suffixes

a. Plural marker *-s*
   girl–girl<u>s</u>
   (*The girls are here*)
b. Possessive marker *'s*
   Mary–Mary<u>'s</u>
   (*Mary's book*)

Verb inflectional suffixes

c. Third person present singular marker *-s*
   bake–bake<u>s</u>
   (*He bakes well*)
d. Past tense marker *-ed*
   wait–wait<u>ed</u>
   (*They waited*)
e. Progressive marker *-ing*
   sing–sing<u>ing</u>
   (*They are singing*)
f. Past participle markers *-en* or *-ed*
   eat–eat<u>en</u>
   (*She has eaten dinner*)
   bake–bak<u>ed</u>
   (*He has baked a cake*)

Adjective inflectional suffixes

g. Comparative marker *-er*
   fast–fast<u>er</u>
   (*She is faster than you*)
h. Superlative marker *-est*
   fast–fast<u>est</u>
   (*She is fastest*)

English has only the inflectional affixes listed above, and all inflectional affixes in English are suffixes (none are prefixes, unlike the situation with derivational affixes, which include both suffixes and prefixes).

The distinction between inflectional and derivational affixes in English is based on a number of factors.

First, inflectional affixes never change the category (part of speech) of the base morpheme (the morpheme to which they are attached). For example, both *eat* and *eats* are verbs; both *girl* and *girls* are nouns. In contrast, derivational affixes often change the part of speech of the base morpheme. Thus, *read* is a verb, but *readable* is an adjective. (As noted earlier, though, some derivational affixes do not change category: for example, derivational prefixes in English generally do not change the part of speech of the base morpheme to which they are attached, so that both *charge* and *recharge*, for instance, are verbs.)

Second, inflectional and derivational suffixes occur in a certain relative order within words: namely, inflectional suffixes follow derivational suffixes. Thus, in *modernize–modernizes* the inflectional -*s* follows the derivational -*ize*. If an inflectional suffix is added to a verb, as with *modernizes*, then no further derivational suffixes can be added. English has no form *modernizesable*, with inflectional -*s* followed by derivational -*able*. For these reasons it is often noted that inflectional affixes mark the "outer" layer of words, whereas derivational affixes mark the "inner" layer. These properties of derivational and inflectional affixes are summarized in table 2.3, which provides a morphological analysis of sample words containing selected English suffixes. (In the table we have ignored certain features of spelling; for example, *read* + *able* + *ity* is spelled *readability*.)

Intuitively, the function of certain derivational affixes is to create new base forms (new stems) that other derivational or inflectional affixes can attach to. Thus, the suffix -*ize* creates verbs from adjectives, and such -*ize* verbs, like other verbs, can have the inflectional ending -*s* attached to them. In this sense, then, certain derivational affixes create new members for a given part-of-speech class, whereas inflectional affixes always attach to already existing members of a given part-of-speech class. This intuitive distinction is reflected in the scheme shown in table 2.3.

Finally, inflectional and derivational affixes can be distinguished in terms of semantic relations. In the case of inflectional affixes, the relation between the meaning of the base morpheme and the meaning of the base + affix is quite regular. Hence, the meaning difference between *tree* and *trees* (singular vs. plural) is paralleled quite regularly in other similar pairs consisting of a noun and a noun + plural affix combination. In contrast, in the case of derivational affixes the relation between the

Table 2.3
Relative order of derivational and inflectional suffixes, with morphological analysis of sample words

Sample word	Base ("stem")	Derivational suffixes ("inner layer")	Inflectional suffixes ("outer layer")
modern	modern		
modernize	modern	ize	
modernizes	modern	ize	s (3rd person)
modernizers	modern	ize + er	s (plural)
write	write		
writer	write	er	
writer's	write	er	's (possessive)
readability	read	able + ity	
reading	read		ing (progressive)
big	big		
bigger	big		er (comparative)
biggest	big		est (superlative)
friend	friend		
friendly	friend	ly	
friendlier	friend	ly	er (comparative)

meaning of the base morpheme and the meaning of the base + affix is sometimes unpredictable, as we have seen. For example, the pair *fix* and *fixable* shows a simple meaning relation ("*X*" and "able to be *X*'d"); but there are also pairs such as *read–readable* and *wash–washable*, where the *-able* form has undergone *semantic drift* and has accrued new elements of meaning beyond the simple combination of the meaning of the base and the meaning of *-able*. Such semantic drift (further discussed in sections 2.2 and 2.6) is generally not found in cases of a base + inflectional affix, so that a word such as *trees* is simply the plural of *tree* and has not accrued any additional meaning.

Note that derivational and inflectional affixes can sometimes be identical in form. For example, *-ing* is an inflectional suffix that is attached to verbs. Thus, *-ing* can be attached to the verb *write* to form the verb *writing*, as in the sentence *I am writing*. However, there is also a derivational suffix *-ing*, which is attached to verbs to form a corresponding noun. For example, the verb *write* can be changed into a noun, *writing*, as in the sentence *Her lucid writings are brilliant*. In this case the suffix *-ing* changes a verb into a noun, and this category change leads us to classify *-ing* as a derivational suffix.

To sum up, then, inflectional affixes indicate certain grammatical functions of words (such as plurality or tense); they occur in a certain order relative to derivational affixes; and they are not associated with certain changes that are associated with derivational affixes (such as category changes or unpredictable meaning changes). Inflectional affixes are often discussed in terms of word sets called *paradigms*. For example, the various forms that verbs can take (*bake–bakes–baking*) form a set of words known as a *verb paradigm*. Verb paradigms in English are rather simple compared to such paradigms in, say, the Romance languages (Italian, French, Spanish, Portuguese, and others) or Latin (in which, for example, a verb such as *amāre* "to love" is said to have at least 100 inflectional forms, including *amō* "I love," *amās* "thou lovest," *amat* "he/she/it loves," *amāmus* "we love," *amem* "I may love," *amāverint* "they will have loved," *amābāmur* "we were being loved," and so on).

2.5   PROBLEMATIC ASPECTS OF MORPHOLOGICAL ANALYSIS

Now we must face one of the hard facts of life in doing morphological analysis, namely, the exceptions or apparent exceptions to many aspects of a given analysis. Three of these problems in isolating the base of a complex word involve *productivity*, *false analysis*, and *bound base morphemes*.

Productivity

We have claimed that the suffix *-able* is attached only to transitive verbs. Yet English does have a small set of nouns that seem to occur with the same suffix *-able*:

(26)

peaceable	actionable
companionable	saleable
marriageable	reasonable
impressionable	fashionable
knowledgeable	

Does this mean that word formation rule (23) is wrong? The answer seems to be no. The nouns listed in (26) form a small, closed set, and as far as anyone can tell, few words, if any, are entering English that consist of *able* attached to a noun. Using more technical terminology, we say that the attachment of *-able* to transitive verbs is *productive*—that is, it happens quite freely—but its attachment to nouns is *not productive*. New V + *able* forms continually enter the language, but the nouns in (26) are now fixed, or dead, expressions that are learned by rote, not formed, or analyzable, by a productive rule. This seems to mean that the mind/brain, when it has identified pairs of words and established a regular relationship between them (e.g., that they are related by a rule of derivational morphology), is able to overlook or ignore words that are apparent counterexamples.

False Analysis

Another general problem we must be sensitive to is the possibility of *false analysis*. Consider the following words:

(27)
hospitable
sizeable

Even though these words end in the phonetic sequence *əbl*, it is unlikely that we would want to analyze this sequence as the suffix *-able*. For one thing, *able* in these words does not seem to have the meaning "to be able," which is certainly a feature of regular (productive) *-able* words. For another thing, the *-able* suffix can itself regularly take the suffix *-ity* to form a noun:

(28)

Adjective	*Noun*
readable	readability
provable	provability
breakable	breakability

But this is not possible with the words listed in (27): *hospitability* and *sizeability* are not possible English words. We do not speak of the *hospitability* of our host or the *sizeability* of the crowd. In two respects, then, *able* in the words of (27) differs significantly from the productive suffix *-able*; hence, it would seem to be a false analysis to claim that the words of (27) contain the productive suffix *-able*. These words simply happen to end in a sequence spelled *able*, and they bear only an accidental resemblance to words with the real suffix *-able*. Finally, put into terms we used earlier, *able* is not the head of a complex word consisting of *size* and *able*.

Returning to the words in (26), we might try to make the case that these words end accidentally in the phonetic sequence *əbl* and that it would be a false analysis to claim that it is the *-able* suffix. Against this idea we note that some of the words do seem to include the meaning "be able" (e.g., *marriageable* "eligible to marry"), and the *-ity* noun form *marriageability* does seem possible (although some speakers of English might well reject it). Other words of (26), however, are not so regular. In any event, in carrying out a morphological analysis we must always be careful to determine whether the processes in question are productive and whether a certain analysis might be a false analysis.

Compositionality also appears to play a major role in determining a morphological analysis. Note that the meaning of *readable* is partially compositional: something is "able to be read." But the meaning of *sizeable* is not based on the verb *size* and the suffix *-able*. The meaning "able to be sized" could exist if one assigned *size* the meaning "to make a certain size, or to group according to size." Thus, *John sized the lumber* might be used to describe John's measuring lumber, or perhaps John's grouping pieces of lumber according to size. But this is not what the adjective *sizeable* means. The meaning "very large" associated with *sizeable* is arbitrarily assigned, much like the meaning "domestic mammal closely related to the common wolf" is assigned to the sequence of sounds *d-o-g*.

Bound Base Morphemes

Closely related to these issues is another classic problem of morphology, namely, the case of a complex word with a recognizable suffix or prefix, attached to a base that is not an existing word of the language. For example, among the *-able* words are words such as *malleable* and *feasible*. In both cases the suffix *-able* (spelled *ible* in the second case because of a different historical origin for the suffix) has the regular meaning "be able," and in both cases the *-ity* form is possible (*malleability* and *feasibility*). We have no reason to suspect that *able/ible* here is not the real suffix *-able*. Yet if it is, then *malleable* must be broken down as *malle + able* and *feasible* as *feas + ible*; but there are no existing words (free morphemes) in English such as *malle* or *feas*, or even *malley* or *fease*. We thus have to allow for the existence of a complex word whose base exists only in that complex word (recall the earlier discussion of the bound base *cran-*, which occurs only in *cranberry* and a few other words).

The problems discussed so far are problems in isolating the base of a complex word: (1) sometimes the base (the form to which the affix is attached) comes from a closed set of forms no longer productive as the base for the word formation rule, (2) sometimes one must be alert to the possibility of a completely false analysis of the base, and (3) sometimes the base may not be an existing word. All of these problems have to do with correctly analyzing how the complex word is structured.

2.6 SPECIAL TOPICS

The Meaning of Complex Words

Another difficulty in morphological analysis is how to analyze the meaning of complex words and how to determine the relation between the meaning of an entire complex word and the meanings of its parts. This relates to the earlier discussion of semantic drift.

First, consider some complex words that appear to have a predictable meaning. For example, *fixable* seems to mean nothing more than "able to be fixed," *mendable* means "able to be mended," and *inflatable* means "able to be inflated." The meaning of these *-able* words seems to be a regular combination of the meaning of the verb stem and the simplest meaning of the *-able* suffix.

However, in other cases certain complications arise. Take, for example, the words *readable, payable, questionable,* and *washable.* The word *readable* does not mean simply "able to be read." When we say that a book is readable, we usually mean that it is well written, has a good style, and in general is a good example of some type of literature. A banker who says that a bill is payable on October 1 does not mean simply that the bill "can be paid" on that date—normally, we would understand *payable* as meaning "should be paid." If a theory or an explanation is *questionable,* it is not merely the case that it can be questioned. After all, any statement can be questioned, even very well established theories. Rather, a questionable theory or account is one that is, in fact, dubious and suspect. Finally, the word *washable* does not mean merely "able to be washed"; we in fact use the word in a very specialized way, to refer to certain types of objects, notably fabrics. Hence, though we can talk about washing a car, it would be somewhat odd to say that the car is washable (even if this is, strictly speaking, true). It is perfectly natural, however, to say that a shirt is washable or that the plastic parts of a table are washable (whereas the wooden parts are not).

These facts illustrate in a particularly clear way that the meanings of many complex words are not merely composites of the meanings of their parts. The word *washable* is more than a composite of *wash* and

-able; rather, it has its own additional elements of meaning. When a word accrues some additional feature of meaning independent from its morphological origin, as *washable* has, we say that the word has undergone *semantic drift*. At least for the cases given here, the additional meaning, over and above the basic meaning of the complex word, involves a narrowing or restricting of the more general meaning of the complex word.

More on Compounds

In section 2.3 we briefly discussed a way to create new words, namely, compounding. Creating complex words by way of combining simpler ones provides a very rich source of new words. Compounding is extremely productive. Consider the following Noun + Noun compounds; *lynx-brush, gin-life, lettuce-dog, house-roach, goat-ghost*. Probably, you have never encountered any of these compounds before. More than likely, they won't be found in any dictionary. Though you may be uncertain about their meanings (indeed, each has a range of reasonable meanings), you will certainly judge them as being plausible words. That is, they are possible, though not necessarily occurring words. As mentioned earlier, there is no limit to the number of compounds that can be produced— more evidence that the dictionary is not a very good representation of our knowledge of words.

In table 2.2 we listed several types of compounds in English. Among these are Noun + Noun (*landlord, snail mail*), Adjective + Adjective (*icy-cold, red-hot*), Adjective + Noun (*blackboard, high chair*), and Noun + Adjective (*earthbound, sky-blue*). All of the examples involve *primary* compounds; that is, each word that makes up the compound is morphologically simple. Speakers create new compounds of this type relatively easily (to use the technical term, such compounding is quite *productive*).

There are also compounds that involve combining morphologically complex words. In particular, we will be looking at *synthetic* (or verbal) compounds: those two-word English compounds in which the second word is *deverbal* (derived from a verb). An example of a deverbal noun is our now familiar example *baker*, a noun derived from a verb by attaching the agentive suffix *-er*. Verbal compounds exhibit some rather interesting properties. Consider the examples in table 2.4. Why are some of these combinations of adjective (noun, or adverb) + deverbal noun good, whereas others are clearly odd? That is, why is *good-looker* well formed,

Table 2.4
Verbal compounds. (Adapted from Roeper and Siegel 1978.)

	Possible	Impossible
I	good-looker odd-seeming clever-sounding	*grim-wanting *clever-supporting
II	fast-mover late-bloomer rapidly-rising	*quick-owner *fast-finding *rapidly-raising
III	wage-earner trend-setter profit-sharing	*child-bloomer *cat-seeming *cake-riser
IV	church-goer cave-dweller opera singer apartment-living	*shortstop-thrower (= throw something to shortstop) *doctor-grafting (= grafting of skin by a doctor)

but not *grim-wanting? In order to tease out the relevant differences, let us turn to the original verbs. Consider the sentences in table 2.5. In groups I–III a certain pattern emerges. Compare *Sarah looks good* with *Sam wants grim*. (The asterisk (*) indicates that the sentence is ill formed (or ungrammatical).) *Good* and *grim* in these sentences are also the first words in their corresponding compounds in group I of table 2.4. *Grim-wanting* is not an acceptable compound, and interestingly, the sentence based on the verb *want* with *grim* adjacent to the verb is also unacceptable. However, *good-looker* is a well-formed compound, and the sentence based on the verb *look* with *good* to its right is also well formed. Each example exhibits this pattern. That is, whenever the compound is well formed, the first word of that compound can appear in a sentence to the immediate right of the verb (ignoring *a*) that corresponds to the second word of the compound.

Many of the examples in group IV illustrate that the first word in the compound can correspond to a noun that occurs in a prepositional phrase immediately following the verb in the sentence (*go to church, dwell in caves*). The compounds in group IV that are ill formed (such as *shortstop-thrower*) do not conform to this pattern. In the example *The*

Table 2.5
Base verbs in a syntactic context

	Possible	Impossible
I	Sarah *looks good.* John *seems odd.* Jill *sounds clever.*	*Sam *wants grim.* *John *supports clever.*
II	The cat *moves fast.* John *bloomed late.* The water is *rising rapidly.*	*The man *owns quick.* *John *found fast.* *Bob is *raising rapidly.*
III	Everyone *earns a wage.* Celebrities *set trends.* Corporations *share profits.*	*The mother *blooms the child.* *It *seems cat.* *Heat *rises the cake.*
IV	Some people *go to church.* Bats *dwell in caves.* Jessye Norman *sings at the opera.* Some people *live in apartments.*	The pitcher *threw* the ball to the *shortstop.* *The doctor grafted* the skin skillfully.

pitcher threw the ball to the shortstop, the noun phrase *the ball* intervenes between the verb and the prepositional phrase containing *shortstop*. In the example *The doctor grafted the skin skillfully*, it is the noun phrase *the skin* that immediately follows *grafted*, not the noun phrase *the doctor*.

The pattern that has emerged can be captured by the following statement (an adaptation of Roeper and Siegel's (1978) *First Sister Principle*):

(29)
All deverbal compounds of the form W1 + W2 (= word 1 + word 2) are formed by taking W1—the first noun, adjective, or adverb that follows the verb (W2) in a sentence—and combining it with W2.

Exactly how to incorporate such a condition in a theory of compounds is the focus of much current research. Our interest here is to illustrate that compounding, like other morphological and grammatical processes, involves referring to such notions as category (here, "verb") and to properties of that category. Verbal compounding does not involve random combinations of words. Quite the contrary: just as the suffix *-able* cannot attach to just any verb, so not just any word can serve as W1 with just any deverbal W2. Thus, compounding is governed by principles that are sensitive to numerous properties of the words involved.

Morphological Anaphora

One very important theme in current linguistic studies concerns *anaphora*. Anaphora involves a relation between, for example, a pronoun and an antecedent noun phrase whereby the two are understood as being used to refer to the same thing. The linguistic system utilizes various mechanisms to signal this phenomenon. Below we examine morphological data related to anaphora.

In English the morpheme *self* functions to signal when two phrases are being used to pick out one individual:

(30)
Mary sees her*self*.

The person who is "seeing," Mary, is the same person who is being "seen." *Self* attaches not only to pronouns but also to other categories of words:

(31)
admirer	self-admirer
denial	self-denial
amusement	self-amusement
deceived	self-deceived
employed	self-employed
employable	self-employable
closing	self-closing
destructive	self-destructive
inhibitory	self-inhibitory

The data in (31) illustrate that *self* may attach to a noun (*admirer, denial, amusement*) or an adjective (*deceived, employed, destructive*). However, *self* does not attach to just any noun or adjective:

(32)
*self-red
*self-cat
*self-chalk

In fact, notice that the nouns and adjectives in the left-hand column of (31) are all morphologically complex and that they are all based on verbs (*employable–employ, inhibitory–inhibit, amusement–amuse*). However, *self* does not attach directly to verbs:

(33)

deceive	*self-deceive(s)
employ	*self-employ(s)
deny	*self-deny(s)
admire	*self-admire(s)

Clearly, there is some kind of dependency between *self* and the verb, yet *self* cannot attach directly to the verb. We can make the following descriptive observation: the deverbal nouns and adjectives in (31) are all based on transitive verbs (note in contrast that *self-fidgety*, based on the intransitive verb *fidget*, is odd):

(34)
admire the child
deny the truth
amuse the class
deceive the public
employ the elderly
close the door
destroy the argument
inhibit the boy

This is not too surprising since *self* functions to indicate that, for example, the subject and the object refer to the same entity. Therefore, a *self-admirer* is someone who admires himself or herself, *self-destruction* involves someone destroying himself or herself, and so on. This is another instance of word formation where the properties of the base word are crucial. In this case the relevant properties may have more to do with whether or not the word is "transitive" than with the category to which the word belongs (though there must be an explanation for why verbs—even though they may be transitive—do not allow *self* to be attached).

In the chapters that follow, we will be looking at other linguistic devices for signaling "coreference."

Classes of Derivational Affixes

In section 2.4 we provided an overview of a distinction that is often made in morphological studies, namely, the distinction between derivational and inflectional affixes. We now present data that many linguists argue reveals that a distinction should be made between types of derivational affixes.

Table 2.6
The noun-forming suffixes -*ity* and -*ness*

Adjective	-*ity* noun	-*ness* noun
luminous	luminosity	luminousness
passive	passivity	passiveness
impetuous	impetuosity	impetuousness

Table 2.7
The suffixes -*ity* and -*ness* compared with respect to location of stress on the base. (Stressed vowels are capitalized.)

Adjective	-*ity* noun	-*ness* noun
lUminous	luminOsity	lUminousness
pAssive	passIvity	pAssiveness
impEtuous	impetuOsity	impEtuousness

Consider the examples in table 2.6. Both -*ity* and -*ness* are affixes that attach to adjectives and derive nouns. The derived nouns in table 2.6, whether ending in -*ity* or in -*ness*, mean roughly "state or quality of being *X*," where *X* stands for the meaning of the adjective (e.g., *luminosity/ luminousness* "state or quality of being luminous"). This is what the two affixes have in common. They differ, however, in important ways. First, consider the data in table 2.7. Notice that the -*ity* nouns exhibit a different stress pattern from both the adjectives and the corresponding -*ness* nouns. In the -*ity* nouns the stress "moves" to the syllable (or vowel) that is to the immediate left of the affix (*luminous–luminosity*), whereas in the -*ness* nouns the stress is the same as in the adjective (*luminous–luminousness*). That is, affixation of -*ity* alters the stress pattern, whereas affixation of -*ness* does not.

For a second difference between the two affixes, consider the data in tables 2.8 and 2.9. Notice that -*ity* cannot attach to any of the derived words in table 2.8 whereas -*ness* can. What accounts for the differing distribution of these two affixes? Many recent analyses involve recognizing that there are two different types of derivational affixes. For our purposes we will refer to -*ity* as belonging to class I and to -*ness*, -*less*, and -*ish* as belonging to class II (see table 2.10). An affix belonging to class II may attach to a morphologically complex word that contains a class I (or a class II) affix, but the reverse is not possible; namely, a class I

Table 2.8
The adjective-forming suffixes -*less* and -*ish*

Base	Adjective
Noun	-*less*
taste	taste*less*
nose	nose*less*
voice	voice*less*
friend	friend*less*
Noun	-*ish*
boy	boy*ish*
bull	bull*ish*
book	book*ish*
lump	lump*ish*
Adjective	-*ish*
blue	blu*ish*
damp	damp*ish*
short	short*ish*
clever	clever*ish*

Table 2.9
The suffixes -*ity* and -*ness* compared with respect to the admissibility of derived adjectival bases

-*less*/-*ish* adjective + -*ity*	-*less*/-*ish* adjective + -*ness*
*tasteless*ity*	tasteless*ness*
*noseless*ity*	noseless*ness*
*voiceless*ity*	voiceless*ness*
*friendless*ity*	friendless*ness*
*boyish*ity*	boyish*ness*
*bullish*ity*	bullish*ness*
*bookish*ity*	bookish*ness*
*lumpish*ity*	lumpish*ness*
*bluish*ity*	bluish*ness*
*dampish*ity*	dampish*ness*
*shortish*ity*	shortish*ness*
*cleverish*ity*	cleverish*ness*

Table 2.10
A partial list of class I and class II affixes in English. (This classification is based on Selkirk 1982, where it is also argued that *-ize*, *-ment*, *-able*, and *un-* belong to both classes.)

Class I	Class II
-ous	-less
-ive	-ish
in-	non-
-ory	-er
-al	-y
-ify	

affix cannot attach to a morphologically complex word that contains a class II affix.

So far we have simply pointed out a distributional puzzle (for *-ness* and *-ity*) and made an assumption about the division of derivational affixes into two classes. To actually justify positing these two classes, much more evidence and analysis is needed; and any proposed solution must be incorporated into morphological theory in general.

Exercises

1. In this chapter we noted that *radar* and *laser* are acronyms. List three other recent English words that are acronyms and state their origin.

2. Below is a list of acronyms. Provide original words for as many of these acronyms as you can.
UNICEF
OPEC
MADD
AIDS
NATO

3. List three recent words that, like *DOB* (date of birth), are alphabetic abbreviations, and state their origin.

4. Consider the word *dissing* in the sentence *Are you dissing me?*
A. What does *dissing* mean?
B. What part of speech does *dissing* belong to? Defend your answer.
C. What is the (social) origin of *dissing* (or *diss*)? That is, what social group first started using this word?

D. How was *diss* formed? (That is, is it a blend? an acronym? a clipping?) Defend your answer.

5. The following quotation is from a *San Francisco Chronicle* opinion piece regarding educational issues by Debra J. Saunders (July 18, 1994):

Politicians and bureaucrats who ignore parents' democratic—small d—rush on this *educrats'* Tiananmen Square may find themselves on the wrong side of a populist rebellion.

A. What is an *educrat*?
B. What kind of word is *educrat*? That is, how was it formed?

6. For the purposes of this exercise, use only the words in the following list:

sidewalk
daughter
laugh
cactus
alligator

A. Using these words, invent five new compounds and state the meaning of each one.
B. What would you guess is a possible meaning of the compound *sidewalk alligator cactus*?
C. What is the "head" of the compound listed in question B? State the reason(s) for your answer.

7. English has a suffix *-en* whose use is illustrated in the following lists:

List A	List B
red	redden
black	blacken
mad	madden
soft	soften
hard	harden
sweet	sweeten
short	shorten
wide	widen
sharp	sharpen

In regard to these data, answer the following questions:

A. What part of speech does the suffix *-en* attach to? That is, what is the part of speech of the words in list A? For evidence to support your answer, consider what other morphemes attach to the words in list A (consult the section "Grammatical Categories (Parts of Speech)").
B. When the suffix *-en* is attached to a word, what part of speech is the resulting word? That is, what part of speech do the words in list B belong to? Give some specific morphological properties of one of the words in list B, in order to justify your answer.
C. In what way does the suffix *-en* change the meaning of the word it is attached to?

8. English also has a prefix *un-*, whose use is illustrated in the following lists:

List A	List B
true	untrue
likely	unlikely
acceptable	unacceptable
wise	unwise
real	unreal
common	uncommon
natural	unnatural
graceful	ungraceful
refined	unrefined
tamed	untamed

A. What part of speech are the words that the prefix *un-* attaches to? That is, what part of speech are the words in list A?

B. When *un-* is prefixed to a word, what part of speech is the resulting new word? That is, what part of speech are the words in list B?

C. In what way does the prefix *un-* change the meaning of the word it attaches to?

D. New words such as *Uncola* (a type of soft drink) and *Uncar* (used in a bus company advertisement to refer to a bus) have been added to the English language. Given the pattern established in lists A and B, why are words such as *Uncola* and *Uncar* "irregular"?

9. Exercise 8 involved examples of a prefix *un-* in English. Now consider a new set of data, involving another prefix *un-*:

List A	List B
tie	untie
wrap	unwrap
cover	uncover
wind	unwind
dress	undress
fold	unfold
buckle	unbuckle
lock	unlock
fasten	unfasten
stick	unstick

How does the prefix *un-* illustrated here differ from the prefix *un-* illustrated in exercise 8? To answer this, answer the following specific questions:

A. What is the part of speech of the words that this second prefix *un-* attaches to? That is, what part of speech are the words in list A? Where a given word could be classified as belonging to more than one part of speech, what is the part of speech that *un-* attaches to?

B. When this prefix *un-* is attached to a word, what part of speech does the resulting new word belong to? That is, what part of speech are the words in list B?

C. In what way does this prefix *un-* change the meaning of the word that it is attached to? Describe this meaning change as carefully as you can.

D. How is the meaning change associated with this prefix *un-* different from the meaning change associated with the prefix *un-* illustrated in exercise 8?

10. Based on the evidence in exercises 8 and 9, we note that English has two prefixes *un-*. Now consider the word *unlockable*. If you think about this word long enough, you will realize that it has two different meanings. Show how these two different meanings are in part determined by the fact that English has two different prefixes *un-*.

11. Consider the word *uninstaller*. Answer the following questions:

A. Which *un-* prefix is involved? Defend your answer.

B. What is the structure of *uninstaller*? That is, which affix attaches first, *un-* or *-er*? Defend your answer.

12. Use the following two lists for this exercise:

List A	*List B*
redo	*rego
rewrite	*recry
rework	*resleep
recook	*resit
reimport	*revanish
rebuild	*rechange
restate	*reelapse
reset	*redie
resharpen	
reshape	

State the word formation rule for the prefix *re-*. Follow the format given for the *-able* rule in this chapter (i.e., (23)). In particular, answer the following questions:

A. What phonological changes, if any, does the prefix *re-* cause in the word or stem to which it attaches?

B. What part(s) of speech does the prefix *re-* attach to? Note the contrast between list A and list B. What is the difference between these sets of words?

C. When *re-* is attached to a word or stem, what is the part of speech of the resulting word or stem?

D. In general, what meaning change(s) are caused by the addition of the prefix *re-*? In the ideal case, what meaning does the prefix *re-* add to the word or stem to which it is attached?

E. Can you find any words with *re-* that have erratic or unexpected meanings? (Are there any *re-* words that systematically mean more than you would expect from the simple meaning of *re-* and the simple meaning of the base?)

F. Why can you *reshoot* a movie but not *reshoot*, say, an animal?

G. Why are the following *re-* words problematic? Discuss three of them: *reduce, reflect, refine, refuse, repeat, relax, release, renew, replicate, revive, remember.*

13. Analyze the following English words, in the manner shown in table 2.3:

a. orderliness   e. fastest
b. capitalizers   f. digestion
c. lengthen   g. employee
d. employer   h. mesmerize

14. In section 2.4 ("Inflectional versus Derivational Morphology") we mentioned that the suffix *-ize* creates a verb from an adjective. As the following example shows, *-ize* is a very productive affix:

Dan Lungren, attorney general of California, was quoted in *Time* (June 6, 1994) as saying, "I call it the *Oprahization* of the jury pool."

A. Discuss what the novel *-ize* word in this quotation means.
B. How does this *-ize* word differ from the examples mentioned in section 2.4?
C. Provide at least three of your own examples that are of the type illustrated in the quotation.

15. On June 19, 1994, the word *"Cops"-ization* appeared in the *San Francisco Chronicle*:

It was the most vivid example yet of the blurring of news and entertainment, another step in the *"Cops"-ization* of TV.

A. What do you think *"Cops"-ization* means?
B. *"Cops"-ization* appears to be a counterexample to the claim that inflectional affixes (*-s* in this case) must appear at the periphery of words and not sandwiched between the base and the derivational affixes. Can you provide an account of *"Cops"-ization* that is consistent with this constraint? That is, how might one analyze *"Cops"-ization* such that it is consistent with the constraint?

16. Compounding provides a common means to create new vocabulary items in most of the world's languages. Consider the following base morphemes from Classical Nahuatl (Aztec):

yaka "nose, point"
o' "road"
kal "house"
a "water"
tepet "hill"
ozca "throat"

Recall that English compounds are right-headed; the meaning of the rightmost member of the compound, its head, is somehow central to the meaning of the whole compound. Thus, a *string apron* is an apron and an *apron string* is a string. Nahuatl compounds are also right-headed. Combine two or more of the Nahuatl morphemes to create a word whose translation corresponds to the English word on the left. The first is done as an example.

"ravine"	tepet-ozca "hill throat"
"boat"	_____
"canal"	_____
"bow of a ship"	_____
"street"	_____

Further Reading

General

For introductions to various background concepts in morphology, see Jespersen 1911, vol. 6; Sapir 1921, chap. 4; Bloomfield 1933, chaps. 13, 14; Adams 1973; Aronoff 1976; Marchand 1969; and Matthews 1991. See Pinker 1999 for an extensive and interesting argument for the *nature of the mental lexicon* and for *combinatorial rules* that enable a person to produce and comprehend novel words and sentences.

Special Topics

For detailed discussions of *compounding*, see Roeper and Siegel 1978, Selkirk 1982, Lieber 1983, Pinker 1995, and references cited there. *Anaphora* phenomena have played a central role in developing and motivating changes in theories of syntax, semantics, morphology, and pragmatics. The literature on this topic is vast. A clear introduction to anaphora from a syntactic perspective can be found in Perlmutter and Soames 1979; see also Reinhart and Reuland 1993 and the references cited there. To review arguments for *classifying derivational affixes* into distinct categories, see Kiparsky 1982, Selkirk 1982, Di Sciullo and Williams 1987, and the references cited there.

Journals

Language, Linguistic Inquiry, Natural Language & Linguistic Theory, The Linguistic Review, The Journal of Linguistic Research, Journal of Linguistics, Linguistic Analysis, Lingua, Studia Linguistica

Bibliography

Adams, V. 1973. *An introduction to Modern English word formation.* London: Longman.

Allen, M. 1978. Morphological investigations. Doctoral dissertation, University of Connecticut, Storrs.

Aronoff, M. 1976. *Word formation in generative grammar.* Cambridge, Mass.: MIT Press.

Bloomfield, L. 1933. *Language.* New York: Holt, Rinehart and Winston.

Bradley, D. C., M. F. Garrett, and E. B. Zurif. 1980. Syntactic deficits in Broca's aphasia. In D. Caplan, ed., *Biological studies of mental processes.* Cambridge, Mass.: MIT Press.

Clark, E., and H. Clark. 1979. When nouns surface as verbs. *Language* 55, 767–811.

Di Sciullo, A. M., and E. Williams. 1987. *On the definition of word*. Cambridge, Mass.: MIT Press.

Jackendoff, R. 1975. Morphological and semantic regularities in the lexicon. *Language* 51, 639–671.

Jespersen, O. 1911. *A Modern English grammar*. London: Allen and Unwin.

Kiparsky, P. 1982. Lexical phonology and morphology. In I. S. Yang, ed., *Linguistics in the morning calm*. Seoul: Hanshin.

Lieber, R. 1983. Argument linking and compounds in English. *Linguistic Inquiry* 14, 251–285.

Marchand, H. 1969. *The categories and types of present-day English word-formation*. 2nd ed. Munich: Beck.

Matthews, P. H. 1972. *Inflectional morphology*. Cambridge: Cambridge University Press.

Matthews, P. H. 1991. *Morphology: An introduction to the theory of word structure*. 2nd ed. Cambridge: Cambridge University Press.

Perlmutter, D., and S. Soames. 1979. *Syntactic argumentation and the structure of English*. Berkeley and Los Angeles: University of California Press.

Pinker, S. 1995. *The language instinct*. New York: HarperPerennial.

Pinker, S. 1999. *Words and rules: The ingredients of language*. New York: Basic Books.

Reinhart, T., and E. Reuland. 1993. Reflexivity. *Linguistic Inquiry* 24, 657–720.

Roeper, T., and M. Siegel. 1978. A lexical transformation for verbal compounds. *Linguistic Inquiry* 9, 199–260.

Sapir, E. 1921. *Language*. New York: Harcourt, Brace & World.

Selkirk, E. O. 1982. *The syntax of words*. Cambridge, Mass.: MIT Press.

Siegel, D. C. 1974. Topics in English morphology. Doctoral dissertation, MIT.

Williams, J. M. 1975. *Origins of the English language*. New York: Free Press.

Zepeda, O. 1983. *A Papago grammar*. Tucson: University of Arizona Press.

Chapter 3

Phonetics and Phonemic Transcription

We take it for granted that we can write a language with discrete symbols (e.g., an alphabet). However, speech is for the most part continuous; neither the acoustic signal (the sound wave) nor the movements of the speech articulators (e.g., the tongue and lips) can be broken down into the kind of discrete units that correspond to the units represented by written symbols. For example, look at the waveform of the word *learn* in figure 3.1. (A waveform graphs changes in the amplitude of the sound wave (vertical axis) against time (horizontal axis).) Like this one, the waveforms of most speech samples have continuous patterns; clearly, the discrete symbols of written speech are not reflected in these acoustic representations.

You can observe an overlap in articulation by comparing the pronunciation of the syllables *bee, bah, boo*. You will find that when you pronounce the *b*, your tongue is already in position to pronounce the "following" vowel. Moreover, you will find that your lips are already pursed when you pronounce the *b* in *boo*, even though the pursing is part of the following vowel.

A writing system, with its set of linearly ordered discrete symbols, turns out to be an idealization of the physical instantiations of speech. So, as we begin our study of the properties of the speech sounds of language, we see that what appears to be the most concrete aspect of speech—alphabetic representation—is actually highly abstract in nature.

3.1 SOME BACKGROUND CONCEPTS

Phonetics is concerned with how speech sounds are produced (articulated) in the vocal tract (a field of study known as *articulatory phonetics*), as well as with the physical properties of the speech sound waves gen-

Figure 3.1
Waveform of the English word *learn*. The vertical axis displays the changes in the amplitude of the sound wave and the horizontal axis measures time.

Table 3.1
Different pronunciations of the plural morpheme

Example word	cat<u>s</u>	dog<u>s</u>	bush<u>es</u>
Pronunciation of plural morpheme for that word	<u>s</u>-sound	<u>z</u>-sound	vowel + <u>z</u>

erated by the larynx and vocal tract (a field known as *acoustic phonetics*). Whereas the term *phonetics* usually refers to the study of the articulatory and acoustic properties of sounds, the term *phonology*, the subject of chapter 4, is often used to refer to the abstract principles that govern the distribution of sounds in a language. In this chapter we will examine the ways in which speech sounds are produced, discussing the articulation of English speech sounds in particular. We will focus on articulation rather than on the acoustic properties of speech sounds; for further information on acoustic phonetics, see Ladefoged 1994 and Johnson 1997.

In chapter 2 we discussed the English plural morpheme *-s*. It turns out that plural nouns formed by attaching the plural morpheme, which is a suffix, do not all end with the same sound (see table 3.1). In chapter 4 we will explore a principled account of the difference, but first we must study the nature of these sounds in order to be equipped with the relevant notions and vocabulary.

Physiology of Speech Production

At its fundamental level the speech signal is a rapidly flowing series of noises that are produced inside the throat, mouth, and nasal passages and that radiate out from the mouth and sometimes the nose. One commonsense view is that learning to speak a language requires only the control of a few muscles that move the lips, jaw, and tongue. These anatomical structures are the most easily observed in any case. In reality the situation is much more complex, for over 100 muscles exercise direct and continuous control during the production of the sound waves that carry speech (Lenneberg 1967). These sound waves are produced by a complex interaction of (1) an outward flow of air from the lungs, (2) modifications of the airflow at the larynx (the Adam's apple or "voice box" in the throat), and (3) additional modifications of the airflow by position and movement of the tongue and other anatomical structures of the vocal tract. We will consider each of these components in turn.

Airflow from the Lungs during Speech
The flow of air from the lungs during speech differs in several important respects from the airflow during quiet breathing. First, during speech, three to four times as much air is exhaled as during quiet breathing. Second, in speech the normal breathing rhythm is changed radically: inhalation is more rapid and exhalation is much more drawn out. Third, the number of breaths per unit time decreases during speech. Fourth, the flow of air is unimpeded during quiet breathing, whereas in speech the airflow encounters resistance from the obstructions and closures that occur in the throat and mouth. While these alterations in the normal breathing pattern are occurring during speech, the function of breathing (exchange of oxygen and carbon dioxide) continues with no discomfort to the speaker.

One of the primary mechanisms for expanding the lungs during both quiet breathing and speech is the contraction of the *diaphragm* (see figure 3.2), a sheet of muscular tissue that separates the chest cavity from the abdominal region. This contraction causes the diaphragm to lower and flatten out, leading to an increase in the size of the chest cavity. The other primary mechanism for the expansion of the chest cavity is the set of muscles between the ribs in the rib cage (the *external intercostals*). Contraction of these muscles causes the ribs to lift up, and because of the way that the ribs are hinged, they swing out, increasing the volume of the chest cavity. Since the lungs are attached to the walls of the chest cavity, when the chest cavity expands, either from diaphragm contraction or from rib movement, the lungs, being elastic, also expand. As the lungs expand, air flows in, up to the point when inhalation is completed. During quiet breathing the diaphragm relaxes at this point, and the

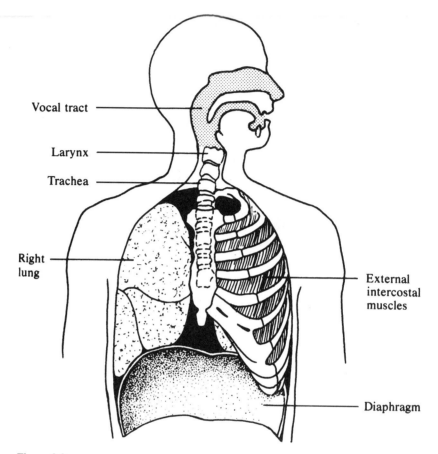

Figure 3.2
Major anatomical structures involved in the production of speech. Air driven
from the lungs through the trachea and the larynx into the vocal tract is the
primary source of the acoustic energy in speech. The lungs are attached to the
chest wall and diaphragm, and when the diaphragm lowers, the size of the chest
cavity is increased, the elastic lungs expand, and air flows inward. Similarly, air
also flows inward when the muscles between the ribs (the *external intercostals*) contract and the rib cage expands outward, thus increasing the size of the chest
cavity. The muscles of the diaphragm and rib cage remain active during speech,
acting as a check on the outward flow of air.

stretched lungs begin to shrink, allowing air to flow out quite rapidly at the beginning, as with air escaping from a filled balloon. During speech, however, the muscles of the diaphragm and the rib cage continue to be active, restraining the lungs from emptying too rapidly. Without this checking force, speech would be loud at first and then become quieter as the lungs emptied. Thus, humans have developed special adaptations for breathing during speech: speech is not merely "added" to the breathing cycle; rather, the breathing cycle is adapted to the needs of speech.

The Role of the Larynx in Speech
The first point where the airflow from the lungs encounters a controlled resistance is at the *larynx*, a structure of muscle and cartilage located at the upper end of the *trachea* (or *windpipe*) (see figure 3.2). The resistance can be controlled by the different positions and tensions in the *vocal cords* (or *vocal folds*), two muscular bands of tissue that stretch from front to back within the larynx (see figure 3.3). During quiet breathing the cords are relaxed and spread apart to allow the free flow of air to and from the lungs. During swallowing, however, the cords are drawn tightly together to keep foreign material from entering the lungs. For speech the most important feature of the vocal cords is that they can be made to vibrate if the airflow between them is sufficiently rapid and if they have the proper tension and proximity to each other. This rapid vibration is called *voicing* (or *phonation*). The *frequency* of vibration determines the perceived *pitch*. Because the vocal cords of adult males are larger in size, their frequency of vibration is relatively lower than the frequency of vibration in females and children. The pitch of adult males' voices is thus lower than that of females and children.

Voicing is the "extra noise," the "buzz" that accompanies the production of the *z*-sound version of the plural morpheme shown in table 3.1. We say that the *z*-sound is *voiced*, whereas the *s*-sound is *voiceless*. The lack of voicing in *s* is due to the fact that the vocal cords are more spread apart and tenser than during the production of *z*, thus creating conditions that inhibit vocal cord vibration.

Other speech sounds found in human language also require other types of vocal cord configurations and movements. We will examine some of these later in the chapter.

Speakers have a high degree of control over the sounds the vocal cords can produce. The ability to sing a melody, for example, depends on being

Figure 3.3
View of the vocal cords. The mechanical vibration of these cords during speech is called *voicing* (or *phonation*). The space between the cords is called the *glottis*.

able to change the vocal cord positions and tensions rapidly and accurately to hit the right notes. Although the ability to sing well is subject to much individual variation, the ability to control the vocal cord positions and tensions necessary for speech is well within the ability of all normal speakers.

Finally, the space between the vocal cords is called the *glottis* (see figure 3.3), and linguists frequently refer to sounds that involve a constriction or closure of this space between the vocal cords as *glottal sounds*.

The Vocal Tract
The *vocal tract*, the region above the vocal cords that includes the (oral) pharynx, the oral cavity, and the nasal cavity, is the space within which the speech sounds of human language are produced (see figure 3.4). We will examine the anatomical features of the vocal tract in the course of discussing how the consonants and vowels of English are formed.

(1) Nasal cavity

(2) Hard palate
(3) Alveolar ridge

(4) Labial region
(lips)

(5) Tongue root

(6) Vocal cords
(glottal region)

(7) Trachea
(tube to lungs)

(8) Velum (soft palate)
(9) Tongue blade
(10) Tongue tip (apex)
(11) Tongue body
(12) Uvula
(13) (Oral) pharynx

(14) Epiglottis

(15) Esophagus
(tube to stomach)

Figure 3.4
Cross section of the human vocal tract

3.2   THE REPRESENTATION OF SPEECH SOUNDS

Phonemic Transcription versus English Orthography

What underlies the continuous flow of human speech is, in fact, a sequence of articulatory configurations that can be represented by a series of discrete units. The basis of the sound component of human language is a *discrete combinatorial* system that is "smeared" together in the overlapping fashion discussed earlier, much like the digital-to-analog conversion that occurs in modern electronic audio devices.

This chapter will introduce you to the discrete units (the *phonemes*) that underlie the articulation of Modern English. In discussing the sounds of English, and the sounds of human language in general, we need a set of symbols to *represent* those sounds. What sort of representational system will be most useful? If we try using the conventional English *orthography* (spelling system) to represent speech sounds, we face problems of two major types: first, a single letter of the alphabet often represents more than one sound; and conversely, a single speech sound is often represented by several different letters (see figure 3.5).

As for problems of the first type, we have already seen that the letter *s* represents a *z*-sound in the word *dogs* and an *s*-sound in the word *cats*.

Figure 3.5
Types of inconsistencies in current English orthography. A single letter can stand for more than one sound, or several letters or groups of letters can stand for the same sound. On the left, the letter *t* represents the *t*-sound in *tin* and the *sh*-sound in *nation*. On the right, the *k*-sound is represented by the letters *k* and *ck* as in the word *kick*, *ch* as in *choir*, *q* as in *quick*, and *c* as in *cow*.

To take another case, the letter *t* can represent a *t*-sound, as in the word *tin*; but it can also represent a *sh*-like sound, as in *nation*.

Conversely, consider the *k*-sound in the word *kick*. This sound is orthographically represented in two different ways: the letter *k* at the beginning of the word and the letters *ck* at the end of the word. The word *cow* also begins with a *k*-sound, but here it is represented by the letter *c*. Similar problems arise with the initial sound in *jug*. This initial sound is represented by the letter *j*, but it is sometimes called "soft *g*" (and is spelled *g*) in words such as *giraffe*. Even the sequence of letters *dge* in words such as *ridge* and *edge* represents the *j*-sound.

In sum, English orthography is inadequate for representing the current speech sounds of American English. This lack of consistency in representing sounds is due in part to the fact that the English writing system became fixed several hundred years ago, although the pronunciation of the words has continuously changed since that period. But what system of symbols should we use to represent the speech sounds of English? More importantly, what should the symbols represent? The writing system we will now introduce uses symbols that represent for the most part the *sounds produced by particular configurations of the vocal tract*. A symbol such as *s* therefore represents the vocal tract configuration in which the tongue tip and/or blade are lightly pressed against the roof of the mouth near the teeth ridge so that when air from the lungs passes between the tongue and the teeth ridge and strikes the teeth, a hissing sound is produced.

The first writing system that we will look at is called a *phonemic transcription system*. Later we will have occasion to discuss and distinguish a *phonetic transcription system*. The crucial property of a phonemic system is that each distinctive speech sound of a language is represented with a unique symbol (or unique combination of symbols). This transcription system therefore overcomes the deficiencies of the current English alphabet. Though we will be discussing English almost exclusively, it is important to note that all human languages have a regular and consistent set of distinctive sounds that can be represented phonemically.

The Consonants of American English

Table 3.2 displays the phonemic consonant symbols of English. A *consonant* is a speech sound produced when the speaker either stops or severely constricts the airflow in the vocal tract. In addition to being classified as *voiceless* (like the *s*-sound in cats) or *voiced* (like the *z*-sound in *dogs*), consonants are described in terms of (1) the *place* and (2) the *manner* of their articulation. The *places* of articulation (see the top of table 3.2) are labeled in terms of anatomical structures, which (moving from the front of the mouth to the back) include the lips and regions along the roof of the mouth. In the production of most consonants, the lower lip or some part of the tongue approaches or touches the designated places of articulation along the roof of the mouth. The *manners* of articulation (see the left-hand side of table 3.2) refer for the most part to how the articulators (lips or tongue) achieve contact with or proximity to the places of articulation. We will see below that the sounds of English are highly regular in their distribution within and along the vocal tract.

We will now describe the consonants of English in terms of the framework given in table 3.2, making use of the anatomical descriptions shown in figure 3.4.

The phonemic symbols we will use here are those of the *International Phonetic Alphabet (IPA)*. We will also include in parentheses alternative symbols commonly used by many linguists. We enclose the IPA symbols in slant lines, a tradition common in linguistics when discussing phonemic symbols.

Stops

Stops are sounds produced when the airflow is completely obstructed during speech.

/p/ A voiceless bilabial stop. The speech sound symbolized by /p/ does not have accompanying vocal cord vibration and is therefore voiceless. The airflow is stopped by the complete closure of the two lips, which

Table 3.2
The consonants of English

MANNER OF ARTICULATION		PLACE OF ARTICULATION						
		Bilabial	Labiodental	Interdental	Alveolar	Alveopalatal	Velar	Glottal
Stops	voiceless	p			t		k	
	voiced	b			d		g	
Fricatives	voiceless		f	θ	s	ʃ		h
	voiced		v	ð	z	ʒ		
Affricates	voiceless					tʃ		
	voiced					dʒ		
Nasals		m			n		ŋ	
Liquids					l			
					ɹ			
Glides		w (ʍ)				j		

gives rise to the term *bilabial* (see 4, figure 3.4). The symbol /p/ represents the first sound in the word *pin*.

/b/   A voiced bilabial stop. The sound represented by /b/ has the same place of articulation as /p/ but is accompanied by voicing. The symbol /b/ represents the first and last sounds in the name *Bob*.

/t/   A voiceless alveolar stop. The *alveolar* consonants of English are produced when the tongue tip (or apex; see 10, figure 3.4) or blade approaches or—in the case of /t/ and /d/—touches the roof of the mouth at or near the alveolar ridge *behind* the upper teeth (see 3, figure 3.4). The English sound represented by the symbol /t/ thus differs from the *t*'s of many European languages in which the tongue tip touches the upper teeth. A Spanish /t/, for example, is a voiceless *dental* stop. The symbol /t/ represents the initial sound in the English word *tin*.

/d/   A voiced alveolar stop. The sound represented by the symbol /d/ has the same place of articulation as /t/ but is accompanied by voicing. The symbol /d/ represents the first and last sounds in the word *Dad*.

/k/   A voiceless velar stop. *Velar* consonants are formed when the body of the tongue approaches or—in the case of /k/ and /g/—touches the roof of the mouth on the *palate* (the soft palate is called the *velum*; see 8, figure 3.4). The symbol /k/ represents the first sound in the word *kite*.

/g/   A voiced velar stop. The sound represented by the symbol /g/ has the same place of articulation as /k/ but is accompanied by voicing. The symbol /g/ represents the first and last sounds in the word *gag*.

Fricatives
Fricatives are sounds produced when the airflow is forced through a narrow opening in the vocal tract so that noise produced by friction is created.

/f/   A voiceless labiodental fricative. The term *labiodental* indicates that the point of contact involves the (lower) lip and the (upper) teeth. The symbol /f/ represents the first sound in the word *fish*.

/v/   A voiced labiodental fricative. The sounds represented by the symbols /f/ and /v/ differ only in voicing, /v/ being voiced. The symbol /v/ represents the first sound in the word *vine*.

/θ/   A voiceless (inter)dental fricative. Both the sound symbolized as /θ/ and its voiced counterpart /ð/ are spelled with *th* in the current English writing system. The *interdental* sounds are produced when the tongue tip is placed against the upper teeth, friction being created by air forced between the upper teeth and the tongue. For most American English speakers, the tongue tip is projected slightly when it rests between the upper and lower teeth. The symbol /θ/ represents the first sound in its own name, the Greek letter *theta*, and in the word *thin*.

/ð/   A voiced interdental fricative. The symbol /ð/ is called *eth* (or *crossed d*). You can hear the difference between the sounds symbolized by /ð/ and /θ/ if you say *then* and *thin* very slowly. You will hear (and feel) the voicing that accompanies the /ð/ at the beginning of *then*, and you will note that the initial consonant of *thin* is not voiced. The symbol /ð/ also represents the first sound of the words *this* and *that*.

/s/   A voiceless alveolar fricative. Note that the fricative sound represented by the symbol /s/ is much harsher than the fricative sound represented by the symbol /θ/. The turbulence for /s/ is created by air passing between either the tongue tip or blade (for some English speakers) and the alveolar ridge, which then strikes the teeth at a high velocity. The symbol /s/ represents the first sound of the word *sit*.

/z/   A voiced alveolar fricative. The sounds represented by /s/ and /z/ differ only in voicing, /z/ being voiced. The symbol /z/ represents the first sound in the name *Zeke*.

/ʃ/   (/š/)   A voiceless alveopalatal fricative. The symbol /ʃ/, usually spelled *sh* in English orthography, represents a fricative similar to /s/, but the region of turbulent airflow lies just behind the alveolar ridge on the hard palate (hence the term *alveopalatal*; see 2 and 3, figure 3.4). During the articulation of /ʃ/ the tongue tip can be positioned either near the alveolar ridge itself (with the tongue blade arched) or just behind the alveolar ridge (in which case the tongue blade does not need to be arched). The symbol /ʃ/ represents the first sound in the word *ship*.

/ʒ/   (/ž/)   A voiced alveopalatal fricative. Unlike /ʃ/, the voiced counterpart /ʒ/ is rare. The symbol /ʒ/ represents the first sound in foreign names such as *Zsa-Zsa* or *Jacques*, but no native English words begin with /ʒ/. More commonly, /ʒ/ occurs in the middle of English words. For example, the letter *s* in *decision* and *measure* is pronounced as the sound represented by /ʒ/.

/h/   A voiceless "glottal" fricative. The /h/ sound is often called a *glottal* fricative because the vocal cords are positioned so that a small amount of turbulent airflow is produced across the glottis. However, the primary noise source for this speech sound is turbulence created at different points along the vocal tract where the tongue body (or blade) approaches the roof of the mouth. The point where the friction is created is determined by the vowel that follows the /h/. In the articulation of the English word *heap*, for example, the tongue body is positioned high and forward, and the fricative noise is produced in the palatal region. The symbol /h/ represents the first sound in the words *how* and *here*.

Affricates

An *affricate* is a single but complex sound, beginning as a stop but releasing secondarily into a fricative.

/tʃ/   (/č/)   A voiceless alveopalatal affricate. The symbol /tʃ/ represents the first sound in the word *chip* (/tʃ/ is usually spelled as *ch*). In articulating this sound, the tongue makes contact at the same point on the roof of the mouth as in the articulation of the sound represented by /ʃ/. Unlike /ʃ/, though, /tʃ/ begins with a complete blockage of the vocal tract (a stop), but then is immediately released into a fricative sound like /ʃ/.

/dʒ/   (/ǰ/)   A voiced alveopalatal affricate. The sounds represented by the symbols /tʃ/ and /dʒ/ differ only in voicing, /dʒ/ being voiced. The symbol /dʒ/ represents the first and last sounds of the word *judge* (/dʒ/ being spelled as both *j* and *dge*, in this case).

Nasals

In English the *nasals* are voiced oral stops, similar to the voiced stops discussed above in that they are voiced and are produced with a complete obstruction in the oral cavity. With nasals, however, the airflow and sound energy are channeled into the nasal passages (see 1, figure 3.4), due to the lowering of the velum (see 8, figure 3.4).

/m/   A bilabial nasal. The sounds represented by the symbols /m/ and /b/ are articulated in the same manner, except that for /m/ the velum is lowered to allow airflow and sound energy into the nasal passages. The symbol /m/ represents the first sound in the word *mice*.

/n/   An alveolar nasal. The sound represented by the symbol /n/ is articulated in the same position as /d/, with the velum lowered. The symbol /n/ represents the first sound in the word *nice*.

/ŋ/   A velar nasal. The symbol /ŋ/ is called *eng* (or even *engma* or *engwa*) and represents the final sound in the word *sing*. The normal English spelling for this single sound is *ng*. In order to hear the sound—and to hear that it *is* only one sound—compare the words *finger* and *singer*. For most speakers of American English the middle consonants of the word *finger* consist of a sequence of the velar nasal /ŋ/ followed by the velar stop /g/. In *singer*, however, only the velar nasal /ŋ/ occurs as the middle consonant, with no following /g/. Similarly, the word *long* ends only in a single consonant, the velar nasal. Note, however, the existence of a dialectal pronunciation of the word *long* in the expression *Long Island*. Certain speakers from the New York City area actually pronounce the final /g/ (*Long Island* = *LonGisland*).

The "*g*-like" quality of /ŋ/ is due to its being articulated in the same way as /g/, except that the velum is lowered. Thus, just as /m/ and /n/ are the nasal counterparts of /b/ and /d/, so /ŋ/ is the nasal counterpart of /g/. The sound represented by the symbol /ŋ/ does not occur in initial position in English words, but only in medial and final positions, as our examples show. A single velar nasal /ŋ/, spelled *Ng* in the United States, is a common surname in Cantonese.

Finally, although English orthography sometimes uses a *digraph* (a combination of two letters) to represent /ŋ/ (namely, *ng*), it should be stressed once again that the velar nasal is a *single* speech sound. Similarly, recall that other consonant sounds of English are represented by two-letter sequences in the current spelling system: *th* for /θ/ and /ð/, *sh* for /ʃ/, and *ch* for /tʃ/. Yet each of these consonants—/ŋ/, /θ/, /ð/, /ʃ/, and /tʃ/—is a single speech sound.

Liquids

Liquid sounds are found in the overwhelming majority of the world's languages, and English has one: /l/. The term *liquid* is a nontechnical, impressionistic expression indicating that the sound is "smooth" and "flows easily." Liquids share properties of both consonants and vowels: as in the articulation of certain consonants, the tongue blade is raised toward the alveolar ridge; as in the articulation of vowels, air is allowed to pass through the oral cavity without great friction.

/l/ An alveolar liquid. In the articulation of English /l/, the tongue blade is raised and the apex makes contact with the alveolar ridge. The sides of the tongue are lowered, permitting the air and sound energy to flow outward. The symbol /l/ represents the first sound in the word *life*.

Glides

Glides are vowel-like articulations that precede and follow true vowels. The term *glide* is based on the observation that the sequence of a glide and a vowel is a smooth, continuous gesture. Because the tongue position in articulating the glides /j/ and /w/ is similar to the tongue position of the vowels in *beet* and *boot*, respectively, these glides are sometimes referred to as *semivowels*.

/w/   A bilabial (velarized) glide. The sound represented by the symbol /w/ is formed with the body of the tongue arched in a high, back position, toward the soft palate (velum). Lip rounding also accompanies the production of this sound. The symbol /w/ represents the first sound in the word *wood*.

/ʍ/   A bilabial (velarized) glide (with a voiceless beginning). Some speakers of English have different initial sounds in the words *which* and *witch*. For these speakers the initial sound in *which* begins as a voiceless sound, followed immediately by the glide /w/. Some linguists write this initial sound as the digraph /hw/.

/ɹ/   An alveolar glide. American English /ɹ/ is produced with a tongue blade that is raised toward the alveolar ridge. Many speakers also curl the apex into a *retroflexed* position (curled upward and backward). Others press the tongue tip against the lower gum (below the teeth) and raise the blade of the tongue toward the roof of the mouth. This sound is also produced with lip rounding (a pursing of the lips) and a retraction of the tongue root (see 5, figure 3.4). The symbol /ɹ/ represents the first sound in the word *red*.

We are following IPA conventions in using the "upside-down *r*" symbol for this English phoneme. The "right-side-up *r*" symbol is reserved for trilled *r*, a sound found in dialects of Scottish English.

Arguments supporting the glide status of /ɹ/ are found in Kahn 1976.

/j/   (/y/)   An alveopalatal glide. The sound represented by the symbol /j/ is formed with the body and the blade of the tongue arched in a high, front position, toward the hard palate. The symbol /j/ represents the first sound in the word *yes*.

The Vowels of American English

Whereas consonants are formed by obstructions—either partial or total —in the vocal tract, vowels are produced with a relatively open vocal tract, which functions as a resonating chamber. The different vowels are

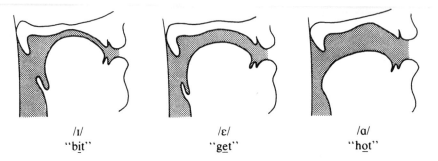

Figure 3.6
Vocal tract shapes for given English vowels

	Front	Back
High	ɪ	(ɨ) ʊ
Mid	ɛ	(ə) ʌ ɔ
Low	æ	ɑ

Figure 3.7
Lax (short) vowels and reduced vowels of American English

formed by the different *shapes* of the open, resonating vocal tract, and the variety of shapes is determined by the position of several anatomical structures: the position of the tongue body and blade, the relative opening of the lips, the relative opening of the oral pharynx (see 13, figure 3.4), and the position of the jaw (see figure 3.6). Although these articulators are, to some extent, anatomically connected, they can be independently controlled to produce the different vowels.

There are three major types of vowels in American English: *lax* (or *short*), *tense* (or *long*), and *reduced*. As the labels suggest, the lax vowels are produced with somewhat less muscular tension than the tense ones and are also somewhat shorter in duration. The reduced vowels could equally well be called the *unstressed* vowels, a point we return to below.

Lax (Short) Vowels
The symbols for the English lax vowels are displayed in figure 3.7. If we imagine this figure superimposed on a cross section of the vocal tract (such as that depicted in figure 3.4), then the positions of the vowels in the chart represent the relative positions of the part of the tongue closest to the roof of the mouth (assume the mouth opening to be on the left, as

in figure 3.4). We can simplify our description of the articulation of vowels by limiting our discussion to this relative position of the highest part of the tongue during vowel production.

/ɪ/   A lax high front vowel. The terms *high* and *front* describe the position of the tongue in the mouth (see figure 3.6). The symbol /ɪ/ represents the vowel sound in the words *bit* /bɪt/ and *wish* /wɪʃ/.

/ɛ/   A lax mid front vowel. The tongue body is relatively forward, as in the production of /ɪ/, but it is slightly lower (see figure 3.6). The symbol /ɛ/ represents the vowel sound in the words *get* /gɛt/ and *mess* /mɛs/.

/æ/   A lax low front vowel. This vowel (and the symbol for it) is called *ash* by many linguists, and the symbol /æ/ represents, in fact, the vowel sound in the word *ash* /æʃ/. It is produced with a front tongue body and with a lowered tongue body and jaw.

/ʊ/   A lax high back vowel. The vowel sound represented by the symbol /ʊ/ is found in words such as *put* /pʊt/ and *foot* /fʊt/. As you start to pronounce the vowel /ʊ/, you can feel your tongue move back and upward toward the velum. You can also feel your lips become rounded (pursed and brought closer together) during the production of this vowel; hence, it is called a *rounded* vowel.

/ʌ/   A lax mid back vowel. The vowel sound represented by the symbol /ʌ/, sometimes called *wedge*, occurs in words such as *putt* /pʌt/ and *luck* /lʌk/. Note that the words *put* and *putt*, which differ in the number of final *t*'s in the English spelling system, actually differ in their vowels, /ʊ/ versus /ʌ/, respectively.

/ɑ/   A lax low back vowel. The position of the tongue is low and retracted in the articulation of the vowel /ɑ/ (see figure 3.6). There are several varieties of /ɑ/-like vowels in English; these vowels constitute one of the most difficult aspects of the study of English vowel sounds. The difficulty is due in part to the fact that there is considerable dialectal variation in the pronunciation of these vowels. We leave it to your instructor to help you assign the appropriate symbols to represent vowels of your own speech or of the English spoken in your area. The vowel sound represented by the symbol /ɑ/ (*script-a*) is the low back vowel shared by most speakers of American English. It is typically found in words such as *hot* /hɑt/ and *pot* /pɑt/.

Notice that the symbol representing this vowel looks more like an italicized *a* than like a roman-style "a."

/ɔ/   A lax low back (rounded) vowel. If you pronounce the words *cot* and *caught* differently, you probably have the vowel /ɔ/ in your pronunciation of *caught*. There is minor lip rounding in the articulation of this vowel.

For many (if not most) speakers of American English the pronunciation of the vowels in the words *father*, *froth*, and *fraught* will be the same. However, you may speak a dialect (e.g., if you are a speaker of some dialects of British English) in which the vowels in the three words may all be different.

Reduced Vowels

There are two so-called *reduced* vowels in English, shown in parentheses in figure 3.7. The most common reduced vowel is called *schwa*, a *mid back* vowel whose symbol is an upside-down and reversed *e* /ə/. It is the last vowel sound in the word *sofa* and sounds very much like the lax vowel represented by the symbol /ʌ/ (some linguists, in fact, use the same symbol for both of these sounds). Schwa /ə/ is called a *reduced* vowel because it is frequently an unstressed variant of a stressed (accented) vowel. Note how the accented vowel /ɛ/ in the base word *democrat* /dɛ́məkɹæt/ "reduces" or "corresponds" to the unaccented vowel /ə/ in the derived word *democracy* /dəmákɹəsi/. Likewise, the vowel /æ/ in *democrat* /dɛ́məkɹæt/ "reduces" or "corresponds" to the second schwa in *democracy* /dəmákɹəsi/.

The other reduced vowel of English is a *high back* vowel represented by the symbol /ɨ/; it is referred to as *barred-i*. It is typically the vowel sound in the second syllable of *chicken* /tʃɪkɨn/. Like /ə/, the vowel /ɨ/ occurs only in unstressed (unaccented) syllables in a word.

There is considerable variation in the pronunciation of these two vowels. Most likely, English has only one basic reduced vowel, and the appearance of one or the other is determined by the surrounding phonetic environment. In chapter 4 we will discuss the reduced vowel and some properties of English words that account for its distribution.

Tense (Long) Vowels and Diphthongs

In addition to its inventory of short and reduced vowels, English has a set of tense vowels (see figure 3.8). The tense vowels are all relatively longer than the lax vowels, and all tense vowels in Standard English end with the tongue body high in the mouth. Tense vowels also sound higher than lax vowels. For example, spectrographic representations (figure 3.9) reveal

	Front	Back
High	i	u
Mid	eɪ	oʊ, ɔɪ
Low	(æʊ)	aʊ, aɪ

(a)

Figure 3.8
Tense (long) vowels and diphthongs of American English

(a) "rid"   (b) "reed"

Figure 3.9
Spectrograms representing the lax vowel /ɪ/ of *rid* (a) and the tense vowel /i/ of *reed* (b). "Δ" marks the vowel's duration: 106 milliseconds (a) and 144 milliseconds (b). Thus, the tense vowel represented here is 38 milliseconds longer than the lax one, a pattern typical of the length difference between tense and lax vowels. The number in angle brackets is the value of the second formant for these vowels. The higher value for /i/ in *reed* (b) reflects a more advanced tongue position, another characteristic of tense vowels.

that the tense vowel /i/ in *reed* is 38 milliseconds longer than the lax vowel /ɪ/ in *rid*; moreover, the second resonant frequency (formant) of /i/ is higher than that of /ɪ/, an acoustic property that corresponds to a more advanced tongue position.

/i/   A tense high front vowel. The symbol /i/ represents the vowel sound in words such as *bead* /bid/ and *three* /θɹi/.

/eɪ/   (alternative IPA transcription /e/; alternative American transcription /ey/)   A tense mid front vowel (with an accompanying high front offglide). This high front offglide is represented in the IPA transcription with the symbol /ɪ/. The vowel is found in words such as *clay* /kleɪ/ and *weigh* /weɪ/.

/u/   A tense high back (rounded) vowel. This transcription represents the vowel sound in words such as *crude* /kɹud/ and *shoe* /ʃu/.

/oʊ/   (alternative IPA transcription /o/; alternative American transcription /ow/)   A tense mid back (rounded) vowel (with an accompanying high back offglide). This high back offglide is represented in the IPA transcription with the symbol /ʊ/. This transcription represents the vowel sound in the words *boat* /boʊt/ and *toe* /toʊ/.

Diphthongs are single vowel sounds that begin in one vowel position and end in another vowel or glide position. Strictly speaking, the vowels /eɪ/ and /oʊ/ are diphthongs, although they have been traditionally classified with the long vowels /i/ and /u/. The following three vowels are unambiguously diphthongs that have substantial tongue movement in their articulation.

/ɔɪ/   (alternative American transcription /oy/)   A tense mid back (rounded) vowel (with an accompanying high front offglide). This transcription represents the vowel sound in words such as *boy* /bɔɪ/ and *Floyd* /flɔɪd/.

/aʊ/   (alternative American transcription /aw/)   A tense low back vowel (with an accompanying high back offglide). This transcription represents the vowel sound in the words *cow* /kaʊ/ and *blouse* /blaʊs/. In some dialects of American English this diphthong begins with a low front vowel and should be transcribed as /æʊ/.

/aɪ/   (alternative American transcription /ay/)   A tense low back vowel (with an accompanying high front offglide). This transcription represents the vowel sound in words such as *my* /maɪ/ and *thigh* /θaɪ/.

East Coast Dialectal Variant

/a/   A tense low vowel. The vowel sound represented by the symbol /a/ (*printed-a*) is found—among other places—in the speech of New England, especially in Maine and eastern Massachusetts. One characteristic expression of the Boston area, "Park the car," contains two instances of the vowel represented by the symbol /a/.

To conclude our discussion of vowels, we point out that one of the reasons that speakers of English have some difficulty in pronouncing the vowels of languages such as Spanish and Italian is that most of the tense (long) vowels of English are diphthongs, whereas the corresponding vowels in Spanish and Italian are not. For example, a native speaker of American English who is learning Italian is likely to pronounce the word *solo* "alone" with two English *o*'s, as shown most clearly in the IPA transcription /soulou/. For this reason, teachers of foreign languages often tell American-English-speaking students to use "pure" vowels—that is, ones without velar offglides—in words such as Italian *solo*.

Consonants and Vowels in Other Languages

All spoken human languages have sound systems made up of consonants and vowels. Nevertheless, languages vary greatly in the number of these sound types. Ignoring dialectal differences, American English has 39 phonemes (24 consonants and 15 vowels); Hawaiian has 13 phonemes (8 consonants and 5 vowels); and Georgian, a Caucasian language spoken in the southwestern part of the former Soviet Union, has 90 phonemes (70 consonants and 20 vowels). All of these languages function successfully as communication systems in spite of their extremely different numbers of speech sounds.

Also despite numerical differences, the vowels found in the world's languages are often quite similar and are produced in similar portions of the mouth. All languages have an /ɑ/-like vowel, and *i*'s and *u*'s are found in the majority of languages. The vowels *a*, *i*, and *u*, being produced at the periphery of the vocal tract, are the maximally distinct vowels. Consonants are subject to more crosslinguistic variation because languages have more consonants than vowels. Nevertheless, languages share a common core of consonant types. Almost all languages have labial stops (such as *p* and *b*), dental/alveolar stops (such as *t* and *d*), and velar stops (such as *k* and *g*), one or more of the nasals (*m* or *n*), a liquid (*r* or *l*), and some kind of fricative (typically an *s*-like sound).

86   Chapter 3

A group of sounds that may be unfamiliar to speakers of English and of European and Asian languages are the so-called click sounds found in several African languages. In the production of clicks, the tongue makes a closure with the roof of the mouth not just at one point, but at two points (both at the velum and at one other point farther forward). The primary airflow is created by making the sealed-off space larger, creating a partial vacuum, usually by lowering the tongue and jaw. When the front stoppage is released and air rushes into the partial vacuum, a click sound results. Some click sounds are made by English speakers, and although they are not part of the English language itself, they are still used for communication. The sound that is written *tsk! tsk! tsk!* is not to be pronounced "tisk, tisk, tisk." The *tsk!* is a single click sound made with air rushing in between the tip of the tongue and the alveolar ridge. In the African language Xhosa, spoken by Nelson Mandela, certain "click" phonemes are an integral part of the consonant system. The click consonant that appears at the beginning of the language name *Xhosa*—a click with a lateral release—is the sound that some people use to signal a horse to "giddy-up." Try pronouncing this lateral click and following it immediately with the sequence *-osa.* If you can do this, you will come very close to pronouncing the name of this language correctly. The official IPA representation for this sequence is /ǁosa/.

The Form of the English Plural Rule: Three Hypotheses

Now that we have a set of symbols that permit us to transcribe the consonant and vowel sounds of English in a precise way, we can reformulate table 3.1, more accurately, as table 3.3. Here the plural morpheme can appear as either /s/, /z/, or /ɨz/.

Even though we can now represent the different pronunciations of the plural morpheme, we are still left with accounting for the *distribution*

Table 3.3
Phonemic transcription of different forms of the plural morpheme

Example word	cat<u>s</u>	dog<u>s</u>	bush<u>es</u>
Phonemic transcription of plural morpheme for that word	/s/	/z/	/ɨz/
Phonemic transcription of that word	/kæts/	/dɑgz/	/bʊʃɨz/

(pattern of occurrence) of the different plural forms. What factors govern, or predict, this distribution? We will pursue this problem by formulating several hypotheses, which we will then test and revise in light of new data.

A given noun can be associated with only one of the three different forms of the plural. Thus, for example, the plural /ɨz/ that is associated with *bush* to make *bushes* cannot be associated with *cat* or *dog*. The result of doing so (/kætɨz/, /dɑgɨz/) sounds "foreign" to a native speaker of English. Thus, there must be some principle governing the occurrence of the different plural shapes. One account for the plural distribution would be to say that the form of the plural morpheme to be used with any given noun is unpredictable, and that we must simply list, for each individual noun of the language, which form it takes. This would amount to saying that speakers of English have simply memorized the phonological form of the plural for each individual noun. The distribution of the forms of the plural would then be given by sets of statements such as the following:

(1)
Hypothesis 1 (Listing of words)
{kæt, kæts} "cat"
{mæp, mæps} "map"
{bæk, bæks} "back"
{dɑg, dɑgz} "dog"
{kæn, kænz} "can"
{tæb, tæbz} "tab"
{buʃ, buʃɨz} "bush"
{dɪʃ, dɪʃɨz} "dish"
{ɹɪdʒ, ɹɪdʒɨz} "ridge"
and so forth

Hypothesis 1 is consistent with the fact that there are nouns such as *child*, *ox*, *sheep*, and *man* for which the shape of the plural ending does seem to be determined by the word itself. However, hypothesis 1 implies that for any new word (not already found in our lists) we will not be able to predict which of the three forms of the plural morpheme it will take. But this is clearly false. Speakers of English can spontaneously and with consensus form the plural for nouns they have never heard before and therefore could not have memorized. We may never have heard the noun *glark* before (since it is a nonsense word), yet we can indeed predict that the form of the plural would be /s/ and not /z/ or /ɨz/; in fact; it seems that every noun that ends in /k/ takes the plural form /s/, whether it is a nonsense word or not. Similarly, every noun that ends in /g/, such as *dog*, takes the plural form /z/; and every noun that ends in /ʃ/, such as *bush*, takes the plural form /ɨz/. It is, in fact, possible to group the nouns that take only /s/ or only /z/ or only /ɨz/ in terms of their last sound. This leads us to a second hypothesis about the distribution of the different forms of the plural morpheme:

(2)

Hypothesis 2 (Listing of final sounds)
The forms of the plural morpheme are distributed according to the following speech sound lists:
a. The plural morpheme takes the form /s/ if the noun ends in /p, t, k, f, or θ/.
b. The plural morpheme takes the form /z/ if the noun ends in /b, m, d, n, g, ŋ, v, ð, l, ɹ, w, j/, or any vowel.
c. The plural morpheme takes the form /ɨz/ if the noun ends in /s, z, ʃ, ʒ, tʃ, or dʒ/.

Notice that hypothesis 2 now reflects a native English speaker's judgments concerning the form that the plural will take for any new word. Accordingly, the task faced by the language learner in learning the distribution of the plural forms is different under hypothesis 2 than under hypothesis 1. That is, language learners do not memorize the particular plural form for every noun; rather, it appears that they acquire a rule to determine what plural form is associated with a particular noun (in terms of its final sound). Of course, there are still nouns whose plural form has to be memorized, as with the exceptional nouns *children*, *oxen*, *sheep*, *men*, and so forth. We can say, then, that there are nouns whose plural follows hypothesis 1 (the exceptional nouns), but the overwhelming majority are subject to hypothesis 2.

To see that hypothesis 2 is still not sufficient to handle all cases of plural formation, we turn to cases in which foreign words are made to undergo English plural formation—in particular, foreign words that contain speech sounds not found in English. Some English speakers, especially announcers on radio stations that play classical music, pronounce the name of the German composer Bach as it is pronounced in German, with a final voiceless velar fricative. This sound, symbolized as /x/, is not part of the English phonemic system. If these English speakers use the name *Bach* (/bɑx/) in the plural, perhaps in referring to two generations of Bachs, it takes /s/ and not /z/ or /ɨz/ (*Bachs* = /bɑxs/). The problem is that the sound /x/ does not appear in the list in hypothesis 2. We therefore need to develop a new hypothesis that reflects the English speaker's ability to assign plurals to words that end in sounds that are foreign to English.

If we compare words that end in, say, /f/ (which take the plural form /s/) and words that end in /v/ (which take the form /z/), we can observe that /f/ and /v/ represent similar sounds that differ only in a single feature—namely, /f/ is *voiceless*, whereas /v/ is *voiced*. Further, words with the final consonant /k/ (which is voiceless) take the plural /s/, whereas words with a final /g/ (which is voiced) take the plural /z/. If we set aside for a moment the nouns that take /ɨz/, we can make the following observation: if a noun ends with a voiceless sound, then it will take the voiceless plural form /s/; but if it ends with a voiced sound, then it will take the voiced plural form /z/. Notice that we now have an account for why hypothesis 2 groups nouns ending in *vowels* with nouns ending in *voiced consonants* such as /b, d, m/ (see hypothesis 2, part (b)): those final sounds are all voiced, and so it follows automatically that all nouns ending in voiced sounds will take the plural form /z/.

Let us now return to the nouns that take the plural form /ɨz/. We note that the final consonants of these nouns (/s, z, ʃ, ʒ, tʃ, or dʒ/) are either *alveolar fricatives*, *alveopalatal fricatives*, or *alveopalatal affricates*.

(3)
Hypothesis 3 (Use of phonetic features)
The forms of the plural morpheme are distributed according to the following conditions:
a. The plural morpheme takes the form /ɨz/ if the last sound in the noun to which it attaches is an alveolar fricative, an alveopalatal fricative, or an alveopalatal affricate.
Otherwise:
b. The plural morpheme takes the voiced form /z/ if the last sound in the noun is voiced.
c. The plural morpheme takes the voiceless form /s/ if the last sound in the noun is voiceless.

English plural formation demonstrates the interaction of two parts of English grammar, where the concept of grammar includes morphology and phonology as well as syntax. English grammar includes a morphological part that specifies that plurals are formed by adding a suffix to nouns, and a phonological part containing rules that determine the actual phonetic shape (or shapes) of that suffix. Linguists hypothesize that grammars of all languages contain a morphological component in which morphemes are combined to form complex or compound words. In this chapter we have seen that combinations of morphemes are often subject to phonological rules that determine the ultimate shape of underlying morphemes, both stems and affixes.

The phonological form of some affixes is invariant. Such a case seems to be the prefix *re-*, which is pronounced /ɹi/ regardless of the phonological shape of the verb to which it is attached. Other affixes may be subject to phonological rules that specify their phonological shape depending on their phonological environment. The English plural morpheme is one of these. Other examples of shape-changing rules are given in the exercises at the end of this chapter and in *A Linguistic Workbook* (Farmer and Demers 2001).

Phonetic Variations on a Phonemic Theme

So far we have assumed that the sounds represented by the phonemic transcription system of English are articulated the same way each time they are produced. This assumption ignores an important aspect of the pronunciation of some phonemes. We discuss below several examples of variation in the pronunciation of certain American English consonants, variations that are common to most speakers of American English.

Types of /t/ in English

Aspirated t. When the sound /t/ occurs at the beginning of a syllable, its pronunciation is accompanied by a puff of air called *aspiration*. You can observe the presence of aspiration if you hold a thin, flexible piece of paper close to the front of your mouth when you say the word *tin*. The paper will flutter immediately after the /t/ is pronounced. You can also place your hand in front of your mouth to feel this puff of air. In contrast, the pronunciation of the /t/'s in the word *stint* is unaspirated; pronouncing these /t/'s will not cause the piece of paper to flutter. Later we will discuss the general conditions under which some English phonemes are aspirated.

In order to represent more detailed aspects of pronunciation (such as aspiration), linguists use a system called (close) *phonetic transcription*. By convention, phonetic symbols are enclosed in square brackets [ ]; the

symbols of the more general transcription system we have been using—
which, when it satisfies conditions to be discussed below, is called a *phonemic transcription*—are enclosed in slant lines / /. For example, in
phonetic transcription *tin* and *stint* are represented as [tʰɪn] and [stɪnt],
respectively (where a superscripted *h* indicates an aspirated sound and its
absence indicates an unaspirated sound). In phonemic transcription they
are represented as /tɪn/ and /stɪnt/. We will discuss the difference between
phonetic and phonemic transcriptions after we have discussed some of
the finer phonetic details of American English speech.

Unreleased t. Final /t/ in words such as *kit* is frequently unreleased in the
pronunciation of many speakers of American English: the tongue touches
the alveolar ridge but does not immediately drop away to "release" the
sound. (In contrast, in most American English dialects the pronunciation
of the final stop /t/ in words such as *fast* is in fact released). For most
speakers of American English, in the pronunciation of the word *kit*, the
voicing ends and the airflow stops *before* the tongue reaches the alveolar
ridge in articulating the final /t/. Where and how is the airflow stopped in
this case? The primary stop articulation in the pronunciation of final /t/
in words such as *kit* occurs in the larynx, rather than in the region of the
alveolar ridge, even though the tongue tip does indeed make contact with
the alveolar ridge immediately *after* the closure of the vocal cords. Recall
that the *glottis* is the space between the vocal cords, and a stop created by
closure at the glottis is called a *glottal stop*, represented as the symbol [ʔ].
A glottal stop appears at the beginning of each of the two *oh*'s of the
expression *oh-oh!*, which we can phonetically transcribe as [ʔʌʔoʊ] or
[oʊʔoʊʔ]. An unreleased /t/ that is produced with a glottal stop immediately preceding the alveolar articulation is symbolized as [ʔt]. Such
sounds are sometimes referred to as *preglottalized*. Thus, the characteristic pronunciation of the word *kit* for most American English dialects is
represented phonetically as [kʰɪʔt].

Glottal stop replacement of t. In certain words the tendency to have a
glottal closure with the articulation of /t/ in certain environments reaches
such an extreme that the glottal stop actually replaces /t/. In many
speakers' pronunciation of words such as *button* and *kitten*, the stop
articulation is actually carried out at the glottis, and the tongue does not,
in fact, move toward the alveolar ridge until the /n/ of the final syllable
is articulated. The /t/ is generally replaced by the glottal stop if the following syllable contains a *syllabic* /n/. The term *syllabic* here refers to

the fact that nasal consonants (such as /n/) can function as syllables by themselves, without an accompanying vowel. In the word *button*, for example, the only sound in the second syllable is the nasal [n̩]—there is no true vowel at all in that syllable. A syllabic /n/ is indicated by placing a straight apostrophe (or tick mark) under the symbol: [n̩]. The phonetic transcription of *kitten* would thus be [kʰɪʔn̩].

Flapped t. In words such as *pitted*, /t/ is regularly pronounced as a voiced "*d*-like" sound by most speakers of American (but not British) English. This sound is articulated by making a quick "tap" with the tongue tip on the alveolar ridge. Because of the rapidity of the articulation of this sound, it is referred to as a *flap* (or a *tap*), transcribed phonetically with the symbol [ɾ]. Thus, a word such as *pitted* is phonetically transcribed as [pʰɪɾɨd]. The flap [ɾ] is always voiced and occurs primarily intervocalically (between vowels).

Alveopalatal t. Children who are learning to write English sometimes spell the word *truck* as *chruk* or *chuk*. In doing so, they reveal that they are quite good phoneticians. What they are noticing is that the /t/ in the word *truck* is pronounced much farther back along the roof of the mouth than is the regular /t/. For many speakers, in fact, the tongue tip touches *behind* the alveolar ridge, at exactly the point where the /tʃ/ phoneme is produced. Moreover, the /ɹ/ phoneme in many dialects is voiceless following /t/ and sounds similar to /ʃ/. Since the combination of the alveopalatal stop followed by the alveopalatal "fricative" (the voiceless *r*) sounds like the /tʃ/ phoneme, it is understandable that children might spell initial *tr* sequences as *ch*. Linguists transcribe this phonetic realization of /t/ as [t̠].

Retraction of an alveolar sound under the influence of a following /ɹ/ also accounts for a dialectal difference in the American English pronunciation of the word *groceries*. In many parts of the eastern United States, speakers pronounce this word as three syllables: /gɹoʊsəɹis/. In the western states, many speakers pronounce this word with two syllables. Under these conditions the word-internal /s/ is adjacent to a following /ɹ/. The /ɹ/ induces retraction of the /s/ and the following pronunciation results: /gɹoʊʃɹis/.

To sum up, there are several phonetic realizations of the phoneme /t/ in American English. These variations and their conditioning environments are shown in table 3.4. These variations are all heard as /t/'s by speakers of English in spite of the wide phonetic variation.

Table 3.4
Phonetic variants of the phoneme /t/ in American English

Articulatory description	Phonetic symbol	Conditioning environments	Example words
Released, aspirated	[tʰ]	when syllable-initial	tin [tʰɪn]
Unreleased, preglottalized	[ˀt]	word-final, after a vowel	kit [kʰɪˀt]
Glottal stop	[ʔ]	before a syllabic *n*	kitten [kʰɪʔn̩]
Flap	[ɾ]	between vowels, when the first vowel is stressed (approximate environment)	pitted [pʰíɾɨd]
Alveopalatal stop	[t̠]	syllable-initial before *r*	truck [t̠ɹʌk]
Released, unaspirated	[t]	when the above conditions are not met first	stint [stɪnt]

Types of /l/ in English

The English language has two types of /l/, referred to informally as *dark-l* and *light-l*. The dark-*l*, which occurs in words such as *luck* and *bell*, has a lower sound than light-*l*, which occurs in words such as *leek*. In English dark-*l* is basic. Its dark quality is due to a coarticulation effect caused by an accompanying raised and retracted tongue body. (Because of this high and back (velar) tongue body, dark-*l* is sometimes referred to as *velarized-l*.) Light-*l* is a positional variant occurring before front vowels such as /ɪ/ and /i/. Before front vowels /l/ is not produced with a retracted tongue body—the body is more forward—and thus the light variant is produced. An English speaker learning French, Spanish, or German must learn to pronounce all of the *l*'s in these languages as light since none of them has dark-*l*. The IPA symbols for light-*l* and dark-*l* are *l* and *ɫ* (or ʟ), respectively.

The Relationship between Phonetic and Phonemic Representation

We have seen that the phoneme /t/ has a number of phonetic variants depending on its *position* in a word. Keeping this in mind, we can see that the phonemic symbol /t/ is actually a *cover symbol* for a range of different sounds (or *phones*) that occur in actual speech. We can refer to all of the sounds/phones for which /t/ is a cover symbol as its *allophones* (sometimes also called *positional variants*, since they occur in specific environments). The positional variants that we transcribe as [t], [tʰ], [ʔt], [ʔ], [t̪], and [ɾ] are all instances of the same phoneme /t/. It is important to stress that every positional variant is represented by a phone. Indeed, every phone is an allophone of some phoneme. Thus, we can refer to the allophones [kʰ], [tʰ], or [t], but we must keep in mind that [kʰ] is an allophone of the phoneme /k/ whereas [t] and [tʰ] are allophones of the phoneme /t/. Criteria for determining whether two or more phones are members of the same phoneme or different phonemes are discussed below.

It is clear, then, that we are using two distinct systems of representation for the sounds of English (and of human language in general) and that different information is encoded in each system. For example, the phonetic representation system explicitly represents information concerning aspiration, preglottalization, and flapping, using notational devices such as superscripted *h* and other special symbols summarized in table 3.4. In contrast, the phonemic representation system is more abstract in nature; it ignores such features as aspiration, preglottalization, and flapping.

Since we are using two representation systems for sounds, the question immediately arises, Why should this be so? How can we justify two systems for encoding phonological information? Why should one representation system ignore (or leave unrepresented) articulatory information encoded by the other system? Why shouldn't we simplify our phonological theory and use only one representation system for sounds?

There are some fairly intuitive ways to answer these questions, and so we must stress that we will provide informal answers here rather than precise definitions. Furthermore, we must point out that part of our discussion will assume certain traditional (or "classical") views on the distinction between phonemic and phonetic representations, in which, for the sake of exposition, we will gloss over a number of problems that have arisen in recent work.

The basic idea behind the distinction between phonetic and phonemic representation systems can be best illustrated by considering pairs of words that linguists refer to as *minimal pairs*: pairs of words that (1) have the same number of phonemes, (2) differ in a single sound in a corresponding position in the two words, and (3) differ in meaning. An example is the pair of words *fine* and *vine*. They differ in meaning, but phonologically they differ only in the contrast between initial /f/ and initial /v/. Thus, /faɪn/ and /vaɪn/ constitute a minimal pair.

Now let us consider two possible pronunciations of the word *kit*: [kʰɪt] and [kʰɪʔt]. As noted earlier, for some speakers of English, the final consonant of *kit* is sometimes released (= [t]) and sometimes unreleased (= [ʔt]). The important point is that no meaning difference is associated with the different pronunciations [kʰɪt] and [kʰɪʔt]: both versions are perceived by native speakers of American English as instances of the same word *kit*. Thus, the distinction between the allophones [t] and [ʔt] in word-final position is not contrastive, and we can say that, for some speakers, these allophones of /t/ are in *free variation* (or of optional occurrence) in that position.

The substitution of /v/ for /f/ can create a minimal pair, as we saw in the case of the words *fine* and *vine*; the sounds /f/ and /v/ are therefore members of different phonemes. By contrast, the substitution of [t] for [ʔt] does not create a minimal pair; they are therefore members of the same phoneme.

The allophones of a phoneme can also occur in what is called *complementary distribution*; that is, one allophone can occur in a position where the other allophone(s) can never appear, and vice versa. The term *complementary distribution* is used because the distribution of one allophone is the complement of the distribution of the other(s). For example, in the position following word-initial /s/, the phoneme /t/ has the obligatory positional variant [t], and the allophones [tʰ] and [ʔt] never occur in this position. Allophones of a single phoneme, then, are always either in free variation or in complementary distribution, but in either case they are not contrastive with one another. To repeat, it is only when phones function contrastively that they are members of different phonemes.

The phoneme is actually more than just a cover symbol for a collection of sounds (its allophones)—it has a psychological aspect as well. The phoneme can be viewed as the speaker's internalized representation of a single speech sound, which, however, can have different phonetic shapes depending on the environment in which it appears. To speakers of American English, for example, the phones [tʰ], [t], [ʔt], and so forth, are all heard as a "single *t*-sound," the phoneme /t/.

Some linguists understand the phoneme somewhat more concretely and view it as a representation of an ideal articulatory target. Because of the effects of the environment in which the phoneme occurs, however, it may be produced in different allophonic versions. In any case, phonemic writing represents the *basic, contrasting sound units* of a language, and many languages use the phonemic principle as the basis of their alphabet.

We write phonemically, then, to represent the minimally contrasting speech sounds of a language. Nevertheless, linguists also have occasion to represent the finer phonetic details of a language. For example, there is often a need to specify just what phonetic features speakers of American English may be carrying over to speaking another language—the features that give them their "American accent." The aspiration of syllable-initial voiceless stops is one such regularly observable feature of English pronunciation, and we want to represent it in some way. To fail to do so would be to fail to give a proper characterization of American English pronunciation. For this reason, we require a phonetic representation system as well as a phonemic representation system in order to characterize the sounds of English (and of human language in general). Speakers of French and Spanish, for example, do not aspirate syllable-initial voiceless stops, and speakers of American English can pronounce these two Romance languages better if they learn to suppress their aspiration rule. Moreover, the fine phonetic details of the pronunciation of /t/ discussed above are typical of American English but not British English. British English does not have the flap rule, nor does it for the most part have the glottal stop reinforcement rule in word-final position. Thus, the word *pity* has the same phonemic representation in both British and American English (/pɪti/), but the phonetic representations differ: [pɪti] in British English, but [pɪɾi] in American English.

So far we have taken care to specify that our phonemic and phonetic generalizations are based on American English. It is important to note that languages can differ with respect to what phonetic features function distinctively. For example, in Hindi, a language spoken in India, the feature of aspiration does in fact function distinctively in voiceless stops. For speakers of Hindi, the consonants /k^h/ (aspirated) and /k/ (unaspirated) are perceived as two completely different consonant sounds, and indeed we can find minimal pairs in Hindi showing the contrast between the two. For example, /k^{h}iil/ means "parched grain," whereas /kiil/ means "nail." Speakers of English tend to hear Hindi /k^h/ and /k/ as free variants of one another, or else they perceive Hindi unaspirated /k/ as English /g/, given that voiced stops in English are unaspirated. But Hindi /k^h/ and /k/ also contrast with Hindi /g/. This example brings up an important point: whether or not a phonetic feature (or the phoneme that contains it) is contrastive (phonemic) is a language-particular phenomenon. That is, a phonetic distinction that functions phonemically in one language may or may not function phonemically in another language. Aspiration functions phonemically in voiceless stops in Hindi, but it has no such function in English.

To take another example, there is no phonemic distinction between an *r*-sound and an *l*-sound in Japanese and Korean. In Korean these two sounds are in complementary distribution; they are allophones of a single phoneme. In Japanese only a single *r*-like phoneme occurs. Speakers of American English are baffled by the fact that to a native Japanese speaker the English words *red* and *led* sound like the same word. How can sounds that seem so different sound the same? The answer is that differences that function phonemically in a language are easy for a native speaker to distinguish. In contrast, differences that do not function distinctively may be hard to distinguish. Speakers of Japanese have trouble distinguishing English /r/ and /l/ in the same way that speakers of English have trouble distinguishing Hindi /k/ and /kʰ/ as two separate phonemes.

In most cases the distinction between phonemic and phonetic representations will not be crucial for our purposes. Generally speaking, we will use phonetic representations, using square brackets ([ ]), when discussing specific details of the pronunciation of a word or syllable, and phonemic representations, using slant lines (/ /), when discussing individual consonants and vowels at a more abstract level, as part of a phonological system. When neither the phonemic nor the phonetic transcription is relevant, we will italicize the letter representing the sound under discussion.

3.3   SPECIAL TOPICS

Vowels before /ɹ/

American English /ɹ/ is often one of the most difficult features of pronunciation for speakers of other languages to learn. It is even hard for native speakers themselves, being one of the last sounds that children acquire when they learn American English. It is also one of the sources of extreme dialectal variation—for instance, imagine the word *fire* being pronounced by Ted Kennedy (U.S. senator from Massachusetts), a country music singer such as George Jones, and Tom Brokaw (NBC Evening News anchor; native of the Midwest). In fact, differences in the pronunciation of /ɹ/ are so complex that we leave it to your instructor to explore with you the features of /ɹ/ in your region.

An interesting aspect of the pronunciation of /ɹ/—one that also has a bearing on dialectal variation, as we will see—lies in the relationship between /ɹ/ and the vowel that precedes it in a word. When beginning students of linguistics transcribe the word *fear*, they often use the tense vowel /i/: /fiɹ/. They notice that the vowel in *fear* sounds higher than the lax vowel /ɪ/ in *bid*, even though they admit that it doesn't seem quite as high as the tense vowel /i/ in *bead* (/bid/). In reality, the vowel in *fear* lies between /ɪ/ and /i/. In fact, the vowel before /ɹ/ is a positional variant—namely, a raised variant of the vowel phoneme /ɪ/, the raising of which is due to the anticipated articulation of the /ɹ/. You can hear that /ɪ/ is the correct vowel by pronouncing both high vowels in the context *s—r*. When you use /ɪ/, the word will sound like *sear* /sɪɹ/. When you use /i/, it will sound like *seer*. Listening to these two words, you will hear that *sear* contains one syllable and *seer* two—the second syllable of *seer* being an *r*-colored vowel transcribed as /ɚ/. The word *seer* is thus written phonemically as /siɚ/. /ɚ/ is an unstressed vowel; when the *r*-colored vowel is stressed, it is transcribed /ɝ/. Thus, to the list of tense vowels in figure 3.8 we must now add the *r*-colored vowel /ɝ/. (As you work through this paragraph, it will help to utter the pair of words *sear* and *seer* several times. Ultimately you will recognize a rhythmical difference in these words. The word *sear* /sɪɹ/ is monosyllabic and has one "beat." The word *seer* /siɚ/ is bisyllabic and has two beats. In section 4.4 we will discuss a difference in the tonal patterns that also accompanies the pronunciation of these two words.)

The term *r-colored vowel* refers to English vocalic sounds that have an *r*-like quality. The *r*-like quality is a consequence of superimposing the articulatory properties of the /ɹ/ glide onto the articulation of a mid central vowel. It is telling that in British English, which does not have *r*-colored vowels, the vowels that correspond to American English *r*-colored vowels are mid central vowels. Thus, the word *brother* is pronounced /bɹʌðə/.

The difference in syllable structure between the two words *sear* and *seer* results from a property of American English that only a lax vowel can appear in the same syllable with a following /ɹ/; if an *r*-sound alone follows a long (or tense) vowel (i.e., an *r*-sound is the only following phoneme), then it must always occur as an *r*-colored vowel in a second, immediately following syllable. The distributional properties of tense and lax vowels and a following *r*-sound can be stated even more strongly: if a

		(a)		
sear	/sɪɹ/		tour	/tʊɹ/
air	/ɛɹ/		for	/fɔɹ/
			far	/fɑɹ/

		(b)				
seer	/siɚ/		fur	/fɝ/	sewer	/suɚ/
Bayer	/beɪɚ/				lower	/loʊɚ/
tire	/taɪɚ/				tower	/taʊɚ/
lawyer	/lɔɪɚ/					

Figure 3.10
Vowels that can appear before an *r*-sound: (a) lax, (b) tense

single *r*-sound follows a lax vowel, then this *r* must be the phoneme /ɹ/, and not the *r*-colored vowel /ɚ/. Figure 3.10 displays words that contain the sequence "vowel + /ɹ/." The lax vowels that do not appear in figure 3.10 are /æ/ and /ʌ/. For most speakers of American English, /æ/ does not occur before /ɹ/. /ʌ/ has actually merged with /r/ to form the *r*-colored vowel written as /ɝ/ or /ɚ/. In chapter 4 we will see why several symbols—/ɹ/, /ɚ/, and /ɝ/—are used to represent *r*-like sounds.

As an example of dialectal variation involving vowels before /ɹ/, consider the words *marry*, *merry*, and *Mary*. Speakers in most parts of the United States, especially in the West, pronounce these words the same: /mɛɹi/. However, many speakers on the East Coast, especially those in New York City, pronounce them all differently: *marry* /mæɹi/, *merry* /mɛɹi/, *Mary* /maɹi/, where the first vowel in the last word is the tense /a/ discussed earlier. Since the tense /a/ does not occur in most dialects, it is not available before /ɹ/.

One additional point needs to be made about the lax vowels that can appear before /ɹ/. Although not all dialects of American English make the /ɑ/–/ɔ/ distinction in pronouncing *cot* and *caught* (/kɑt/–/kɔt/), most, if not all, dialects have the vowel /ɔ/ in monosyllables before /ɹ/. This is the vowel in a word such as *lore* /lɔɹ/. As you pronounce this word, you will perceive that it is a monosyllable, and this monosyllabic pronunciation is consistent with the "lax vowel + *r*" principle discussion above.

The vowel in *lore* may sound like the tense vowel /oʊ/, but it is not. The vowel in *lore* may sound "higher" and more *o*-like, but this raising is due to the influence of the following /ɹ/. Moreover, the vowel in *lore* is not as long as the vowel /oʊ/. In fact, if you pronounce the sequence *l*, followed by /oʊ/, followed by an *r*-sound, you will pronounce the word *lower* /louɚ/. The difference between *lore* and *lower* further underscores the importance of the conditions that govern the occurrence of vowels before *r*-phonemes in English.

Contractions in Casual Spoken English

In discussing the phonetic properties of English, we have so far focused our attention on phonetic details within single words. Now we must note that in casual spoken forms of American English there are a number of phonological contraction processes in which a *sequence* of words is contracted, or reduced, to a shorter sequence. For example, consider the various phonological contractions of forms of the verb *to be*, illustrated in tables 3.5 and 3.6. Taking table 3.5 first, notice that a sequence of words from formal written language such as *she is* will be pronounced in

Table 3.5

Phonetic form of contractions of the verb *to be* with personal pronouns in American English: Bisyllabic forms

Formal written	Formal spoken	Casual spoken bisyllabic forms
I am	/aɪ æm/	/áɪəm/ (or /aɪm̩/)
you are	/ju ɑɹ/	/júɚ/
she is	/ʃi ɪz/	/ʃíɨz/
he is	/hi ɪz/	/híɨz/
it is	/ɪt ɪz/	/íɾɨz/
we are	/wi ɑɹ/	/wíɚ/
they are	/ðeɪ ɑɹ/	/ðéɪɚ/

Table 3.6

Phonetic form of contractions of the verb *to be* with personal pronouns in American English: Monosyllabic forms

Casual written	Casual spoken monosyllabic forms
I'm	[aɪm] or [ɑm]
you're	[jʊɹ] or [jɚ]
she's	[ʃiz]
he's	[hiz]
it's	[ɪts]
we're	[wɪɹ]
they're	[ðɛɹ]

careful, or formal, speech as a sequence of two separate words /ʃi/ /ɪz/, whereas in more casual, rapid speech they are "merged" into a single bisyllabic (two-syllable) form /ʃíɨz/, with stress on the first syllable, indicated by an accent mark, ´, above the first vowel. Notice further that in the bisyllabic form /ʃíɨz/, the vowel /ɪ/ of /ɪz/ is reduced to /ɨ/, a reduction phenomenon that also takes place when the two-word sequence *I am* becomes a single bisyllabic form /áɪəm/, where /æ/ is reduced to /ə/ in the unstressed syllable. Recall that the reduced vowels /ɨ/ and /ə/ occur only in unstressed syllables of a word, as in *sofa* /sóʊfə/ and *chicken* /tʃíkɨn/. In other words, the bisyllabic forms /ʃíɨz/ and /áɪəm/ (or /aɪm̩/) reflect phonetic patterns characteristic of single words, and indeed we can consider such bisyllabic contractions as single phonological words.

To take a final example from table 3.5, consider the sequences with the verb *are: you are, we are, they are*. Notice that in the bisyllabic contracted forms of casual speech, *are* [ɑɹ] is reduced to [ɚ] alone (the vowel [ɑ] having been reduced and merged with the /ɹ/), and in fact this /ɚ/ functions as the second (unstressed) syllable. In the forms /juɚ/, /wiɚ/, and /ðeɪɚ/, notice that the tense vowels /u/, /i/, and /eɪ/ are in the first (stressed) syllable, and /ɚ/ forms the second syllable. This sequence "tense vowel + /ɚ/" reflects the syllabic pattern discussed earlier, which is found quite generally in single words of American English: the two members of the sequence "tense vowel + *r*-sound" must be in different syllables. Therefore, this syllabic pattern is just what we find in the bisyllabic contractions /juɚ/, /wiɚ/, and /ðeɪɚ/.

Notice that in very casual speech the bisyllabic forms of the contractions in table 3.5 can be realized as monosyllabic forms (table 3.6). In these examples we see that *am, are,* and *is* have lost their vowels entirely and have become reduced to /m/, /ɚ/, and /z/, respectively. Thus, *I'm* is pronounced as monosyllabic /aɪm/ or /am/, having lost the schwa (and the glide in the second form) in /áɪəm/. In the forms *you're* (/jʊɹ/), *we're* (/wɪɹ/), and *they're* (/ðɛɹ/), notice that /ɹ/ is now in the same syllable as the preceding vowel; however, the vowel is now a lax vowel (/ʊ, ɪ, ɛ/) and thus /ɹ/ can occur with it as part of the same syllable. There is another variant pronunciation of the contraction *you're*, namely, /jɚ/. In this case the /ʊ/ and the /ɹ/ have merged to create the *r*-colored vowel /ɚ/.

Consonant Clusters

The sequence of English speech sounds in a word is not arbitrary. In fact, there are strict conditions on the order and type of speech sounds that can appear. At the beginning of a word all consonants except /ŋ/ can appear. If two consonants occur at the beginning, however, the possibilities are quite limited. Consider the sequences in (4):

(4)
*bt, *nk, *gb, *pb, *pt, *pk

None of these combinations can begin an English word, even though they can all be found word-internally (e.g., *napkin*). By contrast, all the combinations in (5) are permissible word-initial sequences of English:

(5)
br, dr, gr, bl, gl, pr, tr, kr, pl, kl

Native speakers of English can instantly tell if a combination of sounds is possible, suggesting that speakers have internalized a set of principles that determine well-formedness. To begin to form an idea of what these principles are, note that the difference between the disallowed sequences in (4) and the allowed sequences in (5) is that the former consist of two stops and the latter consist of a stop followed by a /l/ or /r/. In English a word-initial sequence of two stops is not possible, but a sequence of a stop plus /l/ or /r/ is possible (with a couple of exceptions). Conditions of this type are generally referred to as the *phonotactic constraints* (or *phonotactics*) of a language.

Every language has its own set of conditions on consonant sequencing. When a word is borrowed into one language from another, the borrowed word is often restructured to conform to the sequencing conditions in the borrowing language. When English words are borrowed into the Hawaiian language, first, the consonants and vowels in Hawaiian that are closest to the English counterparts are employed, and second, the English words are restructured to conform to Hawaiian phonotactic constraints. The English greeting *Merry Christmas* sounds very different when pronounced by a native speaker of Hawaiian. Figure 3.11 displays the alterations that occur when the English version is converted into Hawaiian.

m ɛ ɹ i k   ɹ ɪ s   m ʌ s
| | | | | | | | | | |
m e l i k a l i k a m a k a

Figure 3.11
How a speaker of Hawaiian pronounces the English expression *Merry Christmas*

Earlier we noted that Hawaiian has 8 consonants (/p, m, n, l, k, h, w, ʔ/) and 5 vowels (/a, e, i, o, u/) and that English has 24 consonants and 15 vowels. There are therefore fewer consonants and vowels available in Hawaiian to represent the consonants and vowels of English. The closest sound to English /r/ is Hawaiian /l/. Somewhat surprising is the fact that the closest consonant to English /s/ is Hawaiian /k/. The other big adjustment in this Hawaiian borrowing is a phonotactic one: Hawaiian does not permit consonant clusters or syllable-final obstruents. As a result, the Hawaiian vowel /a/ is inserted after every consonant that is not immediately followed by a vowel in the borrowed word. *Meli Kalikamaka* is thus the Hawaiian version of *Merry Christmas*.

Exercises

1. George Bernard Shaw, in ridiculing the English spelling system, claimed that a possible spelling for *fish* could be *ghoti*. Why did he claim this? (Hint: The *o* in *women* /wɪmɨn/ is pronounced as an /ɪ/.)

2. Give the English speech sound symbol that corresponds to the following articulatory descriptions:

a. voiceless bilabial stop
b. voiced alveolar stop
c. lax high front vowel
d. voiceless alveolar fricative
e. liquid
f. voiced interdental fricative
g. voiceless alveopalatal affricate
h. tense high back vowel
i. lax low front vowel
j. voiceless velar stop

3. Describe each of the following speech sound symbols using articulatory features:

a. /n/
b. /ʊ/
c. /s/
d. /z/
e. /m/
f. /a/
g. /ɛ/
h. /h/
i. /g/
j. /ʌ/

4. Write the speech sound symbol for the *first* sound in each of the following words. Examples: *fish* /f/, *chagrin* /ʃ/.

a. psychology
b. use
c. thought
d. cow
e. knowledge
f. though
g. pneumonia
h. cybernetics
i. physics
j. memory

5. Write the speech sound symbol for the *last* sound in each of the following words. Examples: *bleach* /tʃ/, *sigh* /aɪ/.

a. cats   f. judge
b. dogs   g. rough
c. bushes   h. tongue
d. sighed   i. garage
e. bleached   j. climb

6. Write the speech sound symbol for the *vowel* in each of the following words. Examples: *fish* /ɪ/, *table* /eɪ/.

a. mood   f. five
b. caught   g. bait
c. cot   h. toy
d. and   i. said
e. tree   j. soot

7. Note the following pairs of words:

a. /bæd/ *bad* and /bæg/ *bag*
b. /sɪn/ *sin* and /sɪŋ/ *sing*
c. /bɛd/ *bed* and /bɛg/ *beg*

You may speak a dialect of American English in which the vowels in the words on the right differ from those in the words on the left. Describe the differences and determine why the vowels are different. (Hint: Consider tongue movement.)

8. Write the following words in the transcription system given in this chapter.

a. 1. through   6. though
    2. rough   7. blink
    3. gouge   8. hinge
    4. Knox   9. hang
    5. draft   10. try
b. 1. miss   6. three
    2. his   7. paste
    3. shoe   8. trash
    4. edge   9. blunt
    5. foot   10. thigh
c. 1. bow (bend at waist)   6. hands
    2. bow (for shooting arrows)   7. loose
    3. hand   8. lose
    4. which   9. tasks
    5. witch   10. chat
d. 1. strengths   6. yeast
    2. halve   7. gym
    3. salve   8. mend
    4. cloths   9. sixths
    5. clothes   10. boil

9. Write the names of the letters of the alphabet using the phonemic symbols given in this chapter. For example, *a* = /eɪ/, *b* = /bi/, *c* = /si/, and so forth. Can

you find any "rhyme or reason" to the vowels that appear with the alphabetic consonants?

10. Write the following words using the phonetic symbols discussed in this chapter:

a. water   f. splat
b. lit   g. tin
c. eaten   h. beading
d. pull   i. beating
e. craft   j. beatin' (casual speech)

11. In some of the following words (e.g., *play*) the *l*'s and the *r*'s are voiceless. Identify these words and try to establish the conditions under which *l* and *r* lose their voicing.

a. Alpo   f. try
b. archive   g. splat
c. black   h. spread
d. play   i. leap
e. dream   j. read

12. Transcribe the following words exhibiting vowels before *r*. (See section 3.3; be aware that dialectal variations will abound in these words.)

a. boor   f. dear
b. bore   g. fir
c. poor   h. mire
d. care   i. sewer
e. car   j. mirror

13. Write the following combinations as contractions (monosyllables, if possible), using the phonetic symbols given in this chapter. Example: *she will* = /ʃɪl/.

a. I will   g. I would
b. you will   h. you would
c. he will   i. she would
d. it will   j. it would
e. we will   k. we would
f. they will   l. they would

14. Using phonetic symbols where possible, write a contracted form (there is more than one version for each of these expressions) for the following sequences, as though they were pronounced in the frame "____ want?" Example: In *What do I want?*, *what do I* = [wʌɾəwaɪ].

a. what do I
b. what do you
c. what does she
d. what does it
e. what do we
f. what do they

15. Nicholas, the 6-year-old son of one of the authors, used the creative spelling *thingck* to spell the word *think*. What assumptions on his part produced this spelling?

Further Reading

General

The study of phonetics is typically divided into *articulatory* and *acoustic phonetics*. Most introductory texts cover both topics: for example, Borden and Harris 1980, MacKay 1987, Lieberman and Blumstein 1988, and Ladefoged 1994. There are also several good books that concentrate on one area; for example, Johnson 1997 and Pickett 1999 cover acoustic phonetics, and Small 1999 is a good practical introduction to English articulation. Fry 1979 and Denes and Pinson 1993 provide a good overview of the physics underlying the acoustic study of language. For a discussion of the *International Phonetic Alphabet* (IPA) and other symbol systems for transcribing speech sounds, see Pullum and Ladusaw 1996.

Special Topics

Kahn 1976 is still an excellent and current discussion of the /ɹ/ *phoneme* and the vowels that co-occur with it. *Consonant clusters in English* are treated in Clements and Keyser 1983.

Journals

Journal of Phonetics, Phonetica, Journal of the Acoustic Society of America, Journal of Speech and Hearing Sciences

Bibliography

Borden, G., and K. Harris. 1980. *Speech science primer*. Baltimore, Md.: Waverly Press.

Chomsky, N., and M. Halle. 1968. *The sound pattern of English*. New York: Harper and Row.

Clements, G. N., and S. J. Keyser. 1983. *CV phonology: A generative theory of the syllable*. Cambridge, Mass.: MIT Press.

Denes, P., and E. Pinson. 1993. *The speech chain: The physics and biology of spoken language*. New York: W. H. Freeman.

Farmer, A. K., and R. A. Demers. 2001. *A linguistics workbook*. 4th ed. Cambridge, Mass.: MIT Press.

Fry, D. 1979. *The physics of speech*. Cambridge: Cambridge University Press.

Johnson, K. 1997. *Acoustic and auditory phonetics*. Cambridge, Mass.: Blackwell.

Kahn, D. 1976. Syllable-based generalizations in English phonology. Doctoral dissertation, MIT.

Ladefoged, P. 1994. *A course in phonetics*. 3rd ed. New York: Harcourt Brace Jovanovich.

Lenneberg, E. 1967. *Biological foundations of language*. New York: Wiley.

Lieberman, P., and S. Blumstein. 1988. *Speech physiology and acoustic phonetics: An introduction*. New York: Cambridge University Press.

MacKay, I. 1987. *Phonetics: The science of speech production*. 2nd ed. Boston: Little Brown.

Pickett, J. M. 1999. *The acoustics of speech communication: Fundamentals, speech perception theory, and technology*. Needham Heights, Mass.: Allyn and Bacon.

Pullum, G. K., and W. A. Ladusaw. 1996. *Phonetic symbol guide*. 2nd ed. Chicago: University of Chicago Press.

Small, L. 1999. *Fundamentals of phonetics: A practical guide for students*. Needham Heights, Mass.: Allyn and Bacon.

Chapter 4

Phonology: The Study of Sound Structure

In the introduction to chapter 3 we noted that the discrete, linear transcription system that we use to write languages is an idealization. There is nothing in the physical realization of speech (articulation and the acoustic signal) that corresponds to the discrete linear properties of our writing system. Speech is continuous and the phonetic segments overlap, yet speakers have little trouble accepting that speech can be represented by a writing system that uses discrete and linearly written symbols. Such writing systems have been in use for more than two thousand years, since the Greeks, inspired by the Phoenician writing system, developed an orthography that represented both vowels and consonants as separable and autonomous units. The idea that the fundamental sound units of a language are consonants and vowels has persisted since that time, and only in the twentieth century was it discovered that consonants and vowels are in turn composed of more basic units, the so-called *distinctive features*. We will discuss the evidence for these features in this chapter.

4.1 WHAT IS PHONOLOGY?

Phonology is the subfield of linguistics that studies the structure and systematic patterning of sounds in human language. The term *phonology* is used in two ways. On the one hand, it refers to a description of the sounds of a particular language and the rules governing the distribution of those sounds. Thus, we can talk about the phonology of English, German, or any other language. On the other hand, it refers to that part of the general theory of human language that is concerned with the universal properties of natural language sound systems (i.e., properties reflected in many, if not all, human languages). In this chapter we will describe a portion of the phonology of English, but we will also discuss some properties of the more general and universal theory of phonology that underlies the sound pattern of all languages. In addition, we will survey some of the phonological rules that are found in most dialects of American English.

As an initial strategy we will take the alternation in pronunciation of the English plural morpheme as an organizing theme for several topics in this chapter. For example, in regard to the plural morpheme, we can ask the following questions:

• What is the proper description of the three different *sounds* of the English plural morpheme shown in table 3.1?
• What are the *conditions on the alternation* that will account for where the different phonological forms of the English plural morpheme occur?

These two questions lead naturally into the more general topics of this chapter:

• What is the proper description of the various sounds that are found generally in human language?
• What is the proper general framework for describing the sound patterns of human language?

We provided tentative answers to the first two questions in chapter 3, but in order to develop all the answers in sufficient detail, we must investigate further properties of the phonology of English as well as of other languages.

4.2   THE INTERNAL STRUCTURE OF SPEECH SOUNDS: DISTINCTIVE FEATURE THEORY

We will see in this section that speech sounds (phones and phonemes) are not the smallest units of phonological systems; rather, the speech sounds themselves are composed of yet smaller features of articulation. We already noted in chapter 3 that generalizations (rules) regarding plural forms are best stated in terms of phonetic features such as voicing. In formulating the English Plural Rule, we made use of the feature of voicing to state an important generalization about the plural shapes: aside from cases where a noun ends in one of the consonants /s, z, ʃ, ʒ, tʃ, dʒ/, the phonological form of the plural morpheme is determined by a general assimilation process, whereby the plural form is voiceless if the final phoneme of the noun is voiceless but is voiced if the final phoneme of the noun is voiced. The feature of voicing, then, allows us to state a generalization that we miss by merely listing phonemes (compare, again, the discussion of hypotheses 2 and 3 of the Plural Rule in chapter 3).

The English Plural Rule exemplifies an important point about determining which phonetic features of a language are in fact the significant ones for a theory of phonology. In English the feature of *voicing* plays two important roles: (1) it plays a crucial role in the statement of phonological regularities, such as the Plural Rule, and (2) it is minimally distinctive in that it serves to distinguish phonemes such as /z/ and /s/ in minimal pairs such as /zɪp/ and /sɪp/. In general, then, the significant phonetic features of human language are those that play a crucial role in the statement of phonological rules and/or distinguish phonemes from one another. Because of the latter function, these features are commonly called *distinctive features*.

Three questions immediately present themselves: What are the correct features? How many are there? Are the same ones found in all languages? We indirectly introduced a feature system in chapter 3. The point- and manner-of-articulation features represent a prima facie acknowledgment that speech sounds can be characterized by the phonetic features that make up these sounds. The features presented in table 3.2 appear to satisfy the criteria of insightfully characterizing phonological regularities and serve to minimally distinguish phonemes. Using these features, we can pick out *classes* of sounds; for example, the manner feature of voicing from table 3.2 was necessary for an insightful characterization of the plural forms.

But the system embodied in table 3.2 is not quite right for a general theory of phonology. This is because the table is stated entirely in terms of the way consonants are articulated in English. For example, the stops /t/ and /d/ are listed as *alveolar*, given that in English these stops are articulated with the tongue tip making contact with the alveolar ridge. But this is not how *t* and *d* are articulated in all languages. For example, in Japanese and in certain continental European languages (such as Spanish) *t* and *d* are *dental* stops: that is, the tongue tip makes contact on the teeth, rather than on the alveolar ridge. Thus, the feature system that forms the basis for table 3.2 would not be accurate for Spanish and Japanese, at least not with respect to the phonemes /t/ and /d/.

This leaves us in an unsatisfactory position: after all, there is an intuitively natural sense in which we want to say that Spanish, Japanese, and English all have the stop consonants *t* and *d*, and whether one type is basically dental and the other type is basically alveolar should not be significant. Furthermore, even in diverse languages the same rules are applicable to both kinds of *t*'s and *d*'s. For example, *t* and *d* become *palatalized* (articulated farther back on the hard palate), typically resulting in the creation of affricates such as /tʃ/ and /dʒ/. Such palatalization processes usually happen in the environment of high front sounds such as /i/ or /j/. For instance, in the English casual speech pronunciation of *don't* plus *you* as *dontcha* /doʊntʃə/, the final /t/ of *don't* becomes /tʃ/ when combined with the glide /j/ of *you*. In Japanese the phoneme /t/ has the positional variant /tʃ/ when followed by the high vowel /i/ or /j/, a palatalization process also found in Brazilian Portuguese, which like Spanish has dental stops. These examples illustrate that despite minor differences in the articulation of *t* that exist across languages, these stops undergo very similar palatalization processes (and other rules as well). Therefore, we want to be able to talk about stops such as *t* and *d* across a number of languages, in a general way that will overlook irrelevant details in articulation.

To this end, a good deal of research in phonology has been aimed at defining a set of phonetic features that will, in fact, allow us to abstract away from English and other languages in such a way that we can refer to consonants and vowels in a general fashion and with crosslinguistic validity. For example, instead of using the phonetic feature *alveolar* to describe /t/ and /d/, phonologists have postulated a feature *coronal* to describe all articulations in which the tongue blade raises to approach or contact the teeth, the alveolar ridge, or the prepalatal region of the roof of the mouth. The feature *coronal* is clearly a more general feature than the feature *alveolar*, in that it includes a wider range of possible articulations. Thus, regardless of the fact that Spanish and Japanese have dental *t*, and that English has alveolar *t*, we can say that these languages all have *(voiceless) coronal stops*. Crosslinguistic considerations have compelled us to propose a feature (coronal) that is more general than the traditional feature(s) (alveolar, dental).

Sometimes, however, we are compelled to propose features that result from decomposition of a traditional feature. We stated in chapter 3 that the phoneme /k/ in English is a voiceless *velar* stop (i.e., it is produced when the tongue touches the soft palate or velum). But in fact it is not always completely velar. Under certain circumstances /k/ is articulated with the body of the tongue making contact with the roof of the mouth at the point where the hard palate joins the velum, producing a prevelar (or postpalatal) *k*. For example, whenever /k/ is followed by the tense vowel diphthong /i/ or the glide /j/, *k* has a prevelar articulation. In words such as *key* /ki/ or *cute* /kjut/, /k/ is prevelar because of a coarticulation effect; in articulating /i/ or /j/, the tongue body must be raised into a high position near the hard palate, and in articulating /k/ before these phonemes, the articulation of /i/ or /j/ is anticipated so that the tongue shifts forward and makes contact in the prevelar region. In contrast, when /k/ is followed by a back vowel, as in *cool* /kul/, it is indeed a velar consonant. However, there is an important feature that all instances of /k/ share: all /k/'s of English are articulated with a *high* tongue body, and they differ only in how far *front* or *back* the high tongue body makes contact with the roof of the mouth. Thus, phonologists have proposed that the features *high* and *back*—the same features used in the description of certain vowels—should characterize /k/, rather than a feature *velar*. The /k/ that precedes front vowels, such as /i/, will be characterized as *high* but *nonback*; the /k/ that precedes back vowels, such as /u/, will be characterized as both *high* and *back*. In other words, /k/ is in both cases *high*, but its specification for *backness* is determined by the adjacent vowel, and therefore the relative backness in the /k/ does not function distinctively. Recall that distinctive features serve to distinguish phonemes. Separating the single feature *velar* into two features *high* and *back* now makes a prediction: there could be a language that has two contrasting /k/ phonemes, one that is high and back and another that is high and nonback. Romanian is just such a language. By replacing a feature such as *velar* with the features *high* and *back*, we can now properly distinguish the /k/ in English from those in other languages, at the same time capturing what all the different types of *k* have in common.

As we examine a range of languages, the need to devise a feature system that has universal validity will become even clearer. This set of features must describe all phonemic contrasts in all languages and must also express all the phonological regularities (rules) in a perspicuous manner.

For the reasons discussed above, it is clear that the manner- and place-of-articulation features listed in table 3.2 are not the optimum set of phonetic features for describing the world's languages. Because of such problems a number of linguists have proposed alternative phonetic feature systems, and we will now examine one of the most influential of these in some detail.

Table 4.1
Distinctive feature composition of English consonants

	p	b	m	t	d	n	k	g	ŋ	f	v
Syllabic	−	−	−	−	−	−	−	−	−	−	−
			(+)			(+)					
Consonantal	+	+	+	+	+	+	+	+	+	+	+
Sonorant	−	−	+	−	−	+	−	−	+	−	−
Voiced	−	+	+	−	+	+	−	+	+	−	+
Continuant	−	−	−	−	−	−	−	−	−	+	+
Nasal	−	−	+	−	−	+	−	−	+	−	−
Strident	−	−	−	−	−	−	−	−	−	+	+
Lateral	−	−	−	−	−	−	−	−	−	−	−
Distributed	−	−	−	−	−	−	−	−	−	−	−
Affricate	−	−	−	−	−	−	−	−	−	−	−
Labial	+	+	+	−	−	−	−	−	−	+	+
Round	−	−	−	−	−	−	−	−	−	−	−
Coronal	−	−	−	+	+	+	−	−	−	−	−
Anterior	+	+	+	+	+	+	−	−	−	+	+
High	−	−	−	−	−	−	+	+	+	−	−
Back	−	−	−	−	−	−	+	+	+	−	−
Low	−	−	−	−	−	−	−	−	−	−	−

An *SPE*-Based System

In tables 4.1 and 4.2 we have listed the consonants and vowels of English as they are classified in a distinctive feature system based on the one proposed by Morris Halle and Noam Chomsky in their 1968 work, *The Sound Pattern of English* (*SPE*). Their proposals in turn build on the pioneering work in distinctive feature theory carried out by Halle and Roman Jakobson (Jakobson and Halle 1956). In the *SPE* system the articulatory features are viewed as basically *binary*, that is, as having one of two values: either a *plus* value (+), which indicates the presence of the feature, or a *minus* value (−), which indicates the absence of the feature.

	s	z	θ	ð	ʃ	ʒ	tʃ	dʒ	l	ɹ	w (ʍ)	j	h
Syllabic	−	−	−	−	−	−	−	−	−	−	−	−	−
									(+)	(+)			
Consonantal	+	+	+	+	+	+	+	+	+	−	−	−	−
Sonorant	−	−	−	−	−	−	−	−	+	+	+	+	+
Voiced	−	+	−	+	−	+	−	+	+	+	+	+	−
Continuant	+	+	+	+	+	+	−	−	+	+	+	+	+
Nasal	−	−	−	−	−	−	−	−	−	−	−	−	−
Strident	+	+	−	−	+	+	+	+	−	−	−	−	−
Lateral	−	−	−	−	−	−	−	−	+	−	−	−	−
Distributed	−	−	−	−	+	+	+	+	−	−	−	−	−
Affricate	−	−	−	−	−	−	+	+	−	−	−	−	−
Labial	−	−	−	−	−	−	−	−	−	−	+	−	−
Round	−	−	−	−	−	−	−	−	−	+	+	−	−
Coronal	+	+	+	+	+	+	+	+	+	+	−	+	−
Anterior	+	+	+	+	−	−	−	−	+	+			
High	−	−	−	−	+	+	+	+	−	−	+	+	−
Back	−	−	−	−	−	−	−	−	−	−	+	−	−
Low	−	−	−	−	−	−	−	−	+	−	−	−	(+)

Each phonetic feature represents an individually controllable aspect of articulation. For example, the feature *nasal* is related to the raising or lowering of the velum. The phoneme /m/ thus has the feature [+nasal], whereas the phoneme /b/ has the feature [−nasal]; this indicates that in the articulation of /m/ the velum is lowered, and in the articulation of /b/ the velum is raised. (Distinctive features, by convention, are enclosed in square brackets [ ], and we will use this convention in the rest of this chapter.) In a similar fashion, all phonemes in the *SPE* system are regarded as *bundles of features*, that is, as groups of binary features with pluses and minuses, as can be seen in tables 4.1 and 4.2. Notice that the

Table 4.2
Distinctive feature composition of English vowels. (ə does in fact differ from ʌ, a difference that is accounted for in the section "Assigning Feet to English Words.")

	i	ɪ	e	ɛ	æ	u	ʊ	ʌ	o	ɔ	ɑ	ə	ɨ
			(eɪ)						(oʊ)				
Syllabic	+	+	+	+	+	+	+	+	+	+	+	+	+
High	+	+	−	−	−	+	+	−	−	−	−	−	+
Back	−	−	−	−	−	+	+	+	+	+	+	+	+
Low	−	−	−	−	+	−	−	−	−	+	+	−	−
Round	−	−	−	−	−	+	+	−	+	+	−	−	−
Tense (long)	+	−	+	−	−	+	−	−	+	−	−	−	−

features allow us to distinguish all the consonant phonemes from one another and at the same time to refer to classes of sounds (e.g., the class of *voiceless consonants*). The distinctive features of the *SPE* system, which we will now briefly describe individually, are proposed as universal features, and not merely as features peculiar to English.

Syllabic The feature [+syllabic] is assigned to phonemes that can function as the head (or peak) of a syllable (we will define "syllable" more accurately in section 4.3). The vowels of English are, of course, syllabic.

Consonantal Phonemes with the feature [+consonantal] are formed in the vocal tract with an obstruction that is at least as narrow as that of a fricative. Note that the glides are therefore not true consonants—nor, as we will see, are they true vowels.

Sonorant "Sonorant sounds are produced with a vocal tract cavity in which spontaneous voicing is possible" (*SPE*, 302). In other words, the vocal tract is not constricted to the extent that airflow across the glottis is inhibited. Vowels, glides, liquids, and nasals are all [+sonorant]. [−sonorant] consonants are frequently referred to as *obstruents.*

Voiced Phonemes are voiced when their articulation is accompanied by a periodic vibration of the vocal cords. All of the phonemes in the word |*bead*| (/bid/) are [+voiced], whereas the phonemes /p/, /t/, and /k/ are [−voiced].

Continuant [−continuant] sounds are made with a complete blockage of the oral cavity. [+continuant] sounds are made without such a blockage.

By this definition nasals are oral [−continuant] stops, although airflow and acoustic energy are shunted through the nasal cavity.

Nasal   Phonemes have the feature [+nasal] when the velum is lowered during speech, thus permitting the airflow and sound energy to activate resonances in the nasal cavity.

Strident   [+strident] sounds are characterized by the high-frequency turbulent noise that accompanies the production of some fricatives and affricates. The phoneme /s/ is [+strident], whereas the phoneme /θ/ is [−strident].

Lateral   If the tip of the tongue is partially blocking the airstream, but the air is allowed to pass along one or both sides of the tongue, the resulting sound is [+lateral]. The phoneme /l/ is the only [+lateral] sound in English.

Distributed   The term *distributed* refers to the relative length of contact that the tongue makes along (not across) the roof of the mouth. The tongue has a relatively longer region of contact along the roof of the mouth in articulating /ʃ/ than in articulating /s/; thus, /ʃ/ is [+distributed] but /s/ is [−distributed]. The terms *laminal* ([+distributed]) and *apical* ([−distributed]) have been used in the past to characterize this articulatory difference.

Affricate (or *Delayed Release*)   Recall that affricates are produced by articulatory gestures during which the airflow is temporarily stopped, but the stoppage is secondarily released into a fricative. This sequence of a stop plus a fricative functions in English as a single phoneme, as in /tʃ/ and /dʒ/.

Labial   A labial articulation involves a bringing together or closing of the lips. The phonemes /f/, /b/, and /m/ are all [+labial].

Round   A round articulation involves an extension and pursing of the lips. All sounds that are [+round] are redundantly [+labial], but [+labial] sounds are not necessarily [+round]. The /b/ in *bead* /bid/, for example, though labial, is produced with no rounding.

Coronal   In articulating a [+coronal] phoneme, the blade of the tongue is raised toward or touches the teeth, the alveolar ridge, or an area along the back of the alveolar ridge. Dental, alveolar, and alveopalatal consonants are [+coronal] phonemes.

Anterior   Anterior sounds are made with the primary constriction in front of the alveopalatal position. Labial, dental, interdental, and alveolar articulations are [+anterior].

High   In articulating a [+high] phoneme, the body of the tongue is raised toward or touches the roof of the mouth. The phonemes /k/, /ŋ/, /tʃ/ are all [+high].

Back   [+back] phonemes are made with the tongue body slightly retracted from the rest (quiet breathing) position. [−back] phonemes (also called front) are made with the tongue body in a relatively forward position. The phoneme /tʃ/ in *chuck* is [−back], whereas the /k/ in that word is [+back].

Low   Phonemes with this feature are made with the tongue body lowered and the root retracted. American English /ɹ/ is [+low] because of its associated pharyngeal constriction.

We now turn to the phonetic features of the vowels given in table 4.2. The features [high], [low], and [back] are the same tongue body features used for characterizing consonants. The gestures associated with these features in vowels are not as extreme, however, as they are for consonants. Two other features found in vowels, [syllabic] and [round], have also already been discussed in connection with vowels. The feature [+tense] is associated with a more extreme articulatory gesture than its [−tense] (lax) counterpart. The [+tense] vowel /i/ is higher and more front than the [−tense] /ɪ/.

The feature [tense] is used to distinguish /ɛ/ and /eɪ/, although we have already noted that there is more than a difference in length and muscle tension between these vowels: /eɪ/ begins in a higher position in the mouth than /ɛ/, and /eɪ/ also has a high offglide. We have therefore listed the tense (long) vowels /eɪ/ and /oʊ/ in terms of the features of their *first* segment. The remaining diphthongs /aɪ/, /aʊ/, and /ɔɪ/ are not listed in table 4.2; they are to be analyzed as clusters of two phonemes: for example /aɪ/ = /a/ + /ɪ/.

Phonemes as Groups of Distinctive Features

As we have seen, the phonemes of all languages may be described in terms of differing subsets of the universally available set of distinctive features, some of which have already been discussed in the description of English phonemes. Although all languages draw from the same universal set of features, individual languages differ in the groups of features that make up their phonemes. For example, the features [coronal], [lateral], [affricate], and [distributed] are all found in English, but they never occur together in a single phoneme. In contrast, in Navajo as well as in many

Table 4.3
Stop and affricate consonants in four unrelated and geographically separated languages

	[labial]	[coronal]	$\begin{bmatrix}+\text{high}\\-\text{back}\end{bmatrix}$	$\begin{bmatrix}+\text{high}\\+\text{back}\end{bmatrix}$
English (Europe, Australia,	p	t	tʃ	k
North America)	b	d	dʒ	g
Navajo (North America)	(missing)	t	tʃ	k
	b	d	dʒ	g
Ganda (Africa)	p	t	c (stop)	k
	b	d	ɟ (stop)	g
Japanese (Asia)	p	t	tʃ	k
	b	d	dʒ	g

other Native American languages of North America, these features do occur together in a single consonant called a *lateral affricate*; the Navajo word *tlah* "ointment" begins with this phoneme, which is represented by the two letters *tl* in the Navajo writing system. To take another example, English does not have the feature of rounding in front vowels, but many European languages do, among them French, German, Hungarian, and Finnish. Thus, the widely differing sounds occurring in the world's languages are actually based on different combinations of a relatively small, restricted set of features such as those given in tables 4.1 and 4.2.

Despite the fact that languages draw upon different features to make up their phonemes, however, there is a surprising amount of convergence in the sound systems of human language. To get a somewhat wider perspective, consider now the consonants listed in table 4.3, drawn from four unrelated, geographically separated languages. Notice that all four languages form their stops at the same general points along the vocal tract: the [labial], the [coronal] (dental/alveolar), the [+high, −back] (palatal), and the [+high, +back] (velar) regions.

It is striking that, despite minor differences in the details of pronunciation, the consonant systems of these diverse languages, and indeed in the majority of the world's languages, cluster around these same regions of articulation. There is intriguing evidence that these particular points of articulation are regions of *acoustic stability* (Stevens 1989). For example, the sound produced by tongue-tip contact throughout the dental and alveolar region is relatively stable acoustically, in that the sound is relatively constant regardless of minor shifts in the position of the tongue within this region. In contrast, the regions of articulation between the commonly occurring points of articulation—for example, the region on the border between the dental/alveolar region and the palatal region—are regions of acoustic instability, where even a small shift in the position of the tongue leads to radical changes in the acoustic properties of the sound. Thus, it is only for articulations made in the vocal tract's regions of acoustic stability that there is considerable "leeway" for tongue position. This leeway permits more rapid speech and coarticulation effects when the target area is larger since an exact articulatory target is not necessary. It is probably not an accident, therefore, that the majority of the world's languages have consonant systems with places of articulation similar to those shown in table 4.3, involving the features [labial], [coronal], [high], and [back].

We do not wish to underemphasize the fact that there are important differences between languages. In chapter 3 we discussed clicks, which are part of the consonant systems of several languages spoken on the African continent. Characteristic of click consonants is that two points of articulation are required to produce them. In addition, there are other, nonclick consonants—also typical of African languages—that are formed with two simultaneous points of contact. The language Igbo (often written *Ibo*), spoken in Nigeria, contains a single sound made with one point of articulation at the lips and the other in the velar region. The language name itself contains this sound, written here as the digraph *gb*. This articulatory combination is not found in English, so it is difficult for an English speaker to coordinate the contact and release of both of these points simultaneously. The sequences *Ig-bo* or *Ib-go* often result instead of the correct *I-g͡bo*. There is an additional complication regarding the airflow during the articulation of this *gb*-sound; it is produced with air flowing inward from the mouth into the vocal tract, a so-called *ingressive* sound.

Consonants with more than one point of articulation are not uncommon. In fact, as noted earlier, English /w/ has both labial and velar constrictions. English /l/ has both a contact coronal and an approximate velar articulation, which gives it its "dark" quality and differentiates it from the *l*'s of French, German, and Spanish, which are never produced with an accompanying velar articulation.

To conclude, the set of universal distinctive features is a set that is *available* to all languages; not all features and combinations of features are actually found in each individual language.

The Role of Distinctive Features in the Expression of Phonological Rules

We have been arguing that the fundamental contrasting units of a language are not the phonemes but the features that make up the phonemes. Additional support for analyzing phonemes into their constituent features comes from the insightful way that phonological regularities can be stated in terms of the features that make up the phonemes.

Let us return one final time to the English Plural Rule and reformulate it in terms of the *SPE* distinctive features.

As part of the reformulation we need to address another point. We assumed in chapter 3 that the plural had "three shapes" (/s/, /z/, /ɨz/) and that these were assigned to a noun depending on the phonetic features of its last phoneme. Recall the final formulation of the Plural Rule from chapter 3:

(1)
Hypothesis 3 (Use of phonetic features)
The forms of the plural morpheme are distributed according to the following conditions:
a. The plural morpheme takes the form /ɨz/ if the last sound in the noun to which it attaches is an *alveolar fricative*, an *alveopalatal fricative*, or an *alveopalatal affricate*.
Otherwise:
b. The plural morpheme takes the voiced form /z/ if the last sound in the noun is *voiced*.
c. The plural morpheme takes the voiceless form /s/ if the last sound in the noun is *voiceless*.

There is no evidence for the assumption that there are three different plural forms, given as a list. In fact, there is an alternative: namely, that the plural morpheme has *one* shape and that there are conditions on pronunciation (or phonological rules) that determine the realization of the different plural shapes. We will incorporate this proposal directly below.

It has been argued (Pinker and Prince 1988) that the basic shape of the plural morpheme is /z/ and that all variations are due to phonological rules of English. If we assume that /z/ is added to all nonexceptional English nouns, then we must have an explanation for the fact that we actually say and hear three different shapes, /s/, /z/, and /ɨz/. Part (a) of hypothesis 3 states that the "plural ending" /ɨz/ follows *alveolar fricatives, alveopalatal fricatives,* and *alveopalatal affricates*. There is nothing in the place and manner features that suggests why the six consonants /s, z, ʃ, ʒ, tʃ, dʒ/ should pattern together. In contrast, the *SPE* distinctive features offer a ready explanation for this grouping: namely, they are uniquely described as the consonants containing the features [+strident, +coronal]. So the *SPE* features have the obvious advantage of making clear the basis for the patterning together of a *natural class* of English phonemes.

Second, the statement in part (a) of hypothesis 3 does not explain *why* the /ɨz/ form of the plural morpheme should appear in the environment of this particular natural class of phonemes. Using *SPE* features, the occurrence of the /ɨz/ form can be understood, if not explained. Note that if the plural morpheme is /z/, then an /ɨ/ must be present between the plural morpheme and the final phoneme of the noun. Such vowel insertion is known as *epenthesis*, a common occurrence in the world's languages. The insertion of the /ɨ/ has the likely function of keeping the [+strident, +coronal] /z/ of the plural ending apart from the final [+strident, +coronal] consonants of the nouns. This separation increases the audibility of the plural ending. Try pronouncing the plural of *bush* with just a /z/ or /s/ instead of the normal /ɨz/. The other two plural endings tend to be lost.

Epenthetic vowels also occur elsewhere in English. Some dialects insert an epenthetic /ə/ between consonants and /l/. Examples are words such as *padlock* /pædəlɑk/ and *athlete* /æθəlit/. This common pronunciation of the latter word often leads to the misspelled form *athelete*.

When the /z/ ending is added to a noun that ends in a ([−strident]) voiceless consonant, the plural ending becomes voiceless to match the ending of the preceding noun. Finally, the /z/ plural form remains unchanged when it is attached to nouns ending in a [−strident] voiced segment.

With the above remarks we are now able to formulate the final version of the Plural Rule, which ironically is not really a plural rule at all, as we will soon see:

(2)

Conditions on plural formation

a. The plural morpheme is /z/ and is subject to the following conditions (rules).

b. If the noun ends in a [+strident, +coronal] consonant, an epenthetic /ɨ/ is inserted between the plural ending and the noun.

c. Otherwise, if the noun ends in a [−voiced] consonant, the feature [−voiced] is spread to the plural morpheme.

Note that we no longer have a "unified" set of statements that specify all of the forms of the plural. The /z/ shape is not the result of a rule at all, but is rather the basic form that is unchanged by rule. It is only /s/ and /ɨz/ (or /ɨ/, actually) that are the result of rules. But these rules are valid for more than plural formation. They are the same rules that apply in the following components of English morphology:

(3)
a. Third person possessive
   John's /z/, Dick's /s/, Butch's /ɨz/
b. Third person verb agreement
   runs /z/, hits /s/, pushes /ɨz/
c. Contraction of the verb *is*
   John's /z/ coming, Dick's /s/ coming, Butch's /ɨz/ coming

If we were to state rules separately for the plural, the third person possessive, third person verb agreement, and contraction, we would miss the generalization that all four of these alternations are subject to *exactly the same principles*, namely, (2b–c).

The patterning of regularities seen in the English plural formation process offers substantial justification for the analysis of phonemes as distinctive feature clusters. The phoneme classes that participate in the formulation of rules can usually be defined by a relatively small number of distinctive features. As we have noted, each of these small lists of phonetic features is the basis for isolating a *natural class* of phonemes (see also Halle 1962), which we can roughly define as follows:

(4)
Natural class (informal definition)
A natural class is a set of phonemes uniquely defined by a small number of distinctive features such that the set plays a significant role in expressing the phonological regularities found in human language.

For example, in the conditions on plural formation (2), the groupings of phonemes used to state the rules are natural classes: the class of phonemes that take the /ɨz/ ending is the class of [+strident, +coronal] consonants; the class of remaining phonemes that condition the [−voiced] feature of the plural ending is defined by their possessing the feature [−voiced].

Another example comes from the "aspiration rule" that characterizes English. Earlier we noted that the phonemes /p, t, k/ participate in this rule. We now can describe this list as the class of [−voiced, −continuant] (stop) consonants. It is important to note here that English does not have three rules that separately specify aspirated allophones for each of the phonemes /p/, /t/, /k/—instead, it has one rule that refers to a natural class.

If you check the feature specifications of the phonemes in table 4.1, you will note that the phoneme /tʃ/ also carries the specification [−voiced, −continuant]. Our rule, as formulated, predicts that aspiration will accompany the release of syllable-initial /tʃ/ in words such as *chip*. You can test for aspiration by placing your hand in front of your mouth as you say the words *chip* and *gym*. You will feel the presence of aspiration in *chip* and its absence in *gym*. The perceived aspiration is less than in the release of stops such as /k/ because the airflow that accompanies the release of /tʃ/ is immediately restricted by the accompanying fricative /ʃ/.

To repeat, the existence of natural classes of distinctive features as the organizing principle of phonological regularities provides empirical support for the position that the mind/brain analyzes phonemes into smaller constituent parts: the distinctive features.

An "unnatural class" is a collection of phonemes that cannot be uniquely specified by a small number of distinctive features. A class of phonemes such as /p, s, l, g/ cannot be described by a small set of features that includes these phonemes and excludes all others. Such unnatural classes are predicted not to participate in phonological rules, and in fact they do not.

Next we present an additional example of a phonological regularity from a distinct language that exhibits further evidence that (1) phonemes pattern in terms of natural classes, and (2) the nature of the phonological regularity is insightfully expressed by a rule written in distinctive features.

Amharic

In Amharic, a language spoken in Ethiopia, the vowel *i* is a variant of the vowel ʌ. Forms showing this alternation are given in (5):

(5)

	Amharic form	*English gloss*
a.	dʒimmāt	"tendon, string"
b.	kʌr	"thread"

c. sʌ̱m   "name"
d. ʔafʌnca   "nose"
e. tʃ'igā̱g   "fog"
f. k'ʌnat   "envy"
g. fʌ̱rē   "nut"
h. tʃ'isɛɲɲā   "tenant"
i. tʌ jji̱t   "sight"
j. bʌrr   "silver"
k. ʃimɛllā   "stork"
l. ʔʌfū̱ɲi̱t   "viper"

This short but representative list reveals that *i* follows the set of consonants /dʒ, tʃ, j, ɲ, ʃ/ and that ʌ follows other consonants. In fact, this is true of all Amharic words: *i* appears only after /dʒ, tʃ, j, ɲ, ʃ/, and ʌ does not appear after these consonants. This nonoverlapping distribution is the *complementary distribution* discussed in chapter 3. (This example also illustrates another point made in chapter 3. The allophones of a phoneme can differ across languages. In Amharic the sounds *i* and ʌ are members of the same phoneme; the basic sound is ʌ, and *i* is derived by rule. In English, of course, these two sounds are distinct phonemes.)

Why do /dʒ, tʃ, j, ɲ, ʃ/ pattern together, and what properties do these consonants have that may account for the change in articulation of the basic /ʌ/ vowel? If you look at table 4.1, you will see that there are two distinctive features, [+coronal] and [+high], that group the consonants /dʒ, tʃ, j, ʃ/ and exclude all others. In other words, these consonants form a natural class according to definition (4). The phoneme /ɲ/, a palatal nasal, does not appear in the chart of English phonemes, but it too possesses the features [+coronal, +high].

Furthermore, the distinctive features are exactly those that permit an insightful description of the vowel change. The vowel /ʌ/ has the features [+back] and [−high], the /vowel/i/ has the features [−back] and [+high], and the consonants /dʒ, tʃ, j, ɲ, ʃ/ also have the features [−back] and [+high]. Thus, the features of the vowels and the preceding consonants tell us that an assimilation process is at work: the [−back] and [+high] features of the consonants appear in the following vowel, thus making it appear as /i/. Here, as in the statement of the English Plural Rule, distinctive features allow the exact nature of the assimilation process between two adjacent phonological segments to be explicitly expressed. Assimilation rules are very common in the world's languages and they are clearly best stated by rules based on distinctive features.

One task currently being carried out by phonologists, then, is to establish the set of distinctive features and the properties of the phonological rules of the world's languages. For further discussion of the issues involved, see the readings listed at the end of this chapter.

4.3   THE EXTERNAL ORGANIZATION OF SPEECH SOUNDS

In this section we survey the principles of organization that govern the combinations of phonemes. Two important organizational units are the syllable and the foot.

Writing polysyllabic English words phonemically is a nontrivial matter, but once you understand the relationship between the occurrence of vowels and their position in metrical feet—a major theme of this section—the task becomes easier. One result of your studying this section is that you will be able to write phonemically any English word you know how to pronounce.

The Syllable

Although native speakers of English can determine, with a high degree of reliability, how many syllables a word has (*cat* has one syllable /kæt/, *catfish* has two syllables /kæt-fɪʃ/, *catalogue* has three syllables /kæ-tə-lɑg/ ([kærəlɑg]), and *catatonic* has four syllables /kæ-tə-tɑ-nɨk/ ([kærətɑnɨk])), there has been little consensus about exactly what a syllable is. In this section we will look at the definition of syllable that guides current research. We will see that the syllable represents a *level of organization* of the speech sounds of a particular language.

We state here "particular language," because languages vary in their syllable structure. Across the world's languages the most common type of syllable has the structure CV(C), that is, a single consonant C followed by a single vowel V, followed in turn (optionally) by a single consonant. As figures 4.1a and 4.1b together show, vowels usually form the "center" or "core" of a syllable, called its *nucleus*; consonants usually form the beginning (the *onset*) and the end (the *coda*) of the syllable. A word such as *napkin* has the syllable structure shown in figure 4.1b.

The properties of syllables are somewhat more complex than just described, however. In the first place, it is not only vowels that can serve as the nucleus of a syllable. We have already seen that /ŋ/ can function as a syllable in English. The consonants /m/ and /l/ also have syllabic variants, as seen in words such as *bottom* [bɑrm̩] and *apple* /æpl̩/. In each case the second syllable (/m/ and /l/, respectively) consists of a consonant.

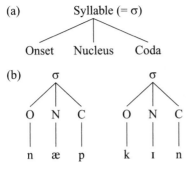

Figure 4.1
(a) Typical syllable structure; (b) syllable grouping of the word *napkin*

Word-internal syllable division is another issue that must be dealt with. In a sequence such as VCV, where V is any vowel and C is any consonant, is the medial C the coda of the first syllable (VC.V) or the onset of the second syllable (V.CV)? We will argue that the second grouping is the correct one, and that this grouping is a consequence of a general property of English syllabification. To see that this is the correct grouping, we can test it with the previously mentioned observation that voiceless stops are subject to a rule, stated in (6), that assigns aspiration in *syllable-initial position*. (Note also that the crucial reference to the syllable in this rule provides additional evidence that syllables are part of the structural properties of English words.)

(6)
Aspiration Rule (informally stated)
Phonemes with the features [−continuant, −voiced] are aspirated in syllable-initial position.

The Aspiration Rule (6) provides a test for determining which syllable an intervocalic consonant is associated with. /p/ is a [−continuant, −voiced] phoneme. If the intervocalic *p* in the sequence *apa* is the onset of the second syllable, it will be aspirated. If it is the coda of the first syllable, it will not be aspirated. Now perform the following experiment. As you pronounce the sequence *apa*, place your hand in front of your mouth. You will feel a small puff of air that accompanies the release of the *p*, regardless of whether you stress the first *a* /ápa/ or the second /apá/. The presence of aspiration is the evidence you need to conclude that *apa* is divided *a-pa*.

The principle that associates an intervocalic consonant with the following vowel is only a special case of a more general rule known as the *Maximal Onset Principle:*

(7)

Maximal Onset Principle
The sequence of consonants that combine to form an onset with the vowel on the right are those that correspond to the maximal sequence that is available at the beginning of a syllable anywhere in the language.

We could also state this principle by saying that the consonants that form a word-internal onset are the maximal sequence that can be found at the *beginning of words.* It is well known that English permits at most three consonants to form an onset; and once the second and third consonants are determined, only one consonant can appear in the first position. For example, if the second and third consonants at the beginning of a word are *pr*, the first consonant can only be *s*, forming *spr* as in *spring*.

To see how the Maximal Onset Principle functions, consider the word *constructs*. Between the two vowels of this bisyllabic word lies the sequence *n-s-t-r*. Which, if any, of these consonants are associated with the second syllable? That is, which ones combine to form an onset for the syllable whose nucleus is *u*? Since the maximal sequence that occurs at the beginning of a syllable in English is *str-* (as seen, for example, in *strike*), the Maximal Onset Principle requires that these consonants form the onset of the syllable whose nucleus is *u*. The word *constructs* is therefore syllabified as *con-structs*. We can adduce evidence that supports this analysis. If the syllabification were *ns-tr*, then the *t* would appear in syllable-initial position, and as we have just seen, syllable-initial *t*'s must be aspirated. But the *t* in the sequence *nstr* is not aspirated, ruling out the putative syllabification *ns-tr*. Other considerations, which we will not discuss here (but consider the domain of the lip rounding caused by the *u*), rule out all but the division *n-str* (see Kahn 1976). This syllabification is the one that assigns the maximal number of "allowable consonants" to the onset of the second syllable.

To return to the Maximal Onset Principle, we note its role in dividing up the following internal sequences: *VnsV, VnstV, VnstrV, VftV,* and *VpV*. Through the application of the Maximal Onset Principle of syllabification, the onset consonants(s) of the second syllable become(s) *Vn-sV, Vn-stV, Vn-strV, Vf-tV,* and *V-pV*. Other possible combinations—*V-nsV* or *Vns-tV*—either represent an impermissible onset sequence (*ns*) or do not incorporate the maximal sequence possible (*t* instead of *st*). Thus, to return to our original example, it is the Maximal Onset Principle that ultimately associates the *p* in *apa* (or indeed any consonant) with the vowel on the right.

This discussion of syllable structure allows us to revisit a topic introduced in chapter 3: conditions on the type and number of allowable consonants at the beginning of a word (phonotactics). These conditions are actually conditions on syllable onsets; therefore, they apply both at the beginning of the word and to any syllable within the word as well. Thus, the Maximal Onset Principle is related to the *sequential constraints* that apply to the series of consonants at the beginning of a word or *syllable*. Not surprisingly, these sequential conditions are best expressed in terms of natural classes of sounds (see Clements and Keyser 1983). The Maximal Onset Principle simply states that within a word, any series of consonants between vowels is divided so that the syllable on the right ends up with the *maximal allowable number that satisfies the conditions of English syllable onsets*.

Whenever someone invents a new word—say, to use as a brand name —this word must conform to the syllable (and word formation) rules of English. The syllable-initial sequence in a word such as **ftik* is not possible in English, although it is possible in other languages. English speakers recognize immediately whether or not a word conforms to the English rules of syllable well-formedness, arguing strongly that they have access to principles of some sort that account for their strong intuitions.

In addition to accounting for how speakers judge whether or not a newly encountered sequence of phonemes is a possible word in their language, sequential constraints on syllables (along with phonological rules) force borrowed words to conform to the principles of that language. In chapter 3 we saw the consequences of the Hawaiian restriction against consonant clusters on that language's version of the English expression *Merry Christmas*. Japanese is another language that allows only a single consonant in onset position. When English words are borrowed into Japanese, Japanese speakers with little knowledge of English insert vowels after all "extra" consonants. (What baseball term do you think *sutoraiku* is?)

In our characterization of the phonology of a language as consisting of *sounds* and *rules*, we see that there are rules that specify the allowable sequences of phonemes, and that the unit in which these combinations are specified is the syllable.

Now that we have established some of the properties of the syllable in English, we can consider how these syllables play a role in patterns of prominence in English words.

Patterns of Prominence (Stress)

The syllables in English words are not all pronounced with the same degree of prominence. They vary in emphasis, length, and (as we will see later) pitch. In a word of four syllables, for example, one syllable is pronounced more prominently than the other three, and typically one of the remaining three is pronounced more prominently than the other two. (For example, in *catamaran* the first syllable is pronounced most prominently, and the last syllable is pronounced more prominently than the middle two.) In order to understand the role of stress and its patterns of occurrence in English words, we need to consider an additional structural unit that organizes English syllables: the foot.

The term *foot* is common in the study of poetry, where it plays an important role in scansion; you are probably familiar with (for example) iambic, trochaic, and dactylic feet. Metrical feet also play a fundamental role in English phonology. And just as *syllables* provide an external organizational framework for *phonemes*, so *feet*, in turn, provide an external organizational framework for *syllables*. We can think of metrical feet as units of prominence and timing: the first element of a foot, the first syllable, carries the strongest "beat" of the foot, and the following syllables within the foot are relatively less prominent. The "beat" of a foot is in fact the property that gives English words their stress patterns.

Types of Feet

For purposes of exposition we will describe English as having the three foot types displayed in figure 4.2, one with one branch (a *unary* foot), one with two branches (a *binary* foot), and one with three branches (a *ternary* foot). Every English word is associated with a metrical foot or a sequence

Figure 4.2
Types of feet that are found in English: (a) unary, (b) binary, (c) ternary

of metrical feet. Every leftmost syllable in a foot carries some degree of stress; every non-leftmost syllable in a foot is unstressed.

Assigning Feet to English Words
In the course of this section we will

• show that English words consist of a foot or sequence of feet,
• discuss additional structural features involving tense vowels that interact with English foot structure,
• discuss a distributional property of English that permits unstressed vowels to occur in the initial syllable in some English words, and
• show the role that metrical feet play in the pronunciation of Modern English words, in phonemic writing, and in changes in pronunciation that have occurred and are still occurring.

Linking Vowels to Foot Structure   For purposes of exposition we will make some simplifying assumptions concerning the underlying form of English words, in particular with respect to phonemes. It is sufficient for our purposes to assume that the lexical form of words consists of *full* vowels (tense and lax) and *reduced* vowels (ə and its variant *i*).

In figure 4.3 we show how the three feet of figure 4.2 are associated with three words. We include the internal structure of the syllable as part of the representation in figure 4.3, although we omit it in all subsequent representations.

It is a property of English feet that the leftmost branch is always associated with (or dominates) a full vowel. In assigning foot structure to

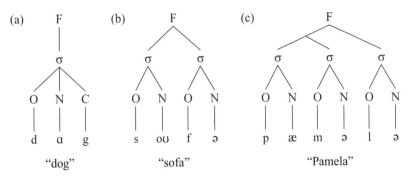

Figure 4.3
The three feet of figure 4.2, assigned to English words: (a) unary, (b) binary, (c) ternary

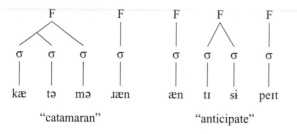

Figure 4.4
Assignment of foot structure to English syllables containing full and reduced vowels

English words, a general rule is that all reduced vowels will be in the nucleus of the right-hand syllables of either binary or ternary metrical feet (with one exception to be discussed below). Because English words consist of sequences of metrical feet and because the longest possible sequence of reduced vowels in a foot is two (i.e., in the nuclei of the two rightmost members of a ternary foot), *the longest sequence of reduced vowels in an English word is two.* Thus, in the foot structure of English words, a single reduced (non-word-initial) vowel is in the nucleus of the right-hand syllable of a binary foot, and two reduced vowels are in the nuclei of the two rightmost syllables of a ternary foot. Examples are displayed in figure 4.4.

Other practical information on assigning foot structure is found in *A Linguistics Workbook* (Farmer and Demers 2001).

Tense Vowels and English Foot Structure   Although the leftmost syllable of a foot always contains a full vowel and never a reduced vowel, it is not the case that a full vowel cannot occur in the right branch of a binary foot and in the two right branches of a ternary foot.

In order for a full vowel to occur in the non-leftmost branch of a metrical foot in English, one of two conditions involving tense vowels must be satisfied. These conditions are exceptionless principles of English, and they interact in a surprising way with foot structure.

(8)
Vowel Sequence Condition
When two vowels are adjacent in an English word, the first vowel must be tense (or long). Examples are numerous: *hiatus* /haɪeɪtəs/, *radio* /ɹeɪdioʊ/, among many others.

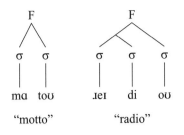

Figure 4.5
Words in which a tense vowel occurs in a non-leftmost member of a metrical foot

(9)

Word-Final Vowel Condition
Only reduced, tense (or long), and short low vowels can appear in word-final position. Examples are numerous: *sofa* /souf<u>ə</u>/, *baby* /beɪb<u>i</u>/, among many others.

The Word-Final Vowel Condition can be stated in another way: the short nonlow vowels cannot appear in word-final position. Thus, English does not have words such as *plɛ, *plʊ, or *plɪ. Even the low vowels are greatly restricted in occurrence; the exclamation *nah* /næ/ meaning "no" is one of the few places a final /æ/ is found. Most speakers, in fact, hear this vowel as lengthened, and it is therefore not a pure short vowel. Something similar may be happening with /ɑ/. It appears in a few expressions such as *baa* (as in "Baa, baa, black sheep, have you any wool?") and the nursery word *ma*, meaning "mother." Again, speakers of English hear this vowel as lengthened, and when pronounced as a short vowel it seems unnatural. So the proper generalization may be that only the reduced or tense (long) vowels can appear in word-final position.

It is a surprising fact that the tense (and not the lax) vowels can appear in the right branch members of metrical feet, especially since right branch members are always metrically weaker than left branch members. Nevertheless, a long vowel appearing in the right branch of a metrical foot must always satisfy one of the two conditions (8) or (9). Some examples will illustrate this point.

Figure 4.5 displays the words *motto* /mɑtoʊ/ and *radio* /ɹeɪdioʊ/. In each of these words the rightmost syllables of a binary or ternary foot not only contain a full vowel, they contain a tense vowel that satisfies one of the two conditions (8) and (9). In *motto* the final /oʊ/ is in word-final position (satisfying condition (9)), and in *radio* the /i/ precedes another "veto"

Figure 4.6
The word *veto*, showing its assignment to two metrical feet

vowel (satisfying condition (8)), and /oʊ/ again is in word-final position (satisfying condition (9)).

How do we know that the word *motto* is indeed composed of a single binary foot, and not a combination of two unary feet, the first of which is more prominent than the second? After all, the latter sequence is also found in English, as the word *veto* in figure 4.6 illustrates.

Evidence for the metrical structure of *motto* comes from what will be the final form of the English Flap Rule. Earlier we described flapping as a process that occurs when *t* or *d* appears between two vowels, the first of which is stressed more than the second. This formulation is not quite correct, although it is consistent with the words in (10):

(10)
water [wɑɾɚ]
attitude [æɾitʰud]
beating [biɾiŋ]

The actual formulation of the Flap Rule involves a reference to foot structure:

(11)
Flap Rule
The English stops /t/ and /d/ are flapped between vowels that are contained in the same metrical foot.

Looking at the word *attitude* in figure 4.7, we see that it consists of two feet. The first /t/ is between vowels that are members of the same foot and thus satisfies the terms of the Flap Rule (11), whereas the second /t/ is between vowels that are members of different feet and thus does not satisfy the terms of the Flap Rule. Note that the form of the Flap Rule

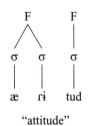

"attitude"

Figure 4.7
Metrical structure of the word *attitude*, showing that the first /t/ is between vowels in a foot, and the second /t/ is not

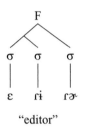

"editor"

Figure 4.8
The ternary foot assigned to *editor* that permits both alveolar stops to be flapped

(11) predicts that if a word contains two alveolar stops and if both stops are intervocalic within a ternary foot, then both will be flapped. This is in fact the case, as the pronunciation of the word *editor* shows (see figure 4.8).

Thus, the foot-based formulation of the Flap Rule overcomes an inadequacy of the earlier formulation (that flapping occurs when a /t/ or /d/ appears between vowels and the first one is stressed). The earlier formulation does account for the lack of flapping in the word *attitude* since the second alveolar stop follows an *unstressed* vowel. On the other hand, the second alveolar stop in *editor* also follows an unstressed vowel, and it is nevertheless flapped. The difference is that the second alveolar stop in *attitude* is between feet and the second alveolar stop in *editor* is inside a ternary foot. The difference in flapping follows from the different metrical structure. We have noticed that if speakers pronounce the final *o* of *editor* as a full vowel ([ɛɾɨtɔɹ] (figure 4.9), then the second alveolar stop is not flapped since it is now between feet.

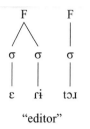

"editor"

Figure 4.9
The lack of flapping on the second alveolar stop in *editor* as a consequence of the last syllable's being assigned its own metrical foot

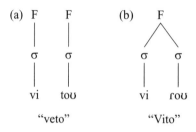

"veto"   "Vito"

Figure 4.10
The lack of flapping in the word *veto* (a) and the appearance of flapping in *Vito* (b) as a consequence of their different metrical structures

Since speakers of English flap the alveolar stop in motto [mɑɾoʊ], we now know that it is not between vowels in two unary feet but between vowels in a single binary foot.

We have seen by looking at *motto* [mɑɾoʊ] that a final /oʊ/ in a two-syllable word can be the nucleus of the rightmost member of a binary foot. Another such word is the Italian name *Vito* [viroʊ], as it is pronounced by many speakers of American English (figure 4.10b). However, a final /oʊ/ in a two-syllable word can sometimes be contained in a unary foot, instead. For many speakers of American English, *veto* [vitoʊ] seems to be such a word (figure 4.10a). From the previous discussion, you can see how the difference in metrical structure illustrated in figure 4.10 leads to the difference in pronunciation between these two words, the *t* in *veto* being mildly aspirated and the *t* in *Vito* being flapped. This difference cannot only be heard; it can be seen in the spectrograms of the two words (figure 4.11). The two unary feet of *veto* are longer than the single binary foot of *Vito*, a fact consistent with their different metrical structures.

(a)   "veto"   (b)   "Vito"

Figure 4.11
Spectrograms showing that *veto* (a), with two unary metrical feet, is longer
(358 milliseconds) than *Vito* (b) (279 milliseconds), with one binary foot

Unstressed Vowels in Word-Initial Syllables   One property of English
metrical structure might appear to be problematic: the presence of word-
initial unstressed vowels in some words (see examples in figure 4.12).

Rather than introduce more types of feet into the description of
English (ones that would permit their leftmost foot to consist of an
unstressed syllable), we propose that English permits a single *unfooted*,
unstressed syllable only at the beginning of a word. Thus, the initial syllables in figure 4.12 are not shown to be associated with a foot.

The Role of Metrical Feet in English Phonology: Three Cases
1. *The variability of length in vowels.* An understanding of the role of
metrical feet permits us to deal with a phonetic property of English that
has previously been handled in various ways. Some phoneticians argue
that English has both long and short sets of tense vowels. These phone-

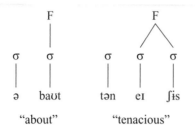

Figure 4.12
Two words showing the lack of foot structure on word-initial syllables that contain unstressed ə

ticians write the name *Fifi* with a long vowel in the first syllable and a shorter tense vowel in the second syllable. However, a basic long versus short distinction in the English tense vowels is unnecessary if we recognize that the first *fi* is the leftmost member of a binary foot, and the second *fi* is the rightmost member of this binary foot and is therefore metrically weaker. Its metrically weaker position causes it to be shorter.

2. *Why vowel pairs such as /ʌ/ and /ə/, /ɪ/ and /ɨ/, /ɝ/ and /ɚ/ are used in phonemic transcription.* As you pronounce the three words *Bubba*, *chicken*, and *murmur*, you will notice that the two vowels in each word "sound the same." However, in phonemic transcription the vowel pairs are written differently: /bʌbə/, /tʃɪkɨn/, and /mɝmɚ/. Why are vowel pairs that sound alike transcribed with different symbols? The answer is that the two different symbol sets—/ʌ, ɪ, ɝ/ versus /ə, ɨ, ɚ/—encode the appearance of vowels in different positions in a metrical foot. The regular lax vowels in the first set occur in the left branch of a metrical foot, and the reduced vowels of the second set occur in the nonleft branch(es) of a metrical foot. The reduced vowel symbols permit linguists to write words phonemically without having to include foot structure as part of the phonemic representation.

3. *Changes in foot structure as a source of changes in pronunciation.* There are three positions where reduced vowels can appear in Modern English: in the initial syllable of a word and as the nonleft members of branching metrical feet. As adjustments are made in the foot structure of certain words, reduced vowels are appearing and the pronunciation of these words is changing. Defooting is one of the most common adjustments, and its effects are seen in the current pronunciation of the words *gymnast* and *assassinate* (figure 4.13).

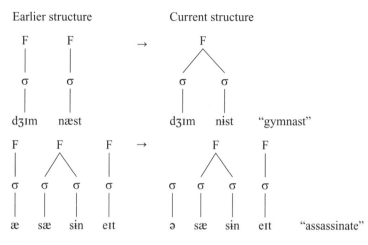

Figure 4.13
Changes in foot structure in two words leading to a change in pronunciation

The structural change from two feet to one binary foot in the word *gymnast* creates the condition for a reduced vowel to appear in the second syllable. Likewise, the loss of the foot on the initial syllable of the word *assassinate* leads this defooted syllable to be pronounced with the reduced vowel ə.

Another example will underscore the role of defooting as a major source of change in the pronunciation of English. Not long ago the word *island* was pronounced like *Thailand*—that is, with an /æ/ in the final syllable. The two unary feet that once were associated with *island* have been replaced with a single binary foot, whose right branch dominates a reduced vowel, leading to the pronunciation /aɪlənd/.

Because of changes in its foot structure, English has more reduced vowels now than it did earlier in its history. These reduced vowels in spoken language often lead to spelling difficulties in written language. For example, the difficulty people have in spelling the words *effect* and *affect* can be traced to the defooting of the initial vowel, as shown in figure 4.14. Because of this defooting, both words are now commonly pronounced /əfɛkt/. Spelling difficulties involving reduced vowels can often be overcome, however, if a related word can be found that has main stress on the vowel in question. In the word [prɛɾɪtɔɹi], the second vowel creates a special spelling problem. Some may be tempted to use the

Earlier structure   Current structure

```
F    F        →              F
|    |                       |
σ    σ              σ    σ
|    |              |    |
i    fɛkt           ə    fɛkt      "effect"

F    F        →              F
|    |                       |
σ    σ              σ    σ
|    |              |    |
æ    fɛkt           ə    fɛkt      "affect"
```

Figure 4.14
The changes in foot structure that led to the homophony of the words *effect* and *affect*

incorrect spelling *preditory* for this word. However, the existence of the word *predation* [pɹɛdeɪʃin] shows that the original vowel was an *a* /eɪ/, and so the correct spelling is *predatory*.

4.4 SPECIAL TOPIC

The Word-Level Tone Contour of English

In addition to differing in loudness because of their position in foot structure, the syllables of an English word differ in pitch (a perception based on the frequency of a sound). Consider the pair *INsult* (noun) and *inSULT* (verb). If you pronounce the noun *insult* several times, you will hear the pitch of your voice change between the two syllables, the first syllable being higher pitched than the second. In fact, you can hum the pitch pattern, high-low, extracting the pitch from the sounds. Now compare the pattern in the verb *insult*. In this case the higher pitch is on the second syllable. Again, humming the pitch pattern reveals a low pitch followed by a higher pitch. The pattern on these two words, then, is High-Low (*INsult*) and Low-High (*inSULT*).

Consider next the pitch patterns in the words in figure 4.15. There seem to be quite a few of them, but in fact they are all instances of a single English pattern (see Goldsmith 1981, 1990). Note first that each word has

```
H L  L          L  H  L          L   L   H
| |  |          |  |  |          |   |   |
ca ta logue     un ra vel        un der neath

H L  L  L       L  H  L  L        L  L  H  L
| |  |  |       |  |  |  |         |  |  |  |
ca ta ma ran    un tou cha ble    Mi ssi ssi ppi
```

Figure 4.15
Different tone patterns on English words. H = high tone, L = low tone

a single high tone and that this high tone is associated with the most prominently stressed syllable. Note also that all of the tones to the right of the high tone are low. Rather than assume that there is a series of patterns in which high tones are followed by one low tone, two low tones, three low tones, and so forth, we make the assumption that there is but a single low tone to the right of the high tone, but that this low tone spreads to all available syllables to the right. What happens to the left of the high tone? It appears that a low tone is also assigned to the left, followed by spreading if possible. Thus, the tone pattern for English words is as shown in (12), and the conditions for linking the tones are as shown in (13):

(12)
English tone pattern
low-high-low

(13)
English Tone Assignment
The high tone links with the most strongly stressed syllable in the word and the low tones spread to any available syllable to the right or left.

There is only one additional detail to consider: namely, the variable behavior of the tone contour (12) when the high tone is assigned to a syllable on the periphery of the word. When main stress falls on the first (leftmost) syllable, there is no evidence of a low tone to its left. In contrast, when main stress falls on the last (rightmost) syllable, there is evidence of a low tone to its right in that a *falling tone* occurs. If you utter the verb *insult* a few times, you will hear the pitch fall off on the last syllable. This fact can be accounted for if we assume that the English tone contour has the following structure:

Figure 4.16
Words exhibiting the spreading of the English tone contour (L)-H-L

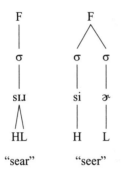

"sear"   "seer"

Figure 4.17
Different syllable structures lead to the different tone contours on the words *sear* (falling HL) and *seer* (HL sequence)

(14)
English tone pattern
(low)-high-low

The parentheses indicate that the first low tone is optional; and if there is no syllable to the left of the stressed syllable with the high tone, this tone will not be realized. In contrast, the low tone on the right must be realized on any syllables present. If no such syllables are present, it will be conjoined with the high tone, forming a high-low falling tone contour, like the one in the word *underneath* in figure 4.16. Words with tone contours assigned by the conditions in (13) are displayed in figure 4.16.

In chapter 3 we noted that the English words *sear* and *seer* are pronounced differently; for one thing, *sear* is monosyllabic (/sɪɹ/) and *seer* (/siɚ/) is bisyllabic. We are now able to point out a consequence of the

English tone assignment principles. The word *sear* has a falling contour HL over its one syllable, whereas the word *seer* has a H-L pattern over its two syllables. These differences are displayed in figure 4.17.

The principles of tone assignment and spreading described above are not just found in English. Similar principles are extremely common in the languages of Africa and are also found in Japanese. In Japanese a single high tone appears on a particular syllable in a word, and all tones to the right of the high tone are low. The fact that so many different languages from different language families have similar tone assignment principles (linking, spreading, etc.) suggests that tone distribution properties are part of the shared language facility in the human species.

Conclusion

At the beginning of this chapter we posed the following questions:

· What is the proper description of the various sounds that are found generally in human language?
· What is the proper general framework for describing the sound patterns of human language?

We are now in a position to provide partial answers for these questions:

· The speech sounds of human language at either the phonemic or the phonetic level of representation are best viewed as complexes of phonetic (distinctive) features, out of which the speech sounds are composed.
· Phonological regularities are best expressed in terms of the phonetic (distinctive) features that make up phonemes. The statements (rules) typically refer to small classes of features that identify natural classes of phonemes.

In recent years a new way of expressing the regularities that characterize human language has gained currency. According to *Optimality Theory* (OT), a phonological representation is well formed if it satisfies an array of ranked, violable, and universal constraints. For more information on this theoretical proposal, see the bibliography at the end of this chapter.

In sum, a phonology consists of two major parts: sounds and conditions on pronunciation (either rules or constraints). As yet linguists have no idea how many constraints or rules are involved in the phonology of English, but the number may be in the hundreds. What is remarkable is that children acquire this system with little conscious effort. Moreover, phonology is but one part of the system of grammar that they must learn.

In the following chapter we will explore the rules that children must learn to create (or understand) a phrase or sentence.

Exercises

Exercises 1–4, which are drawn from English, Tohono O'odham, and Luganda, illustrate the role of natural classes of phonemes in the phonological regularities of these languages. In each exercise a small number of distinctive features will serve to describe the class of segments that condition the change described in that exercise. Assume that the data are representative of the phonological system of the language in question and that the phonemic symbols have the same phonetic feature specifications as the symbols in tables 4.1 and 4.2; refer to the tables in solving these problems. A sample problem and solution are given first, in order to acquaint you with some strategies to follow in solving these problems.

Sample problem: In English, the vowel /ɪ/ becomes long (and is thus written [ɪː], where the colon indicates length) under certain conditions. Consider the examples listed below; then (1) list the phonemes that condition the change of /ɪ/ to [ɪː], and (2) state what feature(s) uniquely specify this class of phonemes.

a. [hɪs]   h. [hɪːd]
b. [wɪʃ]   i. [mɪθ]
c. [pɪːg]   j. [ɹɪːb]
d. [pɪt]   k. [lɪːz]
e. [lɪːm]   l. [snɪp]
f. [tɹɪk]   m. [ɹɪːdʒ]
g. [bɪːl]   n. [kɪːŋ]

We begin with the (ultimately correct) hypothesis that [ɪ] is basic—that short [ɪ] becomes long [ɪː]. The change from short [ɪ] to long [ɪː] is phonologically determined; that is, the lengthening takes place in the presence of certain phonemes. A good strategy is first to list the phonemes to the right of long [ɪː], then to list those to the left. Since [h] is on the left in both item (a) and item (h), it is unlikely that the lengthening in question is solely caused by a phoneme to the left. As an answer to part (1), then, you would next propose that /ɪ/ becomes [ɪː] whenever the phonemes in the list (/d, g, m, l, b, z, dʒ, ŋ/) occur immediately after that vowel. This hypothesis looks promising because, in fact, the short variant [ɪ] never occurs before these segments. The next question is, What is it about the phonemes on the right of the long variant [ɪː] that unifies them as a class? If you look at their feature specifications in table 4.1, you will find that these phonemes are all voiced ([+voiced]), and, in fact, the /ɪ/ never lengthens before voiceless segments. Thus, the answer to part (2) of the problem is that the vowel /ɪ/ is lengthened before (the natural class of) voiced consonants.

1. A particular dialect of English exhibits a predictable variant /ʌɪ/ of the diphthong /aɪ/.

A. What phonetic segments condition this change?
B. What feature(s) uniquely describe the class of conditioning segments?

a. /bʌɪt/ "bite"   i. /fʌɪt/ "fight"
b. /taɪ/ "tie"   j. /baɪ/ "buy"
c. /raɪd/ "ride"   k. /ɹʌɪs/ "rice"
d. /faɪl/ "file"   l. /tʌɪp/ "type"
e. /lʌɪf/ "life"   m. /naɪnθ/ "ninth"
f. /taɪm/ "time"   n. /faɪɚ/ "fire"
g. /ɹaɪz/ "rise"   o. /bʌɪk/ "bike"
h. /ɹʌɪt/ "write"

2. In Tohono O'odham (formerly Papago), a Native American language of the southwestern United States, the phone [tʃ] is a variant of /t/.

A. After looking at the following data, find and list the set of phonemes that condition this change.
B. What feature(s) characterize(s) this class?
C. How would a Tohono O'odham speaker pronounce the word [tuksan] "Black Base (of a mountain)"? This pronunciation is found in southern Arizona, and the word is the source of the city name *Tucson*.

A colon after a vowel symbol indicates that the vowel is long; /ş/ is a voiceless fricative similar to English /s/; and /ɨ/ is a high back unrounded vowel. Other unfamiliar phonemic symbols are not important for the solution to this problem.

a. ta:t "touched"   g. tako "yesterday"
b. to:n "knee"   h. tʃikwo "ankle"
c. tʃiñ "mouth"   i. tʃuʔi "flour"
d. tʃɨm hekid "always"   j. to:bi "rabbit, cottontail"
e. tʃuk "black"   k. taş "sun"
f. tʃikpan "is/was working" l. towa "turkey"

3. In the following words from Luganda, a Bantu language spoken in East Africa, the phone [ř] (a flapped r sound) is a predictable variant of [l].

A. What are the phonemes that condition the change of [l] to [ř]?
B. What feature(s) characterize(s) the class of conditioning segments?

A rising accent mark indicates high pitch; the absence of an accent mark indicates low pitch. Double vowels represent long vowels. Data are from Cole 1967.

a. mukířa "tail"
b. lumóóndé "sweet potato"
c. kulímá "to cultivate"
d. éfířímbí "to whistle"
e. kuwóólá "to scoop or hollow out"
f. kuwólá "to lend money"
g. kutúulá "to sit down"
h. okútábáála "to attach"
i. eříñá "name"
j. oolwééyó "a broom"
k. kwaanířízá "to welcome, invite"
l. kuujjúkířá "to remember"

4. For the following English words, state the conditions under which the different forms of the past tense appear. What determines whether /t/, /d/, or /ɪd/ is used? Hint: Write the past tense marker phonemically in order to discover whether the ending for a given verb is pronounced /t/, /d/, or /ɪd/. For example, *crushed* has final /t/, but *pitted* has final /ɪd/. What distinctive features define each conditioning environment?

a. crushed   k. turned
b. heaped   l. hissed
c. kicked   m. plowed
d. pitted   n. climbed
e. deeded   o. singed
f. bagged   p. hanged
g. killed   q. cinched
h. nabbed   r. played
i. thrived   s. hated
j. breathed   t. branded

5. Write the following words phonemically (using reduced vowels) and group the phonemes into syllables.

a. university   d. congestion
b. cantaloupe   e. fantastic
c. condition   f. contagious

6. Draw feet (unary, binary, or ternary) over the syllables of the following words. (If you find an unfooted syllable, you'll of course draw no foot over it.) First write the words phonemically; then group the phonemes into syllables; and finally link the syllables up to their appropriate feet.

a. anticipate   d. photo
b. anticipation   e. photography
c. anticipatory   f. photogenic

Further Reading

General
For good introductions to the field of phonology, including discussions of *distinctive features* and of the *prosodic features* (syllables, feet, stress, tone) discussed in this chapter, see Hawkins 1984, Kenstowicz 1994, Gussenhoven and Jacobs 1998, Davenport and Hannahs 1998, and Roca and Johnson 1999. A good summary of the principles of *Optimality Theory* as it applies to phonology is found in Archangeli 1999.

Special Topics
Clements and Keyser 1983 provides an excellent overview of the properties of *English syllables*. Good treatments of *English stress* are Halle and Vergnaud 1987, Hayes 1995, as well as the relevant chapters in the books listed above. For a good treatment of the phonological aspects of *tone*, see Goldsmith 1989.

Journals
Linguistic Inquiry, Phonology, Language, Natural Language & Linguistic Theory, Language Analysis

Bibliography and Further Reading

Archangeli, D. 1999. Introducing Optimality Theory. *Annual Review of Anthropology* 28, 531–552.

Chomsky, N., and M. Halle. 1968. *The sound pattern of English*. New York: Harper and Row.

Clements, G. N., and S. J. Keyser. 1983. *CV phonology: A generative theory of the syllable*. Cambridge, Mass.: MIT press.

Cole, D. 1967. *Some features of Ganda linguistic structure*. Johannesburg: Witwatersrand University Press.

Davenport, M., and S. Hannahs. 1998. *Introducing phonetics and phonology*. London: Arnold.

Denes, P., and E. Pinson. 1993. *The speech chain: The physics and biology of spoken language*. New York: W. H. Freeman.

Farmer, A. K., and R. A. Demers. 2001. *A linguistics workbook*. 4th ed. Cambridge, Mass.: MIT Press.

Fodor, J., and J. Katz, eds. 1964. *The structure of language: Readings in the philosophy of language*. Englewood Cliffs, N.J.: Prentice-Hall.

Goldsmith, J. 1981. English as a tone language. In D. Goyvaerts, ed., *Phonology in the 1980's*. Ghent: E. Story-Scientia.

Goldsmith, J. 1990. *Autosegmental and metrical phonology*. Oxford: Blackwell.

Gussenhoven, C., and H. Jacobs. 1998. *Understanding phonology*. London: Arnold.

Halle, M. 1962. Phonology in a generative grammar. *Word* 18, 54–82. Reprinted in Fodor and Katz 1964.

Halle, M., and G. N. Clements. 1982. *Problem book in phonology: A workbook for introductory courses in linguistics and modern phonology*. Cambridge, Mass.: MIT Press.

Halle, M., and J.-R. Vergnaud. 1987. *An essay on stress*. Cambridge, Mass.: MIT Press.

Hawkins, P. 1984. *Introducing phonology*. London: Routledge.

Hayes, B. 1995. *Metrical stress theory: Principles and case studies*. Chicago: University of Chicago Press.

Jakobson, R., and M. Halle. 1956. *Fundamentals of language*. The Hague: Mouton.

Kahn, D. 1976. Syllable-based generalizations in English phonology. Doctoral dissertation, MIT.

Kenstowicz, M. 1994. *Phonology in generative grammar*. Oxford: Blackwell.

Ladefoged, P. 1994. *A course in phonetics*. 3rd ed. New York: Harcourt Brace Jovanovich.

Liberman, M., and A. Prince. 1977. On stress and linguistic rhythm. *Linguistic Inquiry* 8, 249–336.

Pinker, S., and A. Prince. 1988. On language and connectionism: Analysis of a Parallel Distributed Processing model of language acquisition. In S. Pinker and J. Mehler, eds., *Connections and symbols*. Cambridge, Mass.: MIT Press.

Roca, I., and W. Johnson. 1999. *A course in phonology*. Oxford: Blackwell.

Stevens, K. 1989. On the quantal nature of speech. *Journal of Phonetics* 17, 3–45.

Chapter 5

Syntax: The Study of Sentence Structure

5.1 SOME BACKGROUND CONCEPTS

So far in our study of language, we have focused on morphology, phonetics, and phonology, and thus we have been focusing on the level of the word. Now we turn our attention to the analysis of larger structural units of language: phrases and sentences. In focusing on these larger units, we will discover some rather striking properties of the syntax of human language.

Let us begin by considering a sentence that you have never heard before:

(1)
The recent acquisition of MadMouse.com by MKF Corporation raised eyebrows on Wall Street, since all stock options are underwater.

This sentence has probably never before been written or uttered. Yet, as a native speaker of English, you are able to comprehend the sentence (as long as you know the meaning of the individual words, or maybe even if you *don't* know all the words). That is, even if you have not encountered a particular sentence in your previous linguistic experience, you are nevertheless able to understand it because you recognize familiar units (words that you know) combined in a novel but appropriate way. All of us, as native speakers of a language, are able to produce and comprehend an unlimited number of phrases and sentences of that language, many of which we have never heard or produced before. Speakers of a language are enormously creative in their production of novel sentences. We are not just uttering the same sentences over and over again.

Imagine, for a moment, challenging someone to find, in print, occurrences of duplicate sentences. Even with an offer of one dollar for every identical pair, no one is going to get rich—just extremely tired of wading through thousands of unique sentences.

How is it possible that speakers of a language can carry out the impressive task of understanding novel sentences they encounter by the thousands, day in and day out?

One thing is clear: we know that speakers cannot simply have memorized all the phrases and sentences of a language. This is suggested by example (1): if you had simply memorized all the sentences of English, how could you understand a sentence you had never had a chance to commit to memory (because you had never heard it before)? As it turns out, it is in principle impossible for speakers to memorize all the sentences of their native language.

Some simple examples will suffice to show this. Consider first a simple sentence of English: *Jorge is a Portuguese Water Dog*. We can create a longer sentence of English using this first sentence, by *embedding* it within a larger sentence: *Galen suspects that Jorge is a Portuguese Water Dog*. In turn, this sentence can be embedded, yielding an even larger sentence: *Nicholas just reported that Galen suspects that Jorge is a Portuguese Water Dog*. Indeed, there is in principle no limit on this embedding process: *Mary heard that Nicholas just reported that Galen suspects that Jorge is a Portuguese Water Dog*. (In section 5.3 we will return to a more formal discussion of embedding.) Of course, such a long and unwieldy sentence might not ever be uttered in actual speech—it has become long enough to put a strain on our memory—but as native speakers of English we can make an *intuitive* judgment that all of the examples we have discussed so far are well formed: that is, they conform to regular patterns of English syntax that we encounter in many other well-formed sentences and phrases. We will return to a discussion of such intuitive judgments, which form a crucial part of each speaker's linguistic knowledge. But at this point, note that no matter how long we make a certain sentence, we can always embed that sentence, producing a still longer one. This means that the number of (grammatical) sentences in English (or any other language) is *infinite*. Since no matter how many sentences we had on the list there would always be other sentences that were longer that we had not put on the list, it is not possible to exhaustively list all the sentences of a language. Of course, any individual sentence itself is finite in length, but the number of sentences in any language is infinite; that is, the set of sentences is infinite. An infinite set is, in effect, a list that never ends, and for that reason such a list could not possibly be committed to memory.

Since native speakers of a language cannot have memorized each phrase or sentence of their language, given that the set of phrases and sentences is infinite, their linguistic knowledge cannot be characterized as a list of phrases or sentences. (This issue brings up some of the same problems and questions we encountered in chapter 2 in the course of arguing that simply making a list of words inadequately represents our knowledge of words.) If a list of phrases is insufficient, then how can we characterize the native speaker's linguistic knowledge? We will say that a speaker's linguistic knowledge can be characterized as a grammar consisting of a *finite* set of rules and principles that form the basis for the speaker's ability to produce and comprehend the unlimited number of phrases and sentences of the language. The rules and principles of the grammar also serve to capture regularities in the language.

In referring to the linguistic knowledge of the native speaker, we begin to touch upon a distinction between two concepts that have figured prominently in discussions of syntax in recent years: the distinction between *competence* and *performance*. In discussing these concepts, we will be following, in general outline, the work of the linguist Noam Chomsky (see the bibliography at the end of this chapter); indeed, our general approach to syntax in this entire chapter is based on his influential work.

Competence and Performance

Consider the fact that native speakers of a language are able to make numerous *intuitive judgments* about their language. For example, as native speakers of English we can make the intuitive judgment that examples (2a) and (3a–b) are well-formed sentences of English, whereas examples (2b) and (3c) are ill formed (*) or awkward (?):

(2)
a.   The dog bit the horse.
b.   *Dog the horse the bit.

(3)
a.   Who(m) did Mary grow up with?
b.   With whom did Mary grow up?
c.   ?Up with whom did Mary grow?

We do not have to consult grammar books or interview large groups of English speakers in order to determine that (2a) and (3a–b) are all well formed, whereas (2b) and (3c) are not. Rather, as native speakers we are able to make certain judgments, known as *grammaticality judgments*, about whether sentences are well formed or not. Our ability to make such judgments concerning examples like (2a) and (3a–b), on the one hand, and (2b) and (3c), on the other, reflects our linguistic knowledge; by virtue of knowing English, we know that the former examples are fine, whereas the latter are somehow "odd." This knowledge is part of our linguistic competence as native speakers of English.

The competence-performance distinction (see Chomsky 1965) is intended to reflect the difference between the linguistic knowledge of fluent speakers of a language (*competence*) and the actual production and comprehension of speech by those speakers (*performance*). To take a simple example, suppose that a fluent speaker of English has undergone extensive dental surgery on a certain day, which leaves him temporarily unable to talk. Would we want to say that he has lost his knowledge of English? Surely not. That is, in terms of *competence* we would say that the speaker still maintains a fluent grasp of the English language; however, because of *performance limitations* (aching jaw muscles and tooth pain) his vocal apparatus happens to be temporarily afflicted.

We can also observe the competence-performance distinction if we carefully examine the actual speech of native speakers in a conversation. Actual speech is characterized by false starts and stops, hesitations, lapses of memory, coughing, clearing of the throat, and so on. A detailed transcription of actual speech would reveal numerous *uhh*'s and *umm*'s and other extraneous sounds. Although such details reflect the actual performance of a given speaker on a given occasion, they do not necessarily reflect the speaker's competence. In other words, a speaker's competence is his or her *linguistic capacity*, and although that capacity is reflected in actual speech, it may also be obscured by performance factors such as memory limitations, coughing, inebriation, and so on. In a similar fashion, we can say that a Lamborghini sports car has the capacity to travel at 150 miles per hour, even if it happens to be sitting in the shop right now with four flat tires. The point is that we must distinguish between what it can do (under ideal circumstances) and what it is *actually doing* (in the given circumstances of the moment).

Our study of syntax in this chapter will be based on our intuitive judgments as native speakers of English. In the pages that follow we will be examining numerous expressions, some of which we will judge to be ill formed. Hence, the primary data for our study of syntax will come from our own introspection about English sentences—that is, our own linguistic competence. Not only will the rules and principles that we discover from our study be part of the grammar of English, they will also be of a general type found in numerous other languages. We will proceed in our study of syntax first by examining the concept of *syntactic structure*. Having determined some of the central aspects of the concept of structure, we will then examine certain properties of syntactic *rules*. We will not attempt to discuss a wide range of structures or rules; rather, we will focus on a small number of structures and rules in English, in order to get a feel for how syntactic analysis is carried out. But for now, let us begin by examining what we mean by *structure*.

The Concept of Structure

In all languages, sentences are structured in certain specific ways. What is syntactic structure, and what does it mean to say that sentences are structured? Like many other questions that can be posed about human language, it is difficult to answer this one in any direct fashion. In fact, it is impossible to answer the question *What is structure?* without actually constructing a theory of syntax, and indeed one of the central concerns of current theories of syntax is to provide an answer to this question. Thus, it must be stressed that we cannot define the concept of structure before we study syntax; rather, our study of syntax will be an attempt to find a definition (however elaborate) of this concept.

To begin to find such a definition, we will adopt the following strategy: let's assume that sentences are merely unstructured strings of words. That is, given that we can recognize that sentences are made up of individual words (which we can isolate), it would seem that the minimal assumption we could make would be that sentences are nothing more than words strung out in linear order, one after the other. If we examine some of the formal properties of sentences in light of this strategy, we will quickly discover whether our unstructured-string hypothesis is tenable or whether we will be forced to adopt a hypothesis that attributes greater complexity to sentences. That is, we do not want to simply *assume* that sentences are structured; rather, we want to find out whether this hypothesis is *supported* by evidence.

If we adopt the hypothesis that sentences are unstructured strings of words, then almost immediately we must add an important qualification.

One of the first things we notice about the sentences of human languages is that the words in a sentence occur in a *certain* linear order. Although some languages display considerable freedom of word order (standard examples being Latin, Russian, and Aboriginal Australian languages), in no human language may the words of a sentence occur in any random order whatsoever. No matter how free a language is with respect to word order, it will inevitably have some word order constraints (see exercise 11). Furthermore, in many languages the linear order of words plays a crucial role in determining the meaning of sentences: in English, *The horse bit the dog* means something quite different from *The dog bit the horse*, even though the very same words are used in both. Hence, we might say that sentences are unstructured strings of words, but we must ensure that we specify at least *linear order* for those words (see exercise 11).

Structural Ambiguity

Even with the important qualification just made about word order, our unstructured-string hypothesis runs up against an interesting puzzle. Consider the following sentence:

(4)
a. The mother of the boy and the girl will arrive soon.

This sentence is ambiguous; that is, it has more than one meaning. It is either about one person (the mother) or about two people (the mother in addition to the girl). In sentences that contain the verb *is*, the verb *are*, or a tag (see section 5.2), these two possibilities clearly emerge:

(4)
b. The mother of the boy and the girl *is* arriving soon.
c. The mother of the boy and the girl *are* arriving soon.
d. The mother of the boy and the girl will arrive soon, won't *she*?
e. The mother of the boy and the girl will arrive soon, won't *they*?

The interesting feature of sentence (4a) is that the ambiguity cannot be attributed to an ambiguity in any of the words of the sentence. That is, we cannot attribute the ambiguity of the sentence to an ambiguity in *mother* or *boy* or *girl*. In contrast, consider the sentence *I got a mouse today*. This too is ambiguous, but the ambiguity in this case is attributable to an ambiguity in the word *mouse*: it can mean either "any of numerous small rodents of the family Muridae, especially of the genus

Mus, introduced into the United States from the Old World and of wide distribution" or "a pointing device that is used to move the cursor on a computer monitor screen." For (4a), however, we cannot appeal to such an explanation.

At this point, then, we are faced with a puzzle: how is it that a sentence consisting entirely of unambiguous words can nonetheless be ambiguous? Our unstructured-string hypothesis does not lead us to expect this sort of ambiguity, nor does it provide any mechanism for accounting for the phenomenon. Abandoning the unstructured-string hypothesis, let us instead assume that the words in (4a) can be grouped together and furthermore that they can be grouped together in more than one way. If we make this assumption, which is motivated by our example, we can provide an account of the kind of ambiguity exhibited in sentences such as (4a) by saying that although the sentence consists of a single set of unambiguous words, those words can in fact be grouped in two different ways:

(5)
a. The mother (of the boy and the girl) will arrive soon.
b. (The mother of the boy) and the girl will arrive soon.

When *of the boy* and *and the girl* are grouped together as in (5a), the sentence is interpreted to mean that only the mother will arrive. When *of the boy* is instead grouped with *the mother*, as in (5b), the sentence is interpreted to mean that both the mother and the girl will arrive. Thus, depending on how the words are grouped (how they are *structured*), one interpretation rather than the other is possible. One string of words may have more than one well-formed set of groupings, creating a source of ambiguity that is totally separate from lexical (word) ambiguity.

By saying that words in a sentence can be grouped together, we have started to define the concept of sentence structure. Notice that by appealing to a notion of grouping, we have, even with this simple example, already gone beyond superficial observations concerning properties of sentences to postulating abstract, or theoretical, properties. Although the linear order of words is something we can check by direct observation of a sentence, the grouping of words in that sentence is generally not directly observable. Rather, word grouping is a theoretical property that we appeal to in order to account for abstract characteristics of sentences such as structural ambiguity.

Given what we have said so far, it would appear that in specifying the structure of a sentence, we specify (1) the linear order of words and (2) the possible groupings of the words. Indeed, these are two important properties of the structure of sentences, but by no means are they the only important properties. Given that we have initial evidence that requires us to attribute some kind of structure to sentences, let us examine in more detail what is involved in specifying the structure of English sentences (and, more generally, the sentences of many other languages).

5.2   AN INFORMAL THEORY OF SYNTAX

So far we have drawn our evidence for structure from ambiguous sentences that do not contain ambiguous words. We are not limited by such examples. One of the most important ways of discovering why and how sentences must be structured is to try to state explicitly grammatical rules for a given language. For example, consider the following English declarative sentences and their corresponding question (interrogative) forms:

(6)
a. John can lift 500 pounds.
    Can John lift 500 pounds?
b. Gurus are generally thought to be odd.
    Are gurus generally thought to be odd?
c. They will want to reserve two rooms.
    Will they want to reserve two rooms?
d. Mary has proved several theorems.
    Has Mary proved several theorems?

Any native speaker of English knows how to form interrogative and declarative sentences of the sort illustrated in (6). We will now engage in an apparently simple exercise: that is, to state as precisely as we can how such English questions are structured.

The English Question Rule

For the purposes of this discussion, we will assume that interrogative sentences, specifically *yes/no questions* (so called because they are typically answered with "yes" or "no"), are formed from declarative sentences. There is independent evidence that the two sentence types should be related; however, we will not go into those arguments here.

How can we describe the way the questions in (6) are formed from the declarative sentences? One approach would be to number each word of the declarative sentence, as in (7), and state a set of instructions for forming a question based on this sentence, as in (8). Note that the rule in (8) does not refer to structure but refers only to linear order and the notion "word."

(7)
John can lift 500 pounds.
  1   2   3   4   5

(8)
Question Rule I (QR-I)
To form a question from a declarative sentence, place word 2 at the beginning of the sentence.

Given (7) as input, QR-I produces (9) as output:

(9)
Can John lift 500 pounds?
  2   1   3   4   5

Thus, QR-I properly produces the interrogative in (6a). A simple check will reveal that QR-I also works for the other examples in (6).

However, OR-I is inadequate. Though it does account for the sentences in (6), it cannot be extended to other declarative/interrogative pairs. Consider the following declarative sentences:

(10)
a. Yesterday John could lift 500 pounds.
b. Computer gurus are thought to be odd.
c. Those people will want to reserve two rooms.

QR-I predicts that the corresponding questions should be as follows:

(11)
a. John yesterday could lift 500 pounds?
b. *Gurus computer are thought to be odd?
c. *People those will want to reserve two rooms?

Though (11a) might be a possible (albeit awkward) sentence, it is certainly not the question that corresponds to (10a)—which should be *Yesterday, could John lift 500 pounds?* As for (11b) and (11c), they are not the questions corresponding to (10b) and (10c), respectively. Moreover, they are ungrammatical. No native speaker would accept them as being well formed.

It is clear, then, that we must reformulate QR-I so as to account for the counterexamples in (11). We see that English questions are not formed by simply moving the second word of the sentence to the beginning. After all, the second word of an English sentence can be any type of word: a noun, a verb, an adjective, an article, and so on. However, the examples in (6) show that in forming a question in English, it is always a verb that is moved, that is, a word such as *can*, *are*, *will*, and *has*.

In order to state the Question Rule more accurately, we are now forced to suppose that the words of a sentence are not only strung out in some linear order but also classified into different morphological categories— what have traditionally been called *parts of speech*. We have already seen evidence in chapter 2 that words must be classed into parts of speech in order to state word formation rules properly. If we make this assumption for syntax as well as morphology, then we can restate the Question Rule so that it is sensitive to this morphological information:

(12)
Question Rule II (QR-II)
To form a question from a declarative sentence, place the first verb at the beginning of the sentence.

In *John can lift 500 pounds* the first verb is *can*; by placing it at the beginning of the sentence, we derive the question *Can John lift 500 pounds?* Similarly, in *Gurus are thought to be odd* the first verb is *are*; by placing it at the beginning, we derive *Are gurus thought to be odd?* Indeed, the reformulated rule gives the right results for the examples in both (6) and (10), with one exception. For sentence (10a), *Yesterday John could lift 500 pounds*, the first verb is *could*; by placing it at the beginning of the sentence, we derive **Could yesterday John lift 500 pounds?*—which seems to be unnatural. Instead, we want to arrive at the form *Yesterday, could John lift 500 pounds?* We will return to this problem shortly.

We have now been forced to assume that the words in a sentence must be classified into parts of speech. It should be stressed that this classification is not a matter of convenience or conjecture; rather, it turns out to be impossible to state the Question Rule properly if we cannot appeal to such a classification.

Just as we found counterexamples to QR-I, however, we can easily find other counterexamples to QR-II. Consider the following examples:

(13)
a. You know those women.
b. Mary left early.
c. They went to Berkeley.

Here, the first verbs—and the only verb in each case—are *know*, *left*, and *went*, respectively. Applying QR-II yields the following questions:

(14)
a. *Know you those women?
b. *Left Mary early?
c. *Went they to Berkeley?

If QR-II were the correct rule, then the questions in (14) would be well formed. Although English once formed questions of this general sort (similar forms appear in Shakespeare's writings, for example), they are ill formed in present-day English. Why are these sentences different from the ones we considered earlier? Let us review some of the sentences we have examined so far (15a–c, e–f) and add a new one (15d):

(15)
a. John can lift 500 pounds.
   Can John lift 500 pounds?
b. They will want to reserve two rooms.
   Will they want to reserve two rooms?
c. Mary has proved several theorems.
   Has Mary proved several theorems?
d. Bill is doing the dishes.
   Is Bill doing the dishes?
e. You know those women.
   Do you know those women?
f. They went to Berkeley.
   Did they go to Berkeley?

In the pairs of sentences in (15a–d) a verb has changed position in deriving the question from the statement. Note that each of these four sentences has two verbs: an auxiliary verb and a main verb, of which the former is involved in the question formation process. In fact, we may interpret the form of *do* that appears in the questions in (15e–f) as a "placeholder" auxiliary verb.

We will see in the next section that the distinction between main and auxiliary verbs plays a role elsewhere in the grammar. This is important since it further supports the need to draw such a distinction in accounting for the formation of interrogatives.

Auxiliary Verbs versus Main Verbs in English

The auxiliary verbs of English include the following forms:

(16)

a. Forms of the verb *be* (*is, am, are, was, were*)

b. Forms of the verb *have* (*have, has, had*)

c. Forms of the verb *do* (*do, does, did*)

d. The verbs *can, could, will, would, shall, should, may, might, must*, and a few others. Members of this group are usually called *modal auxiliaries*. Modals are "helping verbs" that usually refer to notions such as possibility, necessity, and obligation.

The distinction between auxiliary verbs and main verbs shows up very clearly in several grammatical processes in English, among which are the following:

1. Auxiliary verbs, but not main verbs, are fronted in forming questions:

(17)

a. John *is* running.
   Is John running?

b. They *have* left.
   Have they left?

c. I *can* sing.
   Can I sing?

d. Mary *speaks* Swahili.
   *Speaks Mary Swahili?

When a sentence contains no auxiliary verb but has only a main verb, the auxiliary verb *do* is used in forming questions:

(18)

a. You *know* those women.
   Do you know those women?

b. Mary *left* early.
   Did Mary leave early?

c. They *went* to Berkeley.
   Did they go to Berkeley?

2. The contracted negative form *n't* can attach to auxiliary verbs:

(19)

a. John *is* running.

   John *isn't* running

b. They *have* left.

   They *haven't* left.

c. I *can* sing.

   I *can't* sing.

However, main verbs cannot be negated in this way:

(20)

a. You know those women.

   *You known't those women.

b. Mary left early.

   *Mary leftn't early.

When a sentence contains only a main verb and no auxiliary verb, the auxiliary verb *do* is used in forming the negative version:

(21)

a. You *know* those women.

   You *don't* know those women.

b. Mary *left* early.

   Mary *didn't* leave early.

c. They *went* to Berkeley.

   They *didn't* go to Berkeley.

In addition, auxiliary verbs can be followed by the uncontracted negative *not* (as in *John is not running, They have not left, I cannot sing*). Main verbs cannot be followed by uncontracted *not* in current spoken American English: expressions such as *We know not what we do* and *Ask not what your country can do for you* are possible only in highly stylized forms of English in which an archaic flavor is preserved (as in religious preaching styles and highly formal oratory).

3. Auxiliary verbs, but not main verbs, can appear in tags. A tag occurs at the end of a sentence and contains a repetition of the auxiliary verb found in that sentence:

(22)

John *has* not been here, *has* he?

      main sentence   tag

When the auxiliary verb of the main sentence is positive in form, the repeated auxiliary verb in the tag may be positive or negative in form:

(23)

a. Herman is threatening to leave, is he!

b. Herman is threatening to leave, isn't he?

The positive and negative tags are used under different circumstances (the positive tag often having the force of a challenge; the negative tag being used to request confirmation of the main sentence). But in both cases the auxiliary verb of the tag is a repetition of the auxiliary verb of the main sentence. In addition, when the auxiliary verb of the main sentence is negative in form, the auxiliary verb in the tag is always positive:

(24)

Herman isn't threatening to leave, is he?

In other words, we do not find cases like (25):

(25)

*Herman isn't threatening to leave, isn't he?

Unlike auxiliary verbs, main verbs cannot appear in tags. For a sentence such as *You know those women* there is no corresponding tagged form, *You know those women, know you?* Instead, when a sentence contains only a main verb, the auxiliary verb *do* is used in forming the tag:

(26)

a. You know those women, *do* you!

b. Mary left early, *did* she!

c. They went to Berkeley, *didn't* they?

Thus, auxiliary verbs and main verbs differ not only with respect to question formation but also with respect to negation and tag formation. These differences are summarized in table 5.1.

Given this distinction in English verbs, and given the impossibility of question forms such as those in (14), we must now amend the Question Rule to take account of the new data:

(27)

Question Rule III (QR-III)

a. To form a question from a declarative sentence, place the auxiliary verb at the beginning of the sentence.

Table 5.1
Comparison of auxiliary verbs and main verbs

	Auxiliary verbs	Main verbs
Fronted in forming questions?	Yes: *Is* John running? *Have* they left? *Can* I sing?	No: *Know you those women? *Left Mary early? *Went they to Berkeley? Use *do*: *Do* you know those women? *Did* Mary leave early? *Did* they go to Berkeley?
Negative form can have *n't* attached?	Yes: John *isn't* running. They *haven't* left. I *can't* sing.	No: *You known't those women. *Mary leftn't early. *They wentn't to Berkeley. Use *do*: You *don't* know those women. Mary *didn't* leave early. They *didn't* go to Berkeley.
Can occur in tag sentence?	Yes: John isn't running, *is* he? They haven't left, *have* they? I can't sing, *can* I?	No: *You know those women, know you? *Mary left early, left she? *They went to Berkeley, went they? Use *do*: You know those women, *do* you! Mary left early, *did* she! They went to Berkeley, *didn't* they?

b. If there is no auxiliary verb, but only a main verb, place an appropriate form of the verb *do* at the beginning of the sentence and make appropriate changes in the main verb.

As we can verify, this amended rule covers the cases we have cited so far. For a sentence such as *Mary has left*, the auxiliary verb is *has*; by fronting this, we derive the question form *Has Mary left?* A sentence such as *You knew those women* has no auxiliary verb; thus, we must insert an appropriate form of the auxiliary verb *do*. In this case the appropriate form is *did* (past tense), and we must make appropriate changes in the main verb (changing past tense *knew* to tenseless *know*), thus deriving the question form *Did you know those women?* And so on for the rest of the examples given. We will not be concerned with the details of the use of auxiliary *do*, and thus we leave part (b) of the Question Rule stated in a rather vague way. Since our interest from this point on will be in part (a), we will omit further mention of part (b)—keeping in mind, however, that part (b) is to be understood as being included in further revisions of the rule.

We now have a revised version of the Question Rule, amended to take account of the distinction in English between auxiliary and main verbs. In other words, the Question Rule must be sensitive not only to the distinction among major parts of speech (such as noun vs. verb) but also to the distinction(s) among subcategories of a major category. The Question Rule does not involve just any verb; it involves only a specific subcategory of verbs, namely, the auxiliaries. With this additional refinement, our Question Rule has become more adequate.

Structural Grouping: The Subject Constituent

Question Rule III makes reference to *auxiliary verb*. However, what happens if more than one auxiliary verb occurs in the sentence? Consider the examples in (28):

(28)
a. John *will have* left.
b. Anna *should be* going to Chicago.
c. Galen *has been* studying very hard.

The corresponding interrogative sentences for these are (29a–c)—not (30a–c):

(29)
a. *Will* John have left?
b. *Should* Anna be going to Chicago?
c. *Has* Galen been studying very hard?

(30)
a. *Have John will left?
b. *Be Anna should going to Chicago?
c. *Been Galen has studying very hard?

Have and *be* are (nonmodal) auxiliary verbs in (30). They share all the relevant properties of other auxiliary verbs. To see this, consider the examples in (31):

(31)
a. John has left.
   Has John left?   (interrogative)
   John hasn't left.   (negation)
   John has left, hasn't he?   (tag)
b. Anna is going to Chicago.
   Is Anna going to Chicago?   (interrogative)
   Anna isn't going to Chicago.   (negation)
   Anna is going to Chicago, is she? (tag)
c. Galen is studying very hard.
   Is Galen studying very hard?   (interrogative)
   Galen isn't studying very hard.   (negation)
   Galen is studying very hard, is he? (tag)

As we can see, *have* and *be* (realized here as *has* and *is*) front to form an interrogative, can appear with the negative *n't*, and can appear in tags. Why, then, can these auxiliaries not front when they occur with *will*, *should*, and *has*? What distinguishes "good" fronting of an auxiliary verb from illicit fronting is linear order. The first auxiliary verb in a sequence of auxiliary verbs is the one targeted for fronting. In other words, the rule needs to refer to linear order as well as to categorial information:

(32)
Question Rule IV (QR-IV)
To form a question from a declarative sentence, place the first auxiliary verb at the beginning of the sentence.

Let us look at other sentences containing more than one auxiliary verb. The examples in (33) constitute a class of sentences we have yet to examine:

(33)
a. The people who *are* standing in the room *will* leave soon.
b. Many computer gurus who you *will* meet *are* thought to be odd.
c. Anyone that *can* lift 500 pounds *is* eligible for our club.

Notice that in (33a) the first auxiliary verb is *are*. If we place this first auxiliary verb at the beginning of the sentence, we will derive the following ungrammatical sentence:

(34)
*Are the people who ____ standing in the room will leave soon?

Clearly, in this example it is not the first auxiliary verb that should be moved; instead, it is the second auxiliary verb, *will*:

(35)
Will the people who are standing in the room ____ leave soon?

Is this a counterexample to our previous conclusion? Is this a case where it is really the second auxiliary verb that fronts? To answer this question, we need more data. In the following examples, the auxiliary verb that fronts (which is boxed) does not correspond to any particular number; it can be the third, fourth, or any other number.

(36)
a. The people who *were* saying that John *is* sick $\boxed{\text{will}}$ leave soon.
                   1   2   3
b. The people who *were* saying that Pat *has* told Mary to make Terry
                   1   2

quit trying to persuade David that many computer gurus *are* thought to
                                                        3

be odd $\boxed{\text{will}}$ leave soon.
   4

An important point to notice here is that such examples can be extended indefinitely—as noted earlier in this chapter, there is simply no limit on the length of the sentences we can construct or on the number of auxiliary verbs we can place before the auxiliary verb that fronts. Naturally, when sentences become this long, they become difficult to understand and remember; consequently, they would normally not occur in everyday conversation as single uninterrupted sentences. However, this is a practical problem, a problem of performance limitations on memory, and we will consider sentences such as (36b) as data that our grammar must be able to account for.

In (36a–b) we see that in each instance the auxiliary verb *will* is the correct verb to move to the beginning of the sentence. However, that auxiliary verb does not occupy any particular fixed slot in the linear order of words. Further, it is in principle impossible to specify exactly what can come between that auxiliary and the beginning of the sentence (because there is no limitation on the length of the sentence between the beginning point and the point where the appropriate auxiliary is located). It should be clear that for (36a–b), QR-IV will give the wrong results if we apply it strictly. A more general rule is needed.

If we look more carefully at examples (33a–c), we see that the auxiliary verb that must be moved to the front of the sentence is the auxiliary that immediately follows an intuitively natural grouping of words traditionally referred to as the *subject* of the sentence:

(37)

a. <u>The people who are standing in the room</u>   will …
                Subject   Auxiliary

b. <u>Many computer gurus who you will meet</u>   are …
                Subject   Auxiliary

c. <u>Anyone that can lift 500 pounds</u>   is …
                Subject   Auxiliary

The underlined words in each example of (37) form a unit; that is, they form a single *constituent*. The subject constituent of the sentence (discussed further in the next section) plays an important role in the statement of the Question Rule, since it allows us to locate the appropriate auxiliary verb in the formation of questions. Given the notion of subject constituent, we can now amend QR-IV as follows, to take into account examples such as (33a–c):

(38)
Question Rule V (QR-V)
To form a question from a declarative sentence, locate the first auxiliary verb *that follows the subject of the sentence* and place it at the beginning of the sentence.

Given this reformulation of the Question Rule, we can now pick out the proper auxiliary verb to front in forming questions (you might want to verify that QR-V covers all the cases discussed so far), and we will successfully avoid the problem illustrated by example (34), which plagued QR-IV.

However, it turns out that even QR-V must be further modified. As we have already seen, the appropriate auxiliary verb is not always moved to the front of the sentence. Recall the following examples:

(39)
a.   Yesterday John could lift 500 pounds.
b.   *Could yesterday John lift 500 pounds?
c.   Yesterday, could John lift 500 pounds?

These examples suggest that the appropriate auxiliary verb of the sentence must be placed immediately to the left of the subject, not actually at the beginning of the sentence. This leads to the following modification:

(40)
Question Rule VI (QR-VI)
To form a question from a declarative sentence, locate the first auxiliary verb that follows the subject of the sentence and place it *immediately to the left of the subject.*

This reformulation will cover all the cases we have examined so far.

We began with the minimal assumption that sentences are unstructured strings of words, and we attempted to state an adequate rule for characterizing well-formed questions in English. Successive counterexamples forced us to revise our assumptions about how sentences are structured. For example, notice that the latest statement of the Question Rule forces us to refer to *linear order* (by referring to the *first* auxiliary verb after the subject), to categorize words into *parts of speech* (by referring to auxiliary verbs), and to refer to *constituent structure* (by referring to a structural grouping called *subject*). It is important to note that at each stage the added assumptions were not merely a matter of convenience. For example, we sought independent evidence for the distinction between main verb and auxiliary verb, noting various properties that auxiliary verbs, but not main verbs, share. We have yet to demonstrate the importance of the constituent we referred to as *subject*. We now turn to independent evidence for such a grouping.

The Notion "Subject"

In our latest reformulations of the Question Rule we have referred to the subject of a sentence, and it would be useful here to note that subjects play an important role in other grammatical processes in English (and, indeed, in many other languages). To begin with, what exactly is a *subject*? This notion has never been precisely defined, despite its significant role in linguistic analysis. Like many linguistic notions, it has an intuitive basis. The classic example of a subject comes from simple sentences with action verbs, such as *The farmer fed the duckling*, in which the subject, in this case *the farmer*, is understood as the agent ("the doer") of the action, and the object, in this case *the duckling*, is understood as that which undergoes the action. Not every subject is an agent; in the sentence *Mary resembles her Aunt Bettina*, *Mary* is the subject, but no action is involved. In general, trying to characterize subjects in terms of meaning is an extremely complex undertaking, if indeed it is possible at all.

In any given language we can find grammatical processes that crucially (and uniquely) involve subjects of sentences, however, and we can use these processes as tests for identifying the subject of a sentence in that language. For example, in English, tag questions provide a good test for identifying the subject of a sentence, because the pronoun in the tag agrees with the subject:

(41)

a. You will persuade Aunt Bettina, won't you?

b. John won't sing to Mary, will he?

c. The woman in the photo is feeding the ducks, isn't she?

d. The man who hated everybody didn't leave early, did he?

e. The students in the class voted for me, didn't they?

f. The girl and the boy are playing, aren't they?

The pronouns in the tags illustrated in (41) agree with the subjects of the main sentences in terms of person (first, which is the speaker; second, which is the hearer; or third, which is neither the speaker nor the hearer), number (singular or plural), and gender (masculine, feminine, or neuter). For example, in (41f) the subject, *the girl and the boy*, is third person plural (gender is neutral), and these features are reflected in the pronoun *they* in the tag. The features of person, number, and gender serve to classify the personal pronouns of English, as shown in table 5.2.

In English, then, subjects of sentences have a number of properties:

(42)

a. The subject of a declarative sentence generally precedes the auxiliary and main verb in linear order.

Table 5.2
Classification of English personal pronouns in terms of person, number, and gender

	Singular	Plural
1st person	I	we
2nd person	you	you
3rd person		
Masculine	he	
Feminine	she	they
Neuter	it	

b. It forms the constituent around which an auxiliary is fronted in forming a question (see (40)).

c. It is the constituent with which a pronoun in a tag agrees in terms of person, number, and gender. (See exercise 9 for another grammatical process that makes reference to subjects.)

In languages other than English, subjects can have other grammatical properties. For example, recall the Japanese sentence discussed in section 2.1, *John-ga hon-o yonda* "John read the book." We noted that the subject of the sentence, *John*, has the particle *-ga* attached to it, which serves to indicate the subject function in this particular sentence. (The particle *-o* in turn indicates the object function of *hon* "book.") The subject, then, is overtly marked and is recognized by its marker. It is not recognized by its linear order in the sentence, as in English. In fact, it can occur either before or after the object; the sentence means the same in either case.

Most English pronouns are marked according to their function as subjects or objects (see table 5.3). The pronoun *you* has the same form in all uses (singular and plural, subject and nonsubject), and the pronoun *it* has the same form in subject and nonsubject uses. Otherwise, pronouns in English assume two different forms to reflect their subject or nonsubject function: *I–me, we–us, he–him, she–her,* and *they–them.* The subject pronouns *I, we, she, he,* and *they* are sometimes called *nominative* (or *subjective*) case pronouns; the nonsubject pronouns *me, us, her, him, them* are sometimes called *accusative* (or *objective*) case pronouns. Nonsubject (i.e., nonnominative) pronouns cannot be used in subject position (except in jokes such as *Me Tarzan, you Jane*; expressions such as *What, me worry?*; or conjoined noun phrases such as *Me and Stacy went to the*

Table 5.3
Subject and nonsubject pronouns in English

	SUBJECT PRONOUNS	NONSUBJECT PRONOUNS	
	As subject of sentence	As object of verb	As object of preposition
1st person			
Singular	*I* love movies.	They like *me*.	She spoke to *me*.
Plural	*We* enjoy cars.	You follow *us*.	It ran from *us*.
2nd person			
Singular or Plural	*You* left early.	I found *you*.	I work for *you*.
3rd person			
Singular	*He* collapsed.	Watch *him*!	I'll sit by *him*.
	She won.	I copy *her*.	Go after *her*!
	It blew up.	Why buy *it*?	Look under *it*!
Plural	*They* are nice.	I hired *them*.	It flew over *them*.

mall), and subject pronouns cannot be used in nonsubject positions (note the ungrammatical **You saw I*). Therefore, the form of the pronoun may serve as a clue to the role, subject or object, that the pronoun plays in the sentence.

Aside from the pronouns listed in table 5.3, no other words (nouns) in English change morphological form to reflect subject versus nonsubject function. Thus, in sentences such as *Mary saw the dog* or *The dog saw Mary*, the nouns *dog* and *Mary* have the same shape whether they function as subject or object.

These examples illustrate some of the ways in which subjects can be marked, or function in grammatical processes (also see exercise 9). We have not yet defined the notion "subject." In the section on constituent structure tests we will work out a definition that is structural in nature. In order to understand this definition, we must learn something about constituent structure, a matter to which we now turn.

Constituent Structure and Tree Diagrams

We have now cited two kinds of evidence in favor of the hypothesis that sentences are structured. First, if we do not assume that sentences are structured—that words are grouped into constituents—then we cannot account for how a sentence consisting of a set of unambiguous words can nevertheless be ambiguous. Second, it is impossible to state certain grammatical rules (such as the Question Rule for English) without appealing to constituent structure. Not only can we say that sentences are indeed structured, but we can also indicate (at least partially) how they must be structured. That is, we have found at least three important aspects of sentence structure:

(43)
a. The *linear order* of words in a sentence
b. The categorization of words into *parts of speech*
c. The grouping of words into *structural constituents* of the sentence

These three types of structural information can be encoded into what is called a *tree diagram* (or *phrase marker*) of the sort illustrated in tree 5.1. Note that our "definition" of structure is now a list of (structural) properties that a phrase or sentence must conform to.

Consider the structure in tree 5.1. Such tree diagrams can at first seem quite complicated. But in fact they represent in a simple and straightforward way the kinds of structural information summarized in (43). The trick is learning how to read them (and reading them is an important part

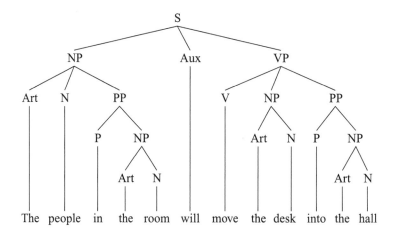

Symbols used: S—sentence; NP—noun phrase; Aux—auxiliary verb; VP—verb phrase; PP—prepositional phrase; Art—article; N—noun; V—verb; P—preposition.

Tree 5.1

of doing syntax). Let's begin by reading tree 5.1, in a step-by-step fashion, to see how it represents structural information. Learning how to decode this particular tree will give you an idea about how to read tree diagrams in general.

Tree 5.1 represents the structure of the sentence *The people in the room will move the desk into the hall.* Beginning at the bottom of the tree, note that each word of the sentence is connected by a line—called a *branch* of the tree—to a certain symbol of the tree:

```
Art     N     P   Art    N    Aux    V    Art    N
 |      |     |    |      |     |     |     |     |       . . .
the   people  in  the   room  will  move  the  desk
```

In this way, each word of the sentence is assigned to a certain lexical category (part of speech). Thus, the word *the* is connected by a branch to the symbol *Art*, standing for *Article*, indicating that *the* is an article. The word *people* is connected by a branch to the symbol *N*, standing for *Noun*, indicating that *people* is a noun. The word *in* is connected by a branch to the symbol *P*, standing for *Preposition*, indicating that *in* is a preposition. Shifting over to the right, the word *move* is connected by a branch to the symbol *V*, standing for *Verb*, indicating that *move* is a verb. In a similar fashion, all the words of the sentence are connected by branches to appropriate symbols indicating their lexical category. Notice that the words, as well as the lexical category symbols *Art*, *N*, *P*, and so on, are all shown in a specific linear order (reading the tree from left to right). Thus, tree 5.1 represents the information cited in (43a) and (43b): the *linear order* of words, and the *categorization* of words into parts of speech.

Now, how do tree diagrams represent structural constituents of a sentence? To see this, we will move up the tree a bit, focusing first on the subject phrase, *the people in the room.* Notice that this string of words is shown as having a certain constituent structure. For example, the sequence of words *the room* is shown as a *noun phrase* (*NP*); that is, the symbols *Art* and *N* are connected by branches to the symbol *NP*:

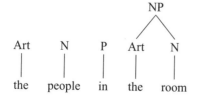

Both *Art* and *N* are connected by branches to the *same* symbol, *NP*;
hence, *Art* and *N* form a single constituent. The NP *the room* and the
preposition *in* are shown as forming a *prepositional phrase* (*PP*); that is,
the symbols *P* (*in*) and *NP* (*the room*) are both connected by branches to
the symbol *PP*:

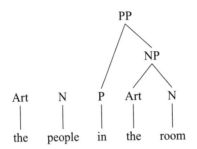

Both *P* and *NP* are connected by branches to the *same* symbol, *PP*;
hence, *P* and *NP* form a single constituent. Thus far, then, in tree 5.1 the
sequence of words *the room* is a single constituent—a noun phrase (NP)
—and the sequence of words *in the room* is a single constituent—a
prepositional phrase (PP).

Finally, let us consider the sequence of words *the people*. This phrase is
structurally similar to the phrase *the room*: it consists of an article followed by a noun, thus forming a noun phrase:

But noun phrases do not only consist of articles followed by nouns.
Sometimes the noun in a noun phrase can be followed by a modifying
phrase. For example, in the phrase *the people in the room*, the prepositional phrase *in the room* is a modifying phrase: that is, it provides additional information about the noun *people*. To put it simply, when we use
the phrase *the people in the room*, we are not talking about any random
group of people; rather, we are talking about the people who are *in the
room*, and in this sense the modifying phrase *in the room* provides
"additional" information about the people. In tree 5.1 this modifying
prepositional phrase is shown as part of the subject noun phrase:

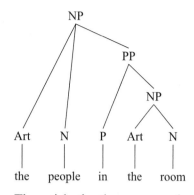

The article *the*, the noun *people*, and the prepositional phrase *in the room* are all connected by branches to the same symbol *NP*; hence, *Art*, *N*, and *PP* all form a single constituent, which functions as the subject of the sentence, *The people in the room will move the desk into the hall*.

Let us now turn to the *verb phrase* (*VP*) of tree 5.1. The symbols *V* (*move*), *NP* (*the desk*), and *PP* (*into the hall*) are all connected by branches to the same symbol, *VP*; this means that the sequence *V-NP-PP* forms a single constituent—namely, the verb phrase *move the desk into the hall*. Finally, moving up to the highest level of the tree, the subject *NP* (*the people in the room*), the auxiliary verb *will* (symbolized as *Aux*), and the *VP* are all connected by branches to the same symbol *S* (standing for *Sentence*); hence, the sequence *NP-Aux-VP* forms a *single constituent*, namely, a *Sentence*. A tree diagram represents syntactic constituent structure in terms of the particular way that its lines branch. The particular points in a tree that are connected by branches to other points are called *nodes* of the tree, and these nodes are labeled with specific symbols such as *S*, *NP*, *Aux*, *VP*, *V*, *N*, *Art*, and *P*. Particular labeled nodes represent single constituents, made up of the items connected to them by branching lines.

In section 5.3 we will discuss how tree diagrams can be *generated* by a type of rule. For the time being, however, it is sufficient merely to know how to read a tree diagram, without worrying yet where the tree "comes from." In decoding tree diagrams, notice that you can start from the top and work your way "down," to see how larger constituents are broken down into their constituent parts. For example, in tree 5.1 you can start at the top, *S*, and trace the branches down from *S* to see what constituents *S* is broken down into (and so on, for other phrases). Or you can start from the bottom of a tree and work your way "up," to see how individual words make up smaller constituents, and how smaller constituents make up larger ones, as we did in our earlier discussion. In any event, with practice you will find that reading tree diagrams becomes quite easy.

Tree 5.1 encodes the important structural properties of a sentence. As we have seen, the various parts of the sentence are shown in a fixed linear order. Each word is assigned a part of speech: *Art*, *N*, *P*, and so on. And different elements in the sentence are shown as being grouped into successively larger constituents of the sentence: *NP*, *Aux*, and *VP* make up a sentence (*S*); *V*, *NP*, and *PP* make up a verb phrase (*VP*); and so on. What is important about this diagram is the information that it encodes, and we must note that the same information could be encoded in other (equivalent) ways. For example, the syntactic constituent structure of phrases and sentences can also be represented in terms of "box diagrams" of the sort illustrated in figure 5.1. This particular box diagram provides a structural analysis of the phrase *the people in the room*: (1) the words are represented in a linear order, (2) each word is assigned to a part-of-speech category, and (3) a hierarchical grouping is defined (the diagram indicates that a Noun Phrase can consist of an Article followed by a Noun followed by a Prepositional Phrase, which in turn consists of a Preposition followed by a Noun Phrase, and so on).

In effect, then, the box diagram of figure 5.1 encodes the same information as the tree structure in tree 5.1 with respect to the subject noun phrase *the people in the room*. In the tree, structural grouping is indicated by branching of the lines, rather than by levels in a box. Even though box diagrams might adequately represent constituent structure information for our purposes at this point, we will continue to represent syntactic structure by means of tree diagrams, since in the theory of syntax

NOUN PHRASE				
Article	Noun	Prepositional Phrase		
		Preposition	Noun Phrase	
			Article	Noun
the	people	in	the	room

Figure 5.1
Constituent structure represented by box diagram

we are adopting in this chapter—the theory known as *transformational grammar*, developed by the linguist Noam Chomsky (see references)—transformational rules are traditionally defined as operating on tree structures. For present purposes, the point is that the same structural information can be encoded in a number of equivalent ways.

The same thing is true for the symbols we have chosen; although we have used the traditional names for the parts of speech, any system of labeling that made the same distinctions would be just as good for our purposes. Hence, we could call articles *class 1 words*, nouns *class 2 words*, and so on. As long as the right distinctions were made and similar words were assigned to similar categories, this system of naming parts of speech would be perfectly adequate.

Constituent Structure Tests: Using Rules, Clefts, and Conjunction

At this point a natural question arises: namely, what evidence do we use to arrive at particular tree diagrams such as tree 5.1? How do we know that the sentence represented by that tree is structured as we have shown it? The answer is that tree diagrams represent hypotheses in our theory of syntax and are motivated by empirical evidence.

One of the ways in which we arrive at a particular formulation of a phrase marker (tree diagram) is to use certain *constituent structure tests*. Such tests usually involve stating a grammatical rule of the language and then formulating the phrase marker (tree) in such a way as to allow the grammatical rule to be stated as simply as possible. For illustration, let us return to tree 5.1. We have good reasons for supposing that the phrase *the people in the room* forms a single NP constituent and is not merely an unstructured string of words. One important reason (but by no means the only one) is that if we represent this set of words as a single NP constituent, we can state the Question Rule in the simplest possible way: we can say simply that the auxiliary verb is to be moved to the left of the subject NP constituent of the sentence, and not, for instance, that the auxiliary verb should be moved to the left of the string of words *the people in the room*. More to the point, however, recall that since there is no limit on the length of the subject of a sentence (see example (36)), it is impossible to state the Question Rule in terms of the linear string of words that make up a subject: we would never be able to exhaustively list all the strings of words that could make up the subject of a sentence. Hence, we are forced to postulate an NP constituent as the subject of a sentence.

In the foregoing discussion, we have used the Question Rule in a constituent structure test. Since grammatical rules (such as the Question Rule) are stated in terms of tree structures, we formulate our tree structures in such a way as to allow the simplest statement of the rules. In a certain sense, then, grammatical rules of a language tell us what the tree structures ought to look like, and for this reason we can use such rules as constituent structure tests.

Cleft Sentences
In addition to using relationships between sentence types (such as declarative and interrogative) as constituent structure tests, we can use certain *sentence frames*. For example, English has a construction referred to as the *cleft sentence*, with the following general form:

(44)
Cleft sentence

It $\left\{ \begin{matrix} \text{is} \\ \text{was} \end{matrix} \right\}$ X that Y

That is, cleft sentences consist of *it* followed by some form of the verb *to be*, followed by some constituent X, followed by a clause introduced by *that* from which X has been "extracted":

(45)
a. It was *the burglar* that ____ broke the lamp.
b. It is *Mary* that I want to meet ____.
c. It was *under the mattress* that we found the money ____.
d. It is *at three o'clock in the afternoon* that they change guards ____.

In these examples X is respectively *the burglar*, *Mary*, *under the mattress*, and *at three o'clock in the afternoon*; Y is *broke the lamp*, *I want to meet*, *we found the money*, and *they change guards*; and ____ is the site from which the material in X has been "extracted."

An important fact about cleft sentences in English is that the phrase that fits into position X of the frame [*It is/was X that ...*] is always (1) a single constituent and (2) either a noun phrase (NP) or a prepositional phrase (PP). Sentences (45a–b) have NPs in position X of the cleft frame; (45c–d) have PPs in that position.

Returning to tree 5.1, we can use the cleft test to determine certain aspects of its constituent structure. Consider the sequences of words *the desk* and *into the hall*. In tree 5.1 *the desk* is shown as a single NP constituent, and *into the hall* is shown as a single PP constituent. Is there any corroborating evidence for this? We can test the validity of the tree by inserting those two phrases into position X of appropriate cleft sentences:

(46)
a. It is *the desk* that the people will move into the hall.
b. It is *into the hall* that the people will move the desk.

Given what we have seen about cleft sentences, (46a) confirms that the phrase *the desk* is a single constituent (an NP) and (46b) confirms that the phrase *into the hall* is a single constituent (a PP). Tree 5.1 accurately reflects this constituent structure by representing *the desk* as an NP and *into the hall* as a PP.

Continuing with tree 5.1, can we determine whether or not the sequence *the desk into the hall* is a single NP (or PP) constituent? The cleft test can help us here:

(47)
*It is *the desk into the hall* that the people will move.

Sentence (47) is ungrammatical. If the sequence *the desk into the hall* were a single NP constituent, then it would be able to occur in position X of the cleft frame [*It is X that* ...]. But it cannot, suggesting that this sequence is *not* a single constituent. Tree 5.1 reflects this property accurately, by representing *the desk* and *into the hall* as two distinct constituents. Those two constituents do not, in themselves, make up another constituent (however, note that those two constituents along with the verb *move* make up a verb phrase constituent). Hence, tree 5.1 assigns a constituent structure in which *move the desk into the hall* is a single constituent (VP) and the three phrases *move* (V), *the desk* (NP), and *into the hall* (PP) are each single constituents, but the sequence *the desk into the hall* is not a single NP constituent. Thus, the constituent structure represented by the tree seems consistent with what we know about the sentence so far.

Conjunction
Another test frame that has been used in linguistic analysis is the *conjunction* test. The assumption underlying this test is that only single constituents of the same type can occur in the frame [_____ and _____] (i.e., only single constituents of the same type can be conjoined with *and*). (This generalization, insofar as it holds, may well follow from other

aspects of the syntax/grammar and may not necessarily involve a rule that constrains the categories that can be conjoined. For our purposes, though, we adopt the constraint as just stated.)

(48)

a. *The teacher* and *the student* argued. (NP and NP)
b. Mary *played the harmonica* and *danced a jig*. (VP and VP)
c. We moved the desk *through the door* and *into the hall*. (PP and PP)

These examples include conjoined noun phases (*the teacher* and *the student*), conjoined verb phrases (*played the harmonica* and *danced a jig*), and conjoined prepositional phrases (*through the door* and *into the hall*). Such examples have been used to show that the conjunction *and* is used to conjoin two constituents of the same type. Indeed, when we attempt to conjoin two constituents not of the same type, a decidedly odd sentence results:

(49)

a.   Mary played the harmonica.
b.   Mary played into the night.
c.   *Mary played the harmonica and into the night.
d.   *Mary played into the night and the harmonica.

In (49c–d) we have conjoined a prepositional phrase with a noun phrase, and the sentence is clearly much less acceptable than any of those in (48). On the basis of the conjunction test, we can establish in English such constituents as NP, PP, and VP: these are all types of expressions that can be conjoined with *and*. Given such a test for constituency, we can assume that structures such as tree 5.1 represent typical constituent structures of English.

There are other aspects of the structure shown in tree 5.1 for which we have presented little or no evidence. For example, we represent the auxiliary verb *will* as a constituent outside the verb phrase. But another logical possibility is to consider the constituent Aux to be part of the verb phrase, as in tree 5.2. This structure may or may not be more adequate than the structure shown in tree 5.1. We have not considered evidence here to support one version over another. It is important to be aware that although the gross outline of the structure shown in tree 5.1 is probably correct, many fine details of the structure are, for the moment, left undetermined.

Tree 5.2

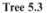

Tree 5.3

We could devote a great deal of space to attempting to justify the various features of the structure shown in tree 5.1; indeed, much work in syntax has been concerned with this sort of issue. Nonetheless, this structure provides a rough illustration of the general sort of structural diagrams used in current syntactic work, and that will suffice for our purposes at the moment. Let us now turn to certain important ideas about phrase markers in general.

Grammatical Relations

We have already alluded to the distinction between *structural concepts* such as noun phrase (NP) and *grammatical relations* such as subject or object. This distinction reflects the fact that we can ask two questions about any given phrase: (1) What is its internal structure? (2) How does it function grammatically within a sentence? Diagrams such as tree 5.1 can also be used to give a structural definition of the grammatical relations *subject* and *object*. In English, the *subject* of a sentence can be structurally defined as the particular NP in the structural configuration that is immediately dominated by S and precedes (Aux) VP, as illustrated in tree 5.3. The *object* of a main verb can be structurally defined as the NP in the structural configuration that is immediately dominated by VP, as shown in tree 5.4.

Trees 5.3 and 5.4 illustrate that the same structural constituent in a sentence can have distinct relational functions. For example, take the phrase *the people in the room*. Structurally, this phrase is an NP, but this NP can function in different ways in different sentences. In tree 5.1 the NP *the people in the room* functions as the subject of the sentence. How-

Tree 5.4

The people in the room frightened the boy

Tree 5.5

ever, in sentence (50) this same NP functions as the object of the main verb:

(50)
The police arrested *the people in the room.*

Hence, the phrase *the people in the room* is structurally an NP and only an NP; but relationally this phrase can be either a subject or an object, depending on its position in the structure of a particular sentence.

The distinction between structural and relational concepts is crucial in determining the meaning of a sentence, as illustrated by the fact that the sentences represented by trees 5.5 and 5.6 have exactly the same structural NP constituents, but those structural constituents have quite different grammatical relations in the two sentences. (Following a common practice, we have used triangles in trees 5.5 and 5.6 to simplify the representation of the internal structure of the NPs.) These two sentences mean different things, and these different meanings result from the fact that the NP that serves as the subject in one tree diagram serves as the object in the other tree diagram.

So far, then, we have isolated the following structural properties and grammatical relations, and we have shown how these can be represented in, or defined on, tree diagrams:

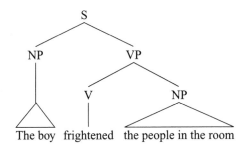

The boy frightened   the people in the room

Tree 5.6

(51)

Structural properties

a. The linear order of elements

b. The labeling of elements into lexical categories (parts of speech)

c. The grouping of elements into structural constituents (phrases)

(52)

Grammatical relations

a. Subject (structural configuration given in tree 5.3)

b. Object (structural configuration given in tree 5.4)

Tree Diagrams and Structural Ambiguity

So far we have seen that tree diagrams (phrase markers) can represent a certain variety of structural and relational concepts. Now we must turn to the question of whether tree diagrams can be used to explain other important linguistic phenomena. To address this issue, let us recall the ambiguous sentence (4a), repeated here as (53):

(53)

The mother of the boy and the girl will arrive soon.

In a theory of syntax using phrase markers to represent syntactic structure, the explanation of the phenomenon of structural ambiguity is straightforward: whereas an unambiguous sentence is associated with just one basic phrase marker, a structurally ambiguous sentence is associated with more than one basic phrase marker. For example, sentence (53) would be assigned two phrase markers, which we could formulate as trees 5.7 and 5.8.

As before, we have simplified the structure in the diagrams by using triangles for certain phrases rather than indicating the internal structure

Tree 5.7

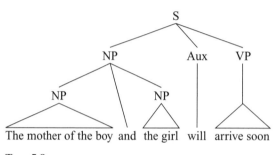

Tree 5.8

of those phrases. But these trees suffice to show the difference in structure that we postulate for the two phrase markers associated with sentence (53). In tree 5.7 the "head" noun of the subject, *mother*, is modified by a prepositional phrase that has a conjoined noun phrase in it: *of the boy and the girl*. In tree 5.8, on the other hand, the subject noun phrase is itself a conjoined noun phrase: *the mother of the boy* followed by *the girl*. We see, then, that a system of representation using phrase markers allows us to account for structurally ambiguous sentences by assigning more than one phrase marker to each ambiguous sentence. In this way the system of tree diagrams can be used to describe instances of ambiguity that are not lexical.

Discontinuous Dependencies

A natural assumption to make about phrase markers is that each sentence of a language is assigned exactly one phrase marker, except for those sentences that are structurally ambiguous. In the latter case, as we have seen, we assign more than one phrase marker—one for each particular meaning of the sentence, roughly speaking. But now let us examine some sentences that are not structurally ambiguous in the sense in which we have been using that term, but that nevertheless display interesting structural properties. Consider the following pairs of sentences:

(54)

a. Mary *stood up* her date.

b. Mary *stood* her date *up*.

(55)

a. The chef *added in* the ingredients.

b. The chef *added* the ingredients *in*.

(56)

a. He *belted down* the drink.

b. He *belted* the drink *down*.

(57)

a. They *batted around* some new ideas.

b. They *batted* some new ideas *around*.

(58)

a. The police *blocked off* the street.

b. The police *blocked* the street *off*.

These sentences illustrate what is known as the *verb + particle construction* in English. In the (a) examples of (54)–(58) the italicized two-word combinations are instances of a verb followed by a particle. For example, in (54a) *stand up* is a verb + particle (where *stand* is the verb and *up* is the particle). (*Stand up* is also referred to as a *phrasal verb*; see Radford 1988.) The interesting feature of this construction is that the particle can occur separated from its verb, as in the (b) examples of (54)–(58). Indeed, in many cases speakers prefer the version in which the particle is separated from the verb, as illustrated in (59) and (60):

(59)

a. ?John threw *down* it.

b. John threw it *down*.

(60)

a. ?Mary called *up* him.

b. Mary called him *up*.

Tree 5.9

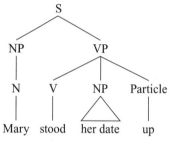

Tree 5.10

It is natural to suppose that the verb + particle sequence is a single constituent in the (b) sentences of (54)–(58). The two words behave as a single unit: for example, *stood ... up* in (54b) means "broke a social engagement without warning." By contrast, *stood* and *near* in (61) do not have an interpretation beyond their respective independent meanings:

(61)
Mary stood near her date.

A good guess at the structure of (54a) would be that shown in tree 5.9.

Now, what phrase marker would we assign to (54b)? The most obvious candidate, in terms of what we have done so far, would be tree 5.10. Because the particle *up* comes last in the linear order of words in (54b), we place it at the end of the VP in tree 5.10. (Keep in mind that we could just as easily have placed the particle at the end directly attached by a branch to S rather than to VP—again, we have not yet looked at any evidence for choosing between these two structures.)

Tree 5.10, though accurate in representing the linear order of words, is inadequate in other ways. Given the codependent nature of *stood* and *up* in *Mary stood her date up*, we know that the particle *up* goes with the verb *stood*: even though the particle is separated from the verb, it is nevertheless the case in (54b), as in (54a), that the verb and the particle together signal a meaning that is not merely the sum of the meanings of the two independent words. That is, it is still the combination of the two items that determines the single meaning. Yet tree 5.10 does not represent this affinity between verb and particle in any way; that diagram gives no indication whatever that *up* is associated with *stood*. Whenever a single constituent of a sentence is broken up in this way, we say that we have a *discontinuous constituent* or, more generally, a *discontinuous dependency*. It turns out that phrase markers, though very useful for representing certain kinds of information about sentences, do not, alone, adequately represent discontinuous dependencies.

For another illustration of the same kind of phenomenon, consider a sentence whose subject contains a modifier:

(62)
Several people who were wearing hats came in.

In this case a phrase, *who were wearing hats*, known as a *modifying clause*, serves to supply additional information about the head noun, *people*. We would assign this sentence a phrase marker such as tree 5.11. (Here the symbol *Mod* indicates a modifying clause; the symbol *Quant* stands for *Quantifier*, the grammatical category that includes words such as *several*, *many*, *few*, and *all*.)

Tree 5.11

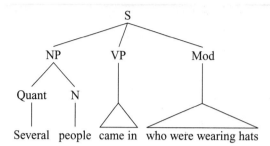

Tree 5.12

In English there is a rather general grammatical process known as *extraposition*, whereby modifying clauses (and other types of clauses that need not concern us) can be shifted to the end of the sentence. Therefore, sentence (63) also has the following version:

(63)
Several people came in who were wearing hats.

This sentence is likely structured as shown in tree 5.12. This diagram correctly indicates that the linear position of the modifying clause is at the end of the sentence. However, it completely fails to show that the modifying clause goes with the subject NP, *several people*. It does not indicate in any way that *who were wearing hats* in fact modifies *several people*. In contrast, in tree 5.11 the head noun (*several people*) and modifying clause (*who were wearing hats*) are shown as part of a single syntactic constituent, indicating that the head noun and the modifier are related. It is not possible to show the relation between the two in tree 5.12, however, because the head noun and the modifier are separated by the verb phrase (*came in*). Consequently, this is another case of a discontinuous dependency, and this dependency is not represented in any way by tree 5.12.

It turns out that discontinuous dependencies are quite common in human language; in fact, such dependencies can be much more complex than we have seen so far. To take just one example, note that the two processes just examined—separation of the verb particle and extraposition of the modifying clause—can interact in the same sentence. To see this, consider (64):

(64)
She stood up all those men who had offered her diamonds.

Recall that the particle *up* can be shifted to the end of the verb phrase:

(65)
She stood ____ all those men who had offered her diamonds up.

This produces an awkward sentence that is difficult to understand: the particle and verb are separated by a constituent that is quite long. But, since modifying clauses can be extraposed in English, we can extrapose the clause here to produce the following perfectly natural sentence:

(66)
She stood all those men ____ up who had offered her diamonds.

In this example the dependencies actually "cross" each other, as illustrated in the final line of figure 5.2. As we see, *up* goes with *stood*, and *who had offered her diamonds* goes with *all those men*; both constituents are broken up in such a way that parts of one constituent intervene between parts of the other (in particular, *up* occurs between *all those men* and its modifying clause). This is a striking example of how sentences of natural language exhibit discontinuous dependencies that may be "interwoven."

Transformational Rules as an Account of Discontinuous Dependencies
The examples we have been discussing show that some properties of sentences in natural language cannot be accounted for in terms of single phrase markers alone, that is, in terms of relations between contiguous words. It turns out that we need to account for relations between items in a sentence that are connected (in some sense), dependent, or related, but that are nonetheless not contiguous in the linear order of words. One way to account for discontinuous dependencies of this sort is to devise a means by which two or more phrase markers can themselves be related to each other in a special way. In this case two (or more) sentences (i.e., two (or more) different phrase markers) need to be related to one another (an interesting contrast to the case of structural ambiguity, in which a single sentence has two (or more) different phrase markers, each corresponding to a different meaning). Relating phrase markers to one another is in fact a fundamental insight of the theory of transformational grammar.

As an illustration, consider again the pair of sentences in (54), repeated here as (67a–b):

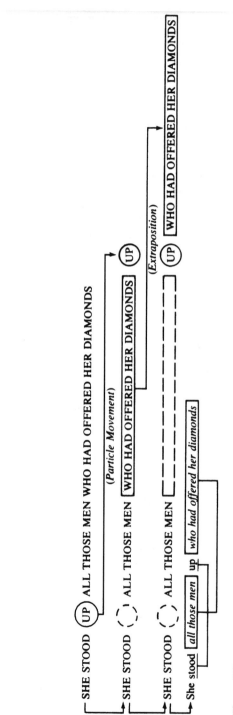

Figure 5.2
Crossing dependencies in Particle Movement and Extraposition

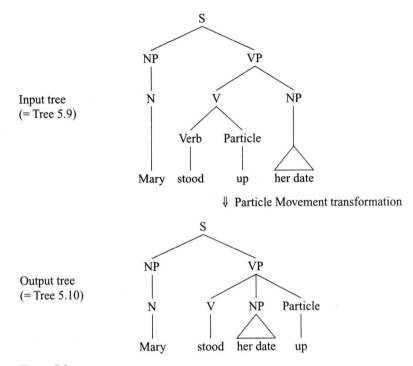

Figure 5.3
Input and output of the Particle Movement transformation

(67)
a. Mary stood up her date.
b. Mary stood her date up.

We will assume as before that sentence (67a) is assigned a single phrase marker, shown as tree 5.9. But what about sentence (67b)? This is the sentence with the discontinuous constituent, *stood ... up*. In order to express the dependency between *stood* and *up* in (67b), let us suppose that this sentence derives from the same phrase marker as (67a), shown as the input tree in figure 5.3. Call this the *input structure* or *base structure* for sentence (67b), *Mary stood her date up*.

Now we postulate a structural operation known as a *transformational rule* (or *transformation*), which we can state informally as follows:

(68)

Particle Movement

Given a verb + particle construction, the particle may be shifted away
from the verb, moved immediately to the right of the object noun
phrase, and attached to the VP node. (This movement is obligatory
when the object noun phrase is a pronoun.)

Transformational rules are operations on tree structures that convert an
input tree structure (or base structure) into an output tree structure (or
derived structure). The operation of the Particle Movement transformation is illustrated in figure 5.3. The output structure in figure 5.3 corresponds to what is called the *surface structure* of sentence (67b); that is,
this output phrase marker correctly represents the actually occurring
word order and structure for the elements of sentence (67b).

We now have a way of accounting for discontinuous dependencies.
The output tree in figure 5.3 is the correct surface phrase marker for the
sentence *Mary stood her date up*: the particle is correctly represented as
following the object NP. Nevertheless, we can account for the dependency between the particle and the verb because we are claiming that the
output tree derives from the input tree in figure 5.3, and in that base
phrase marker the verb and its particle are in fact contiguous and form a
single constituent. Thus, the base (or "underlying") structure of the sentence shows the basic constituency of the verb and its particle, but the
surface structure of the sentence correctly shows the particle as separated
from its verb.

Now let us consider another case involving the other discontinuous
dependency discussed earlier: extraposition of a modifying clause. Once
again, consider pairs of sentences such as (69a–b):

(69)

a. Several people who were wearing hats came in.
b. Several people came in who were wearing hats.

As before, we would assign to sentence (69a) the phrase marker 5.11
(shown as the input tree in figure 5.4). This phrase marker accurately
represents the word order and structure of the elements of sentence (69a).

But what about sentence (69b)? This is the sentence containing the
discontinuous constituent *several people ... who were wearing hats*. We
will account for this sentence in a manner parallel to the case of particle
movement, namely, by postulating that sentence (69b) derives from the
base structure given as the input tree in figure 5.4. In that input structure,

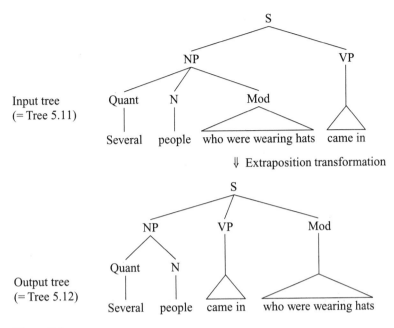

Figure 5.4
Input and output of the Extraposition transformation

then, the head noun and the modifying clause form a single constituent. We will now postulate the following transformational rule:

(70)
Extraposition
Given a noun phrase containing a head noun directly followed by a modifying clause, the modifying clause may be shifted out of the noun phrase to the end of the sentence.

As shown in figure 5.4, by applying this transformation to the input tree, we derive the output tree, which is the correct surface structure for the sentence *Several people came in who were wearing hats.*

We have been able to account for the discontinuous dependency between the modifying clause and the head noun in sentence (69b) by deriving that sentence from the input tree in figure 5.4, in which the discontinuous elements are actually represented as a single constituent. This is another example of a transformational account of a discontinuous dependency. The effect of the transformational rule of Extraposition, like that of Particle Movement, is to set up a relationship between phrase markers: it states, in effect, that for every phrase marker containing a noun phrase with a modifying clause directly following the head noun, there is a corresponding phrase marker in which that same modifying clause has been shifted to the end of the sentence. (Although this is not strictly true—in certain cases extraposition of the modifying clause is prohibited—it is nonetheless quite adequate for present purposes, and we need not add any refinements.)

The kind of analysis we have just sketched is illustrative of a version of the transformational model of syntax. This general sort of model (including numerous variations) has dominated the field of syntax ever since the publication of Noam Chomsky's 1957 book *Syntactic Structures*, the first major work to propose the transformational approach (see Newmeyer 1980, Harris 1993 for discussion). Even though the transformational analysis we have considered is one means of accounting for discontinuous dependencies, the question remains whether there is any reason to suppose it is the best means, or the most insightful means—indeed, many theories have been developed as alternatives to the version of transformational grammar presented here. It is difficult to answer this question in any definitive way, but it is possible to give additional evidence for the model that will serve to illustrate its descriptive power. Any alternative theory must also account for the kinds of observations noted in this chapter.

Interaction between Transformations

We have examined two cases in which a transformational analysis can account for discontinuities, but that in and of itself is not enough to indicate whether the transformational model is a particularly revealing account. It is time to turn to some rather striking evidence for this model. It turns out that individual transformational rules, established for independent reasons, can in fact interact with each other to account for a complex array of surface data in a straightforward and simple fashion.

Consider tree 5.13. One function of this phrase marker is to accurately represent the surface structure of sentence (71):

(71)
She stood up all those men who had offered her diamonds.

However, tree 5.13 also functions in another way, that is, as an input structure from which we can derive another (surface) structure. Notice

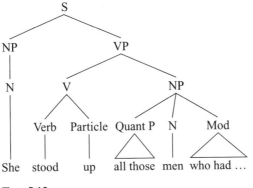

Tree 5.13

that this structure contains both a verb + particle construction and a complex noun phrase composed of a head noun and a modifying clause. Hence, this is a tree to which the Particle Movement transformation (68) may apply (see figure 5.5). If we apply Particle Movement to the top input tree in figure 5.5, we derive the output structure shown as the middle tree in that figure. The particle has been placed after the object noun phrase, as dictated by the rule. This derived structure is not yet a well-formed surface structure (recall the awkwardness and difficulty of the sentence *She stood all those men who had offered her diamonds up*). However, this output tree can, in turn, become a new input tree: we can now apply the Extraposition transformation to yield yet another derived structure, namely, the bottom output tree shown in figure 5.5. We have now arrived at the final (surface) structure for the sentence *She stood all those men up who had offered her diamonds*. Recall that this sentence has two discontinuous dependencies, which actually "cross" each other, as shown in figure 5.2. Yet we can account for this complicated pattern of dependencies in a simple way. We have already postulated the Particle Movement and Extraposition transformations for independent reasons. If we simply allow both rules to apply in sequence, they will automatically interact as shown in figure 5.5. We can now specify precisely what elements of the bottom output tree are dependent upon each other, because we have claimed that it derives from the base structure shown at the top of figure 5.5, and that structure represents the surface discontinuities as underlying constituents.

The important point here, then, is this: individual transformations are postulated to account for certain dependencies; but even stronger evi-

196   Chapter 5

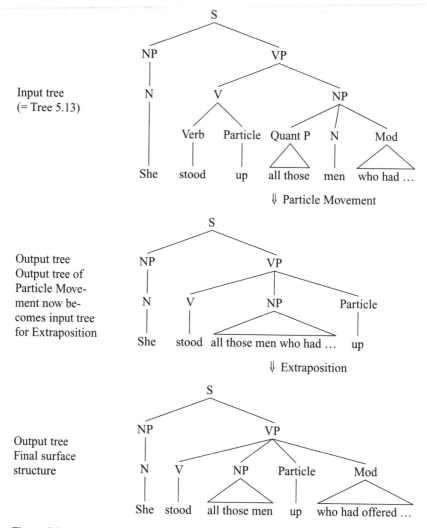

Input tree
(= Tree 5.13)

⇓ Particle Movement

Output tree
Output tree of
Particle Move-
ment now be-
comes input tree
for Extraposition

⇓ Extraposition

Output tree
Final surface
structure

Figure 5.5
Interaction of the Particle Movement and Extraposition transformations

dence comes from the interaction of the independently established transformations. We have seen that the interaction of two transformations applying in sequence automatically leads to a simple account of a complex set of surface structure dependencies.

We began our investigation of syntactic structure by posing the questions, What is structure? and How do we know that sentences are structured? As we have seen, there is no simple answer to these questions nor any way to answer them without actually constructing a theory of syntax. We have provided a partial answer, though, by arriving at the conclusion that sentence structure involves both structural and relational aspects: specification of the linear order of words, classification of words into lexical categories (parts of speech), grouping of words into structural constituents, and assignment of grammatical relations to certain noun phrases in a sentence (such as the subject of the sentence). We did not arrive at this view for the sake of convenience, or because it was handed down to us by ancient grammatical authorities. Rather, we found it impossible to state some of the most fundamental syntactic processes of a language—such as how to form questions—without appealing to these properties. On further investigation we found that in order to account for discontinuous dependencies, we needed to postulate not just structural properties of sentences but structural relations between phrase markers as well. These relationships are stated in terms of formal rules (i.e., transformational rules). In this way our view of what constitutes syntactic structure is very much determined by what phenomena we are trying to explain. Since the appearance of Chomsky's *Syntactic Structures* (1957) linguists have developed increasingly subtle and complex theories in response both to an ever-expanding range of new and heretofore unexplained data on the formal properties of sentences and to the need to constrain evolving models.

Finally, we should note that the constituent structure of sentences is not merely an artifact of syntactic theory; as we will see in chapters 10 and 11, there are compelling reasons to think that aspects of constituent structure have some reality in the minds of both adult speakers and children acquiring their native language.

5.3   A MORE FORMAL ACCOUNT OF SYNTACTIC THEORY

The type of transformational analysis sketched informally in section 5.2 has, in fact, been given a more precise and formal description by theorists

working within the transformational framework. The references at the
end of this chapter give a number of alternative accounts of the more
formal theory (see Kimball 1973 and Wall 1972 for formalizations of
"classical" transformational grammar). In this section we will provide
only a brief description to give some idea of how transformational theory
was developed. It should be stressed that we will present here a description of some of the more basic features of standard, or classical, transformational theory, keeping in mind that at present many linguists are
working on significant modifications and variations of these basic
concepts.

The Formal Statement of Transformations

Recall that a single phrase marker alone cannot account for a discontinuous dependency and that transformational rules are introduced into the
theory in order to express syntactic relations between pairs of phrase
markers. Transformational rules have been formalized in standard transformational theory; to illustrate the formalism used, we restate the Particle Movement transformation:

(72)

Particle Movement

Structural description (SD): X–Verb–Particle–NP–Y

                                                   1   2   3   4 5

Structural change (SC):   1   2 $\emptyset$ 4+3 5

A transformational rule consists, first, of an input: a *structural description*
(SD), which is an instruction to analyze a phrase marker into a sequence
of constituents (in this case, Verb followed by Particle followed by NP).
The variables X and Y indicate that the constituents to the left of the verb
and to the right of the NP (should there be any) are irrelevant to this
transformation—they can represent anything at all. In order for a transformation to be applied, the analysis of a phrase marker must satisfy the
SD of the particular transformation. As we can see, tree 5.14 can be analyzed—that is, can be cut up into chunks—in a way that matches exactly
the sequence of constituents listed in the SD of the Particle Movement
transformation. Hence, this phrase marker satisfies the SD of the rule.

The second part of the transformational rule is the output: a *structural
change* (SC), which in the case of Particle Movement is an instruction to
modify the SD by shifting term 3 (the particle) immediately to the right

Tree 5.14

Tree 5.15

of term 4 (NP), as illustrated in tree 5.15. The particle (term 3) has correctly been placed immediately after the NP (term 4), and the plus sign (+) between them in the SC indicates that these two constituents are to be *sisters*; that is, they are to be attached under the same node (in this case, VP). The symbol ∅ ("zero") indicates that nothing remains in the slot where the particle had been and marks the spot from which the particle was moved.

We can provide independent evidence that the particle is attached under the VP and not, say, under the S. Let us start by considering the examples in (73):

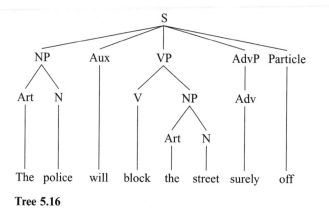

Tree 5.16

(73)

a. Surely the police will block off the street.

b. The police will block off the street, surely.

Surely is a *sentential* adverb (S-adverb). Adverbs of this kind are attached under the S node. Now consider the examples in (74):

(74)

a.   The police will block the street off, surely.

b. *The police will block the street, surely, off.

If *off* were to occur to the right of the S-adverb, as in (74b), it would have to be attached under the S node as in tree 5.16 (not the VP node, since crossing lines are not permitted). (In tree 5.16, *AdvP* = adverb phrase.) However, since (74b) is unacceptable, we know that this structure cannot be correct; *off* cannot be attached under S.

In addition, further data reveal that *off* must be adjacent to the NP object:

(75)

a.   The police will block off the street quickly, *surely*.

b. *The police will block off the street, *surely*, quickly.

c. *The police will block the street quickly *off*.

d.   The police will block the street *off* quickly.

Quickly is a VP-adverb; that is, it is attached under the VP node. (75b) shows that a VP-adverb (*quickly*) cannot occur to the right of an S-adverb (*surely*); this is because the resulting structure would involve

Tree 5.17

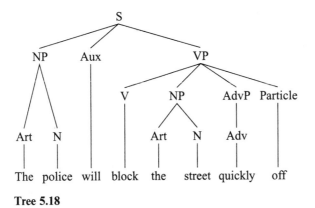

Tree 5.18

crossing lines (see tree 5.17)—a forbidden tree configuration. Turning to (75c), we see that even though the particle is attached under the VP node (see tree 5.18), as required by the transformational rule, it is not adjacent to the NP object. (75d), on the other hand, meets all the requirements specified in the SC of the rule, and consequently it is fine.

There are many other details of transformational formalism that we cannot go into here; for these, see the works listed at the end of the chapter.

Phrase Structure Grammars

Within the early standard transformational models it was assumed that basic phrase markers are generated by *phrase structure rules* (PS rules) of the following sort:

Tree 5.19

Tree 5.20

(76)
a. S   →   NP Aux VP
b. NP   →   Art N
c. VP   →   V NP

Although these particular PS rules are no longer realized as such in more recent theories, they are still instructive. These rules express in a clear way important dependencies that must be captured in any theory of syntax. Each rule is essentially a formula, or specification, for how the constituent represented by a certain symbol—the symbol on the left of the arrow—can be constituted in a tree diagram. For example, PS rule (76a) tells us that S (sentence) can *consist of*, or can be *expanded as*, the sequence NP Aux VP. This is shown in tree form as tree 5.19. The rules also tell us that NP (noun phrase) can be expanded as Art N and that VP (verb phrase) can be expanded as V NP. These expansions are illustrated in tree 5.20. By inserting appropriate words, we derive a structure like tree 5.21.

As noted earlier, each labeled point in a tree is referred to as a *node*; thus, tree 5.21 includes an S node, an NP node, an Aux node, a VP node, and so on. We say that the node S *dominates* the nodes NP, Aux, and VP; the node NP *dominates* the nodes Art and N; the node VP *dominates* the nodes V and NP; and so on. We also use a certain type of genealog-

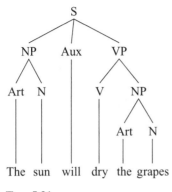

Tree 5.21

ical terminology when discussing the relationships between nodes in a tree. For example, the nodes NP, Aux, and VP in tree 5.21 are referred to as the *daughter* nodes of the node S, which is the *mother* node. Hence, NP, Aux, and VP are *sister* nodes with respect to each other. Notice that the NP node *the sun* and the V node *dry* are not sisters, because the NP is a daughter node of S, whereas the V is a daughter node of VP. In other words, sister nodes must be daughters of the same mother node. (We should note, in passing, that linguistic custom has settled on the mother/daughter/sister terminology, and thus we do not speak of father nodes, brother nodes, and so on.)

Returning to tree 5.20, how do we know what words to insert into that structure? We will assume that part of our grammar consists of a *lexicon*, that is, a list of words of a language. In the lexicon, words are listed with their parts of speech: for example, *the* is listed as an article, *sun* is listed as a noun, *will* is listed as an auxiliary verb, *dry* is listed as a verb, and so on. Given a tree such as tree 5.20, we can insert the word *the* under the node Art, the word *sun* under the node N, the word *will* under the node Aux, the word *dry* under the node V, and so on, as shown in tree 5.21. We could not, for example, insert the word *the* under the node V, because *the* is an article, and not a verb.

It is not the case that every noun phrase of English must contain an article, nor is it the case that every verb phrase must contain an object NP. We say that these are *optional constituents*, and we indicate this by placing them within parentheses:

(77)
a. S   →   NP Aux VP
b. NP   →   (Art) N
c. VP   →   V (NP)

Items in parentheses *may* be chosen in generating a tree structure; the other items *must* be chosen if a structure is to be well formed. Actually, (77b–c) collapse two rules each. The uncollapsed versions are as in (78) and (79).

(78)
NP   →   (Art) N
a. NP   →   N
b. NP   →   Art N

(79)
VP   →   V (NP)
a. VP   →   V
b. VP   →   V NP

The rules in (77a–c) therefore allow us to form both structures like the one in tree 5.21 and structures like the one in tree 5.22.

As we have seen, noun phrases in English may contain various sorts of modifiers after the head noun (e.g., clauses, as in *the men who offered her diamonds*). We have seen that nouns can also be followed by prepositional phrases (PP) as modifiers:

(80)
a. the house *in the woods*
b. the weather *in England*
c. a portrait *of Mary*
d. the prospects *for peace*

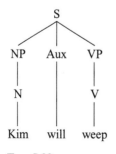

Tree 5.22

In order to form such phrases—or *generate* them, to use the technical term—we can modify our PS rule for NPs as follows:

(81)

NP → (Art) N (PP)

Rule (81) collapses the following rules:

(82)

	Rule		*Example*
a.	NP → N		*Mary* in *Mary is nice.*
b.	NP → Art N		*the boy* in *The boy is nice.*
c.	NP → N PP		*water in the basement* in *Water in the basement is a bad sign.*
d.	NP → Art N PP		*the boy on the swing* in *The boy on the swing fell.*

We now need to add a PS rule to expand prepositional phrases:

(83)

PP → P NP

This set of PS rules, called a *phrase structure grammar*, now generates NPs such as the one in tree 5.23.

Consider again the PS rules in (77), in particular the rules for NP and VP. Notice that an NP must consist at least of an N, which forms the *head* of the NP; and a VP must consist at least of a V, which forms the *head* of the VP. A noun phrase is called a noun phrase because it has a noun as its head; and a verb phrase is called a verb phrase because it has a verb as its head. This has led to the suggestion that for each of the

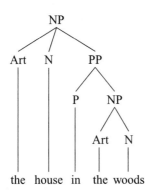

Tree 5.23

lexical categories N (noun), V (verb), A (adjective), and P (preposition), there is a corresponding *phrasal category* NP (noun phrase), VP (verb phrase), AP (adjective phrase), and PP (prepositional phrase). We have already seen how this works for NPs and VPs. What about PPs? Notice that in rule (83) PP is expanded as P NP; in fact, a prepositional phrase *must* contain a preposition, and we say that the preposition is the *head* of the prepositional phrase. (In our discussion we have not touched on PS rules for adjective phrases (AP). See exercise 5 for the structure of these phrases.)

Generally speaking, then, if we let the symbol X stand for the lexical categories N, A, V, and P, and if we let the symbol XP stand for "phrase of the type X," then it seems that we can state a general formula for certain PS rules: $XP \rightarrow \ldots X \ldots$. This says that a phrase of the type XP has a lexical category X as its head, and in this sense it seems that there is a regular relation between lexical categories and phrasal categories (see "Special Topics" at the end of this chapter for further discussion).

Embedding

An interesting consequence of rules (81) and (83) is that we can generate a potentially infinite number of noun phrases. This is because the PS rule for NP may be expanded to contain a PP, which in turn contains an NP, which itself may be expanded to contain a PP; and so on, indefinitely, as in tree 5.24. This is one of the ways in which a finite set of rules—in this case the two rules (81) and (83)—can generate an infinite set of structures. PS grammars containing pairs of rules that "feed" one another are said to be *recursive*.

Suppose that we now allow the rule for VP to include an optional symbol S following V:

(84)
VP   →   V (S)

If we allow such a rule, then the PS rule for S will contain a VP, and the PS rule for VP can contain an S:

(85)
a. S   →   NP Aux VP
b. VP   →   V (S)

This is another instance of recursion, as we can see by examining tree 5.25. Beginning on the very lowest level (on the far right) in this tree,

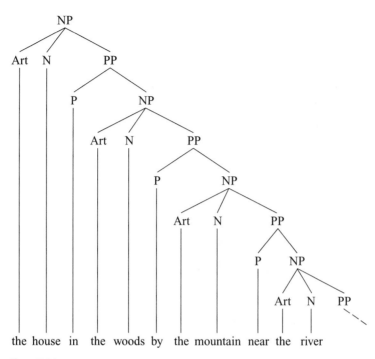

Tree 5.24

notice the sentence, S, *Kim didn't leave*. This sentence is embedded in the VP of a larger sentence, *Bill will say Kim didn't leave*. That S in turn is embedded within the VP of an even larger sentence, *Pat may think Bill will say Kim didn't leave*. A sentence embedded within a larger sentence is referred to as an *embedded clause*, a *subordinate clause*, or just an *embedded sentence*. A sentence that contains an embedded clause is called a *matrix sentence*; in tree 5.25 the sentence *Kim didn't leave* is embedded within the matrix sentence that begins *Bill will ...*, and the sentence *Bill will say Kim didn't leave* is embedded within the matrix sentence that begins *Pat may think ....* The "highest" matrix sentence in tree 5.25 (*Pat may think ...*) is referred to as the *main clause*. A sentence such as *Kim didn't leave* is referred to as a *simple sentence* because it contains no embedded sentences; a sentence such as *Bill will say Kim didn't leave* is referred to as a *complex sentence* because it contains a matrix sentence and an embedded sentence.

The pair of PS rules in (85) thus constitutes another example of recursion: sentences contain verb phrases, which in turn may contain sen-

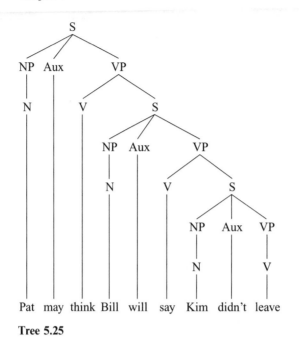

Tree 5.25

tences, which in turn contain verb phrases, and so on. Again, we see how a finite set of rules can generate an infinite number of sentences, and we now have an account for the kinds of examples discussed at the very beginning of this chapter.

We now have the following two PS rules for VP, each of which collapses two rules:

(86)
VP → V (NP)
a. VP → V
b. VP → V NP

(87)
VP → V (S)
a. VP → V
b. VP → V S

Both rules allow for the possibility that the VP contains just a verb (V) (since the NP and S are optional); or the VP may contain a V followed by an NP; or it may contain a V followed by S. We can collapse rules (86) and (87) into a single rule using notation involving braces, { }:

(88)

This rule states that VP must contain at least a V, and that V may optionally be followed by either an NP or an S:

(89)

VP   VP   VP

| /\\   /\\

V   V   NP   V   S

Thus, the parentheses notation, ( ), indicates optionality; the braces notation, {   }, indicates an either-or choice.

Center Embedding

In tree 5.24, beginning at the lowest level (rightmost end), every prepositional phrase (PP) is on the extreme right branch of a noun phrase (NP), which is itself on the extreme right branch of some PP. Structures of this general sort are called *right branching*.

Now consider tree 5.26 (where the symbol *Poss* stands for *Possessive Phrase*). We could generate such a tree with the following PS rules:

(90)

a. NP   →   (Poss) N

b. Poss → NP Poss-Affix

These rules state that an NP may have an optional possessive phrase preceding the head noun. A possessive phrase consists of an NP followed by an Affix (in this case, *'s*). Tree 5.26 once again illustrates the property of recursion, in that an NP may contain a Poss, which in turn contains an NP, which in turn may contain a Poss, and so on. In tree 5.26, beginning at the lowest level (leftmost end), every possessive phrase (Poss) is on the extreme left branch of an NP that is itself on the extreme left branch of a Poss. Structures of this general sort are called *left branching*.

Phrases with right- or left-branching structures are relatively easy to comprehend, provided they are within memory limitations. In other words, the degree of right or left branching itself does not seem to lead to excessive difficulty in comprehension. Of course, if any given phrase becomes very long, we will probably forget what was at the beginning of the phrase by the time we come to the end.

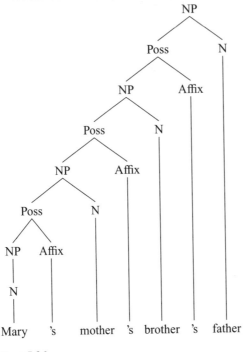

Tree 5.26

Linguists have noted another class of phrases with a property known as *center embedding*, which can pose serious problems for sentence comprehension. Let's begin with the simple sentence *The rat ate the cheese*. Noun phrases such as *the rat* can be modified by clauses (as we have seen in examples of extraposition). In this case, we can modify the noun phrase *the rat* with a clause such as *that the cat chased*, producing the sentence *The rat that the cat chased ate the cheese*. Given that noun phrases can be modified by clauses, there is nothing in principle to prevent us from modifying the noun phrase *the cat* with a clause such as *that the dog bit*:

(91)
The rat that the cat that the dog bit chased ate the cheese.

Notice that the sentence has become extremely difficult to comprehend. If we examine these sentences schematically, a pattern emerges:

(92)

a. The rat ate the cheese

b. The rat (that) the cat chased ate the cheese

c. The rat (that) the cat (that) the dog bit chased ate the cheese

(92a) is a simple sentence, *The rat ate the cheese.* (92b) is an example of center embedding: that is, the modifying sentence *the cat chased* is embedded within the larger sentence *The rat ate the cheese.* With one level of center embedding, as in (92b), the sentence remains comprehensible. However, (92c) involves two center embeddings: the modifying sentence *the dog bit* is embedded within the matrix sentence *the cat chased*, which is in turn embedded within the main sentence *The rat ate the cheese.* We see that two (or more) levels of center embedding (as in (92c)) render the sentence extremely difficult to comprehend. It is not fully understood why center embedding causes such perceptual complexity (i.e., not enough is known about the psychological mechanisms underlying human perceptual abilities); nevertheless, the perceptual difficulties posed by center embedding form an interesting feature of human language processing and comprehension.

5.4   SPECIAL TOPICS

Wh-Questions

In this chapter we investigated the structure of the yes/no question and its relationship to the declarative sentence. Now consider the following pair of sentences:

(93)

a. John will marry *someone.*
b. *Who* will John marry?

(93b) is an example of what is called a *wh-question.* (*Wh* is short for *who, when, which, where, what,* and *how*—words that in traditional grammar are called *interrogative pronouns.*) An appropriate answer to a *wh*-question such as (93b) would be, for example, the name of an individual (and not merely "yes" or "no" as would be appropriate for a yes/no question). Comparing (93b) with (93a), we find two differences: (1) in (93b) the direct object (*who*) of the verb *marry* occurs to the left of the subject (*John*), and (2) in (93b) the auxiliary verb *will* occurs to the left of the subject, as it does in yes/no questions (*Will John marry?*), and not to the right, as in declarative sentences like (93a).

How do we know that *who* is the object of the verb *marry*? Consider (94):

(94)
*Who will John marry someone?

As this example shows, when *who* has been fronted, we cannot place a noun phrase after the verb (i.e., in the object position). This is as bad as placing two noun phrases after the verb:

(95)
*John will marry who someone.

In (93b) the direct object of the verb has been questioned. The subject may be questioned as well:

(96)
a. *Someone* will marry John.
b. *Who* will marry John?

A constituent of an embedded clause can also be questioned. (In (97) the embedded clause is surrounded by brackets. The line, ____, indicates the position that has been questioned.)

(97)
a. *Who* does Mary believe [____ will marry John]?
b. *Who* did Martha say [Mary believed [____ will marry John]]?

In principle there is no limit to the number of embedded clauses that may intervene between *who* and the questioned position. (97a) involves only one level of embedding, whereas (97b) involves two (*will marry John* is embedded under *Mary believed*, which in turn is embedded under *say*).

But this questioning of constituents is not unconstrained. Consider (98)–(101):

(98)
a.   Mary believed that *someone* will marry John.
b. **Who* did Mary believe that ____ will marry John?

(99)
a.   Mary believed the fact that John will marry *someone*.
b. **Who* did Mary believe the fact that John will marry ____?

(100)

a. The minister will marry John and *someone*.

b. **Who will the minister marry John and ____?

(101)

a. That John will marry *someone* is well known.

b. **Who is that John will marry ____ well known?

There are structural situations that prohibit the questioning of a constituent (e.g., subject or object noun phrases in the above examples).
Examples of this sort have intrigued linguists ever since John Robert
Ross's seminal dissertation appeared in 1967. Syntactic theories have
been developed and revised in attempts to best account for the nature of
wh-questions (see references).

Sentence Structure and Anaphora

In chapter 2 we investigated the morpheme *self.* Recall that *self* indicates
when, say, the subject and the direct object are "linked" to the same
entity (*John's self-admiration* means, roughly, "John's admiration of
himself" or "John admires himself"). This is an example of *morphological* anaphora, where the morpheme *self* signals when, for example, the
subject and the object are associated with the same individual. We now
turn to evidence that syntactic *structures* also contribute to anaphora
phenomena. Consider the following examples, where italicized expressions can refer to the same individual:

(102)

a. *Nicholas* left after *he* found the tricycle.

b. He left after Nicholas found the tricycle.

c. After *he* found the tricycle, *Nicholas* left.

In (102a) *Nicholas* and *he* can easily be understood as referring to the
same person. This contrasts with (102b), where *he* and *Nicholas* are presumed to be different people. One difference between (102a) and (102b) is
the order of the two noun phrases. In (102a) *Nicholas* precedes *he* and in
(102b) *he* precedes *Nicholas*. But does linear order account for the difference? (102c) provides evidence that order cannot be the answer. In (102c)
he precedes *Nicholas* and yet they can be interpreted as referring to the
same individual.

  Even though the pronoun *he* precedes the noun phrase *Nicholas* in
both cases, only in (102b) does *he* appear "higher" in the tree than

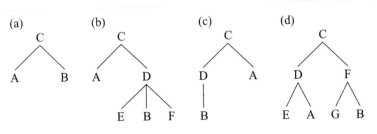

Figure 5.6
C-command configurations

Nicholas. Specifically, in (102b) the pronoun *c(onstituent)-commands* the noun, but in (102c) it does not. C-command is defined as follows:

(103)
A node **A** c-commands a node **B** if and only if the first branching node that dominates **A** also dominates **B**. (Proviso: **A** does not dominate **B** and vice versa.)

Consider the trees in figure 5.6. In figure 5.6a node **A** c-commands node **B** (and vice versa) since the first branching node dominating **A**, which is node **C**, also dominates **B**. In figure 5.6b **A** c-commands **B** because the first branching node that dominates **A** (again **C**) also dominates **B**. But in this case **B** does not c-command **A**. Why? Because the first branching node that dominates **B** is **D**, and **D** does not dominate **A**. In figure 5.6c **A** and **B** bear the same c-command relation to each other as they do in figure 5.6a. The linear order is different, but that is not what is important for c-command. C-command is a relationship between nodes that is *structural* in nature. Notice that in figure 5.6d **A**, though it does precede **B**, does not c-command **B**. Why? Because the first branching node dominating **A**, in this case **D**, does *not* also dominate **B**. It appears, then, that when a pronoun c-commands a nonpronoun noun phrase, as is the case with *he* and *Nicholas* in (102b), the speaker is understood as intending to refer to different individuals. (In chapters 6 and 9 we will consider whether this constraint is semantic or pragmatic in nature.)

More data confirm the importance of c-command in constraining the interpretation of pronouns. (Examples (104) and (105) are from Postal 1971, 20, 24; again, italics indicate coreference.)

(104)
a. If [*he* can], *John* will run.
b. *John* will run if [*he* can].

(105)
a. The man who [investigated *him*] hates *Charley*.
b. The man who investigated *Charley* [hates *him*].

(106)
a. Mary told *John* about the woman who [admired *him*].
b. Mary told him about the woman who admired John.

In (104a–b) and (105a–b) the pronoun does not c-command the nouns *John* and *Charley*. In (104a–b) the first branching node is an S (indicated with brackets) that does not dominate *John*, and in (105a–b) the VP (also indicated with brackets), which is the first branching node dominating *him*, does not dominate *Charley*. In (106a) the first branching node dominating *him* (the VP) does not dominate *John*; therefore, *him* does not c-command *John* and they can be understood as referring to the same individual. However, in (106b) the pronoun *him* does c-command *John* because the first branching node dominating *him* is a VP that also dominates *John*—hence the interpretation that *him* and *John* refer to two different individuals.

The exact nature of the association of pronouns with expressions such as *Nicholas*, *John*, *Mary*, *Charley* is a topic of current debate. Structure does indeed seem to play an important role here, and we have, following one tradition (see Chomsky 1981, Reinhart 1983, and references cited there), captured this by stating the structural contribution in terms of the c-command relations between pairs of nodes.

X-Bar Theory

In "Remarks on Nominalization," Chomsky (1970) proposed an alternative to the kinds of phrase structure (PS) rules presented in this chapter (see Jackendoff 1977, Newmeyer 1980 for a review of Chomsky's arguments). His proposal was an attempt to constrain the set of possible PS rules. Basically, the idea is that phrasal categories (e.g., VP, PP, NP, AP) all have heads that belong to the same category as the phrasal category. Earlier in the chapter we offered an informal description of what a head is—namely, that a phrase (say, PP) has a lexical category (P, for PP) as its head. But what stops us from formulating a rule such as VP → N PP, in which the head of VP would not be V, but N? As yet, nothing we have said blocks such a rule. One response is to impose a constraint on all VPs, NPs, and PPs, for example. One proposal for such a constraint involves the use of variables: under this proposal, the general PS rule

Figure 5.7
In English the head of a phrase is to the left of the complement.

schema for phrasal categories would be *XP* → *X* Comp, where *Comp*,
which stands for *complement*, could be, for example, a PP or an NP, and
X stands for a lexical category (e.g., P, N, V). When *X* equals N, then
XP is an NP; when *X* equals P, then *XP* is a PP; and so on (see figure
5.7). The PS rules must conform to this schema. Notice too that the
rule schema captures a generalization of English syntax, namely, that the
head of a phrase, be it a PP or a VP, is to the left of its complement. We
return to this generalization in the "Special Topics" section of chapter 11.

Another way to capture the endocentric relation between the phrase
and its head (i.e., the relation whereby the category of the head of the
phrase and the category of the phrase itself are the same) was offered by
Farmer (1980, 1984), who proposed that *XP* → *X* Comp is more than a
schema—in fact, is a rule—and that the categorial content is achieved
after words are inserted under the variable nodes, with their category
affiliation replacing the variables (see figure 5.8). A fuller theory adopting
this approach was worked out by Stowell (1981). The development of
X-bar theory (so called because $\bar{X}$ (*X* with an overbar, now generally
replaced by a prime, *X′*) was used instead of *XP*) has advanced considerably since these proposals were first offered and currently constitutes
one of the most lively areas of debate in syntax (see Napoli 1993 and
references cited there).

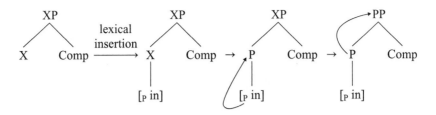

Figure 5.8
The word *in* belongs to the category *preposition*. Thus, *X* becomes P and *XP* becomes PP.

Exercises

1. Consider the following phonemic sequence: /ðʌsʌnzɹeɪzmɪt/ There are at least two meanings that can be associated with this sequence.
A. Identify at least two meanings.
B. Discuss how this example provides further evidence for the importance of the notion of structure.

2. The following tree structures have been left incomplete, in the sense that no words have been filled in. For each structure, list an appropriate sentence that would fit the structure (that is, supply an appropriate word for each blank).

a.

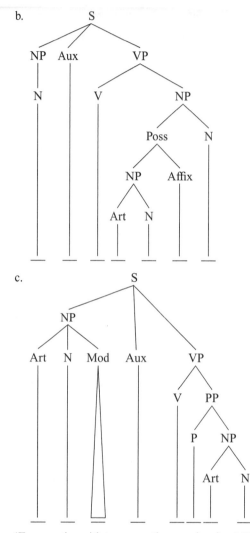

b.

c.

(For practice with trees, see the exercises in *A Linguistics Workbook* (Farmer and Demers 2001) entitled "Simple Phrase Structure Rules," "Simple NPs, VPs, and PPs," "Ill-Formed Trees," and "Possessive NP with a PP.")

3. Using tree 5.1 as your reference, answer the following questions:

A. What are the daughter nodes of the node VP?

B. The subject NP, *the people in the room*, contains a PP node. What are the *sister* nodes of that PP?

C. The phrase structure rule for VP given in (77c) of the text will not generate the VP shown in tree 5.1. Why not (i.e., what constituent is missing from rule (77c))?

How would you reformulate rule (77c) so that it will generate the VP in tree 5.1?
D. Is the sequence of words *the room will move* represented as a *single* constituent in tree 5.1?

4. Draw tree diagrams for the following noun phrases:

a. the weather in England
b. John's uncle in England
c. John's uncle in England's company

5. Adjective phrases have a structure parallel to that of noun phrases, verb phrases, and prepositional phrases. Consider the following italicized adjective phrases:

a. Kim is *angry at Bill's sister.*
b. We're *proud of the invention.*

A. What is the structure of the adjective phrase *angry at Bill's sister*? Draw a tree diagram for this adjective phrase; use the symbol *AP* to stand for *adjective phrase*, and *Adj* to stand for *adjective*. (Hint: A careful study of tree 5.23 should give you any clue you need to draw tree structures for adjectives.)
B. What is the structure of the adjective phrase *proud of the invention*? Draw a tree diagram for this adjective phrase.

6. The sequence of words *light – house – keeper* is structurally ambiguous.

A. How many meanings can you detect for this sequence?
B. What structural groupings would you assign to the phrase, to represent each meaning you have found? (Use parentheses, in the manner of example (5) of the text.) (See the exercise entitled "Tree and Sentence Matching" in *A Linguistics Workbook* for another example of syntactic ambiguity.)

7. In American English the word *so* can be used as an intensifier, or emphasizer, as in the following example:

(i)
a. I can lift this weight.
b. I can *so* lift this weight.

In (ib) *so* functions to indicate emphasis. The following examples show that there is a restriction on the placement of *so* in a sentence (recall that * indicates an ill-formed expression):

(ii)
a. I will pass the test.
b. I will *so* pass the test!

(iii)
a. I know the answer.
b. *I know *so* the answer!
c. I do *so* know the answer!

(iv)

a. Mary is running in tomorrow's race.

b. Mary is *so* running in tomorrow's race!

(v)

a. They took our money.

b. *They took *so* our money!

c. They did *so* take our money!

(vi)

a. He is nice.

b. He is *so* nice.

What is the restriction on the placement of *so*? That is, where can *so* be inserted within a sentence, and when is it impossible to insert *so*? Use yes/no questions, tag formation, and negative placement to support your answer.

8. Example (42) of the text describes a number of properties of the *subject constituent* of English sentences. For example, the pronoun in a tag agrees with the subject of a sentence in person, number, and gender (see example (41)). Now consider the following sentences:

a. That John arrived late annoyed Bill.

b. There were three men in the park.

c. It was Mary who solved the problem.

d. The car, truck, and train collided with each other.

e. Thirty or forty bees have built a hive.

f. That movie, the boys really like a lot.

A. For each sentence, construct an appropriate tag.

B. For each case, indicate what constituent (group of words) of the main sentence the pronoun in the tag *agrees* with. Do this by underlining the relevant words (i.e., the constituent) and connecting it to the tag pronoun (as in example (41)).

C. Based on your results in questions A and B, what is the subject of each sentence?

9. In the text we noted a number of grammatical properties of subjects in English. Now consider the following sentences, focusing in particular on the form of the italicized *verb*:

(i)

a. The boy *likes* that cake.

b. The boys *like* that cake.

c. The boy and the girl *like* that cake.

d. *The boy and the girl *likes* that cake.

(ii)

a. That cake, the boy *likes*.

b. That cake, the boys *like*.

c. *That cake, the boys *likes*.

Many verbs in English *agree in number* with some preceding constituent. That is, the verbs take on a singular form *(likes)* or a plural form *(like)* in the present tense (in the manner illustrated above), depending on whether certain preceding constituents are singular or plural. This process, illustrated in (i) and (ii), is known as *verb agreement*. Now consider the following hypothetical verb agreement rules (iii) and (iv), and answer the questions associated with each:

(iii)
The verb agrees in number with the noun immediately to its left.

A. Why is this rule inaccurate? Use the data in (i) to show that the rule makes a false prediction.

(iv)
The verb agrees in number with the noun phrase that comes at the very beginning of the sentence.

B. Why is this rule inaccurate? Use the data in (ii) to show that the rule makes a false prediction.

Now answer the following question:

C. What constituent of a sentence does the verb agree with in number? That is, what is the proper way to state the verb agreement rule?

10. As we saw in examining the notion "subject," the subject of a sentence can be identified in English by its structural position (see tree 5.3), among other things, and in Japanese by a special marking on the subject noun phrase (*-ga*). There are also languages in which the subject of a sentence can be identified by means of a special marking on the main verb. For example, in Navajo there are two verbal prefixes, *yi-* and *bi-*, illustrated in the following examples:

a. Łį́į́' dzaanééz yiztał   "The horse kicked the mule."
b. Łį́į́' dzaanééz b̄iztał   "The mule kicked the horse."

(The translations of the words *łį́į́'* and *dzaanééz* can be derived from exercise 11.)

A. In Navajo, for sentences of the form *NP1 NP2 yi + Verb*, which NP is interpreted as the subject and which as the object?

B. For sentences of the form *NP1 NP2 bi + Verb*, which NP is interpreted as the subject and which as the object? (For more on the *yi/bi* alternation, see the exercise entitled "Pragmatics: Navajo" in *A Linguistics Workbook*.)

11. Basic word order for English is *Subject-Verb-Object*, as in *Gorillas eat bananas*. For the following two languages, isolate and identify the different words and determine what the basic word order is.

Language 1: Navajo (Native American language of the Southwest)

a. Łį́į́' dzaanééz yiztał   "The horse kicked the mule."
b. Dzaanééz łį́į́' yiztał   "The mule kicked the horse."
c. Ashkii at'ééd yiztsǫs   "The boy kissed the girl."
d. At'ééd ashkii yiztsǫs   "The girl kissed the boy."
e. Ashkii łį́į́' yo'į́   "The boy saw the horse."

horse _____

mule _____

boy _____

girl _____

kicked _____

saw _____

Basic word order: _____

Language 2: Lummi (Native American language of the Pacific Northwest)

a. x̣čits cə-swəyʔqəʔ sə-słeniʔ	"The man knows the woman."
b. x̣čits sə-słeniʔ cə-swəyʔqəʔ	"The woman knows the man."
c. leŋnəs cə-sčətxʷən cə-swəyʔqəʔ	"The bear saw the man."
d. leŋnəs sə-słeniʔ cə-swiʔqoʔəł	"The woman saw the boy."

man _____

woman _____

bear _____

boy _____

know _____

saw _____

Basic word order: _____

12. As noted in the text, in some languages word order is quite free, as, for example, in Tohono O'odham, a Native American language of southern Arizona and northern Mexico. To see the possibilities for word order, consider the following sentence (data from Zepeda 1983):

(i)

Huan	'o	wakon	g-ma:gina.
Subject	Aux	Verb	Object
"John"	"3rd person"	"washing"	"the car"

"John is/was washing the car."

Sentence (i) can have the word order shown, or any of the following word orders:

(ii)

a. Huan 'o g-ma:gina wakon.

b. Wakon 'o g-ma:gina g-Huan.

c. Wakon 'o g-Huan g-ma:gina.

d. Ma:gina 'o wakon g-Huan.

e. Ma:gina 'o g-Huan wakon.

The auxiliary *'o* (which we label *Aux*) indicates a third person subject (in this case, *Huan* "John") and is used in sentences that describe ongoing or incompleted actions. (In the Tohono O'odham sentences, the symbol : is used to indicate a long vowel, and a "prefix" *g-* sometimes appears with nouns and sometimes does not. Both of these features can be ignored in this exercise.) Now answer the following questions:

A. For each sentence in (ii), indicate what the word order is. Use the labels *Subject* (= *Huan*), *Aux* (= *'o*), *Verb* (= *wakon*), and *Object* (= *ma:gina*), in the manner shown in the first example below:

Sentence	*Word order*
a. Huan 'o g-ma:gina wakon.	Subject-Aux-Object-Verb
b. Wakon 'o g-ma:gina g-Huan.	_____
c. Wakon 'o g-Huan g-ma:gina.	_____
d. Ma:gina 'o wakon g-Huan.	_____
e. Ma:gina 'o g-Huan wakon.	_____

B. As your answer to question A will have shown, word order in Tohono O'odham appears to be free (i.e., any order of constituents seems possible), except for one particular constituent of the above sentences, which occurs in the same relative position in every sentence. What is this constituent, and in what position of a sentence must it appear?

C. Given your answer to question B, consider the following ungrammatical sentences of Tohono O'odham:

(iii)
a. *Huan g-ma:gina 'o wakon.
b. *Huan g-ma:gina wakon 'o.

Why are these sentences bad?

(See the exercise entitled "Simple Sentences: Tohono O'odham" in *A Linguistics Workbook* for more relevant data from Tohono O'odham.)

13. Consider the sentence *I kicked the ball into the basket*. Is *the ball into the basket* a single constituent? Show how the cleft construction can be used to answer this question. (Review the discussion of examples (45)–(47); see also the exercise in *A Linguistics Workbook* entitled "Verb-Particle versus Verb-PP Structure.")

14. Under certain circumstances the Particle Movement transformation seems to be obligatory; that is, the particle *must* be separated from the verb:

(i)
a. *She stood up them.
b. She stood them up.

(ii)
a. *I wrote down it.
b. I wrote it down.

(iii)
a. *The bartender kicked out him.
b. The bartender kicked him out.

Under what circumstances must the particle be separated from its verb?

15. The following sentences illustrate cases of extraposition similar to ones discussed in the text:

(i)

a. A review *of the new book by Chomsky* will soon appear.

b. A review will soon appear *of the new book by Chomsky*.

(ii)

a. Several theories *about the structure of language* were presented last night.

b. Several theories were presented last night *about the structure of language*.

The phrases *of the new book by Chomsky* and *about the structure of language* are single constituents that can be shifted to the end of a sentence by the Extraposition transformation.

A. Draw a tree structure for each of the following phrases:

a. a review of the new book by Chomsky

b. several theories about the structure of language

B. Now draw a tree structure for sentence (ia) and a tree structure for sentence (iia) (you will naturally incorporate the structures you have drawn in question A). If you are unsure about details of the verb phrase, simply use triangles to abbreviate the structure, as in trees 5.7, 5.8, 5.11, and 5.12.

C. Finally, draw tree structures for sentences (ib) and (iib). These will be the output trees of Extraposition. (Hint: A careful study of trees 5.11, 5.12, 5.23, and 5.24 should clear up any problems you might have in drawing your trees for this exercise.)

Further Reading

General

For book-length *introductions to syntax*, see Akmajian and Heny 1975, Horrocks 1987, Radford 1988, Baker 1995. For the next level of "introductory syntax," see Napoli 1993, Haegeman 1994, Radford 1997, Cook and Newson 1998. All these works have rich bibliographies from which to draw further reading. For other discussions by Chomsky on the nature of *linguistic competence*, see Chomsky 1976, 1980, 1986, 1995. See also Pinker 1995. For discussion of formal accounts of syntactic theory, see Newmeyer 1980, Radford 1988, Lasnik and Uriagereka 1988, and Napoli 1993.

Special Topics

For a clear introduction to *wh-movement*, see Radford 1988. Napoli 1993 and Haegeman 1994 provide extensive discussion of *wh*-movement, as well as comprehensive bibliographies on the topic. Like *wh*-movement, *anaphora* has played a central role in motivating changes in syntactic theory. The literature on this topic is vast. A clear introduction to anaphora can be found in Perlmutter and Soames 1979. Postal 1971 offers interesting discussion of and an early proposal for handling difficult-to-account-for anaphoric relations. See also Reinhart 1983 and the references cited there.

Journals

Language, Linguistic Inquiry, Natural Language & Linguistic Theory, The Linguistic Review, The Journal of Linguistic Research, Journal of Linguistics, Linguistic Analysis, Linguistics and Philosophy, Lingua, Studia Linguistica

Bibliography

Akmajian, A., and F. W. Heny. 1975. *An introduction to the principles of transformational syntax.* Cambridge, Mass.: MIT Press.

Baker, C. L. 1995. *English syntax.* 2nd ed. Cambridge, Mass.: MIT Press.

Chomsky, N. 1957. *Syntactic structures.* The Hague: Mouton.

Chomsky, N. 1965. *Aspects of the theory of syntax.* Cambridge, Mass.: MIT Press.

Chomsky, N. 1970. Remarks on nominalization. In R. Jacobs and P. Rosenbaum, eds., *Readings in English transformational grammar.* Waltham, Mass.: Ginn.

Chomsky, N. 1976. *Reflections on language.* New York: Pantheon Books.

Chomsky, N. 1980. *Rules and representations.* New York: Columbia University Press.

Chomsky, N. 1981. *Lectures on government and binding.* Dordrecht: Foris.

Chomsky, N. 1986. *Knowledge of language: Its nature, origin, and use.* New York: Praeger.

Chomsky, N. 1995. *The Minimalist Program.* Cambridge, Mass.: MIT Press.

Cook, V. J., and M. Newson. 1998. *Chomsky's Universal Grammar: An introduction.* Oxford: Blackwell.

Farmer, A. K. 1980. On the interaction of morphology and syntax. Doctoral dissertation, MIT. Distributed by the Indiana University Linguistics Club, Bloomington (1985).

Farmer, A. K. 1984. *Modularity in syntax: A study of Japanese and English.* Cambridge, Mass.: MIT Press.

Farmer, A. K., and R. A. Demers. 2001. *A linguistics workbook.* 4th ed. Cambridge, Mass.: MIT Press.

Haegeman, L. 1994. *Introduction to government and binding.* 2nd ed. Oxford: Blackwell.

Harris, R. A. 1993. *The linguistics wars.* New York: Oxford University Press.

Horrocks, G. 1987. *Generative grammar.* London and New York: Longman.

Jackendoff, R. 1977. *X-bar syntax: A study of phrase structure.* Cambridge, Mass.: MIT Press.

Kimball, J. P. 1973. *The formal theory of grammar.* Englewood Cliffs, N.J.: Prentice-Hall.

Lasnik, H., and J. Uriagereka. 1988. *A course in GB syntax.* Cambridge, Mass.: MIT Press.

Napoli, D. J. 1993. *Syntax: Theory and problems.* New York: Oxford University Press.

Newmeyer, F. 1980. *Linguistic theory in America: The first quarter-century of transformational generative grammar.* New York: Academic Press.

Perlmutter, D., and S. Soames. 1979. *Syntactic argumentation and the structure of English.* Berkeley and Los Angeles: University of California Press.

Pinker, S. 1995. *The language instinct.* New York: HarperPerennial.

Postal, P. 1971. *Crossover phenomena.* New York: Holt, Rinehart and Winston.

Radford, A. 1988. *Transformational grammar.* Cambridge: Cambridge University Press.

Radford, A. 1997. *Syntax: A minimalist approach.* Cambridge: Cambridge University Press.

Reinhart, T. 1983. *Anaphora and semantic interpretation.* London: Croom Helm.

Ross, John Robert. 1967. Constraints on variables in syntax. Doctoral dissertation, MIT.

Stowell, T. 1981. Origins of phrase structure. Doctoral dissertation, MIT.

Wall, R. 1972. *Introduction to mathematical linguistics.* Englewood Cliffs, N.J.: Prentice-Hall.

Zepeda, O. 1983. *A Papago grammar.* Tucson: University of Arizona Press.

Chapter 6

Semantics: The Study of Linguistic Meaning

6.1 SEMANTICS AS PART OF A GRAMMAR

The study of linguistic units and their principles of combination would not be complete without an account of what these units mean, what they are used to talk about, and what they are used to communicate. The study of communication is a part of pragmatics, to which we will return in chapter 9. In this chapter we will take up the first two topics, which constitute a major portion of *semantics.*

Semantics has not always enjoyed a prominent role in modern linguistics. From World War I to the early 1960s semantics was viewed, especially in the United States, as not quite respectable: its inclusion in a grammar (as linguists sometimes call a scientific description of a language—see Chomsky 1965) was considered by many as either a sort of methodological impurity or an objective to be reached only in the distant future. But there is as much reason to consider semantics a part of grammar as syntax or phonology. It is often said that a grammar describes what fluent speakers know of their language—their *linguistic competence* (recall chapter 5). If that is so, we can argue that whatever fluent speakers know of their language is a proper part of a description of that language. Given this, then the description of meaning is a necessary part of the description of a speaker's linguistic knowledge (i.e., the grammar of a language must contain a component that describes what speakers know about the semantics of the language). In other words, if appealing to what fluent speakers know about their language counts as motivation for including a phonological fact or a syntactic fact in the grammar of that language, then the same sort of consideration motivates the inclusion of semantic facts.

A more general consideration also motivates us to include semantics in the grammar of a language. A language is often defined as a conventional system for communication, a system for conveying messages. Moreover, communication can be accomplished (in the system) only because words have certain meanings; therefore, to characterize this system —the language—it is necessary to describe these meanings. Hence, if a grammar describes a language, part of it must describe meaning, and thus the grammar must contain a semantics. Taking these two considerations together, it seems reasonable to conclude that semantic information is an integral part of a grammar.

In reading this chapter, though, bear in mind that the subfield of semantics is in a greater state of diversification than phonology or syntax; much that we will discuss is a cautious selection from among possible alternatives. There is no shortage of semantic theories, and it is widely acknowledged that serious open questions still lie at the very foundations of semantics. We suggest consulting the works listed at the end of this chapter, in order to get a general idea of the scope of semantics.

6.2 THEORIES OF MEANING

It would take a whole semantic theory to answer the questions raised below, but in the history of semantics a few "leading ideas" have emerged concerning the nature of meaning, and a brief look at some of these proposals is instructive.

Varieties of Meaning

As a preliminary we should note that in everyday English, the word *mean* has a number of different uses, many of which are not relevant to the study of language:

(1)
a. That was no mean (insignificant) accomplishment.
b. This will mean (result in) the end of our regime.
c. I mean (intend) to help if I can.
d. Keep Off the Grass! This means (refers to) you.
e. His losing his job means (implies) that he will have to look again.
f. Lucky Strike means (indicates) fine tobacco.
g. Those clouds mean (are a sign of) rain.
h. She doesn't mean (believe) what she said.

These uses of the word *mean* can all be paraphrased by other expressions (indicated in parentheses above). None of them is appropriate for our discussion of word meaning. Rather, we will use the terms *mean* and *meaning* as they are used in the following examples:

(2)
a. *Procrastinate* means "to put things off."
b. In saying "It's getting late," she meant that we should leave.

These two uses of the word *mean* exemplify two important types of meaning: *linguistic meaning* (2a) and *speaker meaning* (2b).

This distinction can be illustrated with an example. Suppose that you've been arguing with another person, who exclaims, "The door is right behind you!" You would assume, quite rightly in this context, that the speaker, in uttering this sentence, means that you are to leave—although the speaker's actual words indicate nothing more than the location of the door. This illustrates how a speaker can mean something quite different from what his or her words mean. In general, the *linguistic meaning* of an expression is simply the meaning or meanings of that expression in the language. In contrast, the *speaker meaning* can differ from the linguistic meaning, depending on whether the speaker is speaking *literally* or *nonliterally*. When we speak literally, we mean what our words mean, and in this case there is no important difference between speaker meaning and linguistic meaning. But when we speak nonliterally, we mean something different from what our words mean.

Two nonliteral uses of language are sarcasm or irony, as when someone says of a film, "That movie was a real winner!" uttered in such a way that we understand the speaker to mean that the movie was a flop. Metaphorical uses of language (some of which we discussed in chapter 2) are also types of nonliteral language use, as, for example, when someone is described as having raven hair, ruby lips, emerald eyes, and teeth of pearl. Taken literally, this description would indicate that the person in question is a monstrosity; however, taken metaphorically, it is quite a compliment. As we will see in chapter 9, a crucial feature in human communication is the ability on the part of the hearer to determine whether a speaker is speaking literally or nonliterally.

Returning now to the question of linguistic meaning, it is useful to keep in mind the distinction between the linguistic meaning of an expression and a given speaker's literal or nonliteral use of the expression. Furthermore, in talking about the linguistic meaning of an expression, we must note that meanings can vary across dialects and across individual speakers. To recall an example from chapter 2, in American English the word *bonnet* refers only to a type of hat, whereas in British English it can refer to the hood of a car. Hence, for a word such as *bonnet* we cannot isolate a single meaning valid for all forms of English; rather, our discussion of the meaning of the word will be relative to a specific dialect of English.

The matter is further complicated when we note that meanings of words can vary across individual speakers within the same dialect. For example, the word *infer* seems to have different meanings for different speakers. For some speakers, it has roughly the same meaning as *conclude*, as in *I infer from what you say that you are sick*. For other speakers, it has roughly the same meaning as *imply*, as in *He inferred that he was fed up with us*. The language of a particular individual is referred to as that person's *idiolect* (see chapter 7), and it is clear that the idiolectal meaning of a word can differ from one person to another (even among people who can be said to speak the same dialect). The varieties of meaning we have specified so far are summarized in figure 6.1.

At this point we might ask, How can so many varieties of meaning exist? Isn't it the case, after all, that "official" dictionaries of a language tell us what the meaning of a word is? And isn't it the case that the only "valid" meanings for a word are those listed in the dictionary? In answering these questions, it is important to recall the distinction made earlier between prescriptive and descriptive grammar. Current dictionaries of English (and many other languages as well) derive from a tradition of prescriptive grammar, and almost invariably have focused on the written language. You can probably think of numerous words and

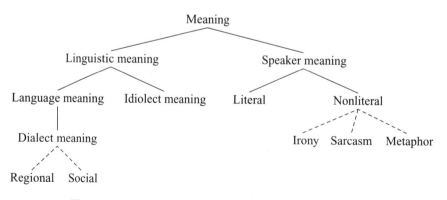

Figure 6.1
Some varieties of meaning

uses of words in current spoken, informal English that do not appear in dictionaries. From a prescriptive point of view these unlisted words and uses might be termed "incorrect" or "improper." From a descriptive point of view, however, the spoken language forms a central source of data for linguistic theory, and linguists are very much concerned with discovering meaning properties and relations in forms of spoken language actually used by speakers (rather than forms of language that prescriptive grammar dictates speakers "should" use). Hence, although dictionaries might be useful in providing certain basic explanations of common words, they do not, by and large, reflect accurately enough the meaning and variations in meaning of words in current use in everyday spoken language. And even where they are useful, they presuppose that the reader is already familiar with all the words used in the definition, which eventually appear in other definitions!

The descriptive point of view is sometimes misinterpreted as advocating "linguistic freedom"—that is, a situation in which speakers are free to use words any way they like and are allowed to "get away with" breaking the rules of proper English. This is, of course, an absurd parody of the descriptive point of view. It turns out that, quite aside from dictionaries and prescriptive grammar books, speakers are indeed not free to use words any way they like. There is tremendous social pressure for speakers of a language to use words in similar ways—successful communication depends on this, in fact—and the need to communicate effectively provides constraints on how "creative" an individual speaker can be in the use of words. What, then, is recorded in language as "meaning"?

What Is Meaning?

Historically, the most compelling idea concerning meaning has been that meaning is some sort of entity or thing. After all, we do speak of words as "having" a meaning, as meaning "something," as having the "same" meaning, as meaning the same "thing," as "sharing" a meaning, as having "many meanings," and so forth. What sort of entity or thing is meaning? Different answers to this question give us a selection of different conceptions of meaning, and a selection of different types of semantic theory.

The Denotational Theory of Meaning

If one focuses on just some of the expressions in a language—for instance, proper names such as *de Gaulle*, *Italy*, or deictics such as *I*, *now*, *that*—one is likely to conclude that their meaning is the thing they refer to. This relation between a linguistic expression and what it refers to is variously called *denotation, linguistic reference,* and *semantic reference.* For convenience we will formulate this conception of meaning in terms of the following slogan:

(D)
The meaning of each expression is the (actual) object it denotes, its *denotation.*

Although (D) does reflect the fact that we use language to talk about the world, there are serious problems with the identification of meaning as denotation.

For instance, if we believe that the meaning of an expression is its denotation, we are committed to at least the following additional claims:

(3)
a. If an expression has a meaning, then it follows that it must have a denotation (meaningfulness).
b. If two expressions have the same denotation, then they have the same meaning (synonymy).

Each of these consequences of (D) turns out to be false. For instance, (3a) requires that for any expression having a meaning there is an actual object that it denotes. But this is surely wrong. What, for instance, is the (actual) object denoted by such expressions as *Pegasus* (the flying horse), *the, empty, and, hello, very,* and *Leave the room*? Next, consider (3b). This says that if two expressions denote the same object, then they mean the same thing; that is, they are synonymous. But many expressions that can be correctly used to denote a single object do not mean the same thing. For instance, *the morning star, the evening star,* and *Venus* all denote the same planet, but they are not synonymous, as can be seen by the fact that the morning star is the last star seen in the morning and the evening star is the first star seen at night. Nor are the expressions *the first person to walk on our moon* and *Neil Armstrong* synonymous, but they denote the same person.

Mentalist Theories of Meaning
Well, we might say, if meanings are not actual objects, perhaps they are mental objects; even if there is no real flying horse for *Pegasus* to denote, there is surely such an *idea,* and maybe this idea is the meaning

of *Pegasus*. A typical example of this view can be seen in the following quotation from Glucksberg and Danks (1975, 50): "The set of possible meanings of any given word is the set of possible feelings, images, ideas, concepts, thoughts, and inferences that a person might produce when that word is heard and processed." As with the denotational theory, this conception of meaning can be formulated in terms of a slogan:

(M)
The meaning of each expression is the *idea* (or ideas) associated with that expression in the minds of speakers.

This sort of theory has a number of problems, but the most serious one can be put in the form of a dilemma: either the notion of an idea is too vague to allow the theory to predict or explain anything specific, and thus the theory is not testable; or if the notion of an idea is made precise enough to test, the theory turns out to make false predictions. The quotation from Glucksberg and Danks illustrates the first problem. How, with such a view of meaning, could one ever determine what an expression means? With such a view, could two expressions be synonymous (have the same meaning), or would there always be feelings and thoughts associated with one expression that are not associated with the other?

Meaning as Images   Suppose we sharpen the notion of an idea by saying that ideas are *mental images* (mental pictures and diagrams). Though this might work for words like *Pegasus* and perhaps *the Eiffel Tower*, it is not obvious how it would work for nouns such as *dog* and *triangle*, or a verb such as *kick*. For instance, if one really does form an image of a dog or a triangle, more than likely the dog will be of some particular species and will not comprise both a Chihuahua and a Saint Bernard; the triangle will be isosceles or equilateral but will not comprise all triangles. Similar problems arise with *kick*. If one really forms an image of X kicking Y, then that image probably will have properties not essential to kicking, such as the sex of the kicker, which leg was used, the kind of thing being kicked, and so forth. In general, mental images are just not abstract enough to be the meanings of even common nouns and verbs. But suppose for the moment that appropriate images could be found for these nouns and verbs. What about other kinds of words? What images are the meanings of words such as *only*, *and*, *hello*, and *not*? Worse still, can the theory apply to units larger than words, such as the sentence *She speaks*

French and Navajo? How, for instance, does an Image Theory of meaning differentiate this sentence from *She speaks French or Navajo*?

Meaning as Concepts   One way around this problem of the excessive specificity of images is to view ideas as *concepts*, that is, as mentally represented categories of things. As we will see in more detail in chapter 10, this version of the idea theory is also problematic. First, concepts also might be too specific in that various speakers' concepts might include information specific to the way they developed the concept, information that is not a part of the meaning of the word that expresses it. There is psychological evidence that our system of cognitive classification is structured in terms of *prototypes*, in that some instances of a concept are more typical (closer to the prototype) than others; robins are more typical birds than penguins, chairs are more typical pieces of furniture than ashtrays, and so on (see chapter 10). Yet these are not features of the meaning of *bird* and *furniture*. And even if concepts work as meanings for some words, such as common nouns, adjectives, and maybe verbs, there are still many other kinds of words that do not have clear conceptual content, such as *elm tree*, *only*, *not*, and *hello*. Furthermore, it is not clear what concept would be assigned to a sentence, though sentences are clearly meaningful. The concept analysis of meaning is at best a theory of a restricted portion of the language. So although this way of understanding the notion "idea" makes the theory as testable as theories in general in cognitive psychology, there is as yet no such theory of meaning in cognitive psychology that is detailed enough to test. To succeed, such a theory must be capable of identifying and distinguishing concepts independently of meaning, which current versions fail to do. In short, theories of meaning as entities, whether they be objects denoted, images in the mind, or concepts, all face various difficulties. Perhaps the trouble lies with the initial assumption that meaning is an entity.

The Sense Theory of Meaning

Frege (1892) argued that ideas cannot be meaning since ideas are subjective and fleeting whereas meaning is objective and (relatively) stable—we use language to pass on information from person to person. And denotations are not enough because if language consisted only of form and denotation, then an identity sentence such as (4a) would carry the same information as (4b):

(4)
a. a = a (the morning star is (=) the morning star)
b. a = b (the morning star is (=) the evening star)

But, said Frege, (4b) does not convey the same information as (4a), since one can believe the first, but not even be aware of the second. Frege's solution was to propose that all referring expressions with a denotation also have what he called a *sense*—a way that the denotation is presented or known to the language user. For instance, you might know a person as "the lady who lives next door" without knowing her as "the principal of Martha Graham Elementary School." Frege also proposed that whole sentences have a sense. For declarative sentences the sense is the conditions that make the sentence true. (Or put another way, a declarative sentence represents the world as being a certain way.) These are called the sentence's *truth conditions* because understanding the sentence is knowing under what conditions the sentence *would be true*. Understanding a declarative sentence such as (5)

(5)
Neil Armstrong was the first person to walk on our moon.

involves knowing how the world must be for the sentence to be true. Note of course that one need not know whether it is *in fact true*. Frege extended this idea to yes/no questions such as (6):

(6)
Was Neil Armstrong the first person to walk on our moon?

He thought that this too expresses a proposition to the effect that Neil Armstrong was the first person to walk on the moon, but that it contains something else as well, an element that carries the force of a *question*. Declaratives also contain an element that carries force, but in their case it is the force of an *assertion*, and imperative sentences contain an element that carries the force of a *request*. However, since interrogatives and imperatives are not true or false, their sense cannot involve truth conditions. What might it involve instead? Contemporary semantics answers by saying that interrogatives are associated with *answerhood conditions*, and imperatives are associated with *compliance conditions*. To understand an interrogative would be to understand what would be an answer to the question it expresses, and to understand an imperative would be to understand what it would be like to comply with the request it expresses. Such conditions (truth conditions, answerhood, conditions, compliance conditions) are collectively called *satisfaction conditions*. The suggestion, then, is that the meaning of a sentence should be analyzed in part in terms of its satisfaction conditions, and the meaning of its constituents should be analyzed in terms of the contributions the constituents make to these conditions:

(S)
The meaning of a sentence is its *sense* satisfaction condition (i.e., its truth condition, compliance condition, answerhood condition), and the meaning of a word or phrase is the contribution it makes to the satisfaction condition of the sentences it occurs in.

This theory has many advantages over earlier denotational and mentalist theories, since (1) it does not equate meaning with either denotation or ideas (images/concepts), and (2) unlike (D) and (M), (S) assigns semantic priority to sentences, in the way that syntax does, and not to words or phrases. In some form or other, this theory is probably the dominant view in linguistic semantics today (see suggested readings).

The Use Theory of Meaning
The idea that meaning should be explained in terms of truth (or more generally, satisfaction) conditions, as well as in terms of any kind of entity, came under attack in the 1930s when Wittgenstein (1933) advanced an alternative conception of meaning as use that influenced Anglo-American theorizing for many decades. Like the previous theories of meaning, the Use Theory of meaning can be formulated as a slogan:

(U)
The meaning of an expression is its *use* in the language community.

One advantage of this theory is that we can just as easily speak about the use of *hello* and of sentences as about the use of *table* or *Pegasus*. The main problem with the Use Theory of meaning is that the relevant conception of *use* must be made precise, and the theory must say how, exactly, meaning is connected to use.

In conclusion, it is fair to say that researchers do not have a very clear idea what meaning is. All of the theories we have surveyed are in various states of disarray. The situation is not hopeless, as there are still promising avenues of approach to this topic. As a student, you should not be deterred by present limitations on understanding, but should consider it a promising area for future research.

6.3   THE SCOPE OF A SEMANTIC THEORY

The foregoing discussion indicates that there are facts for a semantic theory to describe, and it leads us to consider what kinds of information are central to the description of the semantics of a language.

Words and Phrases

Meaning Properties

We now turn our attention to certain *meaning properties* of words that play an important role in the description of human languages. Perhaps the central semantic property of words (and morphemes in general) is the property of being *meaningful* or being *meaningless*. Any adequate account of the lexicon of a language must specify the meaningful words of the language and must represent the meaning of those words (both simple and complex) in some fashion. For example, at the very least an adequate account of the English lexicon must tell us that *procrastinate* means "put things off," *bachelor* means "unmarried adult male," *mother* means "female parent," and so on for numerous other words of the language. Here our earlier distinction between linguistic meaning and speaker meaning is crucial—how could a description of a *language* anticipate all the things a *speaker* might mean in uttering an expression from it on some occasion?

Another important semantic property of words is *ambiguity*, in particular what is referred to as *lexical ambiguity*, as illustrated in the following examples:

(7)
a. He found a *bat*.
    (*bat*: baseball bat; flying mammal)
b. She couldn't *bear* children.
    (*bear*: give birth to; put up with)

In each case the italicized word is ambiguous in that it has more than one meaning. The ability to detect ambiguity is crucial in the communicative process, and successful communication can depend on both speaker and hearer recognizing the same meaning for a potentially ambiguous word.

Similarly for *polysemy*, which is often defined as the property of having more than one related meaning. Thus, *table* can mean a certain kind of furniture, or it can be the act of putting an item at a meeting on hold (*She tabled the motion*). Someone might argue that these are two different words because the same word can't be both a noun and a verb, and so there are no relations here *between* the meanings of a word. Still, there are examples of relations between the meanings of words from just one syntactic category. For instance, *Sports Illustrated* can be bought for 1 dollar or 35 million dollars; the first is something you can read and later start a fire with, the second is a particular company that produces the magazine you just read. Such polysemy can give rise to a special ambiguity (*He left the bank five minutes ago, He left the bank five years ago*). Sometimes dictionaries use history to decide whether a particular entry is a case of one word with two related meanings, or two separate words, but this can be tricky. Even though *pupil* (eye) and *pupil* (student) are historically linked, they are intuitively as unrelated as *bat* (implement) and *bat* (animal).

Another important semantic property of words, in particular words put together into phrases, is *anomaly*. An expression is anomalous when the meanings of its individual words are incompatible:

(8)
a. gradually plummet
b. colorless green idea
c. dream diagonally

Of course, it is almost always possible to impose a meaning on such expressions—indeed, certain forms of poetry demand that the reader impose a meaning on anomalous expressions. For example, *to dream diagonally* might be taken to mean "to lie diagonally in a bed while dreaming," but this is the result of a special (and forced) interpretation, which speakers could argue about at length. The point is that expressions like those in (8) have no conventional interpretation in English. It is important to notice that a semantically anomalous expression can nevertheless be syntactically well formed (e.g., *colorless green idea* is formed on a regular syntactic pattern of English exemplified by phrases such as *colorful red flower*), and this may be a major factor that makes it feasible for speakers to invent meanings for such anomalous expressions.

Meaning Relations

Not only do words have *meaning properties* (such as ambiguity, or having a meaning), they also bear various *meaning relations* to one another. Just as words can be related morphologically (e.g., by word formation rules such as the *-able* rule), so they can also be related semantically, and words related by virtue of meaning form subgroups within the lexicon of a language.

For example, one central meaning relation is *synonymy*, "sameness" of meaning or "paraphrase." Thus, we say that *automobile* is synonymous with *car*, *plane* (in one of its senses) is synonymous with *aircraft*, *kid* (in one of its senses) is synonymous with *child*, and so on.

Words may also be *homophonous*; that is, they may have identical pronunciations but have distinct spellings in the written language, such as *Mary*, *marry*, and *merry*. Two words with the same spelling (and pronunciation) are *homonymous* (i.e., they are *homonyms*). An often-cited example of homonymy is the word *bank* referring to the side of a river, versus the word *bank* referring to a financial institution. Of course, the question immediately arises, Why not say that there is a single word *bank* with two distinct meanings? As we saw in chapter 2, it is by no means easy to resolve the issue of how to count different words, and we can provide no solution here.

Another important meaning relation is *meaning inclusion*, illustrated in (9):

(9)
a. The meaning of *sister* includes the meaning of *female*.
b. The meaning of *kill* includes the meaning of *dead*.

When we put words together that are related by meaning inclusion, we derive expressions that are *redundant* (such as *female sister*), and idiomatic expressions (such as *She killed him dead*).

Even if two expressions are not synonymous and the meaning of one does not include the meaning of the other, they still may be semantically related in that they *overlap*, or *share* some aspect of meaning:

(10)
a. *Father*, *uncle*, *bull*, and *stallion* all express the property "male."
b. *Say*, *speak*, *whisper*, *yell*, *shout*, and *scream* all express the property "vocalization."
c. *Fortunately*, *luckily*, *happily*, and *fortuitously* all express the property "good for" something or someone.

Groups of words in the lexicon can be semantically related by being members of a set known as a *semantic field* (see Lehrer 1974). On a very general and intuitive level, we can say that the words in a semantic field, though not synonymous, are all used to talk about the same general phenomenon, and there is a meaning inclusion relation between the items in the field and the field category itself. Classical examples of semantic fields include color terms (*red, green, blue, yellow*), kinship terms (*mother, father, sister, brother*), and cooking terms (*boil, fry, bake, broil, steam*). The notion of a semantic field can be extended intuitively to any set of terms with a close relation in meaning, all of which can be subsumed under the same general label. Thus, in addition to the specific semantic fields cited, we could refer to labels such as "nautical terms," "plant names," "animal names," "automobile terms," and so on, as specifying semantic fields. It is difficult to be very precise about what counts as a semantic field. Do all time words form a semantic field? How about wearing apparel for the feet, or the things Napoleon thought about the day he died? Although there have been interesting attempts to make the notion of a field more precise (see suggested readings), so far they have not created much consensus for research. The kinds of semantic fields found in the lexicon of any given language (i.e., the kinds of general labels that define the particular semantic fields) may vary from culture to culture, and in fact anthropologists have found the study of semantic fields useful in investigating the nature of belief systems and reasoning in different cultural groups.

Sometimes words can share an aspect of meaning but be "opposite" in some other aspect of meaning. We say that such sets of words are *antonymous*. Typical examples of word antonymy include the following:

(11)
a. *Small* and *large* share the notion "size" but differ in degree.
b. *Cold* and *hot* share the notion "temperature" but differ in degree.

The sense in which words such as *hot* and *cold* are "opposites" is not just that they are incompatible in meaning. Many words are semantically incompatible in the sense that they cannot both be true of something at the same time. For example, the words *cat* and *dog* are semantically incompatible (they cannot both be truly applied to the same thing at the same time); nevertheless, they are not "opposites" in the sense of being antonyms. The examples in (11) are antonyms essentially because there is a scale containing the "opposites" at either end, with a midpoint (or midinterval) between them:

<------------------------|--------------------->

cold   cool   lukewarm   warm   hot

Thus, the words *hot* and *cold* can be said to be antonyms ("opposites") since they define the *extremities* of a scale (of temperature, in this case) that has a midinterval between them (in this case, represented by the word *lukewarm*, a word that can be used to refer to things that are neither hot nor cold). The comparative (*-er*) form of antonyms points in the direction of the scale, and so the midpoint will not take comparison:

(12)
a. smaller – *mediumsizeder – larger
b. colder – cooler – *lukewarmer – warmer – hotter

This completes our initial survey of semantic properties and relations in the area of word (and phrase) meaning. We note, once again, that the study of word meaning reveals that the lexicon of a language is not simply an unorganized list of words. Semantic relations such as synonymy, antonymy, and the relations involved in semantic fields all serve to link certain words with other words, indicating that the overall lexicon of a language has a complex internal structure consisting of subgroups, or "networks," of words sharing significant properties.

Sentences

Since sentences are composed of words and phrases, we can expect that certain semantic properties and relations of words and phrases will carry over to sentences as well. However, as traditional grammarians put it, a sentence (as opposed to a single word or phrase) expresses a "complete thought." This is not a very useful definition of a sentence, but it does suggest that we might expect to find semantic properties and relations that are distinctive to sentences (or expressions that are elliptical for sentences) as opposed to words and phrases.

Meaning Properties and Relations

Among the meaning properties and relations of words and phrases that carry over to sentences are ambiguity and synonymy (paraphrase):

(13)
a. *Synonymy (paraphrase)*
His pants were too small.
His pants were not big enough.

b. *Ambiguity*
   She visited a little girl's school.

Notice that in some cases the ambiguity of a sentence is caused by the ambiguity of a word in it (see (7a–b) again), but in other cases no particular word is ambiguous—the ambiguity is due to structural relations in the sentence (recall the discussion of structural ambiguity in chapter 5). For example, in (13b) it is not clear whether *little* modifies only the word *girl* (*She visited a [little girl's] school*) or modifies the phrase *girl's school* (*She visited a little [girl's school]*). As we will see in chapter 10, speakers often disambiguate such sentences for their hearers by using stress and pauses.

Ambiguity can give rise to humorous double meanings, especially when unintended, as in these newspaper headlines:

BRITISH LEFT WAFFLES ON FALKLANDS
DRUNK GETS NINE MONTHS IN VIOLIN CASE
IRAQI HEAD SEEKS ARMS
TEACHER STRIKES IDLE KIDS
STOLEN PAINTING FOUND BY TREE
TWO SOVIET SHIPS COLLIDE, ONE DIES
TWO SISTERS REUNITED AFTER 18 YEARS IN CHECKOUT COUNTER

Communicative Act Potential
Sentences also exhibit meaning properties and relations that words and phrases may lack.

One important property of a sentence is its *communicative act potential*. Sentences with different structures often have different communicative functions—they are conventionally used to perform different communicative acts in speaking (see "Special Topics," and chapter 9). Thus, a speaker who wants to assert or state that something is true will normally utter a declarative sentence such as *Snow is white*. On the other hand, if the speaker wants to issue an order, request, or command, then an imperative sentence such as *Leave the room!* is appropriate. Finally, if a speaker wants to ask a question, then the obvious choice is an interrogative sentence such as *What time is it?* As a first approximation we could diagram these facts as follows:

(14)

a. Declarative sentence → Used to constate (assert, state, claim, etc.)

b. Imperative sentence → Used to direct (order, request, command, etc.)

c. Interrogative sentence → Used to question

It seems to be a part of the semantics of these structural types (declarative, imperative, interrogative) that they have the distinct communicative functions cited above. In any event, we would not say someone understood sentences of these types unless that person understood the differences in communicative function.

That these different types of sentence have these different normal uses is an important semantic fact. However, the field of semantics has traditionally concentrated on the assertive function of language, concerning itself mainly with the properties and relations that declarative sentences have regarding truth.

Truth Properties

Not only do expressions in a language have meaning and denotation, they are also used to say things that are true or false. Of course, no semantic theory can predict which sentences are used to say something true and which are used to say something false, in part because truth and falsity depend upon what is being referred to and the way the world actually is, and also because the same words can be used in identical sentences to refer to different things. Does this mean that the semantics of natural language cannot deal with truth and falsity? The answer is no, because some truth properties and truth relations hold regardless of reference and the way the world actually is, provided meaning is held constant.

Consider first the property of being *linguistically true* (also called *analytically true* or just *analytic*) or *linguistically false* (also called *contradictory*). A sentence is linguistically true (or linguistically false) if its truth (or falsehood) is determined solely by the semantics of the language and it is not necessary to check any facts about the nonlinguistic world in order to determine its truth or falsehood. A sentence is *empirically true* (or *empirically false*) if it is not linguistically true or false—that is, if it is necessary to check the nonlinguistic world in order to verify or falsify it; knowledge of the language alone does not settle the matter. Semantics is not concerned to explain empirical truths and falsehoods, but it is concerned to explain those sentences that are linguistically true or false. In each of the groups (15), (16), and (17) it is possible to determine truth values (true = T, false = F) without regard to the actual state of the world.

(15)
a. Either it is raining here or it is not raining here. (T)
b. If John is sick and Mary is sick, then John is sick. (T)
c. It is raining here and it is not raining here. (F)
d. If John is sick and Mary is sick, then John is not sick. (F)

(16)
a. All people that are sick are people. (T)
b. If every person is sick, then it is not true that no person is sick. (T)
c. Some people that are sick are not people. (F)
d. Every person is sick, but some person is not (sick). (F)

(17)
a. If John is a bachelor, then John is unmarried. (T)
b. If John killed the bear, then the bear died. (T)
c. If the car is red, then it has a color. (T)
d. John is a bachelor, but he is married. (F)
e. John killed the bear and it's (still) alive. (F)
f. The car is red, but it has no color. (F)

Again, knowing the language seems to be sufficient for knowing the truth or falsity of these sentences, and this being so, the semantics of these sorts of sentences will be relevant to a semantic theory that attempts to characterize knowledge that speakers have about their language.

Truth Relations
We have noted that there are truth relations as well as truth properties that fall within the scope of semantics. The most central truth relation for semantics is *entailment*. One sentence S is said to entail another sentence S′ when the truth of the first guarantees the truth of the second, and the falsity of the second guarantees the falsity of the first, as in (18):

(18)
a. *The car is red* entails *The car has a color.*
b. *The needle is too short* entails *The needle is not long enough.*

We can see that the first sentence in each example, if true, guarantees the truth of the second; and the falsity of the second sentence in each example guarantees the falsity of the first.

Closely related to entailment is another truth relation, *semantic presupposition*. The basic idea behind semantic presupposition is that the falsity of the presupposed sentence causes the presupposing sentence not to have a truth value (T or F). Furthermore, both a sentence and its denial have the same semantic presupposition. Although this truth relation is somewhat controversial, (19) and (20) show typical examples of semantic presupposition in which both the positive (a) and the negative (b) sentences have the same presupposition (c):

(19)
a. The present king of France is bald.
b. The present king of France is not bald.
c. There is a present king of France.

(20)
a. John realizes that his car has been stolen.
b. John does not realize that his car has been stolen.
c. John's car has been stolen.

In sum, in addition to truth properties, there are at least two truth relations that an adequate semantic theory must explain (or explain away), namely, entailment and semantic presupposition. Furthermore, since there are analogues of these properties and relations for nondeclarative sentences, an adequate semantics must ultimately account for how the world can *satisfy* a sentence of any type.

Goals of a Semantic Theory

We now come to the question of the goals of a semantic theory. What should a semantic theory do, and how?

The short answer to the first question is that a semantic theory should attribute to each expression in the language the semantic properties and relations that it actually has; moreover, it should define those properties and relations. Thus, if an expression is meaningful, the semantic theory should say so. If it has a specific set of meanings, the semantic theory should specify them. If it is ambiguous, the semantic theory should record that fact. And so on. Moreover, if two expressions are synonymous, or if one entails the other, the semantic theory should mark these semantic relations. We can organize these constraints on a semantic theory by saying that an adequate theory of a language must generate every true instance of the following schemes for arbitrary expression E:

(21)

a. *Meaning properties and relations*

E means ____.

E is meaningful.

E is ambiguous.

E is polysemous.

E is anomalous (nonsense).

E is redundant.

E and E′ are synonymous.

E and E′ are homonymous.

E includes the meaning of E′.

E and E′ overlap in meaning.

E and E′ are antonymous.

E is conventionally used to ____.

b. *Truth properties and relations*

E is linguistically true (analytic).

E is linguistically false (contradictory).

E entails E′.

E semantically presupposes E′.

We can say in sum that the domain of a semantic theory is at least the set of properties and relations listed in (21); we should not be satisfied with a semantic theory of English that fails to explain them (or to explain them away).

The second question concerning the goals of a semantic theory is, How should the theory handle these semantic properties and relations? What kinds of constraints on a semantic theory are reasonable to impose? We will note just two. First, it is generally conceded that even though a natural language contains an infinite number of phrases and sentences (recall chapters 2 and 5), a semantic theory of a natural language should be *finite*: people are capable of storing only a finite amount of information, but they nevertheless learn the semantics of natural languages. The second constraint on a semantic theory of a natural language is that it should reflect the fact that, except for idioms, phrases and sentences are *compositional*—in other words, that the meaning of a syntactically complex expression is determined by the meaning of its constituents and their grammatical relations. Compositionality rests on the fact that a finite number of familiar words and expressions can be combined in novel ways to form an infinite number of new phrases and sentences; hence, a finite semantic theory that reflects compositionality can describe meanings for an infinite number of complex expressions.

The existence of compositionality is most dramatic when compositional expressions are contrasted with expressions that lack compositionality. In (22a) the expression *kick the bucket* has two meanings:

(22)
a. John kicked the bucket.
b. John kicked the wooden pail.
c. John died.

One of the meanings of (22a) is compositional: it is determined on the basis of the meaning of the words and is approximately synonymous with (22b). The other meaning of (22a) is idiomatic and can be paraphrased as (22c). Idiomatic meanings are not compositional in the sense of being determined from the meaning of the constituent words and their grammatical relations. That is, one could not determine the idiomatic meaning of (22a) by knowing just the meaning of the words and recognizing familiar grammatical structure—an idiomatic meaning must be learned separately as a unit. Idioms behave as though they were syntactically complex words whose meaning cannot be predicted, since their syntactic structure is doing no semantic work.

It would be a mistake to think of the compositionality of a complex expression as simply adding up the meanings and references of its parts. For adjective + noun constructions like that in (23a), adding up sometimes works:

(23)
a. A *bearded sailor* walked by. =
b. Someone who was bearded and a sailor walked by.

But even in such constructions the contributions of syntax can be obscure. In (24), for example, we cannot simply add up the meanings of *occasional* and *sailor*:

(24)
a.   An *occasional sailor* walked by. ≠
b. *Someone who is a sailor and occasional walked by.

Modifiers can create other complications for compositionality, which must also be reflected in a semantic theory of the language. Contrast the arguments in (25) and (26):

(25)

a. That is a *gray* elephant. (T)

b. All elephants are animals. (T)

c. So, that is a *gray* animal. (T)

(26)

a. That is a *small* elephant. (T)

b. All elephants are animals. (T)

c. So, that is a *small* animal. (F)

In (25) the premises (a) and (b) jointly entail the truth of (c), but in (26) the premises (a) and (b) do not jointly entail the truth of (c). The only difference between (25) and (26) is the occurrence of *gray* in (25) and *small* in (26), so clearly there is some difference in the semantics of these two words.

More complicated and interesting examples of the interaction of semantics and syntax come from the functional relations of subject and object in a sentence. In sentences like (27a) and (27c) the words are the same, but the entailments (27b) and (27d) are importantly different.

(27)

a. John killed the snake.

b. The snake died.

c. The snake killed John.

d. John died.

This further illustrates the degree to which a semantic theory must be integrated with a syntactic theory in an adequate description of a natural language.

In conclusion, in this section we have specified and illustrated a number of semantic properties and relations that a complete description of a language must account for, and we have motivated some very general conditions on such an account. At a more advanced level, by reading selections from the bibliography, you can investigate theories that attempt to do just this.

6.4   SPECIAL TOPICS

The issues we have just surveyed represent common ground for most semantic theories. However, many topics are the special concern of particular theories, and the problems they pose for semantics form part of its research agenda for the future.

Mood and Meaning

Traditional grammars say that a verb is in, for example, the subjunctive mood if it has a certain inflection (verbal morphology) and a sentence is in that mood if its main verb is in that mood. We can call this *verbal mood*. Jespersen (1924) championed the alternative idea that moods are best analyzed sententially, as forms with certain conventional communicative functions (what we earlier called "communicative act potential"). We can call these *sentential moods*. In what follows we will be speaking of sentential moods exclusively.

The major moods of English are traditionally said to be the *declarative*, *imperative*, and *interrogative*. For example:

(28)

a. *Declarative*
   Snow is white.

b. *Imperative*
   Leave the room!

c. *Yes/no interrogative*
   Is snow white?
   Snow is WHITE?

d. *Wh-interrogative*
   What time is it?
   You saw WHAT?

But there are also minor moods, exemplified by the following examples:

(29)

a. *Tag declarative*
   You've been drinking again, haven't you.

b. *Tag imperative*
   Leave the room, will you!

c. *Pseudo-imperative*
   Move and I'll shoot!
   Move or I'll shoot!

d. *Alternative question*
   Does John resemble his father or his mother? (with rising intonation on *father* and falling intonation on *mother*)

e. *Exclamative*
   What a nice day!
f. *Optative*
   May he rest in peace.
g. *"One more" sentence*
   One more beer and I'll leave.
h. *Curse*
   You pig, bag of wind, . . . !

The distinction between major and minor mood is not clear-cut, but intuitively minor moods (1) are highly restricted in their productivity, (2) are peripheral to communication, (3) are probably low in their relative frequency of occurrence, and (4) vary widely across languages. This last feature is interesting; there seem to be some regularities across unrelated languages for the major moods, but not the minor moods. For instance, *declaratives* occur marked or unmarked. When they are marked, they have some distinctive characteristic such as word order, a special declarative particle, or declarative inflection. When they are unmarked, they are typically of the same form as dependent clauses. Furthermore, almost all languages have a declarative form devoted to making explicit the force of any sentence. This declarative form is called a *performative* sentence. For example, *I (hereby) order you to leave* makes explicit that the sentence is being used to order, and not request, someone to leave.

Imperatives have been found in almost all languages studied to date. The person being directed to do something is usually referred to via the subject expression (*you*). Typically the verbal morphology of imperatives is simpler than that of other moods, and imperatives resist occurring in dependent clauses. Many languages have a special form for negative imperatives.

As for *interrogatives*, both yes/no and *wh*-interrogatives occur in most languages. Yes/no questions typically are signaled by using rising intonation, although sentence-final or -initial particles, special verbal morphology, and word order are also used. There are three main systems for answering yes/no questions: yes/no systems that use a special particle, such as *yes* or *no*, to answer the question (English, French); agree/disagree systems, where the answer agrees with the proposition expressed (Japanese); and echo systems, where the answer repeats the relevant part of the sentence (Welsh). For example:

(30)
Question
Doesn't John like beans?
a. *Yes/no*
   Yes (he does)./No (he doesn't).
b. *Agree/disagree*
   Yes (he doesn't)./No (he does).
c. *Echo*
   John does./John doesn't.

Finally, some forms seem to have the characteristics of minor moods, but probably are not moods at all. Instead, they are *speech act idioms*— forms that are frozen for a particular use, and so are hardly productive at all (compare *kick the bucket* on its idiomatic and compositional readings). For instance:

(31)
a. How(s) about a beer? (suggestion)
b. Good morning/afternoon/evening. (greeting/leave-taking)
c. Where does he get off saying that? (complaint)

What are the semantics of these various forms? There are two semantic dimensions involved. First, these sentences are all used to perform different types of (communicative) speech acts. Second, connected to each type of speech act are certain satisfaction conditions. The first dimension is sometimes called the *force* of (the utterance of) the sentence; the second is called the *content*. For instance, *Snow is white* has the force of an assertion, and the content of that assertion is that snow is white; *Snow is WHITE?* has the force of a question, and the content (of a question whether) snow is white. Thus, these two sentences have the same content but different forces. *Snow is white* and *Grass is green*, on the other hand, have the same force, but different contents. They are both used to assert, but they are used to assert different things. In general, we would not say someone understood sentences in the various moods unless that person understood both the relevant force and content.

Force and content are intimately related. A sentence with assertive force represents the world to be a certain way, a way indicated by that content, and the sentence is true if the world is that way. These conditions are called the *truth conditions* of the sentences uttered. A true assertion fits the world, and we say it has a *word-to-world* direction of fit.

Imperatives, on the other hand, do not represent the world the way it *is*; instead, they represent the way the world is supposed to *become*. For instance, *Leave the room!* is used to direct the hearer to leave the room, and so comply with that request. We say that imperatives have a *world-to-word* direction of fit. Imperatives have *compliance conditions*. Likewise, interrogatives are used to ask questions, and so have *answerhood conditions*.

In our earlier discussion of the communicative potential of sentences we noted that there are some general correlations between certain types of sentence and certain ranges of speech acts. For instance, declaratives are conventionally used to make statements and other constatives (utterances that are assessable as true or false), whereas imperatives are conventionally used to direct the actions of others, and interrogatives are conventionally used to ask questions. Yet many sentences seem to have the form of a declarative, imperative, or interrogative, but do not have its traditionally defined use:

(32)
Declarative
I promise I'll be there. (promise)

(33)
Imperative
a. Have some more pâté. (offer)
b. Have a nice day! (wish)
c. Break a leg! (traditional Austrian ski leave-taking)
d. Help yourself. (permission)
e. Look out! (warning)
f. Be good! (exhortation)
g. Start, you pile of junk! (exhortation)

(34)
Interrogative
a. When was the battle of Waterloo? (exam question)
b. Which hand is it in? (child's game: request to guess)
c. What should I do now? (request for advice)
d. O Death, where is thy sting? (poetic)
e. Is the Pope Catholic? Can pigs fly? (rhetorical)
f. What should a good theory of mood consist in? (raising the question)

g. Now, how can I put this back together? (wondering aloud)
h. (You've won first prize) Have I? Great! (exclamation-question)
i. Why don't you go to blazes? (curse)

The problem facing existing semantic theories is to account for the force and content of sentences in the various moods in a way that meets four plausible conditions of adequacy:

1. The theory should account for semantic force and content compositionally.
2. It should assign sentences information that is specific enough to enable speakers to communicate literally and directly what we intuitively suppose them to communicate using these sentences.
3. Nevertheless, it must assign sentences information that is general enough that all sentences with the same mood can have the same force potential.
4. It must not postulate implausible or unintuitive ambiguities in sentences of the various moods.

At present no theory of mood and speech acts is able to meet all of these conditions.

Singular and General

The *singular* versus *general* distinction is drawn at two levels—the level of words and phrases ("terms") and the level of what is said (the "proposition expressed") in the utterance—and it signifies something importantly different in each case.

Singular versus General Terms

Denotations are things and events in the world (or groups of them); what words or phrases *denote* are the things and events that the words correctly indicate, name, or describe. For example:

(35)
a. *desk* denotes each and every desk
b. *I* denotes the speaker of this utterance of *I*
c. *the first person to walk on our moon* denotes Neil Armstrong
d. *Richard Nixon* denotes those named Richard Nixon (including the former president of the United States)

These examples reveal a distinction that is important for more advanced work in semantics, and for pragmatics: the distinction between *general terms* such as (35a) and *singular terms* such as (35b–d). General terms —such as common nouns, verbs, adjectives, and phrases that contain them—correctly describe potentially many different things or events. Thus, *red* applies to any red thing (and so denotes them all), and *kick* applies to any act of kicking (and so denotes them all). Singular terms— such as deictics, definite descriptions, and proper names—are used, on particular occasions, to refer to one single thing or collection of things. Thus, *she* is used on an occasion to refer to a contextually specified female, *the dents on the fender* is used on an occasion to refer to a certain collection of dents, *Paris* is used on an occasion to refer to a certain city. Even though there are many persons we can speak of as *she*, and many collections of dents that can be referred to as *the dents on the fender*, and even several different people named *Richard Nixon*, when we use these singular denoting expressions in normal discourse, we are still taken to have just one person or collection of dents in mind.

Singular versus General Propositions

At the level of what is said in uttering a sentence, the distinction between singular and general is a difference drawn *within* the use of singular terms. A *general proposition* is one that could be made true by different particular things. For instance, the property of being the first person to walk on our moon is one that Neil Armstrong in fact has; but had he gotten sick in flight, it might have been had by another member of the crew. So it is true that:

(36)
The first person to walk on our moon might not have been Neil Armstrong.

But in a *singular proposition* the particular referent is a constituent of the proposition expressed. For example, it could not be true that:

(37)
Neil Armstrong might not have been Neil Armstrong.

Notice that even though the first person to walk on our moon is in fact Neil Armstrong, what is said in these utterances is importantly different: (36) involves general descriptive information, (37) involves a single specific individual.

Deictics and Proper Names

So far we have reserved the word *refer* for what speakers do, and the term *denote* for what words or phrases do. Under this terminology, the object (or objects) referred to by a person is called the *referent*, and the object (or objects) semantically referred to by a word or phrase is called the *denotation* of that word or phrase. Two kinds of expression seem to be especially apt for referring to objects we then go on to speak about: so-called deictic expressions and proper names.

Deictics

The word *deictic* comes from the Greek word for pointing, and the idea is that deictic terms pick out their referents like pointers, that is, in virtue of some relation to the context of utterance. In this they are unlike names, which are given to persons, places, and things, and unlike definite descriptions (*the + noun*), which refer by describing their referents. There are two main subdivisions of deictic terms: indexicals and demonstratives.

The expressions in (38) illustrate the purest form of *indexicals*:

(38)
a. I
b. now
c. here

An indexical expression is one that has an indexical use, that is, a literal use to refer to something in virtue of its relation to the actual physical utterance. For example, the word *I* will be used to refer to Sam when Sam utters it, but will be used to refer to Jane when Jane utters it. And every moment the reference of *now* changes. Yet none of these words changes its *meaning* when it changes its reference. If it did, how would we know what it meant, and how could we understand what the speaker was trying to communicate? The semantics of indexicals, on their indexical use, seems to involve rules such as the following:

(39)
a. *I*: used to refer to the speaker of this utterance of *I*
b. *now*: used to refer to the time of this utterance of *now*
c. *here*: used to refer to the place of this utterance of *here*

In these cases the meaning of the indexical plus the context (speaker, time, place, etc.) determines the reference, and that reference alone is what the statement is about.

Some indexicals involve explicit descriptive information as well as indexicality:

(40)
a. yesterday
b. tomorrow

For instance, *yesterday* means something like "the day before the day of this utterance of *yesterday*," and *tomorrow* means something like "the day after the day of this utterance of *tomorrow*."

Demonstratives involve a supplementary gesture (demonstration) or special setting in order to determine reference. Typical examples include:

(41)
a. this, these
b. that, those
c. he, she, it
d. you

Using demonstratives successfully to refer involves more than just the aspects of the context of utterance required by indexicals (speaker, place, time, etc.). In uttering (42),

(42)
He/That man/You are the boss.

it is important to determine who the speaker has in mind or is demonstrating in order to determine who is being claimed to be the boss. Moreover, context can replace gesture in identifying the referent: if a certain man is running for the door, one can, without ambiguity and without gesture, utter (43):

(43)
Stop that man!

Deictic words can have other uses and need not always be used deictically:

(44)
a. *Here* we go again, another bumpy landing.
b. *You* never know./ *You* can't tell a book by its cover.
c. Come on *now*, you don't believe that!
d. I felt *this* crawly thing on my leg.
e. *Everyone* thinks *he* can do something well. (linked)

These uses are not deictic because they are not uses of the expression to refer to something via the actual production of the utterance, nor are they accompanied by a demonstration.

Proper Names

As Kaplan (1989) comments, proper names "may be a practical convenience in our mundane transactions, but they are a theoretician's nightmare. They are like bicycles. Everyone easily learns to ride, but no one can correctly explain how he does it." J. S. Mill (1843) first proposed the Referential Theory of proper names:

(RT)
Proper names are like labels that mean what they name.

As we noted earlier, Frege (1892) claimed that if this were true, then sentences with two names for the same thing should be no more informative than sentences with the same name repeated, but clearly they are indeed more informative:

(45)
a. Bob Dylan is Bob Dylan.
b. Bob Dylan is Robert Zimmerman.

We learn something from the second sentence that we do not learn from the first. But how could that be if names merely introduce their bearer into the proposition expressed? Furthermore, almost all names have many bearers, even historically prominent ones such as *Moses*, *Aristotle*, and *Napoleon*. To which Moses, Aristotle, or Napoleon is the speaker referring? Or consider the issue of *vacuous* names, names that do not name anything. For instance, *Vulcan* was once taken to name a planet just opposite the Sun from Earth (that's why we could never see it). People asked, "Is there life on Vulcan?" But such questions should be as meaningless on the Referential Theory as "Is there life on Csillam?" Neither word names anything; thus, neither makes any semantic contribution to the sentence it is a constituent of. The sentence should therefore fail to have a complete meaning—but intuitively it *does* have a meaning.

These problems led some theorists to propose a *Description Theory* of proper names:

(DT)
Proper names, semantically, are abbreviated definite descriptions of what they name.

This theory explains our ability to refer using names in terms of our ability to refer using definite descriptions. It solves some of the puzzles mentioned for proper names. For instance, sentence (45b) can be informative because the different names abbreviate different descriptions.

Description Theory has come under intense criticism (see Kripke 1980). One problem is how to choose the description we associate with a name. Does each person associate his or her own description? Then how is communication possible? Is there just one description for the whole language? Which one? What is "the" description for *Aristotle*? Furthermore, it seems that no description is necessary because Aristotle might not have been the most famous student of Plato, teacher of Alexander the Great, author of *Metaphysics*, and so on.

According to the Referential Theory of proper names, names contribute only their bearers to what is said, but that seems insufficient to many. According to the Description Theory of reference, names contribute some definite descriptive information to what is said, but no particular information seems motivated or necessary. What are we to think? A compromise has been defended. According to Bach (1987), names have only nominal descriptive content, yielding the Nominal Description Theory of names:

(NDT)
A proper name has the meaning "the bearer of *N*" (*Jane* means "the bearer of *Jane*").

Thus, *Aristotle* means just "the bearer of *Aristotle*." Unlike the Description Theory, this theory does not raise the problem of choosing one description in the language. It explains how sentences with different names for the same thing can be informative. It also explains how we can use a name to refer literally to things that bear that name. Still, it does not yet explain how we can use a name to refer to just one bearer of that name. But settling questions of use of language is the job of *pragmatics*—the study of the use of language in context.

Definite Descriptions: Referential and Attributive

Definite descriptions have the form *the F*, where *F* can be anything appropriate to a noun phrase:

(46)
a. the book on the table
b. the first man to walk on our moon
c. the dent on the fender

By far the most influential theory of the semantics of definite descriptions is Russell's (1905) *Theory of Descriptions*. Russell proposed that sentences containing definite descriptions are to be analyzed as *general* sentences. For instance, (47a) is schematized as (47b), and anything of this form is analyzed as (47c); thus, (47a) is analyzed as (47d):

(47)
a. *The first person to walk on our moon* is *right-handed*.
b. *The F* is *G*.
c. There is just one thing that is F and it is G.
d. There is just one thing that is the first person to walk on our moon and it is right-handed.

Referentiality and Attributivity

Some theorists have objected that Russell's account fails to reflect an important "ambiguity" in descriptions. Consider normal uses of the following sentences:

(48)
a. *The tallest man in the world* must be lonely.
b. *The woman drinking a martini* is a famous linguist.

The first description is naturally used to refer to whatever man is the tallest man, no matter who he may be, and to say of that man that he must be lonely. If there is no single such man, then the statement is false, just as Russell's theory predicts. But in the second case the description is being used to refer to a particular woman, and even if she has ginger ale in her martini glass, the speaker will be saying something true—if the woman is in fact a famous linguist. On the first, *attributive* use of the definite description (as Donnellan (1966) has called it), the role of the description is to set down conditions that determine the referent. In (47a), for example, what the speaker says (the proposition expressed) is completely general in that *whoever* is the first person to walk on our moon is claimed to be right-handed. Indeed, the following is true, since Neil Armstrong might have gotten sick during the flight and had to be replaced by a left-hander:

(49)
The first person to walk on our moon might not have been right-handed.

On the second, *referential* use of the definite description, the description is not essential to picking out the referent, and the important thing is the object or person itself, not how it happens to be described. The description is chosen mainly to help the hearer recognize what or who the speaker has in mind and is referring to, but any device might have done as well: in this case, *that guy over there, him, Neil Armstrong,* and so forth. What one says on the referential use of a description in (47a) is that a single individual—Neil Armstrong—is right-handed:

(50)
Neil Armstrong might not have been right-handed.

The difference between (49) and (50) is the difference between an attributive and a referential use of the definite description *the first person to walk on our moon,* and it is also the difference between a general and a singular proposition.

What Determines Reference?

At present there are two major competing theories of what determines reference: the previously mentioned *Description Theory* and the *Historical Chain Theory.* The basic idea behind the Description Theory, recall, is that an expression refers to its referent because it describes the referent, either uniquely or uniquely enough in the context that the referent can be identified. For instance, the phrase *the first person to walk on our moon* refers to Neil Armstrong by virtue of the fact that the description fits him uniquely. What about other kinds of singular terms, such as the pronouns *he, she, that,* or proper names such as *Charles de Gaulle, America, Fido*? These do not seem to describe anything uniquely, so how does the Description Theory handle them? It says that people using these expressions have *in mind* some description of the thing they intend to refer to. A speaker might say *Close the window,* intending the hearer to pick out the open window as the relevant window. If there are two open and closable windows, then the hearer can reasonably ask which one.

The Historical Chain Theory says, in effect, that an expression refers to its referent by virtue of there being a certain historical relation between the words uttered and some initial dubbing or christening of the object with that name. For instance, on this view, when a speaker uses the name *Charles de Gaulle,* it refers to the person christened by that name, provided there is a chain of uses linking the current speaker's reference with the original christening. This view proposes no unique description to pick out the proper referent; rather, it proposes that referential uses are handed down from speaker to speaker, generation to generation, from the original dubbing or christening. As Kripke (1980, 96), one of the originators of this theory, put it:

> An initial 'baptism' takes place. Here the object may be named by ostension, or the reference of the name may be fixed by a description. When the name is 'passed from link to link', the receiver of the name must, I think, intend when he learns it to use it with the same reference as the man from whom he heard it.

Both theories of reference have strengths and weaknesses. The Description Theory works best for definite descriptions, and perhaps also for indexicals, whereas the Historical Chain Theory works best for proper names, which can be given to persons, places, and things.

Natural Kind Terms, Concepts, and the Division of Linguistic Labor

Putnam (1975, 1988) notes that elm trees are not beech trees and that most speakers know that elm trees are not beech trees. They know that *elm* does not mean the same as *beech*. Yet many of these same speakers cannot tell an elm tree from a beech tree; the knowledge they have in their heads is not sufficient to differentiate these kinds of trees. The same goes for many other *natural kind terms*—common nouns that denote kinds of things in nature, such as aluminum versus molybdenum, gold versus pyrite ("fool's gold"), diamonds versus zircons. We are all confident that these pairs of words are not synonymous, yet many people's concepts contain no information sufficient to distinguish one member of these pairs from the other. Thus, it is clear that normal speakers do not have a determinate concept of the things these words denote. What then fixes their denotation? Putnam suggests that there is a "division of linguistic labor" in language: normal speakers depend on and defer to "experts" in these matters. If one wants to know whether a tree really is an elm or a beech, one calls in a tree specialist. To determine whether a metal is gold or pyrite, one calls in a metallurgist. And so on. These experts have procedures, based on scientific understanding, for determining the category of these samples. Reference with these terms is therefore in part a social phenomenon. In this respect natural kind terms are similar to proper names on the Historical Chain Theory.

Anaphora and Coreference

One phenomenon that has interested linguists and logicians for some time is the relation between pronouns (or pronoun phrases) and a set of "antecedent" noun phrases (see Chomsky 1981 and references cited there). Such relations, known as *anaphoric relations*, can be illustrated as follows:

(51)
Co-linked

a. Reflexives: John shaves himself.

b. Reciprocals: The men liked each other.

c. Idioms: I lost my way.

d. *Wh*-antecedents: Who thinks that he has been cheated?

e. Quantified antecedents: Everyone said that he was tired.

f. Epithets: He stepped on my foot, the creep!

(52)
Disjointly linked

a. Robert saw Michael.

b. He likes Sam.

c. John believes him to be rash.

d. John believes that she is rash.

e. Sam believes that Sam is rash.

In each case the second item is linked to the first item in some way that is relevant to how a speaker and a hearer communicate (there would be a misunderstanding if the speaker intended one linking, but the hearer understood another).

What sorts of linking are we dealing with here? This is a difficult question, and at present any answer would have to be considered tentative, but it seems likely that some of these links are syntactic or semantic, whereas others are pragmatic (see chapter 9 for further discussion). One way of getting a feel for which is which is to ask whether the sentence would be used nonliterally if the link were actually broken. For instance, in (52a) *Robert* and *Michael* are disjointly linked and thus are considered to be distinct in reference. But is this denotation or speaker reference? Well, imagine a person named both *Robert* and *Michael*, who sees himself in a mirror at an arcade. If a speaker were to say *No one saw Michael*, it would be possible to answer literally *That's not so, Robert saw Michael.* Although it can be true that Robert *is* Michael, it is still an odd way of *saying* what we want to say. Why is this so? Probably there is a pragmatic presumption to the effect that unless otherwise indicated, subject and object positions of verbs are to be taken as disjoint in speaker reference. This same principle would account for (52b). A case where the linkage is semantic, and so cannot be overridden pragmatically without being nonliteral, is given in (51a). Here the reflexive pronoun *himself* marks the fact that *him* has the same denotation as the subject of the verb, *John*. If *himself* is changed to *herself*, either one must assume that the speaker is speaking nonliterally in virtue of using the pronoun *her*, or one must assume that *John* is being used to refer to some female. These remarks extend to complex cases such as (52d). Notice that if the name *John* in (52d) is changed to one without gender associations, as in (53), one has to know whether that name is being used to refer to a male or a female in order to determine whether *she* is co-linked with it or not, preserving literality:

(53)
Lee believes that *she* is rash.

In some cases the linking is optional, in that there is another way of construing the sentence literally that does not involve co-linking or disjoint linking. For instance, (54a) and (54b) seem to admit the indicated interpretation:

(54)
a. John thinks that *he* has been cheated. (that man over there)
b. Everyone said that *he* was tired. (that man over there)

Next consider (52e), *Sam believes that Sam is rash*. This sentence has the natural interpretation that two Sams are involved. To account for this, we will first say that when a noun phrase (NP_1) c-commands (see chapter 5) a second noun phrase that is not a pronoun (NP_2), the two noun phrases will be subject to the following presumption:

(55)
Presumption of Disjoint Reference
If a speaker utters a sentence in which NP_1 c-commands NP_2, then the hearer may assume that the speaker intends to refer to two distinct persons (or things).

Given this presumption, sentence (52e) is understood by a hearer to involve references to two different people, unless the context of utterance provides evidence that overrides it. This can happen in cases such as the following:

(56)

Speaker A: Everybody believes Sam is rash.

Speaker B: But does Sam believe *himself* to be rash?

Speaker A: Sure, since *everybody* believes Sam is rash, Sam (pointing to
Sam) must believe that Sam is rash.

This example illustrates again the important difference between semantic constraints and these sorts of pragmatic constraints. If the speaker chooses to override semantic constraints, then he or she will be speaking nonliterally. However, if the pragmatic constraint is overridden, the speaker can still be speaking literally; however, the hearer will now have to figure out what the speaker is referring to, given that the most obvious presumption is not in effect. In this way, we can see that all levels of a grammar can be called upon to explain related aspects of language structure and communication.

Finally, notice that we can use more than one anaphoric device in a sentence and thereby affect its linking. For instance, (57) allows *he* either to be linked to *John* or to refer demonstratively to someone else:

(57)

John said that he was tired.

a. John said that he was tired.

b. John said that he was tired. (that man over there)

However, if we add *as for himself* to the sentence, we block the latter possibility:

(58)

John said that, as for himself, *he* was tired.

How can the phrase *as for himself* contribute to establishing the link between *John* and *he*? These are still matters of current research, but the above examples should serve to illustrate that anaphora is a topic rich in connections among morphology, syntax, semantics, and pragmatics.

Study Questions

1. Give two reasons for including a representation of semantic information in a grammar.

2. What is the Denotational Theory of meaning? Discuss at least one objection to it.

3. On the Denotational Theory of meaning, if an expression has a meaning, it has a denotation. Give at least one example of an expression for which this is false.

4. What is the Mentalist Theory of meaning? What two versions of it are discussed in the text? Discuss the problems with each version.

5. What is the Sense Theory of meaning? Why did Frege think referring expressions have a sense as well as a denotation?

6. What is the Use Theory of meaning? Discuss its major weakness.

7. What semantic properties and relations of words and phrases must a semantic theory account for?

8. What semantic properties and relations of sentences must a semantic theory account for?

9. Why should a semantic theory be finite?

10. What is it for a semantic theory to be compositional?

11. What is verbal mood?

12. What is sentential mood?

13. What are the major moods of English? Give examples.

14. What are some minor moods of English? Give examples.

15. How can we distinguish major and minor moods?

16. What two semantic dimensions are there to mood?

17. What force is standardly associated with each of the major moods?

18. What are some purported counterexamples to these forces?

19. What conditions must an adequate theory of mood meet?

20. At what two levels is the distinction between singular and general drawn?

21. What is the distinction between singular and general terms?

22. What is the distinction between singular and general propositions?

23. What is a "directly referring" expression?

24. What is the general difference in the way deictics, proper names, and descriptions work?

25. What are two major types of deictic terms?

26. What is the major difference between indexicals and demonstratives?

27. What two problems are there for the view that proper names are just labels for what they name?

28. What is the Description Theory of proper names and what problems does it have?

29. What is the Nominal Description Theory of proper names and which problems of the Description Theory does it avoid?

30. What is the distinction between referential and attributive uses of definite descriptions?

31. What are the two major theories about what determines reference?

32. What problems do natural kind terms pose for the Concept Theory of meaning? Discuss.

Exercises

1. Think of a reason, not given in the text, why semantics might be considered a part of a grammar of a language.

2. Can you think of a reason why semantics should not be included in a grammar of a language? Discuss.

3. Think of five words, write down what you think they mean, then look them up in a good dictionary. Is your idiolect at variance with what is recorded in the dictionary?

4. What is *ambiguity* on the Denotational Theory of meaning? How might this semantic property be a problem for the theory? (Hint: Think of the number of possible referents.)

5. What is *ambiguity* on the imagist version of the Mentalist Theory of meaning? How might this be a problem for the theory? Discuss.

6. Suppose someone said that a grammar of a language must describe what a *speaker* means in uttering an expression from the language, and that it must do this for every meaningful expression. What problems are there for this proposal?

7. How might the relevant meaning properties and relations schematized in (21a) be defined for *words*? (Hint: Some of these were defined in the text.)

8. Give examples of homophony for phrases and sentences.

9. Do words or phrases have communicative potential in the way sentences do? Give examples to support your claim.

10. Are there any semantic properties or relations distinctive to *phrases* versus words in the way there are semantic properties and relations distinctive to *sentences* versus words and phrases? If not, why not?

11. Consider the following sentences and state what the referring expression refers to:

a. *The chair you are sitting on* sells all over France for $200.
b. *Time magazine* was bought out by Hearst, so now *it* is good for wrapping your garbage.

12. How many different meanings can you see in the following sentences? (Hint: If you think of the possible meanings of the words in isolation, you may come up with more meanings.)

a. My dogs are very tired today.
b. The green giant is over the hill.
c. Time flies.

13. Interpret the following sentences. What principles do you think you used to interpret them?

a. Ralph may not be a communist, but he's at least a *pinko*.
b. He traded his hot car for a *cold* one.
c. John is studying sociology and other *soft* sciences.
d. Who *killed* Lake Erie?

14. Entailment relations (⇒) are transitive: If *being a cat ⇒ being a mammal*, and *being a mammal ⇒ being an animal*, then *being a cat ⇒ being an animal*. Now consider the "part of" relation. Is it transitive? Defend your answers. If entailment and "part of" are different in this way, why?

a. A second is part of a minute.
   A minute is part of an hour.
   An hour is part of a day.
   Is a second a part of an hour? Part of a day?
b. The toenail is part of the toe.
   The toe is part of the foot.
   The foot is part of the leg.
   Is the toenail part of the leg?
c. Henry's toe is part of Henry.
   Henry is part of the 23rd Battalion.
   Is Henry's toe part of the 23rd Battalion?

15. Analyze each of the humorous newspaper headlines cited in the text, saying what kind of ambiguity is responsible for the double meaning.

16. If a speaker were to utter the following sentences, what might that speaker commonly be taken as intending to communicate? Discuss.

a. Move and I'll shoot!
b. Move or I'll shoot!
c. You've been drinking again, have you!
d. You've been drinking again, haven't you?
e. Marry my daughter, will you!
f. Marry my daughter, will you?
g. What, me worry?

17. Some forms of words do not receive their proper interpretation in any regular way; they are in effect *idiomatic* and must be learned case by case. Here are some typical examples; try to think of more:

Declarative form
a. That just goes to show (you).

Imperative form
a. Take it easy! (meaning: Calm down!)
b. Buzz off! (meaning: Leave!)
c. (Go) Fly a kite! Take a hike! Get lost! (meaning: Leave!)
d. Never mind! Forget it! (meaning: Don't bother doing it!)

Interrogative form
a. Where does he get off saying that?
b. What do you say we leave?
c. How's things?
d. What's up?
e. What's the matter?
f. How about lunch?
g. How about that?

18. Try to paraphrase the declarative and interrogative examples in exercise 17. Why might these cases be so difficult?

19. Can the minor moods be analyzed as compositional compounds of the major moods?

20. Propose a structural analysis (syntactic, intonational) for each of the major and minor moods.

21. Are the purported counterexamples to the standard force of the moods genuine, or can they be explained away? Discuss each case.

22. Can a *singular* term be used to express a *general* proposition? Defend your answer with examples.

23. Can a *general* term be used to express a *singular* proposition? Defend your answer with examples.

24. What other indexical expressions are there besides the ones discussed in the text? (Hint: Think of pronouns in the accusative and possessive.)

25. Find nonindexical uses for all the indexical expressions in the text (except the ones given).

26. Formulate plausible semantic rules for more indexicals on the model of *I* and *now*. For example, try *you*, *this*, *yesterday*, and *here*.

27. How would you describe each of the nonindexical uses given in (44) as a rule? Is this semantic? Discuss.

28. What problems do the following sentences pose for the idea that proper names have no meaning? Discuss.
a. Vulcan exists.
b. Budapest exists.
c. Vulcan does not exist.
d. Budapest does not exist.

29. What are some further problems for the Nominal Description Theory of proper names? Discuss.

30. Consider the following grammatical and ungrammatical sentences containing proper names. Try to formulate a rule (or rules) describing their syntactic distribution. (Words set in capitals are pronounced with heavy stress.)
a.   Paris is beautiful.
b.   *The Paris is beautiful.
c.   THE Paris is beautiful.
d.   The Paris which is in France is beautiful.
e.   The French Paris is beautiful.
f.   Paris the capital is beautiful.
g.   *The Paris the capital is beautiful.
h.   *The Paris, which is in France, is beautiful.
i.   Paris, which is in France, is beautiful.
j.   I saw SOME Sam.
k.   *I saw some Sam.
l.   Sams are all quite similar, you know.
m.   A Sam is usually a funny guy.

31. How does the syntax of proper names differ from that of descriptions?

32. Is there any reason to think that the referential-attributive distinction is a case of semantic ambiguity? Discuss.

33. Is there any reason to think that the referential-attributive distinction is *not* a case of semantic ambiguity? Discuss.

34. What kind of theory of what determines reference do you think is best for deictics? Defend your answer.

35. Think of some natural kind terms that are not nouns (e.g., adjectives, verbs, adverbs).

Further Reading

General

For *article-length* introductions to problems of meaning and semantics, see Alston 1967; Higginbotham 1985; Ladusaw 1988; Chierchia and McConnell-Ginet 1990, chap. 1; Cann 1993, chap. 1; and Larson and Segal 1995, chap. 1. For *books* that survey semantics, see Kempson 1977; Dillon 1977; Fodor 1977; Lyons 1977; Dowty, Wall, and Peters 1981; Allan 1986; Fewley 1992; Saeed 1996; Cruse 1999; and Allan 2000.

Semantics as Part of a Grammar

Katz and Fodor 1963 sets out the original arguments for including a semantic component in a grammar. See also Higginbotham 1985 and Goddard 1998, chap. 1. For software that allows one to do semantics in conjunction with syntax, see Larson et al. 1997.

Theories of Meaning

Good surveys of theories of linguistic meaning can be found in Horwich 1998; Taylor 1998, chaps. 1–4; Goddard 1998, chaps. 2–3; and Lycan 2000, part II. See Katz 1972 for one way of developing the idea that sense is linguistic meaning. Miller 1998 is devoted to developing the Sense Theory of meaning from a historical perspective. Heim and Kratzer 1997 develops Sense Theory within Chomsky's syntactic framework. See Schiffer 1988 and Alston 2000 for discussion of the Use Theory of meaning.

Goals of a Semantic Theory

Marconi 1997 is a recent discussion of *word meaning*. For more on *semantic fields*, see Katz 1972, sec. 7.5; Miller and Johnson-Laird 1976, chaps. 4–5; Grandy 1987; Lehrer and Kittay 1992; and Goddard 1998, chaps. 4–10. Ruhl 1989 takes up issues of *ambiguity* and *polysemy*. Lehrer and Lehrer 1982 contains an interesting discussion of *antonymy*.

Special Topics

For *mood and meaning*, see Sadock and Zwicky 1985 and Harnish 1994b. Kaplan 1978 introduced the distinction between *singular* and *general propositions*. For *deixis*, Fillmore 1997 (originally distributed in 1977) is a linguistic classic, and Kaplan 1989 (originally distributed in 1977) is a philosophical classic. Good survey discussions with an emphasis on linguistics include Levinson 1983, chap. 2, and Anderson and Keenan 1985. For *proper names*, Kripke 1980 is now the classic semantics discussion; and see Sloat 1969 for some important syntactic properties of proper names. For *referential and attributive* uses of *definite descriptions*, the classics are Russell 1905 and Donnellan 1966. An excellent survey discussion is Neale 1990, and Ostertag 1998 is a recent anthology. Evans 1981 is a classic on *reference*. For *natural kind terms* and the *division of linguistic labor*, the classics are Putnam 1975 and Kripke 1980, lecture III. Schwartz 1977 is a useful anthology, and Platts 1997 is a useful recent discussion. Reinhart 1983 is a good early survey of issues in *anaphora* and *coreference*.

Reference Works
Lappin 1996 is a recent and useful survey of specific topics in semantics. Lamarque 1997 and Hale and Wright 1997 contain many entries relevant to semantics.

Journals
Journal of Semantics, Linguistics and Philosophy

Bibliography

Allan, K. 1986. *Linguistic meaning.* 2 vols. London: Routledge and Kegan Paul.

Allan, K. 2000. *Natural language semantics.* London: Routledge.

Alston, W. 1967. Meaning. In P. Edwards, ed., *The encyclopedia of philosophy*, vol. 5. New York: Macmillan.

Alston, W. 2000. *Illocutionary acts and sentence meaning.* Ithaca, N.Y.: Cornell University Press.

Anderson, A., and E. Keenan. 1985. Deixis. In T. Shopen, ed., *Language typology and syntactic description*, vol. 3. Cambridge: Cambridge University Press.

Bach, K. 1987. *Thought and reference.* Oxford: Oxford University Press.

Cann, R. 1993. *Formal semantics.* Cambridge: Cambridge University Press.

Chierchia, G., and S. McConnell-Ginet. 1990. *Meaning and grammar.* Cambridge, Mass.: MIT Press.

Chomsky, N. 1965. *Aspects of the theory of syntax.* Cambridge, Mass.: MIT Press.

Chomsky, N. 1981. *Lectures on government and binding.* Dordrecht: Foris.

Cruse, D. 1986. *Lexical semantics.* Cambridge: Cambridge University Press.

Cruse, D. 1999. *Meaning in language.* Oxford: Oxford University Press.

Devitt, M., and K. Sterelny. 1987. *Language and reality.* Cambridge, Mass.: MIT Press.

Dillon, G. 1977. *Introduction to contemporary linguistic semantics.* Englewood Cliffs, N.J.: Prentice-Hall.

Donnellan, K. 1966. Reference and definite descriptions. *Philosophical Review* 67, 237–242. Reprinted in Harnish 1994a.

Dowty, D., R. Wall, and S. Peters. 1981. *Introduction to Montague semantics.* Dordrecht: Reidel.

Evans, G. 1981. *Varieties of reference.* Oxford: Oxford University Press.

Fawley, W. 1992. *Linguistic semantics*. Hillsdale, N.J.: Lawrence Erlbaum Associates.

Fillmore, C. 1997. *Lectures on deixis*. Stanford, Calif.: CSLI Publications.

Fodor, J. D. 1977. *Semantics: Theories of meaning in generative grammar*. New York: Crowell.

Frege, G. 1892. On sense and reference. Reprinted in Harnish 1994a.

Glucksberg, S., and J. Danks. 1975. *Experimental psycholinguistics*. Hillsdale, N.J.: Lawrence Erlbaum Associates.

Goddard, C. 1998. *Semantic analysis*. Oxford: Oxford University Press.

Grandy, R. 1987. In defense of semantic fields. In Lepore 1987.

Grice, H. P. 1957. Meaning. *Philosophical Review* 66, 377–388. Reprinted in Harnish 1994a.

Grice, H. P. 1968. Utterer's meaning, sentence-meaning, and word-meaning. *Foundations of Language* 4, 225–242.

Grice, H. P. 1969. Utterer's meaning and intentions. *Philosophical Review* 78, 147–177.

Hale, B., and C. Wright, eds. 1997. *A companion to the philosophy of language*. Malden, Mass.: Blackwell.

Harnish, R. M., ed. 1994a. *Basic topics in the philosophy of language*. Englewood Cliffs, N.J.: Prentice-Hall.

Harnish, R. M. 1994b. Mood, meaning and speech acts. In S. L. Tsohatzidis, ed., *Foundations of speech act theory*. London: Routledge.

Heim, I., and A. Kratzer. 1997. *Semantics in generative grammar*. Malden, Mass.: Blackwell.

Higginbotham, J. 1985. On semantics. *Linguistic Inquiry* 16, 547–593.

Horwich, P. 1998. *Meaning*. Oxford: Oxford University Press.

Jackendoff, R. 1972. *Semantic interpretation in generative grammar*. Cambridge, Mass.: MIT Press.

Jackendoff, R. 1983. *Semantics and cognition*. Cambridge, Mass.: MIT Press.

Jespersen, O. 1924. *The philosophy of grammar*. London: Allen and Unwin.

Kaplan, D. 1978. Dthat. In P. Cole, ed., *Syntax and semantics*, vol. 9. New York: Academic Press.

Kaplan, D. 1989. Demonstratives. In J. Almog, J. Perry, and H. Wettstein, eds., *Themes from Kaplan*. New York: Oxford University Press. Selections reprinted in Harnish 1994a.

Katz, J. 1972. *Semantic theory*. New York: Harper and Row.

Katz, J. 1980. *Propositional structure and illocutionary force*. Cambridge, Mass.: Harvard University Press.

Katz, J., and J. Fodor. 1963. The structure of a semantic theory. *Language* 39, 170–210.

Kempson, R. 1977. *Semantic theory*. Cambridge: Cambridge University Press.

Kripke, S. 1977. Speaker's reference and semantic reference. Reprinted in P. French et al., eds., *Contemporary perspectives in the philosophy of language*. Minneapolis: University of Minnesota Press (1979).

Kripke, S. 1980. *Naming and necessity*. Cambridge, Mass.: Harvard University Press. Selections reprinted in Harnish 1994a.

Ladusaw, W. 1988. Semantic theory. In Newmeyer 1988.

Lamarque, P., ed. 1997. *Concise encyclopedia of philosophy of language*. Amsterdam: Elsevier/Pergamon.

Lappin S., ed. 1996. *The handbook of contemporary semantic theory*. Malden, Mass.: Blackwell.

Larson, R., and G. Segal. 1995. *Knowledge of meaning: An introduction to semantics*. Cambridge, Mass.: MIT Press.

Larson, R., D. Warren, J. Freire de Lima e Silva, O. Gomez, and K. Sagonas. 1997. *Semantica*. Cambridge, Mass.: MIT Press.

Lehrer, A. 1974. *Semantic fields and lexical structure*. Amsterdam: North-Holland.

Lehrer, A., and E. Kittay, eds. 1992. *Frames, fields and contrasts*. Hillsdale, N.J.: Lawrence Erlbaum Associates.

Lehrer, K., and A. Lehrer, eds. 1970. *Theory of meaning*. Englewood Cliffs, N.J.: Prentice-Hall.

Lehrer, K., and A. Lehrer. 1982. Antonymy. *Linguistics and Philosophy* 5, 483–501.

Lepore, E., ed. 1987. *New directions in semantics*. New York: Academic Press.

Levinson, S. 1983. *Pragmatics*. Cambridge: Cambridge University Press.

Ludlow, P., ed. 1997. *Readings in the philosophy of language*. Cambridge, Mass.: MIT Press.

Lycan, W. 2000. *Philosophy of language: A contemporary introduction*. New York: Routledge.

Lyons, J. 1977. *Semantics*. 2 vols. Cambridge: Cambridge University Press.

Marconi, D. 1997. *Lexical competence*. Cambridge, Mass.: MIT Press.

Mill, J. S. 1843. *A system of logic*. London.

Miller, A. 1998. *Philosophy of language*. London: McGill–Queen's University Press.

Miller, G., and P. Johnson-Laird. 1976. *Language and perception*. Cambridge, Mass.: Harvard University Press.

Neale, S. 1990. *Descriptions*. Cambridge, Mass.: MIT Press.

Newmeyer, F., ed. 1988. *Linguistics: The Cambridge survey*, vol. 1. Cambridge: Cambridge University Press.

Ostertag, G., ed. 1998. *Definite descriptions: A reader*. Cambridge, Mass.: MIT Press.

Platts, M. 1997. *Ways of meaning*. 2nd ed. Cambridge, Mass.: MIT Press.

Putnam, H. 1975. The meaning of "meaning." In K. Gunderson, ed., *Language, mind and knowledge*. Minneapolis: University of Minnesota Press. Reprinted in Harnish 1994a.

Putnam H. 1988. *Representation and reality*. Cambridge, Mass.: MIT Press.

Reinhart, T. 1983. *Anaphora and semantic interpretation*. London: Croom Helm.

Ruhl, C. 1989. *On monosemy: A study of linguistic semantics*. Albany, N.Y.: State University of New York Press.

Russell, B. 1905. On denoting. *Mind* 14, 479–493. Reprinted in Harnish 1994a.

Sadock, J., and A. Zwicky. 1985. Speech act distinctions in syntax. In T. Shopen, ed., *Language typology and syntactic description*, vol. 1. Cambridge: Cambridge University Press.

Saeed, J. 1996. *Semantics*. Malden, Mass.: Blackwell.

Schiffer, S. 1987. *Remnants of meaning*. Cambridge, Mass.: MIT Press.

Schiffer, S. 1988. *Meaning*. 2nd ed. Oxford: Oxford University Press.

Schwartz, S., ed. 1977. *Naming, necessity and natural kinds*. Ithaca, N.Y.: Cornell University Press.

Sloat, C. 1969. Proper nouns in English. *Language* 45, 26–30.

Taylor, K. 1998. *Truth and meaning: An introduction to the philosophy of language*. Cambridge, Mass.: MIT Press.

Wittgenstein, L. 1958. *The blue and the brown books*. (Written in 1933.) Oxford: Blackwell.

Chapter 7
Language Variation

7.1 LANGUAGE STYLES AND LANGUAGE DIALECTS

Consider the following sentence (from Dillard 1972):

(1)
You makin' sense, but you don' be makin' sense!

Speakers of the standard dialect of English are likely to conclude that
this sentence is ungrammatical. The first clause lacks a (finite) verb (such
as *are*) that the standard dialect requires, and the sequence *do* + *be*
in the second clause is a combination that the standard dialect prohibits.
Speakers of the standard dialect might also question the logic of the sentence (and hence, as has unfortunately happened, the logical abilities of
its utterer). After all, the two clauses appear to contradict each other.
However, we will see in this chapter that the sentence is grammatical in
its dialect (a Washington, D.C., dialect of Inner-City English) and is both
logical and sophisticated. It represents one of the many variations in form
that English can take.

No human language is fixed, uniform, or unvarying; all languages show
internal variation. Actual usage varies from group to group, and speaker
to speaker, in terms of the pronunciation of a language, the choice of words
and the meaning of those words, and even the use of syntactic constructions. To take a well-known example, the speech of Americans is noticeably different from the speech of the British, and the speech of these two
groups in turn is distinct from the speech of Australians. When groups of
speakers differ noticeably in their language, they are often said to speak
different *dialects* of the language.

Dialectal Variation

It is notoriously difficult, however, to define precisely what a dialect is, and in fact the term has come to be used in various ways. The classic example of a dialect is the *regional* dialect: the distinct form of a language spoken in a certain geographical area. For example, we might speak of Ozark dialects or Appalachian dialects, on the grounds that inhabitants of these regions have certain distinct linguistic features that differentiate them from speakers of other forms of English. We can also speak of a *social* dialect: the distinct form of a language spoken by members of a specific socioeconomic class, such as the working-class dialects in England or the ghetto languages in the United States (to which we will return). In addition, certain *ethnic* dialects can be distinguished, such as the form of English sometimes referred to as Yiddish English, historically associated with speakers of Eastern European Jewish ancestry.

It is important to note that dialects are never purely regional, or purely social, or purely ethnic. For example, the distinctive Ozark and Appalachian dialects are not merely dialects spoken by any of the inhabitants. As we will see, regional, social, and ethnic factors combine and intersect in various ways in the identification of dialects.

In popular usage the term *dialect* refers to a form of a language that is regarded as "substandard," "incorrect," or "corrupt," as opposed to the "standard," "correct," or "pure" form of a language. In sharp contrast, the term *dialect*, as a technical term in linguistics, carries no such value judgment and simply refers to a distinct form of a language. Thus, for example, linguists refer to so-called Standard English as a dialect of English, which, from a linguistic point of view, is no more "correct" than any other form of English. From this point of view, the monarchs of England and teenagers in Los Angeles and New York all speak dialects of English.

Although dialects are often said to be regional, social, or ethnic, linguists also use the term *dialect* to refer to language variations that cannot be tied to any geographical area, social class, or ethnic group. Rather, this use of *dialect* simply indicates that speakers show some variation in the way they use elements of the language. For example, some speakers of English are perfectly comfortable using the word *anymore* in sentences such as the following:

(2)
Tools are expensive *anymore*.

Here, *anymore* means roughly the same as *nowadays* or *lately*. Other speakers of English can use *anymore* only if there is a negative element, such as *not*, in the sentence:

(3)
Tools are *not* cheap *anymore*.

As far as we can tell, this difference between speakers cannot be linked to a particular region of the country or to a particular social class or ethnic group.

Language variation does not end with dialects. Each recognizable dialect of a language is itself subject to considerable internal variation: no two speakers of a language, even if they are speakers of the same dialect, produce and use their language in exactly the same way. We are able to recognize different individuals by their distinct speech and language patterns; indeed, a person's language is one of the most fundamental features of self-identity. The form of a language spoken by a single individual is referred to as an *idiolect*, and every speaker of a language has a distinct idiolect.

Once we realize that variation in language is pervasive, it becomes apparent that there is no such thing as a single language used at all times by all speakers. There is no such thing as a single English language; rather, there are many English languages (dialects and idiolects) depending on who is using the language and what the context of use is. Consider the well-known phenomenon of variation in vocabulary words that exists among speakers of English:

(4)
a. *Dope* means "cola" in some parts of the South.
b. *Pocketbook* means "purse" in Boston and in parts of the South.
c. *Fetch up* means "raise" (children) in the South.
d. *Pavement* means "sidewalk" in eastern Pennsylvania and in England.
e. *Happygrass* means "grasshopper" in eastern Virginia.
f. *Bubbler* means "water fountain" in Wisconsin.
g. *Knock up* means "to wake someone up by knocking" in England.
h. *Bonnet* means "hood" (of a car) in England.
i. *Fag* means "cigarette" in England.

As the last three examples indicate, vocabulary differences between American and British English are common and often amusing. Indeed, at one time the Bell Telephone System published a pamphlet entitled

"Getting around the USA: Travel Tips for the British Visitor," which contains a section entitled "How to Say It." This section notes the following correspondences:

(5)

British	American
car park	parking lot
coach	bus
garage	service station
lay by	rest area
lift	elevator
lorry	truck
petrol	gasoline
underground (or tube)	subway
call box	telephone booth
telephonist	switchboard operator
gin and French	dry martini
minerals	soft drinks
suspenders	garters
vest	undershirt

These examples are typical of the sort of dialectal variation found in the vocabulary of British and American English. (For additional examples, see the exercise entitled "British and American English" in *A Linguistics Workbook* (Farmer and Demers 2001).)

Mutual Intelligibility

Given the existence of dialectal and idiolectal variation, what allows us to refer to something called English, as if it were a single, monolithic language? A standard answer to this question rests on the notion of *mutual intelligibility*. That is, even though native speakers of English vary in their use of the language, their various languages are similar enough in pronunciation, vocabulary, and grammar to permit mutual intelligibility. A New Yorker, a Texan, and a Californian may recognize differences in each other's language, but they can understand each other (despite all the jokes to the contrary) and they recognize each other as speaking the "same language." Hence, speaking the "same language" does not depend on two speakers speaking identical languages, but only very similar languages.

In discussing the notion of mutual intelligibility, it is interesting to note, by way of contrast, cases that might be called *one-way intelligibility*, involving speakers of different, but historically related, languages. For example, speakers of Brazilian Portuguese who do not know Spanish can often understand the forms of Spanish spoken in neighboring countries. The analogous Spanish speakers, however, find Portuguese largely unintelligible. A similar situation holds between Danish and Swedish: speakers of Danish can (more or less) comprehend Swedish, but the reverse situation is much less common. Even if one group of speakers can understand another group, they cannot be said to speak the same language unless the second group also understands the first, and thus the notion of *mutual* intelligibility is crucial in specifying when two languages are the "same" language.

Although the notion of mutual intelligibility seems like a reasonable criterion in defining dialects, the situation can be considerably complicated by social and political factors. In China, for example, a northern Chinese speaker of the Beijing dialect (also known as Mandarin) cannot understand the speech of a southern Chinese speaker of Cantonese, and vice versa. For this reason, a linguist might well label Mandarin and Cantonese as two distinct "languages." Nevertheless, in traditional studies of the Chinese language, both Mandarin and Cantonese are regarded as "dialects" of Chinese, given that they are historically related (i.e., they may have been offshoots of several closely related dialects that existed earlier in the history of the Chinese language). Moreover, both Mandarin and Cantonese are spoken in the same nation (they are not languages of two different countries with different governments), and speakers of both "dialects" can use the written language (in the form of Chinese characters) as a common language of communication. For such reasons, the tendency has persisted to use the term *dialect* to refer to various mutually unintelligible forms of the Chinese language.

Historical and political factors can also give rise to the opposite situation, where two mutually intelligible forms are considered not dialects of the same language but two distinct languages. For example, Tohono O'odham (formerly Papago) and Akimel O'odham (formerly Pima) are two Native American languages spoken by members of tribal groups living in the state of Arizona and in northern Mexico. In fact, Tohono O'odham and Akimel O'odham are mutually intelligible and are extremely close phonologically and grammatically, with only minor linguistic differences in pronunciation and syntax (the differences between them being less radical than the differences between American and British English). For this reason, a linguist could well consider Tohono O'odham and Akimel O'odham to be two dialects of the same language. Nevertheless, for historical and political reasons the two tribal groups consider themselves distinct political entities, and they consider their languages to be distinct languages rather than dialectal variations of a single language. Another example is provided by "Dutch" and "Flemish." Speakers of "Dutch" understand speakers of "Flemish" and vice versa. However, there is an important political distinction between the two: "Dutch" is spoken in the Netherlands and "Flemish" is spoken in Belgium.

Having examined some of the complications involved in the term *dialect*, how can we define it? No satisfactory definition of *dialect* has yet been proposed, but for our purposes we will ignore complications and settle on a very general one. A dialect is simply a distinct form of a language, possibly associated with a recognizable regional, social, or ethnic group, differentiated from other forms of the language by specific linguistic features (e.g., pronunciation, or vocabulary, or grammar, or any combination of these). This rough definition is intended to do no more than capture a certain intuitive idea of the term *dialect*, but one that seems useful. In any event, it must be kept in mind that from a linguistic point of view *dialect* is a theoretical concept. In reality, variation in language is so pervasive that each language is actually a continuum of languages from speaker to speaker, and from group to group, and no absolute lines can be drawn between different forms of a language.

Dialects and the Interplay of Regional and Social Factors: New York City /ɹ/

As noted, the classic example of a dialect is the regional dialect, the assumption being that speakers of the dialect form a coherent speech community living in relative isolation from speakers outside the community. Such relative isolation between geographical areas is becoming increasingly rare, and in the United States the population as a whole is so geographically and socially mobile that it is becoming increasingly difficult to speak of regional dialects in any pure sense. Especially in large urban areas, a particular linguistic feature of a regional dialect might well be influenced by social factors.

An interesting example of the effect of "social prestige" on a regional dialect is found in the pronunciation of /ɹ/ in New York City speech. The so-called *r-less* dialect of New York City is so well known that it is often the subject of humor, especially on the part of the New Yorkers who themselves speak it. It is commonly thought that speakers of the dialect completely lack /ɹ/ in words such as *car*, *card*, *four*, *fourth*, and so on, but this is a misconception, as an intriguing study by the sociolinguist William Labov (1972) reveals.

Labov began with the hypothesis that New York City speakers vary in their pronunciation of /ɹ/ according to their social status. Labov interviewed salespeople at several New York City department stores that differed in price range and social prestige. Assuming that salespeople tend to "borrow prestige" from their customers, Labov predicted that the social stratification of customers at different department stores would be mirrored in a similar stratification of salespeople. These assumptions led him to hypothesize that "salespeople in the highest-ranked store will have the highest values of (r) [/ɹ/]; those in the middle-ranked store will have intermediate values of (r) [/ɹ/]; and those in the lowest-ranked store will show the lowest value" (1972, 45).

Labov chose three stores: Saks Fifth Avenue (high prestige), Macy's (middle level), and S. Klein (low prestige). He interviewed salespeople by asking them a question that would elicit the answer *fourth floor*.

The interviewer approached the informant in the role of a customer asking for directions to a particular department. The department was one which was located on the fourth floor. When the interviewer asked, "Excuse me, where are the women's shoes?" the answer would normally be, "Fourth floor."

The interviewer then leaned forward and said, "Excuse me?" He would usually then obtain another utterance, "*Fourth floor*," spoken in careful style under emphatic stress. (1972, 49)

The phrase *fourth floor* has two instances of /ɹ/, both of which are subject to variation in the pronunciation of New York City speakers, and Labov was able to study both casual and careful pronunciations of this phrase.

The result turned out to correlate in an interesting way with the hypothesis. Fox example, Labov found that at Saks, 30 percent of the salespeople interviewed always pronounced both /ɹ/'s in the test phrase; at Macy's 20 percent did so; and at S. Klein only 4 percent did. In addition, Labov found that 32 percent of the interviewed salespeople at Saks had variable pronunciation of /ɹ/ (sometimes /ɹ/ was pronounced and sometimes not, depending on context); at Macy's 31 percent of the interviewees had variable pronunciation; and at S. Klein only 17 percent did. These overall results do suggest that pronunciation of /ɹ/ in New York City is correlated, at least loosely, with social stratification of the speakers.

What about the differences in pronunciation between the casual and the emphatic styles? It turns out that in the casual response the /ɹ/ of *floor* was pronounced by 63 percent of the salespeople at Saks, 44 percent at Macy's, and only 8 percent at S. Klein. In contrast, in the careful, emphatic response the /ɹ/ of *floor* was pronounced by 64 percent at Saks, 61 percent at Macy's (note the jump from 44 percent), and 18 percent at S. Klein. In other words, at Saks there was very little difference between casual and careful pronunciations, whereas at Macy's and S. Klein the difference between these styles was significantly larger. This suggests that speakers at the middle and lower levels of the New York City social scale are perfectly aware that a final /ɹ/ occurs in words such as *floor*. Even though they omit this /ɹ/ in casual pronunciation, it reappears in careful speech.

In emphatic pronunciation of the final (r) [/ɹ/], Macy's employees come very close to the mark set by Saks. It would seem that *r*-pronunciation is the norm at which a majority of Macy employees aim, yet not the one they use most often. In Saks, we see a shift between casual and emphatic pronunciation, but it is much less marked. (1972, 51–52)

As we will see in section 7.2, the difference between casual and careful language styles is important in syntactic variation as well.

Hypercorrection

In connection with the pronunciation of New York City /ɹ/, it is interesting to note that some New York City speakers insert an *r*-sound in words where it does not actually occur in spelling. One can hear *Cuba* pronounced [kjubɚ], *saw* pronounced [sɔɹ], *idea* pronounced [aɪdiɚ], and so on. It seems that the very speakers who drop /ɹ/ in some words and positions will insert an *r*-sound in other words and positions. The cause of this phenomenon is sometimes thought to be *hypercorrection* (i.e., overcorrection): speakers who have been persuaded that it is "incorrect" to drop /ɹ/ will overcompensate or overcorrect for this by inserting an *r*-sound where it does not actually occur in spelling. (Syntactic hypercorrection also occurs—for example, when speakers say *between you and I* instead of *between you and me* on the grounds that *I* is more "correct" and "cultured" than *me*.)

However, we might question whether, for given speakers, inserting an *r*-sound involves only hypercorrection. For one thing, even those speakers who insert an *r*-sound do not always pronounce words such as *idea* with a final *r*-sound: the insertion of an *r*-sound in such words happens only when the next word begins with a vowel (hence, we might hear phrases such as *the idear I heard about* but not **the idear John told me about*). The insertion of an *r*-sound is thus at least partially governed by a phonological principle. In the second place, hypercorrection often involves imitating what is thought to be prestige language. For example, a hypercorrect phrase such as *It is I* is thought to sound more prestigious than *It's me*, even though there is nothing grammatically incorrect about the latter phrase. Returning to words such as *idear*, speakers who insert an *r*-sound in *idear* may not think that such a pronunciation is prestigious. Since insertion of /ɹ/ or /ɚ/ is governed partially by a phonological principle, and since it may not involve imitation of prestige language, for some speakers this insertion of /ɹ/ or /ɚ/ is not strictly a case of hypercorrection.

Labov's study illustrates once again that there is often no absolute or simple distinction between one dialect and another: we cannot simply say that the New York City dialect is *r*-less. Rather, the pronunciation of *r*-sounds in that dialect is variable, and this variation seems to be correlated both with social factors and with context (casual or careful). Thus, just as no language can be said to be unvarying or fixed, so no dialect of a language can be said to be unvarying or fixed either. Finally, not even the language of an individual speaker is unvarying: an individual New Yorker may well show variation in pronouncing *r*-sounds.

"Standard" versus "Nonstandard" Language

A pervasive phenomenon of societies in the contemporary world is the designation of one dialect of a language as the "standard," "correct," or "pure" form of the language. In the contemporary United States, Standard American English (or SAE, for short) is a form of the language used in news programs in the national media (often referred to as "Network English"); it is the language of legal and governmental functions; and it is the language used in the schools as a vehicle for education.

As noted earlier, in linguistic terms no one dialect of a language is any more correct, any better, or any more logical than any other dialect of the language: all dialects are equally effective forms of language, in that any idea or desire that can be expressed in one dialect can be expressed just as easily in any other dialect. This idea that SAE is the correct form of the language is a social attitude—more precisely, a language prejudice —that is just as irrational as social prejudices involving race or gender. In the United States the so-called standard language is perhaps most widely identified with the educated white middle class; hence, a good case can be made that the reverence for the standard language in our schools and official functions is a reflection of the far more general bias in the country toward considering the white middle-class value system the correct or best value system. It is important to realize at the outset that labeling one particular dialect as standard and others as inferior reflects a sociopolitical judgment, not a linguistic judgment. Indeed, in countries throughout the world, the standard national languages is the dialect of the subculture with the most prestige and power.

Inner-City English and the Verb *Be*

A well-known example of a social dialect that has been labeled as nonstandard is Inner-City English. Essentially, the term *Inner-City English* (ICE) refers to an informal style of language used by residents of low-income ghettos in large urban areas of the United States. Although ICE is used by certain Latinos and Whites who live in these ghettos, it is stereotypically associated with African American residents the ghettos. ICE is sometimes referred to as *Black English*, but this term is misleading in that it suggests that all African Americans speak the same dialect and use it all the time. Both impressions are incorrect. African Americans show as much linguistic variation as any other social group in the nation; language is not determined by race. Further, even those who can be said to use ICE do not necessarily use this dialect at all times.

ICE has attracted a good deal of attention from linguists, and recently the Ebonics controversy has revived that interest (see "Further Reading" and references). Linguists' investigations have shown quite clearly that ICE is every bit as rule-governed and as logical as SAE. In a series of important studies Labov (1969a,b, 1973) has demonstrated that there are several important and highly systematic relationships between ICE and SAE. To take what is perhaps the best-known example, consider the frequently noted fact that in ICE present tense forms of the verb *to be* are often dropped in casual speech (examples taken from Labov 1969a):

(6)

a. She the first one started us off.

b. He fast in everything he do.

c. I know, but he wild, though.

d. You out the game.

e. We on tape.

f. But everybody not black.

g. They not caught.

h. Boot always comin' over my house to eat.

i. He gon' try get up.

The omission of the verb *to be* in ICE can easily be misinterpreted by those untrained in linguistics as evidence that ICE is a kind of defective dialect that violates rules of grammar or, worse yet, has no rules of grammar. As Labov (1969b) notes, this has even led to the mistaken view on the part of certain educators and psychologists that African American children entering school have a language deficit and are culturally deprived. Even though the omission of forms of the verb *to be* may at first appear to make ICE quite distinct from SAE, Labov (1969b, 203) points out that

[t]he deletion of the *is* or *are* in [ICE] is not the result of erratic or illogical behavior: it follows the same regular rules as standard English contraction. Wherever standard English can contract, [ICE can] use either the contracted form or (more commonly) the deleted zero form. Thus, *They mine* corresponds to standard *They're mine*, not to the full form *They are mine*. On the other hand, no such deletion is possible in positions where standard English cannot contract: just as one cannot say *That's what they're* in standard English, *That's what they* is equally impossible in the vernacular we are considering.

In the examples already cited, the correspondence between SAE and ICE is as follows:

(7)

SAE: Contraction	*ICE: Deletion*
She's the first one ...	She the first one ...
He's fast ...	He fast ...
You're out ...	You out ...
They're not caught ...	They not caught ...

Both dialects have contraction, but only ICE has the further option of deleting a contractible form of *to be*.

What appears at first to be a significant difference between SAE and ICE actually turns out to be rather minor. Indeed, in both dialects the same general phenomenon is taking place: the verb *to be* (as well as other auxiliary verbs) becomes *reduced* in casual speech when it is unstressed. One dialect reflects the reduction process by contraction alone, the other dialect by contraction or deletion. As we will see, in fact, the deletion of the verb *to be* (and other auxiliary verbs) is by no means limited to ICE but happens quite generally in the informal style in all dialects of American English.

Another grammatical feature of ICE that has been noted in linguistic studies is a certain use of the verb *to be* illustrated by examples such as the following (taken from Fasold 1972, chap. 4):

(8)

a. I get a ball and then some children *be* on one team and some *be* on another team.

b. Christmas Day, well, everybody *be* so choked up over gifts and everything, they don't *be* too hungry anyway.

c. My father *be* the last one to open his presents.

d. Yes, there always *be* fights.

e. On Saturdays, I like to watch cartoons, but I *be* out working.

This use of *be* has been termed *invariant be* (since it does not vary either to reflect past or present tense, or to agree with the subject), and it indicates a habitual and repeatable action, state, or event. Thus, invariant *be* is typically used in general descriptions (as in (8a), a description of a game) and to indicate customary or typical states of affairs. Given this, note that it is unacceptable in ICE to say **He be workin' right now*, since the time expression *right now* does not have a habitual interpretation but instead refers to the specific present. In addition, whereas one can say *He my brother* (SAE *He's my brother*), it is unacceptable to say *He be my brother, since the sibling relation is permanent; that is, it is not repeatable in the way that invariant *be* requires. The sentence *You makin' sense, but you don' be makin' sense* would seem very odd if one did not understand the use of invariant *be*. Dillard (1972, 46) suggests that one could, in uttering such a sentence, mean "You've blundered into making an intelligent statement for once" or "That's a bright remark—but it's not the usual thing for you." The use of invariant *be* has been cited as a grammatical feature unique to ICE, representing what seems to be a genuine difference between ICE and other American English dialects.

In discussions of ICE, there has been an all too unfortunate tendency to compare ICE to SAE without paying sufficient attention to the level of formality of the languages being compared. That is, ICE is an informal-style language used in the ghetto by ghetto residents (within the culture of the ghetto there are more formal styles of language as well: for example, African American religious preaching styles—see Smitherman 1977). ICE has been compared with an "official" language of news broadcasts, governmental functions, and school settings. It is no surprise that significant differences have been found. However, when we examine informal styles of American English, we find similar features across all dialects, and it turns out that certain features of ICE are simply part of the general linguistic features of informal English. It is crucial to distinguish between formal and informal styles of language before one can compare dialects in an accurate way.

Formal and Informal Language Styles

Without being aware of it, each speaker of any language has mastered a number of language styles. To illustrate, in a formal setting someone might offer coffee to a guest by saying *May I offer you some coffee?* or perhaps *Would you care for some coffee?* In an informal setting the same speaker might well say *Want some coffee?* or even *Coffee?* This shift in styles is completely unconscious and automatic; indeed, it takes some concentration and hard introspection to realize that we each use a formal and an informal style on different occasions.

The clearest cases of formal speech occur in social contexts that are formal, serious, often official in some sense, in which speakers feel they must watch their language and in which *manner* of saying something is regarded as socially important. These contexts would include a formal job interview, meeting an important person, and standing before a court of law. Informal speech in our use of that term occurs in casual, relaxed social settings in which speech is spontaneous, rapid, and uncensored by the speaker. Social settings for this style of speech would include chatting with close friends and interacting in an intimate or family environment or in similar relaxed settings.

Some speakers of English, notably self-styled educated speakers, often equate the formal language style with the so-called standard language; the informal style, if discussed at all, is dubbed a form of sloppy speech or even slang, especially in language classes in public schools. But on closer investigation of the actual details of informal language, it turns out that the informal style, far from being merely a sloppy form of language, is governed by rules every bit as precise, logical, and rigorous as the rules governing formal language. (Of course, the informal style also has idiosyncrasies and irregularities—but, then, the formal style does too.) In section 7.2 we will concentrate on some of the rules of the informal style because a detailed study of the syntactic differences between formal and informal language styles reveals a number of important ideas about language variation in general, and about the question of standard versus nonstandard language in particular.

7.2 SOME RULES OF THE GRAMMAR OF INFORMAL STYLE IN ENGLISH

A well-known difference between formal and informal language styles in English (and indeed in many other languages) is that the informal style has a greater amount of abbreviation, shortening, contraction, and deletion. Compare the formal *Would you care for some coffee?* with the informal *Want some coffee?* The formal style is often redundant and verbose, whereas the informal style is brief, to the point, and grammatically streamlined. In this section we will concentrate on two important grammatical features of the informal style, (1) the dropping of the subject of the sentence and (2) the dropping of the auxiliary verb, these being two central features of the *abbreviated* style.

The abbreviated style we will describe here is based on the language of the authors of this book, and all grammatical judgments will be based on our own speech. We have tested and confirmed our judgments with those of numerous other speakers, however. Furthermore, it seems clear that the abbreviation processes we describe are quite general within American English. You may find that your own judgments differ from ours at certain points, and this will be entirely natural; indeed, there could be no better illustration of the topic of this chapter. The important point is that every speaker of English has an abbreviated style in casual speech. Consequently, you will be able to judge for yourself how accurate we are in describing the abbreviated style in general.

Tag-Controlled Deletion

To begin, let us consider sentences that end in tag questions:

(9)

a. You have been sneaking to the movies again, *haven't you?*

b. You are getting pretty excited, *aren't you?*

c. You are not ready to swim fifty laps, *are you?*

d. He is failing his courses, *isn't he?*

e. You will steal my money, *will you!*

As we saw in chapter 5, tag questions—*haven't you*, *are you*, and so on—reflect at least two important properties of a sentence: (1) the tag contains the auxiliary verb found in the main sentence, or (in the case of *do*) the auxiliary appropriate to the main sentence, and (2) the pronoun in the tag agrees with the subject of the sentence. The tag question thus contains, in part, a repetition of some of the information found in the main sentence.

In the informal, abbreviated style, the subject and the auxiliary of the main sentence can in fact be dropped:

(10)
a. Been sneaking to the movies again, haven't you!
b. Getting pretty excited, aren't you?
c. Not ready to swim fifty laps, are you?
d. Failing his courses, isn't he?
e. Steal my money, will you!

Let us refer to the process illustrated here as *Tag-Controlled Deletion*, described as follows: given a sentence with a tag question, the subject and the auxiliary (if any) of the main sentence may be deleted. Tag-Controlled Deletion is a rule of the abbreviated style in informal language.

Notice that there is nothing incomplete about the sentences in (10). That is, even though the subjects and auxiliaries are missing from the main clauses, this information can easily be *recovered* from the tag. Now consider the data in (11), which, as far as we know, are not possible for any speaker:

(11)
a. *Have been sneaking to the movies again, haven't you?
b. *Are getting pretty excited, aren't you?
c. *Are not ready to swim fifty laps, are you?
d. *Is failing his courses, isn't he?
e. *Will steal my money, will you!

(12)
a. *You been sneaking to the movies again, haven't you?
b. *You getting pretty excited, aren't you?
c. *You not ready to swim fifty laps, are you?
d. *He failing his courses, isn't he?
e. *You steal my money, will you!

These examples show another regularity: if the subject is deleted, then the auxiliary must be deleted (11a–e) and vice versa (12a–e). We can make a firm judgment that these sentences are bad, indicating that the abbreviation process is hardly sloppy; that is, not just anything can be deleted or left behind.

How can we account for the fact that the auxiliary verb may not remain behind if the subject of the sentence has been deleted or that the subject cannot be left if the auxiliary is deleted? Labov's observations on contraction suggest that we consider the fact that subjects and auxiliaries are often contracted (compare (13) with (9)):

(13)
a. You*'ve* been sneaking to the movies again.
b. You*'re* getting pretty excited.
c. You*'re* not ready to swim fifty laps.
d. He*'s* failing his courses.
e. You*'ll* steal my money.

If the rule is that the subject of the sentence can be deleted only if the auxiliary verb is contracted onto it, sentences such as those in (11) will never occur: the auxiliary will always be deleted along with the subject. The examples in (12) will never occur since, in Tag-Controlled Deletion, it is the subject that is deleted, not the free-standing auxiliary. To form a sentence such as *Been sneaking to the movies again, haven't you?*, we do not delete the two separate elements *you* and *have*, but the single contracted element *you've*.

This suggests the following descriptive generalization for Tag-Controlled Deletion:

(14)
Tag-Controlled Deletion
The subject of the main sentence may be deleted, under the following conditions:
a. There is a tag.
b. If the main sentence contains an auxiliary, it *must* be contracted onto the subject if it *can* be contracted onto the subject.

We have not addressed examples where the auxiliary is not contractible. As is stands, (14) makes the following prediction: if the auxiliary is not contractible, then it stays behind in Tag-Controlled Deletion. This prediction appears to be correct. For example, consider what happens when the auxiliary is *could*:

(15)
It could get on your nerves, couldn't it.

Since *could* cannot contract onto the subject, the sequence **it'd* would be ill formed. This predicts that (16a) should be odd, whereas (16b) should be fine. This turns out to be correct:

(16)
a. *Get on your nerves, couldn't it.
b. Could get on your nerves, couldn't it.

We have now set up a system wherein the deletion of the subject depends on contraction of the subject with the auxiliary, wherever this is possible. As we saw, in ICE the link between contraction and deletion is crucial, and it turns out that this link is just as crucial in the general abbreviated style of American English.

We have by no means exhausted the topic of Tag-Controlled Deletion. However, the tag cases are only one part of the general deletion processes that affect subject and auxiliary in abbreviated style. We now turn to the deletion of *be* in abbreviated questions.

Deletion of *Be*

Another informal style of English involves abbreviated questions. *Want some coffee?* is an example of one type of abbreviated question; another type, the one we will be examining here, involves the deletion of the verb *be*. The following sentences illustrate cases where deletion is possible:

(17)
a. (You) running a fever?
   (= Are you running a fever?)
b. (You) finally rich now?
   (= Are you finally rich now?)
c. Your car in the garage?
   (= Is your car in the garage?)
d. Satisfied?
   (= Are you satisfied?)
e. John a professor or something?
   (= Is John a professor or something?)
f. (You) gonna leave soon?
   (= Are you going to leave soon?)
g. (You) sposta do that?
   (= Are you supposed to do that?)

Our data show that deletion of the verb *be* and the subject *you* is possible. Note also that the subject *you* cannot be deleted unless the auxiliary verb is deleted as well:

(18)
a. *Are running a fever?
b. *Are finally rich now?
c. *Are satisfied?
d. *Are gonna leave soon?
e. *Are sposta do that?

The verb in question is a contractible verb, just as in the case of Tag-Controlled Deletion. For example, the various forms of *be* can contract with various subjects:

(19)

am I	=	'my	[maɪ]
are you	=	'r you	[ɚju]
is he	=	's he	[zi]
is she	=	's she	[ʃi]
is it	=	's it	[zɪt]
is John	=	's John	[zdʒɑn]
are we	=	'r we	[ɚwi]
are they	=	'r they	[ɚðeɪ]

As noted in chapter 3, *am* shortens and contracts as /m/, *are* contracts as /ɚ/, and *is* as /z/, showing that *be* is a contractible verb and hence can delete. Since the subject *you* is deleted only if *be* is contracted onto it, such ungrammatical cases as *Are running a fever?* can never arise. Thus, in forming an abbreviated question, the second person subject *you* can be deleted as long as *be* is contracted onto it. It turns out that abbreviated questions can be formed with other auxiliary verbs as well, but we will not venture into those cases here.

Deletion and Recoverability of Information

We have seen that abbreviated questions are formed by deleting certain elements (contractible forms of *be* and *you*), and we have posited certain rules to characterize these processes. It is important to realize that apparent abbreviations also occur in the informal style in English. For example, in a situation where we might use the abbreviated question *Want some coffee?*, we might also be able to ask, simply, *Coffee?* To take another example, suppose you see a friend wearing shoes you haven't seen before. You might point to them and ask, *New?* These single-word instances are quite common in casual styles and are perfectly appropriate and comprehensible. The point is that there is no reason whatsoever to suppose that such single-word utterances are derived from whole sentences from which all the other words have been deleted. It is simply that we use many kinds of short expressions (including single words), as long as the context (linguistic or nonlinguistic) makes it clear what we are talking about.

In sharp contrast, the deletion of subjects and contractible verbs in, for example, abbreviated questions is governed by a *systematic rule*, with strict conditions. Not just any kind of deletion of subject and verb is possible, even if the context would make the abbreviation perfectly clear. For example, recall that *Are running a fever?* is impossible. There is nothing incomprehensible about this question; its meaning is clear, and nothing in the context of conversation would rule it out. However, the expression has violated a systematic grammatical rule: if the subject has been deleted, the contractible verb must also be deleted. An important point about grammatical rules is that expressions that violate those rules are ill formed and generally cannot be rescued, or made good, by appealing to meaning or to pragmatic context. In other words, such rules do not have to have logical or commonsense reasons for existing: it is a plain and simple fact that when grammatical rules are violated, an ill-formed expression results. For these reasons, then, we say that an abbreviated question such as *Running a fever?* is in fact the result of a systematic deletion rule, whereas an expression such as *Coffee?* is not.

It turns out that the formation of abbreviated questions involves reference to a small, highly specific set of elements: the subject *you* and the contractible forms of *be* (and *do* and *have* as well, it turns out). It would appear that native speakers of English, as they learn how to form abbreviated questions, come to learn the specific elements that can be missing from these questions. Given that the set of elements is small, we already know what information to "look for" in interpreting abbreviated questions, and in cases of potential ambiguity the conversational (or linguistic) context can resolve the matter.

Inner-City English in Relation to Other American English Dialects

Returning now to the features of Inner-City English that we discussed earlier, it is important to note that certain features of ICE are in fact part of the general set of features for American English dialects in the infor-

Table 7.1
Comparison of formal and informal styles with regard to contraction and deletion of the verb *be*. The informal style sentences in the chart are variations of the formal style sentences at the top. Examples such as *You sick?*, spoken with the rising intonation pattern characteristic of questions, show that deletion of the verb *be* (and other auxiliary verbs) is a feature of all American English dialects, not just Inner-City English. However, in Inner-City English deletion of *be* is allowed in declarative sentences, a possibility not found in other dialects. Thus, Inner-City English actually completes a pattern left incomplete in the informal style of other dialects.

	Questions	Declarative sentences
Formal style	Are you sick?	You are sick.
Informal style: All dialects	'Ryou sick?	You're sick.
Informal style: Inner-City English (deletion)	You sick?	You sick.
Other dialects	You sick?	(not possible)

mal style. In particular, it appears that deletion of the verb *to be* is a property of all dialects in informal style. The difference is that ICE allows deletion of *to be* in declarative sentences as well as abbreviated questions, whereas other dialects limit the deletion of the verb *to be* to abbreviated questions. Hence, ICE has generalized a pattern that other dialects leave incomplete. These results are summarized in table 7.1.

Other features of ICE seem distinctive, however (e.g., recall the use of invariant *be* in examples such as those given in (8)). Hence, not all the features of ICE can be shown to be part of the general features of informal style, and we can speak of ICE as a dialect with certain unique features. Regardless of whether features of ICE turn out to be distinct or part of more general features of American English dialects, the point to be stressed is that this dialect, and other dialects of American English, are in no way defective or illogical.

Where Phonology, Morphology, Syntax, and Pragmatic Context Meet

The rules for the abbreviated informal style that we have discussed here not only provide insight into the nature of language variation; they also provide a concrete example of how different subfields of linguistics are integrated and unified at a broader level. The rules for the abbreviated style must refer to *phonological* information: the deletion process is dependent on the phonological process of contraction: *Morphological* formation also plays a crucial role, since only certain kinds of morphemes can be (phonologically) contracted and then deleted. For example, only contractible verbs can delete, whereas other types of verbs cannot; and both the information about the part of speech and the information about specific words are types of morphological information. The deletion process itself is a *syntactic* process, broadly speaking, since it concerns the way sentences are formed in the abbreviated style. Finally, in order to understand sentences that have undergone deletion, we must be able to infer, or recover, the missing information. The pragmatic context in which the abbreviated sentences are actually used plays a crucial role in this inference process, and hence *pragmatic* information is necessary in our overall account of the abbreviated style.

In other words, linguistic explanations are rarely purely syntactic, or purely morphological, or based on any single component of the grammar. More often than not, to account for linguistic phenomena we require diverse kinds of information from different components of a grammar. Even though various subfields of linguistics are presented in separate chapters of this book—reflecting the need to break down the broad questions about language into more manageable ones—we must not forget that these areas are ultimately integrated when we seek to give complete explanations for linguistic phenomena.

7.3 OTHER LANGUAGE VARIETIES

We have so far examined the phenomenon of language variation in terms of dialects and styles of American English. In this section we will examine certain additional examples of language variation (from other languages, as well as from English) that are of interest to linguists. In our brief survey, we will not attempt to be comprehensive; rather, we will focus on a small number of selected examples in order to give a basic idea of some of the significant ways in which forms of language can vary.

Lingua Francas, Pidgins, and Creoles

For various reasons, groups of people speaking diverse languages are often thrown into social contact. When this occurs, a common language must be found to serve as a medium of communication. Sometimes, by common agreement, a given language (not necessarily a native language of anyone present) known to all the participants is used; a language used in this fashion is known as a *lingua franca*. The term *lingua franca* derives from a trade language of this name used in Mediterranean ports in medieval times, consisting of Italian with elements from French, Spanish, Greek, and Arabic. Until about the eighteenth century, European scholars used Latin as a lingua franca—a common language for treatises on science and other scholarly subjects. In the contemporary world, English serves as a lingua franca in numerous social and political situations where people require a common language. For example, English has become a lingua franca for international scientific journals and international scientific meetings—it is, by common agreement, the language in which scientific results are presented.

Historically, another kind of situation has often arisen in which people come into contact, sharing no common language: namely, when one group is or becomes politically and economically dominant over another. This has been typical of colonial situations, in which the dominant group desires trade with, or colonization of, the subordinate group. In such situations, *pidgin languages* (or *pidgins*) have developed, having the following important properties:

1. The pidgin has no native speakers but is used as a medium of communication between people who are native speakers of other languages.
2. The pidgin is based on linguistic features of one or more other languages and is a *simplified* language with *reduced* vocabulary and grammatical structure.

There have been pidgins based on English, French, Dutch, Spanish, Portuguese, Arabic, and Swahili, among others. Pidgin languages are sometimes called *contact languages* (reflecting the fact that such languages often arise when social groups come into contact) or *marginal languages* (reflecting the reduced grammar and vocabulary of the pidgin).

The word *pidgin* itself is said to derive from the English word *business* as pronounced in Chinese Pidgin English. Pidgin languages have limited vocabulary (most often drawn from the "dominant" language), and in terms of grammatical features they typically lack inflectional morphemes (nouns have no affixes to indicate plurality, and verbs have no affixes to indicate tense or subject agreement). In addition, forms of the verb *to be* are often entirely lacking in pidgins, and prepositions are often limited to a reduced set that serves multiple functions.

In an interesting discussion of Hawaiian Pidgin English, Bickerton (1981) notes that although the vocabulary of the pidgin comes primarily from English, its syntax may vary depending on the original native language of the individual user. For example, Bickerton cites cases such as the following (1981, 11):

(20)
a. da pua pipl   awl poteito it   (pidgin form)
   the poor people only potatoes eat (English gloss)
   "The poor people ate only potatoes." (translation)
b. wok had dis pipl   (pidgin form)
   work hard these people (English gloss)
   "These people work hard." (translation)

Example (20a) is from a Japanese speaker using Hawaiian Pidgin; note that the verb (*it* "eat") comes last in the sentence, just as it does in Japanese. Example (20b) is from a Filipino user of the pidgin; note that the verb (*wok* "work") comes first, just as it does in Philippine languages of the sort this speaker used natively. Although word order in Hawaiian Pidgin is by no means fixed for any given group of speakers, Bickerton notes that the original language of the user of the pidgin is a significant influence on grammatical features of the pidgin. Thus, a pidgin language is not based exclusively on a single language, such as English. It may well have significant features of more than one language.

Although pidgin languages are said to have limited uses, as well as reduced vocabularies and grammars, they can be used in highly expressive ways. Bickerton (1981, 13) cites a striking example from Hawaiian Pidgin English, uttered by a retired bus driver:

(21)
samtaim gud rod get, samtaim, olsem ben get, enguru ["angle"] get, no?
enikain seim. olsem hyuman laif, olsem. gud rodu get, enguru get,
mauntin get—no? awl, enikain, stawmu get, nais dei get—olsem.
enibadi, mi olsem, smawl taim.
"Sometimes there's a good road, sometimes there's, like, bends, corners, right? Everything's like that. Human life's just like that. There's good roads, there's sharp corners, there's mountains—right? All sorts of things, there's storms, nice days—it's like that for everybody, it was for me, too, when I was young."

Although we have not given a word-by-word English gloss of the pidgin, we suggest using the English translation as a basis for isolating words of the pidgin. (Pronouncing the pidgin words makes them easier to understand than seeing them in print.)

It is striking to see how a pidgin—a language with reduced vocabulary and structure—can be used as a vehicle for serious thought. Chinook Jargon, a pidgin used by Native Americans and early Europeans and Americans in the northwestern United States, consisted of a vocabulary of between 500 and 800 words, and users became so skilled that complex communication could take place—even sermons were delivered in Chinook Jargon.

The grammatical structure and basic vocabulary of Chinook Jargon were derived from the Native American languages of the Northwest, although several French words (with Native American adjustments) also were added, for example, *lumuto* "sheep" (from French *le mouton*). A large number of Chinook names for geographical features are still used in the Northwest. For example, river names ending in *-chuck* such as *Pilchuck* and *Skookumchuck* include the Chinook word meaning "rapids, waterfall." Olympia beer containers carry the word *tumwater*, a compound of the Chinook word *tum* and the English word *water* that means "roaring water."

Whereas Chinook Jargon has died out, certain pidgins have become well established, the most notable case being Tok Pisin, a pidgin widely used in Papua New Guinea. Tok Pisin has a writing system, a literature, and even radio programs.

As we have already noted, pidgins are generally used by native speakers of other languages as a medium of communication. Under certain circumstances, however, children may learn a pidgin as their first language. When a pidgin begins to acquire native speakers who use it as their primary language, it greatly expands in vocabulary and grammatical complexity. When this happens, the language is referred to as a *creole language*. Creole languages are said to develop in situations where the adults in a community speak mutually unintelligible native languages and must rely on a pidgin to communicate with each other. As children acquire the pidgin, they use it with playmates and other children in their peer group. Such situations often arose on slave plantations in the Americas, where Africans from linguistically diverse backgrounds could only communicate in a pidgin. Their descendants began to use the pidgin as a first language, and from this sort of development came such creoles as Haitian Creole (based on French), certain forms of Jamaican English, and Gullah (or Sea Island Creole, spoken by descendants of African slaves living on the Sea Islands off the coast of Georgia and South Carolina). Some scholars believe that certain current forms of Inner-City English may have had their origins as a creole language (see Dillard 1972 for discussion), but this is by no means a firmly established conclusion.

When a pidgin becomes creolized—that is, when it comes to be used as a primary language of a group of speakers—it undergoes considerable *expansion* of its vocabulary and grammar and begins to acquire rules comparable in nature and complexity with the rules of any other human language. To take one example, Crowley and Rigsby (1979) have described an interesting English-based creole spoken in the northern part of the Cape York Peninsula in Australia. Some typical vocabulary words of this creole are listed in table 7.2. Among the grammatical features of this creole, common to many other creoles as well, Crowley and Rigsby note a system of marking verb tenses:

(22)
a. Im bin ran.
   "He ran." (*bin* used to mark past)
b. Im ran.
   "He is running."
c. Im go ran.
   "He will run." (*go* used to mark future)

(23)
a. Wan dog i bin singaut.
   "*A* dog was barking."
b. Plenti dog i bin singaut.
   "*Some* dogs were barking."

Wan (originally from the English word *one*) is generally equivalent to the indefinite article *a* in English; and *plenti* (originally from the English word *plenty*) is generally equivalent to the English word *some*. Possession is marked with the preposition *blong* (from the English word *belong*):

(24)
a. stik blong olmaan
   "the old man's stick"
b. dog blong maan
   "the man's dog"

Table 7.2
Some vocabulary words of Cape York Creole. In the Cape York Creole orthography, the vowel *i* is pronounced [ɪ]; *e* is pronounced [ɛ]; *a* is pronounced [ə]; *aa* is pronounced [ɑ]; *o* is pronounced [ɔ], with *oo* having greater length; and *u* is pronounced [ʊ]. (See chapter 3 for explanation of phonetic symbols.) (From Crowley and Rigsby 1979, 206–207.)

English	Cape York Creole
bad	nogud (from "no good")
diarrhea	beliran (from "belly run")
cold (the illness)	koolsik (from "cold sick")
on your back	beliap (from "belly up")
live, stay	stap
a lot	tumach (from "too much")
beach	sanbich (from "sand beach")
return	kambek (from "come back")
other	nadha(wan) (from "another one")
the best	nambawan (from "number one")
the same	seimwei (from "same way")
shout	singaut (from "sing out")
stand	staanap (from "stand up")
sit	sidaun (from "sit down")
run away in anger	stoomwei (from "storm away")
grab, take, get	kech-im (from "catch him")
stingray	tingari
stop a vehicle for a lift	beil-im ap (from "bail it up")
throw	chak-im (from "chuck him")
deaf	talinga nogud (from "telling no good")
blind	ai nogud (from "eye no good")
smoke	faiasmouk (from "fire smoke")
be drunk	spaak (from "spark")
urine, urinate	pipi (from "pee-pee")
lie (tell a lie), pretend	geman (from "gammon")
cheat	blaf (from "bluff")
hide	stoowei (from "stow away")
father's elder brother	big ankl
father's younger brother	litl ankl
maternal grandmother	greni blo madha
Thursday Island	tiai (from "T.I.")
bow of canoe	foored (from "forehead")
Red Island Point	araipi (from "R.I.P.")

Certain morphemes that may function as *concord particles* (among other uses) precede the verb of the sentence and agree with the subject. For example, when the subject is a third person noun (either singular or plural), the concord particle is *i*:

(25)
a. Dog i singaut.
   "The dog is barking."
b. Ol maan i kam ia.
   "The old man is coming here."

Concord particles such as *i* perform the function of "agreement" with the subject and in this way are very similar to the English third person singular morpheme *-s*, which is suffixed to verbs in the present tense (as in *she/he runs* versus *I/you/we/they run*). One difference is that concord particles precede the verb, whereas *-s* is an inflectional suffix on the verb.

To sum up, then, grammatical features such as those illustrated in (22)–(25) often come into existence as a creole evolves from a pidgin.

This evolutionary process has sometimes been described in terms of a broader "creole continuum" (Bickerton 1975). In his study of Guyanese Creole, Bickerton noted that between the pure creole (the *basilect*) and the local variety of Standard English (the *acrolect*), there are a series of *mesolects*: language varieties that form a continuum beginning at the creole and gradually shifting toward Standard English, each successive mesolect approximating Standard English more closely. Individual speakers can often use a range of mesolects from the continuum and are not necessarily limited to a single mesolect. The evolutionary process of pidginization and creolization is concisely summed up by Naro (1979, 888):

In the broadest possible terms, many specialists accept a cyclic concept of pidgin/ creole evolution. The start is some sort of reduction process in both inner and outer form (PIDGINIZATION); this leads to a non-standard linguistic system (a PIDGIN) different from any of the ingredients (SOURCE or SUBSTRATA) existing previously. The middle stage is achieved by re-expansion (CREOLIZA-TION) to a less-limited linguistic system (a CREOLE). The end of the cycle is a stage in which a standard language exerts influence on the creole (DECRE-OLIZATION), producing a result that can range up to a regional variety of the standard.

What "guides" the process of creolization? How can children acquiring a pidgin "expand" the pidgin so that it comes to have grammatical structures on a par with those of other human languages? Some scholars have suggested that the increased complexity of the creole reflects an innate "faculty of language"—that is, a biologically innate linguistic capacity (see Bickerton 1981 for discussion of a "bioprogram" along these general lines). Thus, speakers expanding a pidgin language into a creole are in some intuitive sense constrained by their innate linguistic capacity, and for this reason, perhaps, all creoles are predicted to have very similar structures regardless of where they have developed and what languages are involved. Pinker (1995, 36–37) discusses a creolization process that happened in a Nicaraguan sign language. In a very short time, deaf children who were taught a basic sign vocabulary spontaneously and greatly expanded the vocabulary and expressiveness of their signing system in communicating with each other.

Jargon

In virtually every recognized profession, a special vocabulary evolves to meet the particular needs of the profession. This special, or technical, vocabulary is known as *jargon*. To take well-known examples, physicians and health professionals use medical jargon; lawyers use legal jargon; and linguists use a technical linguistic jargon with vocabulary items such as *phoneme*, *morpheme*, and *transformation*. Jargon is not limited to professional groups, but also exists in what we might term "special-interest" groups. For example, sports enthusiasts, rock climbers, jazz and rock-and-roll fans, custom car hobbyists, art lovers, and many other groups all make use of jargons that are specially suited to the particular interests of the group. Even the criminal underworld has its own jargon, often referred to as *argot*.

Despite its mysterious nature to an "outsider," jargon is not intended to be secret, but, for purely practical reasons, particular jargons are largely incomprehensible to those outside the particular profession or group that uses the jargon. The shared use of jargon is often the basis for a feeling of group solidarity, with the accompanying feeling that those who do not use the jargon are not part of the "elite." Consider the following words, likely to be opaque to many speakers of English but known by all computer programmers: *tweak*, *kluge*, *throughput*, *bitmap*, and hundreds (yes, hundreds) more.

We noted in chapter 2 that several means of creating new words are available to language users: they can abbreviate words, use acronyms, or simply create a word whose shape has never existed before. Medical professionals "prep" (prepare) a patient for an operation; molecular biologists use techniques they refer to as "PCR" (polymerase chain reaction) and the "CAT assay" (chloramphenicol acetyltransferase); theoretical linguists discuss "*wh*-words" and debate the formulation of the "ECP" (Empty Category Principle). Thus, jargon is an instantiation of the creative property of human language: in this case, the expansion of vocabulary to meet new situations using a language's word-building and word-creating feature.

Slang and Taboo Language

It has been said that slang is something that everyone can recognize but no one can define. Speakers show enormous creativity in their use of slang (it is, indeed, one of the most creative areas of language use), and it is often the source of a good deal of humor. Although a precise definition of slang seems extremely difficult (if not impossible), there are, nevertheless, some salient features of this form of language:

1. Slang is part of casual, informal styles of language use. Further, the term *slang* has traditionally carried a negative connotation: it is often perceived as a "low" or "vulgar" form of language and is deemed to be out of place in formal styles of language.
2. Slang, like fashions in clothing and popular music, changes quite rapidly. Slang terms can enter a language rapidly, then fall out of fashion in a matter of a few years or even months. This rate of turnover is much greater than for other areas of the vocabulary of a language.
3. Specific areas of slang are often associated with a particular social group, and hence one can speak of teenage slang, underworld (criminal) slang, the slang of the drug culture, and so on. In this respect slang is a kind of jargon, and its use serves as a mark of membership and solidarity within a given social group. To use outdated slang, or to use current slang inappropriately, is to be hopelessly "out of date" and to be excluded from an "in-group." Consider the slang in table 7.3 and compare it with the slang that you are used to.

Slang is sometimes referred to as *vernacular* (especially when it is associated with a particular social group), and some forms of slang fall under the term *colloquialism*, referring to informal conversational styles of language. These terms do not carry negative connotations; however, for convenience we will continue to use the popular term *slang*.

Table 7.3
Slang expressions used by college students in 2000

Word	Meaning
hangin'	"to relax"
hotty	"physically attractive person"
lamo	"weird person"
phat	"good, cool, neat"
peeps	"parents"

Slang vocabulary often consists of regular vocabulary used in specific ways. For example, the words *turkey* and *banana* are regular vocabulary items in English (and can be used in formal styles with their literal meaning), but in slang they can be used as insults (referring to stupid or foolish people). In addition to the use of regular vocabulary words, however, slang (like jargon) also makes use of regular word formation devices (of the sort discussed in chapter 2) to create new words. For example, slang words can be coined, as was the case for forms such as *diddleysquat* (*He doesn't know diddleysquat*, meaning "He doesn't know anything"). More recently *slam dunk* has become airline pilot slang for plunging an airliner down through congested air traffic, and auto sales slang for getting buyers to pay more than they had to (*Newsweek*, July 3 and August 7, 1987). Blends are common in slang—for example, *absotively* and *posilutely*, both of which are blends based on the words *absolutely* and *positively*. Affixes can be used also, as with the slang suffix *-ski* (or *-sky*), found on such words as *brewski* "beer," *tootski* "a puff on a marijuana cigarette," and *buttinski* "one who butts in." It is interesting to note that *brew* and *toot* (with the same meanings as *brewski* and *tootski*) are recent slang words that are becoming stale or outmoded; the addition of the slang suffix *-ski* "rejuvenates" the words. The origin of this slang use of *-ski* is unknown, but it may be a linguistic parody on Polish or Russian words that end in a similar phonetic sequence.

An interesting, and quite amusing, phenomenon in American slang is the use of the forms *city* and *-ville* to create various compound expressions. For example:

(26)
a. We're in *fat city*.
b. What a bummer! It is, like, *bug city*.

c. You shouda seen all the cars—I mean, *lowrider city!*
d. She cried all night . . . you know, *heartbreak city*.

(27)
a. This place was out in the boonies; I mean, *hicksville*, you know?
b. What a boring place—talk about *nowheresville*.
c. You shouda seen it: those people were so stoned, it was like *drugsville* all the way.
d. That guy's really strange—totally *weirdsville*.

The interpretation of expressions with *city* and *-ville* is clear enough in specific contexts, but not so easy to explicate in general. Such expressions all seem to refer to situations where some maximum concentration or extreme degree is reached: *bug city* means "infested with bugs"; *lowrider city* means something like "lowriders [modified automobiles] everywhere"; *heartbreak city* means something like "maximum heartbreak"; *nowheresville* means something like "really nowhere"; *weirdsville* means something like "very weird." These are only rough paraphrases, and we leave the finer details to the brave reader. Both *city* and *-ville* refer to locations, and it is interesting to note that other words denoting locations can be used in similar ways:

(28)
a. We're on easy *street*.
b. He's in fantasy-*land*.
c. I'm in chocolate *heaven*.

In addition to individual vocabulary items, and expressions on the pattern of *fat city*, there are also longer expressions (with idiomatic meanings) that are characteristic of slang usage, such as the following examples (all used in describing someone who appears unintelligent, foolish, or crazy):

(29)
a. He's got a few screws loose.
b. She doesn't have all her marbles.
c. He's not playing with a full deck.
d. Her elevator doesn't go all the way to the top.
e. He's a few french fries short of a Happy Meal.

These examples contain no grammatical or morphological features that are uniquely slang-related (such as *-ski* or *-ville*). We nevertheless classify them as slang because of their insulting/humorous nature.

Discussion of verbal insults invariably raises the question of obscenity, profanity, "cuss words," and other forms of *taboo language*. Taboo words are those that are to be avoided entirely, or at least avoided in "mixed company" or "polite company." Typical examples involve common swear words such as *Damn!* or *Shit!* The latter is heard more and more in "polite company," and both men and women use both words openly. Many, however, feel that the latter word is absolutely inappropriate in "polite" or formal contexts. In place of these words, certain *euphemisms*—that is, polite substitutes for taboo words—can be used, including words such as *darn* (a euphemism for *damn*), *heck* (a euphemism for *hell*), *gee* or *jeez* (a euphemism for the exclamation *Jesus!*), and so on. An amusing example is the current expression, *the "F" word*, which is a euphemism for that notorious English word that many newspapers spell as *f---*.

Taboo language is not limited to obscenity—sacred language can also be taboo, that is, language to be avoided outside the context of sacred ritual. In many societies the language of religious or magical rites can only be used by certain members of the society (priests or shamans).

What counts as taboo language is something defined by culture, and not by anything inherent in the language itself. There is nothing inherent in the sounds of the expression *Shit!* that makes it "obscene"—it is simply that in our cultural history the word has come to be known and used as a "swear word." Foreigners learning English as a second language will at first find nothing unusual about the word, and will not experience the "emotional charge" that often accompanies the use of a taboo word. For Americans learning French, there is nothing intrinsic in the expression *Merde!* (meaning "Shit!") that seems obscene.

It is interesting to note, however, that bilingual (or multilingual) speakers sometimes avoid words in one language that accidentally resemble taboo words in another language. This phenomenon of *interlingual word taboos* (Haas 1957) can be illustrated in various ways. For example, American students learning Brazilian Portuguese are often embarrassed to learn the word *faca*, meaning "knife," since its pronunciation in Portuguese comes uncomfortably close to sounding like the tabooed English word *fuck*. Haas (1957) cites a case in which a Creek Indian informant avoided using certain words of the Creek language when Whites were around. One of the words was *fakki*, meaning "soil, earth, clay." A particularly interesting case cited by Haas involved a group of Thai students in the United States, who noticed that the Thai word *phrig* (the sequence *ph* pronounced as an aspirated /p/, not as /f/), meaning "pepper," resembled the American English slang word *prick*. It was necessary to use this word frequently when dining in public, and not wanting Americans to overhear a word that sounded like a tabooed word of English, the students sought another term in Thai that could replace the word *phrig*. The substitute that they hit upon was the Thai word *lyn*, which in fact means "phallus" but secondarily came to mean "pepper" in the context of dining out. Ironically, then, the students found a term in Thai that did not sound like a tabooed American English slang word (thus, they could freely talk about pepper with Americans in hearing distance); yet their substitute term had the same meaning as the tabooed English word they were trying to avoid.

Code Switching and Borrowing

The term *code switching* refers to a situation in which a speaker uses a mixture of distinct language varieties as discourse proceeds. This occurs quite commonly in everyday speech with regard to levels of style, as, for example, when speakers mix formal and informal styles:

(30)
We must not permit the State of California to deplete the water supply of the State of Arizona. Ain't no way we're gonna give 'em that water.

The speaker (in this case an Arizona politician) is mixing styles for a certain rhetorical effect: the juxtaposition of formal speech-making style with informal colloquial style adds emphasis to the speaker's position on the water issue; and the use of the informal style in this context is intended by the speaker to increase a feeling of solidarity with the audience.

Code switching can often happen within a single sentence (and at numerous points within a sentence). Among the most interesting cases of this sort of code switching are those in which a speaker mixes distinct (mutually unintelligible) languages, a situation that often arises in bilingual or multilingual areas such as the American Southwest. In the following example, Spanish is mixed with English (the Spanish forms are italicized, with the English glosses in parentheses):

(31)
It's now *ocho y media* ("eight-thirty") on a Saturday night, and we're gonna hear a new artist *con* ("with") his new group. You're in tune with *la maquina ritmica* ("the rhythm machine").

This example (taken from a radio broadcast on station KXEW, "Radio Fiesta," Tucson, Arizona) is predominantly based on English, with a mixture of Spanish words. The reverse situation is also common, where a few English words are mixed in with a predominantly Spanish utterance, as in the following example (where the English word *training* is italicized):

(32)
Estaba *training* para pelear.
"They were training to fight."

In cases of code switching, the speaker is in effect using two distinct language varieties at the same time. We can contrast this situation with that of *borrowing*. When speakers of one language borrow words from another language, the foreign words come to be used as regular vocabulary items. For example, when a speaker of English says, "They have a great deal of *savoir-faire*," we might well recognize that the term *savoir-faire* was originally a borrowed word (or *loanword*) from French, but it has come to be used as a vocabulary item in English (in fact, it is listed in Webster's). In contrast, the Spanish phrase *ocho y media* in (31) is not a borrowed vocabulary item that English speakers now use, but rather is a result of code switching between English and Spanish.

Conclusion

In this chapter we have covered several aspects of variation in language. We would like to conclude with the observation that variation, far from being a "defect" of language, actually reveals its true nature: human language is a rule-governed system within which an enormous amount of flexibility or creativity is possible. Variation is linguistically neutral, and there is no evidence that "nonstandard" dialects *themselves* are less adequate as a means of communication than the so-called standard language. In other words, variation in language does not entail any inferiority in language. Instead, the problem lies in the *attitudes* of the language community toward the *speakers* of these forms. The community as a whole ranks the various forms of language socially, thereby elevating some speakers and stigmatizing others to the point where listeners frequently perform on-the-spot assessments of a speaker's background and abilities based on the selection and pronunciation of a few words! To repeat, then, the fact that dialects occur readily is a natural consequence of humans using language in a creative manner. The force of variation and change in language is such that differentiation within a language will eventually lead to the formation of different languages, a topic to which we turn in the next chapter.

Exercises

1. If you are acquainted with a regional, social, or ethnic dialect, list as many features as you can that distinguish this dialect from the so-called standard language. What are some significant differences in pronunciation, vocabulary words, and syntax?

2. The following types of sentences (originally made famous by *Mad* magazine) are frequently used in the informal style of English:
a. What, me worry?
b. What, John get a job? (Fat chance!)
c. My boss give me a raise? (Are you joking?)
d. Him wear a tuxedo? (He doesn't even own a clean shirt!)

How would you express each of these sentences in formal English? Do these informal sentences express any feeling or idea that is not expressed in the formal style?

3. Several acquaintances who were raised in Brooklyn inform us that the following sentences are informal but grammatical:
a. Let's you and him fight—how about it?
b. Let's you guys shut up, all right?

How does this informal use of *let's* differ from its use in formal English?

4. In the informal style it is quite common to hear sentences such as the following:
a. There's three cars in the garage.
b. There's a lot of problems with this car.
c. There's many ways to do this.

How would these sentences be expressed in formal English, and how do the formal and informal styles differ in the use of *there's*?

5. Sports announcers on TV and radio use a style of English that is both colorful and unique. Listen to a variety of sports broadcasts, paying careful attention to the language, and try to characterize as precisely as you can how this language differs from the formal style or standard language. To get started, you might consider the following sample of sportscaster language: "Smith on third. Jones at bat. Mursky winding up for the pitch." (This language should be reminiscent of the informal style discussed in this chapter.) Remember to include differences (if any) in pronunciation and vocabulary words, as well as syntax.

6. In this chapter we considered abbreviated questions of one type, namely, questions without question words (or *wh*-words) such as *who*, *what*, and *where*.

The following sets of sentences illustrate the differences between *wh*-questions and the abbreviated questions we examined:

(i)
a. Where have you been lately?
b. Where've you been lately?
c. *Where've been lately?
d. Where ya been lately?
e. *Where been lately?

(ii)
a. Who are you taking to the prom?
b. Who're you taking to the prom?
c. *Who're taking to the prom?
d. Who ya takin' to the prom?
e. *Who takin' to the prom?

(iii)
a. What do you want to do?
b. Whattaya wanna do?
c. *Whatta wanna do?
d. Watcha wanna do?
e. *What want to do?

How do these abbreviated *wh*-questions differ from the abbreviated questions studied in the chapter? That is, what are the differences in the rules for forming the two types of abbreviated questions? In answering, pay careful attention to (1) the fact that some of the examples in (i)–(iii) are ungrammatical and (2) the way contraction works in these cases.

7. It is not quite true to say that *be* can never be deleted in the informal speech style of the authors, for the following sentences are good:

a. Odd that Mary never showed up.
b. Good thing you fixed your engine.
c. Too bad (that) she had to leave town so soon.
d. Amazing that he didn't spot that error.

What has been deleted from these sentences? Is this deletion general?

8. Questions typically come from a first person speaker and are addressed to a second person hearer. Can you relate this *use* of questions to the fact that *you* is deleted from abbreviated questions? Can *any* subject be deleted from abbreviated questions as long as use and context make the deletion recoverable?

Further Reading

General

For general background on *dialect studies of American English*, we recommend Francis 1983 and Carver 1987. The following works offer excellent discussions of some of the *dialects spoken by African Americans*: Dillard 1972, Burling 1973,

Labov 1973, and Folb 1980. The Ebonics controversy has recently brought African American dialects to wider public attention. Two good sources are Baugh 2000 and Lakoff 2000. Good surveys of the properties of *pidgins and creoles* can be found in Hymes 1971, Bickerton 1975, Valdman 1977, Crowley and Rigsby 1979, and Holm 1988. The section on pidgins and creoles in Crystal 1987 is also excellent. A good source for issues involving *language and gender* is Tannen 1994.

Journals
American Speech, English Journal, International Journal of the Sociology of Language, Language

Bibliography

Bailey, R. W., and J. L. Robinson, eds. 1973. *Varieties of present-day English.* New York: Macmillan.

Baugh, J. 2000. *Beyond Ebonics: Linguistic pride and racial prejudice.* New York: Oxford University Press.

Bickerton, D. 1975. *The dynamics of a creole system.* Cambridge: Cambridge University Press.

Bickerton, D. 1981. *Roots of language.* Ann Arbor, Mich.: Karoma Publishers.

Bodine, A. 1975. Androcentrism in prescriptive grammar: Singular 'they', sex-indefinite 'he', and 'he' or 'she'. *Language in Society* 4, 129–146.

Burling, R. 1973. *English in black and white.* New York: Holt, Rinehart and Winston.

Carver, C. 1987. *American regional dialects: A word geography.* Ann Arbor: University of Michigan Press.

Crowley, T., and B. Rigsby. 1979. Cape York Creole. In Shopen 1979.

Crystal, D. 1987. *The Cambridge encyclopedia of language.* New York: Cambridge University Press.

Dillard, J. L. 1972. *Black English: Its history and usage in the United States.* New York: Random House.

Dixon, R. M. W. 1971. A method of semantic description. In D. D. Steinberg and L. A. Jakobovits, eds., *Semantics: An interdisciplinary reader in philosophy, linguistics, and psychology.* Cambridge: Cambridge University Press.

Farmer, A. K., and R. A. Demers. 2001. *A linguistics workbook.* 4th ed. Cambridge, Mass.: MIT Press.

Fasold, R. W. 1972. *Tense marking in Black English.* Urban Language Series. Arlington, Va.: Center for Applied Linguistics.

Folb E. A. 1980. *Runnin' down some lines: The language and culture of Black teenagers.* Cambridge, Mass.: Harvard University Press.

Francis, W. N. 1983. *Dialectology: An introduction.* New York: Longman.

Frank, F., and F. Anshen. 1983. *Language and the sexes.* Albany, N.Y.: SUNY Press.

Giglioli, P. O., ed. 1972. *Language and social context.* Baltimore, Md.: Penguin Books.

Glissmeyer, G. 1973. Some characteristics of English in Hawaii. In Bailey and Robinson 1973.

Haas, M. R. 1957. Interlingual word taboos. *American Anthropologist* 53, 338–341. Reprinted in Hymes 1964.

Haviland, J. B. 1979. How to talk to your brother-in-law in Guugu Yimidhirr. In Shopen 1979.

Holm, J. 1988. *Pidgins and creoles,* vol. 1. New York: Cambridge University Press.

Hudson, R. A. 1980. *Sociolinguistics.* Cambridge: Cambridge University Press.

Hymes, D. H., ed. 1964. *Language in culture and society.* New York: Harper and Row.

Hymes, D. H., ed. 1971. *Pidginization and creolization of language.* Cambridge: Cambridge University Press.

Labov, W. 1969a. Contraction, deletion, and inherent variability of the English copula. *Language* 45, 715–762.

Labov, W. 1969b. The logic of nonstandard English. In *Report of the Twentieth Annual Round Table Meeting on Linguistics and Language.* Washington, D.C.: Georgetown University Press. Reprinted in Bailey and Robinson 1973 and Giglioli 1972.

Labov, W. 1972. The social stratification of (r) in New York City department stores. In *Sociolinguistic patterns.* Philadelphia: University of Pennsylvania Press.

Labov, W. 1973. Some features of the English of Black Americans. In Bailey and Robinson 1973.

Lakoff, R. 1973. Language and woman's place. *Language in Society* 2, 45–79.

Lakoff, R. 2000. *The language war.* Berkeley: University of California Press.

Naro, A. 1979. Review of Valdman 1977. *Language* 55, 886–893.

Pinker, S. 1995. *The language instinct.* New York: HarperPerennial.

Pride, J. B., and J. Holmes, eds. 1972. *Sociolinguistics.* Middlesex, England: Penguin Books.

Shopen, T., ed. 1979. *Languages and their status.* Cambridge, Mass.: Winthrop Publishers.

Smitherman, G. 1977. *Talkin and testifyin: The language of Black America.* Boston: Houghton Mifflin.

Tannen, D. 1994. *Gender and discourse.* New York: Oxford University Press.

Thorne, B., and N. Henley, eds. 1975. *Language and sex: Difference and dominance.* Rowley, Mass.: Newbury House.

Valdman, A., ed. 1977. *Pidgin and creole linguistics.* Bloomington: Indiana University Press.

Williams, F., ed. 1970. *Language and poverty.* Chicago: Markham.

Chapter 8
Language Change

8.1 SOME BACKGROUND CONCEPTS

The inherent flexibility of human language, along with its complexity and the creativity with which it is used, causes it to be extremely variable and to change over time. Contemporary speakers of English find the language of Shakespeare's plays in large part intelligible (we can, for instance, extrapolate from the current word *chicken-livered* to guess what the now obsolete word *pigeon-livered* might have meant); nonetheless, small changes are made from time to time in Shakespeare's texts to keep some passages from becoming totally obscure. And our contemporary language will continue this process of change, as well, until eventually there will come a generation that will need subtitles in order to understand the English of twenty-first-century movies. In section 8.3 we will discuss in detail some of the changes that English has undergone in the last fifteen centuries.

Language change is one of the subjects of *historical linguistics*, the subfield of linguistics that studies language in its historical aspects. Sometimes the term *diachronic linguistics* is used instead of *historical linguistics*, as a way of referring to the study of a language (or languages) at various points in time and at various historical stages. *Diachronic* is often used in contrast to *synchronic*, a term referring to the study of a language (or languages) at a single point in time, without reference to earlier (or later) stages. For example, chapter 5 is a synchronic study of current American English syntax, but part of section 8.3 contains a brief diachronic study of syntax, that is, a study of the historical development of certain sentence constructions in English.

In considering the history and development of particular languages, one of the most fascinating questions—and indeed, a question that has

intrigued scholars throughout the ages—concerns the origin and evolution of language in the human species in general. When in the history of
our species did language originate? What was the nature of the first lan-
guage(s)? Often, as in this case, the most fascinating questions in linguistics are the very ones we cannot answer in any definitive way. Let us see
why questions concerning the origin of language have so long resisted
efforts to find clear answers.

The Origin and Evolution of Human Language

Considerable evidence suggests that the capacity for language is a
species-specific, biologically innate trait of human beings. The question
then naturally arises how this capacity may have originated and evolved
in the species. Unfortunately, we have little, if any, solid evidence to
indicate when language may have originated, why it might have developed in our particular species, and how it evolved from its earlier stages.

One idea concerning the origin of human language is that humans
began to mimic the sounds of nature and used these sounds as referents
for the sources of the sound. This theory is sometimes disparagingly
referred to as the *"bow-wow"* theory. The existence of onomatopoeic
words such as *bow-wow, meow, crash, boom* might be taken as evidence
of such mimicking. But onomatopoeic words invariably form a very
small portion of the words of any given language; and even if "imitation
of nature" accounts for some words, we still have no explanation of how
the rest of human language evolved.

According to another speculation, vocal language gradually evolved
from spontaneous cries of pain, pleasure, or other emotions. Once again,
absolutely no evidence has been advanced to show how a full-blown
language—complete with phonology, morphology, syntax, and so on—
could evolve from simple emotional cries. To this day all humans, and
other animals as well, use response cries; and what is left unexplained is
why humans developed language as well.

It has also been suggested that a *gestural language*—that is, a system
of hand gestures and signals—may have preceded vocal language (see
Hewes 1976). This might well be true, but again we are faced with the
problem of understanding how gestural language came to be supplanted
by vocal language, as well as when and why this might have happened.

In addition, it is sometimes speculated that human language gradually
evolved from the need for humans to communicate with each other in
coordinating certain group tasks. The idea here is that people working in

groups can cooperate more efficiently if they can use a vocal language to communicate. But such "functional" theories of the origin of language seem quite dubious. For one thing, it has never been shown that the carrying out of group tasks requires a *vocal* language. Why couldn't a sign language or gestural language suffice as a communication system in the context of groups at work? Further, it has never been shown that group tasks require a communication system anywhere near as complicated as human language. For example, wolf packs are extremely efficient hunting groups and yet have no complex language; further, many farming tasks carried out today by humans require no language and are learned by imitation. Generally speaking, "functional" theories of the origin of language all suffer from a similar defect: human language is vastly more expressive and more powerful than would be dictated by any given functional task involving groups at work. Of course, once human language did evolve, it came to be exploited fully for all kinds of social functions; but the needs involved in such functions cannot be identified as the first cause of language evolution.

At present the most reasonable suggestion about the origin and evolution of human language is that it was intimately linked with the evolution of the human brain. We know, for example, that over roughly the last 5 million years there has been a striking increase in brain size, ranging from about 400 cubic centimeters in our distant hominid ancestors to about 1,400 cubic centimeters in modern *Homo sapiens* (see Miller 1981 for a useful summary). The mere increase in brain size would not necessarily have led to superior intelligence and the evolution of language, since dolphins, for example, have a brain comparable in size to that of humans, yet they have only a rudimentary communication system. Furthermore, even a mere increase in general intelligence might not necessarily have led to the evolution of language. Dolphins and primates, for instance, are considered to be more intelligent than birds, yet their communication systems seem to be no more sophisticated or complex than that of birds. Indeed, as Lenneberg (1964) has pointed out, humans with IQ levels significantly below normal can nevertheless grasp the rudiments of language (see also Yamada 1990). Obviously, brain size is only one factor that may have played a role in the evolution of language; changes in the organization and complexity of the brain must also be supposed to have played a crucial role.

At what point in time language may have originated is far from clear: guesses range from 50,000 to 100,000 years ago and earlier, but such figures are speculative at best. In any event it seems likely that language is a relatively recent development in the human species. There is an abrupt change in the quality and nature of tool development between 50,000 and 100,000 years ago, signaling to some anthropologists the emergence of modern humans. It is plausible that this increased ability may have been associated with a qualitative change in language ability, but we have no evidence at all that this was the case.

The problem in determining the answer to questions concerning the origin and evolution of human language is that we have so little solid evidence on which to base any claims. Attempts have been made to reconstruct the vocal tract of Neanderthal man (see Lieberman 1975 for discussion), and although early reports claimed that Neanderthals had only a limited capacity for speech because their vocal tract was shaped differently from that of modern humans, more recent evidence from Neanderthal remains suggests that they had a vocal tract shaped like ours (*National Geographic*, 1989).

We not only have no idea when language began, we do not even have an idea of what the earlier stages of language might have been like—even in the most recent stage before the modern era. We have stated that language is a biological phenomenon, and in the biological world it is frequently possible to find earlier forms of life existing simultaneously with more evolved forms. For example, the coelacanth was a biologically primitive fish known only in fossil form until a living specimen was discovered and identified in 1938. Might it be possible to encounter a group of people who speak a form of language that can be identified as an earlier form of modern language?

Small, previously unknown groups of people have indeed been discovered from time to time in jungle areas in New Guinea and the Philippines (Molony 1988). These groups have apparently been isolated from other humans for long periods of time and have no knowledge of the modern world. Their existence, then, often gives rise to speculation that they may speak a more primitive language that could be an earlier form of modern human language. But even though the technology of such people is at a Stone Age level, their languages appear to be as developed and as complex as any other human language. So far, then, no natural language (with the possible exception of the pidgin languages discussed in chapter 7) has been shown to be more primitive than any other language in terms of grammatical organization, expressiveness, and so forth.

Hence, it may seem that we are limited to studying the history of languages on the basis of written records, dating back only 6,000 years. It is possible, nevertheless, to make deductions about language at a time that antedates the historical records. This is the subject of the next section.

8.2 THE RECONSTRUCTION OF INDO-EUROPEAN, THE NATURE OF LANGUAGE CHANGE, AND LANGUAGE FAMILIES OF THE WORLD

Similarities among Languages

The discovery in the early nineteenth century that the European languages, such as English, German, and French, were historically related not only to each other, but also to the languages of antiquity, such as Latin, Greek, and Sanskrit (an ancient language of India), led to a revolution in our understanding of the nature and history of language. Linguistic similarities among the different languages of Europe had not gone unnoticed before the nineteenth century. Already in the sixteenth century Filippo Sassetti pointed out similarities between Italian and Sanskrit. Even the philosopher Leibniz observed that Persian and German were grammatically similar. A true understanding of the nature of the relationship among these languages did not come, however, until the early part of the nineteenth century. The person who is credited with the first and clearest statement concerning the relationships among the classical and other ancient languages was Sir William Jones, who wrote in 1786 that

The Sanskrit language, whatever be its antiquity, is of a wonderful structure; more perfect than the Greek, more copious than the Latin ... yet bearing to both of them a stronger affinity, both in the roots of verbs and in the forms of grammar, than could possibly have been produced by accident; so strong indeed, that no philologer could examine them all three, without believing them to have sprung from some common source, which, perhaps, no longer exists: there is a similar reason, though not quite so forcible, for supposing that both the Gothic and the Celtic ... had the same origin with the Sanskrit; and the old Persian might be added to the same family ... (quoted in Lehmann 1967, 15)

This language, "which ... no longer exists," is called *(Proto)-Indo-European* in the English-speaking world, a term reflecting the (earlier) geographical distribution of the speakers of this language family from India to Europe. Note that if it is possible to learn about an earlier form of a language for which no written records exist, then we may also be able to learn about the history of the world's languages and perhaps even something about the geographical origin of language itself. How can we learn about this language that no longer exists and for which no written records are available? In order to see how linguists establish historical relationships among languages, consider the words in (1):

(1)

Language A	Language B	Language C
uno	łáá'ii	eka
dos	naaki	dva
tres	táá'	tri
cuatro	dį́į́'	catur
cinco	ashdla'	pañca
seis	hastą́ą́h	ṣaṣ
siete	tsosts'id	sapta
ocho	tseebíí	aṣṭa
nueve	náhást'éí	nava
diez	neezná	daśa

You may know (or be able to guess) that these are the words for the numerals one through ten in each of the three languages. You will also notice that languages A and C have some phonological similarities: 6 out of 10 words begin with the same (or a similar) consonant; the words for *one* and *eight* are the only ones that begin with vowels; 9 of the words have the same number of syllables; and so forth. Thus, we have some initial evidence that languages A and C (Spanish and Sanskrit, respectively) might be related; but neither of these two seems to be related to language B (Navajo). This brief exercise raises the central questions to be dealt with in this section: (1) How do we establish with a reasonable degree of certainty that two or more languages are related? (2) If languages are related but no longer the same in vocabulary and grammar, how and why did they change? and (3) Does language change involve an improvement or a decay in expressive ability? In attempting to answer these questions, we will be examining some of the most important aspects of *historical* or *comparative linguistics*.

Based on the similarities between Spanish and Sanskrit in the words for *one* through *ten*, we could hypothesize that Spanish and Sanskrit are related languages, meaning that they both are descended from a common ancestor language. However, in order to establish a genetic relationship between or among languages, more is needed than the presence of similar-sounding words. We need to rule out chance overlap in sound and meaning and the presence of borrowed vocabulary. Consider the words in (2) and (3):

(2)

Language A	Language B	Meaning
bhanem	ban	"woman"
alnoba	allaban	"person, immigrant," respectively
lhab	lion-obhair	"netting"
odana	dun	"town"
haʔlwiwi	na h-uile	"everywhere"
kladen	claden	"frost, snowflake"
pados	bata	"boat"
monaden	monadh	"mountain"
aden	ard	"height"
cuiche	cuithe	"gorge"

(3)

Language A	Language B
cuprum	copper
planta	plant
cuppa	cup
discus	dish
coquīna	kitchen
cāseus	cheese

The languages in (2) are Scots Gaelic (language B) and Northeastern Algonquian (language A). Scots Gaelic is a Celtic language of Western Europe, whereas Algonquian is a Native American language of the northeastern United States.

The languages in (3) are Latin (language A) and, of course, Modern English (language B). The meanings of the Latin words are the same as those of their English counterparts, although the pairs of words differ somewhat in pronunciation.

Examples (1), (2), and (3) illustrate three situations in which languages can share a set of words that are individually similar in both sound and meaning. These similarities can be the result of a true historical relationship, of a chance overlap in sound and meaning, or of borrowing from one language to another. We discuss in reverse order these three ways that languages can have words that share sound and meaning.

Borrowing

Many terms relating to Western technology and culture have become part of the vocabulary of the world's languages, and English speakers in turn have borrowed many words from other languages. The vocabularies of Modern Japanese and English, for example, share a significant number of common words, among them *karate*, *sushi*, *hibachi*, *tsunami*, *beer*, and *computer*. This common and shared vocabulary might lead a naive linguist to hypothesize that English and Japanese are somehow related—perhaps they are descended from a common language? (It may be that Japanese and English are in fact descended from a remote common language, but this is unprovable given our present state of knowledge.) In establishing genetic relationships among languages, then, one must exclude words that may have been borrowed and are therefore not part of a common inheritance. The Latin words in (3) were borrowed by (Old) English speakers, and although this vocabulary seems to refer to rather common objects, it does reflect the cultural influence of speakers of Latin in England. Even without records that establish evidence of borrowing, we will see that borrowed words can be distinguished from common inherited words by the principles discussed in the section on establishing genetic relationships among languages.

Chance Overlap in Sound and Meaning

The fact that languages often have similarities in sound structure and have words for common objects yields a significant probability that there will be accidental overlaps in sound-meaning correspondences between them. For example, all languages have a low vowel (such as *a*), and most have *i* and/or *u* vowels; most languages have *t*, *k*, and *p* and the nasal consonants *n* and *m*. Moreover, most languages have words referring to water, the numbers, male and female parents, and other items common to human existence. In Lummi, a Native American language spoken in northwestern Washington State, the word for "father" is /mæn/. In Navajo and Chinese the word for "mother" is /ma/, as in Chinese *mā* and Navajo *shi-má* "my mother." There are a few words in Chinese, Navajo, and Lummi that are phonetically and semantically similar to words in English, but this is insufficient evidence to demonstrate that any of these languages is genetically related to English.

Likewise, there is insufficient linguistic evidence that the languages in (2), Scots Gaelic and Algonquian, are genetically related. The meanings of the phonologically similar words shared by Scots Gaelic and Algonquian are typical of the sort of vocabulary that would suggest a genetic relationship, in that the words generally refer to common objects, words that are unlikely candidates for borrowing. The number of shared words, however, is very small; more importantly, there are no *systematic* sound correspondences between the words of the sort that we will discuss in the next section. We conclude, therefore, that the similarities between Scots Gaelic and Algonquian are due to an accidental overlap in the sound-meaning associations of some of their words.

Establishing Genetic Relationships among Languages

The study of language history and the relationships among languages is one of the tasks of *comparative linguistics*. The traditional procedure that linguists use in determining a true historical (genetic) relationship is called the *comparative method*. It is this method that has led linguists to conclude that Sanskrit and Spanish are, in fact, historically related. The comparative method does not refer to a fixed procedure that is to be followed rigidly. Rather, it refers to the analytical techniques linguists employ in reconstructing the history of languages that are hypothesized to be members of the same language family. We will demonstrate some of the aspects of the comparative method by considering the words in (4), whose phonetic and semantic similarities suggest a historical relationship:

(4)

English	Latin	Greek	Sanskrit
ten	decem	deka	daśa
two	duo	duo	dva
heart	cordia	kardía	hŕd

Limiting ourselves to the word-initial and -final *t* of English, we note that this sound corresponds to the *d*'s of the other languages. The term *correspond* used here means that a particular sound occurring in some position in words of one language appears in the same relative position in semantically similar words of the other languages.

In the case of the forms in (4), we can establish the phonological correspondence set given in (5):

(5)

English	Latin	Greek	Sanskrit
t	d	d	d

Whenever extensive correspondence sets of sounds such as the one in (5)—which could be greatly expanded, if space permitted—can be established among groups of words in different languages, a historical phonological relationship among these languages can be inferred because of the combination of two principles:

(6)
a. Phonological changes are generally regular; that is, within the limits of certain conditions, the changes occur with very few exceptions.
b. The relationship between sound and meaning in a word is arbitrary.

Principle (6a) expresses the fact that speakers of a language can modify their pronunciation in a systematic way. Linguists describe this type of change as the result of *the addition of a phonological rule to a speaker's grammar*. In the examples in (4), the *t*'s in English that correspond to the *d*'s in other languages are the result of some speakers' adding a rule that caused all the original *d*'s to change into *t*'s in their grammars.

That the regular correspondence across different languages occurs in words that are the same or similar in meaning is crucial also. Since a word's meaning is not in any way determined by the sounds making up that word, it is likely that the sound-meaning pairings of each word (principle (6b)) were inherited by each of them from a historically earlier language, because such far-reaching similarities could hardly be due to chance. Put another way, individual pairs of words may be found across languages that exhibit regular phonological relationships. But when these pairs of words from different languages bear the same or related meanings, we can infer that they descended from a common ancestor language in which the arbitrary sound-meaning pairing was already present.

Linguists surmise, then, that Latin, Greek, and Sanskrit have preserved an original *d* articulation, whereas at some point in the history of English, certain speakers changed the pronunciation of their *d*'s into *t*'s. English is not the only language that appears to have undergone the change from *d* to *t*, however. German, Dutch, and the Scandinavian languages also participated in this change. These languages, including English, are all members of the *Germanic language family*, and the change of *d* to *t* most likely occurred within a single Germanic linguistic community before the community separated into the different groups just mentioned. The Germanic languages, then, share several innovations, such as the change of *d* to *t*, that differentiate this group from the other Indo-European languages.

Grimm's Law
The set of correspondences displayed in (4) is in fact only a part of a larger set of correspondences that can be established between English on the one hand and Latin, Greek, and Sanskrit on the other hand. The

underlined portions of the words in (7) indicate the critical consonants involved in the correspondences:

(7)

Germanic (English)	Other languages
a. sli<u>pp</u>ery	lū<u>b</u>ricus (Latin) "slippery"
<u>t</u>en	<u>d</u>ecem (Latin) "ten"
yo<u>k</u>e	iu<u>g</u>um (Latin) "yoke"
b. <u>f</u>ather	<u>p</u>ater (Latin) "father"
<u>th</u>ree	<u>t</u>rēs (Latin) "three"
<u>h</u>orn	<u>c</u>ornū (Latin) "horn"
c. <u>b</u>rother	<u>bh</u>rātar (Sanskrit) "brother"
bin<u>d</u>	ban<u>dh</u> (Sanskrit) "bind"
<u>g</u>uest	<u>h</u>ostis (Latin) "enemy" (note meaning difference)

As noted earlier, the consonants of Latin and Sanskrit are for the most part closer to what is reconstructed as the original Indo-European pronunciation. It is hypothesized that Sanskrit and Latin preserve the original *d*, *b*, and *g* pronunciation of Indo-European, and that these sounds all became voiceless in Germanic. But not all consonants are preserved in their original form in Sanskrit and Latin either, or in any member of the Indo-European language family for that matter. For example, the *g* in English *guest* corresponds to the *h* in Latin *hostis*. Many linguists have hypothesized that the original Indo-European sound was close to a voiced aspirated velar stop, symbolized *gh*. (An asterisk used with transcriptions indicates here that they are hypothetical forms for which no written records are available.) Thus, the original Indo-European *gh* became *g* in Germanic and *h* in the language that was ultimately to become Latin. We display in (8) the set of changes that have been hypothesized to have taken place in Germanic, based on the correspondences represented in (7):

(8)

Grimm's Law

a. b → p
   d → t
   g → k
b. p → f
   t → θ
   k → x (→ h)

c. bh → b
   dh → d
   gh → g

The changes in (8) are known collectively as *Grimm's Law*, because their systematic lawlike character was first stressed by Jacob Grimm (one of the Brothers Grimm, best known in the United States for their collection of German fairy tales). There is some controversy over whether Grimm should be credited for discovering this set of "laws," since the correspondences had already been published by a Dane, Erasmus Rask. Because of his emphasis on their lawlike properties, however, Grimm is usually given credit for the discovery.

The changes that occurred were indeed lawlike, in that all words containing the relevant phonemes underwent the rules, and the changes that occurred applied to natural classes of phonemes, in the sense discussed in chapter 4. For example, the class of phonemes that underwent the changes in (8b) is the class of *voiceless stops*. Thus, after the Germanic languages split off from the other languages, they were subject to a rule that changed all voiceless stops into fricatives (with some minor restrictions that are not important here). This rule is expressed in the following form:

(9)

$$\begin{bmatrix} +\text{consonantal} \\ -\text{voiced} \end{bmatrix} \rightarrow [+\text{continuant}]$$

After rule (9) had applied, words that formerly had *p*, *t*, and *k* then had *f*, *θ*, and *x* (→ *h*), respectively. For Germanic-speaking children acquiring their language after rule (9) had changed the consonants, there would be no evidence for the earlier *p*'s, *t*'s, and *k*'s, and they would simply learn the new consonants. Thus, without evidence from other languages, it would be impossible to tell that Germanic *f*, *θ*, and *x* (→ *h*) were derived from *p*, *t*, *k*. To summarize the thrust of this example, then, we can rephrase the principles in (6) as in (10) and state the conditions under which languages can be said to be genetically related on the basis of their sound systems:

(10)
Principles for establishing genetic relationships
A group of languages can be shown to be genetically related if groups of words can be found in each of the languages such that:

a. They possess *corresponding phonemes* (phonemes in the same position in the word) that are either identical or can be shown to derive from the parent language as the result of regular phonological rules that have applied at some point in the history of each of the languages, and
b. The words that contain the corresponding phonemes have *meanings that are related.*

The Indo-European Language Family

The languages of the Indo-European family also share similar morphological and syntactic properties that support a distant historical relationship. For our purposes, however, the Indo-European languages can be decisively shown to be related because the conditions expressed in (10) are satisfied in sets of shared words. To see how the principles are satisfied, we can begin by considering the set of words and stems meaning "brother" and "bear" (to carry):

(11)

English	Sanskrit	Greek	Latin
brother	bhrátar	phrātēr	frāter
bear	bhar-	pher-	fer-

Based on forms such as these, among many others, scholars have *reconstructed* the original Indo-European forms for "brother" and "bear" to be *bhráter and *bher, respectively. Reconstructed forms such as *bhráter are frequently referred to as *protoforms*. Likewise, a reconstructed "parent" language is often referred to as a *protolanguage*. A reconstructed form is the most plausible hypothetical source from which all of the forms in all the daughter (descendant) languages can be derived. Thus, starting from reconstructed Indo-European forms such as *bhráter and *bher, each of the daughter languages has undergone its own separate and regular changes. Some of these changes are given in figure 8.1. It is important to stress that, when certain conditions are met, *all* Indo-European *bh's changed to *ph* in Greek and to *b* in Germanic; that is, these changes are the result of rules of the sort we considered in chapters 3 and 4. Thus, it is the consistency (or regularity) of the correspondences among the daughter languages of the Indo-European language family (due to rule-governed phonological change) that is decisive in establishing their historical relatedness. Note that none of the descendant languages preserves all of the phonetic features of the hypothesized (parent) protolanguage for the words under consideration. That is, none of the daugh-

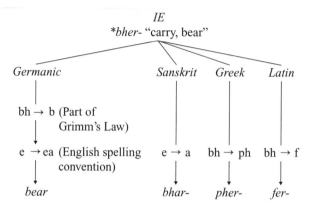

Figure 8.1
The descendant forms from a reconstructed (hypothesized) Indo-European **bher-*
"carry, bear." Each of the "daughter" languages has changed from the "parent"
form in a different way, and thus their common ancestry has been obscured.

ter languages is identical to the protolanguage. Sanskrit turns out to be
more conservative in terms of preserving the original consonants, whereas the other three languages have undergone changes in the consonants,
but have maintained the original *e* vowel.

The considerations that lead to positing original **e* instead of **a* in
forms such as **bher* go beyond the scope of this introductory text, but the
bibliography at the end of this chapter includes several books on historical linguistics in which such issues are discussed.

Language reconstruction and the establishment of language relatedness
involve many additional complications beyond those discussed here, and
much has been learned about the Indo-European language family in the
more than two centuries of research that has been devoted to it. Most of
the languages in Europe, for example, have been shown to be related to
each other historically. Many of these languages are displayed in figure
8.2. Languages on the same "branch" of the tree in the figure share certain features (or changes) not shared by languages on the other branches
of the tree. For example, all the Indic languages underwent the change of
short *e* and *o* to *a*, and all the Germanic languages shared the Grimm's
Law changes in their consonants. Hence, figure 8.2 reflects a classification
system similar to ones used by biologists for plants and animals.

Using techniques of reconstruction such as those discussed here,
linguists have worked out a fair idea of the original Indo-European

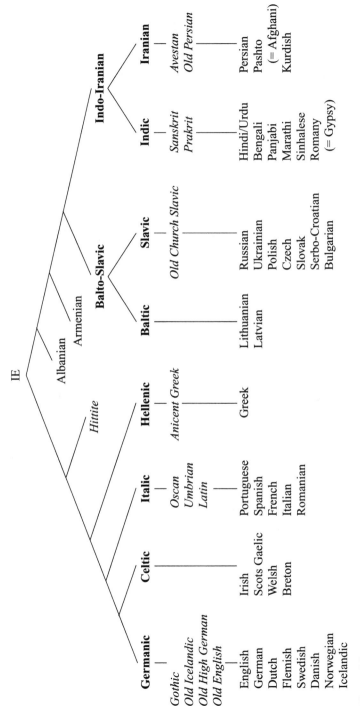

Figure 8.2
The Indo-European language family. Families are listed in boldface type. The oldest attested forms of each family are given in italics, and currently spoken languages are listed in plain roman type at the end of each vertical branch.

language. Many questions remain, however, concerning the original homeland of the Indo-European speakers and the time at which Indo-European began to split up. Until recently the consensus was that the Indo-European homeland was in the steppes of Russia, north of the Black Sea, and that the Indo-Europeans were associated with the Kurgan people (Gimbutas 1970). This theory is supported by archeological as well as linguistic evidence. From this centrally located homeland, some of the Indo-Europeans would have migrated east to India and others would have migrated west toward mainland Europe. Recently an alternative hypothesis has been proposed (Renfrew 1989), placing the Indo-European homeland in what is today Turkey. The expansion of the Indo-Europeans into the surrounding areas is hypothesized to be a consequence of the development of agriculture and the need for new farmland. Whereas earlier theories portrayed the Indo-Europeans as mounted conquerors entering new territory, the most recent theory envisions the offspring from one generation of farmers moving onto adjacent potential farmland, repeating this sequence until all arable land was settled. However, such wavelike settlement is not consistent with the division of Indo-European into its major subfamilies (Germanic, Celtic, and so forth), so it seems clear that much of the history of the migration and settlement of Indo-Europeans is still to be determined.

Whatever the pattern of settlement of the Indo-Europeans, the migrations occurred millennia ago. The Indo-European community of speakers had already split into very different languages more than 4,500 years ago, so the original language could not have been a single language (or group of dialects) fewer than 5,000 to 6,000 years ago. To answer the question of whether this earlier language was more primitive than the languages that descended from it, we can state confidently that there is no evidence that Indo-European was in any sense more primitive than its daughters. Ironically, when the details of Indo-European were first being worked out, it was commonly believed that the daughter languages were "decayed" versions of the pristine original language. The quotation from Sir William Jones at the beginning of this section shows traces of this prejudice. However, it simply does not appear that we can gain any important information about the origin of language from the analytical techniques of reconstructing earlier forms of a language. All reconstructed languages are full-fledged human languages, and there is no evidence that languages have become more expressive or have "improved" in some sense during the past 10,000 years, the most remote time to which we can reconstruct language using the analytical techniques discussed in this section.

Languages of the World

A recent series of articles in *Scientific American* reports a stunning new hypothesis concerning the chronological and geographical origin of human language. This theory places the origin of modern humans (and perhaps human language) in Africa as recently as 100,000 years ago. Under this hypothesis, humans emigrated from Africa and replaced any other hominids in the territory they entered (Neanderthals and possibly descendants of earlier *Homo erectus* populations who left Africa in an earlier migration more than 1 million years earlier). If certain biologists (Wilson and Cann 1992) are correct in their analysis of mitochondrial DNA, not only are all humans descended from relatively recent African populations, but in fact all living humans share an African ancestor, a person whimsically referred to as "Eve." Moreover, the biologists' studies place humans into approximately six groups, based on the degree of similarity in their mitochondrial DNA. There is independent corroboration for these six groups from two additional sources: cellular DNA and blood typing (Cavalli-Sforza 1991).

The relationship of the spread of this African population to the origin of human language is found in our earlier observation that approximately 100,000 years ago a steady increase in the sophistication of human activity (e.g., tool making) began after a long period of stability in the material culture. Scholars (Diamond 1989) hypothesize that the rapid and successful spread of modern humans in the last 100,000 years can be connected to the emergence of language in something like its present form.

The work of the biologists is interesting for historical linguistics since some linguists, using an analytical technique different from the traditional comparative method, have independently proposed language groupings that match the six groupings of the biologists (Shevoroshkin 1990; see figure 8.3). These speculative and controversial linguistic groupings suggest a linguistic relatedness among languages that can be traced back tens of thousands of years. One grouping places the Indo-European languages together with Semitic (the languages of the Middle East, which include Arabic and Hebrew) and the Dravidian languages of India. This protolanguage even has a name: Nostratic.

These proposals for biological and linguistic grouping are controversial, however. Some archeologists (Thorne and Wolpoff 1992) maintain

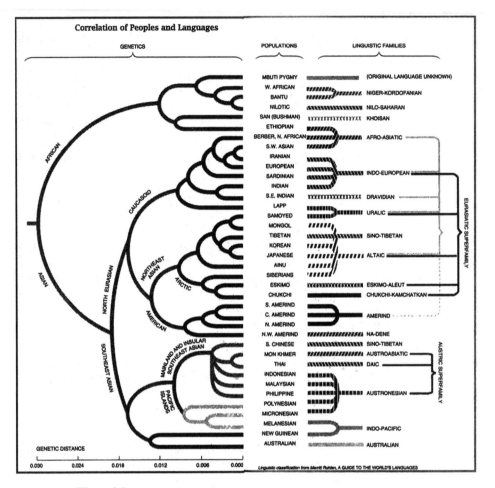

Figure 8.3

The correlation between the biologists' grouping of humans based on shared biological similarities (left side) and the proposed (and not generally accepted) language groupings of some linguists (right side). (Arabic and Hebrew are included in the Afro-Asiatic family.) (From Cavalli-Sforza 1991. Used by permission of the artist.)

that the Eve hypothesis is untenable and contradicted by the physical evidence present in the early Asian skeletons (e.g., Peking man). The linguistic evidence has also been challenged, and the analytical techniques used by the "lumpers" have been the subject of strong attacks (Campbell 1988). Time will tell whether the aggressive groupings of humans and their languages will be analogous to the theories of Wegener regarding continental drift (later proven to be correct) or to the theory of phlogiston (later proven to be incorrect).

Although we cannot yet shed light on the ultimate origin or the ancient history of human language through analytical techniques such as the comparative method, these techniques can illuminate the more recent history of the world's languages by showing that many languages can be grouped together as members of larger families. As noted earlier, most of the languages of Europe are members of the Indo-European language family. Among those that are not members are Finnish, Estonian, and Hungarian, members of the Finno-Ugric family. The Basque language has not been shown to be conclusively related to any other language and is thus termed an *isolate*.

The grouping of other languages of the world—and even their number —is much less clear. Part of the problem in determining the number of languages lies in the differing definitions of dialect, which have a political basis just as often as a linguistic one, as we saw in chapter 7. A commonly cited estimate is that the world's languages number between 4,000 and 5,000, with half of the world's population speaking Indo-European languages. The large number of speakers of Indo-European languages is due in part to the European settlement of the New World. The individual language with the most speakers is Mandarin Chinese. The most common second language—that is, the language learned most frequently as a foreign language—is currently English. Thus, a Japanese pilot landing in Paris communicates with a Russian pilot and the French control tower in English.

Very few of the world's languages are unrelated to other languages; most can be grouped into families. And, as noted earlier, some linguists are becoming quite bold in the grouping of languages. Greenberg (1987) has proposed that the "Indian" languages of the New World can be grouped into three families, a rather striking proposal when one considers that 1,500 languages are involved, covering North, Central, and South America. It has also been proposed that Japanese and Korean are descendants of a common ancestor, and work continues on proving this

Table 8.1
Some non-Indo-European languages of the world

Family	Language	Principal area where spoken	No. of speakers in millions
Afro-Asiatic	Hausa	West Africa	23
	Amharic	East Africa	10
	Arabic	North Africa	155
	Hebrew	Israel	3
Altaic	(Khalkha) Mongolian	Mongolia	2
	Turkish	Turkey	45
Austro-Asiatic	Vietnamese	Vietnam	45
Austronesian	Indonesian-Malay	Indonesia, Malaysia	115
Caucasian	Georgian	Caucasus	3
Dravidian	Kannada	India	32
	Malayalam	India	31
	Tamil	India, Sri Lanka	59
	Telugu	India	60
Finno-Ugric	Finnish	Finland	5
	Hungarian	Hungary	13
Japanese	Japanese	Japan	119
Korean	Korean	Korea	60
Niger-Congo	Swahili	East Africa	32
	Igbo	West Africa	12
	Yoruba	West Africa	14
Sino-Tibetan	Cantonese	Southern China	55
	Mandarin	Northern China	726
	Burmese	Myanmar (Burma)	26
	Tibetan	Tibet	6

hypothesis (Martin 1966). It might appear that we are moving toward collapsing all the world's languages into a single family. Given our present state of knowledge, however, it appears unlikely that all languages will be proven to be descendants of a single ancestor. In table 8.1 we list some of the world's non-Indo-European languages, grouped according to families, giving an approximate number of speakers for each.

Why Languages Change and How Language Change Spreads

Having answered our first question, concerning how to establish historical relationships among languages, we now turn to the second—namely, what are the causes and mechanisms of language change?

Surprisingly perhaps, linguists currently have little understanding of the exact causes of language change. For purposes of discussion, we may divide the topic of language change into two areas: individual and community. By *individual change* we refer to a spontaneous change in a language on the part of a single speaker. *Community change* we may define as the transmission and ultimate sharing of changes among speakers in a linguistic community.

Individual Change

One type of individual change that spontaneously occurs is *grammar simplification*. Modern English has a small class of exceptional nouns in which the final voiceless fricative must be voiced in the plural form (e.g., *leaf* vs. *leaves*). With respect to the regular Plural Rule of English, this change to a voiced fricative is an exception and represents a complication of the regular process of plural formation. Many speakers of English are now regularizing these forms and use plurals such as *handkerchiefs* and *hoofs* instead of the previously used *handkerchieves* and *hooves*. Test yourself with the following expression: *Snow White and the Seven_____*. Not too long ago the common pronunciation was *dwarves*, but now more and more people are using *dwarfs*, the regular form, in the plural. (The title of the Disney movie, which uses the plural *dwarfs*, has supported the use of the new and regular plural.) A good part of the regularization leading to language change is probably carried out by children during language acquisition. Adults may also be a source of change, although very little is known at present about the possible contribution of adults to language change. We simply do not know why a rule such as Grimm's Law applied in Germanic, or why in more recent English, rules for flapped and glottal stop variants of *t* have been added (recall chapter 3). Once a group of speakers have changed their language, however, the change can then spread to other speakers.

Community Change

If a change begins in one area, it is sometimes possible to follow its progress through time and space as it moves *wavelike* through a community of speakers. When two separate areas are the sources of changes, the changes can spread in an overlapping fashion. For example, a difference has been noticed (Joos 1942) in the pronunciation of the word *typewriter* in two dialects of Canadian English: /tʌɪpɹaɪɾɚ/ and /tʌɪpɹʌɪɾɚ/. This difference can be explained in terms of the interaction of two rules, the rule for flapped *t* ([ɾ]) discussed in chapter 3 and the Vowel Centering rule illustrated in exercise 1 of chapter 4. Vowel Centering applies in

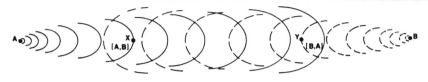

Figure 8.4
Geographic spread of two intersecting rules

some dialects of American and Canadian English, so that the diphthongs /aɪ/ and /aʊ/ become /ʌɪ/ and /ʌʊ/ before voiceless consonants. The pronunciation of the word *typewriter* in the two Canadian dialects can be accounted for by an interesting interaction of the two rules:

(12)
a. *Flap Rule*
/t/ and /d/ become flapped ([ɾ]) between two vowels that are members of the same metrical foot. (See section 4.3 for details.)
b. *Vowel Centering*
The diphthongs /aɪ/ and /aʊ/ become /ʌɪ/ and /ʌʊ/ before voiceless consonants.

Imagine two geographical areas, A and B. In area A, Canadian speakers have rule (12a) in their dialect, but not rule (12b). In area B, on the other hand, speakers have rule (12b), but not rule (12a). What effect might this have on speakers who are located between these two groups? How might their pronunciation be influenced by their neighbors in areas A and B? We know that speakers in one area may have an influence on neighboring speakers, so that features of language such as pronunciation (as well as vocabulary, morphology, and syntax) can be assimilated by the neighboring group. The neighboring group in turn can pass on the feature of pronunciation (which we write as a rule) to further neighbors, so that the rule appears to move "wavelike" through successive groups of speakers. Given this observation, two rules could originate in different areas, but gradually spread. They would eventually "meet" and "cross," creating areas where their effects overlap, as shown in figure 8.4.

Figure 8.4 represents an idealized geographic spread of two rules. At point X, which is close to area A, rule (12a) "arrives" first; however, since X is farther away from area B, rule (12b) "arrives" later. In contrast, point Y is closer to area B, the area of rule (12b), and thus rule (12b) "arrives" at Y before rule (12a) does. This difference in the order of arrival of the rules yields the difference in the pronunciation of the word *typewriter* in the two Canadian dialects, as shown in (13):

(13)

	X-dialect		*Y-dialect*
	taɪpɹaɪtɚ		taɪpɹaɪtɚ
First rule (12a):	taɪpɹaɪɾɚ	First rule (12b):	tʌɪpɹʌɪtɚ
Next rule (12b):	tʌɪpɹaɪɾɚ	Next rule (12a):	tʌɪpɹʌɪɾɚ

This example gives a good indication of how a change in pronunciation can move among dialects. The Flap Rule, which is not found in British English, has spread among most speakers of American English, although there still are American speakers who pronounce *water* with a *t*. The same type of spreading also occurs with lexical, morphological, and syntactic change, and thus radical language change is possible. If one group of speakers becomes isolated or sufficiently separated from another group of speakers of the same language, they may each undergo their own changes and spreading may not take place between the two groups. Under these conditions new, mutually unintelligible languages will eventually arise.

Spread of Changes among Different Languages
An interesting feature of language change is that grammatical properties, especially phonological ones, can spread between adjacent but different languages. For example, the uvular-*r* (an *r*-like sound pronounced in the uvular region of the vocal tract (see figure 3.4)), has been replacing the tongue-tip-*r* in many of the languages of Europe. Uvular-*r* is characteristic of French, but it is now common in many dialects of German as well; it is also replacing the tongue-tip-*r* in dialects of southern Sweden and northern Italy. As might be expected, there is much dispute about where the change started.

One of the more remarkable cases of the spread of a phonological change is found in the Native American languages of the northwestern United States. In Washington State, three distinct language groups were geographically adjacent (or in close social contact) before the contact with the Europeans. These groups are represented by Makah (a language of the Wakashan family), Quileute (a language of the Chemakuan family), and several members of the Salish language family. The relative geographic locations of these languages are indicated in figure 8.5.

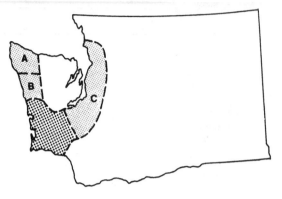

Figure 8.5
Geographical proximity of three distinct language families in the northwestern United States. A = Makah region; B = Quileute region; C = Salish region

What is remarkable about these different languages is that they all lost their nasal consonants by changing them to voiced stops: *m* became *b*, *n* became *d*, and *ŋ* became *g*. Although it is not possible to establish in which language the change began, it is noteworthy that this far-reaching change (indicated by shading in figure 8.5) spread throughout these distinct languages. Almost all of the world's languages have nasal consonants, but these languages are among the few that do not. Notice that the name *Makah* has a nasal consonant—thus appearing to contradict the claim that these languages have no nasals. Also, one of the Puget Sound Salish languages, *Snohomish*, another nasalless language, has *two* nasals in its name. The solution to this apparent contradiction is that the names *Makah* and *Snohomish* were given to these people by neighboring groups that do have nasals in their languages. The Snohomish actually call themselves *sdəhóbʃ* (our spelling), in which *d* corresponds to *n* and *b* corresponds to *m*, according to the regular changes mentioned above.

Language Change: Decay or Improvement?

We now turn to the third question that was posed earlier: does language change lead to a gain or loss in expressiveness?

In the past, language change has been viewed variously as decay and as progress, but at present neither of these views seems appropriate or true. Languages seem to maintain a balance in expressiveness and grammatical complexity over time. If a particular grammatical feature is lost (say, because of a phonological change), some feature may be added in another portion of the grammar (say, in the syntax). For example, when English lost most of its inflectional endings (see section 8.3)—due, it is often claimed, to the deletion of unstressed final syllables as an effect of phonological rules—it was no longer possible to identify the functional role (subject or object) of nouns by their inflectional endings. However, the functional notions of subject and object are now indicated by the syntactic position of nouns, that is, by their position in the linear order of words. In section 8.3 we will also discuss the loss of a morphological rule that created causative verbs from adjectives, a rule that accounts for pairs such as *red* and *redden*. But speakers of English did not lose the notion of causation when this word formation rule was lost. In fact, we can still say "to cause to be blue," for example, even though we cannot say *bluen*. Thus, the expressive possibilities of a language do not appear to be limited by the lack of an overt grammatical structure that carries a particular notion. For example, Chinese has no overt past tense marker, but this does not mean that speakers of Chinese do not have a notion of past time. The idea of past time can be quite clear either from context or from the presence of an adverb that refers to past time.

In the next section we study the changes that have occurred in English during the past fifteen hundred years. The language has changed radically, but there is not a shred of evidence that it has lost any of its powers of expression.

8.3 THE LINGUISTIC HISTORY OF ENGLISH

The English language has undergone extensive changes between the Old and Modern English periods. Changes in grammar, pronunciation, and vocabulary have made Old English no longer understandable to speakers of Modern English. Nonetheless, speakers of Modern English are able to recognize Old English as a relative of their familiar language. For example, in (14b), a word-for-word Modern English translation of (14a) that ignores some meaning differences, many of the words show a strong similarity to the Old English words.

(14)
a. *Old English*
   In þām tūne wǣron þæt hūs and þæt būr þæs eorles.
b. *Modern English*
   In the town were the house and the chamber of-the chief (earl).

As noted earlier, English is part of the Germanic family of languages and is thus historically related to Modern German, Dutch, Swedish, Norwegian, Danish, and Icelandic. The English language began its own separate development in the middle of the fifth century A.D. after a series of invasions of the English islands by Germanic-speaking tribes from what is now northwestern Europe. The invading groups included Saxons, Angles, Jutes, and Frisians. The invaders fought against Celtic-speaking inhabitants, who were eventually overcome. These were not the first Europeans to invade England and do battle with the Celts, however. The Romans had colonized England during the first century A.D., before the migrations of the Angles and Saxons began. As the Roman Empire began to collapse, however, the Roman legions withdrew, making possible the settlement of what was to become England by the Germanic tribes. The remaining Celtic speakers were confined to Wales (Welsh) and Cornwall (Cornish). Welsh is spoken by a small but growing number of people in Wales, and Cornish became extinct in the eighteenth century. The original Celtic language(s) of Scotland became extinct, although Gaelic speakers from Ireland moved to Scotland and developed their own dialect, Scots Gaelic, which is still spoken by a small population. The Irish Gaelic language is also still spoken in Ireland, but only by a minority of its inhabitants.

During the sixth century, the Germanic invasions ended and England entered a period of relative political stability. The island became covered with a patchwork of kingdoms, and during this period of political stability several dialect areas arose. The major dialects were West Saxon, Kentish, Mercian, and Northumbrian, the West Saxon dialect eventually becoming the most important. The differences among these dialects, which mainly involved pronunciation, were similar to differences among dialects in the present-day United States. The language of this period, called Old English (or Anglo-Saxon), was in many ways grammatically similar to Modern German. For instance, the nouns, adjectives, and verbs were highly inflected, as the examples in (15) show:

(15)
Typical Old English nouns, adjectives, and verbs
a. Noun: *cyning* "king"

Singular	Nominative	cyning
	Accusative	cyning
	Genitive	cyninges
	Dative/Instrumental	cyninge

Plural	Nominative	cyningas
	Accusative	cyningas
	Genitive	cyninga
	Dative/Instrumental	cyningum

b. Adjective: *gōd* "good" (weak declension)

		Masculine	Feminine	Neuter
Singular	Nominative	gōda	gōde	gōde
	Accusative	gōdan	gōdan	gōde
	Genitive	gōdan	gōdan	gōdan
	Dative/Instrumental	gōdan	gōdan	gōdan
Plural	(Same plural endings in all genders)			
	Nominative	gōdan		
	Accusative	gōdan		
	Genitive	gōdra		
	Dative/Instrumental	gōdum		

c. Verb: infinitive *dēman* "judge" (compare Modern English *deem, doom*)

Present tense	Singular	1	dēme
		2	dēmst, dēmest
		3	dēmþ, dēmeþ
	Plural	1,2,3	dēmaþ
Past tense	Singular	1	dēmde
		2	dēmdest
		3	dēmde
	Plural	1,2,3	dēmdon

The words in (15) consist of two parts, a base and one of a set of inflectional suffixes. The inflectional morphology of Old English was in fact much more complicated than (15) indicates. The noun *cyning* is an example of a so-called *masculine* noun, but there were two other genders, *feminine* and *neuter*, both of which had different endings. Each of the nominal genders had different subclasses, associated with different sets of inflectional endings. There were, then, about two dozen different types of inflectional endings that could be added to nouns alone.

The adjectives and verbs were also divided into classes that required different endings, so that there were altogether dozens of different classes of inflectional endings that were added to nouns, adjectives, and verbs. One of the major changes between Old English and Modern English, then, was obviously the loss of almost all of these nominal, adjectival, and verbal endings—for the language has very few such suffixes today (recall the discussion of English morphology in chapter 2). In the nouns, only the regular genitive ending -s/es (now the possessive) and the plural ending -s/es have survived. Plurals such as *children* carry on an earlier -en plural ending, and plurals such as *geese* also reflect an earlier class of inflectional ending. (We will discuss the origin of the stem alternation between *goose* and *geese* later.) The adjective endings have also been completely lost, although archaic spellings and phrases such as *ye olde shoppe* or *in the olden days* are relics from this earlier period.

Another indicator of English language history is found in modern words with an initial *sk-* sequence. Old English words containing this sequence underwent a rule that changed an *sk* sequence into a *sh* /ʃ/ sound. Sound changes being very regular (recall principle (10)), Modern English *sk*-initial words cannot be descendants of Old English *sk*-initial words. It turns out that the *sk* sequence found in words such as *sky* and *skirt* is the result of borrowings from the Scandinavian languages. (The Danes in fact controlled northeastern England in the ninth and tenth centuries.) An interesting pair of words is *ship* and *skiff*. The word *ship*, which has come down to us from Old English, would have originally begun with a *sk* sequence that later underwent the change to *sh* (/ʃ/). The word *skiff*, which refers to a small boat, retains the initial *sk* sequence, signaling that it is a borrowing from Scandinavian.

By far the greatest influence on English came from a Continental language—French. The influence of French is of course due to the Norman Conquest of England by William the Conqueror in 1066. The Normans brought with them the French language, and French remained the language of the ruling class for a considerable period. Under its influence the English language changed in terms of vocabulary, phonology, and morphology, as we will see.

Although the changes from Old English to Modern English were continuous and gradual, linguists traditionally distinguish three major periods in this development: the Old English period (fifth to eleventh centuries), the Middle English period (eleventh to fifteenth centuries), and the Modern English period (fifteenth century to the present). Scholars studying the history of English are fortunate in that there are written documents spanning more than 1,200 years that enable them to trace many of the changes that English has undergone during this time. These changes are typical of the changes that all languages undergo. In discussing them, we will concentrate on the three structural components of language—phonology, morphology, and syntax—as well as on vocabulary changes that have occurred between Old and Modern English. Each of these four components can undergo three major types of change: addition, loss, and change in structure.

Lexical Change

Addition

From Old English times to the present, new words have continuously been added to the English language. Surprisingly, only a few Celtic words have found their way into English, even though English speakers have been continuously in contact with Celtic speakers in Wales, Ireland, and Scotland. Personal names such as *Lloyd* and its variant *Floyd* are Welsh borrowings.

By far the greatest number of new words came from French as a result of the Norman invasion. These French words did not always replace Old English words; instead, in many instances they expanded an already existing vocabulary. For example, the words *pork*, *beef*, *veal*, *mutton*, and *venison* are all French words referring respectively to the edible meat of the *swine*, *cow*, *calf*, *sheep*, and *deer*, the latter being Old English words. Formerly, the Anglo-Saxon words were used to refer to both the meat and the animals. Interestingly, the words *beef* and *cow* are both descendants of a common Indo-European word *$g^{wh}ow$-, which, because of the different historical changes in the Germanic and Romance families, has given rise to quite different-sounding words.

Although English has borrowed most heavily from French, other languages have also contributed words. During the Renaissance, for example, a large number of so-called learned (question: when do we say /lɜˈnɪd/ and when do we say /lɜˈnd/?) words from Latin and Greek became part of English (*reverberate* from Latin and *polygon* from Greek are typical examples). From Spanish we have words such as *mesa*, *lariat*, and *taco*. From German we have words such as *kindergarten*, *hamburger*, and *gesundheit*. *Woodchuck* is ultimately an Algonquian word, and *tomato* comes to us from Aztec (via Spanish). English has thus borrowed freely from other languages, a habit that partially accounts for its enormous vocabulary.

In chapter 2 we also noted the many ways that new words can be introduced into English via abbreviations and word formation rules, producing such words as *TV*, *finalize*, and *laser*. Consequently, the number of words that can be added to our language—by borrowing or otherwise—is in principle unbounded.

Loss

Conversely, many words have been lost since the Old English period, though a surprising number of the lost words are still present in compounds. One example is Old English *wer* "man." This word is historically related to the Latin word *vir*, also meaning "man," forms of which (e.g., *virile*) have been borrowed into English. The form *wer*, even though lost as an independent word, still exists in *werewolf*, which originally meant "man-wolf" or "wolfman." The Old English word *rice* "realm, kingdom" has a similar history. This word, which was originally borrowed from a Celtic language, has been lost in the modern language. In contrast, the German language, which also borrowed this word, has preserved it in the word *Reich*. The only relic of this word in Modern English is in the compound word *bishopric*, which originally meant "bishop's realm," a sense close to its present-day meaning.

Change

Many examples of meaning change have already been discussed in chapter 2, which focused on narrowing, broadening, and metaphorical extension of meaning. Another example of semantic narrowing that occurred between Old English and Modern English is seen in the word *hound* (Old English *hund*). This word once referred to any kind of dog, whereas in Modern English the meaning has been narrowed to a particular breed. The word *dog* (Old English *docga*), on the other hand, referred in Old English to the mastiff breed; its meaning now has been broadened to include any dog. The meaning of *dog* has also been extended metaphorically in modern casual speech (slang) to refer to a particularly unattractive person.

Semantic Change and Semantic Fields

We have seen examples of individual words undergoing a meaning change. But semantic change at the word level is not limited to single words—rather, entire groups of words can undergo parallel semantic changes. In her study of *semantic fields* (see chapter 3), Lehrer (1974) noted that words belonging to the same semantic field undergo similar semantic changes. To take an example (Lehrer and Battan 1983), consider the following set of words, drawn from the semantic field of bird names: *goose, cuckoo, pigeon, coot, turkey*. In addition to its literal meaning, each of these words has a metaphorical use indicating "foolishness." According to the *Oxford English Dictionary*, the words *goose, cuckoo,* and *pigeon* were the first of this set to be used in the metaphorical sense in question, and all three acquired their metaphorical meaning at roughly the same time (the first recorded instances dating from the mid-sixteenth century). This could be due to coincidence; but it seems plausible to assume that the simultaneous metaphorical extension of the three words was based on their membership in the same semantic class. Later, the words *coot* and *turkey* came to have the same metaphorical use, again underscoring the idea that words in the same semantic field can undergo similar semantic changes. The word *pigeon*, incidentally, had a metaphorical use indicating "cowardice" in Shakespeare's time—recall *pigeon-livered*—but this use later became obsolete. What bird has taken over this metaphorical meaning of cowardice in Modern English?

It is also the case that the structure of a semantic field plays a role in semantic change. For example, the words *hot* and *cold* are antonyms that describe physical temperature. With pairs of antonyms, if one member undergoes a metaphorical extension, the other tends to change in a parallel fashion. Thus, just as *hot* and *cold* are opposites in describing temperature, so they are also opposites in their metaphorical extension in phrases such as *hot news* (news that is just breaking) versus *cold news* (news that is old). In colloquial style, we can speak of a *hot car* (stolen car); hence, we would not be surprised if speakers began using the phrase *cold car* (one that is not stolen), on the grounds that semantic change tends to affect entire semantic fields in a parallel fashion, and not just single members of the field (for discussion, see Lehrer 1974).

Phonological Change

Rule Addition
There have been many phonological changes between Old English and Modern English, and the rules discussed in chapter 3 (e.g., the rules governing flapped and glottal stop variants of *t*) have been *added* to American English relatively recently. Of course, rules that are added to a language can later be lost as living rules, and only certain effects of the rules remain. For example, an important set of extensive sound changes affecting the long (tense) vowels occurred at the end of the Middle English period, and these changes are the cause of one of the major discrepancies

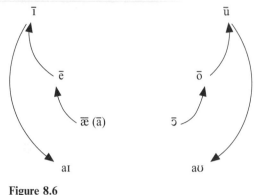

Figure 8.6
The Great Vowel Shift

between the spelling of Modern English and its current pronunciation. Known as the *Great Vowel Shift*, this change had the effects shown in figure 8.6, where the arrows indicate the direction of the changes.

Both of the long (or tense) mid vowels of Middle English, which we can represent by /ē/ and /ō/ (where the *macron* over the vowel indicates length), were raised and diphthongized to yield the current high vowels /i/ and /u/, respectively. The earlier pronunciation of these long mid vowels is still reflected in the spelling of words such as *feet* (once pronounced /fēt/, now pronounced /fit/) and *mood* (once pronounced /mōd/, now pronounced /mud/). The high vowels of Middle English, in turn, became diphthongs, the first part of the vowel "moving down" to become a low vowel. As part of the Great Vowel Shift, then, /ī/ became /aɪ/ and /ū/ became /aʊ/. The current orthography still reflects the former pronunciation in spellings such as *five* (once pronounced /fīv/, now pronounced /faɪv/). Note also the spelling of Old English *tūne* for "town" in (14), the vowel having been pronounced /ū/ before the diphthong /aʊ/ was created. Two of the long low vowels, /æ/ and /ɔ/, were also raised to yield a new set of mid vowels, /eɪ/ and /oʊ/, respectively. Thus, Modern English *mate* /meɪt/ was formerly pronounced /mæt/ and the word *goat* /goʊt/ was formerly pronounced /gɔt/.

The addition of these phonological rules, then, caused a significant change in the pronunciation of English words, and even though the Great Vowel Shift has now been lost from English as a purely phonological rule, its effects are still revealed in the discrepancy between the pronunciation of Modern English and its spelling system.

Rule Loss

Early in the history of English a rule called *i-Mutation* (or *i-Umlaut*) existed that turned back vowels into front vowels when an /i/ or /j/ followed in the next syllable. For example, in a certain class of nouns in the ancestor of Old English, the plural was formed not by adding -*s* but by adding -*i*. Thus, the plural of /gōs/ "goose" was /gōsi/ "geese." Later, when the *i*-Mutation rule was added, the *i*-ending of the plural conditioned the change of /gōsi/ to /gœ̄si/. The /œ/ phoneme is a combination of the /o/ and /e/ phonemes; it is a mid front vowel like /e/ but has lip rounding like /o/. Hence, the effect of *i*-Mutation was to cause back vowels to be articulated in a more forward position in the mouth, but the newly fronted vowels kept the rounding that they had when they were back vowels. Still later, the lip rounding was lost, and the plural /gœ̄s(e)/ became /gēs(e)/. When /gōs/ and /gēs/ finally underwent the Great Vowel Shift, the current pronunciations /gus/ and /gis/ resulted. Thus, *i*-Mutation is an example of a rule that was once present in Old English but has since dropped out of the language, and thanks to the Great Vowel Shift even the effects of *i*-Mutation have been altered.

Change in Rule Applicability

In Old English, fricatives became voiced when they occurred between voiced sounds (i.e., $f \rightarrow v$, $\theta \rightarrow \eth$, $s \rightarrow z$). Since the most common plural ending was formerly -*as*, all nouns ending in fricatives underwent this rule in the plural. The rule causing this voicing is no longer present in Modern English, but its effects can still be observed in pairs such as singular *wife* /waɪf/ and plural *wives* /waɪvz/. This change of the stem in the plural is still the result of a rule, but the form of the rule is quite different from the form that it had in Old English. In Old English the rule was *phonological*: it applied whenever fricatives occurred between voiced sounds. In contrast, the alternation between voiced and voiceless fricatives in Modern English is not phonological but *morphological*: the voicing rule applies only to certain words and not to others. Thus, a particular (and now exceptional) class of nouns must undergo voicing of the final voiceless fricative when used in the plural (e.g., *wife/wives, knife/knives, hoof/hooves*). However, other nouns ending with the same sound do not undergo this process (e.g., *proof/proofs*). The fricative voicing rule of Old English has changed from a phonological rule to a morphological rule in Modern English.

Differences in Phonemic Inventory

Addition of Phonemes

The phonemic system of Old English was similar to that of Modern English, although several differences can be noted. For example, the voiced labiodental fricative [v] was not an independent phoneme in Old English. The [v]'s that did occur were voiced allophonic variants of the phoneme /f/. As a result of subsequent changes between Old English and Middle English, /v/ has become an independent phoneme.

Loss of Phonemes

As noted in the previous section, the mutated (or umlauted) vowels /œ/ and /y/ (front rounded vowels) lost their rounding during the Old English period. The word *thimble*, for example, probably was originally pronounced as [θymbɪl] in very early Old English. Later /y/ (a rounded high front vowel) became unrounded to /ɪ/. (Knowing that the suffix *-il* was used to form nouns with diminutive meaning from other nouns, what can you surmise about the origin of the word *thimble*?)

Morphological Change

Rule Addition

The *-able* rule discussed in chapter 2 is an example of a rule that has been added to English since the Old English period. As a result of the influx of a large number of *-able* words from French into English, English speakers were (and are still) able to extract a productive rule from these words. Words such as *doable* and *washable* have been formed by adding *-able* to the Germanic roots *do* and *wash*.

Rule Loss

An example of a morphological rule that has been lost is the Causative Verb Formation rule of Old English. In Old English, causative verbs could be formed by adding the suffix *-yan* to adjectives. The modern verb *redden* meaning "to cause to be or make red" is a carryover from the time when the Causative Verb Formation rule was present in English, in that the final *-en* of *redden* is a reflex of the earlier *-yan* causative suffix. However, the rule adding a suffix such as *-en* to adjectives to form new verbs has been lost, and thus we can no longer form new causative verbs such as *green-en* "to make green" or *blue-en* "to make blue." (Do you see now how *awake* and *awaken* are related to each other?)

Rule Change

New nouns could be formed in Old English by adding *-ing* not only to verbs, as in Modern English (*sing* + *ing* = *singing*), but also to a large class of nouns. For example, the word *viking* was formed by adding *-ing* to the noun *wic* "bay." (Why might the word for "bay" be used to describe the Vikings?) It turns out that the *-ing* suffix can still be added to a highly restricted class of nouns, carrying the meaning "material used for," as in *roofing*, *carpeting*, and *flooring*. Thus, the rule for creating new nouns with the *-ing* suffix has changed by becoming more restricted in its application, so that a much smaller class of nouns can still have *-ing* attached.

Syntactic Change

Rule Addition

A syntactic rule that has been added to English since the Old English period is the Particle Movement rule discussed in chapter 5. Thus, sentence pairs of the type *John threw out the fish* and *John threw the fish out* did not occur in Old English.

Rule Loss

A syntactic rule that has been lost from English is the morphosyntactic rule of Adjective Agreement. At one time adjectives required endings that had to agree with the head noun in case, number, and gender (see (15)). This rule is no longer found in English, since most of the inflectional endings of English have been lost.

Syntactic Change: Auxiliary Verbs versus Main Verbs

Recall from chapter 5 that contemporary English makes a distinction between auxiliary verbs and main verbs, a distinction reflected in questions (only auxiliary verbs can be fronted in questions, as in *Can you leave?*), negative sentences (only auxiliary verbs can take the contracted negative *n't*, as in *You can't leave*), and tag questions (only auxiliary verbs can appear in tags, as in *You can leave, can't you?*). Focusing now only on so-called modal verbs (*can*, *must*), it is interesting to note that prior to the sixteenth century these syntactic distinctions between main verbs and auxiliary verbs did not exist. At that time it was possible for main verbs to take *not*, and examples such as the following can be found in Shakespeare's writings:

(16)

a. I deny it *not*. ("I don't deny it.")

b. Forbid him *not*. ("Do not forbid him.")

Similarly, main verbs could be fronted in forming questions:

(17)

a. Revolt our subjects? ("Do our subjects revolt?")

b. Gives not the hawthorn-bush a sweeter shade? ("Does the hawthorn-bush not give a sweeter shade?")

However, by Shakespeare's time such patterns were already beginning to disappear as a series of grammatical changes was taking place in the mid-1500s (see Lightfoot 1979 for a summary and discussion). After the sixteenth century the grammar of English had changed so that auxiliary verbs—and never main verbs—had to be used in negation, questions, and other patterns we have noted.

The changes that took place between Old English and Modern English are typical of the kinds of changes that all human languages undergo over time, and after enough years have passed the descendant language (or languages) can be very different from its (their) ancestor language. Moreover, language change offers important indirect evidence about the nature of human language—namely, that it is rule-governed. We have seen that the major changes that the English language underwent between the Old English and Modern English periods are best viewed as changes in the *sets of rules* characterizing the two stages of English. Over time, grammatical rules can be added, lost, or changed; so language has always changed, and indeed, given the complexity of language and the way that humans use it creatively, change is part of the nature of human language.

Study Questions

1. Discuss the various theories for the origin of human language.

2. What is the Indo-European language family?

3. What is one way to establish that languages are descendants of a common ancestor for which no written records exist?

4. What is Grimm's Law? Illustrate its effect with some comparisons between English and Latin or Greek words.

5. What does it mean to say that some language changes move "wavelike" through a community of speakers?

6. What was the Great Vowel Shift? What consequences did this sound change have for contemporary English? Give examples in your answer.

Exercises

1. How can knowledge of Grimm's Law help one remember that a *podiatrist* is a foot doctor?

2. The Indo-European word **ghostis* corresponds to the Latin word *hostis* "enemy" and to the English word *guest*. What is a plausible meaning that **ghostis* could have had that would account for the different meanings in Latin and English?

3. Using the accompanying chart, explain the relationships among the underlined words in the following English sentence: *I turned up the thermostat on my furnace to get warm.*

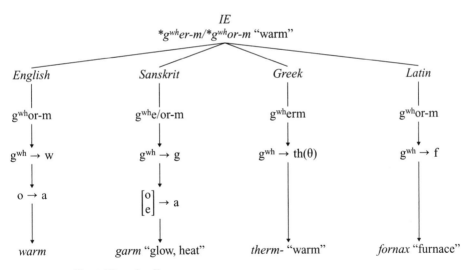

Chart (Exercise 3)
Changes that original Indo-European (IE) **gʷʰer-m/*gʷʰor-m* underwent in several daughter languages. The *n* found in Latin *fornax* is not from IE **m*, but instead is a different suffix that was added to the stem **gʷʰor-*.

4. Each of the Indo-European words in the following list has a cognate in English. You can determine what the words are by (1) applying Grimm's Law to the Indo-European forms and (2) using the meaning of the Latin, Greek, or Sanskrit borrowings as a clue. (Hint: Don't worry about finding regular changes in the vowels for this exercise.)

Indo-European	Words borrowed from classical languages into English
a. *gʰwēn	a. gynecologist (from Greek)
b. *dekm̥	b. decimate (from Latin)
c. *gnō-	c. agnostic (from Greek)
d. *yug(om)	d. yoga (from Sanskrit, means "work")
e. *agrus	e. agriculture (from Latin)

Further Reading

General

The following texts provide a good survey of *historical linguistics* and the *Indo-European language family*: Antilla 1972, Arlotto 1972, Bynon 1977, Ramat and Ramat 1993, and McMahon 1994. Recent discussions of the *origin and dispersal of humans and their languages* are found in Bellwood 1979, 1991, Greenberg 1987, Renfrew 1989, Cavalli-Sforza 1991, Thorne and Wolpoff 1992, and Wilson and Cann 1992. Discussions of the putative *Nostratic superfamily* are found in Kaiser and Shevoroshkin 1988, Bomhard 1992, and Shevoroshkin 1990. Good overviews of the *history of English* are found in Baugh and Cable 1978, Pyles and Algeo 1982, and Hogg 1992.

Journals

Diachronica, Journal of Indo-European Studies, Language, Zeitschrift für Vergleichende Sprachwissenschaft

Bibliography

Antilla, R. 1972. *An introduction to historical and comparative linguistics.* 3rd ed. New York: Harcourt Brace Jovanovich.

Arlotto, A. 1972. *Introduction to historical linguistics.* Boston: Houghton Mifflin.

Baugh, A., and T. Cable. 1978. *A history of the English language.* 3rd ed. Englewood Cliffs, N.J.: Prentice-Hall.

Bellwood, P. 1979. *Man's conquest of the Pacific: The prehistory of Southeast Asia and Polynesia.* New York: Oxford University Press.

Bellwood, P. 1991. The Austronesian dispersal and the origin of languages. *Scientific American* 265.1, 88–93.

Bloomfield, L. 1933. *Language.* New York: Holt, Rinehart and Winston.

Bomhard, A. 1992. The Nostratic macrofamily (with special reference to Indo-European). *Word* 43, 61–83.

Bynon, T. 1977. *Historical linguistics*. Cambridge: Cambridge University Press.

Campbell, L. 1988. Review article on *Language in the Americas*. *Language* 64, 591–615.

Cardona, G., H. M. Hoenigswald, and A. Senn, eds. 1970. *Indo-European and Indo-Europeans*. Philadelphia: University of Pennsylvania Press.

Cavalli-Sforza, L. 1991. Genes, people, and languages. *Scientific American* 265.5, 104–111.

Diamond, J. 1989. The great leap forward. *Discover* 10.5, 50–60.

Fell, B. 1977. *America B.C: Ancient settlers in the New World*. New York: New York Times Book Company.

Gimbutas, M. 1970. Proto-Indo-European culture: The Kurgan culture during the fifth, fourth, and third millennia, B.C. In Cardona, Hoenigswald, and Senn 1970.

Greenberg, J. 1987. *Language in the Americas*. Stanford, Calif.: Stanford University Press.

Greenberg, J. 1989. Classification of American Indian Languages: A reply to Campbell. *Language* 65, 107–114.

Greenberg, J., and M. Ruhlen. 1992. Linguistic origins of Native Americans. *Scientific American* 267.5, 94–99.

Harnad, S., H. Steklis, and J. Lancaster, eds. 1976. *Origins and evolution of language and speech*. Annals of the New York Academy of Science, vol. 280. New York.

Hewes, G. 1976. The current status of the gestural theory of language origins. In Harnad, Steklis, and Lancaster 1976.

Hogg, R. 1992. *The Cambridge history of the English language*. 6 vols. Cambridge: Cambridge University Press.

Joos, M. 1942. A phonological dilemma in Canadian English. *Language* 18, 141–144.

Kaiser, M., and V. Shevoroshkin. 1988. Nostratic. *Annual Review of Anthropology* 17, 309–329.

Lehmann, W. 1967. *A reader in nineteenth-century historical linguistics*. Bloomington: Indiana University Press.

Lehmann, W. 1973. *Historical linguistics: An introduction*. 2nd ed. New York: Holt, Rinehart and Winston.

Lehrer, A. 1974. *Semantic fields and lexical structure*. Amsterdam: North-Holland.

Lehrer, A., and P. Battan. 1983. Semantic fields and semantic change. In *Coyote papers* 4. Department of Linguistics, University of Arizona, Tucson.

Lenneberg, E. 1964. A biological perspective of language. In E. Lenneberg, ed., *New directions in the study of language*. Cambridge, Mass.: MIT Press.

Lieberman, P. 1975. *On the origins of language: An introduction to the evolution of human speech*. New York: Macmillan.

Lightfoot, D. 1979. *Principles of diachronic syntax*. New York: Cambridge University Press.

Martin, S. 1966. Lexical evidence relating Korean to Japanese. *Language* 46, 185–251.

McMahon, A. 1994. *Understanding language change*. Cambridge: Cambridge University Press.

Miller, G. 1981. *Language and speech*. San Francisco: W. H. Freeman.

Molony, C. 1988. The truth about the Tasaday. *Sciences* 28, 12–20.

Moore, S., and T. Knott. 1963. *The elements of Old English*. Ann Arbor, Mich.: George Wahr.

National Geographic Magazine. 1989. Did Neanderthals speak? New bone of contention. October 1989.

Pyles, T., and J. Algeo. 1982. *The origins and development of the English language*. 3rd ed. New York: Harcourt Brace Jovanovich.

Ramat, A., and P. Ramat. 1993. *The Indo-European languages*. New York: Routledge.

Renfrew, C. 1989. The origins of the Indo-European languages. *Scientific American* 261.4, 106–114.

Shevoroshkin, V. 1990. The mother tongue: How linguists have reconstructed the ancestor of all living languages. *Sciences* 30, 20–27.

Sloat, C., S. Taylor, and J. Hoard. 1978. *An introduction to phonology*. Englewood Cliffs, N.J.: Prentice-Hall.

Thorne, A., and M. Wolpoff. 1992. The multiregional evolution of humans. *Scientific American* 266.4, 76–83.

Traugott, E. 1972. *A history of English syntax*. New York: Holt, Rinehart and Winston.

Wilson, A., and R. Cann. 1992. The recent African genesis of humans. *Scientific American* 266.4, 68–73.

Yamada, J. E. 1990. *Laura: A case for the modularity of language*. Cambridge, Mass.: MIT Press.

PART II
COMMUNICATION AND COGNITIVE SCIENCE

INTRODUCTION

In the previous chapters we have explored human language as an abstract system with numerous structural (morphological, phonetic, phonological, syntactic, and semantic) properties. We have seen that human language can be fruitfully analyzed in terms of various units of representation (features, phonemes, morphemes, words, phrases, clauses, sentences, concepts, etc.), along with rules and principles that capture regularities and generalizations among these units. Thus, various "levels" in the description of a language (the morphological, phonetic, phonological, syntactic, and semantic levels) represent regularities in the behavior of the units at that level, and such levels in linguistics are like the levels in other sciences. For instance, chemists describe substances in terms of elements and their principles of combination: water is two parts hydrogen and one part oxygen, combined in a certain way. A physicist might then describe oxygen and hydrogen in terms of their atomic structure, atomic weight, and principles of atomic interaction. Furthermore, it is an important fact about human languages that they are susceptible to variation and change (we do not view the principles that govern the world of physics as varying or changing, though our knowledge of them surely will), and we have seen that often such variation and change are themselves principled in interesting ways.

It is now time to remind ourselves, theoretically, of the importance of the fact that languages are *used* and *learned* by human beings (and many would say *only* by human beings). How could a language change or vary if it were not? Thinking of languages as being used and learned by humans raises still more questions, such as, How do people use language to communicate? How is this knowledge represented in and utilized by the mind/brain? How is it learned?

In chapter 9 we explore the nature of pragmatics, the study of language use in relation to language structure and context of use. As such, the study of pragmatics straddles the boundary between language and the world. Speaking a language involves producing sounds for others to hear, understand, and act upon. How is it possible for a speaker to put thoughts into words and for a hearer to understand them? This, it turns out, is not a trivial or simple accomplishment: a rich and subtle system of principles underlies this apparently facile skill.

It is an important fact about human beings that virtually all of them learn to speak (or sign) a language. Placed in a minimal linguistic environment, all human children with normal brain function will quickly and apparently effortlessly acquire the language spoken (or signed) around them. Thus, we should expect that human language and its use will be interestingly related to human cognition. So far this has proved to be true, and a richly diverse new field called *cognitive science* has developed, incorporating aspects of linguistics, philosophy, psychology, neuroscience, computer science, and artificial intelligence. The basic idea behind cognitive science is that the study of cognition (perception, memory, thought, and action) should be a unified subject of research, drawing on the expertise of many traditional disciplines. For instance, in computer science one learns how to write programs that can perform certain tasks. One also learns how machines can be built that will execute these programs and actually exhibit the capacity written into them. Cognitive science draws on these activities of computer science, using them as an analogy that helps to unify our picture of the human mind. What if the human mind is like a mental "program" and neurons are our "hardware"? Knowing how programs and hardware are related in computer science might help us better understand, by analogy, how our knowledge and our thoughts might be related to the neural structure of our brains. In particular, we might better understand how our knowledge of language and our ability to speak and understand might be related to the structure of our brain. Recent work on "connectionist" models shows that we must not restrict our conception of computers and programming them to just the architectures that happen to be available and commercially viable.

One of the most active areas of psychology is the study of linguistic knowledge, how it is acquired, and how it is used in the production and comprehension of speech. In chapters 10 and 11 we investigate some significant results in the psychology of language (also called psycholinguistics).

Chapter 10 is devoted to exploring issues in the production and comprehension of speech. Here we consider how linguistic knowledge might be represented in the mind and how this information can be put to use in speaking and understanding. Following the flow of information from speaker to hearer, we will both review broad theoretical options and report interesting experimental results.

Chapter 11 is devoted to the study of the acquisition of language. Here we examine the character of normal language development in the (human) child, and the implications this process might have for better understanding human biological endowment. For instance, are human beings preprogrammed to learn (or create) the kind of language system we have been describing? Can the young of another species (such as primates) acquire human language, and if so do they acquire it in the same way? To begin to answer these questions, we first explore the normal course of human language development. We then survey some controversial attempts to teach American Sign Language to primates. Do they learn as human children do, or are there important differences?

Given that human language is clearly unique among communication systems in its richness and complexity, and given the natural disposition children have for mastering it, it is quite reasonable to suppose that there is something special about the human brain, either in capacity or in its structural organization, that makes this distinctively human achievement possible. In spite of the splendid work in the last few decades of a highly dedicated group of neuroscientists, we are still quite ignorant about the structure and functioning of the human brain with respect to such basic cognitive functions as language. In fact, the study of the brain has often been described as the next intellectual frontier. It is certainly true that we understand the rest of the human body a great deal better than we understand the brain. Chapter 12 is devoted to some of the central ideas and controversies to come out of neurolinguistics, the study of the neural basis of language. Since it is hardly feasible to perform experiments on the neuroanatomy of speakers' brains, a crucial source of data about how language might be represented and used by the brain is the experience of patients suffering some loss of speech production or comprehension because of brain injuries.

All in all, it seems that linguists will gain a deeper perspective on their subject matter by seeing exactly how it is related to the neighboring concerns of psychology, neuroscience, and biology. Likewise, these neighboring areas of research can gain something from linguistics; language constitutes the richest and most rigorously described domain of human expertise yet. The structures and regularities discovered by linguists in their analyses of human languages pose a unique challenge to psychological, neurological, and biological theories of human capacities.

Chapter 9

Pragmatics: The Study of Language Use and Communication

9.1 SOME BACKGROUND CONCEPTS

Pragmatics

When Charles Morris proposed his famous trichotomy of syntax, semantics, and pragmatics, he defined the last as "the study of the relation of signs to interpreters" (1938, 6), but he soon generalized this to "the relation of signs to their users" (1938, 29). One year later Rudolf Carnap proposed to "call *pragmatics* the field of all those investigations which take into consideration ... the action, state, and environment of a man who speaks or hears [a linguistic sign]" (1939, 4). However, this characterization of pragmatics is so broad that it includes all studies of language users, from neurolinguistics to sociolinguistics, and would preclude the possibility of formulating contentful general pragmatic principles. Therefore, we will take the term *pragmatics* to cover the study of language use, and in particular the study of linguistic communication, in relation to language structure and context of utterance. For instance, pragmatics must identify central uses of language, it must specify the conditions for linguistic expressions (words, phrases, sentences, discourse) to be used in those ways, and it must seek to uncover general principles of language use. Much of this work was originally done by philosophers of language such as Wittgenstein (1953), Austin (1962), Searle (1969), and Grice (1975), in the years following World War II. In the 1970s linguists such as Ross (1970) and Lakoff (1970) attempted to incorporate much of the work on performatives, felicity conditions, and presupposition into the framework of Generative Semantics (see Newmeyer 1980, Harris 1993). With the breakdown of Generative Semantics, pragmatics was left without a unifying linguistic theory, and research is currently being carried out on a number of topics, many of them surveyed in this chapter, across a number of different disciplines including linguistics, philosophy, psychology, communication, sociology, and anthropology. In what follows we will focus on the central use of language: communication. We will see what problems it poses to pragmatics and what structure it has. Finally we will turn to some special topics in pragmatics.

The Problem

Probably the most pervasive characteristic of human social interaction, so pervasive that we hardly find it remarkable, is that we talk. Sometimes we talk to particular persons, sometimes to anyone who will listen; and when we cannot find anyone to listen, we even talk to ourselves. Although human language fulfills a large variety of functions, from waking someone up in the morning with a cheery *Wake up!* to christening a ship with a solemn *I hereby christen this ship "H. M. S. Britannia,"* we will be focusing here on those uses of language that are instrumental for human communication. Fluent speakers of English, for instance, know facts such as these:

(1)
a. *Hello* is used to greet.
b. *Goodbye* is used to bid farewell.
c. The phrase *that desk* can be correctly used by a speaker on a given occasion to refer to some particular desk.
d. The phrase *is a desk* can be correctly used on a given occasion to characterize any number of desks.
e. *Pass the salt, please* is used to request some salt.
f. *How old are you?* is used to ask someone's age.
g. *It's raining* is used to state that it is raining.
h. *I promise I will be there* is used to promise.

From this list we get a glimpse of the wide variety of possible uses of language, but before we survey these various uses, we must first distinguish between using language *to do* something and using language *in doing* something. It is certainly a very important fact about human beings that we use language *in* much of our thought. It is likely that we could not think some of the thoughts we think, especially abstract thoughts, if we did not have language at our disposal. Central as this fact may be to our cognitive life, it is not central to the pragmatic notion of language use, the use of language to *do* things. When we focus on what people use language to do, we focus on what a person is doing with words in particular situations; we focus on the intentions, purposes, beliefs, and desires that a speaker has in speaking.

As common and effortless as it is to talk, using language successfully is a very complex enterprise, as anyone knows who has tried as an adult to master a second language. Moreover, much goes into using a language besides knowing it and being able to produce and recognize sentences in it. Communication is also a social affair, usually taking place within the context of a fairly well defined social situation. In such a context we rely on one another to share our conception of what the situation is. With people we know, rather than spell everything out, we rely on shared understandings to facilitate communication.

What sort of process is this? Linguistic communication is easily accomplished but, as it turns out, not so easily explained; any theory of linguistic communication worth the title must attempt to answer the following questions:

(2)
What is (successful) linguistic communication? How does (successful) communication work? For example, suppose that a speaker has an intention to report to a hearer that conditions on the road are icy. What makes it possible for the speaker to communicate this to the hearer?

Strangely enough, these questions have not received intensive consideration in the literature of any major discipline. Linguistics, focusing on structural properties of language, has tended to view communicative phenomena as outside its official domain. Likewise, it seems possible to pursue philosophical concerns about meaning, truth, and reference without investigating the details of communication. Traditional psychology of language has focused on the processing of sentences, but without much concern for the specifics of communicative phenomena. Finally, some sociologists and anthropologists concern themselves with conversations, but have bypassed (or assumed an answer to) the question of the nature of communication itself. Thus, what is needed is an integrated approach to communication, where the question of its nature is the focus of investigation. Only recently has the general shape of an adequate theory of communication begun to emerge, and more time and research will be required to explore it in detail.

9.2   THE MESSAGE MODEL OF LINGUISTIC COMMUNICATION

For the last 50 years the most common and popular conception of human linguistic communication has been what we will term the *Message Model*. When the Message Model is applied to human linguistic commu-

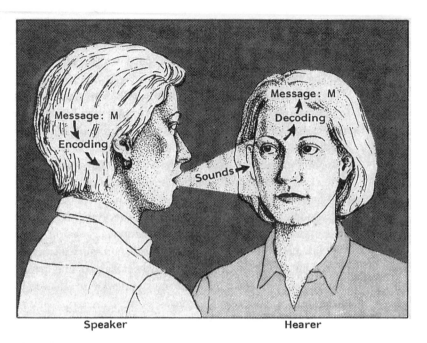

Speaker   **Hearer**

Figure 9.1
The Message Model of communication. A speaker has some message in mind that she wants to communicate to a hearer. The speaker then produces some expression from the language that encodes the message as its meaning. Upon hearing the beginning of the expression, the hearer begins identifying the incoming sounds, syntax, and meanings; then, using her knowledge of language, she composes these meanings in the form of a successfully decoded message.

nication between speakers of a language, the speaker acts as a "transmitter," the hearer acts as a "receiver," and the vocal-auditory path (the sound wave) is the relevant channel. The Message Model for human communication is illustrated in figure 9.1, and summarized later in (6).

This model accounts for certain commonsense features of talk-exchanges: it predicts that communication is successful when the hearer decodes the same message that the speaker encodes; and as a corollary it predicts that communication breaks down if the decoded message is different from the encoded message. Likewise, it portrays language as a bridge between speaker and hearer whereby "private" ideas are communicated by "public" sounds, which function as the vehicle for communicating the relevant message.

Though it has a modern ring, the Message Model goes back over three centuries to the philosopher John Locke, who wrote in 1691 that

[m]an, therefore, had by nature his organs so fashioned, as to be fit to frame articulate sounds, which we call words. But this was not enough to produce language; for parrots, and several other birds, will be taught to make articulate sounds distinct enough, which yet by no means are capable of language.

Besides articulate sounds, therefore, it was further necessary that he should be able to use these sounds as signs of internal conceptions; and to make them stand as marks for the ideas within his own mind, whereby they might be made known to others and the thoughts of men's minds be conveyed from one to another.

The comfort and advantage of society being not to be had without communication of thoughts, it was necessary that man should find out some external sensible signs, whereof those invisible ideas, which his thoughts are made up of, might be made known to others.

There are, moreover, many contemporary statements of essentially this same idea:

The speaker, for reasons that are linguistically irrelevant, chooses some message he wants to convey to his listeners: some thought he wants them to receive or some command he wants to give them or some question he wants to ask. This message is encoded in the form of a phonetic representation of an utterance by means of the system of linguistic rules with which the speaker is equipped. This encoding then becomes a signal to the speaker's articulatory organs, and he vocalizes an utterance of the proper phonetic shape. This, in turn, is picked up by the hearer's auditory organs. The speech sounds that stimulate these organs are then converted into a neural signal from which a phonetic representation equivalent to the one into which the speaker encoded his message is obtained. This representation is decoded into a representation of the same message that the speaker originally chose to convey by the hearer's equivalent system of linguistic rules. Hence, because the hearer employs the same system of rules to decode that the speaker employs to encode, an instance of successful linguistic communication occurs. (Katz 1966, 103–104)

There can be little doubt that this model has fascinated many who are interested in human communication, and it is entrenched, to some extent, in our language. For example, Reddy (1979, 311–316) lists some 80 metaphors built on the idea of language as a "conduit for ideas," among which are the following:

(3)
a. Try to *get* your thoughts *across* better.
b. You still haven't *given* me any idea of what you mean.
c. Try to *pack* more thoughts into fewer words.

d. The sentence was *filled* with emotion.

e. Let me know if you *find* any good ideas *in* this essay.

According to Reddy (1979, 290), the major ideas structuring this metaphor are:

(1) language functions like a conduit, transferring thoughts bodily from one person to another; (2) in writing and speaking, people insert their thoughts or feelings in the words; (3) words accomplish the transfer by containing the thoughts or feelings and conveying them to others; and (4) in listening or reading, people extract the thoughts and feelings once again from the words.

These are clear analogues of the major tenets of the Message Model, and this suggests that our talk about language has come to reflect this conception of communication.

Problems with the Message Model

In order to determine the meaning of expressions, the hearer must be able to mentally process sentences that reflect complex structural properties of human language, such as structural ambiguity and discontinuous dependencies (recall our discussion of these in chapter 5). The decoding of the meaning(s) of a sentence is certainly a crucial part of linguistic communication, but the communicative process does not end with processing structural properties and decoding meaning. Indeed, there is considerably more to the process, and it is here that the Message Model encounters a number of problems. We will briefly outline six typical problems faced by the Message Model, and in so doing we hope to give an idea of how complex the communication process is.

First, since many expressions are linguistically ambiguous, the hearer must determine which of the possible meanings of an expression is the one the speaker intended as operative on that occasion. Thus, as far as the Message Model is concerned, disambiguation is a process that is not governed by any principles, and the Message Model certainly does not supply any such principles. But in actuality, disambiguation is not unprincipled and random; rather, it is usually quite predictable. Although humorous cases of misunderstanding do arise from time to time, in general we do a good job of picking the appropriate reading of an ambiguous expression. To overcome ambiguity, the hearer presumes the speaker's remarks to be *contextually appropriate*. For example, at an airport zoning meeting the sentence *Flying planes can be dangerous* would naturally be taken as a remark about the danger of planes flying overhead; but at a meeting of the Pilots' Insurance Board it would naturally be taken as a reminder of the risk of piloting planes. To take another example, imagine the following conversation:

(4)
A: We lived in Illinois, but we got Milwaukee's weather.
B: Which was worse

Notice that without some extra optional cue (such as exaggerated intonation), A does not know whether B was making an assertion or asking a question:

(5)
Assertion: It was worse getting Milwaukee's weather!
Question: Which weather was it worse to get?

Hence, the Message Model must be supplemented by principles of contextual appropriateness to compensate for the pervasive ambiguity of natural language. This is the problem of *ambiguity*.

Second, the Message Model does not account for the fact that the message often contains information about particular things being referred to, and such reference is rarely uniquely determined by the meaning of expressions. For example, the phrase *the shrewd politician* can be used on different occasions to refer to different people such as Winston Churchill or Richard Nixon. Yet the phrase always means one thing ("politician who is shrewd"). A hearer who thinks of Richard Nixon when the speaker's intended referent is Winston Churchill will not have understood the message correctly. So the Message Model must be supplemented by mechanisms for successfully recognizing the intention to refer to a specific person, place, or thing. This is the problem of the *underdetermination of reference (by meaning)*.

Third, the Message Model represents successful communication as simply producing, hearing, and understanding meaningful expressions. But this is not all there is to communication. What is missing in the model so far is an account of the speaker's *communicative intention*, which is not, in general, uniquely determined by the meaning of the expression uttered, but is part of the message communicated. For example, *I'll be there tonight* might be a prediction, a promise, or even a threat, depending upon the speaker's intentions in the appropriate circumstances. Despite these various intentions on the part of the speaker, the sentence has only one relevant meaning. This is the problem of the *underdetermination of communicative intention (by meaning)*.

Fourth, the Message Model does not account for the additional fact that we often speak *nonliterally*; that is, we may not mean what our words mean. Common cases of this are irony, sarcasm, and figurative uses of language such as metaphor. Thus, a speaker who says *Oh, that's just great* can, in the appropriate context, be taken to mean the opposite of what the words mean. (Think of discovering a flat tire on your way to class in the morning.) Nonliteral cases are especially difficult for the Message Model to accommodate, since in nonliteral communication the message conveyed by the speaker does not incorporate the literal meaning at all. Rather, the hearer is intended to *use* the literal meaning in figuring out what the speaker actually intends to communicate. This is the problem of *nonliterality*.

Fifth, the Message Model does not account for the fact that we sometimes mean to communicate more than what our sentences mean. We sometimes speak *indirectly*; that is, we sometimes intend to perform one communicative act by means of performing another communicative act. For example, it would be quite natural to say *My car has a flat tire* to a gas station attendant, with the intention that he repair the tire: in this case we are *requesting* the hearer to *do* something. But how can the speaker mean that the hearer is to do something if the sentence she utters merely reports on the state of her car? The answer is that in uttering the sentence the speaker is (literally and) *directly* reporting a state of affairs presumed to be unsatisfactory and is *indirectly* requesting the hearer to rectify the situation. How does a hearer know if a speaker is speaking indirectly as well as directly? Again, the answer is contextual appropriateness. In the above case, it would be contextually inappropriate to be only reporting a flat tire at a gas station. In contrast, if a police officer asks why a motorist's car is illegally parked, a simple report of a flat tire would be a contextually appropriate response. In the latter circumstance, the hearer (the police officer) would certainly not take the speaker's words as a request to fix the tire. Again, we see the surprisingly pervasive role that presumptions of contextual appropriateness play in successful communication. A speaker can use the very same sentence to convey quite different messages depending on the context. This is the problem of *indirection*.

The sixth and final problem with the Message Model is that communicating a message is not always the purpose of our remarks, and this model does not connect at all with these other uses. For example there are *institutional* acts such as firing or baptizing someone, whose function is to change the institutional status of that person. There are also institutional speech acts such as calling a base runner out or finding a defendant guilty, which involve judgments of truth with institutional and social consequences. Communicative success is not the point of such utterances since the runner is out, the employee is fired, and the baby is baptized, whether or not they recognize it at the time. Thus, it is not necessary to recognize any communicative intention for these acts to succeed. Likewise, there are speech acts (called *perlocutionary* acts; see "Special Topics") involving the causing of an effect in a hearer. For instance, a speaker might say things with an intent to persuade, impress, or deceive an audience, but the members of the audience may well not be persuaded, impressed, or deceived if they happen to recognize the speaker's intention to do these things. In contrast, communicative intentions are always intended to be recognized. This is the problem of *noncommunicative acts*.

To summarize, the Message Model would answer the questions in (2) as follows:

(6)
Successful communication according to the Message Model
Linguistic communication is successful if the hearer receives the speaker's message. It works because messages have been conventionalized as the meaning of expressions, and by sharing knowledge of the meaning of an expression, the hearer can recognize a speaker's message—the speaker's communicative intention.

We have seen that this answer to the central question of communication is seriously defective, in that it does not accommodate most of the common cases of successful linguistic communication. For instance, in order to recover a determinate message, the Message Model of communication must assume that (1) the language is unambiguous, (2) what the speaker is referring to is determined by the meaning of the referring expressions uttered, (3) the communicative intention is determined by the meaning of the sentence, (4) speakers only speak literally, and (5) speakers only speak directly; and it suggests that (6) speakers use words, phrases, and sentences only to communicate.

The six problem areas discussed above show why the simple Message Model of talk-exchanges does not even begin to be adequate to account for the full richness of normal human language use. Clearly, more than just a common language is required to enable the hearer to identify the speaker's communicative intentions on the basis of the speaker's utterances. A *shared system of beliefs and inferences* must be operating, which function in effect as communicative strategies.

9.3   THE INFERENTIAL MODEL OF LINGUISTIC COMMUNICATION

If the connection between a speaker's communicative intention (message) and a sentence is *not* one of conventional coding of the message into the sentence via its meaning, then what is it? What is the connection between sounds and communicative intentions that makes communication in all its forms possible?

Basically, the connection is *inferential*. According to the theory of communication to be presented here, linguistic communication is successful when the hearer, upon hearing an expression, recognizes the speaker's communicative intention. Thus, the *Inferential Model* of linguistic communication would propose the following answers to the questions posed in (2):

(7)
Successful communication according to the Inferential Model
Linguistic communication is successful if the hearer recognizes the speaker's communicative intention. Linguistic communication works because the speaker and the hearer share a system of inferential strategies leading from the utterance of an expression to the hearer's recognition of the speaker's communicative intent.

If this is the correct approach to take to communication, then we need to know more about the system of inferential strategies; we want to know how such a system can account for successful communication, while avoiding the limitations of the Message Model. In particular, we want to know how it (1) incorporates the notion of communicative intentions, (2) does not make these communicative intentions uniquely determined by the meaning of the expression uttered, and (3) accounts for literal, non-literal, direct, and indirect ways of communicating.

The Message Model of linguistic communication applies, if at all, only to a highly idealized form of communication—which hardly ever actually takes place! However, if one tries to construct a theory of actual, normal communication, then the idea that *rules* or *conventions* of language connect sounds with messages (see (6)) is replaced by the idea that systems of *intended inference* and *shared beliefs* are at work, and that therefore the real job of the communicative part of pragmatics is to investigate these systems.

In what follows we will do just that. The basic idea is quite simple: linguistic communication is a kind of cooperative problem solving. The speaker faces the problem of getting the hearer to recognize the speaker's communicative intentions; so the speaker must choose an expression that will facilitate such recognition, given the context of utterance. From the hearer's point of view the problem is to successfully recognize the speaker's communicative intention on the basis of the words the speaker has chosen and the context of utterance.

The *Inferential Model* of communication proposes that in the course of learning to speak our language we also learn how to communicate in that language, and learning this involves acquiring a variety of shared beliefs or *presumptions*, as well as a system of inferential *strategies*. The presumptions allow us to presume certain helpful things about potential hearers (or speakers), and the inference strategies provide communicants with short, effective patterns of inference from what someone utters to what that person might be trying to communicate. Taken together, the presumptions and strategies provide the basis for an account of successful linguistic communication.

Presumptions

Linguistic Presumption
Unless there is evidence to the contrary, the hearer is presumed capable of determining the meaning and the referents of the expression in the context of utterance.

Communicative Presumption
Unless there is evidence to the contrary, a speaker is assumed to be speaking with some identifiable communicative intent.

Presumption of Literalness
Unless there is evidence to the contrary, the speaker is assumed to be speaking literally.

Conversational Presumptions
Relevance: The speaker's remarks are relevant to the conversation.
Sincerity: The speaker is being sincere.
Truthfulness: The speaker is attempting to say something true.
Quantity: The speaker contributes the appropriate amount of information.
Quality: The speaker has adequate evidence for what she says.

If a speaker and hearer share these presumptions on a given occasion, then the problem of successful communication is easier to solve, since

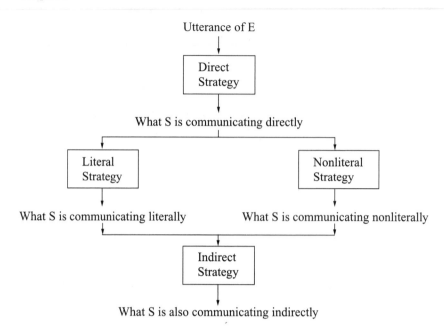

Figure 9.2
The system of inferential strategies. S = speaker, E = expression

the hearer already has a fairly specific set of conversational expectations: hearers expect speakers to mean just what they say (to speak literally and directly), to not mean what they say (to speak nonliterally), or to mean more than they say (to speak indirectly). We will propose that, in order to accomplish this, the speaker and the hearer share a system of inference strategies, each of which handles one of the inadequacies in the Message Model. Thus, there will be strategies not only for direct and literal communication, but also for indirect and nonliteral communication. We can "flowchart" these strategies as shown in figure 9.2.

Direct and Literal Communication

When we communicate directly, we perform just one communicative act; and when we communicate literally, what we say is compatible with what we mean. Crudely put, in direct and literal communication we say what we mean and mean what we say. We have been advocating the idea that even the "simplest" forms of linguistic communication are complicated affairs, and that once we drop the idealizations that the Message Model imposes, we can see that we need more than just rules of language.

Rather, we need notions like *intended inference, shared contextual beliefs,* and various *presumptions* to explicate the connection between sounds and communicative intents. We now want to put these ingredients together into inferential *strategies* for literal and direct communication. That is, we want to represent the patterns of inference, presumption, and shared beliefs that go into this form of communication.

Direct Strategy

Our first strategy, the *Direct Strategy*, will enable the hearer to infer from what he hears the speaker utter to what the speaker is directly communicating. Any alternative to the Message Model of linguistic communication must represent any information the hearer is intended to make use of in order to understand the speaker, in spite of ambiguity. It may seem trivial, but clearly one of the most basic pieces of information the hearer needs for communication to be successful is to know what expression the speaker uttered. If the hearer misses the words, it is unlikely the message will be understood. So the first step in successful communication is for the hearer to recognize the speaker's utterance:

(Step 1)
Utterance act
The hearer recognizes what expression the speaker has uttered.

Recall that the first failure of the Message Model involves ambiguity. The Message Model makes no allowance for the fact that the expression uttered may be ambiguous and that the hearer will usually be expected (by the speaker) to realize which meaning was intended to be operative on that occasion. Often, one meaning is contextually inappropriate, and the speaker will be assumed to mean only the appropriate one. For instance, the sentence *Give me a cheap gas can* has the potential for meaning either *Give me a can for cheap gas* or *Give me a gas can which is cheap*. (We normally take it to mean only the latter because we use the same cans for cheap and expensive gas. However, it is possible that in the future cheap gas will require a different kind of can, and then the former meaning will be an equally strong option. Still, even though one meaning is currently more salient because of real-world conditions, the expression itself is structurally fully ambiguous). Thus, once having heard the expression, the hearer must decide which meaning of the expression is the relevant intended one. This process is still not well understood, so we will simply represent the hearer's success as step 2:

(Step 2)

Operative meaning

The hearer recognizes which meaning of the expression is intended to be operative on this occasion.

However, even after the hearer has disambiguated the expression in the context, another task usually remains before it is possible to determine what communicative act has been performed. As noted before, this involves determining what, if anything, the speaker is referring to. This is a problem because reference is rarely determined solely by the meaning of the utterance. This is clearer if we remember that a message is often about a particular person, place, or thing in the world, but the *meaning* of an expression in the language rarely, if ever, determines exactly *which* person, place, or thing. Even "singular" referring expressions like *the book I left at your house* and *he* can be used to refer to endless different objects without changing their meaning. In normal communication we presume that the hearer can use the operative meaning of the expression as well as the context to determine our references. Thus, the next step of the hearer's inference will be to identify what it is that the speaker is referring to:

(Step 3)

Speaker reference

The hearer recognizes what the speaker is referring to.

The third problem for the Message Model involves the "message." Just because a speaker produces some sounds (an *utterance*) does not guarantee that something is being communicated, since it is possible to utter words without communicating anything: we can talk in our sleep, give examples of grammatical sentences, practice our pronunciation, or just recite a poem or a pleasant-sounding phrase. Moreover, we do not expect hearers to figure out that we are intending to communicate each time we say something; rather, we rely on the Communicative Presumption to alert the hearer to the possible presence of a communicative intent.

One of the most interesting facts about communicative intentions is that they are intended to be recognized, and when they are recognized, they are fulfilled. Most intentions do not have this characteristic. If A recognizes B's intention to shoot a basket, it is not the case that B thereby shoots the basket. When speakers try to communicate something, they intend to be understood as trying to communicate, and they are successful in communicating when the hearer recognizes that intention. Thus, for a speaker to request hearers to do something and be successful in that communication, hearers must understand not only *what* is being requested, but also *that* they are being requested. If a speaker utters the sentence *I'll be there tonight*, then if it is a promise, the hearer must recognize the utterance *as* a promise in order for communication to be successful. If the speaker instead intends the utterance to be a threat, then the hearer must take it *as* a threat for communication to be successful. Communication breaks down if the speaker intends the utterance one way and the hearer takes it another way.

Given this, it is easy to see that in successful communication the hearer can use the Communicative Presumption as well as contextual information and the operative meaning to infer what it is that the speaker might be *doing*—what *communicative act* the speaker might be performing. If the inference is correct, the speaker's communicative intention will be recognized and communication will be successful:

(Step 4)
Direct
The hearer recognizes what the speaker is intending to communicate directly.

The *Direct Strategy* is therefore simply this: from step 1, infer steps 2, 3, and 4. We diagram this strategy in figure 9.3.

Literal Strategy
The next strategy, the *Literal Strategy*, will enable the hearer to infer from what the speaker would be directly communicating, if speaking literally, to what the speaker is literally (and directly) communicating. Recall that the fourth failure of the Message Model involves the nature of the connection between the message and the meaning of the expression uttered. The fact is that we do not always mean (to communicate)

(Step 1) Utterance of E

(Step 4) What S is communicating directly

Figure 9.3
The Direct Strategy

just what our words mean. The Message Model of communication has no way of handling cases requiring the message to be distinct from the meaning of the expression uttered. To accommodate nonliteral utterances, we must elaborate the above communicative step, since the hearer really has a choice to make upon hearing an utterance: is the speaker speaking literally (and if not, what *is* she trying to communicate)? Thus, the next step in the hearer's communicative inference would be to recognize the fact that it would be contextually appropriate for the speaker to be speaking literally:

(Step 5)
Contextual appropriateness
The hearer recognizes that it would be contextually appropriate for the speaker to be speaking literally.

However, we do not seem to always be in a quandary about how to take people's words. According to the Presumption of Literalness, literal utterances seem to have a certain communicative priority in that we presume a person to be speaking literally unless there is some reason to suppose the contrary (for some psychological evidence, see chapter 10). Given this presumption, the hearer can infer what the speaker is communicating literally:

(Step 6)
Literal
The hearer recognizes what the speaker is intending to communicate literally (and directly).

The hearer who reasons to step 6 will take the speaker to be speaking literally simply on the basis that there is nothing contextually inappropriate in doing so. But what is it to be contextually appropriate? Many things can contribute to this, but among the most important are the shared beliefs about the nature, stage, and direction of the talk-exchange that we earlier called "Conversational Presumptions." There are also Conversational Presumptions that speakers will speak clearly, politely, and ethically. The violation of any of these presumptions, when they are thought to be in effect, can constitute a case of contextual inappropriateness.

In conclusion, the *Literal Strategy* is simply this: from step 4 of the Direct Strategy, infer steps 5 and 6, given the Presumption of Literalness and the Conversational Presumptions. We diagram this strategy in figure 9.4, adding it to the previously illustrated Direct Strategy. A hearer who follows these strategies can infer what the speaker is literally and

(Step 1) Utterance of E

(Step 4) What S is communicating directly

(Step 6) What S is communicating literally (and directly)

Figure 9.4
The Direct and Literal Strategies

directly communicating, from what the hearer hears the speaker utter. If the hearer is correct in this inference, communication will have been successful; but if the hearer fails, so will communication.

Nonliteral Communication

Sometimes when we speak, we do mean something other than what our words mean. When what we mean to communicate is not compatible with what our expression literally means, then we are speaking nonliterally. Here are typical examples of expressions that are sometimes uttered nonliterally:

Overstatement
(8)
a. No one understands me. (Not enough people understand me.)
b. A pig wouldn't eat this food. (A person, given a choice, wouldn't eat it.)
c. Her eyes opened as wide as saucers. (Her eyes opened very wide.)
d. I can't make a shot today. (I'm making very few.)

(9)
That was the worst food I've ever had. (It was very bad.)

(10)
a. Paul Newman *is* Jesse James. (Paul Newman plays the part convincingly, or with conviction.)

b. We do it all for you. (We look after your interests.)

c. When you say "Bud," you've said it all. (All that needs to be said about beer.)

d. If it's not Schlitz, it's not beer. (Not the way beer should be.)

e. The future is now. (You should prepare now for the future.)

Irony, sarcasm

(11)

a. Boy, this food is terrific! (terrible)

b. That argument is a real winner. (loser)

Figures of speech

(12)

a. I've got three *hands* (workers) here to help.

b. Look at the *TV Guide* and see what's on the *tube* (TV)!

c. Down in Texas, cattle are only $200 a *head* (animal).

If one thing bears a very close association to another, the utterance is sometimes classified as a case of *metonymy*:

(13)

a. The White House (the president or staff) denounced the agreement.

b. The Crown (the monarch or staff) issued a statement.

c. I have read all of Chomsky (Chomsky's works).

If the connection is some kind of similarity or comparison, then the utterance is sometimes classified as a *metaphor*:

(14)

a. He punted the idea away. (He totally rejected the idea.)

b. Kim is a block of ice. (Kim is cold and unresponsive.)

c. She's a ball of fire. (She's got a lot of energy.)

d. Time is money. (Time is valuable.)

Note that these examples differ in one crucial respect: some are rare or novel or in some way have to be figured out (e.g., (14a)), whereas others are often heard and verge on being cliches (e.g., (14b–d)). The crucial difference is that in the novel cases we must not only reason from various cues and context that the utterance is in fact nonliteral, but also use these cues and contextual information to figure out *what the speaker means*— what the speaker's message is. We will say that these forms of communication are *nonstandardized*. Owing to prior exposure, precedence, or training, however, the other forms are *standardized* for a particular nonliteral interpretation (or a narrow range of such interpretations). With standardized forms, such as (11a–b) uttered with that distinctive bratty and sarcastic intonation, or (14c), it is only necessary to know from context *that* the speaker is speaking nonliterally—the hearer then automatically knows what the speaker is communicating because that expression is standardized for that alternative message. In general, standardized forms are often on their way to getting new meanings, but they have not yet lost all vestiges of their origins and still require some rudimentary reasoning to figure out.

In the case of (mainly nonstandardized) nonliteral communication, the hearer must figure out what the speaker is trying to communicate, given that the speaker is speaking nonliterally. Why should the hearer suppose that the speaker is not speaking literally—that is, meaning what the expression means? A glance back at examples (8)–(14) will reveal that utterances of these (and similar) expressions would, if taken literally, violate Conversational Presumptions that are supposed to be in effect. For instance, if the speaker were being sincere and truthful, and generally had beliefs similar to ours, then the speaker could not *literally* mean

(10a)
Paul Newman is Jesse James.

(10e)
The future is now.

(14a)
He punted the idea away.

In these cases there is conflict between the literal meaning of the expression and the Conversational Presumptions, *if* the speaker is speaking literally. Since the hearer has no reason to suppose that the speaker is still not abiding by the presumptions, the hearer will infer that the speaker is speaking *nonliterally*. In short, contextual inappropriateness can lead the hearer to take the speaker nonliterally. So instead of step 5, which records contextual appropriateness, we have alternative step 5′, which records contextual *in*appropriateness:

(Step 5′)
Contextual inappropriateness
The hearer recognizes that it would be contextually inappropriate for the speaker to be speaking literally.

Once the hearer realizes that the speaker cannot plausibly mean what she says, there is the problem of figuring out what *was* meant. At this point the hearer must make an intelligent guess as to what the speaker's communicative intent might be, based on shared background information as well as the literal meaning of the expression uttered.

The literal meaning of the expression helps the hearer in a number of different ways. From examples (8)–(14) we can infer some very general shared principles that can help the hearer make this inference:

(P1)
Sarcasm, irony
The opposite of what is said

(P2)
Metaphor
Some relation of salient similarity

(P3)
Exaggeration
The next evaluation toward the midpoint of the relevant scale

Notice how a normal hearer might use (P1)–(P3) to interpret the examples of nonliteral communication given earlier. Suppose that the speaker and the hearer have just seen a movie and they share the belief that it was terrible. Under these circumstances it would be contextually inappropriate for one to say *That was a real winner* and mean it literally. So the hearer will conclude that it is nonliteral, and that (P1) is the appropriate principle connecting what the speaker said literally with what she meant nonliterally. If the hearer does this correctly, he will conclude that the speaker was intending to communicate *That was a real loser*, which is just the message we wanted to account for.

Thus, the information a hearer must recognize in order to make nonliteral communication possible is that the speaker does not mean what she has said, but rather means something related to it:

(Step 6′)
Nonliteral
The hearer recognizes what the speaker is communicating nonliterally (and directly).

When a hearer reaches step 6′ correctly, nonliteral communication is successful.

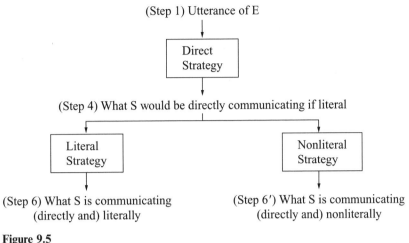

Figure 9.5
The Literal and Nonliteral Direct Strategies

Strategies for Nonliteral Communication

As with literal and direct communication, in order to account for a common type of talk-exchange we have had to supplement considerably the resources of the Message Model. We will now add to our previous strategies the *Nonliteral Strategy*: from step 4 of the Direct Strategy, infer steps 5' and 6'. Our system of strategies is summarized in figure 9.5.

Indirect Communication

Sometimes when we speak we are not only performing some direct form of communication but also speaking indirectly—we mean something *more* than what we mean directly. For instance:

(15)
a. The door is over there. (used to request someone to leave)
b. I want 10 gallons of regular. (used to request 10 gallons of regular)
c. I'm sure the cat likes having its tail pulled. (used to request the hearer to stop pulling the cat's tail)
d. You're the boss. (used to agree to do what the speaker says)
e. I should never have done that. (used to apologize)
f. Did you bring any tennis balls? (used to inform the hearer that the speaker did not bring any)
g. It's getting late. (used to request the hearer to hurry)

Notice that indirect acts can be performed by means of either literal or nonliteral direct acts. Examples (15a) and (15b) are cases of indirect acts being performed by means of literal direct acts—the speaker really does mean what is said, but also means *more*. In case (15c) this is not so; the speaker does not, presumably, really mean that the cat likes having its tail pulled. Instead, the speaker is being sarcastic—she means directly, but nonliterally, that the cat does *not* like having its tail pulled, and she wants the hearer to conclude that he should stop it.

How does the hearer know that the speaker is not speaking merely directly? How does the hearer know to seek an indirect use of language as well as a direct one? Mainly, again, by virtue of contextual inappropriateness. For instance, it would be strange if, on driving into a gas station, the speaker of (15b) had only been reporting her wants and was not also making a polite request for some gas. A mere report of what one now wants is relevant to the taking of a poll, perhaps, but is not contextually appropriate at a gas station. Thus, the same sort of contextual information and presumptions used in recognizing previous communicative intentions and acts are also used with indirect acts.

The hearer is also able to use context and the Conversational Presumptions to *find* the speaker's indirect communicative intent. Once the hearer identifies why the speaker cannot merely be speaking directly, he is able to use this information to aid in recognizing her indirect intent. Thus, reporting a desire for a tank of gas at a service station would be contextually inappropriate if that were all the speaker was doing. Since requesting expresses the desire that the hearer do something, it would be natural in the circumstances for him to conclude that in reporting this desire the speaker was also requesting the gas, since requesting would be the contextually appropriate thing to do.

Once we are aware of such forms of communication, it becomes obvious how often we talk indirectly. (In fact, we do it so often that certain forms have become standardized for their *indirect* use. Such forms as "Could you lend me five dollars?" and "Why don't you try the other key?" are rarely used literally and directly in normal circumstances.) To account for the possibility of indirect communication, we must supplement our (literal and nonliteral) direct strategies with *indirect* strategies. To see how (nonstandardized) indirect communication works in the Inferential Model, we will examine one of the examples given earlier.

Suppose that the speaker utters (15a), *The door is over there*, to the hearer, thereby indirectly requesting the hearer to leave. How might the

hearer reason? The first thing he must notice is that it would be contextually inappropriate for the speaker to be merely reporting the location of the door, assuming that the speaker and the hearer both already
know the location of the door, and this is not relevant to the conversation.
Thus, step 7 of the Inferential Model will be relevant to initiating a search
for the indirect message; the hearer will note the following information:

(Step 7)
Contextual inappropriateness
The hearer recognizes that it would be contextually inappropriate for
the speaker to be speaking merely directly.

As with nonliteral communication, the hearer now faces a problem-
solving situation; if the speaker means something *more* than what is
directly communicated, what is it? In the above example we might suppose that the speaker and the hearer were having a dispute, and in that
case it would be clear that the speaker was requesting the hearer to leave.
Unfortunately, little is known at present about the actual mental processes that take place during indirect communication, so we will represent
only the result of an indirect inference:

(Step 8)
Indirect
The hearer recognizes what the speaker is also communicating
indirectly.

In example (15a) the communication has both a direct and an indirect
component. Moreover, the direct component is literal—the speaker does
really mean that the door is over there, though this is not all that she
means.

Strategies for Indirect Communication

We can now supplement the existing direct strategies with strategies for
indirect communication. The *Indirect Strategy* says: from step 6 or 6′,
infer steps 7 and 8. The augmented system of strategies is shown in figure
9.6.

Looking back at (15c), we see an example of communication that has
both a direct and an indirect component. The direct component in this
case is *non*literal, however, in that the speaker does not really mean that
the cat likes having its tail pulled. In this case communication is success-

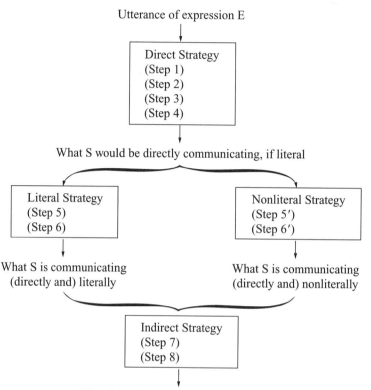

Figure 9.6
Strategies for direct and indirect communication

ful only if the hearer first applies the Direct Strategy and the Nonliteral Strategy, then the Indirect Strategy. That is, the hearer must first reach step 6′:

(Step 6′)
Nonliteral
The hearer recognizes what the speaker is communicating nonliterally and directly—in particular, that the speaker is nonliterally and directly claiming that the cat does not like having its tail pulled.

However, since the direct act would be conversationally inappropriate if it was the only communicative act being performed, the hearer infers step 7:

(Step 7)
Contextual inappropriateness
The hearer recognizes that it would be contextually inappropriate for the speaker to be speaking merely directly—in particular, merely claiming that the cat does not like having its tail pulled.

The hearer must recognize the indirect communicative intent as well and will therefore go on to step 8:

(Step 8)
Indirect
The hearer recognizes what the speaker is also communicating indirectly—in particular, that she is requesting the hearer to quit pulling the cat's tail.

When the hearer reaches step 8, communication is complete and successful.

Proverbs

Proverbs offer an interesting challenge to theories of language use. Consider:

(16)
Imperative
a. Let sleeping dogs lie.
b. Don't cry over spilled milk.
c. Look before you leap.

(17)
Declarative
a. He who hesitates is lost.
b. Absence makes the heart grow fonder.
c. Every cloud has a silver lining.

Proverbs are traditional sayings having a fixed general sentential form, alluding to a common truth or general wisdom, with some (rudimentary) literary value, used to guide action, explain a situation, or induce a feeling or attitude. For example, suppose Sheila has a wasp's nest that she wants to remove from her garage and she is approaching it with a broom. Harry says, "Let sleeping dogs lie." Harry has communicated something—what and how? First, Harry advised Sheila not to whack the nest with the broom. Second, he did this by alluding to a common truth or general wisdom associated with the words, something like "Sometimes it is better to leave things alone." Sheila is expected to equate *sleeping dogs* in the proverb with the wasp's nest, and to equate *let lie* in the proverb with not hitting the nest with the broom. Putting these together, Sheila gets "Don't hit the wasp's nest with the broom—it's better to leave it alone."

It seems that proverbs are not used both literally and directly, and they are often used both nonliterally and indirectly. If a proverb is used literally, it is used indirectly as well; and if a proverb is used directly, it is also used nonliterally. We seem to avoid bluntly directing our audience, and we often use proverbs to soften the effect by distancing ourselves from the advice—we let the common truth or general wisdom do the talking.

Conclusion: The Inferential Model versus the Message Model

The crucial defect of the Message Model of linguistic communication is that it equates the message a speaker intends to communicate with the meaning of some expression in the language. As we have seen, this leads to six specific defects: the Message Model cannot account for (1) the use of ambiguous expressions, (2) real-world reference, (3) communicative intentions, (4) nonliteral communication, (5) indirect communication, and (6) noncommunicative uses of language.

To account for these sorts of facts, an Inferential Model is called for —that is, a model that connects the message with the meaning of the uttered expression by a sequence of inferences. This model involves a series of inference strategies that, if followed, take the hearer from hearing the expression uttered to the speaker's communicative intent. Moreover, each major step in the inference accounts for some failure of the Message Model. For instance, to infer step 2 is to infer the operative meaning, which is to contextually disambiguate the utterance and so avoid the first objection to the Message Model. The Inferential Model also includes referential, nonliteral, and indirect strategies, thereby avoiding the second, fourth, and fifth objections; and it provides an account of communicative intentions and noncommunicative uses of language, thereby avoiding problems three and six.

If the Inferential Model is correct, communicative competence consists, in part, of the mastery of certain pragmatic strategies, such as the ones given above. Each strategy contains a pattern of inference and an appeal to various presumptions and shared contextual beliefs. These are the real building blocks of a theory of language use and communication. It is up to cognitive science to discover the actual principles of inference; linguistics and philosophy can only constrain the correct answers.

9.4   DISCOURSE AND CONVERSATION

Even a casual survey of normal linguistic communication will reveal an important fact: the unit of communication is not always a single complete sentence. Often we speak in single words, phrases, and fragments of sentences:

(18)
A: Want to see a movie tonight?
B: Uh, well, uh ...
A: Do you?
B: No.

At other times we speak in units of two or more connected sentences:

(19)
A: Let me tell you about my ski accident. You see, I was ...

Broadly speaking, the study of *discourse* is the study of units of language and language use consisting of more than a single sentence, but connected by some system of related topics. The study of discourse is sometimes more narrowly construed as the study of connected sequences of sentences (or sentence fragments) produced by a single speaker. In what follows we will construe the term *discourse* narrowly, and when more than one person is involved, we will speak of a *conversation* or more generally a *talk-exchange*. There are many forms of discourse and many forms of talk-exchange. Letters, jokes, stories, lectures, sermons, speeches, and so on, are all categories of discourse; arguments, interviews, business dealings, instruction, and conversations are categories of talk-exchanges.

Conversations (and talk-exchanges in general) are usually structured sequences of expressions by more than a single speaker. This structure is rarely consciously apparent to speakers. However, we need only recall a conversation that has "gone wrong" in some sense, in order to become aware of the conversational expectations we have acquired. Although the structure of conversations (and other talk-exchanges) has not been exhaustively described, being presently under intense investigation, we can summarize some of their major properties here. First, any reasonable number of people can participate, and there are principles that govern how and when people can take a turn. Second, there are principles that make certain aspects of the conversation socially obligatory, such as greeting and leave-taking. Third, as we have already seen, there are principles making contributions to conversations relevant to each other, such as answering questions or justifying refusals.

We will first illustrate some cases where English provides devices that are sensitive to communicative contexts and are therefore useful in the study of both discourse in general and conversation in particular. We will then look at some of the salient features of conversational openings, turn taking, and closings.

Language and Context

The "context" of an utterance is an expandable notion. Sometimes the relevant context is linguistic—just the previous and anticipated utterances in the discourse or conversation. But context can extend to the immediate physical and social environment as well; and finally, it can encompass general knowledge. Each of these concentric circles of "context" can play a role in the interpretation of an utterance. Our contributions to conversations both *reflect* and *affect* the linguistic and nonlinguistic context of utterance.

Our comments can *reflect* features of the context of utterance in that we often "watch our language" by avoiding certain words or phrases. More subtly, our language also has structural devices, often called *stylistic variants*, that allow us to merge more easily into the flow of conversation. Consider the following simple conversation:

(20)
A: Who shot the bear?
B: John. John shot it. John shot the bear.
B': *It* was a bear *that* John shot.
B": *What* John shot *was* a bear.

In (20) speaker A's utterance focuses on John, but the answers given by speakers B' and B" focus on the bear, and this disruption in continuity of topic makes these contributions inappropriate and more difficult to follow.

Our comments also can *affect* the context by making it appropriate for the same speaker to go on and say one sort of thing rather than another. For instance, it would be appropriate for the speaker to tell a joke after asking whether the hearer had heard the one about the traveling salesman, or to tell a story after remarking that she had recently had some adventure.

Thus, language structure can both reflect and affect the structure of the discourse by a single speaker. In the sections that follow we will elaborate on the structure of talk-exchanges involving more than one speaker.

Openings

There are many ways of beginning a conversation or other talk-exchange. One is to start out with no preliminaries whatsoever: "Something's wrong with the fax machine." Another is to preface our remarks with an *opening*. For instance, there are a number of attention-getters (called *vocatives*) used at the beginning of a conversation, such as "Hey," "Hey, John," "Excuse me," "Say,..." Once we have the hearer's attention, we might then use a conversational parenthetical such as "You know," "Listen," "Know what?" But probably the most common opening in casual conversations is the *greeting*. Basically, a greeting is an expression of pleasure at meeting someone. But these expressions can vary enormously in complexity and formality. Consider, for instance, the following sample:

(21)
Casual
Hello! Good morning! Ahoy!
How are you? How have you been?
Look who just walked in! What a pleasant surprise!

(22)
Informal
Howdy! Hi! Greetings!
How y'doing? What's up?
Go ahead, don't say hello! (ironic)
Long time no see!

(23)
Formal
Good day, Mrs. Smith.
To what do I owe this lucky meeting?

Greetings tend to be highly ritualized in form, in that we generally use a small number of them over and over again. They serve mostly to give everyone in the conversation a turn at saying something (notice that it would be odd if, halfway through the introductions, someone were to launch into a long narration on some topic). However, after a round of greetings it is normally quite proper for someone to take the floor and either begin the substance of the talk-exchange or initiate closings.

Turn Taking

The person who starts speaking after the greetings are over in fact initiates the substance of the conversation by taking the next turn. How did that person get the conversational baton, and how is it passed on? One influential analysis has proposed that turn taking is controlled by three principles:

(P1)
The speaker "selects" the next speaker.

(P2)
The first to talk becomes the speaker.

(P3)
The speaker continues her own remarks.

The current speaker "selects" the next speaker in various ways, one of which, of course, is to ask someone a question. Generally the person being asked has the next turn, though someone else could, in accordance with (P2), simply break in and start talking. Clearly, unless these remarks were urgent in some way, we would consider such an act rude. The same is true if the speaker asks someone a question and then keeps on talking, in accordance with (P3). These observations suggest that (P1) overrides (P2) and (P3) in the sense that (P1) has conversational priority. A speaker who wants to violate that principle needs to have a good reason, on pain of being considered rude, ignorant, or insensitive. This in itself suggests that we have the sort of expectations about conversations that these principles describe. But are these principles (P1)–(P3) really *rules* that speakers follow, or are they merely convenient summaries ("rules of thumb") of conversational behavior, viewed from the outside, as it were? This is a hotly debated issue. Why do we have such principles governing conversations? One reason is that for information to get through, everyone cannot be talking at once, and sequencing principles help minimize the chances of disruptive overlap. When disruptive overlap does happen for any length of time, the result is usually embarrassing to other members of the conversation.

Closings

Just as conversations rarely begin with their central topic, so they rarely come to an abrupt end. Participants don't simply quit talking; they have a highly ritualized way of bringing normal conversations to an end. On one proposal, the end of normal conversations consists of a *pre-closing* sequence, where the participants more or less agree to close, followed by a *closing section*, where they actually do close. These two stages have some characteristic ways of being completed. Consider the following examples:

(24)
Pre-closing
We-ell, it's been nice talking to you . . .
Say hello to Joan for me . . .
Closing
See you.
Goodbye. Bye-bye. Bye. Cheerio. Ciao.

Except for special circumstances, such as forgetting something important, once the closing phase has been reached, the conversation should be brought to a conclusion. A speaker can do this either collectively with one remark or a glance at everybody, or separately with appropriate closings to each person or group of persons.

Conclusion

Normal conversations have a discernible structure. They tend to begin and end in certain ritualistic ways. The change of speakers tends to be orderly and based on principles of turn taking. There tend to be recognizable levels of formality, informality, and familiarity in such interchanges. Moreover, the language seems to make available devices for smoothly integrating one's remarks into the flow of words. It should not be surprising that conversations reflect both social and linguistic principles; they are, after all, both social and linguistic events, and as such they vary to some extent from culture to culture.

9.5   SPECIAL TOPICS

Performatives

Austin (1961, 220) introduced *performative* as a "new and ugly word" into philosophy and linguistics. Here is part of what he said:

I want to discuss a kind of utterance which looks like a statement ... and yet is not true or false ... in the first person singular present indicative active ... if a person makes an utterance of this sort we would say that he is *doing* something rather than merely *saying* something.

Revealingly, he gives the following example:

When I say *I do* (take this woman to be my lawful wedded wife), I am not reporting on a marriage, I am indulging in it.

Austin gives other examples, such as uttering *Three no trumps* to make a bid in bridge. Thus, the original idea of a performative utterance was that uttering certain words, in the appropriate circumstances, by and to the appropriate people constitutes *doing something* (think again of the marriage). Such utterances are not reports of doings (the speaker is not asserting anything), so they are not true or false. But as Austin explored these utterances, he found what he called *explicit performatives*, sentences that make explicit what one is *doing with words*:

(25)
a. I (hereby) promise to be there.
b. I (hereby) apologize for that.
c. I (hereby) advise you to leave.
d. I (hereby) declare this meeting adjourned.

However, Austin soon came to realize that the category of explicit performatives was suspect. First, not all explicit performatives are of the above form—explicit performatives can take other persons and voices:

(26)
a. Passengers are (hereby) warned to cross the tracks by the bridge.
b. You are (hereby) authorized to conduct negotiations for us.

Second, some explicit performatives also can be viewed as true or false:

(27)
I state once and for all that I am innocent.

And finally, explicit performatives seem to be both sayings *and* doings:

(28)
A: I promise to be there.
B: Is that true—do you promise?
A: Yes.

In the opening remark, speaker A seems to be both promising and saying that she is promising. These and other observations led Austin (1962) to propose a general theory of uses of language or *speech acts* in which the category of performatives played no special role. But that did not solve the problem of how performatives work. One suggestion is that when a speaker uses performatives, such acts are governed by special pragmatic rules, and by sharing such rules, speakers and hearers are able to communicate. This proposal has the virtue of extending our view of language as rule-governed beyond the study of language structure to the study of function and use. If such a theory could be made to mesh with the present components of a grammar (phonology, syntax, semantics), it would add significantly to our ability to explain the creative aspect of language use.

Recall that the simplest and most straightforward sort of speech act is performed literally and directly. By being literal and direct, a speaker imposes a minimal load on the hearer in understanding what is said. With nonliteral and indirect acts, more inferences are required on the part of the hearer; breakdowns and misunderstanding can result whenever these extra inferences are required.

The major problem with treating sentences such as (25a–d) as being literally and directly used to perform the acts named in the sentences themselves is that the performative verb does not have its normal meaning and does not make its normal contribution to the meaning of the sentence it occurs in—it does not have a compositionally determined meaning (recall the discussion of compositionality in chapter 6). For instance, if the word *promise* in (25a) conventionally indicates that the speaker is promising in uttering it, then why isn't a speaker promising in uttering (29a) or (29b)?

(29)
a. I promised that I would be there.
b. I promise too much to too many.

In these cases the speaker is reporting a promise, not indulging in one. Yet we still need an account of how (25a), and not (29a) or (29b), can be used to promise.

In the face of these difficulties some theorists have proposed that performatives such as (25) are not *directly* used to promise, apologize, and so on, but rather are directly used to do what declarative sentences normally do—declare or state. They are only *indirectly* used to promise, apologize, and so on. For example, (30) might be used to request the hearer to move:

(30)
You're standing on my foot.

We analyze this request as *indirect* by saying that *directly* the speaker uses (30) to state that the hearer is standing on the speaker's foot. Likewise, on this account (25a) is used *directly* to state or declare that the speaker is promising, and it is used *indirectly* to promise that the speaker will be there. How might the hearer be expected to recognize the speaker's intention to promise in stating that she is promising? Given the pragmatic presumptions and especially the Presumption of Truthfulness, the hearer might be expected to reason as follows:

1. The speaker is stating that she is promising to be there.
2. If her statement is true, then she must be promising to be there.
3. Presumably the speaker is being truthful.
4. So the speaker must be promising to be there in saying *I promise to be there*.

The chief advantage of this approach is that since the performative sentence is directly used to state, not to promise, the word *promise* can mean the same thing in performative as well as in nonperformative sentences, and so there is no problem of compositionality either below or above the level of the phrase.

Speech Acts

Speech acts are acts performed in uttering expressions. When they began exploring speech acts, theorists found no appropriate terminology already available for labeling different types, so they had to invent one. The terminology we use here comes, in large part, from the work of Austin (1962) and Searle (1969). According to the theory they have developed, there are four important categories of speech acts, illustrated in figure 9.7.

Utterance acts are simply acts *of* uttering sounds, syllables, words, phrases, and sentences from a language. From a speech act point of view, these are not very interesting acts because an utterance act per se is not communicative; it can be performed by a parrot, tape recorder, or voice synthesizer. The main interest of utterance acts derives from the fact that in performing an utterance act, we usually perform either an *illocutionary act* (an act performed *in* uttering something) or a *perlocutionary act* (an act performed *by* uttering something—an act that produces an *effect* on the hearer). It is illocutionary acts that interest speech act theorists most.

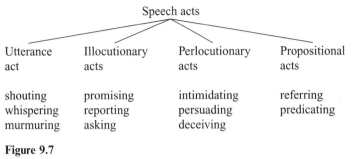

Figure 9.7
Types of speech acts

Austin (1962) characterized the *illocutionary act* as an act performed *in* saying something. For instance, in saying *Sampras can beat Agassi*, one might perform the act of asserting that Sampras can beat Agassi. Some other examples of illocutionary acts are given in (31):

(31)
promising	threatening
reporting	requesting
stating	suggesting
asking	ordering
telling	proposing

What are some of the important characteristics of illocutionary (as opposed to perlocutionary) acts? First, illocutionary acts can often be successfully performed simply by uttering the right explicit performative sentence, with the right intentions and beliefs, and under the right circumstances. Second, illocutionary acts (unlike perlocutionary acts) are central to linguistic communication. Our normal conversations are composed in large part of statements, suggestions, requests, proposals, greetings, and the like. When we do perform perlocutionary acts such as persuading or intimidating, we do so by performing illocutionary acts such as stating or threatening.

Third, and most important, unlike perlocutionary acts, most illocutionary acts used to communicate have the feature that one performs them successfully simply by getting one's illocutionary intentions recognized. For example, if A says

(32)
Sampras can beat Agassi.

and if B recognizes A's intention to tell B that Sampras can beat Agassi, then A will have succeeded in telling B, and B will have understood A. But if A is attempting to persuade B that Sampras can beat Agassi, it is not sufficient for B just to recognize A's intention to persuade B; B must also believe what A said.

Austin characterizes *perlocutionary acts* as acts performed *by* saying something. For instance, suppose John believes everything a certain sportscaster says; then by saying *Sampras can beat Agassi*, that sportscaster could convince John that Sampras can beat Agassi. Some typical examples of perlocutionary acts are these:

(33)

inspiring	embarrassing
persuading	misleading
impressing	intimidating
deceiving	irritating

What are some important characteristics of perlocutionary acts? First, perlocutionary acts (unlike illocutionary acts) are not performed by uttering explicit performative sentences. We do not perform the perlocutionary act of convincing someone that Sampras can beat Agassi by uttering (34):

(34)
I (hereby) convince you that Sampras can beat Agassi.

Second, perlocutionary acts seem to involve the *effects* of utterance acts and illocutionary acts on the thoughts, feelings, and actions of the hearer, whereas illocutionary acts do not. Thus, perlocutionary acts can be represented as an illocutionary act of the speaker (S) plus its effects on the hearer (H):

(35)
a. S tells + H believes ... = S persuades H that ...
b. S tells + H intends ... = S persuades H to ...

Illocutionary acts are therefore means to perlocutionary acts, and not the converse. Perlocutionary acts have not been investigated to the extent that illocutionary acts have been, partly because they are not as intimately related to linguistic structure, semantics, and communication as are illocutionary acts.

Looking again at illocutionary acts such as asserting, questioning, requesting, and promising, note that there can be an overlap in *what* is asserted, questioned, requested, and promised. For instance, suppose a speaker utters the following sentences and thereby performs the indicated acts:

(36)
a. Agassi beat Sampras. (statement)
b. Agassi beat Sampras? (question)
c. Agassi beat Sampras! (request, demand)

All of these illocutionary acts are concerned with Agassi's beating Sampras, which is called the *propositional content* of the illocutionary act. As (36) illustrates, different types of illocutionary acts can have the same propositional content. Furthermore, each type of illocutionary act can have different propositional contents. For example, the illocutionary act of stating can have a wide variety of propositional contents in that a wide variety of propositions can be stated:

(37)
a. The earth is flat.
b. Nobody is perfect.

The simplest type of propositional content is expressed by means of acts of *referring* and *predicating*, wherein a speaker refers to something and then characterizes it. Suppose that a speaker utters the sentence *Agassi is tired* and thereby asserts that Agassi is tired. In making this assertion, the speaker would also be performing the *propositional acts* of referring to Agassi with the name *Agassi* and of characterizing him with the predicate *is tired* (see Searle 1969).

We have now delineated four major types of speech acts: utterance acts, illocutionary acts, perlocutionary acts, and propositional acts—the last including the subacts of referring and predicating. Although a speaker's purposes in talking may require the performance of any one or more of these types of acts, communication seems centrally bound up with illocutionary acts and propositional acts, and these acts have received the major portion of our attention.

Meaning, Saying, and Implicating

Speakers can mean what they say, not mean what they say, or mean more than they say. But when does a speaker mean, say, or implicate something by an utterance, and what determines what is meant, said, or implicated?

Meaning

In chapter 6 we distinguished speaker meaning from linguistic (word, phrase, sentence) meaning and concentrated on theories of linguistic meaning. Now, what about speaker meaning? The most influential analysis is that of H. P. Grice (1957). For a speaker to mean something by an utterance (or any act), at least in the sense of meaning to communicate something, the speaker must intend, by that utterance, to produce some effect in an audience, for instance a belief or an action. But that is not enough; A might leave B's wallet at the scene of the crime, intending the police to think B committed the crime, without meaning to communicate, in the relevant sense, that B did it. To mean (to communicate) something, Grice adds that this intention must be intended to be recognized by the audience. Since this was not true in the wallet example, it would not be a case of meaning something. But that is still not enough. A child might show her mother her pallor, intending her mother to believe that she is sick and intending that intention to be recognized by her mother. Grice is still not satisfied that the child means that she is sick by the display (you may disagree). The problem, he thinks, is that the recognition of the intention to produce the effect plays no role in actually producing that effect—the pallor alone might be sufficient to cause the mother to believe the child is sick. So the final ingredient in speaker meaning is that the intention should play such a role:

(38)
Speaker meaning
The agent meant something by x is (roughly) equivalent to "The agent intended the utterance of x to produce some effect in an audience by means of the recognition of this intention." And to ask what the agent meant is to ask for a specification of the intended effect.

Although Grice and others went on to suggest refinements and revisions of this definition, most theorists agree that Grice had discovered something essential to meaning (to communicate) something, namely, that communicative intentions are "open" or "overt" and not hidden or deceptive—they are intended to be recognized, and when the audience does recognize them, communication is successful.

Saying

Grice (1975) thought that the notion of what is said that would be useful to pragmatics would involve three ideas: the operative meaning of the expression uttered, the time of utterance, and the reference(s) made in the utterance. If a speaker uttered (39),

(39)
He's in the grip of a vice.

an audience would know what was said if the audience could determine the operative meaning of *vice* (character defect or mechanical apparatus), the time of its utterance, and who *he* is being used to refer to.

Implicating

As we have seen, speakers can mean to communicate more than they say. A special and interesting type of communication has been explored by Grice under the label of *conversational implicature*, so called because what is implied (or as Grice prefers to say, *implicated*) is implicated by virtue of the fact that the speaker and hearer are cooperatively contributing to a conversation. According to Grice (1975), such conversations are governed by the Cooperative Principle:

Cooperative Principle
Make your conversational contribution such as is required, at the stage at which it occurs, by the accepted purpose or direction of the talk-exchange in which you are engaged.

But what does cooperating amount to? Grice suggests that for stretches of conversation involving mainly transfer of information, cooperating amounts to obeying (if only implicitly) certain *conversational maxims* such as those given in (40).

(40)
Quantity
Be informative:
1. Make your contribution as informative as is required (for the current purposes of the conversation).
2. Do not make your contribution more informative than is required.
Quality
Try to make your contribution one that is true:
1. Do not say what you believe to be false.
2. Do not say that for which you lack adequate evidence.
Relevance
Be relevant.

Manner

Be perspicuous:

1. Avoid obscurity of expression.
2. Avoid unnecessary ambiguity.
3. Be brief (avoid unnecessary prolixity).
4. Be orderly.

(These maxims inspired the Conversational Presumptions given earlier.) Grice proposes that conversations are cooperative endeavors where participants may be expected (unless they indicate otherwise) to comply with general principles of cooperation, such as making the appropriate contribution to the conversation. Now, imagine the following interchange between friends:

(41)

a. Questioner: Where is your husband?
b. Speaker: He is in the living room or the kitchen.
c. Implication: The speaker does not know which room he is in.

In this case the speaker in saying (41b) implies that (41c) is true, though she does not say that it is. This implication arises because, since the speaker has not indicated noncooperation, she may be assumed to be cooperating and so to be giving all of the relevant and requested information. Since the speaker has said (41b) and may be presumed to be cooperative, she has implied (41c). Of course, the speaker may know exactly where her husband is; in that case she would be misleading the hearer in that she is pretending to cooperate in the conversation but is not really doing so.

The categories of meaning, saying, and implicating are not yet strictly defined, and some phenomena are hard to categorize:

(42)

a. It is raining (here, now).
b. I've had breakfast (today).

What is the status of the parenthetical (unspoken) information? It seems to be communicated, but no words mean it, so it is not said. Is it implicated? No conversational maxims seem to be required.

Pragmatic Presupposition

In the everyday sense of *presuppose*, to presuppose something is to assume something, or to take it for granted in advance, but not to say it. Since assuming something is not normally considered an act but rather a state, presupposing is best viewed as a state and not an act. Related to (pragmatic) presupposing is (pragmatic) *presupposition*: that which is assumed or taken for granted. Clearly, presuppositions are not acts, though they are related to them. This characterization is pretty vague, but the phenomena cited in current linguistics under the label of (pragmatic) presupposition are quite varied, and our characterization has at least the virtue of reflecting a common denominator among many different kinds of cases. To simplify matters, we will identify three main types of phenomena that go by the label of (pragmatic) presupposition in current discussions.

According to one conception, *presupposition*$_1$, a speaker's assumptions (beliefs) about the speech context are presuppositions. As one author (Lakoff 1970, 175) writes:

Natural language is used for communication in a context, and every time a speaker uses a sentence of his language ... he is making certain assumptions about that context.

Some typical examples of (pragmatic) presupposition$_1$ are the following:

(43)
a. Sam realizes that Irv is a Martian.
b. Sam does not realize that Irv is a Martian.
c. Irv is a Martian.

(44)
a. Sam has stopped kissing his wife.
b. Sam has not stopped kissing his wife.
c. Sam was kissing his wife.

In (43) and (44), the (a) and (b) sentences are said to presuppose the truth of the (c) sentence. Notice that on this pragmatic conception of presupposition, as with the semantic notion of presupposition, both a sentence and its negation have the same presupposition.

A more restrictive notion, (pragmatic) *presupposition*$_2$, is this: the (pragmatic) presupposition$_2$ of a sentence is the set of conditions that have to be satisfied in order for the intended speech act to be appropriate in the circumstances, or to be felicitous. As one author (Keenan 1971, 49) writes:

Many sentences require that certain culturally defined conditions or contexts be satisfied in order for an utterance of a sentence to be understood ... these conditions are naturally called presuppositions of the sentence.... An utterance of a sentence pragmatically presupposes that its context is appropriate.

This view is echoed by another linguist (Fillmore 1971, 276):

By the presuppositional aspects of a speech communication situation, I mean those conditions which must be satisfied in order for a particular illocutionary act to be effectively performed in saying particular sentences.

Some typical examples of presupposition$_2$ are these:

(45)
a. John accused Harry of writing the letter.
b. John did not accuse Harry of writing the letter.
c. There was something blameworthy about writing the letter.

(46)
a. John criticized Harry for writing the letter.
b. John did not criticize Harry for writing the letter.
c. Harry wrote the letter.

(47)
a. Tu es dégoûtant. ("You are disgusting.")
b. Tu n'est pas dégoûtant. ("You are not disgusting.")
c. The addressee is an animal or child, is socially inferior to the speaker, or is intimate with the speaker (signaled by the use of the familiar pronoun *tu* rather than the more formal *vous*).

Again, in each of (45)–(47) it is claimed that the (c) sentence is presupposed by both the (a) sentence and the (b) sentence.

A final notion, (pragmatic) *presupposition$_3$*, is that of shared background information, which one author (Jackendoff 1972, 230) characterizes as follows:

We will use ... "presupposition of a sentence" to denote the information in the sentence that is assumed by the speaker to be shared by him and the hearer.

Typical examples of presupposition$_3$ are such sentences as the following:

(48)
a. Was it Margaret that Paul married?
b. Wasn't it Margaret that Paul married?
c. Paul married someone.

(49)
a. Betty remembered to take her medicine.
b. Betty did not remember to take her medicine.
c. Betty was supposed to take her medicine.

(50)

a. That Sioux Indian he befriended represented the chief.

b. That Sioux Indian he befriended did not represent the chief.

c. He had befriended a Sioux Indian.

Again, in (48)–(50), the (a) and (b) sentences are said to presuppose the (c) sentence in that the conditions mentioned in (c) must be shared information. It may be disputed whether or not it is useful to apply the term *presupposition* to all of the phenomena just listed, but it cannot be disputed that these data must be explained (or explained away) by an adequate pragmatic theory.

Speaker Reference

In chapter 6 we distinguished between speaker reference and denotation, only to put speaker reference aside. We now focus our attention on these acts of referring to things in the world. Although speakers can (in some sense) refer in speaking to themselves, or to nobody in particular, normally we refer communicatively; we refer to objects and intend our audience to recognize our reference to those very things.

Linguists tend to work with a *broad* conception of speaker reference, where the speaker has some particular thing in mind and utters something that will enable the hearer to also have that thing in mind. Under the broad usage, sentence (51) could be used to refer to a particular beer:

(51)
There's a beer in the refrigerator.

Notice that nothing in the sentence denotes a single beer. Philosophers tend to work with a *narrow* conception of speaker reference, where the speaker has some particular thing in mind and uses a singular term to refer to that thing:

(52)
The *Bohemia* in the refrigerator is cold.

Let's concentrate on the narrow conception and see how literal, non-literal, and indirect reference works with the singular terms we investigated in chapter 6: indexicals, definite descriptions, and proper names.

Literal Singular Reference

To use a singular term literally is to refer to something that the term denotes. For example:

(53)

He is tired.

a. A particular *male* is being referred to.

b. *He* denotes *males*.

(54)

The first person to walk on our moon is right-handed.

a. A particular person who is *the first person to walk on our moon* is being referred to.

b. *The first person to walk on our moon* denotes Neil Armstrong.

(55)

Neil Armstrong is right-handed.

a. A particular person named *Neil Armstrong* is being referred to.

b. *Neil Armstrong* denotes all people named *Neil Armstrong*.

In each case the speaker uses the singular term literally to refer the hearer to the particular person or thing the speaker has in mind, which is a part of the denotation of the singular term. By referring literally, the speaker makes communication easier because the hearer need only find the particular thing from among the objects in the denotation of the singular term.

Nonliteral Singular Reference

In the case of nonliteral singular reference the speaker intends to refer to some particular thing that the singular term does *not* denote. This can make communication more difficult because the hearer cannot use the denotation to cut down the class of potential referents. What the hearer must do is use the meaning of the singular term as a clue to what the speaker has in mind, then use contextual information to determine the referent. For example, someone might use *he* to refer to a masculine woman, or one might use *Napoleon* to refer to a diminutive megalomaniac, or one might use *the world's most famous linguist* to refer to a presumptuous colleague.

Indirect Singular Reference

In the case of indirect singular reference the speaker refers to one thing by first referring the hearer to another. For instance, pointing to a dot on a map of Australia, a speaker might say,

(56)
Here is the town we should stay in when we visit the Uluru.

By referring the hearer directly to a point on the map (with, say, the name *Curtain Springs*), the speaker could be referring indirectly to the town of Curtain Springs. Indirect reference can even become ritualized when the identity of the indirect referent is not as important as the direct referent. Thus, a waiter might turn in an order by saying,

(57)
The fillet of sole (the person who ordered it) at table four wants a glass of Chablis.

Conclusion

We have briefly surveyed five special topics in pragmatics: performatives; speech acts; meaning, saying, and implicating; pragmatic presupposition; and speaker reference. Any adequate general pragmatic theory will have to incorporate an account of these phenomena. The exciting thing about pragmatics at present is that there is broad consensus on the general shape of a pragmatic theory, and much interesting and hard work to be done within that theory.

Study Questions

1. What was pragmatics originally taken to be? What problem was there with the original formulation? What revision was made?

2. What are some uses of language that fluent speakers know?

3. What are the problems of linguistic communication as formulated in the text?

4. What is the Message Model of linguistic communication?

5. What six problems does the Message Model have? (Illustrate each with an example.)

6. What is the inferential answer to the original problem of linguistic communication?

7. What presumptions does the Inferential Model utilize?

8. What are the four major types of communication?

9. How has each type been characterized?

10. State the strategies for direct and literal communication.

11. What varieties of nonliteral communication were surveyed in the text? Give an example of each.

12. State the strategy for nonliteral communication.

13. What are some examples of indirection? State the strategy for indirect communication.

14. How does the Inferential Model meet the first five objections to the Message Model? Discuss.

15. What is the broad notion of discourse? What is the narrow notion of discourse?

16. What is a greeting?

17. State three principles of turn taking.

18. What are the two major steps in closing a conversation?

19. What is the main problem with treating performatives as *directly* used to perform the acts they denote?

20. What is the indirect analysis of performatives?

21. What are four basic categories of speech acts?

22. What three things distinguish illocutionary from perlocutionary acts?

23. What was Grice's original analysis of a speaker meaning something by an utterance?

24. What, according to Grice, determines what is said?

25. What are the maxims of conversation?

26. What is the difference between conversationally implicating something and saying it?

27. How is something conversationally implicated?

28. What three notions of presupposition were surveyed in the text? Give an example of each.

29. What is the difference between the broad and the narrow conceptions of speaker reference?

30. What are literal, nonliteral, and indirect reference? Give an example of each.

Exercises

1. Find sentences and a use of them that might conform to the Message Model. Discuss.

2. Think of three different sentences for performing each of the following acts literally and directly: congratulating someone on a promotion, apologizing for spilling the soup, firing someone.

3. Consider two of the examples of figures of speech given in the text:

a. The White House (the president or staff) denounced the agreement.
b. I have read all of Chomsky (Chomsky's works).

Are these also cases of (nonliteral) indirect reference? Discuss.

4. Consider the following sentences, then state what you take the speaker's intended meaning to be.

a. I'm all thumbs today!
b. He's plowing his profits back into the business.
c. Cat got your tongue?
d. That movie was a real turkey!
e. You took the words right out of my mouth.
f. She's got something on her mind.

5. Which, if any, of the sentences in exercise 4 involve lexical or syntactic ambiguity? Identify the nonliteral word or phrase. Defend your answer.

6. Find five everyday, commonplace examples of nonliteral language use. Try to include an imperative and an interrogative example in your list. Paraphrase the intended nonliteral interpretation as best you can.

7. Find five typical, commonplace cases of speaking *indirectly* that are not given in the text. Say what the direct communicative message is (is it literal or nonliteral?) and also say what the indirect message is. Try to include an example from each major mood of English: declarative, imperative, and interrogative.

8. Consider the following proverbs:

a. A rolling stone gathers no moss.
b. Look before you leap.
c. A stitch in time saves nine.

How would you paraphrase the intended message behind each of them?

9. Can proverbs be nonliteral, indirect, literal, and (only) direct? Defend your answers by giving examples.

10. Say how the Inferential Model tries to overcome each of the first five inadequacies of the Message Model. How about the sixth? Discuss.

11. When is it normal not to open a talk-exchange with a greeting? Discuss.

12. Can you think of any modifications or additions that might be made to the three principles of turn taking discussed in the text? Elaborate.

13. Which of the following words can be performative?

a. adjourn
b. explain
c. baptize
d. intend
e. conclude
f. nominate

Give examples to illustrate.

14. Try to give an explicit definition of a *performative sentence*, keeping all of Austin's examples in mind.

15. Is an utterance of *I (hereby) promise to be there* literally and directly a promise, or is it literally and directly a statement that you promise to be there, and only indirectly a promise? Defend your answer.

16. Compare and contrast the direct and indirect analyses of how we communicate with performatives.

17. What differences in utterance acts are indicated by words such as *whisper* and *shout*? Think of five more words that report utterance acts and say how they differ.

18. Give five verbs indicating *illocutionary* acts to add to the list in the text.

19. Give five verbs indicating *perlocutionary* acts to add to the list in the text.

20. What is the relation between conversational implicature, nonliterality, and indirection? Discuss.

21. What is the relation between conversational implicature and presupposition? Are they different? The same? Discuss.

22. We sometimes use *she* to refer to countries, boats, guns, and so on. Are these uses nonliteral? Discuss.

23. Give three new examples each of nonliteral and indirect (singular speaker) reference; use a definite description, pronoun, and proper name.

Further Reading

General
For *article-length introductions to pragmatics*, see Horn 1989, Recanati 1996, Travis 1997, and the entries for "Pragmatics" in Mey 1998. For *book-length introductions to pragmatics*, see Levinson 1983, Leech 1983, Blakemore 1988, Green 1989, Mey 1993, Thomas 1995, Yule 1996, Verschueren 1999, and Grundy 2000. See Jucker 1995, Nerlich and Clarke 1996, and Arnovick 1999 for *historical material on pragmatics*, and Hauser 1996 for more on the *biology of communication*.

The Message Model and Its Problems

For more detailed discussion of the Message Model and historical references, see Bach and Harnish 1979, introduction; Akmajian, Demers, and Harnish 1980; Sperber and Wilson 1986, chap. 1; and Peters 1989.

Inferential Approaches to Communication

The origin of contemporary *inferential* approaches to communication is found in Grice 1957, 1975. Two different elaborations of Grice's inferential approach to communication were worked out in Bach and Harnish 1979 and in Sperber and Wilson 1986. Turner 1995 and 1996 survey and extend inferential principles. For more on *nonliteral* communication and *metaphor* in particular, see Searle 1979a, Ortony 1979 (an influential early anthology), Moran 1997, the entry "Metaphor" in Mey 1998, and Nogales 1999 (a concise survey). For more on *indirect* communication, see Sadock 1974 and Searle 1975. For more on *standardization*, see Morgan 1978 and Bach and Harnish 1979, chaps. 9–10.

Discourse and Conversation

Discourse and conversation is now a vast topic, which we barely touched on. Good article-length surveys include Levinson 1983, chap. 6; Heritage 1984, chap. 8; Blakemore 1988; Schiffrin 1988; Jacobs 1994; and Yule 1996, chaps. 8–9. See also the "Discourse" entries in Mey 1998. Good book-length introductions include Coulthard 1977, Brown and Yule 1983, Stubbs 1983, Taylor and Cameron 1987, Blakemore 1988, Aijmer 1996, Gee 1999, and Markee 2000. Halliday and Hasan 1976 is the classic work on discourse cohesion. Van Dijk 1997 is a useful recent collection. For original work on *openings*, see Schegloff 1972. On *turn taking*, see Sacks, Schegloff, and Jefferson 1974, and for critical discussion, see Searle et al. 1992. For *closings*, see Schegloff and Sacks 1973. Sacks 1992 is a provocative compilation by one of the originators of conversational analysis. Schenkein 1978 is an important early collection in this tradition. The series "Advances in Discourse Processes" (editor R. Freedle, Ablex Publishing Co.) emphasizes the psychological dimension.

Special Topics

For more on *performatives*, see the first half of Austin 1962. For constative indirect analyses, see Bach and Harnish 1979, sec. 10.1, and Bach and Harnish 1992. For declarational analyses, see Recanati 1987 and Searle 1989. The original work on *speech acts* was Austin 1962; others are Searle 1969, 1979b, Bach and Harnish 1979, Sperber and Wilson 1986, Vanderveken 1990, Geis 1995, Clark 1996, and Alston 2000. Searle 1969, chaps. 4–5, discusses propositional acts of *reference* and *predication*. Verschueren 1985 and Wierzbicka 1987 provide an analysis of many central speech act verbs. For *meaning*, *saying*, and *implicating*, see Grice 1957, 1975, Carston 1988, Recanati 1989, and Bach 1994. For a critical discussion of Grice's theory of speaker meaning, see chapter 2 of Avramides 1989. Davis 1998 and Asher 1999 are recent critiques of Grice's theory of implicature, Atlas 2000 is a recent discussion, and Levinson 2000 elaborates Grice's theory. For a recent survey article on *pragmatic presupposition*, see the entry "Presupposition, pragmatic" in Mey 1998. Also see Levinson 1983, chap. 4; the papers in Fillmore and Langendoen 1971; and Davis 1991, part IV. Book-length treatments include Kempson 1975, Wilson 1975, and van der Sandt 1988. Horn 1996 relates presupposition to implicature. For *speaker reference*, see Bertolet 1987, Kronfeld 1990, and Roberts 1993. *Pragmatics and Cognition* 1998, vol. 6, is a special issue on reference.

Reference Works
Verschueren 1978; Nuyts and Verschueren 1987; Davis 1991; Verschueren, Ostman, and Blommaert 1995; Lamarque 1997, sec. VIII; Kasher 1998; Mey 1998

Journals
Journal of Pragmatics, Pragmatics, Pragmatics and Cognition, Language and Communication, Discourse Processes, Discourse Studies, Language in Society

Bibliography

Aijmer, K. 1996. *Conversational routines in English: Convention and creativity.* New York: Longman.

Akmajian, A., R. Demers, and R. Harnish. 1980. Overcoming inadequacies in the "Message-Model" of linguistic communication. *Communication and Cognition* 13, 317–336. Reprinted in Kasher 1998.

Alston, W. 2000. *Illocutionary acts and sentence meaning.* Ithaca, N.Y.: Cornell University Press.

Arnovick, L. 1999. *Diachronic pragmatics: Seven case studies in English illocutionary development.* Amsterdam: John Benjamins.

Asher, N. 1999. Discourse structure and the nature of conversation. In K. Turner, ed., *The semantics/pragmatics interface from different points of view.* New York: Elsevier.

Atlas, J. 2000. *Logic, meaning and conversation.* Oxford: Oxford University Press.

Austin, J. L. 1961. *Philosophical papers.* Oxford: Oxford University Press.

Austin, J. L. 1962. *How to do things with words.* Oxford: Oxford University Press.

Avramides, A. 1989. *Meaning and mind.* Cambridge, Mass.: MIT Press.

Bach, K. 1987. *Thought and reference.* Oxford: Oxford University Press.

Bach, K. 1994. Conversational implicature. *Mind and Language* 9(2), 124–162.

Bach, K., and R. Harnish. 1979. *Linguistic communication and speech acts.* Cambridge, Mass.: MIT Press.

Bach, K., and R. Harnish. 1992. How performatives really work: A reply to Searle. *Linguistics and Philosophy* 15, 93–110. Reprinted in Kasher 1998.

Bertolet, R. 1987. Speaker reference. *Philosophical Studies* 52, 199–226.

Blakemore, D. 1988. The organization of discourse. In Newmeyer 1988.

Blakemore, D. 1992. *Understanding utterances*. Oxford: Blackwell.

Brown, G., and G. Yule. 1983. *Discourse analysis*. Cambridge: Cambridge University Press.

Carnap, R. 1939. *Foundations of logic and mathematics*. Chicago: University of Chicago Press.

Carston, R. 1988. Implicature, explicature, and truth-theoretic semantics. In R. Kempson, ed., *Mental representations*. Cambridge: Cambridge University Press.

Clark, H. 1996. *Using language*. Cambridge: Cambridge University Press.

Cole, P., ed. 1978. *Syntax and semantics 9: Speech acts*. New York: Academic Press.

Cole, P., ed. 1981. *Radical pragmatics*. New York: Academic Press.

Cole, P., and J. Morgan, eds. 1975. *Syntax and semantics 3: Pragmatics*. New York: Academic Press.

Coulthard, M. 1977. *An introduction to discourse analysis*. London: Longman.

Davis, S., ed. 1991. *Pragmatics: A reader*. Oxford: Oxford University Press.

Davis, W. 1998. *Implicature*. Cambridge: Cambridge University Press.

Dijk, T. van, ed. 1997. *Discourse studies*. 2 vols. Thousand Oaks, Calif.: Sage.

Fillmore, C. 1971. Verbs of judging. In Fillmore and Langendoen 1971.

Fillmore, C., and D. T. Langendoen, eds. 1971. *Studies in linguistic semantics*. New York: Holt, Rinehart and Winston.

Gazdar, G. 1979. *Pragmatics: Implicature, presupposition and logical form*. New York: Academic Press.

Gee, J. 1999. *An introduction to discourse analysis*. London: Routledge.

Geis, M. 1995. *Speech acts and conversational interaction*. Cambridge: Cambridge University Press.

Green, G. 1989. *Pragmatics and natural language understanding*. Hillsdale, N.J.: Lawrence Erlbaum Associates.

Grice, H. P. 1957. Meaning. *Philosophical Review* 66, 377–388. Reprinted in Harnish 1994a.

Grice, H. P. 1975. Logic and conversation. In Cole and Morgan 1975. Reprinted in Grice 1989 and Harnish 1994a.

Grice, H. P. 1989. *Studies in the way of words*. Cambridge, Mass.: Harvard University Press.

Grundy, P. 2000. *Doing pragmatics.* 2nd ed. Oxford: Oxford University Press.

Hale, B., and C. Wright, eds. 1997. *A companion to the philosophy of language.* Malden, Mass.: Blackwell.

Halliday, M., and R. Hasan. 1976. *Cohesion in English.* London: Longmans.

Harnish, R. M., ed. 1994a. *Basic topics in the philosophy of language.* Englewood Cliffs, N.J.: Prentice-Hall.

Harnish, R. M. 1994b. Communicating with proverbs. *Communication and Cognition* 26(3/4), 265–290.

Harris, R. 1993. *The linguistics wars.* Oxford: Oxford University Press.

Hauser, M. 1996. *The evolution of communication.* Cambridge, Mass.: MIT Press.

Heritage, J. 1984. *Garfinkel and ethnomethodology.* Cambridge: Polity Press.

Holdcroft, D. 1978. *Words and deeds.* Oxford: Oxford University Press.

Horn, L. 1989. Pragmatic theory. In Newmeyer 1988.

Horn, L. 1996. Presupposition and conversational implicature. In S. Lappin, ed., *The handbook of contemporary semantic theory.* Malden, Mass.: Blackwell.

Jackendoff, R. 1972. *Semantic interpretation in generative grammar.* Cambridge, Mass.: MIT Press.

Jacobs, S. 1994. Language and interpersonal communication. In M. Knapp and G. Miller, eds., *Handbook of interpersonal communication.* 2nd ed. Thousand Oaks, Calif.: Sage.

Jucker, A. 1995. *Historical pragmatics.* Amsterdam: John Benjamins.

Kasher, A., ed. 1998. *Pragmatics: Critical concepts.* 6 vols. New York: Routledge.

Katz, J. 1966. *The philosophy of language.* New York: Harper and Row.

Katz, J. 1980. *Propositional structure and illocutionary force.* Cambridge, Mass.: Harvard University Press.

Keenan, E. 1971. Two kinds of presupposition in natural language. In Fillmore and Langendoen 1971.

Kempson, R. 1975. *Presupposition and the delimination of semantics.* Cambridge: Cambridge University Press.

Kronfeld, A. 1990. *Reference and computation.* Cambridge: Cambridge University Press.

Lakoff, G. 1970. Linguistics and natural logic. *Synthese* 22, 151–271.

Lamarque, P., ed. 1997. *Concise encyclopedia of philosophy of language.* New York: Pergamon.

Leech, G. 1983. *Principles of pragmatics.* New York: Longman.

Levinson, S. 1983. *Pragmatics*. Cambridge: Cambridge University Press.

Levinson, S. 2000. *Presumptive meanings*. Cambridge, Mass.: MIT Press.

Locke, J. 1691. *An essay concerning human understanding*. New York: Dover Publications (1959).

Markee, N. 2000. *Conversation analysis*. Mahwah, N.J.: Lawrence Erlbaum Associates.

Mey, J. 1993. *Pragmatics: An introduction*. Malden, Mass.: Blackwell.

Mey, J., ed. 1998. *Concise encyclopedia of pragmatics*. Amsterdam: Elsevier/ Pergamon.

Moran, R. 1997. Metaphor. In Hale and Wright 1997.

Morgan, J. 1978. Two types of convention in indirect speech acts. In Cole 1978.

Morris, C. 1938. *Foundations of the theory of signs*. Chicago: University of Chicago Press.

Nerlich, B., and D. Clarke. 1996. *Language, action and context: The early history of pragmatics in Europe and America 1780–1930*. Amsterdam: John Benjamins.

Newmeyer, F. 1980. *Linguistic theory in America: The first quarter century of transformational generative grammar*. New York: Academic Press.

Newmeyer, F., ed. 1988. *Linguistics: The Cambridge survey*, vol. 4. Cambridge: Cambridge University Press.

Nogales, P. 1999. *Metaphorically speaking*. Stanford, Calif.: CSLI Publications.

Nunberg, G. 1978. *The pragmatics of reference*. Bloomington: Indiana University Linguistics Club.

Nuyts, J., and J. Verschueren, eds. 1987. *A comprehensive bibliography of pragmatics*. Amsterdam: John Benjamins.

Ortony, A., ed. 1979. *Metaphor and thought*. Cambridge: Cambridge University Press.

Peters, J. 1989. John Locke, the individual, and the origin of communication. *Quarterly Journal of Speech* 75, 387–399.

Pragmatics and Cognition [special issue on reference]. 1996. Vol. 6.

Recanati, F. 1987. *Meaning and force: The pragmatics of performative utterances*. Cambridge: Cambridge University Press.

Recanati, F. 1989. The pragmatics of what is said. *Mind and Language* 4, 295–329. Reprinted in Davis 1991.

Recanati, F. 1996. Pragmatics. In *The Routledge encyclopedia of philosophy*. London: Routledge.

Reddy, M. 1979. The conduit metaphor: A case of frame conflict in our language about language. In Ortony 1979.

Roberts, L. 1993. *How reference works*. Albany, N.Y.: State University of New York Press.

Ross, J. R. 1970. On declarative sentences. In R. Jacobs and P. Rosenbaum, eds., *Readings in English transformational grammar*. Waltham, Mass.: Ginn.

Ruhl, C. 1989. *On monosemy*. Albany, N.Y.: State University of New York Press.

Sacks, H. 1992. *Lectures on conversation*. 2 vols. Oxford: Blackwell.

Sacks, H., E. Schegloff, and G. Jefferson. 1974. A simplest systematics for the organization of turn-taking for conversation. Reprinted in Schenkein 1978.

Sadock, J. 1974. *Toward a linguistic theory of speech acts*. New York: Academic Press.

Sandt, R. van der. 1988. *Context and presupposition*. London: Croom Helm.

Schegloff, E. 1972. Sequencing in conversational openings. In J. Gumperz and D. Hymes, eds., *Directions in sociolinguistics: The ethnography of communication*. New York: Holt, Rinehart and Winston.

Schegloff, E., and H. Sacks. 1973. Opening up closing. *Semiotica* 8, 289–327.

Schenkein, J., ed. 1978. *Studies in the organization of conversational interaction*. New York: Academic Press.

Schiffrin, D. 1988. Conversation analysis. In Newmeyer 1988.

Searle, J. 1969. *Speech acts*. Cambridge: Cambridge University Press.

Searle, J. 1975. Indirect speech acts. Reprinted in Searle 1979b.

Searle, J. 1979a. Metaphor. Reprinted in Searle 1979b.

Searle, J. 1979b. *Expression and meaning*. Cambridge: Cambridge University Press.

Searle, J. R. 1989. How performatives work. *Linguistics and Philosophy* 12, 535–558. Reprinted in Harnish 1994a and Kasher 1998.

Searle, J., et al. 1992. *(On) Searle on conversation*. Amsterdam: John Benjamins.

Smith, N., ed. 1982. *Mutual knowledge*. New York: Academic Press.

Sperber, D., and D. Wilson. 1986. *Relevance*. Cambridge, Mass.: Harvard University Press. 2nd ed. Malden, Mass.: Blackwell (1995).

Stubbs, M. 1983. *Discourse analysis*. Chicago: University of Chicago Press.

Taylor, T., and D. Cameron. 1987. *Analyzing conversation: Rules and units in the structure of talk*. New York: Pergamon.

Thomas, J. 1995. *Meaning in interaction: An introduction to pragmatics*. New York: Longman.

Travis, C. 1997. Pragmatics. In Hale and Wright 1997.

Turner, K. 1995. The principles of pragmatic inference: Co-operation. *Language Teaching* 28, 67–86.

Turner, K. 1996. The principles of pragmatic inference: Politeness. *Language Teaching* 29, 1–13.

Vanderveken, D. 1990. *Meaning and speech acts.* Cambridge: Cambridge University Press.

Verschueren, J. 1978. *Pragmatics: An annotated bibliography.* Amsterdam: John Benjamins.

Verschueren, J. 1985. *What people say they do with words.* Norwood, N.J.: Ablex.

Verschueren, J. 1999. *Understanding pragmatics.* New York: Arnold.

Verschueren, J., J. Ostman, and J. Blommaert, eds. 1995. *Handbook of pragmatics.* Amsterdam: John Benjamins.

Wierzbicka, A. 1987. *English speech act verbs.* New York: Academic Press.

Wilson, D. 1975. *Presupposition and non-truth-conditional semantics.* New York: Academic Press.

Wittgenstein, L. 1953. *Philosophical investigations.* New York: Macmillan.

Yule, G. 1996. *Pragmatics.* Oxford: Oxford University Press.

Chapter 10

Psychology of Language: Speech Production and Comprehension

10.1 PSYCHOLINGUISTICS: COMPETENCE, PERFORMANCE, AND ACQUISITION

We have seen that it is possible to analyze a natural language at a number of different levels: sounds (phonology), words (morphology), sentence structure (syntax), meaning (semantics), and use (pragmatics). The task of linguistics is in part to discover the appropriate units of analysis at each level and to state generalizations in terms of these units that capture the regularities inherent in the language itself. But languages are not just abstract structured systems. They are also used in thought and communication, and it is the task of *psycholinguistics* (or *psychology of language*) to discover how knowledge of language is represented in the mind/brain of a fluent speaker, how this information is utilized in the production and comprehension of expressions, and how speakers acquire these abilities.

Chomsky (1972) proposes that we construct three models. The first reflects what a fluent speaker knows (what information is stored) about the sound-meaning relations in the language—it is a model of the speaker's linguistic *competence* (figure 10.1). This is to be distinguished from a *performance model*, which reflects the actual processes that go into producing and understanding language (figure 10.2).

Finally, a language *acquisition model* (or device) reflects the changes in the competence and performance of a child during the acquisition period and thus provides a model of the child's language-learning achievements (figure 10.3).

In the remainder of this chapter we will explore some of the central issues surrounding current attempts to build a *performance* model. In section 10.2 we will look at some empirical constraints on the production side

Figure 10.1
A competence model

Figure 10.2
A performance model

Figure 10.3
An acquisition model

of a performance model, and in section 10.3 at constraints on the comprehension side. In chapter 11 we will investigate language acquisition.

10.2   SPEECH PRODUCTION

The easiest way of thinking about theories of speech production is to imagine building a device that will simulate the flow of information from message to sounds—in other words, a model of the phenomenon of a speaker expressing a message to a hearer: the speaker thinks of a message, "plans" how to express it, and finally articulates the expression with the vocal tract.

Conceiving the Message

A speaker brings to the communication situation a wide variety of general beliefs about the world, about the past, present, and future course of the talk-exchange, and about the hearer's beliefs about these things as well. Accompanying these beliefs are the speaker's desires, hopes, intentions, and so forth. In the course of the talk-exchange many of these beliefs, desires, and intentions not only affect what is said, but themselves change as a result of what is said. We will organize our discussion of speech production around the idea that these mental states form the *cognitive background* for normal language processing:

(1)
Cognitive background
The speaker has a variety of beliefs and desires concerning such factors as
a. the nature and direction of the talk-exchange,
b. the social and physical context of the utterance,
c. the hearer's beliefs in general, beliefs pertinent to the speaker's impending remark in particular, and whatever contextual beliefs the hearer shares with the speaker.

Given these cognitive states, the speaker next must formulate the beginnings of the message to be communicated, as well as the manner in which it is to be communicated. In light of our discussion in chapter 9, we will refer to these as *pragmatic intentions*:

(2)
Pragmatic intentions
On the basis of the cognitive background, the speaker begins to form pragmatic intentions to
a. refer to something (referential intent),
b. perform some communicative act(s) (communicative intent),
c. perform these acts literally, nonliterally, directly, or indirectly,
d. have various effects on the thought or actions of the hearer (perlocutionary intent).

We know very little at present about the psychological mechanisms underlying the storage of background information and the formation of pragmatic intentions, in part because there are serious methodological problems with studying speech production. The standard methodology in psycholinguistics is to test for regular relationships between what subjects perceive and how they respond to it. Studying comprehension, the experimenter can manipulate characteristics of the input (such as the rate of the speech coming in) and look for regularities in the subjects' responses (such as the kinds of errors they make), but with speech production there is no good way of controlling the input, since the input is the subjects' *thoughts*. Psychologists know of no effective and ethically permissible way of controlling thoughts for experimental purposes, and so researchers in speech production must rely on very different kinds of phenomena, such as the analysis of hesitations, speech errors (both spontaneous and induced), evoked potentials, and language disorders.

Planning the Expression: Speech Errors

Having begun to formulate at least some of the above pragmatic intentions, how does the speaker put them into words? What sort of process is this? The Message Model suggests one possibility: that expression is basically a word-by-word encoding of the message from beginning to end. For instance, as the concept THE PLUMBER ... comes into the speaker's mind as the beginning of the message, the words "The plumber ..." might begin to come out. Furthermore, when a word itself requires planning, the procedure is the same: build it up from left to right out of phonemes and syllables.

However, there is considerable evidence against this picture of speech planning, some of which comes from the study of speech errors. Speech errors have been the subject of both casual and scientific interest for centuries, partly because of their relative infrequency, given the complexity of the task (see the discussion of articulation in chapter 3). It has been estimated that there is one error in about every 1,000 spoken words of an English speaker (Bock and Loebell 1988).

Probably the most famous speech error maker of all time was the Reverend William A. Spooner (1844–1930) of Oxford University, who lent his name (spoonerisms) to such classics as these:

(3)

a. "Work is the curse of the drinking class" for "Drink is the curse of the working class"

b. "Noble tons of soil" for "Noble sons of toil"

c. "You have hissed all my mystery lectures. I saw you fight a liar in the back quad; in fact, you have tasted the whole worm" (try your own hand at paraphrasing this one)

From a casual inspection of these errors, one might conclude that they are unsystematic, that errors are virtually a random phenomenon. But students of the subject agree that certain types of errors predominate; in fact, the kinds of errors that predominate are those that involve *linguistic constituents* in some way. (Klima and Bellugi (1979, chap. 5), show that

the same is true for "slips of the hand" in American Sign Language.)
These include:

(4)
a. *Exchange errors*
   h̲issed all my m̲ystery lectures
b. *Anticipation errors*
   a l̲eading l̲ist (reading list)
c. *Perseveration errors*
   a p̲honological f̲ool (phonological rule)
d. *Blends*
   mo̲inly (mostly, mainly), imp̲ostin̲ator (imposter, impersonator)
e. *Shifts*
   Mermaid__ moves̲ (mermaids move) their legs together.
f. *Substitutions*
   sympathy for symphony (form), finger for toe (meaning)

We have illustrated these types of error with mainly phonological segments, but they happen with all sorts of linguistic units, though rarely
with nonunits. Consider, for instance, the following samples:

(5)
a. *Phonetic features (voicing)*
   g̲lear p̲lue s̲ky (clear blue sky)
   p̲ig and v̲at (big and fat)
b. *Stress*
   Stop beating your **BRICK** against a h̲ead wall. (Stop beating your
   HEAD against a brick wall.)
c. *Syntactic features (indefinite)*
   a m̲eeting __arathon (an eating marathon)
d. *Stem and affix*
   He favors pushing busters. (busting pushers)
e. *Negation*
   I d̲isregard this as precise. (I regard this as imprecise.)
f. *Past tense*
   Rosa always date__ shra̲nks. (dated shrinks)

These examples illustrate important features of speech errors as evidence for the speech-planning process. First, errors usually involve the
alteration of some linguistic unit. Rarely are the speech error data completely random, and this suggests that *the speech-planning process uses*

linguistic units in its planning operations. Second, the errors reveal that the planning system must be looking ahead. A system that did not look ahead could hardly make the errors shown in (5a); the voicing feature appears to have moved backward in the first example (though forward in the second).

Consider next example (5b). The words *brick* and *head* were interchanged, but notice that the stress (indicated with capitals) did not move with the originally intended stressed word (*head*). Instead, it stayed in its original location, suggesting that there must be a level of representation for stress that is abstract and detached from the words themselves.

In the case of the indefinite article (5c) the speaker had intended to say *an eating marathon*, but when the /m/ moved forward and was attached to *eating*, the indefinite article changed from *an* to *a* to accommodate the error: the subject did not say *an meeting arathon*. This means that during the planning process there was a stage where the /m/ could move forward and a later stage where the indefinite article *a* could adjust to the next vowel by the addition of /n/. Again, the error indicates that the processor has planned ahead.

The examples involving stem and affix, negation, and the past tense emphasize the point that the processor might work in stages and is able to anticipate, using information about what is coming three or four words ahead. Consider (5e), *I disregard this as precise*: not only was negation anticipated three words ahead, but the form of the negation was adjusted to conform to morphological constraints as well; the subject did not say *I imregard this as precise*. Finally, the past tense example (5f) is interesting in that the tense feature moved onto a word that is homophonic with a verb (*to shrink*), but is in this occurrence a noun (*a shrink* "psychiatrist"). However, the speech-planning system apparently could not use this information at this stage; it treated the word as a verb in the past tense, producing *shrank*. The challenge for theories of speech production is not only to account for these errors, but also to account for these *patterns* of errors.

One influential proposal is that of Garrett (1975, 1980), who noticed certain patterns in his error corpus that could be accounted for if the production system contains at least two important levels of planning activity: what he calls the *functional* level and the *positional* level (see figure 10.4). Functional level planning deals with multiphrasal representations of the functional roles of words—their semantic values and syntactic relations. Positional level planning deals with single-phrase rep-

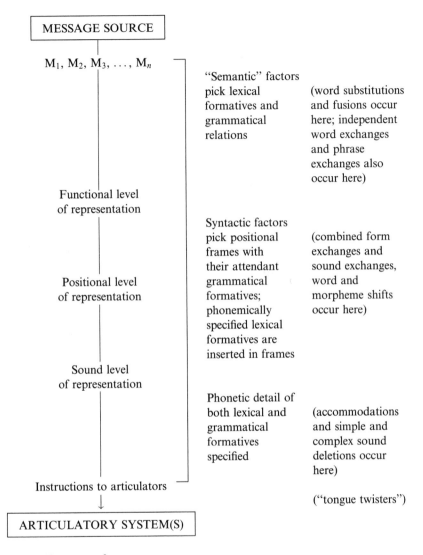

MESSAGE SOURCE

$M_1, M_2, M_3, \ldots, M_n$

"Semantic" factors
pick lexical
formatives and
grammatical
relations

(word substitutions
and fusions occur
here; independent
word exchanges
and phrase
exchanges also
occur here)

Functional level
of representation

Syntactic factors
pick positional
frames with
their attendant
grammatical
formatives;
phonemically
specified lexical
formatives are
inserted in frames

(combined form
exchanges and
sound exchanges,
word and
morpheme shifts
occur here)

Positional level
of representation

Sound level
of representation

Phonetic detail of
both lexical and
grammatical
formatives
specified

(accommodations
and simple and
complex sound
deletions occur
here)

Instructions to articulators

("tongue twisters")

ARTICULATORY SYSTEM(S)

Utterance of a sentence

Figure 10.4
Garrett's model of levels of speech production. (From Garrett 1975.)

resentations of the sound structure and serial ordering of the elements of the sentence. The patterns of error can be summarized as follows:

1. *Word* exchange errors occur predominantly *between* phrases, and in fact between words of the same syntactic category (noun, verb, etc.).
2. *Sound* exchange errors occur predominantly *within* phrases and do not respect syntactic categories.
3. *Morpheme* exchange errors are of both types. If they occur between phrases, then the morphemes are from words of the same category. If they occur within phrases, then the morphemes are rarely from words of the same category.
4. *Exchange* errors for words, morphemes, and sounds are restricted mainly to major (open, content) categories such as noun, verb, adjective.
5. *Shift* errors are restricted mainly to minor (closed, function) categories.
6. *Substitution* errors can be either form-related or meaning-related.

These regularities can be accounted for if the planning process involves the two levels just described; the idea is that items can get scrambled *at a level* because information about them is simultaneously available, but items cannot become scrambled *between* levels because information about items at these two levels is not simultaneously available. Thus, words can exchange across phrasal boundaries at the functional level, but sounds can only exchange within a phrase at the positional level, and so on for the other error regularities (see Dell and Reich 1981, for another analysis).

Slips of the Ear

Speech error studies have some distinctive methodological pitfalls that must be avoided if the data are to be reliable. One interesting class of mistakes has been called *slips of the ear*. Cutler (1982, 12) and Pinker (1995, 186) report examples such as those in (6a–c) and (6d–f), respectively.

(6)
a. Do you know about reflexes?
   Perceived: Do you know about Reith lectures?
b. It's about time Robert May was here.
   Perceived: It's about time to drop my brassiere.
c. If you think you have any clips of the type shown ...
   Perceived: If you think you have an eclipse ...
d. A girl with kaleidoscope eyes
   Perceived: A girl with colitis goes by

    e. Our father which art in Heaven; hallowed be thy name ... Lead us not into temptation ...
       Perceived: Our father wishart in heaven; Harold be they name ... Lead us not into Penn Station ...
    f. He is trampling out the vintage where the grapes of wrath are stored.
       Perceived: ... where the grapes are wrapped and stored.

Researchers take a number of precautions to guard against mishearing examples, such as requiring witnesses or tape recordings. Clearly, also, these errors can be the source of communication breakdowns, as noted in chapter 9.

10.3   LANGUAGE COMPREHENSION

The study of the processes of comprehension, from signal to understanding, does not suffer from the problems of identifying and manipulating the input. If anything it is the output, understanding, that is the problem in this case. On reflection it is not so clear what we really mean when we say that a hearer understood what a speaker said, or what a speaker meant (to communicate). For the time being we will leave the issue of the nature of understanding at the intuitive level, and we will begin our review with the input to speech comprehension, the speech signal itself. The entire process of comprehension is summarized in figure 10.5.

It is generally assumed that the speech recognition capacity identifies as much about the speech sounds as it can from the sound wave. The syntactic parsing capacity identifies the words by their sounds and analyzes the structure of the sentence, and the semantic interpretation capacity puts the meaning of the words together in accordance with these syntactic relations. The pragmatic interpretation capacity selects a particular speech act or communicative intent as the most likely. If the hearer is right, communication is successful; if not, there has been a breakdown.

It should not be assumed that these different processes are carried out either by different "areas of the brain" or necessarily one after the other. Many of them can overlap both in time and in brain activity. The question of the neurological realization of these linguistic capacities is the province of the field of neurolinguistics, which is the subject of chapter 12.

Modularity

When the "cognitive" perspective replaced behaviorism in the 1960s, it brought with it a conception of mental functioning as mental computa-

Figure 10.5
Functional analysis of comprehension into subcapacities

tion. The most pervasive example of computational devices at the time
was the standard stored program von Neumann machine, the kind of
machine your PC is. This traditional model, sometimes called a *unitary*
architecture, represents minds as constructed out of two principal components: input (sensory data) and output (motor response) processors and
a central processing unit. All higher-level cognitive functions were
thought to be explainable by a single (hence "unitary") set of principles
in the central processor. On this conception, incoming stimuli are first
processed by sensory systems such as the machinery of the eye or the ear,
and the data are then turned over to the central cognitive processor.
Everything is treated the same: language, visual recognition, reasoning,

Figure 10.6
The Müller-Lyer illusion

memory, and so on. There is no place for special perceptual processing between sensory input and central cognitive processing.

More recently another cognitive organization, utilizing special-purpose perceptual processors, has been proposed. These processors are called *modules*, and systems containing them are said to be *modular*; hence, the architecture itself is sometimes called *modular*. We can expect differences between perceptual systems and cognition when we consider that the purpose of perceptual systems is to *track the ever-changing environment*, whereas the purpose of central cognitive systems is to *make considered judgments*. Because of these differences in purpose there are important differences in the way these systems function. Consider input systems. First, such special-purpose computational systems are *fast*. Typically, perceptual processes are completed within a few tenths of a second. Second, there seems to be *special neural circuitry* devoted to the various perceptual processes. Third, perceptual systems are sensitive to *specific domains* of information. The language system responds to language input, but not to sneezes, and the face recognition system responds to upright faces, but not to inverted faces (or to photographic negatives of faces). Fourth, perceptual systems are *mandatory*: once they begin processing, they cannot be turned off by knowledge or decision. Fifth, perceptual systems are *informationally encapsulated*: they can utilize only certain information and do not make use of all of the information available to the person as a whole. Consider illusions. Knowing that the line segments in figure 10.6 are actually the same length (measure them) does not cause the illusion of difference to go away. Finally, the inner workings of perceptual systems are *not available to introspection*.

These features make perceptual systems like special-purpose computers, well suited for tracking the environment—they are fast and relatively reliable. Central processes, on the other hand, trade off speed for accuracy. They are relatively slow (think about the processes of deciding where to go to college, or what to major in), but they allow us to consider lots of available information, from a wide variety of sources. Central processes typically involve processes of deductive and probabilistic reasoning.

Is the language processor a module? Fodor (1983) and others contend that language processing is indeed modular, like (other) perceptual systems (but see Marslen-Wilson and Tyler 1987). Language functions to *pick up information about the environment*: it is not infallible in this, but neither are other perceptual systems. Also, the language processor seems *specific to language* input, regardless of the sensory modality (see the discussion of the curious "McGurk effect" in section 10.4). It is *fast* enough that we can recognize syllables and even activate semantic information within $\frac{3}{10}$ second, and it is *mandatory* or *automatic* in that we cannot just decide to turn it off once it has started. Language processing is *not accessible to introspection*, and there is considerable evidence (see chapter 12) that language is processed directly on *specific neural circuits* in the brain. When these areas are damaged, specific language capacities can be affected. The most controversial claim of language modularity is *information encapsulation*. After surveying some central topics, we will return to this issue.

This raises the question of the general architectural structure of the language-processing mechanisms, and their relation to the rest of cognition. First, there is the strong "autonomy" claim (Forster 1979) that each component of the language processor functions like a little module—it works autonomously on its input. Second, there is the claim that there can be interaction between components *within* the language faculty, but there can be no influences on the module from central systems. Since this second position allows for interaction inside the module, it is important where such a theory draws the line between language processing and general cognition. Some, such as proponents of cohort theory, draw the line quite early and include only lexical access—the process of contacting lexical information in memory. Others suggest that basic mechanisms of parsing (and semantic interpretation) are also a part of the language module. Third, contrasting with these positions are highly *interactive* theories such as the artificial intelligence model HEARSAY II (see Lesser et al. 1977) and current connectionist models (see section 10.4).

Speech Perception

The hearer, having heard an expression uttered by the speaker, must now recover its meaning(s). For a fluent speaker of a given language this might seem like a trivial task. After all, what is there to understanding sentences of our native language aside from knowing the individual words of the language plus a few simple word order rules for forming word sequences that "make sense"?

A serious problem with this view is that in actual speech, sentences are, physically, continuous streams of sound, not broken down into the convenient discrete units that we call words. A good illustration of this is the experience of a traveler in a foreign land who does not know the local language. The traveler does not hear neatly arranged sequences of individual words—the sentences and phrases of the language all sound like streams of unintelligible noise. The idea that we *do* hear such sequences as discrete, linearly ordered units is only an illusion that results from the fact that in knowing a language, we perceptually analyze a physical continuum into individual sounds (as well as words and phrases). A striking aspect of this perceptual analysis of sounds was demonstrated in a set of experiments by Schatz (1954). Tape recordings of various consonant-vowel combinations were made, then cut and respliced to create new consonant-vowel combinations. In one case, the word *ski* was cut between the *k* and the *i*, and the initial *sk* was then combined with other sounds to form the new consonant-vowel sequences. When the *sk* from *ski* was combined with a new sequence *ar* and played to English speakers, the subjects did not hear the word *scar*, as we might expect. Instead, they reported hearing the word *star* 96 percent of the time. Further, when the *sk* from *ski* was combined with the sequence *ool*, the word *spool* was heard 87 percent of the time, rather than the expected *school*. Thus, the acoustic signal corresponding to the *k* in the word *ski* can be perceived as a *k* (as in *ski*), *t* (as in *star*), or *p* (as in *spool*), depending on the following vowel. These cases show that a single acoustic signal can be perceived as different consonants, which cannot be identified until the following vowel is known.

A particularly striking example of context effects in speech perception is the *phoneme restoration effect* discovered by Warren and Warren (1970). Subjects were presented with the word *legislature* in the context of the sentence *The state governors met with their respective legislatures convening in the capitals*, but with the /dʒɨs/-sounds removed, and replaced by a cough. However, subjects do not hear something like *le-cough-latures*; rather, they hear the word *legislatures* with a cough in the background. This works with a variety of other noises as well—tones, buzzes, and so forth—but if silence is presented in place of the /dʒɨs/-sound, then the /dʒɨs/-sound is not restored.

Another illustration of the nonlinearity of speech processing comes from an experiment by Pollack and Pickett (1963). Speech sequences were created by excising portions of conversations via an electronic "gate" of variable width. Individual words that were excised from the tape were rarely intelligible when the gate was so narrow that the preceding and following words were not included. However, as the gate was widened to allow more and more of the original utterance, the entire sequence eventually became intelligible. As reported by Lieberman (1966), the excised portion does not become gradually more intelligible as the gate width increases; rather, the signal remains unintelligible until a particular gate width is reached, and at this point the entire sequence suddenly becomes intelligible. Later work (see Grosjean and Gee 1987) extended this idea to prosodic information. The implication is that "letter by letter" models of speech perception apply rarely if ever to speech phenomena. Although an enormous amount of interesting work has been done on speech perception in the last 30 years, the fundamental problem of saying how the speech signal is converted into meaningful units remains unsolved.

Lexical Access and Syntactic Analysis

The output of the speech recognition capacity is a representation of as much information as it can obtain about the speech sounds of the utterance, based on the sound wave alone. In most cases information about some of the segments will be missing, as will information concerning aspects of intonation and word or phrase boundaries. It is the job of the syntactic parsing capacity to identify the relevant words and relate them syntactically. It is the job of the semantic interpretation capacity to produce a representation of the meaning of the sentence (or other expressions). We will follow this process from words to sentence to meaning as best we can, though current research shows that very little is known about many of these operations.

Lexical Access and Word Recognition

If we are to understand what speakers are saying, we must understand the sentences they utter; and to do this, we must recognize (at least some of) the words that make up these sentences. The psycholinguistic literature often distinguishes two processes here: *lexical access*, in which the language processor unconsciously "accesses" or makes contact with the information stored at an address in the mental lexicon, and *word recognition*, in which one of the accessed words (and its meaning) is selected and made available to introspection. There are at least two prominent experimental techniques for investigating lexical access and word recognition. *Lexical decision* requires subjects to decide whether or not a displayed series of letters constitutes a word. *Naming* requires subjects to pronounce the displayed series of letters. By presenting words and nonwords to subjects and timing their responses in these tasks, researchers can test different aspects of models of word recognition. Since these two tasks are sensitive to different aspects of this process, results that generalize across both tasks are probably more reliable.

Given the speed at which language comprehension is possible (over 4 words per second), it is clear that the time it takes to identify words need not be very long at all, perhaps an average of about $\frac{1}{5}$ second (Rohrman and Gough 1967). Thus, it would be implausible to suppose that a hearer searches randomly through a mental dictionary (lexicon) of 50,000 words to find the word (with its syntactic and semantic properties) that is associated with the sounds that are heard. In fact, it appears that accessing the mental lexicon is systematic.

First, the mental lexicon appears to some extent to be ordered by sounds—much as a normal dictionary is ordered by the alphabet (Fay and Cutler 1977). Second, lexical access also seems sensitive to how *frequently* one has heard the word (Forster and Chambers 1973) and how *recently* one has heard the word (Scarborough, Cortese, and Scarborough 1977). If frequent or recent words are more easily accessed, then the more likely a word is to occur in one's experience, the more likely it is to be accessed easily. This is the *frequency* (or *recency*) *effect*. Third, as we will see shortly (see also section 10.4), various kinds of prior context can favorably influence the speed and accuracy of lexical access (*priming*): repeated words prime themselves, *doctor* primes *nurse*, *banjo* primes *harp*, and even *couch* primes *touch* (orthographic priming) (Meyer and Schvaneveldt 1971). Fourth, an interesting side effect of lexical access involves the *word superiority effect*: letters are more quickly and accurately recognized in the context of words than they are by themselves or in the context of nonwords (Reicher 1969). This suggests that lexical access is implicated in the recognition of the very letters that make up the word being recognized. (How could this be so?) Finally, possible but nonactual words such as *obttle* are rejected more slowly (about 650 milliseconds) than clear nonwords such as *xnit*, which are rejected in about the same time as it takes to recognize actual words (500 milliseconds).

As a theory of word recognition, Forster (1978) proposed the influential *search model*, which resembles the search method for a book in a library: get a reference to a book; go to the card catalogue; find the card for the

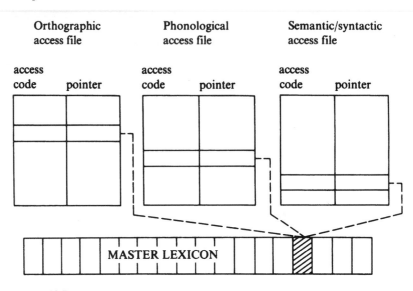

Figure 10.7
Organization of peripheral access files and master lexicon. (From Forster 1978.)

book (the cards being organized in different ways—by author, title, subject); from the card, get the number that points to the book's location in the stacks. According to Forster's model (see figure 10.7), when a word is first perceived, it activates the appropriate *access code*, which is orthographic if the word is read, phonological if it is heard. (The syntactic/semantic code is used primarily for finding words to speak, and we ignore it for now.) The system next begins searching the relevant access file, which is arranged so that the most frequent/recent items are compared first. If the perceived word is sufficiently close to an item in the access file, the search will stop and the system will follow the pointer to the location in the master lexicon where the full entry for the word is given. The system then does a *postaccess check* to verify all information.

This model neatly explains some of the basic findings. For instance, it explains why frequent/recent words are recognized faster than infrequent words, since frequent words are searched first. The model also predicts that nonwords should take longer to reject than actual words do to be accepted, because the system will continue to look for a nonword until the file (or some bins in the file) have been exhausted, whereas the search will terminate whenever a word is found. Nonwords that are similar to words will trick the system momentarily (perhaps until the postaccess check) and so will take even longer to reject.

Ambiguity and Disambiguation

Let's suppose that a word has been recognized. How about its meaning(s)? Not only are most of the words in English ambiguous; many of the words in each speaker's idiolect are ambiguous as well. This poses an interesting problem for the speech understander—should it note all of the meanings of each word, or only some (normally one), and if so, which one? (Note that it does seem that we normally hit on the right or appropriate meaning most of the time). Since this process is so fast, we should not expect introspection to answer this question.

Research suggests that more processing is going on than introspection may reveal. One early sequence of studies (Bever, Garrett, and Hurtig 1973) found evidence that hearers typically access *all* of the meanings of the words they hear; by the end of a clause, the most plausible meaning is selected and the processing continues. If this should turn out to be the wrong choice, as in so-called *garden path sentences* such as (7), then the processor must go back and try again:

(7)
He gave the girl the ring impressed the watch. (put *whom* after *girl*)

It is still not clear exactly what causes a meaning to be selected: is it memory limitations, or time limitations, or the arrival of some structural unit (such as the end of the clause)? One study (Tanenhaus, Leiman, and Seidenberg 1979) found that up to about $\frac{1}{4}$ second, both meanings of ambiguous noun-verb words (such as *watch*) were activated, but after that period of time one reading was selected. A related study (Swinney 1979) found that by three syllables after an ambiguous word, a decision had been made on the appropriate meaning. Seidenberg et al. (1982) found that the language processor will activate the "flower" meaning of *rose* not only in the context of (8a) but also, surprisingly, in the context of (8b):

(8)
a. He handed her a *rose*.
b. The balloon *rose* into the clouds.

All of this suggests that when we process sentences, all known meanings of each word are first automatically activated, then some as yet poorly understood process selects the most appropriate one based on various cues.

In some cases the speaker can help the hearer out. In one study (Lehiste 1973) subjects were asked to listen to ambiguous sentences such as (9), where the speaker had a particular meaning in mind:

(9)

The steward (*greeted* [*the* girl) with a smile].

It was found that when hearers disambiguated the sentence correctly and got the intended smiling-girl meaning, the speakers paused (by as much as $\frac{1}{6}$ second) between the crucial words (italicized in (9)), thus giving the hearers a cue as to what was meant.

Syntactic Strategies

Imagine that the speech comprehension capacity has determined which words it is presently hearing and it has looked up their idiosyncratic syntactic and semantic characteristics. What does it do now? Recall that one goal is to figure out the meaning(s) of the whole sentence on the basis of the meaning(s) of its words and their syntactic relations. So it must begin to determine those relations.

One very influential proposal about how this is done was made by Bever (1970). He proposed that part of this system consists of perceptual *strategies.* These strategies tell the system how to make decisions about syntactic structures in the face of uncertainty and incomplete information. For instance, given the rate of speech comprehension, it is unlikely that *all* possibilities are investigated at every level of analysis; rather, hearers use strategies as rules of thumb to make intelligent guesses. Of course, if these principles are only strategies, and not exhaustive searches, then it should be possible for the speech comprehension capacity to err— we should be able to trick it. And trick it we can. Consider one of Bever's strategies:

(10)

Main Clause Strategy (MCS)

The first NP + V + (NP) sequence is the main clause of the sentence, unless the verb is marked as subordinate.

Such a strategy works well for sentences such as (11a), but it is tricked by sentences such as (11b), which should be read as (11c):

(11)

a. The horse raced the car, and won.

b. The horse raced past the barn fell.

c. The horse (which was) raced past the barn fell.

Thus, it would seem that something like the MCS is operating in understanding. But might the MCS be simply a special case of more general processes? In fact, it has been proposed (Frazier and Fodor 1978) that the parsing capacity involves two stages. The first stage, because of (short-term) memory limitations, looks at about six words of the sentence at a time, attempting to categorize the words as nouns, verbs, and so on, and to group as many of them together in a phrase as its limited capacity allows. The second stage takes these structured phrasal "packages" and attempts to build a coherent syntactic structure for the whole sentence. On this view, many errors can be accounted for by the operating characteristics of the two stages. In particular, these errors can, in many cases, be attributed to the "short-sightedness" of the first stage; it will follow the principle of Minimal Attachment:

(12)
Minimal Attachment (MA)
Try to group the latest words received together under existing category nodes; otherwise, build a new category.

This parsing strategy explains many intuitive and experimental results. Frazier (1979) reports a sequence of experiments in which such sentences were presented to subjects visually one word at a time (at the rate of about 3 words per second) and the subjects were asked to judge their grammaticality. If comprehension tends to follow the principles of the two-stage model, then sentences like (13b) will take longer to process than sentences like (13a). (The extra embedded pair of brackets indicates the new node that is required. MA = minimal attachment; NMA = nonminimal attachment.)

(13)
a. (MA) We gave [the man the grant proposal we wrote] because he had written a similar proposal last year.
b. (NMA) We gave [the man [the grant proposal was written by last year]] a copy of this year's proposal.

The model (and intuition) predicts (13b) to be more difficult to process because *the man* is not minimally attached. The experiment confirmed this; on average, it took over twice as long to process sentences like (13b) than sentences like (13a). This result was confirmed by Rayner, Carlson, and Frazier (1983) by tracking eye movements of readers of sentences such as (14a) and (14b):

(14)
a. (MA) The kids [played all the albums *on the stereo*] before they went to bed.

b. (NMA) The kids played all [the albums [*on the shelf*]] before they went to bed.

Even though general knowledge makes it clear that *on the shelf* modifies *albums* and not *play* in (14b), the difficulty normally associated with non-minimal attachment was in fact observed in eye movement patterns; relevant world knowledge was not consulted during the parse. This again suggests modularity.

Constituent structure of sentences in not merely an artifact of syntactic theory; there is reason to think that gross constituent structure in fact has reality in the minds of speakers. In various experiments that have come to be known as the *click experiments*, Fodor, Bever, and Garrett (1974) tried to show that test subjects utilize major constituent boundaries in their perception of sentences. Subjects wearing headphones heard a tape-recorded sentence in one ear, while in the other ear they heard a "click" noise simultaneously superimposed on some part of the sentence. They were asked to write down each sentence they had heard and to indicate where in the sentence they had heard the click sound. A typical sentence in this experiment was (15), where the dots underneath words indicate the various locations of the superimposed click noises:

(15)
That the girl was . happy | was evident from the way she laughed.

The major constituent break in this sentence occurs between *happy* and *was*, and clicks were superimposed both before this major break and after it. The subjects in the experiment showed a definite tendency to "mis-hear" the location of the click: when the click actually occurred *before* the major break, subjects reported hearing it *later* (closer to the major break); when the click actually occurred *after* the major break, subjects reported hearing it *earlier* (again closer to the major break). When the click was located at the major break itself, the tendency to "mis-hear" its location was much lower.

This experiment has been interpreted as showing that hearers process sentences in terms of major *clauses* of a sentence, and that these major constituents *resist interruption*. Hence, when a click was placed within a major clause (say, at the word *was* in (15)), hearers tended to report it as occurring in the break, and not in the clause itself, suggesting that on a perceptual level major clauses are integrated units that resist being broken up. The results of the click experiments are by no means uncontroversial. If these results hold up, however, then it appears that major constituent structure is both a theoretical device used by linguists to explain syntactic phenomena and a psychologically real unit of perception on the part of hearers.

The picture of parsing that emerges from these and other studies is that as words are heard and identified, their meanings are activated and the comprehension device begins to try to put them together into phrases. As comprehension proceeds, the device runs out of immediate memory and must group the words together as best it can. As words come in, this process continues, and the comprehension device also tries to connect these phrases into a total coherent sentential structure. The details of this process are the topic of much current research.

Context/Interaction Effects and Modularity

As we have seen, the hypothesis that lexical access is modular is heavily supported by the fact that even in the face of sentential contexts that favor one reading, more than one meaning of a word is briefly activated (recall the *rose* example). This suggests that highly interactive models are wrong in predicting that context guides the processor away from contextually inappropriate interpretations. There is even evidence that *hearing* a word will activate information about its *spelling*, even though this could not be relevant in the context. Seidenberg and Tanenhaus (1979) found that in an auditory rhyme detection task, similarly spelled words (*tie, pie*) were detected faster than dissimilarly spelled words (*rye, pie*).

Fishler and Bloom (1979) found that subjects in a lexical decision task responded more quickly to *teeth* than to *tree* or *truth* in contexts such as these:

(16)
a. John brushed his teeth.
b. John brushed his tree.
c. John brushed his truth.

A modularity theorist must account for this without supposing that our general knowledge that one brushes teeth more often than trees is affecting the lexical access.

Putting highly interactive theories temporarily aside, how are we to decide between the strong "autonomy" conception, "cohort" theory, and Fodor's modular input system conception of language processing? This proves quite difficult since each type of theory has the resources to accommodate a wide number of effects (see Norris 1986).

Garden Path Sentences

If the language module extends beyond lexical access to parsing, then the assignment of structure ought to be mandatory and encapsulated; we already saw some evidence from eye movement studies of reading that this is so. Crain and Steedman (1985) argue that such sentences indicate encapsulation only because they are being studied in isolation. Normally, they claim, there is a pragmatic principle at work:

(17)

Principle of Referential Success (PRS)
If there is a reading that succeeds in referring to an entity already established in the hearer's mental model of the domain of discourse, then it is favored over one that is not.

Crain and Steedman argue that if there is a relevant set of horses in the hearer's discourse model, then (11b) will not be misanalyzed; the hearer will not be led down the garden path. They found that on a sentence classification task, subjects could be influenced by prior context as well as the nature of the lexical items in the sentence. For instance, (18a) was misclassified as ungrammatical more frequently than (18b).

(18)
a. The teachers taught by the Berlitz method passed the test.
b. The children taught by the Berlitz method passed the test.

How could this be if the parser treats these as structurally identical? The first answer comes from the fact that *teacher* and *children* differ in their semantics, and semantic information is in principle available to the syntax in Fodor's version of modularity (though not in the autonomy version). The second comes from an experiment that tested the PRS (Clifton and Ferreira 1987). Subjects were given the following types of sentences in contexts that established discourse referents and so should have facilitated processing:

(19)
a. (NMA) [The editor [played the tape]] agreed the story was big.
b. (MA) [The editor played the tape] and agreed the story was big.
(control sentence)

Here, the nonminimally attached structure should have been computed first, as it is for (19b). If, however, hearers follow the Minimal Attachment principle *regardless* of context, then they should have had trouble with (19a), compared to (19b). This is the result reported, indicating that although the PRS was available to guide the parser (subjects used it to answer true/false questions about these sentences), the parser was incapable of utilizing this information—in short, it is informationally encapsulated.

Semantic Interpretation: Mental Representation of Meaning

How does the mind represent the meaning of words or morphemes, and how does it combine these to represent the meaning of phrases and sentences? These are the central questions in this area of research, and although much interesting work has been done, we are only beginning to glimpse what the answers might look like.

Word and Phrase Meaning: Concepts

The problem of word meaning for psychology is finding a psychological state that could plausibly be the state of knowing the meaning of a word. We saw in chapter 6 that images are not the answer, at least not the whole answer. The most popular and influential theory in psychology at present is that the mental representation of meaning involves *concepts*. But how are we to think of concepts? One way to think of them is in terms of their *role* in thought; another is in terms of their *internal structure*.

Probably the most pervasive role for concepts to play in thought is *categorization*. Concepts allow us to group things that are similar in some respect into classes. We are able to abstract away from irrelevant details to the properties that are important for thought and action. The stability of our everyday mental life depends to a great extent on our capacity to categorize and conceptualize particular objects and events.

Concepts also combine to form *complex concepts* and ultimately *complete thoughts*. For example, we might have the concepts MISCHIEVOUS and BOYS, and form the complex concept MISCHIEVOUS BOYS. Or we might form the thought that BOYS ARE MISCHIEVOUS, the wish that BOYS NOT BE MISCHIEVOUS, and so on. From the point of view of semantics, some concepts are taken to be the mental representation of the meaning of *words* (following Fodor 1981, we call these *lexical concepts*), some concepts are taken to be the mental representation of the meaning of *phrases* (*phrasal concepts*), and thoughts are taken to be the mental representation of the meaning of (declarative) *sentences*. How may we describe the internal structure of concepts, especially the internal structure of lexical concepts? We will now look at the traditional view of concepts, some criticisms of this view, and an alternative view of concepts that has recently become popular.

Concepts: The Traditional View   The traditional view of the mental representation of the meaning of words, dating from the seventeenth-century British Empiricists, holds that there are two sorts of concepts: simple and complex. Simple concepts, such as RED, are thought to be the result of (innate) sensory and perceptual processes. Complex concepts, on the other hand, are generally learned and are the result of combining simple concepts in accordance with various principles such as conjunction and negation. For instance, the concept TRIANGLE might be learned by conjoining the concepts PLANE, CLOSED, FIGURE, WITH, THREE, STRAIGHT, SIDES. Or, to take another example, BACHELOR might be learned by conjoining ADULT and MALE with the negative NOT MARRIED. Sometimes the traditional view is called the *definitional view* because the concepts associated with a word or phrase as its meaning are said to *define* it. This view can be summarized as follows:

(20)
The traditional view of concepts
a. Concepts can be either *simple* or *complex*.
b. Simple concepts are derived from *sensation* and *perception*.
c. Complex concepts are composed ultimately out of simple concepts.
d. Each of these simpler concepts is equally *necessary* for the complex concept, and the simpler concepts together are jointly *sufficient* for the complex concept.
e. Something is an *instance* of a complex concept just when it is an instance of the simpler constituent concepts.
f. Concepts are the *meaning* of words and phrases; and *understanding* a word or phrase is grasping its associated concept.

The traditional theory is intuitively plausible in many ways. For instance, it explains how *concepts can be learned* (one combines simpler concepts one already knows), how *concepts can correctly apply* to things (by those things falling under the simpler constituent concepts), and how *communication can be successful* (if a speaker uses a word that the hearer also knows, then speaker and hearer must share the defining concepts and so they both will know what things it correctly applies to).

Problems with the Traditional View of Concepts: Decomposition and Typicality Effects This traditional view, despite its considerable virtues, has been under serious attack for at least three decades. First, it is very implausible that *all* complex concepts can be analyzed or *decomposed* into sensory or perceptual properties. Consider the concept of a CHAIR or a HAT. Clearly, chairs and hats have certain structural characteristics that can be represented perceptually. However, they also have certain important *functions* or *uses*, which are not perceptual properties—we do not see "sittability" or "wearability." Even worse, think of BACHELOR: what is the *perceptual* property of being NOT MARRIED? There is also evidence from the acquisition of perceptual language by blind children that more than sensation and perception must form the basis of word meaning (see Landau and Gleitman 1985).

Second, there is experimental evidence against the idea that understanding words, phrases, and sentences involves activating the kinds of complex defining concepts that the traditional view requires. For instance, Fodor, Fodor, and Garrett (1975) asked subjects to evaluate the validity of arguments such as the following:

(21)
a. If practically all of the men in the room are *not married*, then few of the men in the room have wives.
b. If practically all of the men in the room are *bachelors*, then few of the men in the room have wives.

Notice that (21b) contains *bachelors*, which is commonly thought to be definable in terms of NOT MARRIED. Since experiments have shown that negation adds significantly to comprehension time, we would expect that if *bachelor* is in fact decomposed into concepts including NOT MARRIED, then (21b) should take at least as much time on average to process as (21a). However, subjects processed sentences like (21b) significantly *faster* than sentences like (21a), suggesting that the definitional decomposition posited by the traditional view was not taking place.

A more elaborate study (Fodor et al. 1980) has provided further evidence against definitional decomposition. First it was established that subjects are experimentally sensitive to differences or "shifts" between surface grammatical relations and deeper grammatical relations. For example, consider (22a) and (22b):

(22)
a. John expected Mary to write a poem.
b. John persuaded Mary to write a poem.

These sentences have the same surface structure, but they differ in their underlying grammatical relations in that *Mary* is both the object of *persuade* and the subject of *write* in (22b), but only the subject of *write* in (22a). To see this, contrast the meaning of the following passives:

(23)
a. John expected a poem to be written by Mary.
b. *John persuaded a poem to be written by Mary.

Given that these differences are experimentally detectable, Fodor et al. gave subjects sentences like (24a) and (24b):

(24)
a. John saw the glass.
b. John broke the glass.

On the traditional view, these should have very different conceptual structures. In (24a) *the glass* is the object of *saw*, but in (24b) *the glass* is really the subject, not the object, of *break*. According to the traditional view, (24b) is *really* stored as something like (25):

(25)
John caused the glass to break.

This "shift" should be detectable with the tests just described, but it was not, thereby providing further evidence against the traditional view.

Third, there is experimental evidence that the internal structure of many lexical concepts does not resemble that of definitions (i.e., of equally necessary and sufficient conditions). In an influential series of studies Rosch and her associates (Rosch 1973, Rosch and Mervis 1975) have provided evidence that the categorization process exhibits "typicality effects," suggesting that concepts possess an internal structure favoring typical members over less typical ones. Let us look at two of these effects.

First, people are quite consistent in rating certain kinds of objects as more or less typical of a kind. For instance, in one experiment Rosch (1973, experiment 3) asked over 100 subjects to rank members of eight assorted categories with regard to typicality or exemplariness. Table 10.1 gives these categories, their members, and their ranking. On the basis of these results and similar ones from other experiments, it is possible to see

Table 10.1
Judgments of "goodness of category membership." (From Rosch 1973.)

Category	Member	B & M[a] frequency	"Exemplariness" rank	Category	Member	B & M[a] frequency	"Exemplariness" rank
Fruit	Apple	429	1.3	Vehicle	Car	407	1.0
	Plum	167	2.3		Boat	145	2.7
	Pineapple	98	2.3		Scooter	99	2.5
	Strawberry	58	2.3		Tricycle	43	3.5
	Fig	16	4.7		Horse	14	5.9
	Olive	3	6.2		Skis	3	5.7
Science	Chemistry	367	1.0	Crime	Murder	387	1.0
	Botany	242	1.7		Assault	132	1.4
	Geology	76	2.6		Stealing	95	1.3
	Sociology	46	4.6		Embezzling	40	1.8
	Anatomy	19	1.7		Blackmail	16	1.7
	History	3	5.9		Vagrancy	3	5.3
Sport	Football	396	1.2	Disease	Cancer	316	1.2
	Hockey	130	1.8		Measles	168	2.8
	Wrestling	87	3.0		Cold	90	4.7
	Archery	49	3.9		Malaria	54	1.4
	Gymnastics	16	2.6		Muscular dystrophy	15	1.9
	Weight lifting	3	4.7		Rheumatism	3	3.5
Bird	Robin	377	1.1	Vegetable	Carrot	316	1.1
	Eagle	161	1.2		Asparagus	138	1.3
	Wren	83	1.4		Celery	96	1.7
	Chicken	40	3.8		Onion	47	2.7
	Ostrich	17	3.3		Parsley	15	3.8
	Bat	3	5.8		Pickle	2	4.4

[a] Frequency with which the member was listed in response to the category name from Battig and Montague 1969.

Table 10.2
Categories and members used in reaction time experiment. (From Rosch 1973.)

Category	Member	
	Central	Peripheral
Toy	Doll	Skates
	Ball	Swing
Bird	Robin	Chicken
	Sparrow	Duck
Fruit	Pear	Strawberry
	Banana	Prune
Sickness	Cancer	Rheumatism
	Measles	Rickets
Relative	Aunt	Wife
	Uncle	Daughter
Metal	Copper	Magnesium
	Aluminum	Platinum
Crime	Rape	Treason
	Robbery	Fraud
Sport	Baseball	Fishing
	Basketball	Diving
Vehicle	Car	Tank
	Bus	Carriage
Science	Chemistry	Medicine
	Physics	Engineering
Vegetable	Carrot	Onion
	Spinach	Mushroom
Part of the body	Arm	Lips
	Leg	Skin

whether "typical" members of a category behave differently in thought from "atypical" members. For instance, Rosch (1973, experiment 4) constructed sentences such as (26a) and (26b) from the list in table 10.2:

(26)

a. A *doll* is a *toy*. (typical)

b. A *skate* is a *toy*. (atypical)

Subjects took significantly less time to judge a "typical" sentence true than an "atypical" sentence—they could decide that a doll is a toy faster than that a skate is a toy. This was found to be true not only for adults, but also for children. Moreover, these results have proved quite reliable in many such experiments using a wide variety of materials.

Typical versus atypical members of a class tend to be (1) more likely categorized correctly, (2) learned first by children, (3) recalled first from memory, (4) more likely to serve as cognitive reference points (e.g., an ellipse is judged "almost" a circle, rather than a circle being judged "almost an ellipse"), and (5) likely to share more characteristics and so have a high "family resemblance." These results (see Smith and Medin 1981 for a good survey) are generally thought to imply that concepts are structured in ways incompatible with the traditional view. In particular, on the traditional view component concepts are *equally* and *exhaustively defining*. Thus, the component concepts that define BIRD are all necessary for something to be correctly categorized BIRD. And if something is correctly represented as falling under all of the defining concepts, then it is correctly categorized BIRD. Yet when features of concepts for various birds are actually evoked from subjects (see table 10.3), it is clear that a trivial feature such as "says 'who'" can be sufficient to pick out one bird (an owl), and that no feature is necessary for all birds.

New Theories: Prototypes and Fuzzy Concepts   These experimental findings have evoked a variety of responses. Some theorists (see Miller and Johnson-Laird 1976) have attempted to revise the traditional view by distinguishing a conceptual *core* of defining concepts from an *identification procedure* that is sensitive to typicality characteristics.

Other theorists (Smith, Shoben, and Rips 1974) have moved to a *probabilistic* model of concepts. On this view, component concepts are given a certain probability of applying correctly, as shown in table 10.4.

An object is categorized as (for instance) a robin rather than a chicken if it reaches some critical sum of probabilities.

Still others (Rosch and Mervis 1975) have proposed a *prototype* or *exemplar* model of concepts, wherein concepts are structured around descriptions or images of typical/focal instances of the concept. As Rosch and Mervis (1975, 112) put it:

Categories are composed of a "core meaning" which consists of the "clearest cases" (best examples) of the category, "surrounded" by other category members of decreasing similarity to that core meaning.

None of these theories has been worked out to the point where it can be evaluated in detail, though all can handle the typicality effects. Unfortunately, each theory has difficulties at present. Of particular interest and concern is the apparent failure of probabilistic and exemplar models to

Table 10.3
Feature listings for 12 concepts. (Adapted from Smith and Medin 1981.)

Features	Bird				
	Bluebird	Chicken	Falcon	Flamingo	Owl
Eats fish	0	0	0	0	0
Flies	12	0	7	0	0
Ugly	0	0	0	0	0
Eats insects	9	0	0	0	0
Eats dead	0	0	0	0	0
Is food	0	17	0	0	0
Pink	0	0	0	23	0
Stands on one leg	0	0	0	13	0
Says "who"	0	0	0	0	24
Tuxedo	0	0	0	0	0

provide a general account of *phrasal* concepts. What, for instance, is the exemplar for the concept GRANDMOTHER LIVING IN A LARGE AMERICAN CITY? Without such an exemplar we do not have a concept and without a concept, no meaning. But surely such phrases do have meaning, and we do have such concepts (see Fodor 1981).

Versions of the prototype theory have encountered both experimental and theoretical problems. Armstrong, Gleitman, and Gleitman (1983) ran a series of "typicality" experiments that seem to show that subjects respond to such well-defined concepts as "even number," "odd number," and "plane geometry figure" with the same graded responses that Rosch found for notions like "sport" and "bird." A sample of their results is shown in table 10.5. Clearly, it makes no sense to structure the concept of an *even number* around the number 2 rather than 6, because there is no numerical difference in their "evenness." If some numbers were "more even than others," then balancing a checkbook would be a lot harder than it already is. (How would you add, subtract, and divide by both very even numbers and not-so-even numbers?) As Armstrong, Gleitman, and Gleitman comment:

What they [these results] do suggest is that we are back at square one in discovering the structure of everyday categories *experimentally* ... the study of conceptual structure has not been put on an experimental footing, and the structure of those concepts studied by current techniques remains unknown.

Concepts are mental categories, and so the items in the world that the concept applies to are the members of that mental category. With tradi-

Table 10.3

(continued)

Bird

Penguin	Robin	Sandpiper	Seagull	Starling	Swallow	Vulture
11	0	0	18	0	0	0
0	9	5	9	6	7	2
0	0	0	0	0	0	15
0	20	8	0	4	5	0
0	0	0	0	0	0	22
0	0	0	0	0	0	0
0	0	0	0	0	0	0
0	0	0	0	0	0	0
0	0	0	0	0	0	0
11	0	0	0	0	0	0

Table 10.4

The probabilistic view: featural approach. (See Smith and Medin 1981.)

Robin	Chicken	Bird	Animal
1.0 moves	1.0 moves	1.0 moves	1.0 moves
1.0 winged	1.0 winged	1.0 winged	.7 walks
1.0 feathered	1.0 feathered	1.0 feathered	.5 large size
1.0 flies	1.0 walks	.8 flies	
.9 sings	.7 medium size	.6 sings	
.7 small size		.5 small size	

tional concepts these items form a set picked out by the definition: the denotation of the mental category (concept) TRIANGLE would be the set of all closed, three-sided, plane geometry figures. But what about the denotation of nontraditional categories? The most common idea is to combine nontraditional theories of concept structure with *fuzzy set* theories of their denotation. In fuzzy set theory (Zadeh 1965), objects belong to a set *to a certain extent*, and the notion of set membership is a *graded* notion. Thus, Rover's membership in the class of dogs might be .85, and his membership in the class of females might be .10 (he might have some female characteristics).

The problem for conceptual combination arises when we look at the principles for combining fuzzy sets (see Osherson and Smith 1981). For instance, the rule for conjunction (intersection) says that the membership

Table 10.5
Categories, category exemplars, and exemplariness ratings for prototype and well-defined categories. Under each category label, category exemplars and mean exemplariness ratings are displayed (N = 32). (Adapted from Armstrong, Gleitman, and Gleitman 1983.)

Category	Exemplar	Exemplariness rating	Category	Exemplar	Exemplariness rating
Even number			Female		
Group A	4	1.1	Group A	Mother	1.7
	8	1.5		Housewife	2.4
	10	1.7		Princess	3.0
	18	2.6		Waitress	3.2
	34	3.4		Policewoman	3.9
	106	3.9		Comedienne	4.5
Group B	2	1.0	Group B	Sister	1.8
	6	1.7		Ballerina	2.0
	42	2.6		Actress	2.1
	1000	2.8		Hostess	2.7
	34	3.1		Chairwoman	3.4
	806	3.9		Cowgirl	4.5
Odd number			Plane geometry figure		
Group A	3	1.6	Group A	Square	1.3
	7	1.9		Triangle	1.5
	23	2.4		Rectangle	1.9
	57	2.6		Circle	2.1
	501	3.5		Trapezoid	3.1
	447	3.7		Ellipse	3.4
Group B	7	1.4	Group B	Square	1.5
	11	1.7		Triangle	1.4
	13	1.8		Rectangle	1.6
	9	1.9		Circle	1.3
	57	3.4		Trapezoid	2.9
	91	3.7		Ellipse	3.5

of the resulting conjoined set is equal to the *lower* membership rating of the component sets or classes C_1 and C_2:

(27)
Rule for &
Membership of $(C_1 \& C_2)$ = the lower of C_1, C_2.

Thus, Rover's membership rating in the combined class of FEMALE DOGS is .10, since his membership in FEMALE is .10, and that is the lower of the two.

But this rule for conjunction is problematic with any concept whose intuitive prototype rating is *greater* for the conjunctive concept than for the minimal constituent concept. Thus, a guppy is low on typicality for fish and low on typicality for pets, but it is relatively high on typicality for the conjoined concept PET FISH, thus contradicting the rule for conjoining fuzzy sets. Similar examples can be found for other rules of fuzzy set theory as well. In the words of Osherson and Smith (1981, 55):

Amalgamation of any of a number of current versions of prototype theory with Zadeh's ... fuzzy set theory will not handle strong intuitions about the way concepts combine to form complex concepts and propositions. This is an important failing because the ability to construct thoughts and complex concepts out of some basic stock of concepts seems to lie near the heart of human mentation.

Later Smith and Osherson (1984) proposed an alternative account of conceptual combination with prototype concepts that conforms to experimental results on typicality judgments of conjoined concepts.

We have concentrated on the representation of lexical meaning because that is currently an area of intense study. But as can be seen from our discussion, much work needs to be done before we have a theory of concepts that is adequate as an account of word meaning. In particular, such an account must (1) relate to categorization, typicality effects, and so forth, (2) relate to how words apply to objects and events in the world, and (3) relate to how words and concepts can combine to form more complex expressions, concepts, and thoughts.

Sentence Meaning and Pragmatic Interpretation

How do the meanings of words and phrases combine to form the meaning of sentences, and how are the meanings of sentences represented in the mind? These are hard questions that psychology of language is still grappling with. Here we will look briefly at three sentence-level phenomena: given-new information, nonliteral interpretations, and indirection and politeness.

Presupposition and Given-New Information   We noted in chapter 9 that it may be helpful for a speaker to distinguish information that is presupposed, unfocused, or *given*, from information that is asserted, focused, or *new*. Languages make available a number of different devices that can be used to mark this distinction. English speakers often use the definite article (*the*), passive voice, repeating adverbs (*again*), cleft constructions, and various topicalization constructions to make the focus of their thoughts clear:

(28)

a. A boy came for the money.

b. *The* boy came for the money.

(29)

a. A friend of ours met Sam at the airport.

b. Sam *was* met at the airport *by* a friend of ours.

(30)

a. This Christmas Eugene got drunk.

b. This Christmas Eugene got drunk *again*.

(31)

a. Eugene got drunk at Christmas.

b. *It was* Eugene *who* got drunk at Christmas.

c. *What* Eugene *did was to* get drunk at Christmas.

b. *As for* Eugene, *he* got drunk at Christmas.

Thus, in (28b) the speaker may take the identity of the boy as known. In (29b) Sam is already the focus or a topic of conversation. In (30b) it is assumed that Eugene has been drunk at Christmas before. In (31b) it is assumed that someone got drunk at Christmas. In (31c) it is assumed that Eugene did something. And in (31d) Eugene is the focus or a topic of conversation. On the basis of such examples, Haviland and Clark (1974) have proposed that speakers and hearers share the Given-New Strategy:

(32)

Given-New Strategy

(GN1)

Divide the sentence into given and new information.

(GN2)

Match the given information in memory.

(GN3)
Integrate new information into memory.

Experimental evidence in fact exists for something like the Given-New Strategy. For instance, Haviland and Clark (1974) report a sequence of experiments designed to test (GN2). Subjects were given sentences such as (33)–(35):

(33)
a. Last Christmas Eugene became absolutely smashed.
b. This Christmas he got very drunk again. (984 milliseconds)

(34)
a. Last Christmas Eugene went to a lot of parties.
b. This Christmas he got very drunk again. (1040 milliseconds)

(35)
a. Last Christmas Eugene couldn't stay sober.
b. This Christmas he got very drunk again. (1063 milliseconds)

In the first example, the context sentence (33a) provides an appropriate antecedent for *again* in sentence (33b), and the match at step (GN2) should be quite direct. In the second example, the context sentence (34a) provides only the basis for an inference to an appropriate match, so step (GN2) should be less directly or immediately carried out. In the third example, the context sentence (35a) specifies the appropriate condition negatively; an inference involving negation is required and thus (35) is also less direct than (33). The average amount of time that elapsed between the subjects' beginning to read the second sentence and their understanding it is given in parentheses for each case. These figures confirm the plausibility of step (GN2) of the Given-New Strategy.

Nonliteral Communication   Research on the development of linguistic abilities suggests that children up to the age of about 10 have considerable difficulty giving the figurative meaning of even the most common proverbs (Richardson and Church 1959). Since these children obviously have their literal linguistic abilities, we might suppose that understanding novel nonliterality is an additional layer of processing and as such takes additional time, even in adults.

Unfortunately, the situation is very unclear at the moment. Brewer, Harris, and Brewer (1974, 3) did find evidence that "unfamiliar proverbs are understood in two sequentially ordered steps, with comprehension of the literal level of meaning preceding comprehension of the figurative level." On the other hand, Gibbs (1986, 3) found evidence that "people do not need to process the literal meaning of sarcastic expressions ... before deriving their nonliteral sarcastic interpretations." In one experiment subjects were given sentences such as *You're a big help* at the end of passages that would lead one to interpret them either just literally or sarcastically, and it took them about the same amount of time to identify each. In another experiment subjects' memory for sarcastic occurrences of the same expressions used in the first study was superior to their memory for literal occurrences. These results are suggestive, but because the tasks the subjects were asked to perform in these experiments were so distantly related to the processes of comprehension they are supposed to inform us about, we must be hesitant about drawing processing conclusions here.

Indirection and Politeness   As noted in chapter 9, when we speak indirectly, we mean more than we say, and we expect our audience to infer what we mean on the basis of what we have said plus contextual information. Is there any experimental support for such processes? Some evidence for inferential strategies in comprehension comes from work on politeness. After all, one of the main reasons for indirection is either to be polite, to avoid being rude, or to show deference and respect. Unfortunately, the notion of politeness is not all that clear, and to use it as an experimental tool requires that it be made more precise. Clark and Schunk (1980) proposed to treat requests as polite to the extent that the *cost* to the hearer of complying with the request goes *down* and/or the *benefits* to the hearer go *up*. On the hearer's side, Clark and Schunk suggest the Attentiveness Hypothesis:

(36)
Attentiveness Hypothesis
The more attentive the hearer is to all aspects of the speaker's remark, within limits, the more polite it is.

In a pair of experiments, subjects were asked to rate various indirect requests, such as (37a–c), and various possible replies, such as (38a–c), for politeness:

(37)
a. May I ask you where Jordan Hall is?
b. Do you know where Jordan Hall is?
c. Do you want to tell me where Jordan Hall is?

(38)

a. Certainly, it's around the corner.
b. It's around the corner.
c. No.

The replies in (38) are decreasingly "attentive" to the question-request structure of the utterances in (37). It was found that the Attentiveness Hypothesis could account for a significant amount of the correlation in these rankings, and to that extent these experiments support the view that the literal meaning is being processed in such cases.

Of course, a hearer need not always wait until the end of a sentence to figure out that it is being used indirectly. Prior context can bias the hearer in favor of *expecting* indirect communication. In a pair of experiments, Gibbs (1979) gave subjects sentences such as *Must you open the window?* embedded in two different contexts: one that biased the interpretation toward the literal and direct message, and one that biased the interpretation toward the indirect message:

(39)

Literal and direct context: Mrs. Smith was watering her garden one afternoon. She saw that the house painter was pushing a window open. She didn't understand why he needed to have it open. A bit worried, she went over and politely asked, "Must you open the window?"
Paraphrase: "Need you open the window?"

(40)

Indirect context: One morning John felt too sick to go to school. The night before he and his friends had gotten very drunk. Then they had gone surfing without their wetsuits. Because of this he caught a bad cold. He was lying in bed when his mother stormed in. When she started to open the window, John groaned, "Must you open the window?"
Paraphrase: "Do not open the window."

Subjects were to judge whether the paraphrase was true or false. It was found that subjects took less or equal time to judge the indirect interpretations in context compared to the time they took to judge the literal ones. How could this be if the literal meaning is computed first?

Conclusion

This completes our brief survey of some of the main areas of current work on the psychology of language. We have followed the flow of information from thoughts to sounds; from sounds to words, phrases, and sentences; and from sentences to the communicative intentions of speakers. Along the way we have found not only alternative conceptions of the right answer to crucial questions, but also huge gaps in our understanding of them. The psychology of language has all the signs of being a vital and active area of scientific research.

10.4 SPECIAL TOPICS

The following topics do not fit naturally into the preceding survey of psycholinguistics, but they are interesting areas of research and have important consequences for the field.

The McGurk Effect

In 1976 McGurk and McDonald reported a short but striking experiment on the sort of stimuli that can switch on the language processor. In this experiment a videotape was made of a woman uttering various syllables, such as *ba-ba* and *ga-ga*. The sound track was then spliced onto the visual track so that for each syllable, viewers saw the woman saying one syllable, but they heard her saying a different one. These tapes were then shown to 21 preschool children (3–5 years), 28 elementary school children (7–8 years), and 54 adults (18–40 years). The subjects heard the sound track by itself, saw and heard the audiovisual combination, and in each case were asked to repeat what they heard.

Subjects were quite accurate when listening to the sound track alone: preschool children 91 percent, elementary school children 97 percent, and adults 99 percent. But for the audiovisual combination the error rate was high, and the interaction of the audio and the visual components was quite interesting. The left-hand columns of table 10.6 list the various possible auditory and visual stimuli, and the right-hand columns list the various responses subjects gave to what they thought they heard. The percentages of these responses for the different age groups are given in table 10.7. Of particular interest are the "fused" responses, where the subject hears a speech sound that is not on the audio portion of the tape. The experienced sound seems to arise from the interaction of the visual and the auditory systems. As anyone who has experienced the "McGurk effect" will testify, it is quite disorienting to change what you hear by opening and closing your eyes—to watch a tape of someone speaking a

Table 10.6
Stimulus conditions and definition of response categories from auditory-visual condition. (From McGurk and McDonald 1976.)

Stimuli		Response categories				
Auditory component	Visual component	Auditory	Visual	Fused	Combination	Other
ba-ba	ga-ga	ba-ba	ga-ga	da-da	—	—
ga-ga	ba-ba	ga-ga	ba-ba	da-da	gabga bagba baga gaba	dabda gagla etc.
pa-pa	ka-ka	pa-pa	ka-ka	ta-ta	—	tapa pta kafta etc.
ka-ka	pa-pa	ka-ka	pa-pa	—	kapka pakpa paka kapa	kat kafa kakpat etc.

familiar sound, close your eyes and hear a different sound, then open your eyes and hear the original sound again! And these effects do not disappear even after seeing and hearing hundreds of tapes. It is also interesting that adults tend to be more influenced by the visual input than the younger subjects. Subsequent work has broadened our understanding of these effects and how they are produced, but many aspects of the McGurk effect are still not understood.

Open- and Closed-Class Items

Many processes we have been discussing seem to be sensitive to the distinction drawn in chapter 2 between two kinds of words and morphemes: open-class items and closed-class items (see table 10.8). Open- and closed-class items differ in several respects. (1) As noted in chapter 2, open-class items are typically words belonging to categories than can be and frequently are added to over time (hence "open"), whereas closed-class items belong to categories that are rarely added to (hence relatively "closed" over time). (2) Open-class items have explicit *descriptive* content, whereas closed-class items help define the syntactic *structure* of the

Table 10.7
Percentage of responses in each category in the auditory-visual condition. (From McGurk and McDonald 1976.)

Stimuli			Responses				
Auditory	Visual	Subjects	Auditory	Visual	Fused	Combination	Other
ba-ba	ga-ga	3–5 yr (n = 21)	19	0	81	0	0
		7–8 yr (n = 28)	36	0	64	0	0
		18–40 yr (n = 54)	2	0	98	0	0
ga-ga	ba-ba	3–5 yr (n = 21)	57	10	0	19	14
		7–8 yr (n = 28)	36	21	11	32	0
		18–40 yr (n = 54)	11	31	0	54	4
pa-pa	ka-ka	3–5 yr (n = 21)	24	0	52	0	24
		7–8 yr (n = 28)	50	0	50	0	0
		18–40 yr (n = 54)	6	7	81	0	6
ka-ka	pa-pa	3–5 yr (n = 21)	62	9	0	5	24
		7–8 yr (n = 28)	68	0	0	32	0
		18–40 yr (n = 54)	13	37	0	44	6

Table 10.8
Open-class and closed-class items

Open-class items (content words)	Closed-class items (function words)
nouns	auxiliaries
verbs	pronouns
adjectives	conjunctions
	determiners
	pronouns
	prepositions

expressions they are a part of. This makes the distinction potentially important to any process that is sensitive to such structure. (3) Educated speakers of English know about 60,000 open-class items, but there are only about 200 closed-class items. (4) Closed-class items have fewer syntactic category ambiguities (such as the noun-verb ambiguity of *jump*) than open-class items. (5) Closed-class items average much higher frequencies of occurrence than open-class items. (6) Closed-class items take contrastive, but not sentential, stress.

As we might expect, these differences have certain consequences for processing; we will look at two of them. First, the processing consequences of the open-class/closed-class distinction show up in speech errors. In general, open-class items occur often in exchange errors, but rarely in shift errors, whereas closed-class items occur rarely in exchange errors, but often in shift errors. It is interesting and important to note that inflectional affixes pattern like closed-class items. Thus, exchanges have been observed in which endings are stranded as in (41a), but not as in (41b):

(41)
a.   She's already <u>trunk</u>ed two <u>pack</u>s.
b.   *She's already pack<u>s</u> two trunk<u>ed</u>.

Second, recall that the time needed to recognize a word decreases sharply as its frequency of occurrence increases. However, this does not seem to hold for closed-class items (see Bradley, Garrett, and Zurif 1982; but see also Gordon and Caramazza 1982).

These results extend to another finding. A nonword beginning with an open-class word (such as *glasset*) is recognized as a nonword more slowly than a comparable item beginning with a sequence that is not a word (such as *slasset*). However, if the word occurs at the end of the nonword (such as *teglass*), then recognition time is the same as that for nonwords. The recognition system is working from left to right; when it hits a part of a nonword that is a word, it is fooled momentarily into thinking it has found a word, and it needs extra time to recover from this interference. Interestingly, none of this seems to be true of closed-class items. Nonwords with closed-class initial segments (such as *inslet*) are not significantly harder to recognize than nonwords without them (such as *enslet*). This indicates that sentence processing seems to be sensitive in various surprising ways to the open- versus closed-class distinction, a distinction drawn in morphology on linguistic grounds.

The Psychological Reality of Empty Categories

Certain experimental work indicates that linguistic categories might be psychologically real. To understand the following experiment, recall that a word like *doctor* primes recognition of a word like *nurse*. This technique of activating one item by means of previously activating semantically related items is called *semantic priming*. Recall that there are other varieties of priming as well. For instance, *APPLE* primes *apple* (font), *hair* primes *bare* (sound), *couch* primes *touch* (spelling), and a word primes itself (repetition priming).

We can now describe an experiment on empty categories using priming. In a sentence such as (42), what is the object of the verb *control*? (The expression [e] will be explained shortly).

(42)
The astute lawyer was hard for the judge to control [e] during the very long trial.

Who was hard for the judge to control during the trial? Clearly it was *the astute lawyer*. But how could that phrase be the object of *control* in sentence (42)? It is not even in object position—it is at the beginning of the sentence, separated from *control* by intervening words. Various current theories claim that there really *is* a syntactic object after *control*; however, this element is not pronounced and is therefore phonologically "empty." Hence, it constitutes an *empty category*, symbolized in some cases as [e] and in others as [PRO] (see Chomsky 1981). Here the empty category is the object of *control*. This category, in its location after *control*, is also semantically linked to the meaning of *the astute lawyer*. Bever and

McElree (1988) argue that if the semantic information is there, then that location after *control* should show priming effects for semantically related words, and it does. In Bever and McElree's experiments subjects first read sentences such as these:

(43)
The astute lawyer who faced the female judge hated the long speech during the trial. (nonanaphor construction)

(44)
The astute lawyer who faced the female judge hoped he would speak during the trial. (pronoun construction)

At the end of each sentence there was a probe word (such as *astute*). The subject had to decide whether it occurred in the sentence or not. The amount of time subjects took was measured, as well as the number of errors they made. The results (displayed in table 10.9) suggest that the task was sensitive to the presence of the anaphoric pronoun *he* in (44). The technique was then extended to sentences without explicit pronouns, but with gaps and empty categories that access their antecedents in the same way:

(45)
The astute lawyer who faced the female judge strongly hoped [PRO] to argue during the trial. (PRO construction)

(46)
The astute lawyer who faced the female judge was certain [e] to argue during the trial. (NP-raising)

Table 10.9
Response times (seconds) to recognize that the probe word was in the preceding sentence (error response times are not included in the mean reaction times). % error rates are in (parentheses); % subjects with at least 1 error on a given construction are in [brackets]. (From Bever and McElree 1988.)

Experiment	1		
Nonanaphor (type [(43)])	1.05	(12)	[43]
Pronoun (type [(44)])	0.93	(6)	[33]
PRO (type [(45)])	0.96	(15)	[50]
NP-raising (type [(46)])	0.92	(7)	[27]
Tough-movement (type [(47)])	0.87	(7)	[27]

(47)
The astute lawyer was hard for the judge to control [e] during the very
long trial. (*tough*-movement construction)

Again, the results indicate that these elements are processed just as overt
pronouns are. Decision times and error rates are both significantly better
than for sentence (43) used as a control. Thus, the linguistic evidence
and the psycholinguistic evidence converge on the same analysis of these
sentences.

Connectionist Models of Lexical Access and Letter Recognition

The idea that cognition is computation has suggested to some that humans are cognitively organized like a normal production line computer.
Neuroscience, on the other hand, seems to suggest a rather different
organization. In recent years this second, *connectionist* trend has been
gaining popularity as a framework within which to pursue a wide variety of psychological studies, including work on language processing (see
Rumelhart, McClelland, and the PDP Research Group 1986). The reason
for this increase in popularity is twofold: dissatisfaction with traditional
models, and the discovery of virtues of the new models (see Churchland
and Sejnowski 1989).

One of the striking facts about current attempts to program computers
to do "intelligent" tasks (tasks we would say require intelligence in a
human) is the complementarity between what computers do well or badly
and what brains do well or badly (see table 10.10). Why such a disparity?
Partisans of traditional views on artificial intelligence claim that bigger,
faster machines and better programming techniques will eventually erase
the difference. Critics think the problem runs deeper: that the brain's
architecture is simply different from that of standard computers. After
all, unlike hardware technology, biological computation has been around
for millions of years and has evolved its architecture to deal with problems
posed by our environment. Perhaps it is this difference in architecture that
accounts for the complementary differences in abilities. Connectionists
often describe their models as brainlike, but there is no claim that they
exactly model the known behavior of networks of neurons (see Smolensky
1988, 1989).

Connectionist Models

At its simplest a connectionist model consists of a collection of *units* or
nodes that can have varying degrees of *activation*, say between 0 and 1.

Table 10.10
People versus computers: strengths and weaknesses

	Well	Badly
Computer	extended logical and arithmetic reasoning	pattern recognition (language, vision) motor coordination spontaneous generalization learning
People	pattern recognition (language and vision) motor coordination spontaneous generalization learning	extended logical and arithmetic reasoning

These units are *connected* to other units in a *network*. Each connection has a certain *weight* or *strength*. When a node is activated, it *passes activation* to the nodes it is connected to according to the strength of those connections. This activation can be either *excitatory* (causes connected nodes to become more active) or *inhibitory* (causes connected nodes to become less active). Connectionist networks can *learn* by changing the strength of the connections between different nodes.

There are a wide variety of possibilities in assembling a network. How highly activated must a node be to fire? Which nodes are connected to which nodes? Are they excitatory or inhibitory? How does the system represent its environment? How is its output to be interpreted? How does the system learn from experience? We will look first at a sample connectionist network and then at the virtues of such networks and the problems they pose.

In a pair of influential papers McClelland and Rumelhart proposed a connectionist model of letter recognition in four-letter words and defended its psychological plausibility (see McClelland and Rumelhart 1981, Rumelhart and McClelland 1982). By investigating its structure and operation in some detail, we can get a feel for how connectionist models work in general. Consider the fragment of the network shown in figure 10.8. This device operates at three distinct levels: the feature level, at which nodes represent parts of letters; the letter level, at which nodes represent parts of words (i.e., letters); and the word level, at which nodes represent words. The feature level can excite or inhibit nodes at the letter

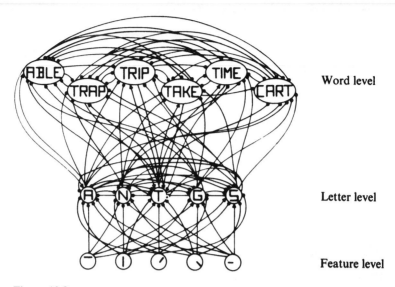

Word level

Letter level

Feature level

Figure 10.8
A connectionist model of letter recognition. Excitatory connections are symbolized by arrowheads and inhibitory connections by dots. (From McClelland and Rumelhart 1981.)

level, and these can in turn excite or inhibit nodes at the word level—and be excited or inhibited by them.

Suppose we present the letter T to the network. T is made up of the features ‾ and |, so it will activate the first two feature detectors. Notice that *these and only these* feature-detecting nodes excite the T-node at the letter level. The remaining features *inhibit* the other letter nodes. Thus, only the T-node is activated by a T. Activating the T-node also partially excites the words beginning with a T, such as TAKE, but it inhibits other words (remember, this is just a fragment of the network). The system *recognizes* a letter (or word) when (1) it settles down into a stable pattern, and (2) a particular node is activated above the proper threshold.

McClelland and Rumelhart were able to show that the behavior of this model conforms to many experimental results in word recognition. Consider the so-called word superiority effect reviewed earlier: letters are recognized faster and more reliably in the context of words than alone or in nonword letter strings. The model accounts for this because as the letters for, say, TAKE are recognized, more and more activation builds

Table 10.11

A comparison of standard computer models and connectionist models

STRUCTURAL DIFFERENCES	
Standard computer models	Connectionist models
Fast (millionths of a second)	Slow (hundredths of a second)
Few components	Many components (e.g., brain = 10^{11})
Few connections in all	Many connections in all (e.g., brain = 10^{15})
Few connections per unit (= 10s)	Many connections per unit (e.g., brain = 10^4)
Location-addressable memory	Content-addressable memory

FUNCTIONAL DIFFERENCES	
Standard computer models	Connectionist models
Described by algorithms	Described by differential equations
Serial processing	Parallel processing
Brittle, fault-intolerant	Gracefully degrading
Sensitive to noise	Tolerant of noise
Do not learn, generalize, or extract central tendencies naturally	Learn, generalize, and extract central tendencies naturally

up on the TAKE-node and it passes this activation back to its constituent letter nodes (look at the network again). This is a kind of priming that facilitates the recognition of these letters, resulting in the word superiority effect.

As this simple example illustrates, and as summarized in table 10.11, connectionist models can have some very different properties from standard computational models. Probably the basic difference is this: standard machines compute by executing a program on symbolic structures (both stored in memory) in a serial fashion, whereas connectionist machines compute via the simultaneous interactivation of many connected nodes, each of which passes on only very limited information.

In spite of these obvious virtues, doubts and open questions concerning connectionist models abound in the literature. There are two main kinds of criticism. First, concerning connectionist models in general, Fodor and Pylyshyn (1988) argue that much of cognition involves a languagelike representation system—a language of thought—and they claim connectionism offers no way of accounting for the combinatorial and compositional nature of thought (for a reply, see Smolensky 1991). Second, concerning specific models, especially of language, Rumelhart and McClelland (1986) argue that a connectionist model can learn the past tenses of English verbs in the way children learn them, without being given, or learning, any linguistic rules. However, Pinker and Prince (1988) and Lachter and Bever (1988) argue that the model only appears to do this: that linguistic information was actually built in and that the training program was unnatural. By consulting the references in this section, you can decide for yourself whether connectionism is an exciting new prospect or just old associationism with new terminology.

Study Questions

1. What is psycholinguistics? (Illustrate with Chomsky's three models.)

2. What methodological problems arise in the study of speech production?

3. What is a "spoonerism"? Give examples.

4. What are the six major types of speech error? Give examples of each.

5. What two important features of the speech-planning process do speech errors (such as examples (4) and (5) in the text) illustrate?

6. What are the functional level and the positional level in Garrett's model of speech production?

7. What six patterns of speech errors do we find?

8. How might these be accounted for on Garrett's model?

9. What might researchers do to ensure that speech errors in their collections are genuine? (Illustrate with "slips of the ear.")

10. What are the major subcapacities in speech comprehension?

11. What are the differences in function/purpose between perception and cognition?

12. What are the six main properties of input systems (modules)?

13. What are the three major comprehension architectures?

14. What is the "phoneme restoration effect"? What are its implications for modularity?

15. What two processes are involved in processing at the word level?

16. What are the two main experimental tasks used in lexical access studies?

17. Why suppose that the mental lexicon is systematically organized?

18. What are five basic findings in the study of lexical access?

19. Describe the main features of Forster's "search model" of word recognition. How might it account for the five basic findings?

20. What evidence is there that hearers normally process (subconsciously) all of the meanings of an expression they know? How does this bear on the issue of modularity?

21. What is the Main Clause Strategy (MCS)?

22. What two stages do Frazier and Fodor propose for parsing? What principle is proposed for the first stage? What evidence is there for it?

23. What are the "click experiments"? What do they purport to show?

24. What are some experimental results that might pose a problem for modularity?

25. What is a "garden path" sentence?

26. What is the Principle of Referential Success (PRS)? What is the evidence for and against it?

27. What is the traditional doctrine of concepts?

28. What two problems does the traditional doctrine have?

29. What is the prototype theory of concept structure? How does it handle the typicality effects?

30. What are two problems with the prototype theory of concepts?

31. What is a "fuzzy" set? What is the rule for conjoining fuzzy sets?

32. What problem does this rule have?

33. What is the Given-New Strategy? What evidence is there for it?

34. What is the Attentiveness Hypothesis? What evidence is there for it?

35. What is the "McGurk effect"? What implications does it have for modularity?

36. What is the distinction between open-class and closed-class items? What implications does this distinction have for language processing?

37. What evidence is there that unspoken words or phrases may still be constituents of a sentence, in some sense?

38. What is a connectionist model?

39. What are the strengths and weaknesses of traditional models of mental capacities and connectionist models of mental capacities?

Further Reading

General

For an *article*-length overview of the psychology of language and psycholin-
guistics, see Tanenhaus 1988. There are many good *book*-length introductions:
Fodor, Bever, and Garrett 1974; Clark and Clark 1977; Foss and Hakes 1978;
Garnham 1985; Garman 1990; Altmann 1997; Scovel 1998; Carroll 1999; and
Cairns 1999. For a useful anthology on the cognitive science of language, see
Gleitman and Liberman 1995.

Speech Production

For survey *articles* or *chapters* on speech production, see Fodor, Bever, and
Garrett 1974, chap. 7; Clark and Clark 1977, chaps. 5–6; Foss and Hakes 1978,
chaps. 6–7; Garnham 1985, chap. 9; Garrett 1988; Garman 1990, chap. 7; Carroll
1999, chap. 8; Bock and Levelt 1994; Altmann 1997, chap. 10; Scovel 1998, chap.
3; Cairns 1999, chap. 5; Garrett 2000. For detailed proposals on how pragmatic
factors can affect what is uttered, see Gazdar 1980. For more on lexical access in
speech production, see Levelt, Roelofs, and Meyer 1999. For more on speech
errors and speech production, see Garrett 1993 and Dell 1995. For *book*-length
treatments, Levelt 1989 is a comprehensive survey, and Butterworth 1980 is a
useful anthology.

Language Comprehension

For survey *articles* or *chapters* on language comprehension, see Fodor, Bever, and
Garrett 1974, chap. 6; Clark and Clark 1977, chaps. 2–4; Garnham 1985, chaps.
3–6; Garman 1990, chaps. 4–8; Trueswell and Tanenhaus 1994; Altmann 1997,
chaps. 7–8; Scovel 1998, chap. 4; Cairns 1999, chaps. 6–7. An early influential
text on cognition that takes a generally *computational* view of the mind is Neisser
1967. Introductions to cognitive science from a computational perspective include
von Eckardt 1993 and Dawson 1998. An influential work within the class of *unitary* architectures is Anderson 1983. *Modular* architectures were introduced in
Fodor 1983. Fodor 1985 is a summary with commentaries and replies. Garfield
1987 is an early collection devoted to modularity; Gunnar and Maratsos 1992
focuses on language. Regarding *speech perception*, see Clark and Clark 1977, chap.
5; Foss and Hakes 1987, chap. 4; Pisoni and Luce 1987; Miller 1990; Garman
1990, chap. 4; Carroll 1999, chap. 4. Regarding the *mental lexicon* and *lexical
access*, see Garnham 1985, chap. 3; Emmorey and Fromkin 1988; Forster 1990;
Garman 1990, chap. 5; Altmann 1997, chaps. 5–6; and Carroll 1999, chap. 5. See
Dell et al. 1997 for lexical access and aphasia. See Marslen-Wilson 1987 for a
critical discussion of Forster's theory and the alternative *cohort model*. For a
survey of the psychology of *word meaning*, see Garnham 1985, chap. 5; Johnson-
Laird 1987; and Schwanenflugel 1991. Tsohatzidis 1990 is a useful anthology on
prototypes and meaning. There has recently been an explosion of work on *concepts*. For the beginning of contemporary work on concepts and concept formation, see Bruner, Goodnow, and Austin 1956. Smith and Medin 1981 is still the

best book-length survey of theories of concepts. Margolis and Lawrence 1999 is an up-to-date anthology of central writings on concepts with a valuable comprehensive introduction. For recent criticism of classical and prototype theories of concepts, and the proposal of a provocative alternative, see Fodor 1998. See Fodor, Bever, and Garrett 1974 and Clark and Clark 1977 for a review of many of the *click experiments*, and of the problems and controversy that surround them. For recent developments in *sentence interpretation*, see Frazier 1999. For more on the psychology of *nonliterality*, see Gibbs 1994.

Special Topics

For a survey of the *McGurk effect*, see Summerfield 1987. For more on *open- and closed-class items*, see Garrett 1982. For more on *empty categories*, see Cloitre and Bever 1988, McElree and Bever 1989, and Fodor 1989. For a good recent introduction to *connectionist modeling* (with a diskette for doing your own simulations), see McLeod, Plunkett, and Rolls 1998. Chapters 8 and 9 survey recent connectionist studies of language. Plunkett and Marchmann 1991, 1993, update the *past tense debate*.

Reference Works

Gernsbacher 1994 is one of the most comprehensive surveys of psycholinguistics available. See also the chapters in Eysenke and Keane 1990 on language processing.

Journals

Journal of Psycholinguistics Research, Journal of Memory and Language (formerly *Journal of Verbal Learning and Verbal Behavior*), *Language and Cognitive Processes, Brain and Language, Mind and Language*

Bibliography

Altmann, G. 1997. *The ascent of Babel*. Oxford: Oxford University Press.

Anderson, J. 1983. *The architecture of cognition*. Cambridge, Mass.: Harvard University Press.

Armstrong, S., L. Gleitman, and H. Gleitman. 1983. On what some concepts might not be. *Cognition* 13, 263–308.

Batting, W., and W. Montague. 1969. Category norms for verbal items in 56 categories: A replication and extension of the Connecticut category norms. *Journal of Experimental Psychology* 80 (Monograph supplement 3, Part 2).

Bever, T. 1970. The cognitive basis for linguistic structures. In J. Hayes, ed., *Cognition and the development of language*. New York: Wiley.

Bever, T., M. Garrett, and R. Hurtig. 1973. The interaction of perceptual processes and ambiguous sentences. *Memory and Cognition* 1, 277–286.

Bever, T., and B. McElree. 1988. Empty categories access their antecedents during comprehension. *Linguistic Inquiry* 19, 35–43.

Bock, K., and P. Levelt. 1994. Language production: Grammatical encoding. In Gernsbacher 1994.

Bock, K., and H. Loebell. 1990. Framing sentences. *Cognition* 35, 1–39.

Bradley, D., M. Garrett, and E. Zurif. 1982. Syntactic deficits in Broca's aphasia. In D. Caplan, ed., *Biological studies of mental processes.* Cambridge, Mass.: MIT Press.

Brewer, W., R. Harris, and E. Brewer. 1974. Comprehension of literal and figurative meaning. Paper presented at the meeting of the Midwestern Psychological Association.

Brown, F., and S. Levinson. 1978. Universals in language usage: Politeness phenomena. In E. Goody, ed., *Questions and politeness.* Cambridge: Cambridge University Press.

Bruner, J., J. Goodnow, and G. Austin. 1956. *A study of thinking.* New York: Wiley.

Butterworth, B., ed. 1980. *Language production*, vol. 1. New York: Academic Press.

Cairns, H. 1999. *Psycholinguistics.* Austin, Tex.: Pro-Ed.

Carroll, D. 1999. *Psychology of language.* 3rd ed. Pacific Grove, Calif.: Brooks/Cole.

Chomsky, N. 1965. *Aspects of the theory of syntax.* Cambridge, Mass.: MIT Press.

Chomsky, N. 1972. *Language and mind.* Enlarged ed. New York: Harcourt Brace Jovanovich.

Chomsky, N. 1981. *Lectures on government and binding.* Dordrecht: Foris.

Churchland, P. S., and T. Sejnowski. 1989. Neural representation and neural computation. In Nadel et al. 1989.

Clark, H., and E. Clark. 1977. *Psychology and language.* New York: Harcourt Brace Jovanovich.

Clark, H., and D. Schunk. 1980. Polite responses to polite requests. *Cognition* 8, 111–143.

Clifton, C., and F. Ferreira. 1987. Modularity in sentence comprehension. In Garfield 1987.

Cloitre, M., and T. Bever. 1988. Linguistic anaphors, levels of representation and discourse. *Language and Cognitive Processes* 3, 293–322.

Cooper, W., and E. Walker, eds. 1979. *Sentence processing: Psycholinguistic studies presented to Merrill Garrett.* Hillsdale, N.J.: Lawrence Erlbaum Associates.

Crain, S., and M. S. Steedman. 1985. On not being led up the garden path: The use of context of the psychological parser. In D. Dowty, L. Karttunen, and

A. Zwicky, eds., *Natural language parsing*. Cambridge: Cambridge University Press.

Cutler, A. 1982. The reliability of speech error data. In A. Cutler, ed., *Slips of the tongue*. The Hague: Mouton.

Dawson, M. 1998. *Understanding cognitive science*. Malden, Mass.: Blackwell.

Dell, G. 1995. Speaking and misspeaking. In Gleitman and Liberman 1995.

Dell, G., and P. Reich. 1981. Stages in sentence production: An analysis of speech error data. *Journal of Verbal Learning and Verbal Behavior* 20, 611–629.

Dell, G., M. Schwartz, M. Martin, N. Saffran, and D. Gagnon. 1997. Lexical access in aphasic and nonaphasic speakers. *Psychological Review* 104, 801–838.

Emmorey, K., and V. Fromkin. 1988. The mental lexicon. In Newmeyer 1988.

Eysenke, M., and M. Keane. 1990. *Cognitive psychology: A student's handbook*. Hillsdale, N.J.: Lawrence Erlbaum Associates.

Fay, D., and A. Cutler. 1977. Malapropisms and the structure of the mental lexicon. *Linguistic Inquiry* 8, 505–520.

Fishler, I., and P. Bloom. 1979. Automatic and attentional processes in the effects of sentence contexts on word recognition. *Journal of Verbal Learning and Verbal Behavior* 18, 1–20.

Fodor, J. A. 1981. Current status of the innateness controversy. In *Representations*. Cambridge, Mass.: MIT Press.

Fodor, J. A. 1983. *The modularity of mind*. Cambridge, Mass.: MIT Press.

Fodor, J. A. 1985. Precis of *The modularity of mind*. *The Behavioral and Brain Sciences* 8, 1–6.

Fodor, J. A. 1998. *Concepts: Where cognitive science went wrong*. Oxford: Oxford University Press.

Fodor, J. A., T. Bever, and M. Garrett. 1974. *The psychology of language*. New York: McGraw-Hill.

Fodor, J. A., M. Garrett, E. Walker, and C. Parkes. 1980. Against definitions. *Cognition* 8, 263–367.

Fodor, J. A., and Z. Pylyshyn. 1988. Connectionism and cognitive architecture. In Pinker and Mehler 1988.

Fodor, J. D. 1989. Empty categories in sentence processing. *Language and Cognitive Processes* 4(3/4), 155–209.

Fodor, J. D., J. A. Fodor, and M. Garrett. 1975. The psychological unreality of semantic representation. *Linguistic Inquiry* 6, 515–531.

Forster, K. 1978. Accessing the mental lexicon. In E. Walker, ed., *Explorations in the biology of language*. Cambridge, Mass.: MIT Press.

Forster, K. 1979. Levels of processing and the structure of the language processor. In Cooper and Walker 1979.

Forster, K. 1990. Lexical processing. In Osherson and Lasnik 1990.

Forster, K., and S. Chambers. 1973. Lexical access and naming time. *Journal of Verbal Learning and Verbal Behavior* 12, 627–635.

Foss, D. 1969. Decision processes during sentence comprehension: Effects of lexical item difficulty and position upon decision times. *Journal of Verbal Learning and Verbal Behavior* 8, 457–462.

Foss, D., and D. Hakes. 1978. *Psycholinguistics*. Englewood Cliffs, N.J.: Prentice-Hall.

Frauenfelder, U., and L. Tyler, eds. 1987. *Spoken word recognition*. Cambridge, Mass.: MIT Press.

Frazier, L. 1979. *On comprehending sentences*. Distributed by the Indiana University Linguistics Club, Bloomington.

Frazier, L. 1999. *On sentence interpretation*. Dordrecht: Kluwer.

Frazier, L., and J. D. Fodor. 1978. The sausage machine: A new two-stage parsing model. *Cognition* 6, 291–325.

Fromkin, V. 1973a. Slips of the tongue. *Scientific American* 229.6, 110–116.

Fromkin, V., ed. 1973b. *Speech errors as linguistic evidence*. The Hague: Mouton.

Garfield, J., ed. 1987. *Modularity in knowledge representation and natural language understanding*. Cambridge, Mass.: MIT Press.

Garman, M. 1990. *Psycholinguistics*. Cambridge: Cambridge University Press.

Garnham, A. 1985. *Psycholinguistics: Central topics*. New York: Methuen.

Garrett, M. 1975. The analysis of sentence production. In G. Bower, ed., *The psychology of learning and motivation*. New York: Academic Press.

Garrett, M. 1980. Levels of processing in sentence production. In Butterworth 1980.

Garrett, M. 1982. Production of speech: Observations from normal and pathological language use. In A. Ellis, ed., *Normality and pathology in cognitive functions*. New York: Academic Press.

Garrett, M. 1988. Processes in language production. In Newmeyer 1988.

Garrett, M. 1990. Sentence processing. In Osherson and Lasnik 1990.

Garrett, M. 1993. Errors and their relevance for theories of language production. In G. Blandken, J. Dittmann, H. Grimm, J. Marshall, and C. Wallesch, eds., *Linguistic disorders and pathologies: An international handbook*. Berlin: de Gruyter.

Garrett, M. 2000. Remarks on the architecture of language processing systems. In Y. Grodzinsky, L. Shapiro, and D. Swinney, eds., *Language and the brain: Representation and processing*. San Diego, Calif.: Academic Press.

Gazdar, G. 1980. Pragmatic constraints on linguistic production. In Butterworth 1980.

Gernsbacher, M. ed. 1994. *Handbook of psycholinguistics* San Diego, Calif.: Academic Press.

Gibbs, R. 1979. Contextual effects in understanding indirect requests. *Discourse Processes* 2, 1–10.

Gibbs, R. 1986. On the psycholinguistics of sarcasm. *Journal of Experimental Psychology: General* 115, 3–15.

Gibbs, R. 1994. *The poetics of mind*. Cambridge: Cambridge University Press.

Gleitman, L., and M. Liberman, eds. 1995. *An invitation to cognitive science*, vol. 1. 2nd ed. Cambridge, Mass.: MIT Press.

Gordon, B., and A. Caramazza. 1982. Lexical decision for open and closed class: Failure to replicate differential frequency sensitivity. *Brain and Language* 15, 143–160.

Grosjean, F., and J. Gee. 1987. Prosodic structure and spoken word recognition. In Frauenfelder and Tyler 1987.

Gunnar, W., and M. Maratsos, eds. 1992. *Modularity and constraints in language and cognition*. Hillsdale, N.J.: Lawrence Erlbaum Associates.

Haviland, S., and H. Clark. 1974. What's new? Acquiring new information as a process in comprehension. *Journal of Verbal Learning and Verbal Behavior* 13, 512–521.

Johnson-Laird, P. 1987. The mental representation of the meaning of words. *Cognition* 25, 189–211.

Joshi, A., and B. Webber, eds. 1980. *Elements of discourse understanding*. Cambridge: Cambridge University Press.

Klima, E., and U. Bellugi. 1979. *The signs of language*. Cambridge, Mass.: Harvard University Press.

Lachter, J., and T. Bever. 1988. The relation between linguistic structure and associative theories of language acquisition: A constructive critique of some connectionist learning models. In Pinker and Mehler 1988.

Landau, B., and L. Gleitman. 1985. *Language and experience: Evidence from the blind child.* Cambridge, Mass.: Harvard University Press.

Lehiste, I. 1973. Phonetic disambiguation of syntactic ambiguity. *Glossa* 7, 107–122.

Lesser, V., R. Fennel, L. Erman, and R. Reddy. 1977. Organization of the Hearsay II speech understanding system. *IEEE Transactions*. ASSP 23, 11–23.

Levelt, W. 1989. *Speaking: From intention to articulation*. Cambridge, Mass.: MIT Press.

Levelt, W., A. Roelofs, and A. Meyer. 1999. A theory of lexical access in speech production. *Behavioral and Brain Sciences* 22, 1–85.

Liberman, A. M. 1970. The grammars of speech and language. *Cognitive Psychology* 1, 301–323.

Lieberman, P. 1966. *Intonation, perception, and language*. Cambridge, Mass.: MIT Press.

Margolis, E., and S. Laurence, eds. 1999. *Concepts*. Cambridge, Mass.: MIT Press.

Marslen-Wilson, W. 1987. Functional parallelism in spoken word-recognition. In Frauenfelder and Tyler 1987.

Marslen-Wilson, W., and K. Tyler. 1987. Against modularity. In Garfield 1987.

McClelland, J., and D. Rumelhart. 1981. An interactive activation model of context effects in letter perception: Part 1. An account of basic findings. *Psychological Review* 88, 375–407.

McElree, B., and T. Bever. 1989. The psychological reality of linguistically defined gaps. *Journal of Psycholinguistic Research* 18, 21–35.

McGurk, H., and J. McDonald. 1976. Hearing lips and seeing voices. *Nature* 264, 746–848.

McLeod, P., K. Plunkett, and E. Rolls. 1998. *Introduction to connectionist modelling of cognitive processes*. Oxford: Oxford University Press.

Meyer, D., and R. Schvaneveldt. 1971. Facilitation in recognizing pairs of words: Evidence of a dependence between retrieval operations. *Journal of Experimental Psychology* 90, 227–234.

Miller, G., and P. Johnson-Laird. 1976. *Language and perception*. Cambridge, Mass.: Harvard University Press.

Miller, J. 1990. Speed perception. In Osherson and Lasnik 1990.

Munro, A. 1979. Indirect speech acts are not strictly conventional. *Linguistic Inquiry* 10, 353–356.

Nadel, L., L. Cooper, P. Culicover, and R. Harnish, eds. 1989. *Neural connections, mental computation*. Cambridge, Mass.: MIT Press.

Neisser, U. 1967. *Cognitive psychology*. New York: Appleton-Century-Crofts.

Newmeyer, F., ed. 1988. *Linguistics: The Cambridge survey*. Cambridge: Cambridge University Press.

Norris, D. 1986. Word recognition: Context effects without priming. *Cognition* 22, 93–136.

Osherson, D., and H. Lasnik, eds. 1990. *Language: An invitation to cognitive science*, vol. 1. Cambridge, Mass.: MIT Press.

Osherson, D., and E. Smith. 1981. On the adequacy of prototype theory as a theory of concepts. *Cognition* 9, 35–58.

Pinker, S. 1995. *The language instinct*. New York: HarperPerennial.

Pinker, S., and J. Mehler, eds. 1988. *Connections and symbols*. Cambridge, Mass.: MIT Press.

Pinker, S., and A. Prince. 1988. On language and connectionism: Analysis of a Parallel Distributed Processing model of language acquisition. In Pinker and Mehler 1988.

Pisoni, D., and P. Luce. 1987. Acoustic-phonetic representation in word recognition. In Frauenfelder and Tyler 1987.

Plunkett, K., and V. Marchmann. 1991. U-shaped learning and frequency effects in a multi-layered perceptron: Implications for child language acquisition. *Cognition* 38, 43–102.

Plunkett, K., and V. Marchmann. 1993. From rote learning to system building: Acquiring verb morphology in children and connectionist nets. *Cognition* 48, 1–49.

Pollack, I., and J. Pickett. 1963. The intelligibility of excerpts from conversation. *Language and Speech* 6, 165–171.

Rayner, K., M. Carlson, and L. Frazier. 1983. The interaction of syntax and semantics during sentence processing: Eye movements in the analysis of semantically biased sentences. *Journal of Verbal Learning and Verbal Behavior* 22, 358–374.

Reicher, G. 1969. Perceptual recognition as a function of the meaningfulness of the stimulus material. *Journal of Experimental Psychology* 81, 275–280.

Richardson, C., and J. Church. 1959. A developmental analysis of proverb interpretations. *Journal of Genetic Psychology* 94, 169–179.

Rohrman, N., and P. Gough. 1967. Forewarning, meaning and semantic decision latency. *Psychonomic Science* 9, 217–218.

Rosch, E. 1973. On the internal structure of perceptual and semantic categories. In T. Moore, ed., *Cognitive development and the acquisition of language*. New York: Academic Press.

Rosch, E., and C. Mervis. 1975. Family resemblance studies in the internal structure of categories. *Cognitive Psychology* 7, 575–605.

Rumelhart, D., and J. McClelland. 1982. An interactive activation model of context effects in letter perception: Part 2. The contextual enhancement effect and some tests and extensions of the model. *Psychological Review* 89, 60–94.

Rumelhart, D., and J. McClelland. 1986. On learning the past tenses of English verbs. In Rumelhart, McClelland, and the PDP Research Group 1986.

Rumelhart, D., J. McClelland, and the PDP Research Group. 1986. *Parallel Distributed Processing*. 2 vols. Cambridge, Mass.: MIT Press.

Scarborough, D. L., C. Cortese, and H. S. Scarborough. 1977. Frequency and repetition effects in lexical memory. *Journal of Experimental Psychology: Human Perception and Performance* 3, 1–17.

Schatz, C. 1954. The role of context in the perception of stops. *Language* 30, 47–56.

Schwanenflugel, P., ed. 1991. *The psychology of word meaning*. Hillsdale, N.J.: Lawrence Erlbaum Associates.

Scovel, T. 1998. *Psycholinguistics*. Oxford: Oxford University Press.

Seidenberg, M., and M. Tanenhaus. 1979. Orthographic effects on rhyme monitoring. *Journal of Experimental Psychology: Human Learning and Memory* 5, 546–554.

Seidenberg, M., and M. Tanenhaus. 1986. Modularity and lexical access. In I. Gopnik and M. Gopnik, eds., *From models to modules*. Norwood, N.J.: Ablex.

Seidenberg, M., M. Tanenhaus, J. Leiman, and M. Bienkowski. 1982. Automatic access of the meanings of ambiguous words in context. *Cognitive Psychology* 14, 489–537.

Shattuck-Hufnagel, S. 1979. Speech errors as evidence for a serial-ordering mechanism in sentence production. In Cooper and Walker 1979.

Smith, E., and D. Medin. 1981. *Categories and concepts*. Cambridge, Mass.: Harvard University Press.

Smith, E., and D. Osherson. 1984. Conceptual combination with prototype concepts. *Cognitive Science* 8, 337–361.

Smith, E., E. Shoben, and L. Rips. 1974. Structure and process in semantic memory: A featural model for semantic decisions. *Psychological Review* 81, 214–241.

Smolensky, P. 1988. On the proper treatment of connectionism. *The Behavioral and Brain Sciences* 11, 1–84.

Smolensky, P. 1989. Connectionist modeling: Neural computation/mental connections. In Nadel et al. 1989.

Smolensky, P. 1991. Connectionism, constituency, and the language of thought. In B. Loewer and G. Rey, eds., *Meaning in mind: Fodor and his critics*. Oxford: Blackwell.

Summerfield, Q. 1987. Some preliminaries to a comprehensive account of audio-visual speech perception. In B. Dodd and R. Campbell, eds., *Hearing by eye*. Hillsdale, N.J.: Lawrence Erlbaum Associates.

Swinney, D. 1979. Lexical access during sentence comprehension: (Re)consideration of context effects. *Journal of Verbal Learning and Verbal Behavior* 18, 645–659.

Tanenhaus, M. 1988. Psycholinguistics: An overview. In Newmeyer 1988.

Tanenhaus, M., J. Leiman, and M. Seidenberg. 1979. Evidence for multiple stages in the processing of ambiguous words in syntactic contexts. *Journal of Verbal Learning and Verbal Behavior* 18, 427–440.

Trueswell, J., and M. Tanenhaus. 1994. Towards a lexicalist framework for constraint based syntactic ambiguity resolution. In C. Clifton, K. Rayner, and L. Frazier, eds., *Perspectives in sentence processing*. Hillsdale, N.J.: Lawrence Erlbaum Associates.

Tsohatzidis, S., ed. 1990. *Meaning and prototypes*. London: Routledge.

von Eckardt, B. 1993. *What is cognitive science?* Cambridge, Mass.: MIT Press.

Wanner, E., and M. Maratsos. 1978. An ATN approach to comprehension. In M. Halle, J. Bresnan, and G. Miller, eds., *Linguistic theory and psychological reality*. Cambridge, Mass.: MIT Press.

Warren, R., and R. Warren. 1970. Auditory illusions and confusions. *Scientific American* 223.6, 30–36.

Zadeh, L. 1965. Fuzzy sets. *Information and Control* 8, 338–353.

Chapter 11
Language Acquisition in Children

11.1 SOME BACKGROUND CONCEPTS

> How comes it that human beings, whose contacts with the world are brief and personal and limited, are nevertheless able to know as much as they do?
>
> Bertrand Russell

One need only study a foreign language, or take a course in linguistics, to begin to appreciate the enormous complexity of human language. At every level—phonetic, phonological, morphological, syntactic, semantic, and pragmatic—human language is an intricate system of abstract units, structures, and rules, used in a powerful system of communication. Once we appreciate the nature of language and the true depth of its complexity, we can also appreciate the remarkable, and in many ways fascinating, feat that children accomplish in mastering it so easily.

Language development occurs in all children with normal brain function, regardless of race, culture, or general intelligence. In other words, the capacity to acquire language is a capacity of the human species as a whole. A position held by many linguists is that even though different groups of people speak different languages, all human languages have a similar level of detail and complexity, and all languages share general abstract properties; for example, all human languages can be analyzed as systems consisting of discrete structural units, with rules for combining those units in various ways. That is, even though languages differ superficially, they all reflect general properties of a common linguistic system typical of the human species.

Any theory of language acquisition must account for what children do and do not do in the course of achieving adult linguistic competence. On the one hand, small children produce expressions that do not occur in adult speech; on the other hand, they do *not* produce ill-formed expressions that one might think they would. Consider the following examples (from Pinker 1990):

(1)
a.   John saw Mary with her best friend's husband.
b.   Who did John see Mary with ____?
c.   John saw Mary and her best friend's husband.
d.   *Who did John see Mary and ____?

In (1b) the position corresponding to *her best friend's husband* in (1a) is questioned, and the resulting *wh*-question is fine. By contrast, in (1d) the position corresponding to *her best friend's husband* in (1c) is questioned, and the resulting *wh*-question is ungrammatical (see "Special Topics" in chapter 5 for more examples of ill-formed *wh*-questions). Interestingly, children do not produce ill-formed sentences such as (1d), whereas they do produce well-formed sentences like (1b). And why do young children typically produce the word *breaked*, for example, as opposed to *broke*? *Breaked* (not to be confused with *braked*) is not the past tense form of *break* in the adult grammar of speakers of English. Here are some other examples noted by Pinker (1999, 15):

(2)
a. I *buyed* a fire dog for a grillion dollars.
b. Hey, Horton *heared* a Who.
c. My teacher *holded* the baby rabbits and we patted them.
d. Daddy, I *stealed* some of the people out of the boat.
e. Once upon a time a alligator was eating a dinosaur and the dinosaur was eating the alligator and the dinosaur was eaten by the alligator and the alligator *goed* kerplunk.

How can this pattern of behavior be accounted for? We will look at two rather different approaches to answering this important question.

How Important Is the Environment in Language Acquisition?

The first approach we will consider is *behaviorism*. Behaviorists (most notably B. F. Skinner) assert that the behavior of an organism can be accounted for by theories based solely on observing its interaction with the environment. Under this view, the child is endowed at birth with general learning abilities but not with any language-specific knowledge; linguistic behavior is molded (i.e., externally reinforced) by adult speakers (a child "learning" a language is corrected when "wrong" and rewarded when "right"); and imitation plays an important role (children are viewed as imitating others' speech).

Directly opposed to the behaviorist position is an alternative approach proposed by Noam Chomsky. Chomsky argues that language acquisition cannot be accounted for without positing a linguistically specific system of principles and parameters that every healthy (in the relevant sense) child is genetically endowed with, a system he refers to as *Universal Grammar* (UG) or as the *Language Acquisition Device* (LAD). (This is not to say that under this view, children's environment plays no role at all in acquiring their native language; such an assertion would be unreasonable. Children clearly need to be exposed to linguistic data in order to eventually attain adult competence. However, in Chomsky's approach the role of the environment is to be a source of data.)

Chomsky argues that an account of language acquisition constrained by behaviorist principles falls short for many reasons. For example, he claims that the linguistic data available to the child are themselves impoverished and not sufficient for a child to inductively arrive at a grammar capable of producing well-formed novel expressions yet at the same time not producing ill-formed expressions. (One must keep in mind that the linguistic data that the child is exposed to are streams of sound (or hand gestures in the case of American Sign Language) that may consist of one or more words during any given acoustic event. The acquired grammar is, then, underdetermined by the data (i.e., streams of sound, available to the child.) Furthermore, language development in children occurs spontaneously and does not require conscious instruction or reinforcement on the part of adults. In a very short period of time (a span of four to five years) children are able to develop very complex linguistic systems, moving from a one-word stage to multiword stages, on the basis of limited and often fragmentary data. Although adults often imagine that they are "teaching" children how to speak, there is no convincing evidence that children need such instruction. Indeed, as many a parent has discovered, the attempt to instruct children in language can produce frustrating results:

(3)
Child: I taked a cookie.
Parent: Oh, you mean you took a cookie.
Child: Yes, that's right, I taked it.

A striking example of the insufficiency of overt instruction in facilitating language acquisition can be gleaned from the following story offered by a 4-year-old boy. The story is accompanied by the picture in figure 11.1.

One day the dog ate his food and the rooster ate his food and then the duck did. Then the hay got into the hay putter and the hay putter put the hay where it belonged.

First, note the novel word *hay putter*, which the child did not learn from adult speech but simply made up himself. Next, note his use of pronouns, both present and absent. In the first sentence he uses the possessive pronoun *his* twice, to refer first to "the dog" and then to "the rooster." We understand that the duck is eating his *own* food too (as illustrated in the picture), not the dog's or the rooster's, even though the child does not use an overt possessive pronoun in that case. In fact, the child has produced an example of what the linguistics literature terms *sloppy identity*. There is nothing "sloppy" about the construction itself. In fact, it involves mastery of a structure whose properties are not at all transparent. Most speakers are totally unaware of these properties and are certainly not in a position to explain to the child that, for example, "The sentence *Mary loves her cat and Susie does too* is ambiguous between *Susie loves Mary's cat* (the 'strict identity' case) and *Susie loves her own cat* (the 'sloppy identity' case), and in order for the hearer to get the 'sloppy' interpretation, the abstract possessive pronoun has to be able to be a bound variable." Children are not taught how to produce such constructions—indeed, linguists are still trying to account for exactly how they work!

Another mechanism that is important in the behaviorist theory of language learning, but in fact seems to play little or no role in the child's mastery of language, is imitation. Indeed, children show enormous creativity in their use of language. They utter words, phrases, and sentences they have never heard before; they also understand utterances they have never heard before. Anyone who has studied child language, or has observed children, can recount examples such as the following:

(4)
a. Parent: Did you like the doctor?
b. Child: No, he took a needle and shotted my arm.

(5)
Luke Skywalker, Han Solo, and crew have made a Death Star more powerful than the other two and have stolen a Star Destroyer.

One day the dog
ate his food and
the rooster ate his food
and then the duck did.
Then the hay got into
the hay putter and
the hay putter put the
hay where it belonged.

Figure 11.1
Nicholas's picture

In (4b) the child (a 6-year-old girl) has spontaneously created a new verb in this context, one that makes perfect sense, and one that she could not have learned by imitating adult speakers. And in (5), although the 6-year-old boy's imagination is fired up by a popular movie, the sentence is his own.

This is all not to say that imitation and instruction play no role whatsoever in learning one's native language—for example, it may be a factor in learning some vocabulary and pragmatic functions—but the point, again, is that imitation and overt teaching play at best a very minor role in the child's mastery of grammar. The child, simply by exposure to a language, is able to master its linguistic features. We return to this issue in the section on acquisition of pragmatic competence.

In part on the basis of these kinds of examples, Chomsky has concluded that children deductively arrive at a grammar that enables them to both produce and understand novel expressions.

Early Stages in the Development of Language

Studies of linguistic development have revealed that children pass through a series of recognizable stages as they master their native language. Although the age at which children will pass through a given stage can vary significantly from child to child, the particular sequence of stages seems to be the same for all children acquiring a given language. Here we will review some of the better-known stages of language development for children learning English (see the bibliography at the end of the chapter for more detailed summaries).

Babbling

Prior to the development of language, all children, regardless of the language they will ultimately learn, pass through a stage referred to as *babbling*. In this stage, which begins at around 5 to 6 months, the child utters sounds and sound sequences (syllables such as *ba*, *ma*, *ga*) that are as yet meaningless but nevertheless recognizable as being more language-like than earlier infant cries. Indeed, a number of sounds and syllables of the babbling stage will occur later as the child develops language. It has also been noted that certain sounds that occur in babbling appear to be lost when the child begins to use language (see Jakobson 1968) but appear again at a later stage. As Clark and Clark (1977, 390) note:

... when children start to use their first words, they no longer seem able to produce some of the very sounds they used when babbling. One striking example can be found in their use of *l* and *r*: although these are very frequent in babbling, they rarely appear in children's first words and are among the latest sounds that children master.

It seems, then, that in the babbling stage children produce languagelike sounds quite freely, but as they develop their native language, they must master a systematic set of rules and patterns and they must, in effect, learn how to fit given sounds into those patterns. It has been argued, however, that babbling is not unrelated to the development of linguistic abilities (see Sachs 1985 and references cited there).

The fact that all children (including the congenitally deaf) go through a babbling stage, regardless of language and culture, and make very similar kinds of sounds at this time suggests that humans are biologically predisposed to go through this phase.

The One-Word Stage

The babbling phase, which lasts for some six to eight months, gradually gives way to the earliest recognizable stage of language, often called the *one-word stage*. At some point in the late part of the first year of life or the early part of the second year, children begin using recognizable words of their native language. These words are usually the names of familiar people, animals, and objects in the child's environment (*mama*, *dada*, *kitty*, *doggie*, *ball*, *bottle*, *cup*) and words indicating certain actions and demands (*More!*, *No!*). Viewed from the perspective of adult grammar, the kinds of words that occur at this stage include simple nouns and verbs; there are as yet very few so-called function words (prepositions, articles, auxiliary verbs, interrogative words) in the child's language (see Brown 1973).

In evaluating children's language at the one-word stage, one must be extremely cautious about comparisons between the child's language and the adult language. For example, it is not clear that a given word uttered by a child at this stage has the same use that it would have in the adult language. Children's use of words sometimes shows an *overextension* or *underextension* of reference. For example, a certain child might use the word *doggie* to refer not just to dogs but to all common animals in the environment (an example of overextension). In contrast, a child might use the word *doggie* to refer not to all dogs (i.e., all animals that could properly be referred to by the word *doggie*) but only to certain specific dogs (an example of underextension). It is not clear exactly what children's early words mean to them. For example, what do *mommy* and *baby* mean to a child who uses these words to refer to inanimate objects? For obvious reasons we cannot interview a young child to find out. The fact that adults (especially parents) claim to understand these early utterances should not be taken as evidence that children's utterances mean what adults' utterances mean. Adults have a strong ability to interpret utterances in terms of the nonlinguistic context of the utterance (the time, place, situation, and participants involved), and based on this nonlinguistic context a child's utterances can be assigned an appropriate meaning by the adult. This method of *rich interpretation*, as it has sometimes been called, allows the adult to arrive at a certain understanding of the child's utterances, but this, in and of itself, does not reveal what the child might actually have in mind, nor does it reveal what the expression means to the child. For such reasons, it is difficult to determine whether an individual word uttered by the child is to be understood as *holophrastic* (as standing for an entire sentence or proposition), or whether it is to be taken as simply expressing a concept that is somehow relevant to the particular context of the utterance.

Multiword Stages

At some point during the second year of life, the child's utterances gradually become longer, and the one-word stage gives way to multiword stages. As noted earlier, the exact age at which children pass through a given stage varies significantly from child to child. For example, one child might enter the two-word stage at 20 months of age, and another might enter the same stage at 27 months. In general, the multiword stages we will describe here begin roughly in the second half of the child's second year and extend roughly to the child's fifth year. Although age varies, the particular sequence of stages described below is quite similar for all children.

As shown in table 11.1, during the early multiword stage—at roughly the two-word stage—children begin to express a variety of grammatical and conceptual relations. It is during this stage that children learning English begin to use word order to indicate certain relations—for example, Possessor followed by Possessed, or Subject followed by Predicate (again see table 11.1). In addition, the child's language begins to reflect the distinction between sentence types, such as negative sentences, imperatives, and questions. In this stage of linguistic development, we see the beginnings of a structured language (e.g., subject + predicate structure), and it is clear that the child is beginning to master the broader grammatical features of the language. As the length of the child's utterances increases beyond the two-word stage, the major grammatical constructions of the native language begin to develop in more detail. Two constructions of English that have been studied from the point of view of their development are negative sentences and questions. This development is summarized in table 11.2. Beginning with negative sentences, we see that at the one-word stage negation is simply expressed by single words with negative meaning, such as *no* or *allgone*. In the early multiword stage, these negative words occur at the beginning (or, more rarely, at the end) of expressions—for example, *no eat*, *allgone milk* (see also table 11.1, section 8). At this stage the negative word does not intervene between other words; that is, it does not occur "internally" within an expression. However, in later multiword stages the negative word begins to occur within expressions, between subject and predicate (*Mommy no play*).

Recall from the discussion of questions in chapter 5 that English draws a distinction between auxiliary verbs and main verbs. For example, in the adult grammar, the negative *not* (or the contracted *n't*) occurs with auxiliary verbs such as *do*, *does*, *did*, *is*, *am*, *are*, *have*, *has*, *can*, *could*, *may*, *might*, *shall*, *should*, *will*, *would*, *must*, and a few others. Thus, Modern English has no sentences of the form **I drink not*, but instead has sentences of the form *I don't drink*, *I won't drink*, *I mustn't drink*, and so on. In mastering English, then, children must become aware that a special class of auxiliary verbs functions both to "carry" the negative and to invert with the subject to form questions. At the stage where the negative word begins to appear internally in expressions (as in *Mommy no play*), we find the first negative auxiliary verbs in the child's language, usually the auxiliaries *can't* and *don't* (as in *I can't do that*, *I don't know him*). At this stage auxiliaries do not yet occur in the positive form. That is, although we find *can't* and *don't*, we do not yet find *can*, *does*, or *did*.

In the following stages a wider range of negative auxiliaries begins to appear, and auxiliaries finally begin to appear in positive sentences as well as negative sentences. Thus, it seems that mastery of the system of negation in English is dependent upon, or at least tightly connected with, the mastery of auxiliary verbs.

The same connection is found in the development of questions, for auxiliary verbs play an important role here as well. Beginning with the one-word stage (see table 11.2), questioning is indicated solely by into-

Table 11.1
Common types of utterances found in the early multiword stage. (From Foss and Hakes 1978.)

Semantic characterization	Syntactic characterization	Forms	Examples
1. Nomination (naming, noticing)	Existential	here it there's this see } + Noun that hi	there book that car see doggie hi spoon
2. Possession	Noun Phrase	Noun } + Noun Pronoun	my stool baby book Mommy sock
3. Attribution	Noun Phrase	Adjective + Noun	pretty boat party hat big step
	or		
	Predicate Adjective	Noun } + Adjective Pronoun	carriage broken that dirty Mommy tired
4. Plurality	Noun Phrase	Quantifier + Noun	two cup all cars
5. Actor-Action	a. Subject + Predicate	Noun + Verb	Bambi go Mommy push (Kathryn) airplane by
	b. Subject + Predicate	Noun + Noun	Mommy (wash) jacket Lois (play) baby record
	c. Predicate	Verb + Noun	pick glove pull hat helping Mommy

Category		Syntactic Structure	Examples
6. Location			
	a. object location	Subject + Prepositional Phrase	Noun + Prep P	sweater chair lady home baby room
	b. action toward location	Verb + Prepositional Phrase	Verb + Prep P	sat wall walk street
7. Requests and Imperatives	a. Verb + Object	Verb + Noun	want milk gimme ball
	b. Quantifier + Object	{more / 'nother} + Noun	more nut 'nother milk
8. Negation			
	a. nonexistence	Neg + Sentence	Neg + {Noun / Verb / Adjective}	allgone milk no hot nomore light any more play
	b. rejection	Neg + Sentence	Neg + {Verb / Noun}	no dirty soap no meat no go outside
	c. denial	Neg + Sentence	Neg + {Noun / Verb / Adjective}	no morning (it was afternoon) no Daddy hungry no truck
9. Questions			
	a. requests and imperatives	*Yes/No* Question	Same word order as statements and imperatives; signaled only by rising intonation	
	b. information requests	*Wh*-Question	Fixed forms with *wh*-	What dat? What (NP) do? Where (NP) go?

Table 11.2
Development of negative sentences and questions in child language. (Adapted from Foss and Hakes 1978 and Clark and Clark 1977.)

Stage	Negative sentences	Questions	
		Yes/no questions	*Wh*-questions
One-word stage	Negation expressed by single negative word: no allgone	Questioning indicated by intonation and/or context	
Early multiword stage	Negative word occurs at beginning of expression; does not occur between other words: No eat No sit down Allgone milk No hot No mommy go	Auxiliaries have not developed; no inversion of word order; only intonation is used: That mine? See baby? Drink baba?	Very limited; *where* and *what* are predominant forms, used at beginning of expressions: Where doggie? Where Daddy go? What dat?
Later multiword stage	Negative word occurs inside expression, between subject and predicate; negative auxiliaries *can't* and *don't* appear: There no milk He not big Mommy no play I can't do that I don't know him	Continued use of intonation; no inversion of word order; auxiliaries do not yet occur in positive sentences: You can't fix it? She no play? See doggie? Dolly go boom?	Additional *wh*-words develop to include *why*; no inversion of word order: Why mommy go? What dolly do? Why kitty sleep?

Wider range of negative auxiliaries appears; auxiliaries begin to appear in positive as well as negative sentences:

I didn't do it
He doesn't like it
I'm not a baby
I won't read the book
Mommy can't find dolly

Auxiliaries begin to appear in positive sentences; inversion of auxiliary appears:

Can't you get it?
Will you help me?
Did you see him?

Additional *wh*-words develop to include *how*; still no inversion of word order:

What she did?
Why doggy run?
What he can do?
How she can do that?

nation and/or nonlinguistic cues in the context of utterance. As the child proceeds to an early multiword stage, auxiliary verbs have not yet developed, and yes/no questions (questions that can be answered "yes" or "no") are indicated by rising intonation at the end of the expression. So-called *wh*-questions (questions that begin with one of the "*wh*-words," such as *who*, *what*, *when*, *where*, *why*, and *how*) are quite limited at this early multiword stage (*Where doggie?*, *What dat?*).

As children enter later multiword stages, additional *wh*-words (such as *why*, *who*) begin to enter their language. Yes/no questions continue to be indicated by intonation until the stage is reached where auxiliary verbs develop in positive sentences as well as negative sentences. With the development of auxiliary verbs, inversion of subject and auxiliary begins to appear in children's yes/no questions (*Can't you get it?*, *Will you help me?*). However, even at this stage the inversion of word order has not yet begun to occur in *wh*-questions, which continue to be marked by *wh*-words at the beginning of expressions (as in *What she did?*, *What he can do?*, etc.). The inversion of auxiliaries in *wh*-questions (*What did she do?*, *What can he do?*) develops at a stage later than the stage where inversion of auxiliaries occurs in yes/no questions.

The above examples, though brief, illustrate the fact that children develop their native language in a sequence of identifiable stages. Further, we see that specific constructions of a language develop in an interrelated way: the development of negative sentences and questions in English is intimately connected with the development of the auxiliary verb system.

11.2   IS THERE A "LANGUAGE ACQUISITION DEVICE"?

In this section we will examine data and analyses that linguists have marshaled to support the LAD view of language acquisition. Throughout this discussion we must keep in mind the question of the balance between what aspects of a child's native language acquisition crucially depend upon modeling adults' behavior and what aspects are attributable to the child's own inner resources (e.g., an LAD). We will review studies in the areas of phonetics/phonology, morphology, syntax, and pragmatics.

Acquisition of Phonetic/Phonological Principles

As exemplified below, small children are unable to produce all the sounds of their native language with equal facility. (We display all children's expressions in square brackets to remain consistent with the conventions of child language researchers cited here. We also preserve their transcription systems.) Smith (1973, 10) cites the following exchange:

(6)
Father: "Say 'jump'"
Son: [d̪ʌp]
Father: "No, 'jump'"
Son: [d̪ʌp]
Father: "No, 'jummp'"
Son: [uːli: d̪ɛdi: gæn d̪eː d̪ʌp]
        (Only Daddy can say "jump.")

The collective results of Olmsted (1971), Templin (1957), and Wellman et al. (1931), as cited by Owens (1984), reveal that sounds classed by manner of articulation are acquired in roughly the following order: nasals, glides, stops, liquids, fricatives, and finally affricates. Sounds classed by point of articulation are acquired in the order: labials, velars, alveolars, dentals, palatals (Owens 1984, 179). Therefore, /m/, which is a labial nasal, is expected to be among the first consonants acquired, and the affricate /dʒ/ is expected to be one of the last.

Individual case studies of children's pronunciation of words (see, e.g., Smith 1973) reveal many examples of substitution. That is, a child often substitutes one sound in a word for another. For example, *Ken* is pronounced [tɛn] instead of [kɛn] (fronting); *light* is pronounced [yait] (a liquid is replaced by a glide); *this* becomes [dɪs] (a fricative is replaced by a stop); *glove* becomes [gwʌm] (/m/ is substituted for /v/, maintaining the labial feature).

A child may also change a sound in anticipation of another sound (*anticipatory assimilation*). Smith (1973, 20) cites the examples in (7), in which an initial sound becomes labial in anticipation of a following labial:

(7)
knife	→	[maip]
nipple	→	[mibu]
stop	→	[bɔp]
table	→	[beːbu]
room	→	[wum]
rubber	→	[b̪ʌbə]
shopping	→	[wɔbin]
zebra	→	[wiːbə]

Menn (1985, 82) notes that her subject (Daniel) replaced initial labial stops with [g] when the word ended with a velar stop:

(8)

bug	→ [gʌg]	("gug")
big	→ [gɪg]	("gig")
book	→ [gʊk]	("gook")
bike	→ [gajk]	("gike")
pig	→ [gɪg]	("gig")

Other examples that we have noticed (with our own children) are *popcorn* → [kɑkɔɹn], *octopus* → [apəpʊs]. Assimilation may go the other way as well (*regressive assimilation*): *cooperate* → [kɑkɑkɹeɪ], *zebra* → [zizɹə], *popsicle* → [pɑpsɨpʊ].

Syllable structure starts out quite simply CV. When confronted with a word with CVC syllable structure, the child may delete the final consonant (*ball* → [bɑ]) or insert a vowel (*good* → [gʊdə]). Either strategy serves to "open up" the syllable. When a word is particularly long, syllables may be deleted, though the stressed syllable is always retained (*hippopotamus* → [hɪpánɨs], *Jennifer* → [dɛ́fɚ], *elephant* → [ɛ́fɑn], *Nicholas* → [níkəs]. Consonant clusters tend to be eliminated (*jump* → [dʌp]). Smith (1973, 166) notes that there are certain universal tendencies:

The most clear-cut tendency is where one member of the cluster is a stop and the other is not, in which case the cluster is almost invariably reduced to the stop alone. This seems to obtain whether the stop is the first or second element concerned.

He offers the following examples (p. 166):

(9)

stop	→ [d̥ɔp]
play	→ [b̥ei]
tree	→ [d̥iː]
piano	→ [pænəu]
clean	→ [ġiːn]
queen	→ [kiːm]
milk	→ [mik]

These data reveal that children do not substitute randomly in pronouncing words that are hard for them. Rather, their substitutions appear to be sensitive to properties of the syllable as well as to the properties of the segments in the word.

Smith (1973) discusses several arguments from language acquisition that support the reality of distinctive features. One argument involves *metathesis* (transposition). Examples of metathesis involving segments are *desk* → [dɛks], *animal* → [æmɨnɑl]. An example involving the metathesis of a feature is *difficult* → [gipətul] (Smith 1973, 187). In *difficult* the first and third consonants are targeted: /d/ → /g/ and /k/ → /t/. However, this is not a segment-for-segment exchange; rather, certain features are exchanged, and others remain in their original position. Voicing, for instance, remains in place (/d/ and /g/ are both voiced and /k/ and /t/ are both voiceless). What metathesizes is backness and coronality ([+back, −coronal] → [−back, +coronal] and [−back, +coronal] → [+back, −coronal]). Smith notes (p. 187) "that [it would appear] these metatheses can only be satisfactorily explained in terms of the feature composition of the segments involved and not merely in terms of the segments as such."

Acquisition of Morphology

In the realm of morphology, as well, there is evidence that children develop creative principles—in this case for word formation. A commonly cited piece of evidence for this is the phenomenon of *overgeneralization*, in which the child extends a rule-governed pattern to forms that do not follow the rule (see Ervin 1964, Slobin 1971). For example, the regular past tense in English is formed by adding the suffix *-ed* to the verb stem: *talk–talked*. However, there are numerous verbs in English with irregular past tenses, such as *take–took*, *break–broke*. A child who says *taked* is overgeneralizing the rule for the regular past tense by using the regular past ending with an irregular verb. One explanation for the "error" is that the child has mastered a rule for forming the regular past tense.

In this regard, the form *shotted*, cited in (4b), provides a particularly interesting example. Here, the child has created a new verb (presumably the verb *to shot*, which is probably a denominal verb based on *shot*—a noun meaning "hypodermic injection"; the verb *to shoot* already existed in the child's vocabulary and was used exclusively in situations involving toy guns and playing dead). However, having created a new verb stem, the child nevertheless assimilated it into the regular morphology of English and provided it with the regular *-ed* past tense ending.

The young boy who wrote about Luke Skywalker and company produced the word *scaredness* while describing the adventures of these characters. The derivational affix *-ness* attaches to adjectives to create nouns;

and *scared* can be an adjective (as well as the past tense of the verb *scare*), as in *a scared child* or *He is very scared*. The boy produced a novel word based on his knowledge of the properties of both *scared* and the suffix *-ness*.

The English Plural

In a well-known experiment involving English morphology, Berko (1958) provided nonsense words to children aged 4–7 and asked them to give a variation of the nonsense word reflecting certain morphological properties, such as the plural morpheme. For example, children were presented with test frames like the following:

(10)
This is a wug. (accompanied by a picture of an imaginary birdlike animal)

Now there is another one.

There are two of them. (accompanied by a picture of two of the imaginary animals)

There are two ____.

The idea is to provide the plural form of the nonsense word *wug. If children have mastered a rule for forming plurals, they should be able to answer *wugs*. As Berko put it:

> If knowledge of English consisted of no more than the storing up of many memorized words, the child might be expected to refuse to answer our questions on the grounds that he had never before heard of a *wug, for instance, and could not possibly give us the plural form since no one had ever told him what it was. This was decidedly not the case. The children answered the questions; in some instances they pronounced the inflectional endings they had added with exaggerated care, so that it was obvious they understood the problem and wanted no mistake made about their solution. (1958, 164)

Compounds

A study carried out by Gordon (1985) provides compelling evidence for positing specific morphological principles as part of an LAD. Gordon's results bear on whether or not there is psychological evidence (based on acquisition) for a particular linguistic theory of word formation, namely, the *Level-Ordering Hypothesis*, proposed by Kiparsky (1982). According to the theory, the formation of complex words is constrained by the individual properties of three levels of word formation (see figure 11.2) plus a restriction on the interaction of these levels. Level I is where

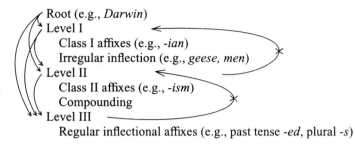

Figure 11.2
Kiparsky's Level-Ordering Hypothesis

derivational affixes of class I (see chapter 2, "Special Topics") are attached to a root, or base morpheme. Derivational affixes applying at level I affect the phonology of the sound sequence they attach to. For example, in the word *Darwin*, stress is on the first syllable (*DARwin*). When -*ian* is attached, stress shifts to the second syllable from the left, yielding *DarWINian*. Thus, -*ian* qualifies as a level I affix. Level II includes both compounding (e.g., *loudspeaker*) and derivational affixes that do not affect the phonology of the sound sequence to which they attach. For example, -*ism* is a level II affix; when it attaches to *Darwin*, the stress remains on the first syllable: *DARwinism*. Level III is where the inflectional affixes (e.g., tense, plurality) are added.

Morphologically complex words are structured in such a way that level I affixes are innermost, level II affixes medial, and level III affixes outermost in the word. The following constraint is crucial: The output of level III word building *cannot* be the input to either level II or level I, and the output of level II *cannot* be the input to level I. Thus, *Darwinianism* is fine (where the output of level I, *Darwinian*, is the input to level II, the attachment of -*ism*), but *Darwinismian (where the output of level II is the input to level I) is hopeless.

As noted above, compounding involves level II word building. Irregular inflection (e.g., irregular plurals: *geese, mice, women, men*) is a level I phenomenon. For present purposes we are interested in the compounds *mouse-eater, mice-eater, rat-eater, rats-eater*. Native speakers of English characterize the first three as well formed and the fourth as ill formed. Why is *mice-eater* admitted and *rats-eater* rejected? The reason, according to the Level-Ordering Hypothesis, is that *mice*, having come from level I, is available for the purposes of compounding at level II, whereas *rats* is not available until level III (where inflectional affixes are added), at which point it is too late to perform the level II process of compounding *rats* with *eater*.

Gordon demonstrates that when asked "What do you call someone who eats mice?" (p. 79), children (ages 3–5) responded *mice-eater* 36 out of 40 times (or 90 percent of the time). By contrast, when asked "What do you call someone who eats rats?" they responded *rats-eater* only 3 out of 164 times (or 2 percent of the time). These are very striking results in light of the fact that children are not exposed to many examples of irregular plurals occurring in compounds, *teethmarks* being one of the notable instances. (This is an interesting example of "impoverished data.") One can conclude that these results support the view that the Level-Ordering Hypothesis reflects knowledge that may well be innate.

Acquisition of Syntax

Recursion

Turning now to syntax, consider that all native speakers of English have learned how to interpret expressions such as the following:

(11)
a. the child
b. the child who is reading the book
c. the child who is reading the book which was written by Dr. Seuss

As noted in the discussion of recursion in chapter 5, phrases such as these can be iterated indefinitely—there is no upper bound on the length they can attain. The syntactic rules of English allow us to add modifiers to nouns as shown in (11), and no matter how long such phrases were to become, at no point could we say that they violated the rules of English syntax (even if such phrases were stylistically awkward or difficult to comprehend because of performance factors). Such examples show that it is impossible in principle to have been exposed to—much less memorize —all the expressions of a language. This is yet more evidence that we have mastered rules or principles—not simply individual expressions— that allow us to associate sound and meaning for a potentially infinite set of expressions.

Yes/No Questions

In chapter 5 we argued for an account of yes/no questions in English that involves a rule that is defined over a highly structured string of words and does not just make reference to the linear order of the words. We demonstrated that without recognizing that sentences are structured, we cannot hope to distinguish between strings of words that are acceptable yes/no questions and those that are not. Crain and Nakayama (1987, 542) demonstrate "that hypotheses based on serial order [akin to hypothesis II in chapter 5] are not entertained in children's formation of the rule of subject/AUX inversion ... [and] ... that only structure-dependent rules are formulated in language acquisition." Recall examples such as (12a–b) (Crain and Nakayama's (5a)):

(12)
a. The man is tall.
b. Is the man tall?

A rule for forming yes/no questions that simply stated, "Identify the first verb and move it to the beginning of the sentence" would work in the case of (12) but would predict both (13a) and (13b) (Crain and Nakayama's (6) and (7)) to be well formed:

(13)
a. The man who is tall is in the room.
b. *Is the man who tall is in the room?

Children do not produce questions like the ill-formed (13b). Therefore, it appears that children know that structure, and not just the more salient linear order property of sentences, is relevant in the formation of yes/no questions.

C-Command and Control
In this section we will see yet again that a principle based on linear order is insufficient when accounting for the acquisition of a complex syntactic construction, in this case a construction involving "control" (to be discussed below). Indeed, children appear to make use of an abstract structural relation (c-command) when interpreting control structures.

Consider the following sentences (from Chomsky 1969, 10, (12a–c), (13a–c)):

(14)
a. John wanted Bill to leave.
b. John begged Bill to leave.
c. John expected Bill to leave.

(15)
a. John wanted to leave.
b. John begged to leave.
c. John expected to leave.

In (14a–c) and (15a–c) the subject of the verb *leave* does not appear overtly in the embedded clause. In (14a–c) *Bill* is syntactically the object of *wanted*, *begged*, and *expected*, respectively; that is, it is an NP immediately dominated by VP. It is also the understood subject of *leave*. In these cases the object NP, *Bill*, controls the subject argument of *leave*. When *want*, *beg*, and *expect* do not have an object NP, as in (15a–c), then it is their subject that controls the subject argument of *leave*. This distribution can be characterized in terms of the *Minimal Distance Principle* (MDP), as cited by Chomsky (1969, 10): "[T]he implicit subject of the complement verb [*leave*] is the NP most closely preceding it." Chomsky demonstrates that children between the ages of 5 and 10 appear to be following the MDP even when to do so yields the wrong interpretation. Consider (16a–b) (from Chomsky 1969, 36):

(16)
a. Donald tells Bozo to lie down.
b. Donald promises Bozo to lie down.

(16a) follows the MDP: *Bozo* is understood as the controller of the subject argument of *lie down*. But (16b) yields a different result: *Donald* and not the closer NP, *Bozo*, is the controller. The difference between (16b) and the examples in (14), (15), and (16a) is due to the verb *promise*. The control properties of *promise* are not determined by the MDP. Chomsky tested children on examples like (16a–b) and found some interesting results. The children clustered into four groups, which Chomsky characterizes as reflecting four stages in acquisition (see table 11.3). At stage 1 the child has learned the MDP, applies it across the board, and is unaware of any exceptions (such as *promise*). At stage 2 the child realizes the MDP does not always apply but does not yet know why—now making mistakes with MDP-conforming *tell*-type verbs as well as with "exceptional" *promise*. At stage 3 the child consistently treats *tell*-type verbs correctly but has not yet quite figured out *promise*. Finally, by stage 4 the child "gains complete control over his new rule for *promise*, and applies it consistently" (Chomsky 1969, 38).

Table 11.3
Children's interpretations of test constructions with *promise* and *tell*. The chart shows the children's assignment of subject to complement verb following *promise/ tell* in 8 constructions of the type

Donald	Duck	promises/tells	Bozo	to	do	a	somersault.
NP$_1$		pr/tell	NP$_2$	to inf vb			...

Incorrect interpretations (stages 1, 2, 3) assign wrong subjects as indicated. Correct interpretation (stage 4) assigns NP$_2$ following *tell*, NP$_1$ following *promise*. (From Chomsky 1969, 37.)

Incorrect interpretations	**Stage 1.** 10 children *tell*—all correct *promise*—all wrong Assigned NP$_2$ as subject throughout. Boys: 5.0, 5.1, 5.3′, 6.10, 7.6 Girls: 6.5, 6.6, 7.1, 8.7, 8.10 **Stage 2.** 4 children *tell*—mixed *promise*—mixed Assigned both NP$_1$ and NP$_2$ as subject following both words. Boys: 6.9 Girls: 5.1′, 5.3, 6.9′ **Stage 3.** 5 children *tell*—all correct *promise*—mixed Assigned NP$_2$ as subject consistently following *tell* and both NP$_1$ and NP$_2$ following *promise*. Boys: 8.2, 9.2, 9.7′ Girls: 6.5′, 8.8′
Correct interpretation	**Stage 4.** 21 children *tell*—all correct *promise*—all correct Assigned NP$_2$ as subject following *tell*, and NP$_1$ following *promise*. Boys: 5.2, 5.2′, 5.3″, 5.10, 6.7, 7.3, 7.9, 8.4, 8.5, 8.8, 9.7″, 9.8, 9.9 Girls: 7.0, 7.0′, 7.2, 8.6, 9.1, 9.7, 9.8′, 10.0

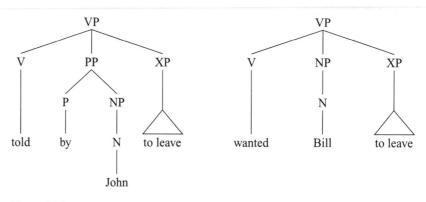

Figure 11.3
VP structure of (17), *Mary was told by John to leave*, and (14a), *John wanted Bill to leave*. Since we have not presented arguments for how to represent the structure of *to leave*, we leave this structure indeterminate by using the variable *XP* and the shorthand triangle.

But the MDP is not sufficient to account for further data:

(17)
Mary was told by John to leave.

The MDP predicts that the NP *John* should be the controller of the subject argument of *leave*. But this is incorrect: *Mary* is the controller. Maratsos (1974) demonstrates that children who understand passive sentences (e.g., *John was kissed by Mary*) interpret *Mary* and not *John* as the controller, which is the correct interpretation but is inconsistent with the MDP. Note that an important structural difference holds between the NP *John* in (17) and the NP *Bill* in (14a–c). The NP *John* is in a prepositional phrase, which is in turn dominated by VP, whereas the NP *Bill* is directly dominated by VP (see figure 11.3). Notice also that the NP *John* does not c-command *leave*. (Recall from chapter 5, "Special Topics," that c-command is a structural relation that may hold between a pair of nodes. A node A (e.g., *Bill*) c-commands another node B (e.g., *leave*) if and only if the first branching node that dominates A also dominates B.) The first branching node that dominates *John* is the PP node. This PP node, however, does not dominate *leave*; therefore, *John* does not c-command *leave*. *Bill*, on the other hand, does c-command *leave* since the first branching node (VP) dominating *Bill* also dominates *leave*. What these examples show is that in order for a noun phrase to be a controller, it

Figure 11.4
The speaker has a multidimensional image of what he wants to say and wants to communicate this image to his friend. His image has to be serialized into speech sounds arranged in such a way that the content of his image can be transmitted to his friend. The rules of transmission that allow for his friend to hear and decode the string of sound is grammar. Every language has its own grammar at one level of analysis. But as linguists have shown us, there is a deep structure to the grammar that is common across all languages. (From Gazzaniga 1992, fig. 4.5.)

must c-command the embedded verb; in other words, linear order is not sufficient to account for the cases of control cited here, even for children. Thus, children appear to have a deeper understanding of structure and the role it plays in constraining the interpretation of sentences than one might first expect. (See Pinker 1990 for discussion of these issues.)

Acquisition of Pragmatic Competence

We now arrive at the interface domain of linguistic competence. Though individuals may have a systematic grammar of their native language, does it follow that they know how to use linguistic expressions in a contextually appropriate manner? To what extent can we rely on the grammar in order to communicate successfully? Gazzaniga (1992, 83) implies that that is all we need:

One way of looking at language is as a solution to the problem of how to take one of these levels [reference to predication, quantification, tense, modality, illocutionary force] (which has a multidimensional topology), and encode it into a linear channel so as to get it into someone else's head [figure 11.4]. Grammar is a device, a way of giving a standardized code, to that kind of information.

We are already quite familiar with this view: it is an example of the Message Model of communication discussed in chapter 9. As outlined there, such a theory faces numerous problems. To review a few of them: (1) A linguistic expression rarely, if ever, uniquely identifies the referent (e.g., *Mary* could be used to refer to anyone named Mary). (2) An expression such as *My flight will arrive at 6:00 p.m.* could be used to indirectly request that the hearer pick the speaker up at the airport, but this is not linguistically encoded in the expression. (3) Crucial to successful communication is the hearer's recognition of the speaker's communicative intent; however, not all linguistic expressions are used to communicate (e.g., Ronald Reagan's "The economy is in a hell of a mess," uttered while testing a microphone), and not all speech acts, to be successful, require that the hearer recognize the speaker's intent (e.g., acts of deceiving and persuading). It does not follow, then, that grammatical competence guarantees communicative competence.

A child is faced with the task of figuring out how expressions are *used* in a communicative context. This requires, for example, figuring out that sentences like *It is hot* are directly used to state and that they are either true or false, whereas sentences like *Where is it hot?* are used to request information and require compliance—the hearer is to supply the information. The child also must learn when it is socially appropriate to utter certain expressions. In Japanese, for example, different verb forms must be used depending on the speaker's relationship to the hearer (e.g., parent-child, student-teacher, friend-friend). What is appropriate in one context is totally inappropriate in another.

Clearly, the environment plays a crucial role in acquiring communicative competence. If children did not at least witness how linguistic expressions are used, it is hard to imagine that they would know when it is and is not appropriate to use these expressions. Certainly in the course of achieving grammatical competence children are interacting with their environment in appropriate and inappropriate ways.

To what extent this interaction informs the acquisition of grammatical concepts as well is a topic of lively debate (recall the discussion of the role of the environment in section 11.1, and see Lenneberg 1967, Gleason and Ratner 1993, chap. 8, and references cited there). An interesting individual whose language development bears on this issue (Yamada 1990) is a young woman ("Laura") who, even though severely retarded (full scale IQ of 41 at age 14 using the Wechsler Intelligence Scale for Children – Revised), nevertheless has the ability to produce complex sentences requiring fairly sophisticated grammatical competence. Yamada (1990, 113) notes that

Laura's performance ... challenges claims that pragmatic factors play a primary role in the acquisition process and that social and communicative functions are the basis for language structures and features (Givón 1979; Bates and MacWhinney 1979, 1982). The sentiment that interaction with the environment crucially affects and shapes language development is also found in social-interactive approaches to language acquisition (Snow 1972, 1977; Snow and Ferguson 1977; Dore 1974; Bruner 1974, 1975; Ochs and Schieffelin 1979; Zukow, Reilly, and Greenfield 1979). Although her pragmatic functions were extremely impoverished, Laura used syntactic structures such as relatives and passives that some claim to be functionally motivated by pragmatic factors....

According to the view represented by Yamada, pragmatic information gleaned from interacting with the environment informs the "acquisition of communicative skills" but does not determine the acquisition of grammatical competence.

Is There a Critical Period for Language Acquisition?

Language development takes place during a very specific maturational stage of human development. Sometime during the second year of life (at roughly anywhere from 12 to 18 months), children begin uttering their first words. During the following 4 to 5 years, linguistic development occurs quite rapidly. By the time children enter school, they have mastered the major structural features of their language. Refinements of the major features continue to appear, and the ability to learn language (one's native language or foreign languages) continues to be strong until the onset of puberty. At this point, for reasons that are not fully understood, the "knack for languages" begins to decline, to a greater or lesser extent depending on the individual. The optimal period of time for language acquisition (2 years to puberty) is sometimes referred to as the *critical period*.

Lenneberg (1967, 178) notes that

Primary language cannot be acquired with equal facility within the period from childhood to senescence [old age]. At the same time that cerebral lateralization becomes firmly established (about puberty) the symptoms of acquired aphasia tend to become irreversible within about three to six months after their onset. Prognosis for complete recovery rapidly deteriorates with advancing age after the early teens. Limitation to the acquisition of primary language around puberty is further demonstrated by the mentally retarded who can frequently make slow and modest beginnings in the acquisition of language until their early teens, at which time their speech and language status becomes permanently consolidated.

These observations are consistent with the view that there is a biologically determined critical period for language acquisition.

Evidence that maturation plays a role in a child's ability to acquire language may be drawn from the experience of "Genie." Genie (not her real name) was kept in total isolation by her parents until she was discovered by the outside world at the age of 13 years 7 months. Her father had not permitted anyone to speak to her (or around her, for that matter). When Genie was found, there was no evidence that she had any linguistic capabilities whatsoever. A central question was, To what extent could Genie be rehabilitated? Was she beyond the critical period for acquiring language? Interestingly, within seven months she was able to count (to five), she knew some color terms as well as a couple of verbs, and she was able to name most objects in her surroundings. However, she had considerable trouble with syntax. Curtiss (1977, 31) reports:

There were attempts to teach her … rituals, for example, to ask specific questions. This attempt failed. Genie could not memorize a well-formed WH-question. She would respond to "What do you say?" demands with ungrammatical, bizarre phrases that included WH-question words, but she was unable to come up with a phrase she had been trained to say. For example, instead of saying the requested "Where are the graham crackers?" she would say "I where is graham cracker," or "I where is graham cracker on top shelf." In addition, under pressure to use WH-question words, she came out with sentences such as:

Where is tomorrow Mrs L.?
Where is stop spitting?
Where is May I have ten pennies?
When is stop spitting?

These problems are significant, for they illustrate, as Curtiss points out, "that Genie, like normal children, was unable to imitate or even retain in memory, syntactic structures which were not in keeping with her grammatical development" (p. 31).

Despite Genie's lack of grammatical competence she was an avid communicator. In an interview Curtiss talks about the child: "She told us her feelings. She shared her heart and mind. From that perspective, who cares about grammar?" (Rymer 1993, 220).

Other evidence for a critical period for language acquisition comes from the varied experiences of deaf children. Gazzaniga (1992) reports on research by Elissa Newport that indicates that deaf children who are not exposed to sign language until late adolescence (and have no other language) "can learn it. Yet, when the sign language of people who have learned language as adults is compared with the language of signers who have learned sign language as children, there are noticeable differences in the extent to which their communication follows the rules of American Sign Language" (p. 79). In fact, Calvin and Ojemann (1994) point out the special problems facing the deaf child of hearing parents; in these families deafness may not be immediately recognized and the child's exposure to language may be delayed. The later these events happen, the greater the risk that the child will fail to acquire the grammar of that crucial first language. Deaf children of deaf parents are exposed to fluent sign language from birth; they develop normally and are not linguistically at risk.

That there is a biological basis for this critical period for language acquisition has been both championed and assailed. The issue is perhaps more one of emphasis. Just which aspects of language acquisition are attributable to how humans are "hard-wired" and which depend on social interaction is yet to be determined and the topic of much lively debate.

Conclusion

The properties of language development that we have cited—a spontaneous maturational development typical of the human species as a whole —strongly suggest that the linguistic capacity is part of the genetic endowment of human beings. The hypothesis of biological innateness of the language faculty has been most vigorously advanced by Noam Chomsky, who has put it this way (1986, 4):

Consider ... the idea that there is a language faculty, a component of the mind/ brain that yields knowledge of language given presented experience. It is not at issue that humans attain knowledge of English, Japanese, and so forth, while rocks, birds, or apes do not under the same (or indeed any) conditions. There is, then, some property of the mind/brain that differentiates humans from rocks, birds, or apes. Is this a distinct "language faculty" with specific structure and properties, or, as some believe, is it the case that humans acquire language merely by applying generalized learning mechanisms of some sort, perhaps with greater efficiency or scope than other organisms? These are not topics for speculation or *a priori* reasoning but for empirical inquiry, and it is clear enough how to proceed: namely, by facing the questions of (1) [What constitutes knowledge of language? How is knowledge of language acquired? and How is knowledge of language put to use?]. We try to determine what is the system of knowledge that has been attained and what properties must be attributed to the initial state of the mind/ brain to account for its attainment. Insofar as these properties are language-specific, either individually or in the way they are organized and composed, there is a distinct language faculty.

From this point of view, then, the development of language in children is guided by a set of "innate ideas and principles," that is, a genetically determined linguistic capacity that all humans are endowed with at birth. From this point of view, all children are biologically programmed with the capacity to develop language—namely, the language(s) they are significantly exposed to during the appropriate maturational stage. Language development can thus be regarded as analogous to other biological developments in human growth and maturation. In this way, the traditional view that language is unique to human beings may in fact have a sound biological basis. Just as other biological characteristics can be unique to a certain species (such as the shape of the body or the structure of internal organs), so too the capacity for language and other properties of human mental functioning may well be a unique part of the genetic endowment of human beings.

Our discussion of language development in children has focused on two important and intimately interconnected properties of human language. First, it is *rule-governed*; that is, humans master and follow rules for forming and using expressions of their native language. Second, it is *creative*; that is, humans spontaneously produce and understand expressions they have never encountered before in their linguistic experience. These are both properties that have been stressed in putting forth the claim that the human linguistic capacity is unique.

11.3   IS THE HUMAN LINGUISTIC CAPACITY UNIQUE? CHILDREN AND PRIMATES COMPARED

In recent years, in a fascinating set of experiments, the traditional idea that language is unique to the human species has been challenged. Psychologists, working in teams, have attempted to teach chimpanzees and gorillas various communication systems (e.g., sign language) that are thought to reflect certain essential properties of human language. Such projects have raised an intriguing possibility: even if a primate species (such as the chimpanzee) has a very rudimentary natural communication system in the wild, perhaps a member of this species could be taught a communication system not natural to the species, with complex properties on a par with certain properties of human spoken language.

Are primates in fact able to acquire and use language in a way similar to the way humans do? Primates have often been compared with children with respect to the acquisition of language, yet the contrast between the two is striking. Young children acquire complicated linguistic systems apparently effortlessly, whereas primates have required massive training efforts to master quite rudimentary communication systems. From one point of view—the traditional one referred to above—this would hardly be surprising. Humans, after all, are predisposed to learn language, whereas chimpanzees and gorillas are not. From this perspective, comparing children and primates with respect to language development is quite instructive, and the contrast between the two serves to clarify the nature of the task that children carry out in mastering their native language.

In asking whether any other species can be shown to use a communicative system in a way similar to the way humans use language, we will need to pay particular attention to the two just-mentioned properties of human language use that supposedly set it apart from other animal communication systems. Can these properties be shown to exist in the communication systems that have been taught to primates? To put it another way, are primates and children comparable in their acquisition and use of language? To answer this, we will consider some of the chimpanzee and gorilla projects that have attracted notice in recent years.

Washoe

In June 1966, Alan and Beatrice Gardner began a project that was to have immediate popular appeal, if not immediate academic acceptance. Their project was to teach a young (approximately 1-year-old) female chimpanzee named Washoe to communicate in American Sign Language (ASL). Although their avowed purpose was to probe "the extent to which another species might be able to use human language" (Gardner and Gardner 1969, 664), it is evident that they were challenging claims that animals were incapable of learning any communication system that approached human language. As might well be expected, the success of the project quickly became a hotly debated issue. The popular press concluded almost immediately that Washoe was able to converse in ASL, and articles began appearing with titles such as "First Message from the Planet of the Apes." This kind of reaction put the skeptic in a position comparable, in the public mind, with that of seventeenth-century defenders of the uniqueness of man, who argued that "brutes" (animals), unlike man, have no souls. It is unfortunate that the skeptic was placed in this position, because the Gardners' project is interesting and important enough to deserve serious intellectual consideration, and such consideration requires that we carefully scrutinize all claims about the linguistic proficiency of chimps. We will review Washoe's basic accomplishments, inviting you to consider for yourself some of the central questions raised by these studies (see the exercises at the end of the chapter).

The problem of teaching a member of another species a human language presents the investigator with two fundamental preliminary decisions: what species to pick, and what language to use. The Gardners' choice in these matters was inspired. First and foremost, chimpanzees are among the most intelligent creatures of the animal world. Combining this with the fact that they are notoriously imitative and quite sociable with their human cousins (humans and chimpanzees share 96 percent of their DNA), one gets a promising picture of a prospective language learner. Chimps have other important characteristics as well. They are manually adept; they are sociable with members of their own species; and they develop through a sequence of phases that are comparable to those in human development. These latter characteristics are important in that they allow the possibility of investigating communication among members of the species as well as allowing comparison of the chimp's acquisition of language with that of a normal child.

Why did the Gardners choose to teach Washoe ASL? Attempts to teach chimps spoken English have not been at all encouraging. For instance, Keith and Catherine Hayes attempted to teach spoken English to a chimp named Viki (Hayes 1951). They raised Viki like a human child, in an optimal home environment. Yet after 6 years of training, Viki's speaking vocabulary was barely four words: *mamma*, *pappa*, *cup*, and *up*. The main problem seemed to be that a chimp's vocal apparatus is not suited to the production of many human speech sounds. Recalling the dexterous and imitative nature of chimps (who will occasionally gesture spontaneously to humans), the Gardners hit upon the idea of using a gestural language as the test system. A number of gestural systems of communication are available, but ASL was a natural choice for a number of reasons. Most important, it is a system used naturally by many people; it therefore affords a good basis of comparison for such things as acquisition rate, proficiency, and comprehension. It is also a system with structure comparable in many ways to spoken human language. Finally, there is an iconic aspect to many signs that may be of some value at early stages of instruction. We will see examples of this iconicity in Washoe's acquisition of the signs for *bib*.

Unlike Viki (the Hayes's chimp), Washoe was not raised in a home like a child. She was not raised in a conventional laboratory, either. Most of

Table 11.4
Washoe chronology

Date	Event
1965 (c. June)	Washoe is born in the wild
1966 (June)	Is brought to Nevada and begins training
1966 (December)	Has acquired her first 4 signs
1967 (April)	Signs her first combinations
1967 (July)	Has acquired her first 13 signs
1968 (April)	Has acquired her first 34 signs
1969 (c. June)	Has acquired 85 signs; end of first 3 years of training
1970	Is sent to the Institute for Primate Studies in Norman, Oklahoma
1975	Is reported to have 160 signs

her time with the Gardners was spent in a two-and-a-half room house trailer supplied with the usual trappings of human life and surrounded by a pleasant yard, 5,000 square feet in area. Washoe spent her nights alone, but during the day she was provided with an environment that was as stimulating as possible for learning ASL. She never lacked an ASL communicant, and there was opportunity for plenty of conversation, play, and outings. To follow Washoe's progress, see the chronology provided in table 11.4.

How Washoe Learned

Since the goal of the Gardners' experiment with Washoe was to assess the extent of her ability to learn ASL, and not to test any particular theory of learning, virtually any teaching method thought to work was tried on occasion. In spite of this variation, the Gardners were able to keep track of how Washoe learned at least some of her signs.

Just as human children do a great deal of verbal babbling, so chimps do a certain amount of manual babbling, that is, natural and spontaneous gesturing. The Gardners thought that some of these natural gestures might form the basis of meaningful signs. But this hope was thwarted: probably only one of Washoe's signs was based on her natural gestures (the sign for *funny*), and this sign proved to be unstable. Babbling shades easily into invention, and it is possible to describe Washoe's acquisition of signs for *come/gimme* and *hurry* either as modified babbling or as invention. However, the Gardners describe a less controversial example of an invented sign when they write:

Sometimes we could not find an ASL equivalent for an English word in any of our manuals of ASL and no informant was available to supplement the manuals. In these cases we would adapt a sign of ASL for the purpose. The sign for *bib* was one of these cases and we chose to use the ASL sign for *napkin* or *wiper* to refer to bibs as well. This sign is made by touching the mouth region with an open hand and a wiping movement. During Month 18 Washoe had begun to use this sign appropriately for bibs, but it was still unreliable. One evening at dinner time, a human companion was holding up a bib and asking her to name it. Washoe tried *come-gimme* and *please*, but did not seem to be able to remember the bib sign that we had taught her. Then, she did something very interesting. With the index fingers of both hands she drew an outline of a bib on her chest—starting from behind her neck where a bib should be tied, moving her index fingers down along the outer edge of her chest, and bringing them together again just above her navel.

We could see that Washoe's invented sign for *bib* was at least as good as ours, and both were inventions. At the next meeting of the human participants in the project, we discussed the possibility of adopting Washoe's invention as an alternative to ours, but decided against it. The purpose of the project was, after all, to see if Washoe could learn a human system of two-way communication, and not to see if human beings could learn a system devised by an infant chimpanzee. We continued to insist on the napkin-wiper sign for bibs, until this became a reliable item in Washoe's repertoire. Five months later, when we were presenting films on Washoe's signing to fluent signers at the School for the Deaf in Berkeley, we learned that drawing an outline of a bib on the chest with both index fingers is the correct sign for *bib*. (Gardner and Gardner 1971, 39)

As a further possible case of innovation, Washoe was later reported (in Oklahoma) to have signed *water bird* for *swans*, though her attendant used the sign for *duck*.

Some signs—for instance, *sweet*, *flower*, *toothbrush*, and *smoke*—were acquired by imitation. On the other hand, *more* and *open* were selectively shaped from gestures that were similar in some respect to these signs.

Finally, *tickle* and many other signs were the result of guidance (also called *molding*). In these cases Washoe's hand was formed or molded into the proper shape and then brought through the motion required for the sign.

There is some evidence that Washoe was able to generalize the use of a sign from its original referent to new cases, and thus an important feature of human language acquisition may have been present in her case. The sign for *key* is a relevant example:

A great many cupboards and doors in Washoe's quarters have been kept secure by small padlocks that can all be opened by the same simple key. Because she was immature and awkward, Washoe had great difficulty in learning to use these keys and locks. Because we wanted her to improve her manual dexterity, we let her practice with these keys until she could open the locks quite easily (then we had to hide the keys). Washoe soon transferred this skill to all manner of locks and keys, including ignition keys. At about the same time, we taught her the sign for "key," using the original padlock key as a referent. Washoe came to use this sign both to name keys that were presented to her and to ask for the keys to various locks when no key was in sight. She readily transferred the sign to all varieties of keys and locks. (Gardner and Gardner 1971, 162)

What Washoe Learned

Although it has been reported that by 1975 Washoe had a vocabulary of at least 160 signs (Fouts 1975), the most detailed report of her vocabulary is by Gardner and Gardner (1975), who describe Washoe's first 85 signs in the order of acquisition. These signs passed the test of being used spontaneously and appropriately on 15 consecutive days.

As Washoe's chronology indicates, her first combinations (such as *gimme sweet* and *come open*) were observed after about 10 months of training. Over the next 26 months she was observed to make 294 different two-sign combinations. By the spring of 1968, after about 2 years of training, Washoe was appropriately using four- and five-sign combinations such as *you me go out* and *you me go out hurry*. Does this mean that Washoe was spontaneously creating new combinations, the way children spontaneously create new multiword sentences? The Gardners' evidence does not establish this, and studies of other chimpanzees strongly suggest that multisign combinations used by chimpanzees are quite different in character from sentences used by children.

The Gardners have attempted to establish that in Washoe's idiolect the signs are grouped into such categories as proper names, common nouns, pronouns, modifiers, verbs, and locatives (Gardner and Gardner 1975). However, the evidence for this categorization comes mainly from comparing Washoe's question-and-answer sequences with those of young children; such comparison leaves open a number of issues that might call the conclusions into question. In particular, this procedure assumes that one can really motivate these syntactic categories in the analysis of child language, which, as we have already noted, is not obviously the case, because many of these tests are semantic and pragmatic, not syntactic.

Washoe Compared with Children

Part of the attractiveness of ASL as a language to teach Washoe was that it is a human language and thus it might be possible to compare

Washoe's progress against that made by children. We know of no detailed comparison of Washoe's development and that of deaf children acquiring ASL, but the Gardners (1971) have compared her two-sign combinations with the earliest two-word utterances of hearing children as shown in table 11.5.

As can be seen, the two schemes resemble each other closely. Curiously, though, there are no reports of Washoe spontaneously asking questions, and this distinguishes her in one important respect from the normal child.

What is one to conclude about Washoe's linguistic ability? Does she use ASL? Has she learned to communicate in a human language? These are extremely difficult questions to answer. It is important to keep in mind that chimps are quite clever, and care should be taken not to be too impressed by their ability to figure out complicated ways of getting what they want. Further, it should be noted that the Nim Chimpsky project (see Terrace 1979), carried out after the Washoe project, raised serious questions about the interpretation of data in chimpanzee projects, and at present there is little convincing evidence from the Washoe project (or others) for a linguistic ability among chimpanzees that is comparable to that of human children.

Koko and Kanzi

Two other significant experiments have been undertaken: one involving a gorilla named Koko (Patterson 1978, 1981) and another involving pygmy chimpanzees (Savage-Rumbaugh et al. 1986).

Koko has been raised in an environment similar to Washoe's. She lives among humans and has been taught ASL. She has learned more than 600 signs and is purported to sign combinations that are similar to human language compounds. For example, when shown a Pinocchio doll with a long nose, she signed *elephant doll*; when shown a mask, she signed *eye hat*; and when shown a zebra, she signed *tiger horse*. These combinations are different in quality from Washoe's *water bird* since Washoe may have been signing a combination of two things in view, *water* (the lake) and *bird* (the duck). Koko's combinations are more abstract and in fact, if accurate, reveal a conceptual structure that is strikingly human. Koko has lied on occasion—for example, naming one of her trainers as the one who pulled a sink from the wall. She has also been claimed to have conversations (Patterson 1978, 459).

Table 11.5
Parallel descriptive schemes for the earliest combinations by children and Washoe. (Thorpe 1974, from Gardner and Gardner 1971.)

Brown's (1970) scheme for children		Scheme for Washoe	
Types	Examples	Types	Examples
Attributive: Adj + N	big train, red book	Object-Attribute Agent-Attribute	drink red, comb black Washoe sorry, Naomi good
Possessive: N + N	Adam checker, mommy lunch	Agent-Object Object-Attribute	clothes Mrs. G., you hat baby mine, clothes yours
N + V	walk street, go store	Action-Location Action-Object Object-Location	go in, look out go flower, pants tickle baby down, in hat
Locative: N + N	sweater chair, book table		
Agent-Action: N + V	Adam put, Eve read	Agent-Action	Roger tickle, you drink
Action-Object: V + N	put book, hit ball	Action-Object	tickle Washoe, open blanket
Agent-Object: N + N	mommy sock, mommy lunch	Appeal-Action Appeal-Object	please tickle, hug hurry gimme flower, more fruit

Me: "What did you do to Penny?"
Koko: "Bite." (Koko, at the time of the incident, called it a scratch.)
Me: "You admit it?"
Koko: "Sorry bite scratch."

(At this point I showed Koko the mark on my hand—it really did look like a scratch.)

Koko: "Wrong bite."
Me: "Why bite?"
Koko: "Because mad."
Me: "Why mad?"
Koko: "Don't know."

The pygmy chimpanzee (*Pan paniscus*) has proven to be most like humans in its ability to acquire a communication system (Savage-Rumbaugh et al. 1986). The pygmy chimp, also called the bonobo (chimp), is a different species from the common chimp (*Pan troglodytes*) that has been the object of earlier studies (e.g., Washoe). Physically the pygmy chimp is very similar to (and, despite its name, only slightly smaller than) the common chimp. Behaviorally, however, the pygmy chimp is strikingly different. Males participate in child raising, and social groups are much more cohesive and stable. Males occasionally bring fruit to a female to initiate copulation, which often takes place face to face. Pygmy chimps also have an exceptional ability to respond to spoken English. Kanzi, one of the first pygmy chimps studied, could respond to 150 spoken English words in 1986 (Savage-Rumbaugh et al. 1986).

An extremely important difference between pygmy chimps and other primates is that language acquisition by pygmy chimps does not require intense operant conditioning. In fact, the pygmy chimp's learning is best described as spontaneous acquisition—the same process that occurs with human children. Pygmy chimps first learn the meaning of words and respond to them appropriately in a receptive manner; that is, they learn to identify objects and carry out actions from spoken commands of their trainers. (Researchers claim that they talk to the young pygmy chimps much as human parents talk to their children.) Later, they learn to "produce" these words by touching a geometric symbol (lexigram) on a specially constructed keyboard that lights up and activates a speech synthesizer that produces the English word that has been linked to that keystroke. Finally, they are able to find words (i.e., their symbols) on the keyboard and use them appropriately.

Although no syntax was taught to Kanzi, he spontaneously enters sequences such as action-object, agent-action, entity-location, and action-action. His trainer hypothesizes that this is because Kanzi has learned the structure of the English sentences that he constantly hears. A three-lexigram sequence is about as long an expression as he produces, although he has shown the ability to respond appropriately to longer sentences. For example, when given the sentence, "Let's go to the gullywashers and look for turtles," Kanzi responded by traveling to the gullywashers and looking at places where turtles had been seen earlier.

The promising results reported in Savage-Rumbaugh et al. 1986 have continued to be supported in subsequent research. As reported in Savage-Rumbaugh, Shanker, and Taylor 1998, Kanzi has acquired a form of communication that mirrors important properties of human language; for example, he can both understand (when spoken) and produce novel combinations of signs in a determined order. Further research with this species will doubtless lead to clarifying the nature of the hypothesized Language Acquisition Device in the human species.

Is Language a Uniquely Human Cognitive Ability?

The chimpanzee and gorilla projects we have discussed in this chapter, as well as other primate projects we have not reviewed (such as the Sarah project (Premack and Premack 1972), the Nim Chimpsky project (Terrace 1979), and the Lana project (Rumbaugh 1977)), represent important research on interspecies communication. In the last three decades, the idea of systematic communication between humans and nonhuman species has become more than just a fanciful speculation. Whether or not the primate projects can ever show that apes are able to use a linguistic system in the way humans do, such research has indeed shown that apes can manipulate symbols and that they can learn simple communication systems that are not natural to their species. Building on these results, future research may well be able to give us an overall picture of how primate intelligence is structured, and this information in turn may provide interesting points of comparison and contrast with human intelligence.

To sum up, the promising work on the bonobo chimpanzee suggests that a simplified form of a human-type language can be learned by another closely related species. What is clear, nevertheless, is that the enormous complexity of language structure and the richness of the use of language is a uniquely human cognitive ability, and the development of language in children continues to be a cognitive development that is unparalleled in any other species.

11.4 SPECIAL TOPIC

Principles and Parameters

We have reviewed numerous reasons for concluding that the child has special capabilities for acquiring a language, and we have noted the proposal that children are endowed genetically with "Universal Grammar" (UG) (or the "Language Acquisition Device" (LAD)), which is said to account for these capabilities. But just what does UG/LAD consist of? Chomsky (e.g., Chomsky 1986) proposes that UG/LAD consists of a set of innate principles and parameters that are universal (i.e., the same for all individuals) at what he calls the "initial state" (the stage before the child begins to construct a specific grammar for the language he or she is exposed to). Note that this view has the consequence that all human languages are alike in a fundamental way. That is, because all specific human languages are the product precisely of human speakers, whose genetic faculty for language (in the general, abstract sense; i.e., their UG/LAD) is equipped with the same principles and parameters, all human languages incorporate the principles and parameters and thus share basic properties at an abstract level. The variety found in the world's languages, though not insignificant, is thus relatively superficial. Let us now explore some principles and a parameter that have been hypothesized to be included in UG/LAD. We will then return briefly to the relation between UG/LAD and specific languages.

Binding Principles

Consider the patterns of reference in the following sentences, where an italicized pair of nouns can be used to refer to the same individual (coreference) or not (noncoreference), an italicized pair that is underlined refers to the same individual(s), and nonitalicized, nonunderlined nouns are not being used to refer to the same individual:

(18)

a. *Nicholas* left after *he* found the tricycle.

b. He left after Nicholas found the tricycle.

c. After *he* found the tricycle, *Nicholas* left.

(19)

Robert saw Michael.

(20)

Tom believes that Sam likes *him*.

(21)

a. *John* shaves *himself*.
b. *They* saw *themselves* on TV.
c. ?*John* believes that the girl was pointing the camera at *himself*.

Chomsky (1981) proposes the following principles—termed *binding principles*—to account for the intuitions concerning reference in these kinds of examples:

(22)

Binding principles

A. An anaphor (e.g., *herself*, *each other*) must be bound in its governing category.

B. A pronoun (e.g., *he*, *she*, *him*, *her*) must be free in its governing category.

C. An R-expression (referring expression; e.g., *Mary*, *the child*) must be free.

The terms *bound* and *free* involve structural information we will not go into here. For our purposes, *bound* means that coreference is obligatory (i.e., under the right structural conditions, an anaphor must be associated with another noun phrase that it can be coreferential with), and *free* means that the noun phrase is not coreferential with any c-commanding noun phrase within a particular domain, depending on whether Principle C or Principle B is operative.

Principle C does not allow an R-expression like *Nicholas* (*John*, *Robert*, *Michael*, etc.) to be coreferential with another noun phrase when the other noun phrase c-commands the R-expression. In (18a, c) (and (20)) the pronoun *he* (*him*) does not c-command *Nicholas* (*Tom*); therefore, Principle C in effect allows the two to be coreferential. By contrast, in (18b) the pronoun *he* does c-command *Nicholas*; therefore, the two cannot be coreferential. In (19) *Michael* cannot be coreferential with *Robert* since *Robert* c-commands *Michael*.

Principle B constrains the interpretation of pronouns. A pronoun cannot be coreferential with another noun phrase that both c-commands it and is in the same governing category. For present purposes, assume that the governing category is the clause that immediately contains the pronoun. In (20) the governing category for the pronoun *him* is the embedded clause *Sam likes him*. Thus, *him* cannot be coreferential with *Sam* but can be coreferential with *Tom*, which is "outside" the governing category for *him*.

Principle A governs the interpretation of anaphors. Principle A stipulates that an anaphor such as *himself* must be coreferential with a noun phrase that both c-commands and occurs within the same governing category as the anaphor. In (21a) *John* both c-commands and is in the same governing category as *himself*; hence, *himself* has the required antecedent. However, in (21c) the governing category for *himself* is the clause *the girl was pointing the camera at himself*. *John* is outside this domain, so that even though it c-commands *himself*, it does not qualify as an antecedent. Since there is a gender mismatch between *the girl* and *himself*, *the girl* (although it is in the correct position structurally) is not available literally to serve as the antecedent; hence, the sentence is perceived as quite odd.

Chomsky offers these principles as an example of what may well be a universal set of constraints. This is not to say that the particular statements in (22) are correct as they stand; indeed, the precise formulation of the binding principles has been the topic of much debate. Rather, they constitute a hypothesis that is subject to modification based on empirical data and further refinements.

Obviously, the words that are in fact the pronouns and anaphors of a language are not universal; these the child has to figure out. But if the binding principles are universal, as proposed, then these need not be learned.

The Head Parameter

Parameters, unlike for example the principles of binding, involve fixing a value (or resetting a default option) based on experience (i.e., exposure to linguistic data). The parameter discussed here involves fixing a value for the head of a phrase. Recall that the *head* of a phrase is the node that shares the same category as the phrase (a noun is the head of a noun phrase; a preposition is the head of a prepositional phrase; etc.). In chapter 5 we briefly explored X-bar theory. The schema offered there for English was $XP \rightarrow X$ Comp (alternatively written $XP \rightarrow X\ YP$). That is, in English the head of a phrase always appears to the left of the comple-

Table 11.6
The Head Parameter

Language	Head Parameter setting	Examples	
English	$XP \rightarrow X\ YP$	V + Complement = VP	see [the watch]
		P + Complement = PP	in [the room]
		N + Complement = NP	watch [that Mary saw]
Japanese	$XP \rightarrow YP\ X$	Complement + V = VP	[tokei-o] miru
			watch-ACC see
			("see (the) watch")
		Complement + P = PP	[heya] ni
			room in
			("in (the) room")
		Complement + N = NP	[Hanako-ga mita] tokei
			Hanako-NOM saw watch
			("(the) watch (that)
			Hanako saw")

ment (hereafter indicated as *YP* in X-bar schemata). Other languages, such as Korean and Japanese, exhibit an alternative order: $XP \rightarrow YP\ X$, where the head appears to the right of its complement (see table 11.6).

Assume that it is given as part of UG that the head of a phrase is either to the left or to the right of its complement. This principle the child need not learn. What the child does need to figure out is which setting of the so-called Head Parameter—left or right—is correct for the particular language he or she is learning. And if X-bar theory holds—that is, if it is correct that there is a general schema for phrases rather than a separate phrase structure rule for each type of phrase—then the child need figure out the relative order of only one type of head and complement; the others will all be ordered the same way. Say that an English-learning child figures out that the head-complement order in English verb phrases is V Comp. Since this is an instance of the X-bar schema $XP \rightarrow X\ YP$, the child will automatically know that heads are to the left of complements in the other phrasal types as well (N Comp, P Comp, A Comp). By exposure to the speech of those around them, children learning Japanese will figure out the relative order of head and complement of a particular phrasal type in that language—say, NP $\rightarrow$ Comp N—and, by X-bar theory, will therefore know that the setting of the Head Parameter for Japanese is to the right: $XP \rightarrow YP\ X$.

To return to the relation between UG and specific languages, we note Chomsky's (1982, 7) explanation that

[t]he grammar of a language can be regarded as a particular set of values for these parameters, while the overall system of rules, principles, and parameters is UG, which we may take to be one element of human biological endowment, namely, the "language faculty."

One key question in this regard is, How much of the rule system must actually be specified in a particular grammar? Or equivalently, What aspects of the rule system must actually be learned, as knowledge of language is acquired? What is the actual set of parameters associated with the rule system (e.g., phrase structure rules (X-bar theory), transformational component), and how freely can they be assigned values? Ideally, the choice of values for parameters should be as limited as possible, so as to maximize the explanatory power of linguistic theory and to account for the possibility of acquiring knowledge of grammar ("language learning").

The challenge, then, is to answer Bertrand Russell's query,

How comes it that human beings, whose contacts with the world are brief and personal and limited, are nevertheless able to know as much as they do?

as it relates to language acquisition. Indeed, how do children acquire such an incredibly rich and complex system in such a short time and in such an effortless manner?

Study Questions

1. What is the evidence that children acquiring language do not simply memorize words and sentences?

2. Who are "Laura" and "Genie" and what linguistic issues do their cases address?

3. Discuss the experiment that demonstrated that children have not simply memorized the plural forms of all nouns in English.

4. What is the *Level-Ordering Hypothesis*? How is *rats-eater* relevant to this hypothesis? (That is, what predictions does the hypothesis make with respect to this example?) How does this example bear on the issue of language acquisition?

5. In what way is infant babbling different from the earliest forms of "real" language that the child begins to speak?

6. What is a *holophrastic expression* in child language?

7. What is *overextension*? What is *overgeneralization*?

8. What is *anticipatory assimilation*?

9. Why does Chomsky posit *Universal Grammar* (or the *Language Acquisition Device*)?

10. What is the *Minimal Distance Principle*? What example shows this principle to be inadequate? How is all this relevant to the nature of language acquisition?

11. What position does Gazzaniga state on the role of grammar in communication? What are the problems with this view?

12. What is the *critical period* for language acquisition? What evidence is brought to bear on this issue?

13. What evidence is there that Washoe produces and understands ASL (American Sign Language)?

14. Recall, from chapter 5, four important aspects of syntactic structure. What evidence is there that Washoe's dialect has syntactic structure?

Exercises

1. Compare and contrast the sentence types found in table 11.1 (children's language) with the sentence types found in table 11.5 (children's language and Washoe's language).

2. Why might Washoe have called miniatures, but not pictures, *baby*? (Could *baby* also mean to Washoe "small example of"?)

3. Design an experiment (a thought experiment) that could show, to your satisfaction, whether Washoe can use ASL as a human does.

4. What semantic similarities and differences are there between Washoe's sign language and natural spoken languages? Can we attribute meaning to Washoe's code?

5. What are some similarities and some differences between the way Washoe was instructed in sign language and the way normal children learn their first language?

6. Suppose Washoe were to successfully pass a suitable language test. What would this tell us about the answers to such questions as

A. Is the capacity for language acquisition innate?
B. Is the capacity for language acquisition specific to the human species?
C. Is the capacity for language acquisition innate in the human species?

Further Reading

General
The 18 articles on language acquisition in Bloom 1994 provide an excellent follow-up to the presentation here. For more on the role of *imitation*, see Ervin 1964 and Bloom, Hood, and Lightbown 1974. For more on *sloppy identity*, from

a purely theoretical point of view, see Ross 1967 and Reinhart 1983. For discussion of *overextension* and *underextension*, see Leopold 1970, Clark 1973, Bowerman 1994, and Huttenlocher and Smiley 1994. For more discussion of *overgeneraliza- tion*, see Ervin 1964, Slobin 1971, and Pinker 1999. Regarding the *Level-Ordering Hypothesis*, see Pinker 1990 and Gazzaniga 1992 (the latter includes interesting discussions of Gordon's results). As for the position that language is *rule-governed* and that humans master and follow rules for forming and using expressions, see Rumelhart and McClelland 1986 (where this view is challenged) and Pinker and Prince 1998 (where it is defended). The most promising research on *interspecies communication* involves the bonobo (pygmy) chimpanzee. For a good overview, see Savage-Rumbaugh et al. 1993; Savage-Rumbaugh and Lewin 1994; Savage-Rumbaugh, Shanker, and Taylor 1998; and Burling 1999.

Special Topic
For more detail on the debates regarding the formulation of the *binding princi- ples*, see Reinhart and Reuland 1993.

Journals
Cognitive Psychology, Cognition, Journal of Child Language, Journal of Psycho- linguistic Research, Journal of Experimental Psychology, Language

Bibliography

Anisfeld, M. 1984. *Language development from birth to three*. Hillsdale, N.J.: Lawrence Erlbaum Associates.

Atkinson-King, K. 1973. Children's acquisition of phonological stress contrasts. Working Papers in Phonetics 25. UCLA.

Bates, E., and B. MacWhinney. 1979. The functionalist approach to the acquisi- tion of grammar. In Ochs and Schieffelin 1979.

Bates, E., and B. MacWhinney. 1982. Functionalist approaches to grammar. In Wanner and Gleitman 1982.

Berko, J. 1958. The child's learning of English morphology. *Word* 14, 150–177.

Bloom, L., L. Hood, and W. F. Lightbown. 1974. Imitation in language devel- opment: If, when, and why. *Cognitive Psychology* 6, 380–420.

Bloom, P., ed. 1994. *Language acquisition: Core readings*. Cambridge, Mass.: MIT Press.

Bowerman, M. 1994. Learning a semantic system: What role do cognitive pre- dispositions play? In Bloom 1994.

Brown, R. 1970. The first sentences of child and chimpanzee. In *Selected psycho- linguistics papers*. New York: Free Press.

Brown, R. 1973. *A first language*. Cambridge, Mass.: Harvard University Press.

Bruner, J. S. 1974. From communication to language: A psychological perspective. *Cognition* 3, 255–287.

Bruner, J. S. 1975. The ontogenesis of speech acts. *Journal of Child Language* 2, 1–19.

Burling, R. 1999. Review of *Apes, language, and the human mind* (Savage-Rumbaugh, Shanker, and Taylor 1998). *Language* 75, 591–593.

Cairns, H. S., D. McDaniels, J. R. Hsu, and M. Rapp. 1994. A longitudinal study of principles of control and pronominal reference in child English. *Language* 70, 260–288.

Calvin, W. H., and G. A. Ojemann. 1994. *Conversations with Neil's brain: The neural nature of thought and language.* Reading, Mass.: Addison-Wesley.

Chomsky, C. S. 1969. *The acquisition of syntax in children from 5 to 10.* Cambridge, Mass.: MIT Press.

Chomsky, N. 1981. *Lectures on government and binding.* Dordrecht: Foris.

Chomsky, N. 1982. *Some concepts and consequences of the theory of government and binding.* Cambridge, Mass.: MIT Press.

Chomsky, N. 1986. *Knowledge of language: Its nature, origin, and use.* New York: Praeger.

Chomsky, N. 1988. *Language and problems of knowledge: The Managua lectures.* Cambridge, Mass.: MIT Press.

Chomsky, N. 1993. A minimalist program for linguistic theory. In K. Hale and S. J. Keyser, eds., *The view from Building 20: Essays in linguistics in honor of Sylvain Bromberger.* Cambridge, Mass.: MIT Press.

Clark, E. 1973. What's in a word? On the child's acquisition of semantics in his first language. In T. E. Moore, ed., *Cognitive development and the acquisition of language.* New York: Academic Press.

Clark, H., and E. Clark. 1977. *Psychology and language: An introduction to psycholinguistics.* New York: Harcourt Brace Jovanovich.

Crain, S., and M. Nakayama. 1987. Structure dependence in children's language. *Language* 63, 522–543.

Curtiss, S. 1977. *Genie: A psycholinguistic study of a modern-day "wild child."* New York: Academic Press.

Dale, P. S. 1976. *Language development: Structure and function.* 2nd ed. New York: Holt, Rinehart and Winston.

de Villiers, J. G., and P. A. de Villiers. 1978. *Language acquisition.* Cambridge, Mass.: Harvard University Press.

Dore, J. 1974. A pragmatic description of early language development. *Journal of Psycholinguistic Research* 4, 423–430.

Ervin, S. M. 1964. Imitation and structural change in children's language. In Lenneberg 1964.

Ferguson, C. A., and D. I. Slobin. 1973. *Studies of child language development.* New York: Holt, Rinehart and Winston.

Foss, D., and D. Hakes. 1978. *Psycholinguistics.* Englewood Cliffs, N.J.: Prentice-Hall.

Fouts, R. 1975. Capacity for language in great apes. In R. Tuttle, ed., *Socioecology and psychology of primates.* The Hague: Mouton.

Gardner, B., and R. Gardner. 1971. Two way communication with an infant chimpanzee. In A. Schrier, H. Harlow, and F. Stollnitz, eds., *Behavior of nonhuman primates.* New York: Academic Press.

Gardner, H. 1991. *The unschooled mind.* New York: Basic Books.

Gardner, R., and B. Gardner. 1969. Teaching sign language to a chimpanzee. *Science* 165, 664–672.

Gardner, R., and B. Gardner. 1975. Evidence for sentence constituents in early utterances of child and chimpanzee. *Journal of Experimental Psychology* 104, 244–267.

Gazzaniga, M. 1992. *Nature's mind.* New York: Basic Books.

Givón, T. 1979. *On understanding grammar.* New York: Academic Press.

Gleason, J. B., and N. B. Ratner, eds. 1993. *Psycholinguistics.* New York: Holt, Rinehart and Winston.

Gordon, P. 1985. Level ordering in lexical development. *Cognition* 21, 73–93.

Hayes, C. 1951. *The ape in our house.* New York: Harper and Row.

Huttenlocher, J., and P. Smiley. 1994. Early word meanings: The case of object names. In Bloom 1994.

Jakobson, R. 1968. *Child language, aphasia,* and phonological universals. The Hague: Mouton. (Originally published in German, 1941.)

Kiparsky, P. 1982. From cyclic phonology to lexical phonology. In H. van der Hulst and N. Smith, eds., *The structure of phonological representations.* Dordrecht: Foris.

Lenneberg, E. H., ed. 1964. *New directions in the study of language.* Cambridge, Mass.: MIT Press.

Lenneberg, E. H. 1967. *Biological foundations of language.* New York: Wiley.

Leopold, W. F. 1970. *Speech development of a bilingual child: A linguist's record.* Vol. 3, *Grammar and general problems in the first two years.* New York: AMS Press. (Originally published 1949.)

Maratsos, M. P. 1974. How preschool children understand missing complement subjects. *Child Development* 45, 700–706.

Menn, L. 1985. Phonological development: Learning sounds and sound patterns. In J. B. Gleason, ed., *The development of language*. Columbus, Ohio: Charles E. Merrill.

Ochs, E., and B. Schieffelin, eds. 1979. *Developmental pragmatics*. New York: Academic Press.

Olmsted, D. 1971. *Out of the mouth of babes*. The Hague: Mouton.

Owens, R. E. 1984. *Language development: An introduction*. Columbus, Ohio: Charles E. Merrill.

Patterson, F. 1978. Conversations with a gorilla. *National Geographic* 154, 438–465.

Patterson, F. 1981. *The education of Koko*. New York: Holt, Rinehart and Winston.

Pinker, S. 1990. Language acquisition. In D. N. Osherson and H. Lasnik, eds., *Language: An invitation to cognitive science, vol. 1*. Cambridge, Mass.: MIT Press.

Pinker, S. 1995. *The language instinct*. New York: HarperPerennial.

Pinker, S. 1999. *Words and rules: The ingredients of language*. New York: Basic Books.

Pinker, S., and A. Prince. 1988. On language and connectionism: Analysis of a Parallel Distributed Processing model of language acquisition. In S. Pinker and J. Mehler, eds., *Connections and symbols*. Cambridge, Mass.: MIT Press.

Premack, A., and D. Premack. 1972. Teaching language to an ape. *Scientific American* 227.4, 92–99.

Reinhart, T. 1983. *Anaphora and semantic interpretation*. London: Croom Helm.

Reinhart, T., and E. Reuland. 1993. Reflexivity. *Linguistic Inquiry* 24, 657–720.

Ross, J. R. 1967. Constraints on variables in syntax. Doctoral dissertation, MIT.

Rumbaugh, D. 1977. *Language learning by a chimpanzee: The Lana project*. New York: Academic Press.

Rumelhart, D., and J. McClelland. 1986. On learning the past tenses of English verbs. In J. McClelland, D. Rumelhart, and the PDP Research Group, *Parallel Distributed Processing: Explorations in the microstructure of cognition*. Vol. 2, *Psychological and biological models*. Cambridge, Mass.: MIT Press.

Rymer, R. 1993. *Genie: A scientific tragedy*. New York: HarperPerennial.

Sachs, J. 1985. Prelinguistic development. In J. B. Gleason, ed., *The development of language*. Columbus, Ohio: Charles E. Merrill.

Savage-Rumbaugh, S., K. McDonald, R. Sevcik, W. Hopkins, and E. Rubert. 1986. Spontaneous symbol acquisition and communicative use by pygmy chimpanzees (*Pan paniscus*). *Journal of Experimental Psychology* 115, 211–235.

Savage-Rumbaugh, E. S., J. Murphy, R. Sevcik, K. Brakke, S. L. Williams, and D. M. Rumbaugh. 1993. *Language comprehension in ape and child*. Monographs of the Society for Research in Child Development 58, nos. 3–4.

Savage-Rumbaugh, E. S., and R. Levin. 1994. *Kanzi: An ape at the brink of language*. New York: Wiley.

Savage-Rumbaugh, E. S., S. Shanker, and T. J. Taylor. 1998. *Apes, language, and the human mind*. Oxford: Oxford University Press.

Slobin, D. 1971. On the learning of morphological rules: A reply to Palermo and Eberhart. In D. I. Slobin, ed., *The ontogenesis of grammar: A theoretical symposium*. New York: Academic Press.

Smith, N. V. 1973. *The acquisition of phonology*. Cambridge: Cambridge University Press.

Snow, C. E. 1972. Mothers' speech to children learning language. *Child Development* 43, 549–565.

Snow, C. E. 1977. Mothers' speech research: From input to interaction. In Snow and Ferguson 1977.

Snow, C. E., and C. A. Ferguson. 1977. *Talking to children: Language input and acquisition*. Cambridge: Cambridge University Press.

Templin, M. 1957. *Certain language skills in children*. Minneapolis, Minn.: University of Minnesota Press.

Terrace, H. S. 1979. *Nim*. New York: Alfred A. Knopf.

Thorpe, W. H. 1974. *Animal nature and human nature*. Garden City, N.Y.: Doubleday.

Wanner, E., and L. R. Gleitman, eds. 1982. *Language acquisition: The state of the art*. New York: Cambridge University Press.

Wellman, B., I. Case, I. Mengert, and D. Bradbury. 1931. Speech sounds of young children. University of Iowa Studies in Child Welfare 1931, 5.

Yamada, J. E. 1990. *Laura: A case for the modularity of language*. Cambridge, Mass.: MIT Press.

Zukow, P. G., J. Reilly, and P. M. Greenfield. 1979. Making the absent present: Facilitating the transition from sensorimotor to linguistic communication. In K. Nelson, ed., *Children's language*, vol. 2. New York: Gardner Press.

Chapter 12

Language and the Brain

The biological side of language is the subject of increasing research, and advances are possible because of the growing sophistication of available experimental techniques and equipment. It is somewhat ironic that until recently, progress in our understanding of brain functions has come not from the study of normal individuals but largely from the study of individuals with injured brains. Whenever disease or injury affects the left side of the brain, some aspect of the ability to perceive, process, or produce language may be disturbed. Individuals with such brain disease or injury are said to be *aphasic*, and their brain disturbances can give us insight into how the human brain carries out its language-related tasks.

Aphasia is a broad term encompassing numerous syndromes of communicative impairment. Some aphasics labor to speak a single word, whereas others effortlessly produce long but meaningless utterances. By studying the effect of brain damage on speech and comprehension, researchers have obtained invaluable clues to the organization of speech and language in the human nervous system. *Neurolinguists* are interested in the correlation between brain damage and speech and language deficits. These language and brain specialists believe that the study of language form and use will reveal principles of brain function, and that the study of brain function may support or refute specific linguistic theories.

Of the many questions of interest to neurolinguists, three are fundamental: (1) Where in the brain are speech and language localized? (2) How does the nervous system function to encode and decode speech and language? and (3) Are the components of language—phonology, syntax, semantics—neuroanatomically distinct and therefore vulnerable to separate impairment?

Sections 12.1, 12.2, and 12.3 were written by Kathryn Bayles, Department of Speech and Hearing Sciences, University of Arizona.

12.1 WHERE IS LANGUAGE LOCALIZED IN THE BRAIN?

Language: A Left Hemisphere Phenomenon

For nearly a century and a half, scholars have debated the question of speech and language localization within the brain. In the 1860s, scientists known as localizationists speculated that the functioning of specific regions in the brain was responsible for language. Antilocalizationists argued that speech and language were the consequence of the brain functioning as a whole.

In 1861, Paul Broca, a French surgeon and anatomist, described to the Société d'Anthropologie in Paris a patient who in life had had extreme difficulty in producing speech. Later, at autopsy, the patient was found to have damage in the posterior inferior part of the *frontal lobe* in the left cerebral hemisphere, now known as *Broca's area* (the *motor speech area*; see figure 12.1). With the publication of this report Broca became the first individual to substantiate the claim that damage to a specific area of the brain results in a speech deficit. In 1865, Broca extended his claim about speech localization by reporting that damage to sites in the left cerebral hemisphere produced aphasia, whereas destruction of corresponding sites in the right hemisphere left linguistic capacities intact.

In 1874, Carl Wernicke, a young German physician, published a monograph describing patients with speech comprehension deficits who had damage (lesions) outside Broca's area, in the left posterior temporal lobe. Wernicke's work strengthened Broca's claim that left hemispheric structures are essential for speech and generated intense interest in the hypothesis that different areas within the left hemisphere fulfill different linguistic functions.

Today scientists agree that specific neuroanatomic structures, generally of the left hemisphere, are vital for speech and language, but debate continues as to which structures are committed to the various linguistic capacities. For most individuals the left cerebral hemisphere is dominant for language, regardless of handedness. Approximately 70 percent of all individuals with damage to the left hemisphere will experience some type of aphasia, as compared with only 1 percent of those with right hemispheric lesions.

Confirmation of left cerebral language dominance has come from many research techniques, one of which was introduced by J. Wada in 1949. Wada reported that the injection of sodium amytal into the main (carotid) artery on the language-dominant side of the brain induces a

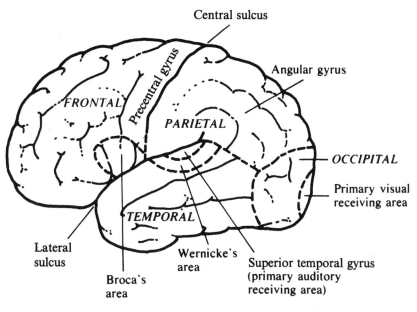

Figure 12.1
Landmarks of the left cerebral hemisphere

temporary aphasia. Physicians have subsequently used this technique as a means of determining cerebral dominance in patients facing neurosurgery; in this way, they can avoid damaging the language centers during surgery.

Substantially adding to our knowledge of the neurology was a report published in 1959 by Wilder Penfield and LaMar Roberts, neurosurgeons at the Montreal Neurological Institute. Penfield and Roberts had been studying the brain as well as treating its infirmities. To provide relief from intractable seizures in patients with epilepsy, Penfield and Roberts surgically removed portions of the brain. Because of the threat of producing aphasia by removing regions subserving speech and language, they used electrical stimulation to map the functions of the exposed brains of their patients.

Electrical current applied to a spot on the brain can sometimes activate involuntary expression of the function associated with that brain site. Stimulation may also interfere with a function being performed by the conscious patient. For example, electrical stimulation applied to areas on one side of the brain associated with motor function can produce limb twitching, numbness, and movement on the opposite side of the body.

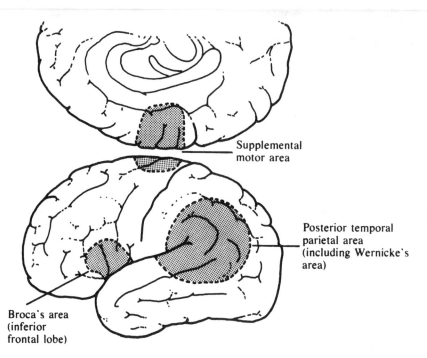

Supplemental
motor area

Posterior temporal
parietal area
(including Wernicke's
area)

Broca's area
(inferior
frontal lobe)

Figure 12.2
Primary cortical areas involved in speech and language function. (After Penfield
and Roberts 1959.)

Penfield and Roberts discovered that when electrical current was applied
to a brain area involved in speech, one of two things occurred: the patient
either had trouble talking or uttered a vowel-like cry. However, no patient
ever produced an intelligible word as a result of electrical stimulation.

Through the cooperation of hundreds of courageous patients, who
remained conscious during surgery, Penfield and Roberts were able to
conclude that three areas of the left hemisphere are vital to speech and
language: *Broca's area*, *Wernicke's area*, and the supplemental *motor
area* (see figure 12.2).

As evidence accumulated verifying left cerebral speech dominance,
researchers sought to discover whether the left hemisphere speech areas
were structurally unique. Geschwind and Levitsky (1968) were the first to
report that a region in the left temporal lobe was larger than the same
area on the right in 65 percent of the brains they studied. This area,
called the *planum temporale*, has also been found to be larger even in fetal

brains, a finding that suggests the readiness of the left hemisphere for language dominance at birth (Wada, Clarke, and Hamm 1975, Witelson and Pallie 1973).

In order to understand the details of localization theory, it is first necessary to become familiar with some basic concepts about the structure and function of the nervous system.

The Nervous System

The central and peripheral nervous systems form an intricate communication network through which the behavior of the body is governed. The brain and spinal cord constitute the *central nervous system* (CNS) and are linked to the *peripheral nervous system* by bundles of nerve fibers that extend to all parts of the body. Impulses received from peripheral receptors are sorted, interpreted, and responded to by the CNS.

The basic cellular unit of the nervous system is the *neuron*, of which there are an estimated 12 billion. Each neuron is structurally distinct and composed of (1) a *cell body*, (2) receptors known as *dendrites*, and (3) a conductive mechanism, or *axon*. The dendrites receive input from other neurons and transmit *away from* the cell body. Some nerve fibers transmit sensory information to the CNS, others carry information from the CNS to the limbs and body parts, and still others form communicative links between the different parts of the nervous system.

Levels of the Central Nervous System

The central nervous system is hierarchically organized, higher structures being more complex than lower ones (see figure 12.3). At the lowest level is the spinal cord, which acts as a cable through which streams of neuronal messages between the body and the brain are transmitted. Above the spinal cord is the brain stem, the regulator of such things as breathing, muscle tone, posture, sleep, and body temperature. Lower nervous system structures, such as the spinal cord and lower brain stem, are primarily reflexive and controlled by higher centers. At the highest level of the nervous system are the cerebral hemispheres, responsible for voluntary activity.

The cerebral hemispheres emerge from the higher brain stem and are covered with a convoluted sheath of gray matter, called the *cortex*, which is approximately $\frac{1}{4}$ inch thick. Within the cortex are approximately 10 billion neurons arranged in at least six layers. The degree of connectivity in this three-dimensional cellular network is almost beyond comprehen-

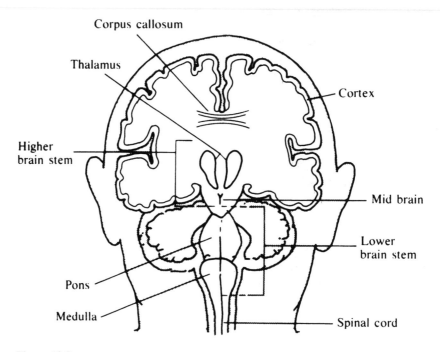

Corpus callosum

Thalamus

Cortex

Higher
brain stem

Mid brain

Lower
brain stem

Pons

Medulla

Spinal cord

Figure 12.3
Hierarchical arrangement of the central nervous system

sion. Sholl (1956), a noted neuroanatomist, writes that the cortex contains fields of neurons where a single axon may influence up to 4,000 other neurons.

The Cerebral Cortex: General Characteristics

In outward appearance the two cerebral hemispheres are roughly similar, being composed of convolutions, called *gyri*, and depressions or fissures, known as *sulci*. Certain gyri and sulci serve as landmarks helping to differentiate the boundaries of the four lobes of each hemisphere. The structures are illustrated in figure 12.1.

The *lateral sulcus* (= fissure of Sylvius) separates the frontal lobe from the temporal; the *central sulcus* (= fissure of Rolando) separates the frontal lobe from the parietal. (Here and below, the terms enclosed in parentheses are ones formerly used for the brain's anatomical structures.) No fissure separates the parietal and occipital lobes; these two lobes can be distinguished only by microscopic examination of cell structures.

Located in the parietal lobe, at the upper end of the lateral sulcus, is the cortical area known as the *angular gyrus*, in which functions necessary to speech, reading, and writing are interrelated.

Within each hemisphere are areas known to serve specific functions. In front of, and running parallel to, the central sulcus is a strip of cortex known as the *precentral gyrus* (= motor strip), which controls fine, highly skilled, voluntary motor movements. This area is also referred to as the *primary motor area* or the *primary motor cortex*. Sections of the primary motor area are related to voluntary movements in particular parts of the body; for example, the facial and laryngeal muscles are represented in the lower end, in close proximity to Broca's area.

Next to Wernicke's area, in the temporal lobe, is the *superior temporal gyrus* (= Heschl's gyrus), known also as the *primary auditory cortex*. When auditory impulses arrive at the superior temporal gyrus, a noise is perceived, but meaningful interpretation must be made by the adjacent auditory association area (Wernicke's area). This pattern of cortical organization, consisting of interpretive regions of the cortex lying adjacent to sensory receiving areas, is repeated in the visual cortical system and in the system receiving sensations from the body.

Cortical Conduction

The bulk of the cerebral hemispheres, beneath the outer layer of gray matter, is composed of three basic types of nerve fiber tracts that form a neural communication network of astonishing complexity. Association nerve fibers connect different portions of the same hemisphere. Projection fibers connect the cortex with lower portions of the brain and spinal cord, and transverse fibers interconnect the cerebral hemispheres.

Of particular importance to speech and language function is the massive transverse fiber tract called the *corpus callosum* (see figure 12.3). By means of the corpus callosum the two hemispheres are able to communicate with each other in the form of electrical impulses. Eccles (1972) estimated that if one assumes that each of the approximately 200 million nerve fibers constituting the corpus callosum has an average firing capacity of 20 impulses per second, then the corpus callosum can carry the astronomical number of 4 billion impulses per second.

You may wonder why, if speech is localized in the left hemisphere, it is necessary for the cerebral hemispheres to communicate with each other for speech to function normally. The reason is that sensations from right and left halves of the body go primarily to the *contralateral* (opposite) hemisphere. If, for example, an object is held in the left hand, impulses travel from the left side of the body to the *right* hemisphere, and although the right hemisphere would recognize the object, verbalizing the name of the object would require involvement of the speech center in the left hemisphere.

The importance of the corpus callosum has been made strikingly clear through split-brain research. Gazzaniga and associates studied the effect of disruption of communication between the hemispheres in patients who had had them disconnected surgically by severing the corpus callosum, an operation that is performed to reduce the frequency and severity of incapacitating seizures. Once the cerebral hemispheres are disconnected, there are techniques whereby stimuli can be visually presented to a single hemisphere. When Gazzaniga and Sperry (1967) presented stimuli in the form of written words, letters, and numbers to the left hemisphere alone, patients were able to describe them orally. But information perceived exclusively by the right hemisphere could not be verbalized, either orally or in writing. The right hemisphere was mute.

To investigate the possibility that even though split-brain subjects could not describe visual stimuli presented to their right hemispheres, they nevertheless comprehended them, Gazzaniga and Sperry gave the patients a nonverbal means of responding. For instance, subjects were asked to match a written word with its referent by pointing to the object when it was displayed as one item in a group of assorted items. Under these conditions the right hemisphere was found to be capable of recognizing letters, short words, and numbers.

To discover whether the right hemisphere could also comprehend spoken words, Gazzaniga and Sperry asked patients to identify words presented auditorily. Because auditory stimuli are received by both sides of the brain, Gazzaniga and Sperry limited the available answers to the right hemisphere. Subjects were instructed to push a button when they saw that one of a set of nouns projected serially to the left visual field (the right hemisphere) matched one previously spoken. Results with split-brain patients showed that the right hemisphere can understand oral (as well as written) language, although the limits of its comprehension have yet to be determined.

Recent research suggests that the right hemisphere may be limited in its linguistic competence. Split-brain subjects have been observed to have difficulty responding appropriately to verbal commands, simple active and passive subject-verb-object sentences, and word sequences when they were presented visually to the right hemisphere.

Thus, although the right hemisphere is generally unimpaired in grasping the meaning of single words, it performs poorly with phrases. Perhaps only certain kinds of linguistic stimuli can be comprehended by the right hemisphere. More research is needed to explore its decoding capacities.

12.2   HOW DOES THE BRAIN ENCODE AND DECODE SPEECH AND LANGUAGE?

Speech and Language: A Cortical and Subcortical System

What the silence of the isolated right hemisphere has dramatized is that speech is not solely a cortical function. Subcortical fiber tracts as well as gray matter areas deep within the brain—particularly the *thalamus*—also participate in speech and language. The thalamus can be conceived of as a great relay station, receiving nerve fiber projections from the cortex and lower nervous system structures and radiating fibers to all parts of the cortex (see figure 12.4).

Emerging as especially important to speech and language function is the left thalamus. Damage to portions of this structure produces invol-

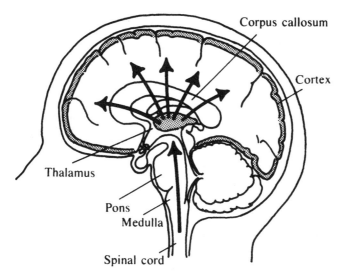

Figure 12.4
Fiber radiations from the thalamus to the cortex

untary repetition of words and disturbs the patient's ability to name objects. The thalamus is thought to be involved in the focusing of attention by temporarily heightening the receptivity of certain cortical sensory areas. Ojemann and Ward (1971) observed that information presented to patients during left thalamic stimulation was more easily retrieved, both during and after stimulation, than information that had been presented prior to stimulation. They speculated that the thalamus may provide an interaction between language and memory mechanisms.

Neurolinguists are far from being certain which neuroanatomical structures are essential to the encoding and decoding of linguistic stimuli, but they agree that speech results from an integrated cortical and subcortical system. An awareness that the neural sensory, motor, and associative mechanisms are interconnected is basic to understanding how the brain functions to encode and decode language.

A simple model can represent our knowledge of the transmission of signals to the language mechanism. In figure 12.5, the dark band between the semicircles (which represent coronal sections of the cerebral hemispheres) represents the hemispheric connection. Notice that impulses coming from the right side of the body have direct access to the dominant speech center, whereas those from the left must touch base with the right hemisphere before passing over the corpus callosum for processing. The left hemisphere is not dominant, however, for the processing of *all* auditory signals. Nonspeech environmental sounds do not have to be passed on to the left hemisphere but are processed primarily in the right hemisphere. How do we know this?

Evidence from Dichotic Listening Research

By means of a research technique called *dichotic listening*, we can analyze the characteristics of incoming stimuli processed by the individual hemispheres. During a dichotic listening task two different stimuli are presented simultaneously, through earphones, to the left and right ears. For example, the right ear may be given the word *base* and the left ear *ball*. The listeners are instructed to say what they hear. Interestingly, certain types of stimuli delivered to a particular ear will be more accurately reported by the listener. This is because the nervous system is capable of scanning incoming stimuli and routing them to that area of the brain specialized for their interpretation. Kimura (1961) was the first to observe that when two digits were presented simultaneously, one to each ear, the listener more accurately identified those presented to the right ear. How-

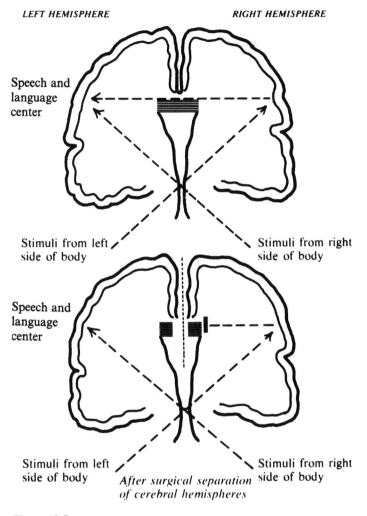

LEFT HEMISPHERE   *RIGHT HEMISPHERE*

Speech and
language
center

Stimuli from left
side of body

Stimuli from right
side of body

Speech and
language
center

Stimuli from left
side of body

After surgical separation Stimuli from right
of cerebral hemispheres side of body

Figure 12.5
Callosal connection

ever, when the listener was known to have the less common right hemispheric dominance for speech, Kimura observed a left ear advantage. In
other words, the ear having more direct access to the language center had
an advantage. Although there is some auditory input to each cortex from
the ear on the same side of the body, these uncrossed (or *ipsilateral*)
inputs are thought to be suppressed.

The right ear advantage (REA) was originally thought to exist only for
linguistically meaningful stimuli, but the same advantage has been found
for nonsense syllables, speech played backward, consonant-vowel syllables, and even small units of speech such as fricatives. Intrigued by these
findings, investigators have sought to discover those features of speech
likely to trigger left hemisphere processing. One hypothesis was that an
REA would be found for any sound produced by the vocal tract muscu-
lature. Research results have disconfirmed this explanation, for REAs
have been found for synthetic speech and Morse code, but not for laugh-
ing and coughing.

The REA associated with Morse code stimuli suggests that the left
hemisphere may be dominant for more than the phonetic structure of
language. In fact, the left hemisphere may be dominant for a number
of nonlinguistic functions. For example, several investigators have noted
that the ability to perform fine judgments of temporal order is a function
of the left hemisphere: aphasics perform poorly, compared with controls and subjects with right hemisphere damage, on nonlinguistic tasks
requiring temporal order judgments (Brookshire 1972, Swisher and Hirsh
1972). Lackner and Teuber (1973) have proposed that the left hemisphere
has an advantage in temporal acuity and, as a consequence, language
processing may have been drawn to the left hemisphere since speech is
temporally ordered.

Much evidence implies that left hemisphere damage also impairs the
ability to program complex motor sequences such as playing a violin. A
disorder known as *oral nonverbal apraxia* is commonly associated with left
hemisphere damage. DeRenzi, Pieczuro, and Vignolo (1966, 51) defined
the disorder as "the inability to perform voluntary movements with the
muscles of the larynx, pharynx, tongue, lips, and cheeks, although automatic movements of the same muscles are preserved." Patients have
trouble voluntarily performing simple gestures such as whistling, blow-
ing, clearing the throat, or sticking out the tongue. It has been argued
that if the left hemisphere is dominant for programming motor sequences, it is logical that this special ability would be used to program the

extremely complex motor sequences associated with speech, which, as pointed out in chapter 3, requires the simultaneous coordination of at least 100 muscles.

Besides having a superior capacity for processing temporally ordered stimuli and programming complex motor sequences, the left hemisphere is believed to be specialized for associative thought. Two notable studies support this hypothesis. DeRenzi, Scotti, and Spinnler (1969) observed that patients with left hemisphere damage performed more poorly than right-lesioned patients in an object-matching task. Patients were handed an object and required to match it to 1 of 10 on display in front of them; the held object differed in form and color from its displayed match. The left hemisphere was found to be superior at recognizing the same object in a different form. In the second study, by Faglioni, Spinnler, and Vignolo (1969), subjects with left hemisphere damage exhibited significantly greater difficulty than both right-damaged individuals and controls in matching a sound, such as a bell, with a picture of its source.

It may be the case, as some investigators theorize, that speech and language function is not cognitively unique but is imposed in the left hemisphere because speech and language functions require the special nonlinguistic capacities of this hemisphere.

Complementary Specialization of the Cerebral Hemispheres

For some time the view prevailed that the left hemisphere was superior, overall, to the right; but this misconception has recently been corrected. The research techniques providing insight into speech and language function have unveiled functions for which the right hemisphere is dominant, particularly those functions requiring spatial ability.

Injury to the right hemisphere can result in visuospatial impairment. An affected individual may have trouble getting from one place to another, drawing objects, assembling puzzles, or recognizing faces. Such an individual may disregard anything on the left side of the body, even to the extent that when asked to draw the face of a clock, the patient may squeeze all the numbers in on the right side of the face.

Psychological research suggests that the two hemispheres differ in the manner in which they treat incoming stimuli, the right hemisphere processing stimuli holistically (as wholes) and the left analytically (by parts). For example, Kimura (1966) exposed 3 to 10 dots to each visual half-field for 80 milliseconds. Subjects exhibited a left visual field superiority in guessing the number of dots. The brevity of the exposure time prevented subjects from counting the dots, lending support to the notion that the right hemisphere (associated with the left visual field) is superior at grasping the whole without a complete analysis of its parts.

Some musical skills are thought to be right hemisphere dependent. Although musical deficits are likely to exist after damage to the language-dominant (left) hemisphere, people with right hemisphere damage show deficits in discriminating complex sounds, timbres, and melodies. In a dichotic listening task, Kimura (1973) played a different melody to each ear simultaneously. Subjects were then asked to pick out these two melodies from among four melodies, each of which was played, individually, to both ears. Normal subjects were able to pick out the melody that had been presented to the left ear (right hemisphere) better than the one presented to the right ear.

Bever (1975) discussed Kimura's findings and suggested that to musically naive subjects the perception of melody is a holistic phenomenon, thereby generating a left ear advantage for those subjects. In his own experiments, however, Bever discovered that musically sophisticated subjects experienced a musical sequence better in the right ear (left hemisphere), because, he argued, they approached the task analytically.

Inasmuch as each cerebral hemisphere has unique functional superiorities (summarized in figure 12.6), it seems inappropriate to refer to the language-dominant left hemisphere as the major one. It is more accurate to conceive of the hemispheres as complementarily specialized. The degree of hemispheric specialization, however, varies among individuals. Right-handed individuals who have a family history of right-handedness will show the greatest hemispheric specialization. Least likely to show hemispheric specialization are left-handed individuals with a family history of left-handedness. Some of these individuals are thought to have bilateral representation of basic skills. The possibility of bilateral representation is not surprising when we remember that each hemisphere has the capacity to replicate functions of the other; indeed, one hemisphere may take over for the other when it is injured or removed.

Right hemisphere language dominance is not uncommon in adults who sustained injury to the left hemisphere early in life. The literature is replete with documented cases of the development of language by the right hemisphere after injury to the left. Nonetheless, the adaptability of the nervous system decreases with age, and when left hemisphere injury occurs after puberty, the danger of permanent aphasia is great.

LEFT HEMISPHERE   RIGHT HEMISPHERE

Speech   Holistic processing
Writing   Stereognosis
Temporal-order   Nonverbal
judgments   environmental sounds
Language   Visuospatial skills
Reading   Nonverbal ideation
Associative thought   Recognition and
Calculation   memory of melodies
Analytic processing   Left visual field
Right visual field

Figure 12.6
Complementary specialization of cerebral hemispheres

Do the Hemispheres Equally Support the Development of Speech and Language?

Although speech and language function can be taken over by the right hemisphere if necessary, there is evidence that the right hemisphere does not have the same potential for speech and language specialization as the left has.

Dennis and Whitaker (1976) monitored the development of three children in whom one hemisphere of the brain was surgically removed during infancy (hemispherectomy) to arrest seizures associated with Sturge-Weber-Dimitri syndrome. Of the three children, two (SM and CA) had only the right hemisphere and one (MW) only the left. At the age of 10 these children were given psychological and psycholinguistic tests. Intelligence was found to be comparable among the three, as shown in table 12.1. However, other differences emerged. When given a variety of complex verbal commands varying in information and syntactic complexity, only MW, the child with the left hemisphere, was able to maintain proficient performance. Syntactic rather than semantic complexity appeared to impair the performance of SM and CA. By contrast, as might be

Table 12.1
IQ scores of children in the Dennis and Whitaker study (1976)

IQ test	MW	SM	CA
Verbal	96	94	91
Performance	92	87	108
Full scale	93	90	99

expected, the isolated left hemisphere (MW) performed more poorly on visuospatial tasks.

Functional asymmetry of the cerebral hemispheres is economical, enabling brain tissue to perform a wider variety of functions than would be possible if each hemisphere were a replica of the other. On the other hand, the potential of each hemisphere to replicate the functions of the other, in a developing nervous system, provides a prudent backup system. As we conclude the discussion of how the brain functions to encode and decode speech and language, it seems appropriate to pose the question of whether the areas within the left hemisphere speech and language system are functionally divisible in phonological, semantic, and syntactic subsystems. This is the topic of the next section.

12.3   ARE THE COMPONENTS OF LANGUAGE NEUROANATOMICALLY DISTINCT?

Within the left hemisphere there is neither uniform nor equal representation of linguistic functions. Damage to a small area in the hemisphere does not result in the impairment of *all* linguistic capabilities. On the contrary, lesions in different areas of the hemisphere lead to qualitatively distinct aphasia syndromes. A review of the language and speech behaviors associated with the different aphasia syndromes will suggest a crude definition of the boundaries of the various linguistic domains.

Aphasiologists have no uniform criteria for classifying types of aphasia, the consequence of which is considerable terminological diversity. Widely accepted, however, as distinct aphasia syndromes are the following: Broca's aphasia, Wernicke's aphasia, conduction aphasia, and anomia.

Broca's Aphasia

Broca's aphasia, named for Paul Broca, who first described its symptoms, is known also as *expressive* or *motor aphasia*. It follows from a lesion in the motor speech area (posterior part of the inferior frontal gyrus), or Broca's area (see figure 12.1). However, according to Mohr (1976) the cluster of symptoms traditionally associated with Broca's aphasia results from a more extensive lesion than the one described by Broca. Ironically, even Broca's own patient had a more diffuse lesion, but Broca focused on the more circumscribed area in the inferior frontal region because of the view of his contemporaries that large strokes always begin as a smaller focus.

The symptoms of Broca's aphasia will seem logical if we note the proximity of Broca's area to the cortical region of the brain controlling the muscles of speech (see figure 12.1). The foremost symptom is the inability of the affected individual to speak fluently. Great effort is required to utter short halting phrases, described as telegraphic because of the absence of function words (words such as *the*, *by*, *but*). Literal *paraphasias*— substitutions, omissions, or distortions of sounds—are both frequent and inconsistent, and when the aphasic is permitted several repetitions of misarticulated phrases, articulation usually improves.

Bound morphemes such as tense, plural, and comparative markers are frequently missing. Surface word order is usually appropriate, however, and the verbal output makes sense. The characteristics of the spoken language are mirrored in the patient's reading and writing. Although comprehension of language may not be normal, it is usually good enough for these individuals to grasp the meaning of what they hear. In fact, most of Broca's aphasics are painfully aware of their own mistakes. As you read the following samples of utterances produced by Broca's aphasics, remember that there is no way to reproduce in print the intense effort these individuals must make to produce even a few words.

Examiner: Tell me, what did you do before you retired?
Aphasic: Uh, uh, uh, puh, par, partender, no.
Examiner: Carpenter?
Aphasic: (shaking head yes) Carpenter, tuh, tuh tenty [20] year.
Examiner: Tell me about this picture.
Aphasic: Boy . . . cook . . . cookie . . . took . . . cookie.

Neurolinguists agree that Broca's aphasics have suffered impairment to the phonological system but debate whether the syntactic component of language is impaired. Linguistic observations of aphasic language have a rather recent history compared with clinical studies. More research will be required to settle the issue of whether phonological theory can account for all of the linguistic aberrations displayed by Broca's aphasics when the lesion is confined to the frontal lobe.

Wernicke's Aphasia

Wernicke's aphasia, known also as *sensory aphasia* or *receptive aphasia*, is the consequence of a lesion in the auditory association cortex of the temporal lobe (see figure 12.1). This area is adjacent to the region that receives auditory stimuli. Predictably, the primary characteristic of this type of aphasia is impairment in the ability to understand spoken and written language. Wernicke's aphasics may suffer a severe loss of understanding even though their hearing is normal. Great variation in symptoms occurs in Wernicke's aphasia.

Fluency is usually not a problem, although interruptions in the flow of speech occur when the patient cannot retrieve a specific word. Often patients speak very rapidly, the content of what they say ranging from mildly inappropriate to complete nonsense, as in the following example:

Examiner: Do you like it here in Kansas City?
Aphasic:　Yes, I am.
Examiner: I'd like to have you tell me something about your problem.
Aphasic:　Yes, I ugh can't hill all of my way. I can't talk all of the things I do, and part of the part I can go alright, but I can't tell from the other people. I usually most of my things. I know what can I talk and know what they are but I can't always come back even though I know they should be in, and I know should something eely I should know what I'm doing . . .

Circumlocutions are numerous: Wernicke's aphasics talk in circles about objects they are unable to name, as when a patient says *what you drink* for *water*. Patients with word retrieval deficits overuse empty words like *thing* and *one*. Language alterations in the form of word substitutions may be numerous. At times the substitution bears a relation to the intended word, as when someone says *slipper* for *shoe* or *corn flakes* for *cereal*. At other times there is no apparent connection between the intended and substituted words. In extreme cases, patients use unrecognizable words called neologisms.

For patients with severe comprehension deficits the prognosis for recovery is poorer than for Broca's aphasics, who have better comprehension. Aphasiologists speculate that Wernicke's aphasics have damaged feedback systems, limiting their ability to monitor what they say and thus limiting their ability to correct themselves.

Whereas Broca's aphasia is primarily a deficit in the phonological component of language, Wernicke's aphasia affects the semantic and syntactic components. The lateral sulcus separating Broca's and Wernicke's areas may represent a neuroanatomical boundary separating the phonological from the syntactic and semantic components at the cortical level. It must be pointed out, however, that Broca's and Wernicke's areas are connected subcortically by a bundle of nerve fibers called the *arcuate fasciculus*. This may serve as a transmission line carrying signals received in the auditory reception cortex to the auditory association cortex for interpretation and, subsequently, to the speech production cortex for verbalization. Should the arcuate fasciculus be damaged, the affected individual would be expected to have difficulty repeating auditory information. And that is exactly what happens in conduction aphasia.

Conduction Aphasia

Conduction aphasia follows from localized lesions in the temporoparietal regions that serve to synthesize meaning and form. All avenues of expression are affected. Spontaneous speech is fluent but circumlocutory and inadequately structured. Similar defects are found in spontaneous writing. Reading aloud is difficult, and repeating is severely disturbed. Comprehension of oral and written material is normal or only mildly affected.

Conduction aphasics can be differentiated from Broca's aphasics by their fluent spontaneous speech; Broca's aphasics find spontaneous speech harder than repetition. Conduction aphasics are like Wernicke's aphasics in that they are fluent, but unlike Wernicke's they have good speech comprehension. Conduction aphasia is not a problem of receptive or expressive mechanisms as much as it is a problem of the transmission between the two.

Anomia

In classic *anomia* the patient has difficulty finding words, both during the flow of speech and in naming on confrontation. That is, when presented with a stimulus object, the individual is unable to retrieve its name. Yet when these individuals are offered the correct name of the stimulus item, they instantly recognize it. Further, they can usually select the correct name from a group of names.

Comprehension and repetition of speech are normal, and speech is fluent although filled with circumlocutions. The following selected responses made by anomic aphasics aptly illustrate word-finding difficulties:

Examiner: Who is the president of the United States?

Aphasic: I can't say his name. I know the man, but I can't come out and say ... I'm very sorry, I just can't come out and say. I just can't write it to me now.

Examiner: Can you tell me a girl's name?

Aphasic: Of a girl's name, by mean, by which weight, I mean how old or young?

Examiner: On what do we sleep?

Aphasic: Of the week, er, of the night, oh from about 10:00, about 11:00 o'clock at night until about uh 7:00 in the morning.

The brain lesions associated with classical anomia involve the dominant angular gyrus (see figure 12.1), that area of the brain thought to be necessary for the formation of association between the sensory modalities.

To sum up, the different forms of aphasia show that representation of linguistic functions in the left hemisphere is by no means uniform or equal. We have seen that lesions in different areas of the left hemisphere lead to distinct aphasia syndromes. Future research on these distinctions is certain to be both interesting and important.

12.4 SPECIAL TOPICS

PET and MRI Imaging

Using techniques known as *positron emission tomography* (PET) and *magnetic resonance imaging* (MRI), researchers can study visual displays of the locations in the brain that are active during a variety of tasks, including those tasks involved in language use.

In a PET scan a substance such as blood or glucose is tagged with a radioactive marker and then injected into the bloodstream. The radioactive marker gives off positrons (positively charged electrons), and when a positron collides with an electron in the body, the two particles annihilate each other, producing gamma rays. It is these gamma rays that are detected and provide information concerning the location and strength of the blood flow.

Once the radioactively tagged substance has been injected into the subject's arm, it reaches the brain within a few seconds. This experimen-

Figure 12.7
Representation of the bright spots that are generated by positron emission tomography (PET). The spot at the back appears during reading. The upper spot appears during speech. The more forward spot appears when a subject is asked to think about what a word means. (Figure based on Montgomery 1989, 59.)

tal technique depends crucially on the fact that more blood is delivered to the parts of the brain that undergo increased metabolic activity than to the parts that are relatively inactive. The extra blood produces an increase in the number of collisions between positrons and electrons, which in turn produce increased gamma radiation, measured by detectors surrounding the head. The parts of the brain that play a role in a particular activity can then be displayed on a computer screen.

Figure 12.7 shows a cross section of a brain with superimposed PET scans, revealing locations that are active during different language tasks. The most forward location shows the part of the brain that is active when the subject is asked to think about the meaning of a word. The location at the top shows the part of the brain that is active when the subject pronounces a word. Finally, the location at the back shows the part of the brain that is active when the subject reads a word.

In order to determine which parts of the brain are active during a particular task, the researcher first obtains a brain activity baseline by having the subject, who is lying down, quietly gaze at a mark on an overhead computer screen. If the researcher is studying brain activity during silent reading, for instance, the subject is next asked to read silently a word that appears on a screen. A computer program then subtracts the data from the first activity (silent gazing) from the data from the second activity (silent reading). Since reading words and looking at a mark on a computer screen require different cortical activity, the result of the subtraction highlights the additional brain activities that occur in silent reading.

If the subject is next asked to pronounce words as they are presented by earphone, the location where the auditory signal is processed and where the articulation is controlled also exhibit increased gamma radiation, each time as measured against an appropriate control for the subtraction procedure. Proceeding in this way, experimenters can map out the areas of the brain that are active in various isolatable tasks. What is important is that these experiments support the position that there are centers or local areas that are active in the control and processing of language.

One important result of PET research is that language information of a visual nature can be transferred from the occipital lobe directly to anterior portions of the brain for semantic processing without necessarily passing through the auditory association components (Petersen et al. 1988). At one time it was thought that the reading of a word required that information first be passed forward through the superior temporal gyrus, where it would receive an auditory interpretation. From the auditory area it would pass to Broca's area, where it would receive a phonetic interpretation, and to other centers for semantic processing. In reading short and common words, one interpretation (still not proven) is that the information can be received in the visual area and then directly transferred to the more forward comprehension areas, bypassing the intervening auditory areas. This is shown by the fact that during silent reading gamma radiation shows up in the posterior visual area and the more forward comprehension areas, but not in Broca's area. As figure 12.8 illustrates, when subjects are given a word visually and then asked to determine its rhyming properties, the auditory centers do "light up" as well as the centers seen in figure 12.7 that are active in silent reading. Researchers hypothesize that as children learn to read, their "sounding out" of the pronunciation will always involve the auditory area and Broca's area (Petersen et al. 1988). Later, the visual information is able

Figure 12.8
Part (a) represents the parts of the brain that are activated when we hear words.
Part (b) shows what parts light up when a subject is asked whether two written
words rhyme. Note that the part of the brain indicated by the arrow, the word
sound area, lights up in (b), even though no speaking is taking place. This area
does not light up, in fact, when adults read familiar words. (Figure based on
Montgomery 1989, 64.)

to be passed directly forward to the comprehension areas. There are thus at least two paths from the visual cortex to the more forward comprehension areas.

Research using magnetic resonance imaging (MRI) has proved very useful since this technique can detect and measure some signals that are inaccessible to PET scans.

The method depends on the fact that many atoms behave as little compass needles in the presence of a magnetic field. By skillfully manipulating the magnetic field, scientists can align the atoms. Applying radio wave pulses to the sample under these conditions perturbs the atoms in a precise manner. As a result they emit detectable radio signals unique to the number and state of the particular atoms in the sample.... Specifically, it [MRI] can detect an increase in oxygen that occurs in an area of heightened neuronal activity. (Raichle 1994, 63)

Thus, the parts of the brain that are active in certain tasks can be studied.

An important result (Raichle 1994) is that learning can have a restructuring effect on the brain, in the form of simplification in neural activity. Subjects were asked to generate verbs appropriate for use with nouns displayed on a computer screen. For example, they might see the noun *dog*, for which the verbs *bark* and *run* would be possible responses. At first, the production of the verb following the noun prompt was accompanied by characteristic patterns of neural activity. After subjects performed this association task for as short a time as 15 minutes, their neural activity revealed by the MRI scans became restructured and simpler: in fact, it was the same as when they read single words without an association task.

Event-Related Potentials

Yet another means of measuring brain activity is related to electroencephalograms (EEGs). When a subject's brain waves are being monitored during an EEG, computer technology makes it possible to isolate differences in brain activity that happen between tasks that differ in a controlled feature over very short periods of time (milliseconds); that is, it enables researchers to measure the unique voltage changes, or responses, associated with a particular psychological event. These changes in potential associated with experimental tasks are referred to as *event-related potentials* (ERPs).

What is important about ERPs from the linguist's perspective is that characteristic differences in response to linguistic stimuli correspond to the distinctions that linguists make in analyzing language. We discuss two examples here, from the realms of semantics and syntax (Neville et al. 1991).

Semantic anomaly effects are one of the most robustly reduplicated results in language-based ERP research (Kutas and Hillyard 1983, Neville et al. 1991). A typical sentence pair is the following:

(1)
a.   The scientist criticized Max's *proof* of the theorem.
b.   *The scientist criticized Max's *event* of the theorem.

Subjects encountering a semantically anomalous sentence such as (1b) display a characteristic brain pattern, a strikingly negative voltage dip that generally peaks 400 milliseconds after the anomalous word is encountered (the *negative-400 milliseconds* or *N400* response). This dip does not occur when semantically well formed sentences such as (1a) are encountered. This characteristic pattern is displayed in figure 12.9.

The ERPs to syntactic anomalies have also been studied. Just like semantic anomalies, syntactic violations trigger what are now predictable ERP patterns. What is noteworthy is that different types of syntactic violations trigger different ERPs, which in turn all differ from the N400 potentials that appear with semantically anomalous sentences like (1b). Two of these are the *sustained positive shift* or *SPS*, a significant positive increase in potential after a certain class of violations is noted by the subject, and the *left anterior negative* (shift) or *LAN*, a downward movement of the potential in the area of the left front side of the brain. (The detectors surround the scalp, and the left side of the brain is generally the side where most language-related activities take place.) These ERPs are found in subjects presented with the following three syntactic violations.

In the first case the word order of the sentence violates the phrase structure rules of English (see chapter 5). Sentence (2) is typical of the kind of sentence used in this experiment:

(2)
*The scientist admired Max's *of proof* the theorem.

Subjects exposed to this sentence display three ERPs: a drop in potential at 125 milliseconds (N125); a LAN, which occurs between 300 and 500 milliseconds (LAN 300–500); and an SPS, which occurs between 500 and 700 milliseconds (SPS 500–800).

Another type of syntactic violation involves the illicit extraction of *wh-*phrases from certain environments. In chapter 5 we noted that certain

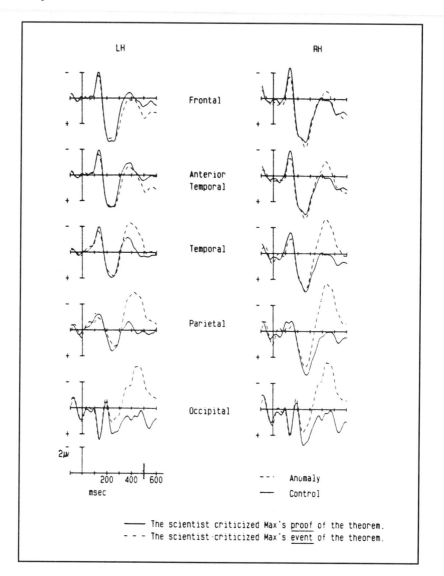

Figure 12.9
Graph showing drop in negative potential at 400 milliseconds for semantic anomalies. Measurements are given at positions along the left and right hemispheres. (From Neville et al. 1991.)

Table 12.2
ERPs elicited by different types of deviant sentences

	N	SPS	LAN
Semantic anomaly	400		
Phrase structure violation	125	500–700	300–500
Specificity Condition violation	125		300–500
Subjacency Condition violation		500–700	

conditions block the extraction of *wh*-phrases (i.e., the transformational rule that moves a *wh*-expression to the beginning of a sentence to form a *wh*-question); when these conditions are violated, the resulting sentence is ill formed. Two different types of violations are displayed in (3):

(3)
a. *What did the scientist criticize Max's proof of ____?
b. *What was a proof of ____ criticized by the scientist?

The condition that blocks extraction of *what* in (3a) is the Specificity Condition, which prohibits extraction of a *wh*-phrase from a specific or definite NP; the condition that blocks extraction in (3b) is the Subjacency Condition, which has as a consequence that extraction from subjects is more difficult than extraction from objects. (In the unacceptable (3b) *what* is extracted from the subject *a proof of what*; compare extraction from the object *a picture of what* in *What did the newspaper print a picture of ____?*, which is acceptable to most speakers of English.)

Subjects exposed to sentences such as (3a), the Specificity Condition violation, displayed the ERPs N125 and LAN 300–500. When exposed to sentences such as (3b), the Subjacency Condition violation, they displayed only the SPS reaction. A summary of these ERP patterns is given in table 12.2.

As research continues, the understanding of ERPs is becoming more refined. For example, Hagoort, Brown, and Groothusen (1993) reported that subjects exposed to sentences like (4) displayed SPSs:

(4)
*The spoilt child *are* throwing the toy on the ground.

Recent work (Hagoort, Brown, and Osterhout 2000) has demonstrated that this SPS is independent of semantic/pragmatic factors. This is shown by the fact that the same SPS evoked by sentence (4) is also evoked by (5b), but not by (5a):

(5)

a. *The boiled watering-can *smokes* the telephone in the cat.

b. *The boiled watering-can *smoke* the telephone in the cat.

Garrett (2000, 43) summarizes the current results of ERP research as follows:

• Semantic integration of lexical elements into their context is distinct from syntactic integration of lexical elements into their structural frame.

• More than a single syntactic signature is demonstrable and they span a substantial time range—approximately 150 ms. to 700+ ms.

• Earlier responses to syntax are inflexible and are localized to a substantial degree in classic language processing areas associated with syntactic processing (viz., based both on language impairment data and brain imaging data).

• Later responses to syntax show greater sensitivity to interpretive factors than do the early responses and are much more broadly distributed.

• Though the dissociation of the processing types cannot tell us how syntactic processing fits into the overall language processor, it does rather convincingly indicate that the identification of such a structural type is not an artifact of linguistic analysis.

Investigations into ERPs are well underway, and experiments are leading to increasingly significant results. ERP studies, then, provide one of the most promising types of instrumental evidence that bears on linguistic theories.

Japanese Orthography and Graphic Aphasia

The Japanese language is primarily written with two types of symbols (ignoring romaji, the Latin-alphabet-based script): *kanji* and *kana*. The kanji writing uses borrowed Chinese characters (about 3,000 of them), which are associated arbitrarily with their sound. In other words, the logographic writing characteristic of Chinese is carried over into Japanese (see the appendix). The kana script is a phonetic script (based on the syllable) for which there is a regular sound/symbol correlation. For examples of both scripts, see figure 12.10. Japanese writing consists of a mixture of these two writing systems, although the language could be written entirely in kana since the sound associated with any kanji character can be represented in writing with the kana syllables. These two different writing systems permit two different types of graphic aphasia to appear. If damage occurs to Broca's area, the patient loses the ability to

Kanji	Kana
一月	いちがつ
二月	にがつ
三月	さんがつ
四月	しがつ
五月	ごがつ
六月	ろくがつ
七月	しちがつ
八月	はちがつ
九月	くがつ
十月	じゅうがつ
十一月	じゅういちがつ
十二月	じゅうにがつ

Figure 12.10
The kanji characters of Japanese (borrowed from Chinese) on the left can all be
written in the kana script on the right. Represented are the names of the months.

process the kana (phonetic) script, although the ability to read and write
kanji may remain intact. If part of Wernicke's area is injured, the ability
to write kanji script may be preserved, but the expressions are meaningless. Some experimental data concerning these two different kinds of
aphasia are shown in table 12.3.

Conclusion

Progress continues to be made with respect to understanding how language is stored and processed by the brain. PET scans and MRI have
greatly increased our ability to look inside the working brain, but as
sophisticated as these techniques are, they merely measure blood flow.
ERP research offers a new and exciting approach to the study of the

Table 12.3
Two types of agraphia in Japanese. Japanese aphasics display some characteristics rarely found in Western patients because of the unique writing system used in Japan. There are two separate forms of such writing. One is kana, which is syllabic. The other is kanji, which is ideographic. Kana words are articulated syllable by syllable and are not easily identified at a glance, whereas each kanji character simultaneously represents both a sound and a meaning. A patient with Broca's aphasia, studied by Tsuneo Imura and his colleagues at the Nihon University College of Medicine, was able to write a dictated word correctly in kanji but not in kana (top left). When the patient was asked to write the word *ink*, even though there is no kanji character for the word, his first effort was the kanji character "sumi," which means "india ink." When required to write in kana, the symbols he produced were correct but the word was wrong. Another patient who had Wernicke's aphasia wrote kanji quickly and without hesitation. He was completely unaware that he was producing meaningless ideograms, as are patients who exhibit paraphasias in speech. Only two of the characters had meaning (top right). (From N. Geschwind, "Language and the Brain." Copyright © 1972 by Scientific American, Inc. All rights reserved.)

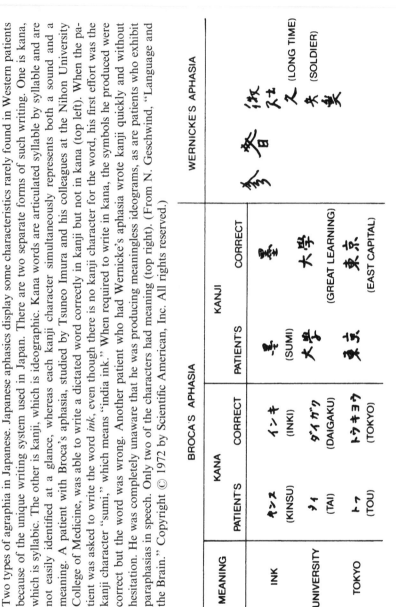

	BROCA'S APHASIA				WERNICKE'S APHASIA
	KANA		KANJI		
MEANING	PATIENT'S	CORRECT	PATIENT'S	CORRECT	
INK	キンス (KINSU)	インキ (INKI)	髪 (SUMI)	髪	
UNIVERSITY	ダイ (TAI)	ダイガク (DAIGAKU)	大学	大学 (GREAT LEARNING)	
TOKYO	トウ (TOU)	トウキヨウ (TOKYO)	東京	東京 (EAST CAPITAL)	

(LONG TIME) (SOLDIER)

electrical activity of the brain, data from which can be linked to specific structural and meaning properties of human language. One of the guiding principles for future research will be to expand our knowledge of *how* the brain takes, stores, and processes information (knowledge). It may well be that questions about the storing and processing of human language will provide the most accessible features for studying the structure and functioning of the human mind.

Study Questions

1. Many technical terms appeared in this chapter. Compose a definition for each of the following:

a. aphasia	g. Wernicke's area
b. neurolinguistics	h. dichotic listening
c. corpus callosum	i. ipsilateral
d. temporal lobe	j. arcuate fasciculus
e. neuron	k. anomia
f. Broca's area	l. cortex

2. In what cortical regions are speech and language thought to be localized?

3. What is the corpus callosum, and how is it relevant to speech and language function?

4. Compare and contrast research techniques that have provided neurolinguists with information about where speech and language are located in the brain.

5. Suppose you were holding a pencil in your left hand and you wished to describe it. Discuss the chain of events occurring in the nervous system that would enable you to describe the pencil.

6. Discuss the complementary specialization of the cerebral hemispheres.

7. Why is it thought that speech and language function may not be cognitively unique?

8. Discuss how the ability to read and write kanji symbols may be preserved, whereas the ability to read the kana script is lost in some Japanese stroke victims.

9. "Lip movement" does occur when some people read. Discuss how this may occur using what you have learned in this chapter.

Further Reading

General
For general discussions of *brain asymmetry* and *language localization*, see Witelson and Pallie 1973; Wada, Clarke, and Hamm 1975; Springer and Deutsch 1985; and Kean 1988.

Special Topics
Introductory treatments of *PET* (positron emission tomography) and *MRI* (magnetic resonance imaging) can be found in Montgomery 1989 and Raichle 1994. Among the more recent publications in the area of *ERPs* (event-related potentials) are Friederici, Hahne, and Mecklinger 1996; Coulsen, King, and Kutas 1998; Friederici 1998; Hagoort et al., in press; and Hahne and Friederici, in press.

Journals
Brain, Brain and Language, Cortex, Journal of Cognitive Neuroscience, Language and Cognitive Processes

Bibliography

Bever, T. 1975. Cerebral asymmetries in humans due to differentiation of two incompatible processes: Holistic and analytic. In D. Aaronson and R. Rieber, eds., *Developmental psycholinguistics and communication disorders*. New York Academy of Sciences, vol. 263, p. 251.

Brookshire, R. 1972. Visual and auditory sequencing by aphasic subjects. *Journal of Communication Disorders* 5, 259–269.

Coulsen, S., M. King, and M. Kutas. 1998. Expect the unexpected: Event related response to morphosyntactic violations. *Language and Cognitive Processes* 13, 21–58.

Dennis, M., and H. Whitaker. 1976. Hemispheric equipotentiality and language acquisition. In *Language development and neurological theory*. Brock University Conference, May 1975. New York: Academic Press.

DeRenzi, E., A. Pieczuro, and L. Vignolo. 1966. Oral apraxia and aphasia. *Cortex* 2, 50–83.

DeRenzi, E., G. Scotti, and H. Spinnler. 1969. Perceptual and associative disorders and visual recognition. *Neurology* 19, 634–642.

Eccles, J. 1972. *The understanding of the brain*. New York: McGraw-Hill.

Faglioni, P., H. Spinnler, and L. Vignolo. 1969. Contrasting behavior of right and left hemisphere-damaged patients on a discriminative and a semantic task of auditory recognition. *Cortex* 5, 366–389.

Friederici, A. 1998. Diagnosis and reanalysis. In J. D. Fodor and F. Ferreira, eds., *Reanalysis in sentence processing*. Dordrecht: Kluwer.

Friederici, A., A. Hahne, and A. Mecklinger. 1996. Temporal structure of syntactic parsing: Early and late event related potential effects. *Journal of Experimental Psychology: Learning, Memory, and Cognition* 22, 1219–1248.

Garrett, M. 2000. Remarks on the architecture of language processing systems. In Y. Grodzinsky, ed., *Language and the brain*. San Diego, Calif.: Academic Press.

Gazzaniga, M., J. Bogen, and R. Sperry. 1963. Laterality effects in somesthesis following cerebral commissurotomy in man. *Neuropsychologia* 1, 209–215.

Gazzaniga, M., and R. Sperry. 1967. Language after section of the cerebral commissures. *Brain* 90, 131–148.

Geschwind, N. 1972. Language and the brain. *Scientific American* 226.4, 76–83.

Geschwind, N., and W. Levitsky. 1968. Human brain: Left-right asymmetries in temporal speech region. *Science* 161, 186–187.

Hagoort, P., C. Brown, and J. Groothusen. 1993. The syntactic positive shift as an ERP-measure of syntactic processing. *Language and Cognitive Processes* 8, 439–483.

Hagoort, P., C. Brown, and L. Osterhout. 2000. The neurocognition of syntactic processing. In C. Brown and P. Hagoort, eds., *The neurocognition of language*. Oxford: Oxford University Press.

Hahne, A., and A. Friederici. In press. Language comprehension: The brain dissociates early automatic and late controlled processes. *Journal of Cognitive Neuroscience*.

Kean, M.-L. 1988. Brain structures and linguistic capacity. In F. Newmeyer, ed., *Linguistics: The Cambridge survey*, vol. 2. Cambridge; Cambridge University Press.

Kertesz, A., S. Blank, M. Polk, and J. Howell. 1986. Cerebral asymmetries on magnetic resonance imaging. *Cortex* 22, 117–127.

Kimura, D. 1961. Cerebral dominance and the perception of verbal stimuli. *Canadian Journal of Psychology* 15, 166–177.

Kimura, D. 1966. Dual functional asymmetry of the brain in visual perception. *Neuropsychologia* 4, 275–285.

Kimura, D. 1973. The asymmetry of the human brain. *Scientific American* 228.3, 70–80.

Kutas, M., and S. A. Hillyard. 1983. Event-related brain potentials to grammatical errors and semantic anomalies. *Memory and Cognition* 11, 539–550.

Lackner, J., and H. Teuber. 1973. Alterations in auditory fusion thresholds after cerebral injury in man. *Neuropsychologia* 11, 409–415.

Levy, R. 1976. The question of electrophysiological asymmetries preceding speech. In H. Whitaker and H. Whitaker, eds., *Studies in neurolinguistics and psycholinguistics*. New York: Academic Press.

McAdam, D., and L. H. Whitaker. 1971a. Language production: Electroencephalographic localization in the normal human brain. *Science* 172, 499–502.

McAdam, D., and L. H. Whitaker. 1971b. Electrocortical localization of language production. *Science* 174, 1359–1360.

Mohr, J. 1976. Broca's area and Broca's aphasia. In H. Whitaker and H. Whitaker, eds., *Studies in neurolinguistics and psycholinguistics*. New York: Academic Press.

Montgomery, G. 1989. The mind in motion. *Discover* 10.3, 58–68.

Neville, H., J. Nocil, A. Barss, K. Forster, and M. Garrett. 1991. Syntactically based sentence processing classes: Evidence from event-related potentials. *Journal of Cognitive Neurosciences* 3.2, 151–165.

Ojemann, G., and A. Ward, Jr. 1971. Speech representation in ventrolateral thalamus. *Brain* 94, 669–680.

Penfield, W., and L. Roberts. 1959. *Speech and brain mechanisms*. Princeton, N.J.: Princeton University Press.

Petersen, S., et al. 1988. Positron emission tomographic studies of the cortical anatomy of single word processing. *Nature* 331, 585–589.

Raichle, M. 1994. Visualizing the mind. *Scientific American* 270.4, 58–65.

Sholl, D. 1956. *The organization of the cerebral cortex*. New York: Wiley.

Springer, S. P., and G. Deutsch. 1985. *Left brain, right brain*. Rev. ed. San Francisco: W. H. Freeman.

Swisher, L., and I. Hirsh. 1972. Brain damage and the ordering of two temporally successive stimuli. *Neuropsychologia* 10, 137–152.

Wada, J. 1949. A new method for the determination of the side of cerebral speech dominance: A preliminary report on the intracarotid injections of sodium amytal in man. *Medical Biology* (Tokyo) 14, 221–222.

Wada, J., R. Clarke, and A. Hamm. 1975. Cerebral hemispheric asymmetry in humans. *Archives of Neurology* 32, 239–246.

Witelson, S., and W. Pallie. 1973. Left hemispheric specialization for language in the newborn: Neuroanatomical evidence of asymmetry. *Brain* 96, 641–646.

Appendix

The Written Representation of Language

Systematic writing developed in the Near East about 6,000 years ago and was originally *pictographic* or *ideographic*. Pictographs represent objects and are thus *iconic*, whereas ideographs represent ideas or sets of related ideas and are thus *symbolic*. For example, a circle ○ used as an ideograph might represent the sun, summer, light, heat, and so forth. What is crucial is that this type of writing system did not represent either words or the sounds making up the words. When the individual symbols come to be associated with certain words in a standardized fashion, the writing system is said to be *logographic*. A partially logographic writing system is used today in China. For the most part the Chinese characters represent a linking of a meaning concept and a phonetic syllable (see figure A1). Throughout China the phonetic representation of a particular character may vary, but the meaning will remain relatively invariant. This lack of a constant sound-meaning association is advantageous in China because there exist so many different dialects of spoken Chinese. Mandarin, a form of Chinese spoken in the north, and Cantonese, a form spoken in the south, are mutually unintelligible. But since Mandarin speakers associate their Mandarin pronunciations with the individual characters and Cantonese speakers associate their Cantonese pronunciations with these same characters, and since both groups assign essentially the same meanings to the characters, Mandarin and Cantonese speakers can communicate via their common writing system (which functions as a lingua franca). European languages share some logographic symbols, the Arabic numerals being perhaps the most common example. For the numbers 3, 4, 5, for example, French speakers say *trois, quatre, cinq*, German speakers *drei, vier, fünf*, and English speakers *three, four, five*.

An extension of the logographic system occurs when a symbol that represents a word comes to be associated with the sound (pronunciation)

Figure A1
Chinese characters, an example of logographic writing. These "compounds" have the form of a puzzle and are to be interpreted according to the following instruction: What is a word that sounds like *kung* "work" and is associated with the key word? Thus, *hung* "big belly" is a word that sounds like *kung* and can be associated with a human being. These Chinese compounds show that the Chinese writing system is not purely logographic. (From H. Pedersen, *The Discovery of Language*, 1962. Reprinted by permission of Harvard University Press.)

of that word and is used to represent other words that contain the same sound. We can illustrate this type of writing with an example from English. Noting that the symbol *4* is pronounced /fɔɹ/, we can use this symbol to represent the preposition *for* as in the expression *4 me* "for me." It can even be used to form part of a longer word, as in *4-ground* "foreground." This type of writing is found in Egyptian hieroglyphics and is still used today in the type of children's puzzle called the *rebus*.

As soon as symbols became associated with sounds, new possibilities for representing language became available. A common writing system, one that many languages still use, is *syllabic writing*. The earliest writing of this type was done in *cuneiform* (from Latin *cuneus* "wedge"). The name reflects the fact that a wedge-shaped stylus was used to make marks on soft clay tablets that were dried or even baked in kilns. The cuneiform symbols (see figure A2) were derived from pictographs and ultimately came to represent combinations of sounds and in some cases single sounds. The Sumerians first developed this writing system more than 5,000 years ago, and it soon spread to other people such as the Babylonians and Akkadians, who used these symbols to write their own languages. Some early writing systems of Semitic (the language family that includes Arabic and Hebrew) were basically syllabic, but they did not represent the vowels (sch sntncs cn stll b ndrstd).

Egyptian hieroglyphics are also basically syllabic even though they appear to be ideographic or even pictographic. A Frenchman, Jean-François Champollion, is credited with the earliest comprehensive decipherment of these Egyptian symbols. Using the Rosetta stone, on which a bilingual inscription in Greek and two forms of Egyptian writing, hieroglyphic and demotic, were found, Champollion discovered that the hieroglyphics represented sounds (see figure A3). *Hieroglyphics* are a very ornate writing system that eventually became limited to use in writing religious inscriptions on monuments. For common religious writing, a script called *hieratic* was developed, a simplified form of the original hieroglyphics. The hieratic script was better suited for writing quickly with pen on papyrus. The hieratic script remained in general use for religious writing, and from it an even simpler form, *demotic*, was developed for everyday use. Examples of the three writing systems are displayed in figure A4.

Another type of syllabic writing system uses a different symbol for each consonant + vowel combination. Such a system was invented by Sequoia in the nineteenth century for use in writing his native Cherokee lan-

1.

𒀭𒈾𒊹𒆠𒂊𒄀𒍝𒑖 𒐈𒍝𒈾𒆠𒅎𒈾𒆠 𒂊𒑖𒐊𒂊𒑕 𒐈𒍝𒈾𒆠𒅎𒈾𒆠 𒐈𒍝𒈾 𒆠𒅎𒈾𒆠𒈾𒂍𒈾𒐋 𒐈𒍝𒈾𒆠𒅎𒈾𒆠 𒀭𒂍𒆠𒀭𒂍𒈾𒐋 𒃶𒈾𒍝𒀀𒈾𒈾𒂖𒈾𒂍𒆠𒈾𒑖𒋾𒀭𒈾𒑖𒂍𒆠𒐋𒂍𒈾𒐋𒂍𒆠𒑖𒈾𒐋𒐋𒀀𒐋𒈾𒂊𒂊𒐋𒈾𒐋𒈾𒐈𒀭𒂍𒈾𒀭𒍝

2.

𒐈𒍝𒆠𒈾𒂊𒍝𒈾𒑖 𒐈𒍝𒈾𒆠𒅎𒈾𒆠𒑖𒂊𒑖𒐊𒂊𒑕𒑖𒐈𒍝𒈾𒆠𒅎𒈾𒆠𒑖𒐈𒍝𒈾𒆠𒅎𒈾𒆠𒈾𒂍𒈾𒐋𒀭𒈾𒊹𒆠𒂊𒂍𒀭𒍝𒑖𒐈𒍝𒈾𒆠𒅎𒈾𒆠𒂍𒆠𒈾𒑖𒃶𒀭𒃶𒑖𒂍𒐈𒈾𒐋𒂍𒑖𒍝𒑖𒈾𒆠𒑖

In transcription the inscriptions read thus (I add an interlinear translation):

1.

Dārayavahuš	xšayaþiya	vazarka	xšayaþiya	xšayaþiyānām
Darius	king	great,	king	of kings,
xšayaþiya	dahyunām	Vištāspahya	puþʾa	Haxāmanišiya
king	of countries,	Hystaspes's	son,	the Achæmenid,
hya	imam	tačaram	akunauš.	
who	this	palace	made.	

2.

Xšayāršā	xšayaþiya	vazarka	xšayaþiya	xšayaþiyānām
Xerxes	king	great,	king	of kings,
Dārayavahauš	xšayaþiyahyā	puþʾa	Haxāmanišiya [1]	
Darius's	the king's	son,	the Achæmenid.	

Figure A2
Cuneiform, one of the earliest writing systems. The above transcription, dated from about 2400 B.P., is Old Persian, a language distantly related to English. What punctuation can you see in this example of cuneiform writing? (From H. Pedersen, *The Discovery of Language*, 1962. Reprinted by permission of Harvard University Press.)

Cartouche of Ptolmess and its analysis

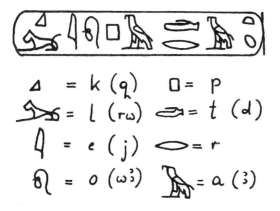

$\triangle$ Feminine ending

O Determinative after feminine name

Cartouche of Cleopatra and its analysis

Figure A3
Examples of Egyptian hieroglyphic writing with accompanying sound-symbol correspondences. What does the hieroglyph for *l* look like that would help you remember this symbol? (From J. Ober, *Writing: Man's Great Invention*, 1965. Courtesy of the Peabody Institute of the Johns Hopkins University.)

Figure A4
Examples of the three kinds of script used in ancient Egypt: hieroglyphic (top), hieratic (center), and demotic (bottom). Note the increasing abstractness that accompanies the evolution of Egyptian writing. (From J. Ober, *Writing: Man's Great Invention*, 1965. Courtesy of the Peabody Institute of the Johns Hopkins University.)

guage (see figure A5). Yet another variant of syllabic writing uses a single symbol for each consonant and a different diacritic (a mark added to the symbol) to indicate which vowel occurs with the consonant (see figure A5). An example of this type of syllabic writing is the *Devanagari* script that was used to write ancient Sanskrit and is still used in writing modern Indian languages. The Devanagari syllabary is generally believed to have descended from an early Semitic writing system.

The oldest writing system in the New World is that of the Mayans (see figure A6). This writing system, which dates from at least 700 B.C., has only recently been satisfactorily deciphered (Stuart and Houston 1989). It shares a similarity with Japanese writing in that it has both a logographic form (Japanese kanji) and a syllabic form (Japanese kana). There is no evidence, however, that the creation of this writing system was not indigenous to what is now Mexico and Central America.

The ancient Greeks adopted and revised the writing system of the Phoenicians, Semitic people who were sea-traders in the Mediterranean.

Figure A5
Two examples of syllabic writing systems. The Cherokee syllabary (top) uses a different symbol for each vowel + consonant combination. The Devanagari system (bottom) has a single symbol for each consonant but adds diacritics (extra marks) to indicate the various vowels following the consonant. (Cherokee syllabary from Sloat, Taylor, and Hoard 1978. Devanagari syllabary from H. Pedersen, *The Discovery of Language*, 1962. Reprinted by permission of Harvard University Press.)

a	e	i	o	u	ʌ
ga	ge	gi	go	gu	gʌ
ha	he	hi	ho	hu	hʌ
la	le	li	lo	lu	lʌ
ma	me	mi	mo	mu	
na	ne	ni	no	nu	nʌ
kwa	kwe	kwi	kwo	kwu	kwʌ
sa	se	si	so	su	sʌ
da	de	di	do	du	dʌ
dla	tle	tli	tlo	tlu	tlʌ
tsa	tse	tsi	tso	tsu	tsʌ
wa	we	wi	wo	wu	wʌ
ya	ye	yi	yo	yu	yʌ
ka	hna	nah	s	ta	ti
tla	te				

SPECIMEN OF DEVANĀGARĪ

समादिशत्पिता पुवं लिख लेखं ममाज्ञया

sa mā di śa tpi tā pu tram̐ li kha lē kham ma mā jña yā

नतेनलिखितोलेखः पितुराज्ञानखण्डिता

na tē na li khi tō lē khaḥ pi tu rā jñā na kha ndi tā

Figure A6

Graphic variation enabled Maya scribes to write each word in several ways. Shown here are three variants of the verb *ts'apah* "was set upright." Each example includes signs for three syllables: *ts'a*, *pa*, and *ha*. In the first (left) the signs are in conventional order. In the second (middle) the *pa* sign has been inserted into the *ts'a* sign, which is vertical. In the third variant (right) the scribe has made use of a "full-figure" glyph for *pa*: a seated man with a bulbous nose who cradles a *ts'a* sign. (From D. Stuart and S. Houston, "Maya Writing." Copyright © 1989 by Scientific American, Inc. All rights reserved.)

This writing system represented vowels and consonants as separate symbols. Such writing systems are called *alphabetic* (a name formed by combining the first two letters of the Greek alphabet: *alpha* and *beta*).

Thus, we can trace the development of writing systems from ideographic to alphabetic, each step representing an increased economy in the inventory of symbols needed. Whereas logographic writing requires thousands of different symbols, alphabetic writing requires from as few as 13 (for Hawaiian) to at most several dozen.

The Greek alphabet is the ultimate source for all the alphabets used today to write modern European languages, including English. There is still controversy over what the alphabetic symbols should represent, however. Should English be written with symbols that are phonetic? In this case the word *democrat* /démǝkɹæt/ would have different vowels from the word *democracy* /dǝmákɹǝsi/, a word to which it is closely related. Likewise, insisting that English be written with purely phonetic symbols would require that the plural morpheme be written as either *s*, *z*, or *ɨz*, depending on the nature of the final phoneme of the noun to which the plural morpheme is attached. Another type of writing system, the *morphophonemic* system, in which all phonological detail that can be predicted by general rules is not symbolized, would require the plural morpheme to be written as a single shape. A discussion of the relative merits of these different writing systems is beyond the scope of this text (but can be found in Reed 1970).

We conclude this appendix with the observation that writing systems do not seem to be able to halt language change. On the contrary, language change has been one of the historical causes for changes that occur in writing systems. Even though spellings such as *thru* for *through* are becoming more common, it cannot be foreseen whether the current writing system of American English will be revised in the near future. Such revisions are as much a political issue as a practical one. Language change is inexorable because of the nature of language itself. Language is extremely complicated, speakers have enormous flexibility in its use, and children must recreate the whole adult grammar when they acquire a language. We should be amazed that language stays as stable as it does and that writing systems stay in use as long as they do.

Bibliography

Ober, J. 1965. *Writing: Man's great invention.* Baltimore, Md.: The Peabody Institute.

Pedersen, H. 1962. *The discovery of language.* Bloomington: Indiana University Press.

Reed, D. 1970. A theory of language, speech, and writing. In M. Lester, ed., *Readings in applied transformational grammar.* New York: Holt, Rinehart and Winston.

Sloat, C., S. Taylor, and J. Hoard. 1978. *Introduction to phonology.* Englewood Cliffs, N.J.: Prentice-Hall.

Stuart, D., and S. Houston. 1989. Maya writing. *Scientific American* 261.2, 82–89.

Glossary

acoustic phonetics The study of the physical properties of the speech sound waves generated by the larynx and the vocal tract.

acronym formation A process for creating new words from existing words, by taking the first letter (or letters) of a sequence of words to spell a new word (e.g., *disk operating system = DOS*). An acronym differs from an alphabetic abbreviation in that it is pronounced as a word, not as a sequence of letters (*DOS* is pronounced "doss").

affix A bound morpheme that is attached to a stem and modifies its meaning in some way or indicates, for example, person, number, gender, tense. Prefixes and suffixes are two common kinds of affixes.

affricate 1. A single consonant sound that consists of a stop followed by a secondary fricative release at the same point of articulation. The English words *chip* and *jump* begin with affricates. 2. A feature assigned to single phonemes that consist of a stop followed by a secondary fricative release.

algorithm (See *effective procedure*.)

allophone A positional or free variant of a phoneme.

alphabetic abbreviation A process for creating new words from existing words, by taking the first letter of a sequence of words, where each letter receives its alphabetic pronunciation (e.g., *personal computer = PC*).

alternation The existence of two or more variant pronunciations for a given morpheme, each of which occurs under different conditions.

alveolar Formed by means of a constriction or blockage between the tongue tip or blade and the ridge just behind the upper teeth. The English words *too, see, now*, and *lie* begin with alveolar consonants.

alveolar ridge The bony projection located just behind the upper teeth.

alveopalatal Formed by means of a constriction or blockage between the tongue tip or blade and the area just behind the alveolar ridge. The English words *ship* and *chip* begin with alveopalatal consonants.

ambiguity   The property of having more than one linguistic meaning.

American Sign Language (ASL)   A system of manually produced visual signals, analogous to words, used by the deaf in the United States. ASL is not the same as signed English; that is, it is not a representation of the letters, sounds, words, or syntax of English but is rather a completely separate language. The signs of ASL have been analyzed into about 55 constituents, some involving the configuration of the hand(s), some the position of the hand(s) with respect to the rest of the body, and some the action or movement of the hand(s).

anaphora   The referential linking found between pairs of constituents in sentences such as *All people* think *they have talent.*

Anglo-Saxon   Another name for *Old English.*

anterior   A feature assigned to phonemes that are formed at the alveolar ridge or anywhere in front of it.

anticipatory assimilation   An assimilation process in which one sound affects a following sound. Antonym: *regressive assimilation.* Synonym: *perseverative coarticulation.*

anticipatory coarticulation   A coarticulation effect in which some motion of the vocal tract needed for one sound begins during an earlier sound. Antonym: *perseverative coarticulation.*

apex   In phonetics, refers to the tip of the tongue.

aphasia   A cover term for various kinds of communicative impairment that occur as a result of brain damage.

aphasic   Suffering from a brain disease or injury that impairs communicative ability.

apical   Formed with the tip of the tongue.

argot   A variety of jargon, especially the jargon used by criminals.

article   A member of the closed-class set of elements. English has both definite (*the*) and indefinite (*a, an*) articles. Syntactically, articles combine with nouns to form noun phrases (e.g., *the dog*).

articulation   The formation of a speech sound by positioning some part of the vocal tract.

articulatory phonetics   The study of how speech sounds are produced by the speech organs, in particular the vocal tract.

aspiration   The puff of air that sometimes follows the pronunciation of a stop consonant. The *p* in English *pill* is aspirated.

assimilation   A process by which the phonetic features of one sound are transferred to a neighboring sound.

attributive use of a singular term   The use of a singular term to express a general proposition. Antonym: *referential use*.

back   1. Formed by placing the body of the tongue slightly behind the resting position. The English words *boot* and *boat* have back vowels. Antonym: *front*. 2. A feature assigned to vowel and consonant phonemes that are formed with the tongue body slightly in back of the resting position.

backformation   The process of creating new words by removing some part of a morphologically simple word that is incorrectly analyzed as a morpheme, especially an affix.

base   1. In syntax, the part of a grammar that contains only phrase structure rules, before any transformational rules apply. 2. In morphology, another name for *stem*. A free base morpheme is a morpheme to which other morphemes (e.g., affixes) optionally attach. A bound base morpheme requires another morpheme (e.g., *cran* requires *berry*, *apple*, etc.).

bilabial   Formed by means of a constriction between the two lips. The English words *pay*, *bay*, and *may* begin with bilabial consonants.

blade   The large part of the tongue just behind the tip.

blend(ing)   The process of creating a new word from existing words, typically by combining the beginning of one word with the end of another (e.g., *in̲f̲o̲r̲m̲a̲t̲i̲o̲n̲*, *commercial → infomercial*).

borrowing   The incorporation of words (or some other characteristic) from one language into another language.

bound morpheme   A morpheme that does not constitute an independent word, but must be combined with some other morpheme. All affixes and some stems are bound morphemes.

Broca's area   Part of the frontal lobe of the left cerebral hemisphere of the brain. Damage to this area results in a kind of aphasia characterized by lack of fluency in producing speech.

calque   An expression from one language that is translated literally into another language. The terms *firewater* and *iron horse* are calques from Native American languages into English.

chance overlap   Accidental similarities between languages that are not genetically related.

cleft sentence   A kind of English sentence that consists of *it*, some form of the verb *to be*, a noun phrase or prepositional phrase, *that*, and a clause that modifies the noun (e.g., *It was Mary that I saw*, *It was in the park that I saw Mary*).

clipping   A process of creating new words from existing words by shortening them (e.g., *professor → prof*).

closed class   A group of morphemes whose membership is small and that does not readily accept new members. Articles, conjunctions, and affixes are examples of closed classes. Synonym: *function word*. Antonym: *open class*.

coarticulation   The process by which some of the motions of the vocal tract needed for one sound take place during neighboring sounds.

coda   Within a syllable, the consonant or sequence of consonants that follows the nucleus.

code switching   A situation in which a speaker uses a mixture of different languages or different varieties of a single language in the same sentence or discourse.

coined word   A new word that is made up and added to the lexicon of a language.

communicative act   An act whereby a speaker succeeds in conveying a message by having his or her communicative intent recognized.

communicative intention   An intention that a speaker intends to be recognized and that is fulfilled when it is so recognized.

comparative linguistics   The subfield of linguistics that studies related languages in order to learn about their historical development.

comparative method   A collection of analytical techniques used by linguists to reconstruct the history of two or more related languages.

competence (linguistic)   Knowledge of language; the linguistic capacity of a fluent speaker of a language. Antonym: *performance*.

complement   In X-bar theory, a syntactic unit that is defined as the sister to the head of a phrase.

complementary distribution   A relation between two speech sounds such that each occurs in one or more positions where the other one never does. Two sounds that are phonetically similar and that are in complementary distribution are usually allophones of the same phoneme.

complex word   A word that can be broken down into two or more meaningful or recognizable parts.

compositionality   The property by which the meaning of a complex expression is determined by the meaning of its constituents plus their grammatical relations.

compound   A word that is formed by combining two or more words or stems.

concept   A way of categorizing things, events, etc., into sets.

conjunction   The coordination, or combining, of two or more phrases (e.g., [the boy who laughed] *and* [the girl who smiled]).

connectionism   The doctrine that connectionist models of cognitive capacities will prove correct. (See *connectionist model*.)

connectionist model   A model of cognitive capacity utilizing a network of simple units with weighted connections.

consonant   A speech sound produced with the vocal tract relatively constricted.

consonantal   A feature assigned to phonemes that are formed with a considerable degree of obstruction in the vocal tract.

constative   The category of illocutionary acts that produce something true or false: stating, asserting, reporting, etc.

constituent   A word or an intuitively natural grouping of words that behaves as a unit with respect to some grammatical rules.

constituent command (c-command)   A syntactic relationship defined as follows: A node A c-commands a node B if and only if the first branching node that dominates A also dominates B. (Proviso: A does not dominate B and vice versa.)

constituent structure   The way in which the words of a sentence group together into phrases of various types.

constriction   The narrowing or closing off of some part of the vocal tract to produce a speech sound.

content   What an expression (or a mental state) is about—its meaning, sense, reference.

content word   Synonym: *open-class word*. Antonym: *closed-class word*.

continuant   A feature assigned to phonemes that are formed without a complete blockage of the airflow in the oral cavity. Noncontinuants are stops.

contrast   A relation between two speech sounds such that replacing one by the other sometimes makes a difference in the meaning of a word. Two sounds that are in *contrast* are allophones of *different* phonemes.

control   A syntactic construction in which the object (or subject) of a verb is understood as the subject of another (complement) verb (e.g., *John persuaded Mary to leave*, where the object of *persuaded*—namely, *Mary*—is understood as the subject of *leave*).

conversation   Any set of connected utterances by more than one speaker that has the structure characterized by greetings, turn takings, and closings.

conversational implicature   The act of implicating something via the conversational maxims. (See *conversational maxims*.)

conversational maxims   Grice's principles of Quantity, Quality, Relevance, and Manner that govern cooperative talk-exchanges.

coronal   A feature assigned to phonemes that are formed by a constriction between the tongue blade and the teeth, the alveolar ridge, or the area just behind the alveolar ridge.

correspondence set   A regular pattern of relationship among similar sounds in a group of related languages; such patterns are arrived at by comparing sets of related words.

creole   A language that developed from a pidgin by expanding its vocabulary and acquiring a more complex grammatical structure. Unlike pidgins, creoles have native speakers.

critical period   The developmental period (between infancy and puberty) during which a child can acquire language with the fluency of a native speaker (e.g., without an accent).

decoding   The process of converting a signal in some communication system back into the original message. Antonym: *encoding*.

definite description   Expression of the form *the F* (e.g., *the dog*).

defooting   The loss of a metrical foot. In English a unary foot may become defooted only when adjacent to another foot in a word.

deictic   Expression used to refer in virtue of properties of its physical production. Subtypes: indexicals (e.g., *I*) and demonstratives (e.g., *this*).

demonstrative   Expression used to refer in virtue of an accompanying demonstration (e.g., *this* accompanied by an act of pointing).

denotation   Another name for *semantic reference*.

dental   1. Formed by means of a constriction between the tongue tip or blade and the upper teeth. 2. Can also be used to describe interdental sounds.

derivation   1. In morphology, the process by which affixes combine with words or stems to create new words or stems (as, for example, the *-able* suffix of English derives an adjective from a verb). Contrasts with *inflection*. 2. In syntax, the successive stages in the generation of a sentence that result from applying the rules of the grammar.

diachronic   Concerned with changes taking place over a period of time. Antonym: *synchronic*.

diachronic linguistics   Another name for *historical linguistics*.

dialect   A distinct form of a language (or other communication system) that differs from other forms of that language in specific linguistic features (pronunciation, vocabulary, and/or grammar), possibly associated with some regional, social, or ethnic group, but that is nevertheless mutually intelligible with them.

dichotic listening   A research technique in which two different stimuli are presented simultaneously (through earphones) to the left and right ears. This technique is used to investigate the roles of the two hemispheres of the brain.

digraph   A sequence of two letters used to spell a single sound. Two common digraphs in English are *sh* and *ng* for the final sounds of *hash* and *hang*.

diphthong   A vowel that consists of two parts, a louder vowel and either an onglide or an offglide, which together serve as the nucleus of a single syllable. The English words *buy*, *boy*, and *cow* end in diphthongs.

discontinuous dependency   The situation in which a single constituent is broken into two parts that are separated by material from outside that constituent.

discourse   Narrowly construed, any set of connected utterances by a single speaker.

distinctive   (See *contrast*.)

distinctive feature   A phonetic property that distinguishes phonemes from one another and that plays a crucial role in the statement of phonological rules. (See also *feature*.)

distributed   A feature assigned to phonemes that are formed with a relatively long area of contact or approximation between the tongue and the roof of the mouth.

domination   The relationship between a node and the material that branches down from it in a tree diagram.

effective procedure   A finite step-by-step procedure for doing something.

embedding   The occurrence of one sentence (or other grammatical construction) within another one.

encoding   The process of converting a message into a signal by means of which it can be communicated to other individuals. Antonym: *decoding*.

entailment   A relation between sentences S and S′ such that if S is true, then S′ must also be true, and if S′ is false, then S must also be false.

euphemism   A polite expression used as a substitute for taboo language or to refer to some topic regarded as delicate, such as death, sex, or certain body functions.

event-related potential (ERP)   A voltage value isolated by computer analysis of electroencephalogram (EEG; brain scan) patterns that can be associated with a particular psychological event.

extraposition   The process of separating a modifying clause from the noun it belongs with by moving the clause to the end of the sentence.

feature   Any of several articulatory characteristics into which speech sounds can be analyzed.

flap   A consonant sound formed by making a quick tap with the tip of the tongue against the roof of the mouth. In American English, the *t* in the word *better* is usually pronounced with a flap.

force   The type of illocutionary act performed in the utterance of an expression, as in *That had the force of a promise.*

formal language style   A variety of a language that is used in official contexts, for example, making a speech in a courtroom. Antonym: *informal language style.*

free morpheme   A morpheme that constitutes an independent word.

free variation   A relation between two speech sounds such that either one can occur in a certain position, and the substitution of one for the other never makes any difference in the meaning of a word. Two sounds that are in free variation are allophones of the same phoneme.

frequency effect   The finding that high-frequency words are recognized faster than low-frequency words.

fricative   A consonant sound in which the airflow is channeled through a narrow opening in the vocal tract, producing turbulence. The English words *fill* and *soup* begin with fricatives.

front   Formed by placing the body of the tongue slightly forward from the resting position. The English words *beet* and *bet* have front vowels. Antonym: *back.*

function word   Synonym: *closed-class word.* Antonym: *open-class word.*

garden path sentence   A sentence such as *The horse raced past the barn fell* that leads the parser down a "garden path" to a (momentarily) incorrect analysis.

general proposition   A proposition containing only properties or concepts. Antonym: *singular proposition.*

general term   An expression that applies to an indefinitely large group of things.

generate   In syntax, to specify the grammatical sentences of a language by applying a set of rules.

generification   The process by which a word for a brand name is extended in use to denote a class of items no matter who the manufacturer is (e.g., brand name *Band-Aid* extended to denote any adhesive strip used in minor first aid situations; *Vaseline* extended to denote any brand of petroleum jelly).

glide   A vowel-like sound that precedes or follows a true vowel. The English words *you, we,* and *red* begin with glides.

glottal   Formed by means of a constriction at the vocal cords. A glottal stop appears at the beginning of each of the two *oh*'s of the English exclamation *oh-oh!.*

glottis   The space between the two vocal cords.

grammatical relation   The way a constituent of a sentence functions within that sentence. Two common grammatical relations for noun phrase constituents are subject and object.

Great Vowel Shift   A set of regular sound changes affecting the long (tense) vowels of English that took place around the fifteenth century. These changes account for many of the discrepancies between the pronunciation of English words and their spelling, which was established before the Great Vowel Shift took place.

Grimm's Law   A set of regular sound changes that took place in Proto-Germanic, in which Indo-European voiceless stops became voiceless fricatives, voiced stops became voiceless stops, and voiced aspirated stops became simple voiced stops.

hard palate   Another name for *palate*.

head of a phrase   The node that belongs to the same category as the phrase. For example, a noun phrase is headed by a noun; a prepositional phrase is headed by a preposition.

high   1. Formed by placing the body of the tongue relatively close to the roof of the mouth (said of vowels). The English words *see* and *Sue* have high vowels. 2. A feature assigned to vowel and consonant phonemes that are formed with the body of the tongue near the roof of the mouth.

historical linguistics   The subfield of linguistics that studies how languages change over time.

holophrastic speech   The utterance of a single word that expresses a thought usually expressed by an entire sentence.

hypercorrection   Overcorrection; the attempted rectification of a supposed error by introducing something that was never part of the original form, using as a model some other pattern in the language.

iconic   A term used to characterize the relationship between an object and a representation of that object when the representation physically resembles the object in some way.

ideograph   A character in a writing system that represents some idea and is a picture of some object related to that idea.

idiolect   The variety of a language spoken by a single individual.

idiom   An expression whose meaning is noncompositional. (See *compositionality*.)

illocutionary act   1. Narrowly viewed, any utterance act that is also a communicative act. 2. Widely viewed, any utterance act that is either a communicative act or an institutional act.

implicature   The act of communicating one thing while saying another.

indexical   An expression used to refer in virtue of the relation of its physical production to the context of utterance (e.g., *I*).

indirect utterance   An utterance in which the speaker performs one illocutionary act by means of performing another (e.g., *requesting* the heat to be turned up by *stating* that it is cold in here).

Indo-European A large group of historically related languages that includes many of the languages of northern India and Iran and most of the languages of Europe.

Inferential Model A theory of communication in which speaker and hearer share a system of inferential strategies that lead from the speaker's utterance to the hearer's recognition of the speaker's communicative intention.

inflection The process by which affixes combine with words or stems to indicate such grammatical categories as tense or plurality (e.g., the *-ed* and *-s* suffixes of English). Contrasts with *derivation*.

informal language style A variety of a language that is used in casual conversations, typically with friends. Antonym: *formal language style*.

innate Determined by the genetic makeup of an organism, rather than acquired by experience. Antonym: *learned*.

Inner-City English An informal style of English typically (though not exclusively) used by African American residents of ghettos in large urban areas of the United States.

input system A module for analyzing sensory and perceptual information.

institutional act An act that consists in affecting the institutional status (social relations) of some person or thing.

interdental Formed by placing the tongue tip between the upper and lower teeth. For many English speakers, the words *thin* and *this* begin with interdental consonants.

International Phonetic Alphabet A standardized phonemic transcription system that is intended for transcribing any spoken human language.

jargon A set of special vocabulary items used by members of some profession or specialized social group.

labeled bracketing A linear representation of the information found in a tree diagram that uses nested brackets to show constituent groupings and subscript labels to show categories (e.g., [$_{NP}$] is a noun phrase constituent).

labial A manner of articulation (or distinctive feature) that characterizes speech sounds that involve bringing together or closing of the lips.

labialized Another name for *rounded*.

labiodental Formed by means of a constriction between the lower lip and the upper teeth. The English words *fee* and *vow* begin with labiodental consonants.

laminal Formed with the blade of the tongue.

Language Acquisition Device (See *Universal Grammar*.)

language universal Any property that is shared by most, if not all, human languages.

larynx   The voice box, that is, the structure of muscle and cartilage at the upper end of the windpipe that contains the vocal cords.

lateral   A feature assigned to phonemes that are formed with the tongue tip touching the roof of the mouth, but in which air passes along one or both sides of the tongue.

lax   1. Pronounced with relatively little muscular tension. Antonym: *tense*. 2. In describing English vowels, another name for *short*.

learned   Acquired by experience, rather than determined by genetic makeup. Antonym: *innate*.

lexical access   The process of contacting a word in the mental lexicon.

lexical ambiguity   The situation in which a word has two or more linguistic meanings. Contrasts with *structural ambiguity*.

lexical category   Another name for *part of speech*.

lexical decision task   The task of deciding as quickly as possible whether or not a string of letters is a word.

lexicon   A listing of all the words in a given language, each with its form, its meaning, and its part-of-speech classification.

lingua franca   Trade language; a language that is used by general agreement as the means of communication among speakers of different languages.

linguistic labor, division of   The idea that different members of the linguistic community have different competence, especially with respect to natural kind terms.

linguistic meaning   The meaning(s) that an expression has simply as a part of the language it belongs to.

liquid   A consonant sound in which the vocal tract is neither closed off nor constricted to a degree that produces friction. The English word *low* begins with a liquid.

literal utterance   An utterance in which the speaker means at least what the expression uttered means. Antonym: *nonliteral utterance*.

logical form   The representation of those aspects of a sentence that determine its logical relations.

logograph   A character in a writing system that represents a complete word. The Arabic numerals are logographs, and the Chinese writing system is heavily logographic.

long   1. In English, a term applied to vowels of stressed syllables that have a relatively greater duration, have offglides to a higher vowel position, and are pronounced with relatively great muscular tension. The vowels of *feed*, *made*, and *mode* are long. Antonym: *short*. 2. A feature assigned to phonemes that have a relatively greater duration than average.

low   1. Formed by placing the body of the tongue relatively far from the roof of the mouth (said of vowels). The English words *cat* and *cod* have low vowels. 2. A feature assigned to vowel and consonant phonemes that are formed with the body of the tongue far from the roof of the mouth and somewhat retracted.

magnetic resonance imaging (MRI)   A means of observing the internal properties of objects (typically the human body) by measuring the electrical activity associated with molecules stimulated by strong magnetic fields.

manner of articulation   The way in which a sound is formed, usually specifying the type of constriction in the mouth. Contrasts with *place of articulation*.

matrix sentence   A sentence that contains another sentence embedded within it.

Message Model   A theory of communication in which the sender sequentially encodes the information he or she wants to communicate into a signal that travels to a receiver, who then sequentially decodes it to recover the original message.

metaphorical extension   The process of describing objects, ideas, or events from one realm by using words from a different realm (usually one that is more familiar or concrete), on the basis of some perceived similarity.

metrical foot   A structural unit that organizes syllables. In English, the leftmost syllable is the "head" of the foot and carries the main stress.

mid   Formed with the body of the tongue neither close to nor far from the roof of the mouth (said of vowels). The English words *bet* and *code* have mid vowels.

minimal pair   Two words that have different meanings and differ in form only in having different phonemes in one corresponding position. The English words *sip* and *zip* are a minimal pair; they differ in meaning and have different phonemes in initial position.

module   A special-purpose psychological capacity.

mood   A sentential form associated with a specific communicative function (e.g., declarative, interrogative, imperative).

morpheme   The parts into which a complex word can be divided; in other words, any part of a word that cannot be broken down further into meaningful or recognizable parts.

morphology   The subfield of linguistics that studies the internal structure of words and the relationships among words.

morphophonemic transcription   A writing system in which all phonological detail that can be predicated by general rules is not symbolized.

mutual intelligibility   The situation that holds between two varieties of a language when speakers of either one are able to understand the other.

naming task   The task of pronouncing a string of letters as quickly as possible.

nasal   1. A consonant sound made by blocking the airflow in the mouth, but allowing it to pass through the nasal passages. The English word *man* begins and ends with nasals. 2. A feature assigned to vowel and consonant phonemes in which the velum is lowered, enabling the natural resonances of the nasal passages to be excited.

native speaker   A person who speaks a language fluently, typically because that person has been brought up speaking that language as a child.

natural class   A grouping of phonemes uniquely defined by a small number of distinctive features such that that grouping plays a significant role in expressing the phonological regularities found in natural languages.

natural kind term   An expression that denotes kinds of things in nature, such as *gold* or *tiger*.

neologism   Narrowly construed, a neologism is a new word that has been added to a language. More broadly, new words and words that have undergone meaning change have been described as neologisms.

neurolinguistics   The subfield of linguistics that studies the relation between language and the brain, especially the correlation between brain damage and speech and language deficits.

node   A point in a tree diagram at which lines connecting different constituents are connected.

nonliteral utterance   An utterance in which the speaker does not mean at least some of what the words uttered mean. Antonym: *literal utterance*.

nonstandard language   Any variety of a language that lacks social prestige and is not considered acceptable in official contexts. Antonym: *standard language*.

nucleus   The loudest part of a syllable, usually consisting of a vowel or a diphthong.

obstruent   (See *sonorant*.)

Old English   The Germanic language spoken in Britain from the fifth to the eleventh centuries A.D. that is the ancestor of Modern English.

onset   Within a syllable, the consonant or sequence of consonants that precedes the nucleus.

open class   A class of words whose membership is large and that readily accepts new members, for example, nouns, verbs, and adjectives. Members of this class are sometimes referred to as *content words*. Antonym: *closed class*.

operative meaning   The linguistic meaning of an utterance that the speaker expects to lead the hearer to the speaker's communicative intent.

Optimality Theory   A model of grammar according to which a representation is well formed if it satisfies an array of ranked, violable, and universal constraints.

orthographic abbreviation   The type of abbreviation that results when the spelling of a word has been shortened but the pronunciation has not necessarily been altered (e.g., *mister → Mr.*).

orthography   Any writing system that is widely used by the members of a given society to write their language. Most orthographies do not represent the speech sounds of the language in a systematic way. For example, this sentence is written in English orthography.

overextension   The use of a word to refer to more than what that word conventionally refers to. Antonym: *underextension*.

palatal   Formed by means of a constriction between the body of the tongue and the (hard) palate. The English word *you* begins with a palatal sound.

palate   The front part of the roof of the mouth, often referred to as the hard palate since there is bone underneath.

particle   1. In English, a word that combines with a verb to create an expression with an idiomatic meaning (e.g., *up* in *call up*). 2. In other languages, various kinds of affixes or function words; the class of particles must be defined separately for each language.

part of speech   A group of words that share certain grammatical properties, such as the kinds of affixes they take and the kinds of syntactic constructions they occur in.

performance (linguistic)   1. What a speaker actually does in uttering or comprehending an expression. 2. The speech that is actually produced by native speakers, in which some of their linguistic capacity may be obscured by such factors as coughing, memory limitations, or inebriation. Antonym: *competence*.

performative   An expression such as *I promise to be there* that describes the act being performed in its utterance.

performative utterance   The act of sincerely uttering a performative.

perlocutionary act   An act of intentionally affecting the thought or action of the hearer by performing an utterance act. Need not be recognized to be successful.

perseverative coarticulation   The kind of coarticulation effect in which some motion of the vocal tract needed for one sound continues on into a later sound or sounds. Antonym: *anticipatory coarticulation*.

phonation   Another term for *voicing*.

phone   A speech sound. This term is generally used to avoid making any claim about the phonemic or allophonic status of the sound.

phoneme   A speech sound that is psychologically a single unit, in contrast with other such units, but is often realized by two or more allophones that are in either complementary distribution or free variation with each other.

phoneme restoration effect   The phenomenon of hearing (and so "restoring") a phoneme in a word even though that phoneme has been removed from the signal and replaced with some other noise.

phonemic transcription   A writing system for representing speech sounds that omits phonetic details that can be predicted by general rules. Each distinctive speech sound of a language is represented with a unique symbol (or combination of symbols.)

phonetics   The study of speech sounds.

phonetic transcription   A writing system for representing speech sounds that includes much detail.

phonology   The subfield of linguistics that studies the structure and systematic patterning of sounds in human language.

phonotactics   The patterns into which phonemes (or distinctive features) can be arranged to form syllables and words in a given language.

phrasal category   A constituent of a tree diagram that is potentially larger than a single word. Phrasal categories are (usually) named according to the lexical categories that serve as their heads.

phrase marker   Another name for *tree diagram*.

phrase structure grammar   A description of the syntax of a language that contains only phrase structure rules.

phrase structure rule   A statement of an operation that expands a single symbol into two or more parts (e.g., S → NP Aux VP).

pictograph   A character in a writing system that represents some object by a schematic, physical representation of that object.

pidgin   A simplified version of some language, often augmented by features from other languages. A pidgin typically arises in colonial situations and is used at the beginning primarily as a trade language.

pitch   In speech, the perception of the frequency of vibration of the vocal cords.

place of articulation   The part of the mouth, throat, or larynx where the airflow meets the greatest degree of constriction in the production of speech sounds. Contrasts with *manner of articulation*.

polysemy   The property of having multiple meanings that are semantically related.

positional variant   A phonetic form that predictably occurs in a specifiable environment. The aspirated $[p^h]$ that predictably occurs in syllable-initial position is a positional variant of the phoneme /p/ in English.

positron emission tomography (PET) scan   A experimental technique that permits researchers and physicians to measure and map active areas of the brain and other organs.

pragmatic presupposition   Something that is assumed or taken for granted in saying something.

pragmatics   The study of language use and its relation to language structure and context of utterance.

preglottalized   Preceded by a glottal stop or glottal constriction.

presumption   A special sort of shared belief in which speaker and hearer share the expectation that something is the case, but in which that expectation can be overridden at any time by new evidence.

productive   In morphology this word identifies a word formation rule that can be used to create new vocabulary. The adjective-forming *-able* rule is productive because it can be used to create new words. In contrast, the verb-forming *-en* suffix (e.g., *redden*) is no longer productive because it cannot be used to form new words (e.g., **greenen*).

program   An effective procedure written in a programming language.

programming language   A language executable directly or indirectly by a computer.

propositional act   1. Widely viewed, the act of expressing a proposition. 2. Narrowly viewed, the act of referring to something and predicating something of it.

protoform   A reconstructed word or stem that is hypothesized to be the ancestor of a set of related words or stems in daughter languages.

protolanguage   A reconstructed language that is hypothesized to be the ancestor of some group of related languages.

prototype   A typical or representative instance of a concept.

prototype theory   Any theory that claims that concepts have an internal structure that reflects which members are prototypes of that concept.

psycholinguistics   The subfield of linguistics whose goal is to discover the psychological principles that underlie the ability of humans to comprehend, produce, and acquire language.

reconstruction   The process of determining the probable forms of some earlier stage of a language by comparing related forms in two or more present-day languages.

recursivity   A property of grammars whereby a finite set of rules with the ability to apply repeatedly can generate an infinite set of structures.

reduced   Weakened to the point where it loses its distinctive quality (usually said of vowels in unstressed syllables). The English word *sofa* ends in a reduced vowel.

reduplication   The repetition of all or part of a word in order to modify its meaning in some way.

referential use of a singular term   The use of a singular term to express a singular proposition. Antonym: *attributive use*.

regressive assimilation   An assimilation process in which one sound affects a preceding sound. Antonym: *anticipatory assimilation*. Synonym: *anticipatory coarticulation*.

retroflexed   Formed by curling the tip of the tongue upward and backward. The English word *red* begins with a retroflexed consonant for some speakers.

round   A feature assigned to phonemes whose formation is accompanied by a pursing and extension of the lips.

rounded   Formed by pursing the lips in addition to a primary constriction elsewhere in the vocal tract.

satisfaction conditions   The conditions under which the statement made with a declarative sentence is true, the question asked with an interrogative sentence is answered, and the directive issued with an imperative sentence is complied with.

schwa   A nondistinct (mid back) vowel often found in unstressed syllables in English. The final sound of *sofa* is a schwa.

semantic decomposition   The analysis of a single word or morpheme into a set of semantic primitives that define it.

semantic drift   The process whereby a word accrues or loses features of meaning independent of its morphological origin.

semantic field   A group of words with related meanings, for example, kinship terms or color terms.

semantic presupposition   A relation between sentences S and S′ such that S would not be true *or* false unless S′ were true.

semantic priming   The phenomenon whereby a word is recognized faster if a semantically related word was recognized earlier.

semantic reference/referent   The object, event, etc., that an expression applies to by virtue of the meaning of the expression. Antonym: *speaker referent*.

semantics   The study of meaning, reference, truth, and related notions.

semivowel   Another name for *glide*.

sense   The sense of an expression determines its reference and constitutes its cognitive significance.

shared beliefs   A speaker and a hearer share a belief when they both have the belief, each believes the other has the belief, and each believes the other believes they each have the belief.

short   In English, a term applied to vowels of stressed syllables that have a brief duration, lack offglides, and are pronounced with relatively little muscular tension. The vowels of *bit*, *bet*, and *bat* are short. Antonym: *long*.

simple word   A word that cannot be broken down into smaller meaningful parts.

singular proposition   A proposition containing the single object referred to by a singular term. Antonym: *general proposition*.

singular term   An expression used to refer on an occasion to just one thing.

slang   A set of expressions that is characteristic of informal language style, tends to change rapidly, and often serves to indicate solidarity within a given social group.

sonorant   A feature that characterizes speech sounds whose articulation is not so narrow that the airflow across the glottis is appreciably inhibited; thus, sonorants are typically voiced. Nonsonorants are frequently referred to as *obstruents*.

speaker meaning   What the speaker means or intends to communicate in uttering an expression.

speaker reference   The speaker's act of referring to some object, event, etc. Antonym: *semantic reference*.

speaker referent   The object, event, etc., that a speaker is referring to. Antonym: *semantic referent*.

speech act   An act performed in uttering a linguistic expression.

speech comprehension model   An explicit representation of the processes leading from the hearing of speech sounds to the recognition of the speaker's communicative intent.

speech production model   An explicit representation of the processes leading from a pragmatic intent to the sounds that a speaker produces.

standard language   The variety of a language that has social prestige and that is used in official contexts. Antonym: *nonstandard language*.

stem   A morpheme that serves as a base for forming new words by the addition of affixes.

stop   A consonant sound made by temporarily blocking the airflow completely. The English words *pin* and *dog* begin with stops.

strident   A feature assigned to phonemes that are characterized by high-frequency turbulent noise.

structural ambiguity   The situation in which a sentence has two or more different linguistic meanings even though none of the individual words is ambiguous. The ambiguity of such sentences resides in their different constituent structures. Contrasts with *lexical ambiguity*.

structural change   The operation carried out by a transformational rule.

structural description   A description that characterizes the analysis of a phrase marker into a sequence of constituents that serve as input to a transformational rule.

syllabic   A feature assigned to phonemes that occur as the nucleus of a syllable; such phonemes are usually vowels, but are occasionally consonants.

syllable   A unit of phonological structure that usually consists of a vowel preceded and/or followed by various consonants.

symbolic   A term used to characterize the relationship between an object and a representation of that object when there is no resemblance between the two.

synchronic   Concerned only with a single stage or time period. Antonym: *diachronic*.

syntactic parsing   The process of assigning the correct syntactic structure to a string of words by scanning it from beginning to end.

syntax   The subfield of linguistics that studies the internal structure of sentences and the relationship among their component parts.

taboo language   A set of expressions that are considered inappropriate in certain contexts. For example, profanity and obscenity are considered inappropriate in formal language contexts.

tag   Structured material added at the end of a statement; a tag contains an auxiliary verb, a pronoun that agrees with the subject of the sentence, and sometimes the word *not* or its contracted form *n't*.

tense   1. In phonetics, a speech sound pronounced with relatively great muscular tension. Antonym: *lax*. 2. In describing English vowels, another name for *long*. 3. Verbal affix indicating time.

transcription   Any system of writing used by linguists that represents the speech sounds of a language in a systematic way.

transformational grammar   A description of a language that contains both phrase structure rules and transformational rules.

transformational rule   An operation that converts an input tree structure into a different structure by adding, deleting, or rearranging material. Transformational rules consist of a structural description of the input and the structural change that they effect.

tree diagram   A graphic representation of syntactic constituent structure that uses branching lines and nodes that have category labels.

truth   A relation between a sentence and the world such that the world is the way the sentence represents it as being.

truth condition   A condition that the world must meet for an expression that has that truth condition to be true.

underextension   The use of a word to refer to less than what that word conventionally refers to. Antonym: *overextension*.

Universal Grammar   The genetically endowed information consisting of principles and parameters that enable the child to deduce a grammar from the primary linguistic data.

utterance act   The production of an expression from a language.

velar   Formed by means of a constriction between the body of the tongue and the velum. The English words *coo* and *go* begin with velar consonants.

velum   The back part of the roof of the mouth, often referred to as the soft palate since there is no bone underneath.

verb   1. (transitive) A verb that takes a direct object (e.g., *John ate his dinner*, where *his dinner* is the direct object). 2. (intransitive) A verb that does not take a direct object (e.g., *Time elapsed* and not **Time elapsed the day*).

vocal cords   The two muscular bands of tissue that stretch from front to back within the larynx. The vocal cords vibrate periodically to produce voiced sounds.

vocal folds   Another name for the *vocal cords.*

vocal tract   The region above the vocal cords that produces speech sounds; it consists of the (oral) pharynx, oral cavity, and nasal cavity.

voiced   1. Accompanied by vocal cord vibration. Antonym: *voiceless*. 2. A feature assigned to phonemes that are accompanied by periodic vibration of the vocal cords.

voiceless   Not accompanied by vocal cord vibration. Antonym: *voiced.*

voicing   The sound made by the vibration of the vocal cords. This sound is heard during the production of vowels and some consonants.

Wernicke's area   Part of the left posterior temporal lobe of the brain. Damage to this area results in a kind of aphasia characterized by fluent, but meaningless, speech and the apparent inability to comprehend language.

***wh*-question**   An interrogative sentence beginning with one of the so-called *wh*-words: *who, when, which, where, what, how* (e.g., *Who is John paying?*).

word formation rule   A process by which an affix is added to a word or stem to create a new word, and the meaning of the word is modified in some way.

word recognition   The process of selecting an accessed word and promoting it to consciousness.

X-bar theory   A theory of phrase structure that enables a structural definition of *head of a phrase* and facilitates cross-categorial generalizations (e.g., the location of the head with respect to the complement).

yes/no question   An interrogative sentence characterized either by rising intonation or inversion of subject and auxiliary (e.g., *John can play?, Can John play?*), which can be answered "yes" or "no."

Index

Abbreviated questions, 291–293
Abbreviated style. *See* Language style, abbreviated
Abbreviations. *See* Words, alphabetic abbreviations
-able, 36–39, 40–42, 45, 47–48, 49–50
-able rule, 36–39, 348
Accidental overlap, 322–323
Accusative case. *See* Case, accusative
Acoustic phonetics, 65–66
Acoustic stability, 119
Acquisition of speech by children, 490–493
Acquisition model, 417, 418, 477–506
Acrolect, 301
Acrolect, 301
Acronym. *See* Words, acronyms
Adjectival endings, 341–342
Adjective Agreement rule, 349
Adjective Agreement rule, 349
Adjectives, 13, 19, 20, 24, 33
Adverbs, 19, 20, 24
  adverb phrase (AdvP), 200
Affixes, 421, 422, 495–496
  derivational, 25, 32, 35–42, 43, 44, 45, 54–57
  inflectional, 43, 44, 46, 341, 457
  prefix, 18
  suffix, 18, 19
Affricate, 74, 77, 89, 112, 114–115, 117, 491
Afghani, 329
Afro-Asiatic, 334
Agent, 169
Agentive nouns, 35
Agraphia, 556
Agreement, 288, 301, 349
Airflow, 67
Akimel O'odham, 279–280
Albanian, 329
Algonquian, 321, 322, 323, 343
Allophones, 93–94, 95, 348
Alphabet, 65, 568

Alphabetic abbreviations. *See* Words, alphabetic abbreviations
Altaic, 334
Alveolar, 74, 76, 77, 79, 85, 89, 111, 112, 117, 119, 120, 135
Alveolar ridge, 71, 78, 91, 92, 111, 117
Alveopalatal, 74, 76, 77, 79, 89, 92, 93, 117
Ambiguity, 237, 241–242, 245, 246, 293, 367, 373, 386, 433, 434
  lexical, 155, 237
  structural, 154–156, 183–184, 189, 366
American English, 14, 26, 42, 85, 90, 92, 96, 98, 100, 161, 229, 277, 280, 288, 307, 315, 336, 337
American Sign Language, 359, 421, 479, 505, 507–512
Amharic, 124–125, 334
Anaphora, 53, 213, 261–264, 518
Ancient Greek, 329
Ancient Greek, 329
Anglo-Saxon. *See* Old English
Animal communication, 506–507
Anomaly, 238, 246
Anomia, 545–546
Answerhood condition, 235, 252
Antecedent, 53, 261–262, 450, 459, 518
Anterior, 114–115, 117. *See also* Distinctive features, anterior
Anticipation errors, 421–422
Anticipatory coarticulation, 492
Antonymy, 240–241, 246, 345
anymore, 276–277
Apex, 78, 79
Aphasia, 527, 554–555, 556
Appalachian dialect, 276
Arabic, 296, 331, 334, 561, 563
Arbitrary pairing, 15–16
Arcuate fasciculus, 545
Argot, 302
Armenian, 329
Armstrong, S., 446, 448

Articles (Art), 21, 22–23, 24, 172, 173, 176, 203, 221, 222
Articulators, 73
Articulatory phonetics, 65
Arytenoid cartilages, 70
Aspirated *t*, 90–91, 93, 127
Aspiration, 90, 94, 96
Aspiration rule, 124, 127
Assertion, 235
Assimilation, 110, 125
  anticipatory, 491
  regressive, 492
Association nerve fibers, 533
Associative thought, 539
Attentiveness Hypothesis, 452
Attributivity, 259–260
Austin, J., 361, 391, 392–393, 394
Austro-Asiatic, 334
Austronesian, 334
Avestan, 329
Axon, 531
Aztec, 27, 61, 343

Babbling
  children's, 482–483
  Washoe's, 509
Bach, K., 258
Back. *See* Vowels, back
Backformation, 40–42
Balto-Slavic, 329
Barred-*i*, 82
Base. *See* Morphemes, base
Base structure. *See* Input tree
Basilect, 301
Basque, 333
Bates, E., 503
Battan, P., 334–335
Battig, W., 443
Bayles, K., 257
Be, 100–101, 178, 284–287, 291–292, 296
Behaviorism, 478, 480
Bellugi, U., 420
Bengali, 329
Berko, J., 494
Bever, T., 433, 434, 436, 458, 459, 464, 540
Bickerton, D., 297, 301, 302
Bilabial, 68, 71
Bilingual, 307
Binary, 114
Binding Principles, 516–518
Biological innateness of linguistic capacity, 515
Bisyllabic, 98, 100–101
Blends. *See* Words, blends
Bloom, L., 437

Bock, K., 258, 420
Bonobo, 512, 514–515
Bontoc Igorot, 18, 24
Borrowing. *See* Words, borrowing
Bound affix. *See* Morphemes, bound
Bound base. *See* Morphemes, bound base
Box diagram, 176–177
Braces, 209
Bradley, D. C., 457
Brain stem, 531, 532
Branching node, 214–215
Brand names. *See* Words, generified
Brazilian Portuguese, 112, 279, 306
Breton, 329
Brewer, E., 451
Brewer, W., 451
British Empiricists, 440
British English, 14, 82, 92, 96, 98, 230, 276, 280, 337
Broadening. *See* Words, broadening
Broca, P., 528, 542
Broca's aphasia, 542–544, 545, 556
Broca's area, 528, 529, 530, 533, 543, 548, 554
Brookshire, R., 538
Brown, C., 553
Brown, R., 483, 513
Bruner, J., 503
Bulgarian, 329
Burmese, 334

Calques, 28
Calvin, W., 505
Campbell, L., 333
Canadian English, 335–336
Cann, R., 331
Cantonese, 78, 279, 334, 561
Cape York Creole, 300
Caramazza, A., 457
Carlson, M., 435
Carnap, R., 361
Case
  accusative, 170, 340–341
  dative/instrumental, 340–341
  genitive, 340–341, 342
  nominative, 170, 340–341
  objective, 170
  subjective, 170
Casual speech. *See* Language style, casual
Category
  lexical. *See* Parts of speech
  phrasal, 206
Categorization, 439
Caucasian languages, 334
Causative Verb Formation rule, 348–349
Cavallie-Sforza, L., 331, 332

C-command (Constituent command), 214, 215, 497–501
Celtic, 329, 340, 343, 344
Center embedding, 209–211
Central nervous system (CNS), 531
Cerebral cortex, 531, 532, 535
Chambers, S., 431
Champollion, J. F., 563
Chance overlap, 322–323
Chemakuan, 337
Cherokee, 563, 566
Chest cavity, 67
Child language
  rule governed nature of, 506
  stages in development of, 482–491
Chimpanzees, 507–515
Chinese, 8, 279, 322, 339, 554–555, 561, 562
Chinese Pidgin English, 296
Chinook Jargon, 298
Chomsky, C., 497, 498, 499
Chomsky, N., 4, 9, 114, 151, 152, 177, 194, 197, 215, 227, 262, 417, 458, 479, 482, 505, 517–518
Church, J., 451
Churchland, P. S., 460
Circumlocutions, 544
Clark, E., 482, 488
Clark, H., 450, 451, 452, 482, 488
Clarke, R., 531
Clause
  embedded, 207, 212
  main, 289
  modifying, 187
  subordinate, 207
Cleft sentences, 177–179, 450
Clements, G. N., 129
Click experiments, 436–437
Clicks, 86, 120
Clifton, 438
Clippings, 26, 32
Closed class. See Words, closed class
Closings, 390, 391
Coarticulation effect, 93, 113
Coda, 126–127
Code-switching, 307–308
Cognitive background, 419
Cognitive science, 5, 358
Coined words. See Words, coined
Cole, D., 145
Cole, D., 145
Colloquialism, 303
Colloquial style, 327
Commands, 242
Communication, 5–6, 228, 232–233, 258, 362–363
Communicative act, 368

Communicative contexts, 502
Communicative intention, 367, 369, 370, 371, 374–375, 382, 386, 398
Communicative function, 242
Communicative potential, 242–243
Communicative Presumption, 371, 374, 375
Comparative, 24
Comparative linguistics, 320–323
Comparative method, 323
Competence, 151–153, 227, 501–503
Competence model, 417–418
Complement, 216, 579
Complementary distribution, 95, 125
Compliancy condition, 235, 252
Compositionality, 32, 34–35, 246–248
Compounds, 32, 34–35, 246–248
  deverbal, 52
  headless, 35
  primary, 50
  stress patterns of, 34
  synthetic, 50
  verbal, 50
Comprehension, 419, 425, 433, 451–452
Concepts, 234, 439–449
  complex concepts, 439, 440
Concord particles, 301
Conduction aphasia, 545
Conjunctions, 22–23, 24, 177
Conjunction test, 179–181
Connectionist Models, 460–464
Consonant clusters, 101–102, 492
Consonant, 73–79, 85–86, 103, 114–116
  ambisyllabic, 115
  of American English, 73–79, 114
  definition of, 73
Constituent-command. See C-command
Constituents, 167, 420
  optional, 203–204
Constituent structure, 171, 172, 197, 436
  tests for, 177–178
Contact languages, 296
Context, 388–389, 437, 453
Contextual appropriateness, 368, 383, 385
Contextual inappropriateness, 368, 379–380
Continuant, 114–116
Contracted forms, 18, 24
Contradiction, 235
Control, 497–501
Conversation, 15, 387, 389
Conversational Implicatures, 399
Conversational Maxims, 399
Conversational Presumptions, 371, 376, 379, 382, 400
Cooperative Principle, 399
Coreference, 54, 261–264, 516–517
Core meaning, 445

Cornish, 340
Coronal, 112, 114–115, 117, 119, 120
Corpus callosum, 532, 533, 535
Correspondence (sound), 323–327
Cortese, C., 431
Cortex. *See* Cerebral cortex
Cortical conduction, 533–535
Crain, S., 438, 497
Cran-, 18, 42, 48–49
Creativity, 480, 506
Creek, 306
Creole continuum, 301
Creoles, 295, 298–302
Critical Period, 503–505
Crowley, T., 299, 300
Cuneiform, 563
Curtiss, S., 504
Culter, A., 424, 431
Czech, 329

Danish, 279, 340
Danks, J., 233
Daughter nodes, 203
Declarative, 156, 157, 169, 211, 212, 235,
    242, 249, 250, 252, 385
Decomposition, 441–442
Definite article, 450
Definite descriptions, 254, 255, 404
Definitional decomposition, 441
Deictic expressions, 254, 255–257
Dell, G., 424
Demers, R. A., 90, 132, 218, 278
Demonstratives, 22–23, 24, 255, 256–257
Demotic writing, 563, 566
Dennis, M., 541, 542
Denotation, 232, 234, 235, 243, 253, 255,
    404
Denotational theory (of meaning), 231–
    232
Dental, 111, 112, 117, 119, 120
Dental stops, 111
DeRenzi, E., 538, 539
Derivational affixes. *See* Affixes,
    derivational
Derivational morphology, 28–29, 36–39
Derived structure. *See* Output tree
Description Theory, 257–258, 260–261
Descriptive grammar, 230–231
Devanagari script, 566
Deverbal, 52
Diacritic, 566
Diachronic linguistics, 315
Dialectal variation, 97–100, 276–278
Dialects, 275–295
  mutual intelligibility of, 278–280
  regional, 276

  social, and ethnic, 276
  standard and nonstandard, 275, 283–284
Diamond, J., 331
Diaphragm, 67, 68, 69
Dichotic listening, 536
Dictionary entry, 13–14
Digraph, 78
Dillard, J., 275, 286, 299
Diminutive suffix, 40
Diphthongs. *See* Vowels, diphthongs
Direct communication, 368, 370, 372–373
Direct strategy, 372–375, 376, 377, 381,
    382, 384
Disambiguation, 366
Discontinuous constituent, 187
Discontinuous dependencies, 184–189, 192,
    193, 195, 196, 366
Discourse, 13, 109, 110–126, 143, 387, 389
Discrete combinatorial system, 71
Distinctive features, 493
Distributed, 114–115
Distribution, 86
dontcha, 112
Dore, J., 503
Dravidian, 331, 334
Dutch, 280, 296, 324, 329, 340

Ebonics, 284
Eccles, J., 533
-ed. *See* Past participle *-en/-ed*
Effability, 7
Embedded clause, 207, 212
Embedded sentence, 207
Embedding, 150, 206–209
Empty categories, 458–460
Engma, 77, 78
Entailment, 244–245, 246, 248
Epenthesis, 122
Epiglottis, 71
-er agentive suffix, 13–14, 35–36, 41, 50
-er comparative suffix, 43, 45, 241
ERP. *See* Event-Related Potentials
Ervin, S. M., 493
Esophagus, 71
-est superlative suffix, 43, 45
Estonian, 333
Euphemisms, 306
Event-Related Potentials, 257, 258–261,
    550–554, 555
Evolution of language, 316–319
Exaggeration, 380
Exchange errors, 421, 423, 424
Exclamative, 350
External intercostal muscles, 67, 68
Extraposition, 188, 189, 190, 192, 193, 195,
    196

Faglioni, P., 539
False analysis, 46, 47–48
Farmer, A. K., 90, 132, 216, 218, 278
Fasold, R. W., 286
Fay, D., 431
Features, 493
Ferguson, C., 503
Figurative meaning, 451
Figures of speech, 378
Filipino, 297
Fillmore, C., 402
Finnish, 119, 333, 334
Finno-Ugric, 334
Fishler, I., 437
Flapped *t*, 92, 93, 94, 335
Flap Rule, 134–136, 336–337
Flemish, 280, 329
Focus, 388
Fodor, J. A., 428, 436, 441, 442, 446, 463
Fodor, J. D., 435, 441
Foot,
　assignment, 131
　types, 130–131
Force of utterance, 251
Formal style, 290, 372
Forster, K., 428, 431, 432
Foss, D., 486, 488
Fouts, R., 511
Frazier, L., 435
Free Variation, 95
Frege, G., 234, 235, 257
French, 8, 12, 16, 27, 46, 93, 96, 119, 120, 234, 250, 296, 298, 299
Frequency effect, 431
Fricatives, 74, 75–77, 85, 89, 491
Front (consonant), 74, 113
Front (vowel). *See* Vowels, front
Frontal lobe, 528
Full vowels, 131
Function words, 22, 483
Fuzzy concept, 445–449
Fuzzy set theory, 447, 449

Ganda, 119
Garden path sentences, 433–434, 438–439
Gardner, A., 507–512
Gardner, B., 507–512
Garrett, M., 422, 423, 433, 436, 441, 457, 554
Gazzaniga, M., 501, 504, 534
Gee, J., 430
Gender, 169, 170, 341, 349
General Proposition, 254
General terms, 254
Generified words, 26, 27
Genetic (historical) relationship, 323–334

Genie, 504
Genitive. *See* Case, genitive
Georgian, 109, 119, 120, 334
German, 21, 27, 34, 88, 93, 319, 324, 329, 340, 343, 344, 561
Germanic language family, 324–327, 329, 335, 340, 343, 348
Geschwind, N., 530, 556
Gestural language, 316, 317
Gibbs, R., 452, 453
Gimbutas, M., 330
Given-new information, 450–451
Givon, T., 503
Gleason, J., 502
Gleitman, H., 446, 448
Gleitman, L., 441, 446, 448
Glides, 74, 79, 101, 491
Glottal sounds, 71, 76
Glottal stop, 91, 93
Glottis, 70, 91
Glucksberg, S., 233
Goldsmith, J., 140
Gordon, B., 457, 494, 496
Gothic, 319, 329
Gough, P., 431
Governing Category, 518
Grammar simplification, 335
Grammaticality judgments, 150, 151–152
Grammatical relations, 181–183, 197, 441
Graphic aphasia, 554–555
Great Vowel Shift, 345–347, 351
Greek, 296, 319, 323, 324, 327–330, 343, 351, 352, 563
Greek alphabet, 568
Greenberg, J., 333
Greetings, 389–390
Grice, H. P., 361, 396, 399
Grimm, J., 326
Grimm's Law, 324–327, 328, 335, 351
Groothusen, J., 553
Grosjean, F., 430
Gullah, 299
Guyanese creole, 301
Gypsy. *See* Romany
Gyrus, 532–533

Haas, M. R., 306
Hagoort, P., 553
Haitian Creole, 299
Hakes, D., 486, 488
Halle, M., 114, 123
Hamm, A., 531
Hard palate, 71, 79, 112
Harris, R., 194, 451
Hausa, 334
Haviland, S., 450, 451

Hawaiian, 27, 85, 102–103, 129, 568
Hawaiian Pidgin English, 297
Hayes, C., 508
Hayes, K., 508
Head (of a phrase), 205, 206, 215
Head Parameters, 518–519
Hebrew, 331, 334, 563
Hellenic, 329
Hemispherectomy, 541
Hesitations, 420
Hewes, G., 316
Hieratic script, 563, 566
Hieroglyphics, 563, 565, 566
High. *See* Vowels, high
Hillyard, S., 551
Hindi, 96–97
Hindi/Urdu, 329
Hirsh, I., 538
Historical Chain Theory, 260–261
Historical Linguistics, 315, 320
Historical relationship, 323–334
Hittite, 329
Hoard, J., 566
Holophrastic utterances, 484
Homophonous words, 239, 246
Houston, S., 566, 568
Hungarian, 119, 333, 334
Hurtig, R., 433
Hypercorrection, 282–283
Hyphenated words, 33–34

ICE. *See* Inner-City English
Icelandic, 329, 340
Iconic, 561
Ideographic systems. *See* Pictographic
    systems
Idiolect, 230, 277, 278, 433
Idioms, 247
Igbo, 120, 334
Illocutionary act, 394, 395, 396, 397
Imitation, 482
Imperatives, 242–243, 249, 250, 252,
    385
Imura, T., 556
i-mutation, 347
Indefinites, 421, 422
Indexical expressions, 255–256
Indic, 329
Indirect communication, 368, 370, 372,
    381–383, 386, 452, 453
Indirect singular inference, 404
Indirect Strategy, 383–386
Indo-European, 319, 324–333, 350–352
Indonesian-Malay, 334
Inferences (pragmatic), 373
Inferential model, 370–387

Inferential strategies, 370, 371–372, 373,
    452
Infix, 18
Infixation, 18–19
Inflectional affixes. *See* Affixes, inflectional
Inflectional morphology, 301, 341
Informal style. *See* Language style, informal
-*ing* progressive, 20, 43, 45
Inner-City English (ICE), 275, 284, 285,
    286, 291, 293, 299
Input tree, 191, 192, 193, 196
Intended inference, 370
Intentions (pragmatic), 419
Interdental, 74, 75, 76
International Phonetic Alphabet (IPA), 673,
    79, 84, 86, 93
Interrogatives, 156–157, 160, 164, 165, 242–
    243, 249, 250, 252
Interrogative pronoun, 211
Intuitive judgment. *See* Grammaticality
    judgments
Invariant *be*, 286
-*ion*, 42
Ipsilateral, 538
Irish, 329
Irish Gaelic, 340
Irony, 229, 230, 368, 378, 380
Isolate, 333
Italian, 46, 85, 296, 319, 329
Italic, 329
-*ity*, 47–49
i-umlaut, 347

Jackendoff, R., 215, 402
Jakobson, R., 114, 482
Jamaican English, 299
Japanese, 12, 16, 21, 22, 27, 97, 111, 119,
    129, 143, 170, 221, 250, 297, 322, 333,
    334, 554–555, 556, 566
Jargon, 302–303, 304
Jespersen, O., 249
Johnson, K., 66
Johnson-Liard, P., 445
Jones, Sir William, 319, 330
Joos, M., 335
Judgments (grammaticality). *See* Gram-
    maticality judgments

Kahn, D., 79, 128
Kana script (Japanese), 554–555, 556, 566
Kanji script (Japanese), 554–555, 556, 566
Kannada, 334
Kanzi (pygmy chimpanzee), 514–515
Kaplan, D., 527
Katz, J., 365
Keenan, E., 401

Kentish, 340
Keyser, S. J., 183
Kimball, J. P., 198
Kimura, D., 536, 538, 539, 540
Kiparsky, P., 494–495
Kleenex, 26–27
Klima, E., 420
Koko, 512, 514
Korean, 97, 333, 334, 519
Kripke, S., 258, 261
Kurdish, 329
Kutas, M., 551

Labial, 71, 85, 114–115, 117, 119, 120
Labialization. *See* Vowels, rounded
Labiodental, 74, 75
Labov, W., 281, 284, 285, 290
Lachter, J., 464
Lackner, J., 538
Ladefoged, P., 66
Lakoff, G., 361, 401
Laminal, 114–115
LAN. *See* Left Anterior Negative Shift
Lana project, 515
Landau, B., 441
Language Acquisition Device (LAD), 479,
   490, 494, 515, 516
Language change, 334–350
  community, 335–336, 337–338
  individual, 335
Language families, 327–334
Language localization (in brain), 528
Language processor, 454
Language reconstruction, 327–328
Language style
  abbreviated, 288, 289, 294–295
  casual, 265–266, 286, 389
  colloquial style, 327
  informal, 287–288, 303, 389
  formal, 290, 372
Larynx, 67, 68, 69, 91, 538
Lateral, 74, 114–115, 117
Lateral affricate, 119
Latin, 154, 296, 319, 321, 322, 323, 324,
   325, 327–330, 343, 344, 351, 352
Latvian, 329
Laura, 502–503
Lax vowels. *See* Vowels, lax (short)
Left Anterior Negative Shift (LAN), 551,
   553
Left branching, 209
Lehiste, I., 433
Lehmann, W., 319
Lehrer, A., 236, 344–345
Lehrer, K., 236
Leiman, J., 433

Lenneberg, E., 67, 317, 502, 503
Lesser, V., 428
Level-Ordering Hypothesis, 494–496
Levitsky, W., 530
Lexical access, 430–432
Lexical ambiguity, 155, 237
Lexical categories. *See* Parts of speech
Lexical change, 343–344
Lexical concepts, 439
Lexical decision, 431
Lexicon, 203, 241, 431
Lexigram, 515
Lieberman, P., 318, 430
Lightfoot, D., 350
Lingua francas, 295–269, 561
Linguistic capacity, 151
Linguistic knowledge, 150–151
Linguistic Presumption, 371
Linguistic Reference. *See* Denotation
Liquids, 74, 78, 85, 491
Literal communication, 370, 372–373
Literal meaning, 229, 368, 453
Literal singular reference, 403–404
Literal strategy, 375–377, 381, 382, 384,
   386
Literalness (Presumption of), 371, 376
Lithuanian, 329
'll, 19, 24
Loanword. *See* Words, borrowings
Localization theory, 528–531
Locke, J., 366
Loebell, H., 420
Logographic systems, 554, 561, 562, 566,
   568
Long. *See* Vowels, tense (long)
Low. *See* Vowels, low
Luganda, 144, 145
Lummi, 222, 322
Lungs, 67, 69

Macron, 346
MacWhinney, B., 503
Magnetic resonance imaging (MRI), 546,
   550, 555
Makah, 337, 338
Main clause, 289
Main Clause Strategy, 434
Main verbs. *See* Verbs, main
Malayalam, 334
Mandarin, 333, 334, 561
Manner of Articulation, 111, 113, 491
Maratho, 329, 500
Marginal languages, 296
Marslen-Wilson, W., 428
Martin, S., 334
Maturational stage, 503

Maximal onset principle, 128–129
Mayan script, 566, 568
McClelland, J. L., 460, 461, 462, 463
McDonald, J., 454, 455, 456
McElree, B., 459
McGurk, H., 454, 455, 456
McGurk effect, 428, 454–456
Meaning
  as concepts, 234
  as images, 233–234
  lexical, 449
  linguistic, 229, 230, 237
  sentence, 449–452
  speaker's, 229, 230, 237, 398
  theories of, 228–236
  varieties of, 228–231
  word, 439
Meaning inclusion, 239
Meaning overlap, 239
Meaning properties, 237
Meaning relations, 238–241
Medin, D., 445, 446, 447
Medulla, 532, 535
Menn, L., 492
Mental images, 439
Mentalist Theories (of meaning), 232–233
Mercian, 340
Mervis, C., 442, 445
Mesolects, 301
Message Model, 372, 373–375, 381, 386–
  387, 418, 420, 501
Metaphor, 229, 378, 380
Metaphorical extension. See Words, meta-
  phorical extension
Metathesis, 493
Metonymy, 378
Metrical feet, 130–132, 137–139
Meyer, D., 431
Mid. See Vowels, mid
Middle English, 342, 346, 348
Mill, J. S., 257
Miller, G., 317, 445
Minimal Attachment Principle, 435, 438–
  439
Minimal Distance Principle, 498–500
Minimal pair, 94, 95, 111
Modal auxiliaries, 160
Modifying clauses, 187
Modularity, 425–428, 437, 438
Mohr, J., 543
Molony, C., 318
Mongolian, 334
Monosyllabic, 98–101
Montague, W., 443
Montgomery, G., 547, 549
Mood, 249–253

sentential, 249
verbal, 249
Morphemes, 17
  base, 18, 19, 44, 45, 56
  bound, 18, 24
  bound base, 18, 24, 48–49
  contracted form, 18, 24
  free, 18, 24
  grammatical, 23
  independent base, 18
  stem (see base)
Morphological acquisition, 493–496
Morphological change, 348–349
Morphophonemic writing systems, 568
Mother node, 203
Motor speech area. See Broca's area
MRI. See Magnetic resonance imaging
Muller-Lyer illusion, 427
Multiword stage, 484–490
Mutual intelligibility, 278–280

Nakayama, M., 497
Naming, 431
Napoli, D., 216
Naro, A., 301
Narrowing. See Words, narrowing
Nasals, 74, 77–78, 85, 114–115, 117, 122–
  124, 337–338, 491
Nasal cavity, 70, 71, 77
Natural class, 122–123, 326
Natural-kind terms, 261
Navajo, 12, 118, 119, 212, 222, 234, 320,
  322
Neanderthal man, 318
Negation, 161, 163, 165, 285, 349, 350, 422,
  485, 488
Neologism. See Words, neologism
Network (connection), 461, 462
Network English. See Standard American
  English
Neurolinguistics, 424, 527
Neville, H., 551, 552
Newmeyer, F. J., 194, 215
Newport, E., 504
New York City English, 280–282
New York City /r/, 280–282
Nicaraguan Sign Language, 302
Niger-Congo, 334
Nim Chimpsky project, 512, 515
Nodes (of a tree diagram), 202
  branching, 214–215
  daughter, 203
  mother, 203
Noncommunicative acts, 369
Nonliteral communication, 368, 370, 372,
  377–381, 384, 386, 451–452

Nonliteral meaning, 229–230
Nonliteral singular refence, 404
Nonliteral strategy, 381, 382, 384, 386
Northumbrian, 340
Norwegian, 329, 340
Nostratic, 331
Noun (N), 19, 21, 24, 33, 172, 173, 176, 180,
   203
 deverbal, 50
Noun phrase (NP), 158, 164, 165, 190
Nucleus (of a syllable), 126–127
Number, 169, 170, 349

Ober, J., 565, 566
Object, 21, 39, 169–171, 181–183, 203, 212
Obstruent, 103
Occipital lobe, 532
Ochs, E., 503
Off-glide, 84
Ojemann, G., 505, 536
Old Church Slavic, 329
Old English, 339–342, 344, 346–350
Old High German, 329
Old Icelandic, 329
Old Persian, 319, 329, 564
Olmsted, D., 491
One-way intelligibility, 279
One-word stage, 483–484, 488
Onomatopoeic words, 16, 316
Onset, 126–129
Open class. See Words, open class
Openings, 389–390
Operative meaning, 374
Optative, 250
Optimality Theory, 143
Oral cavity, 70
Oral nonverbal apraxia, 538
Oral pharynx. See Pharynx
Origin of language, 316–319
Orthography, 71–72, 78, 109, 119, 139, 300,
   346, 437, 554–555
Oscan, 329
Osherson, D., 447, 447
Osterhout, L., 553
Output tree, 191, 193, 195, 196
Overextension (of reference), 483
Overgeneralization, 493–494
Overlap (chance), 322–323
Overstatement, 377–378
Owens, R. E., 491
Ozark dialect, 276

Palatal, 119–120
Palatalization, 112
Palate. See Hard palate; Velum
Pallie, W., 531

Panjebi, 329
Papago. See Tohono O'odham
Paradigms, 46
Paraphasia, 543
Paraphrase, 454
Parietal Lobe, 532, 533
Parkes, C., 441
Parsing, 428, 430, 434, 436, 437, 438
Particle Movement rules, 185–189, 190–
   196, 198, 348, 349
Particles, 21
Parts of speech, 19–22, 158, 168, 172, 173,
   197, 209
Pashto, 329
Passive, 450
Past participle -en/-ed, 43
Past tense (English), 421, 422
Patterson, F., 512
Pedersen, H., 562, 564, 566
Penfield, W., 529–530
Perceptual strategies, 434
Perceptual systems, 425–427
Performance, 151–153, 417
 limitations, 152
 model, 417, 418
Performatives, 250, 391–394, 396, 405
Peripheral nervous system, 531
Perlocutionary acts, 369, 394, 395, 396, 397
Perseveration errors, 421
Persian, 319, 329
Person, 169, 170
PET. See Positron emission tomography
Petersen, S., 548
Pharynx, 70, 71, 80, 538
Phonation. See Voicing
Phone, 93
Phoneme, 71, 94, 95, 110, 111, 348
 acquisition of, 491
Phoneme addition, 348
Phoneme loss, 348
Phoneme restoration effect, 429
Phonemic transcription, 71–72, 86, 90, 91
Phonetic features, 111–113, 421
Phonetics, 65–66
Phonetic symbols, 93–97
Phonetic transcription, 71–72, 90
Phonetic variation, 90–93
Phonological change, 345–347
 change in rule applicability, 347
 rule addition, 345–347
 rule loss, 347
Phonology, definition of, 66, 109
Phonotactics, 102–103, 129
Phrasal category, 206
Phrasal concepts, 439
Phrase marker. See Tree diagrams

Phrase structure rules (PSR), 201–206, 207, 208, 215
Phrase structure violation, 551–553
Pickett, J., 430
Pictographic systems, 556, 561, 563, 568
Pidgins, 295, 296–298
Pieczuro, A., 538
Pima. *See* Akimel O'odham,
Pinker, S., 11, 12, 120, 302, 424, 464, 478, 501
Pitch, 69, 140
Place of articulation, 73, 113, 491
Planum temporal, 530
Plural morpheme, 16, 18, 19
Plural rule (of English), 78–82, 100, 110–112
Plural -*s*, 12, 16, 19, 34, 35, 36, 60
Point of articulation. *See* Place of articulation
Polish, 304, 329
Politeness, 452
Pollack, I., 430
Polysemy, 237–238, 246
Pons, 532, 535
Portuguese, 46, 279, 296, 329
Positional variants. *See* Allophones
Positron emission tomography (PET), 546–550, 555
Possessive phrase, 209
Possessive *'s*, 43, 342
Postal, P., 214
Posterior temporal lobe, 528
Pragmatic intentions, 419
Pragmatic interpretation capacity, 425, 426
Pragmatics, 258, 361
 acquisition of, 501–503
Prefix, 18
Preglottalization, 91, 93, 94
Premack, A., 515
Premack, D., 515
Prepositional phrase (PP), 172, 174, 176, 180, 204
Preposition (P), 19, 20, 22–23, 24, 33, 171, 172, 173, 296, 563
Prescriptive grammar, 230–231
Prescriptive rules, 7
Presumptions, 371–372, 373, 382, 386
Presupposition (pragmatic), 400–403, 405, 450
Prevelar *k*, 112–113
Primates, 506–516
Priming (semantic), 431, 458
Prince, A., 120, 464
Principle of referential success, 438–439
Principles and Parameters, 516–520
Productivity, 46–47, 50

Progressive. *See* Assimilation
Projection nerve fiber, 533
Pronouns, 169–171, 214, 215, 459, 517
Proper names, 254, 255, 257–258
Propositional Acts, 395, 397
Propositional content, 397
Proto-forms, 327
Proto-Indo-European, 319
Proto-language, 327
Prototypes, 234, 445, 448–449
Proverbs, 385–386
Pseudo-imperative, 249
Putnam, H., 261
Pygmy chimpanzee. *See* Bonobo; Kanzi
Pylyshyn, Z., 463

Quality (Presumption of), 371
Quantifier, 187
Quantity (Presumption of), 371
Question Rule, 156–160, 162, 163–168, 172, 178, 211, 212
Questions, 235, 349, 485–490, 496–497
 alternative, 249
Quileute, 337, 337

Radar, 25
Radford, A., 185
Raichle, M., 550
Rask, E., 326
Ratner, N. B., 502
Rayner, K., 435
r-colored vowel, 97–100
re-, 60–61
Reanalysis, 17–18
Rebus, 563
Reconstruction, 327, 328
Recursion, 206, 496
Reddy, M., 365–366
Reduced vowels. *See* Vowels, reduced
Redundancy, 246
Reduplication, 21
Reed, D., 569
Reference, 367, 386
 disjoint, 262–263
 linguistic, 255–257
 speaker's, 262, 403–405
Referent, 255
Referential intent, 419
Referentiality, 259–260
Referential Theory, 257–258
Regional dialects, 276
Reich, P., 424
Reicher, G., 431
Reilly, J., 503
Reinhart, T., 215
Released-*t*, 93

Relevance (Presumption of), 371
Renfrew, C., 330
Requests, 235
Retroflex, 79
R-expression, 235, 517
Reversals. *See* Words, reversals
Richardson, C., 451
Rich interpretation, 484
Right branching, 209
Right ear advantage, 538
Rigsby, B., 299, 300
Rips, L., 445
r-less dialect. *See* New York City English
Roberts, L., 529–530
Roeper, T., 51, 52
Rohrman, N., 431
Romance languages, 46, 96, 343
Romanian, 329
Romany, 329
Rosch, E., 442, 442, 444, 445
Rosetta stone, 563
Ross, J., 213, 361
Round. *See* Vowels, rounded
Rule governed, 67, 506
Rumbaugh, D., 515
Rumelhart, D. E., 460, 461, 462, 463
Russell, B., 249, 477, 520
Russian, 8, 154, 304, 329
Rymer, R., 504

Sachs, J., 483
Sacred language, 306
SAE. *See* Standard American English
Salish, 337–338
Sanskrit, 319, 320, 323, 324, 325, 327–330, 352, 566
Sapir, E., 18
Sarah Project, 515
Sarcasm, 229, 230, 368, 378, 380, 382, 452
Sassetti, F., 319
Satisfaction Condition, 236
Savage-Rumbugh, S., 512, 514, 515
Scansion, 130
Scarborough, D. L., 431
Scarborough, H. S., 431
Schatz, C., 429
Schieffelin, 503
Schunk, D., 452
Schvaneveldt, R., 431
Schwa, 82, 101
Scots Gaelic, 321, 322, 323, 329, 340
Scotti, G., 539
Sea Island Creole, 299
Search Model, 431–432
Searle, J., 361, 397

Seidenberg, M., 433, 437
Sejnowski, T., 460
self, 53–54, 213
Selkirk, E. O., 57
Semantic anomaly effect, 551, 553
Semantic drift. *See* Words, semantic drift
Semantic fields, 239–240, 344–345
Semantic interpretation, 439–452
Semantic interpretation capacity, 425, 426
Semantic presupposition, 245, 246
Semantic reference. *See* Denotation
Semitic, 331, 563, 566
Semivowels. *See* Glides
Sense Theory, 234–236
Sentence (S), 429
  complex, 207
  matrix, 207
  simple, 207
Sentence frames, 178
Sentence meaning, 449–453
Sequoia, 563
Serbo-croatian, 329
Shakespeare, W., 159, 315
Shanker, S., 515
Shared (contextual) beliefs, 373, 386. *See also* Presumptions
Shaw, G. B., 103
Shifts, 421, 424
Shoben, E., 445
Sholl, D., 532
Short-term memory, 434
Short vowels. *See* Vowels, lax (short)
Siegel, M., 51, 52
Sincerity (Presumption of), 371
Singular Proposition, 254
Sinhalese, 329
Sino-Tibetan, 334
Sister constituents, 199
Skinner, B. F., 478
Slang, 303–305, 307
Slavic, 329
Slips of the ear, 424–425
Sloat, C., 566
Slobin, D., 493
Sloppy Identity, 480
Slovak, 329
Smith, E., 445, 446, 447, 449
Smith, N. V., 491, 492
Smitherman, G., 286
Smolensky, P., 460, 463
Snohomish, 338
Snow, C., 503
Social dialects. *See* Dialects, social
Soft palate. *See* Velum
Sonorant, 114–116
Sound waves, 66

Spanish, 17, 46, 85, 93, 96, 111, 112, 120,
    279, 296, 307, 308, 319, 323, 329, 343
Speaker Reference, 374, 403–405
SPE-based system, 114–118, 121–122
Specificity condition violation, 553
Spectrogram, 83
Speech acts, 251, 369, 393, 394–403, 405
Speech errors, 420–424, 457
Speech perception, 428–430
Speech planning, 421–422
Speech recognition capacity, 425, 426
Spelling. *See* Orthography
Sperry, R., 534
Spinal cord, 531, 532, 535
Spinnler, H., 539
Spooner, W., 420
Spoonerisms, 420
SPS. *See* Sustained poitive shift
Standard American English (SAE), 276,
    283–286
Steedman, M. S., 438
Stems. *See* Morphemes, base
Stevens, K., 119
-*s* (third person singular), 20, 43, 45, 301
Stops, 73–75, 491
Stowell, T., 216
Stress, 130–131, 421, 422
  assignment, 130–131
Strident, 114–115, 117
Structural ambiguity. *See* Ambiguity,
    structural
Structural change (SC), 198–199
Structural constituents. *See* Constituents
Structural description (SD), 198
Structural linguistics, 4
Stuart, D., 566, 568
Stylistic variants, 388
Subjacency condition violation, 553
Subject, 21, 39, 175, 181–183, 212
  constituent, 168–171
  deletion of, 289–291
Subordinate clause, 207
Substitution, 421, 424, 491–492
Suffix, 18, 19
Sulcus, 352–353
Supplemental motor area, 530
Surface structure, 192, 194, 195, 196, 442
Sustained positive shift (SPS), 551, 553
Swahili, 18, 296, 334
Swedish, 279, 329, 340
Swinney, D., 433
Swisher, L., 538
Syllabic, 91, 114–116, 556, 566
  consonants, 91
Syllabic writing, 563
Syllabification, 126–130

Syllable, 92, 98, 126–127, 140
Syllable Structure, 126–127, 492
Symbolic, 561
Synchronic linguistics, 315
Synonymy, 232, 233, 239, 241, 245, 246, 261
Syntactic acquisition, 496–501
Syntactic anomaly effect, 557
Syntactic change, 349–350
Syntactic parsing. *See* Parsing
Syntactic parsing capacity, 425, 426
Syntactic strategies, 434–437
Syntactic structure, 153–156
Systematic rule, 293
Systematic sound correspondence, 323

Taboo language, 303, 306–307
Tag-controlled deletion, 288–292
Tag declarative, 249
Tag questions, 154, 161–163, 165, 169, 288–
    289, 349
Talk-exchanges, 369–370, 387, 389, 390,
    418
Tamil, 334
Tanenhaus, M., 433, 437
Taylor, S., 515, 566
Telegraphic speech, 23, 543
Telegu, 334
Templin, M., 491
Tense vowels. *See* Vowels, tense (long)
Terrace, H. S., 512, 515
Teuber, H., 538
Thalamus, 532, 535–536
Thorne, A., 331
Thorpe, W., 513
Tibetan, 334
Tohono O'odham, 15, 21, 144, 145, 222,
    223, 279–280
Tok Pisan, 298
Tone, 140–143
  English tone assignment, 414–143
Tongue
  apex, 78, 79
  blade, 71, 76, 77
  body, 71, 78
  root, 71, 79
  tip, 71, 76
Topic, 388
Topicalization, 388
Trachea, 68, 69, 71
Transcription. *See* Phonemic transcription;
    Phonetic transcription
Transformational (generative) linguistics, 4
Transformational grammar, 177, 198
Transformational rules, 189–194
  interaction between, 194–197
Tree diagrams, 171–175, 182, 184

Truth
  analytic, 243, 246
  empirical, 243
  linguistic, 243, 246
Truth conditions, 235, 251
Truth properties, 243–244
Truth relations, 244–245
Truthfulness (Presumption of), 371
Turkish, 334
Turn taking, 390
Tyler, 427
Typicality effects, 441, 442–445

Ukranian, 329
Umbrian, 329
Umlaut. *See i*-mutation
un-, 59–60
Unboundednesss, 7
Underextension (of reference), 483–484
Universal Grammar, 479, 516, 519–520
Unreleased *t*, 91–92, 93
Use Theory (of meaning), 236
Utterance Act, 373, 394, 395, 397
Uvula, 71
Uvular-*r*, 337

Velar, 71, 75, 77, 85, 112, 113, 119, 491
Velum, 71, 77, 79, 112
Verb paradigm, 46
Verb-particle construction. *See* Particle
  movement rules; Particles.
Verb phrase (VP), 172, 175, 180, 203
Verbs (V), 13, 19, 20, 21, 24, 33, 172, 173,
  203
  intransitive, 38, 54
  main, 159–164, 169, 349–350
  modal, 160
  transitive, 38, 39, 54
Vernacular, 303
Vicki (chimpanzee), 508
Vietnamese, 334
Vignolo, L., 538, 539
Visuospatial impairment, 539
Vocal cords, 69, 70, 71, 91
Vocal tract, 67, 68, 70, 79, 119, 318
  cross section of, 80
Vocative, 389
Voicing, 69, 73, 74, 75, 76, 77, 79, 89, 111,
  114–116, 121, 347, 421
Vowel Centering Rule, 335–336
Vowels, 79–86, 113
  back, 80, 81, 82, 83, 84, 113, 119, 120, 347
  central, 98
  diphthongs, 82, 83, 84, 118, 346
  front, 80, 81, 83, 84, 347, 348
  full, 131
  high, 80, 81, 82, 83, 84, 98, 113, 114–116,
    118, 119, 120, 346, 348
  lax (short), 80–82, 83, 98, 99, 101, 131
  low, 80, 81, 82, 83, 84, 346
  mid, 80, 81, 82, 83, 84, 98, 346, 347
  of American English, 79–85
  reduced, 80, 82, 100–101, 131, 133, 138
  rounded, 81, 82, 84, 116, 117, 347, 348
  unstressed, 80, 98, 135, 137
  tense (long), 80, 82–84, 98, 99, 101, 116,
    118, 131, 132, 133, 137–138, 346

Wada, J., 528–529, 531
Wakashan, 337
Walker, E., 441
Wall, R., 198
Ward, A., 536
Warren, R., 429
Washoe, 507–512, 513
Wellman, B., 491
Welsh, 250, 329, 340, 343
Wernicke, C., 528
Wernicke's aphasia, 544–545, 556
Wernicke's area, 529, 530, 533, 555
West Saxon, 340
Whitaker, H., 541, 542
Wh-questions, 211–213, 478, 488
Wh-words, 490
Williams, J. M., 40, 41
Wilson, A., 331
Witelson, S., 531
Wittgenstein, L., 236, 361
Wolpoff, 331
Word-final vowel condition, 133
Word formation rules, 25, 32–42, 343
  category change, 37, 39
  phonological change, 36–37, 39
  productivity of, 46–47
  semantic change, 37–38, 39
Word meaning, 439–449
Word order, 21, 154, 543
Word recognition, 430, 431
Words, 12–13, 16, 127, 365, 366
  acronyms, 25, 32, 57, 302
  alphabetic abbreviations, 26, 32, 95, 288,
    302, 343
  backformation, 40–42
  blends, 26, 32, 304, 421
  borrowings, 102, 307, 308, 344
    direct, 27–28, 32
    indirect, 28, 32
  broadening, 28, 30, 32, 344
  clipping, 26, 32
  closed class, 22–23, 24, 455–458
  coined, 25, 32, 304
  complex, 15–16, 19, 28

Words (cont.)
  content, 22
  function, 22, 483
  generified, 26–27
  metaphorical extension, 29, 229, 230, 344,
    345
  narrowing, 28, 30, 32, 344
  neologism, 23, 25, 32, 544
  onomatopoeic, 16, 316
  open class, 22, 24, 455–458
  proper nouns, 27
  reversals, 28, 31, 32
  semantic drift, 28, 30–31, 32, 45, 49–50
  simple, 16, 19
Writing systems. *See* Orthography

X-bar Theory, 215–217, 518–519
Xerox, 26–27, 35, 40
Xhosa, 86

Yamada, J., 317, 502–503
Yes/No questions. *See* Question rule
Yiddish English, 276
Yoruba, 334

Zadeh, L., 447, 449
Zepeda, O., 222
Zukow, P., 503
Zurif, E. B., 457